The History of Futurism

The History of Futurism

The Precursors, Protagonists, and Legacies

Edited by
Geert Buelens, Harald Hendrix, and Monica Jansen

LEXINGTON BOOKS
Lanham • Boulder • New York • Toronto • Plymouth, UK

Published by Lexington Books
A wholly owned subsidiary of The Rowman & Littlefield Publishing Group, Inc.
4501 Forbes Boulevard, Suite 200, Lanham, Maryland 20706
www.rowman.com

10 Thornbury Road, Plymouth PL6 7PP, United Kingdom

British Library Cataloguing in Publication Information Available

Library of Congress Cataloging-in-Publication Data

The history of futurism : the precursors, protagonists, and legacies / edited by Geert
Buelens, Harald Hendrix, and Monica Jansen.
    p. cm.
  Includes bibliographical references and index.
  ISBN 978-0-7391-7386-2 (cloth : alk. paper) — ISBN 978-0-7391-7388-6 (pbk. : alk.
paper) — ISBN 978-0-7391-7387-9 (electronic)
  1. Futurism (Literary movement) 2. Futurism (Art) 3. Art and literature. I. Buelens,
Geert, 1971– II. Hendrix, Harald. III. Jansen, Michelangela Monica, 1966–
  PN56.F8H57 2012
  809'.9114—dc23   2012022248

Printed in the United States of America

Contents

Text Credits

Chapter 3

All poetry from same source. Published in 1912, translated by author in 2012.

Chapter 4

"Città terribili." Published in 1903/1906, translated by Claudia Clemente 2012.

"Les émeutes." Published in 1903/1906, translated by Claudia Clemente 2012.

"Royère having rolled." Published in 1909, translated by Claudia Clemente 2012.

"Les villes terribles." Published in 1903/1906, translated by Claudia Clemente 2012.

"Regarding F.T. Marinetti." Published in 1909, translated by Claudia Clemente 2012.

"One wishes that." Published in 1909, translated by Claudia Clemente 2012.

"La strada." Published in 1903/1906, translated by Claudia Clemente 2012.

Chapter 5

"The Blacksmith." Published in 1901, translated by Claudia Clemente 2012.

"La Passione." Published in 1907, translated by Claudia Clemente 2012.

"Saffica pagana." Published in 1907, translated by Claudia Clemente 2012.

"Inno al sole." Published in 1907, translated by Claudia Clemente 2012.

"I humbly publish." Published in 1903, translated by Claudia Clemente 2012.

"Beautiful still." Published in 1907, translated by Claudia Clemente 2012.

"Abissi azzurri." Published in 1907, translated by Claudia Clemente 2012.

"Al vento." Published in 1909, translated by Claudia Clemente 2012.

"Remain / always anonymous." Published in 1907, translated by Claudia Clemente 2012.

"To the man of tomorrow." Published in 1935, translated by Claudia Clemente 2012.

Chapter 8

"Traffic police chief." Published in 1925, translated by author, on the basis of extant translation by Willard Bohn, modified by Marella Feltrin-Morris in 2005/2012.

"Perhaps tomorrow." Published in 1914, translated by author.

"I am not speaking." Published in 1925, translated by Willard Bohn in 2005.

"Dawn." Published in 1937, translated by Willard Bohn, modified by Marella Feltrin-Morris in 2005.

"The moon smiles." Published in 1920, translated by Willard Bohn in 2005.

"I'd like." Published in 1925, translated by Marella Feltrin-Morris in 2012.

"For a long, long time." Published in 1910, translated by Marella Feltrin-Morris in 2012.

"I want to give a man a knife." Published in 1916/1919, translated by author and Marella Feltrin-Morris in 2012.

"Today I see before me." Published in 1910, translated by Nicholas Benson in 2010.

"Shall we go?" Published in 1913, translated by Marella Feltrin-Morris in 2012.

Chapter 9

"In the fields." Published in 1908, translated by author.

Chapter 13

"Tomorrow, no more wagons." Published in 1912, translated by Claudia Clemente 2012.

"Midnight rain." Published before 1919, translated by Claudia Clemente 2012.

"Today is Saturday." Published in 1926, translated by Claudia Clemente 2012.

"Pioggia sul cappello." Published in 1922, translated by Claudia Clemente 2012.

"Colourings of autumn." Published in 1926, translated by Claudia Clemente 2012.

"Tre stracci ad asciugare." Published in 1904, translated by Claudia Clemente 2012.

"They mourn the talc lanterns." Published in 1912, translated by Claudia Clemente 2012.

"Am I a poet?" Published before 1909, translated by Claudia Clemente 2012.

"Portrait from within." Published in 1926, translated by Claudia Clemente 2012.

"Against myself." Published in 1926, translated by Claudia Clemente 2012.

"Speak poetry you all will." Published in 1965, translated by Claudia Clemente 2012.

CHAPTER ONE

~

Futurisms

An Introduction

GEERT BUELENS AND MONICA JANSEN

There is no such thing as "Futurism." Any definition of the futurist movement should try to take into account its diverse goals and results in space and
time. Futurism is always in the plural. This text aims not just to attest to the
multiplication of the movement's outcomes, but to clarify its internal contradictions introducing an order that distinguishes precursors, protagonists,
and legacies. Indeed, though Futurism remains very much a relevant force in
our contemporary world, it is one of the main claims of this book that the
movement was deeply rooted in nineteenth-century romantic and symbolist
sensibilities. In a similar vein, an attempt is made to broaden the scope of
who is internationally associated with (literary) Futurism. Despite the fact
that Marinetti is still widely seen as both the original and surviving futurist,
by no means was he the only one who could rightfully claim the title. What
exactly that title means today is also discussed. Futurism is not only that
infamous avant-garde movement which became tainted by fascism, it also
proved to be an enduring artistic force in postwar, democratic Italy and in
other places in the world where the theory and praxis of modern life and art
were and are explored.

The History of Futurism focuses mainly on Italian Futurism and leaves other
important currents like its Portuguese and Russian counterparts aside—though
Marjorie Perloff addresses the latter in relation to the futurist manifesto. The
aim and scope of the book are international, nevertheless, in that it makes
available relevant Italian scholarship to an international audience. It treats

1

Futurism as a multidisciplinary movement, Italian based but basically internationally orientated, mixing aesthetics, politics and science. The main focus of the book is literary, although in connection to audiovisual media, since non-language based articulations of futurist aesthetics like painting and architecture are generally better known internationally.

The year 2009 marked the centenary of the *Founding and Manifesto of Futurism*, published on February 20, 1909, in the Paris newspaper *Le Figaro*. To commemorate this event all over the world exhibitions, *serate* and public readings were staged, journal issues, catalogs, anthologies and scholarly books were published, and festivals, conferences and panel discussions were organized. The Utrecht conference of December 1–3 on which this book is based came rather late in the year—more attuned to the sixty-fifth anniversary of Marinetti's death on December 2, 1944, than to the manifesto's centenary.[1] Our intention, of course, was not to veil the events in a mournful nostalgia, but to look back and assess the state of Futurism Studies in order to create an open and forward looking view on both its legacies and potentials. Furthermore, the focus on Marinetti's role offered the occasion to go into the essentiality (or not) of the movement's founder.

Despite the current academic boom in *memory* and *heritage studies*, the forward looking stance of Futurism never fails to fascinate. This success might be due to the buoyant, boyish enthusiasm that was the basic stance of so many futurist interventions and which seems to have resisted most attempts to deconstruct it, despite the sobering fact that we all know too well how that specific energy was politically channeled up to the 1940s. That we are living in a profoundly populist climate might be another part of the explanation. It is not an overstatement to label many of the futurists' actions outrageous. Finely attuned as they were to the obsessions of the twentieth century the futurists knew they had to be loud, extreme and persistent. Whereas the orthodox modernist aesthetic would claim that less was actually more, the futurists quite systematically opted for a "Why go for less if you can get more?" approach. Consequently, a typical futurist *serata*, or evening performance, would consist of political speeches, poetry and manifesto readings, fist-shaking by the barrel-chested athlete poet Armando Mazza, a traveling picture show and the performance of various pieces of music. Their irredentism actions to provoke the Italian government to reclaim Italian territories from Austria and, after August 1914, to enter the First World War in order to win these regions back from the Austrian enemy would include flyers, parades, fist fighting, Austrian flag burning, the wearing of futuristically designed green-white-red nationalist costumes and the sensational enrolling of the Italian flag from the top balcony of a Milan opera house during a Puccini opening night. Their preferred podiums were both the traditional Italian theater stage and the public squares and streets of major cities, as is shown in this volume by Patricia Gaborik's attempt to map Futurism. The futurists knew that in the modern time, the forum belongs to whoever is forceful and inventive enough to take it.

Precursors

As stated before, in this book that forum consists of three parts, preceded by Marjorie Perloff's contrastive reflection on the futurist manifestos. The first one is both commonplace and heresy. Futurism wanted the future to begin now and discarding what went before was central to its tactics. The futurists had no greater enemies than what they called *passeists*, those artists, thinkers, bourgeois and women who were stuck in a romantic and decadent past and who seemed intrinsically unable to explore the possibilities and dynamism of new forms of art, science and politics. Yet, as early critical witnesses like Apollinaire already pointed out (not without nationalist self-interest, by the way) many of the Italian movement's revolutionary techniques were firmly rooted not so much in traditional as in romantic and symbolist sensibilities— those nineteenth-century currents in other words that before the futurists had reveled in forceful yet ambivalent reactions to modernity. As Jeffrey Schnapp reminds us, the romantics developed an all encompassing vision in which *Dichtung* would top all the arts and sciences. The symbolists opened up the field of art and poetry not only to what had generally been considered as bad taste (the low, the vulgar, the abject and morally defective) but in the works of the Belgian poet Emile Verhaeren also to the *machinerie* of the modern industrial world. In "We Abjure Our Symbolist Masters, the Last Lovers of the Moon" (1911) Marinetti would include Verhaeren in a list of a handful of "great precursors,"[2] but the essays in this section of the book show that Marinetti's dealings with especially symbolist culture went much further. For quite some time, futurist poetry not so much broke with symbolist techniques and themes, but extended them into a new era. This is particularly evident in Davide Podavini's treatment of *Poeti Futuristi* (1912), Marinetti's threshold anthology of futurist poetry. The author suggests that we speak of a poetry of transition that connects Italian and French symbolist with futurist poetry. Eleonora Conti confirms, with her analysis of the satirical Provence literary journal *Les Guêpes* (Wasp's Sting), Marinetti's mediating role between Italian and French culture. These fluid lines between tradition and innovation are confounded also in another sense, with the anticipation of the futurist manifesto in Palermo as early as 1905. As Laura Greco shows, in 1905 Sicilian writer Federico De Maria founded *La fronda*, a journal that was already futurist in its intents and outcomes. Although revolutionary, it is not yet transgressive as was the futurist avant-garde. A movement obsessed by the magic of numbers as is shown by Jeffrey Schnapp, and which follows an order of its own against the grain of chronologies; or a movement with such a widespread network that it covered the whole peninsula and put the desire for simultaneity into practice. The "practical" dimension of Futurism penetrated Italy's provinces rather than its metropoles, as Patricia Gaborik shows in her chapter on mapping Futurism across Italy.

Protagonists

A century after its birth Futurism to many still means Marinetti. He was the one who supposedly made it all up, who directed, defended and distributed it, who decided upon its political alliances and, one could argue, took it to its (his) grave. The strength of his personality, his multi-artistic explorations and his extraordinary talent for public relations tend to obscure the basic fact that crucial contributions to both the theory and praxis of Futurism were created by artists like Umberto Boccioni, Carlo Carrà, Luigi Russolo, Giacomo Balla, Gino Severini, Francesco Balilla Pratella, Valentine de Saint-Point, Ardengo Soffici, Giovanni Papini, Bruno Corra, Emilio Settimelli, Antonio Sant'Elia, Fortunato Depero, Enrico Prampolini, Arnaldo Ginna, Remo Chiti, Rosa Rosà, Giovanni Fiorentino, Enif Robert (Enif Angiolini), Futurluce (Elda Norchi), Volt (Vincenzo Fani Ciotti), Francesco Cangiullo, Ivo Pannaggi and Vinicio Paladini—to name only those who in Yale's 2009 *Futurism* anthology are featured as coauthors of manifestos from before the 1922 so-called March on Rome.

The central *Protagonist* section proves that Futurism was much more than Marinetti's idiosyncratic obsession. Many of the other futurists are internationally only known as names, signatories of one or more of the many futurist manifestos. Yet, their theoretical and multi-artistic contributions were vital to the origins and the development of the movement. Paolo Buzzi, for example, is not only the race driver who is made "the driver of the world" in Marinetti's April 1909 "Let's Kill Off the Moonlight," but also a highly inventive writer and artist in his own right. Together with chapters about some lesser known aspects of Marinetti's artistic and political endeavors, essays on Paolo Buzzi's Great War collages, Ardengo Soffici's words-in-freedom, Rosa Rosà's feminist prose, Volt's protofascist SF (sci-fi) experiments, Luciano Folgore's poetic parodies and Fortunato Depero's radiophonic lyrics greatly complement our knowledge about this multifaceted phenomenon that was Futurism.

Numerology is present also in Futurism's obsession with time, both as a theme and a technical writing issue, as is shown by Beatrice Sica with an analysis of the creative writings of Marinetti, Palazzeschi and others. Another key concept is war. Monica Biasiolo shows how the multimedial works by Paolo Buzzi, whose artistic project *Conflagrazione* is composed of *papier collé* and newspaper scraps, connects new artistic languages with political messages on the Italian participation in the Great War. The female question is put on the futurist agenda by women writers Rosa Rosà and Enif Robert, who write novels in which they imagine a transmutation into new, futurist women, staying however within the limits of the futurist programme. Silvia Contarini argues that Marinetti's manual *Come si seducono le donne* (How to Seduce Women) represents a step backwards, an attempt to close off the way towards emancipation within the futurist movement, while female creative power could have been turned into a vital force for the artistic movement. Aspects of conservatorism are also present in projects to revolutionize genre literature. Kyle Hall demonstrates, in his chapter on Vincenzo Ciotti Fani (Volt in art), author of the futurist apocalyptic SF novel *La fine del mondo* (The End of the World), that the futurists did not necessarily identify with revolutionary politics, but rather with some conservative aspects of fascism. And not all protagonists identified without criticism with a future-oriented poetics, and in the end showed more affinities with tradition than with innovation. Experiments of self-reflection are to be found in Ardengo Soffici's poetry collection *BÏf§Zf+18* (pronounce as *bizzeffe*), analyzed by Dirk Vanden Berghe, and the stylistic parodies of different futurists in various poetry collections by Luciano Folgore, studied by Stefano Magni. Innovation is to be found rather in the medium than in the message? Depero's innovative use of the medium of radio to create a universal language—Depero invented the "onomalingua"—is explored by Francesca Bravi, while Federico Luisetti, in his philosophical treatment of Marinetti's radio syntheses, makes a distinction between the technological substance of the medium, the radio, and its creative potential, the "radia," which can be caught in the space of the interval, in the *in-between*, and which transcends the life time of the movement.

Legacies

In terms of canonized authors or artists it produced, the legacy of Futurism at first does not look impressive. Marinetti was not a great novelist, nor an important poet or cook. Carrà and Severini are interesting painters, but not as groundbreaking as Picasso, Kandinsky or Mondrian were. Russolo's *art of noise* ideas proved very fruitful in later years, but compared to the contributions of contemporaries like Stravinsky or Schönberg, his *intonarumori* enjoyed more of a *novelty* success. The futurists introduced startling ideas about photography, film and the theater, but they did not produce artists as seminal as Man Ray, Sergej Eisenstein or Bertolt Brecht. The artists who might have had the greatest potential in their respective fields (Boccioni as a sculptor, Sant'Elia as an architect) died during the First World War. So perhaps the futurists' legacy should be framed differently. Marcel Duchamp is often credited as the father of conceptual art, but on so many levels the futurists could claim that title with equal rights. The central contributions of Futurism to our culture are to be situated in those modern obsessions *par excellence*, the ideas of energy and "cool." Tellingly, their scope—manifestos about literature and art, but also about sexuality, violence, war, politics, fashion, advertising and mathematics—aims at covering just about every aspect of modern life, as if they wanted to ask their audience *Wollt ihr die totale Kunst?*

Which, inevitably, brings up Futurism's dealings with Mussolini and Italian fascism. As Günter Berghaus stressed during the conference debates, we must not forget that Marinetti was also the founder of a fascist political party. But whether this party embraced fascist or rather reactionary ideologies is still a question open for discussion. The question put forward by Berghaus, if the move towards politics is at odds with the movement's creative anarchy, is addressed by Walter Adamson in his reflection on the meaning of the "end" of an avant-garde. Futurism's poetics was marked by an oft-neglected irony, continually putting itself into discussion and transforming itself into a multiuse and multi-formed praxis. This is true for its aesthetics as well as for its functioning as a cultural and political agent. A similar argument is developed by Sascha Bru, who argues that action art is rooted in Futurism and lives on in artistic life experiments by Beuys and the Yes Men collective. From cases like these we understand that Futurism's aesthetic programme is gradually re-integrated in the neo-avant-gardes that sprung up after World War II. In the 1960s the Futurist Manifesto resurfaces in the programmatic and literary writings of the Italian neo-avant-garde Gruppo 63, as Florian Mussgnug illustrates in his chapter, and in the 1970s the so-called "word-image poetry" by artists belonging to the Florence-based Gruppo 70 still echoes, as Teresa Spignoli argues, the futurist words-in-freedom.

This multiple approach calls for a reframing of research on Futurism, both in a historical sense, in order to get hold on its diversified outputs and connotations in time through concrete archival investigation—Günter Berghaus gives the first move in this book with his chapter on the postwar reception of Futurism— and in a meta-historical sense, in order to discover continuities in the aesthetic dynamics of modernity.

In a world obsessed by multimedia tools like the iPad or wireless data repositories such as the Cloud, Futurism has become very much a reality, be it more in the realm of mainstream consumerism than in that of oppositional culture. Technology is not only there to facilitate our lives, it is increasingly supposed to be beautiful. When it comes to aesthetics most people today might prefer their iPhone over the *Victory of Samothrace*. This, one could argue, is the pop triumph of Futurism. Its general cultural and political legacy is much more difficult to assess. Marinetti's wish to be the head and center of Futurism, which made him an easy target for parodies abroad, is obstructed by the very essence of the avant-garde's project, to supply the life sphere with artistic anarchy as an alternative to democracy. Or the other way round: every alternative is inevitably related to Marinetti, which confirms the centrality of the founder for the future of the movement. This book offers arguments for both readings.

Note

1. This book has its starting point in an international conference on *Futurisms: Precursors, Protagonists, Legacies*, organized by Geert Buelens, Harald Hendrix, Monica Jansen, and Wanda Strauven, and hosted at Utrecht University, December 1–3, 2009.

2. Lawrence Rainey, Christine Poggi, and Laura Wittman, eds. *Futurism: An Anthology* (New Haven: Yale University Press, 2009), 95.

CHAPTER TWO

~

The Audacity of Hope

The Foundational Futurist Manifestos

MARJORIE PERLOFF

Every pine woods madly in love with the moon has a futurist road that crosses it from end to end.

—Filippo Tommaso Marinetti, *Le Futurisme*, 1911[1]

We rang for room service and the year 1913 answered: it gave Planet Earth a valiant new race of people, the heroic Futurians.

—Velimir Khlebnikov, "Futurian!"[2]

A hundred years after its inception, Futurism remains a curiously misunderstood movement. When the San Francisco Museum of Modern Art announced its impending futurist festival in the fall of 2009, a number of bloggers wrote in protest, declaring that they were not about to "celebrate" the one hundreth anniversary of a manifesto that disturbingly called for war as "the hygiene of the people" and for the "contempt for woman." In London, James Hall, the *Times Literary Supplement*'s reviewer of the big Futurism exhibition at the Tate Modern, asked peevishly, "Can anything now be salvaged from the futurist movement?" His own answer: "It is badly dented by its indiscriminate addiction to new technologies, and its hatred of anything old ("Museums: cemeteries!"). It is seriously crumpled by its love of war . . . by its active support of Italian imperialism and for fascism." The *Guardian*'s review was titled "Futurism Falls Flat at

Tate Modern"; its author, Adrian Searle, remarking that "None of the key figures in the movement—Giacomo Balla, Luigi Russolo, Boccioni, Carrà, and Severini—were artists of the first rank." As for Malevich [the Tate exhibition had a Russian section], his 1914 Aviator, Searle quipped, "seems inexplicably to be clutching a *ghostly white sturgeon*"—a reference to rural life as well as to Christianity that seems, so the reviewer thinks, to have no place in this futurist composition. In a more generalizing vein, Lawrence Rainey, the editor of a new definitive anthology of futurist writings and art work for Yale University Press (2009) concludes his Introduction with the statement, "Alluring, vulgar, ludicrous, chilling, monstrous, farcical, grim—[Futurism] remains one of the great dead ends of modernism."[3]

How do we reconcile such statements with the astonishing number of anniversary symposia, festivals, and exhibitions commemorating the First Futurist Manifesto and its progeny? RoseLee Goldberg's *Performa 2009*, for example, with its three-weeks worth of events all in New York City, had Futurism as its theme, thus seeming to confirm the claim of the organizers of the Utrecht Futurist Symposium that prompted this volume that "Futurism seems to be the one avant-garde movement that was most successful in enduringly inspiring artists and writers around the world and in thus bridging the gap between theory and praxis."

Dead end of modernism or enduring inspiration? It all depends on whose Futurism we have in mind. For there was not one monolithic Futurism but two: the Russian, long little known in the West because of the language barrier and the difficulty of access to Soviet archives, now understood to be at least as important as the Italian. Secondly, in its Italian manifestation, the term Futurism is generally used to cover the entire period from the publication of Marinetti's 1909 manifesto in *Le Figaro* to the impresario's death in 1944. Never mind that two of the most prominent artists of the movement, the painter-sculptor Boccioni and the architect Sant'Elia, were killed in battle in 1916, that a third, Carlo Carrà, had detached himself from Futurism by the end of World War I, adopting a mode of figurative realism, even as the painters Balla and Depero became predominantly designers, the latter finding work in New York, producing covers for *Vanity Fair* and *Vogue*, as well as designing the 1932 Campari soda bottle that became the company's logo. Never mind that Luigi Russolo, the author of the famed 1913 manifesto "The Art of Noises," whose *intonarumori* were featured at concerts in 1913–1914 and influenced composers from Satie to Cage and Tudor as well as a generation of sound poets, refused in 1922 to join the fascist party and broke with the futurists completely. The one member of the original *cénacle* who continued to preach the gospel of a now reconceived Futurism was Marinetti himself, who tried for the next two decades to align "futurist" principles to fascist realities—a project doomed to failure: it was, for example, impossible to reconcile the key concept of *parole in libertà* with the new authoritarianism. Indeed, after the war, and increasingly in the late 1920s and 1930s, futurist manifestos and writings largely lost their shock value, the poets either reshuffling the now familiar encomia to speed and mechanization, or, as in the case of the talented women poets like Benedetta, returning to the lyric mode Marinetti had attacked so vehemently.

Like most artistic movements, Futurism was, in fact, short-lived. Marinetti himself declared, on the last page of the first manifesto, that his was a young person's sport: "The oldest of us is thirty: so we have at least a decade for finishing our work. When we are forty, other younger and stronger men will probably throw us into the wastebasket like useless manuscripts—we want it to happen!"[4] When he wrote these words, Marinetti had no way of knowing, of course, that, by the end of the decade, his prophecy would have come true, that the original futurist impetus would have largely evaporated. But it is not only a question of history. Think of the Oxford Movement and the PRB (*Pre-Raphaelite Brotherhood*), of Anglo-American Imagism or the German *Die Brücke*, Zurich Dada or French *Lettrisme*, Minimalist Art or Objectivism or Language Poetry. By definition, the *oppositional* stance of a given avant-garde movement cannot last, given that political and cultural change is ongoing, and a subsequent generation coming of age inevitably feels, as did Apollinaire in a remark Gertrude Stein adopted as her epigraph for *The Making of Americans*, "On ne peut pas porter partout avec soi le cadavre de son père."[5] Indeed, the inevitable dissolution of avant-garde movements deserves much more attention than we have given it.

In my 1986 book on the subject, I preferred the term Futurist Moment to Movement, although now I would go further and say that even as *movements*, the Futurisms, both in Italy and in Russia, were the affair primarily of the *avant-guerre*, culminating in the war years and the Communist Revolution of 1917. Retroactively, we may well find the seeds of fascism—or, for that matter, of Stalinism—in the aggressive nationalism and jingoism that paradoxically co-existed with the utopian cosmopolitanism of the futurists. But such retroactive claims are always questionable: suppose, after all, the war had broken out, not in 1914 but a decade later, or suppose Russia had not become involved and the Bolshevik Revolution had been deferred? "Everything we see," as Wittgenstein wrote when he was at the front with the Austrian army, "could always be otherwise."[6]

My focus, then, will be on the foundational years of the Futurisms, specifically on the *language* of the early manifestos within the particular contexts in which they came into being. Here geography is central. Futurism was born, not in the "advanced" capitals of Europe—Paris, London, Berlin—where bourgeois culture was firmly established, but in what were only recently industrialized and still markedly backward nation-states on the periphery. Italy, after all, became a unified nation only in 1861, the same year serfdom was abolished in Russia. The citizens of both nations were regarded by the French and Germans, and especially by the British, as not quite civilized. In 1908, the year Marinetti was drafting the first manifesto, E. M. Forster published *A Room with a View*, a novel about clashing social values among middle-class English tourists in Florence, the native Italians providing no more than a colorful, folkloric backdrop. In chapter 2, for example, the newly arrived heroine, Lucy Honeychurch, is taken for a stroll on the Lungarno by a certain Miss Lavish, a fellow guest at the Pensione Bertolini:

> Miss Lavish darted under the archway of the white bullocks, and she stopped and, she cried:
> "A smell! A true Florentine smell! Every city, let me teach you, has its own smell."
> "Is it a very nice smell?" said Lucy, who had inherited from her mother a distaste for dirt.
> "One doesn't come to Italy for niceness," was the retort; "one comes for life. Buon giorno! Buon giorno!" bowing right and left. "Look at that adorable wine-cart! How the driver stares at us, dear, simple soul!"[7]

Such "kind" condescension to the "simple" Italian worker has its sinister side: witness the treatment of gondoliers, shopkeepers, and hotel personnel in Thomas Mann's 1912 *Death in Venice*. Either way, the stereotype of an inferior, still-primitive Italy was one Marinetti set himself to overturn in the 1909 *Founding and Manifesto of Futurism*.

What Marinetti called *l'arte di far manifesti* was, as Martin Puchner has shown, an aestheticized descendant of Marx and Engels's *Communist Manifesto*, whose opening declaration, "A spectre is haunting Europe, the spectre of Communism," moves rapidly through a series of short, numbered propositions, beginning with the explosive, "The history of all hitherto existing society is the history of class struggle," to prepare the ground for its final exhortation "Workers of the world, unite!" "Throughout its subsequent history," writes Puchner, the manifesto will be defined by this impatience, by the attempt to undo the distinction between speech and action, between words and the revolution."[8] An effective manifesto, Marinetti explained to a painter friend in 1909, depends on the fusion of "violence and precision"— "l'accusation *précise*, l'insulte bien *définie*."[9] inherited from Marx and Engels.

The precise insult, the well-defined accusation: this was the formula that made its debut in the *Fondation et manifeste du futurisme*, published in Paris on the front page of *Le Figaro* on February 20, 1909. The headnote in the left column reads:

> M. Marinetti, the young Italian and French poet, whose remarkable and fiery talent has been made known throughout the Latin countries by his notorious demonstrations and who has a galaxy of enthusiastic disciples, has just founded the school of "Futurism," whose theories surpass in daring all previous and contemporary schools. The *Figaro*, which has already provided a nostrum for a number of these schools . . . today offers its readers the Manifesto of the "Futurists." Is it necessary to say that we assign to the author himself full responsibility for his singularly audacious ideas and his frequently unwarranted extravagance in the face of things that are eminently respectable and happily, everywhere respected? But we thought it interesting to reserve for our readers the first publication of this manifesto, whatever their judgment of it will be.[10]

This bit of mythmaking sets the tone for the brilliant propaganda machine to come. I say mythmaking because the fact is that Marinetti became a public figure as a result of, not prior to, the publication of the first futurist manifesto. Even more ironic, the bilingual Marinetti whose "theories" were ostensibly more "daring" than those of "all previous and contemporary schools," was writing, as late as 1909, decadent love poems in French like *Le dompteur* ("The Vanquisher"), with its apostrophe to *Ta chair, ta chair et sa chaleur nue tout entière* ("Your flesh, your flesh and all its naked warmth").[11] But Marinetti understood that the launch of a new movement was a form of theatre, of performance art, of media manipulation. For an Italian poet to publish a manifesto on the front page of a leading Paris newspaper was already a major coup.[12]

But it didn't happen overnight. The 1909 manifesto, originally called *Elettricismo* or *Dinamismo*—Marinetti evidently hit on the more general title *Futurismo* while making revisions in December 1908—was delayed by an unforeseen event that took place at the turn of 1909. On January 2, two hundred thousand people were killed in an earthquake in Sicily. As Günter Berghaus, tells us:

> Marinetti realized that this was hardly an opportune moment for startling the world with a literary manifesto, so he delayed publication until he could be sure he would get front-page coverage for his incendiary appeal to lay waste to cultural traditions and institutions. Several Italian newspapers published the manifesto in early February 1909 or reported its content. Toward the middle of February, Marinetti traveled to Paris, where in the Grand Hotel, he composed

the introductory paragraphs and submitted the full text to the editors of the prestigious newspaper *Le Figaro*.[13]

The earthquake story is significant because it points to a central paradox that animates the 1909 manifesto as well as its futurist successors. On the one hand, Marinetti's Milan had been rapidly industrialized during the first decade of the century: it was now, as Berghaus reminds us, a city of banks, theatres, department stores, and music halls, in which old buildings were rapidly demolished so that large roads could be cut through the urban center. Streets were illuminated with powerful arc lamps and bore heavy traffic: buses, trams, automobiles, as well as the familiar bicycles were everywhere. But natural disasters like the earthquake were reminders of the precarious foothold the new technology had in the Italian provinces. Then, too, there was as yet no cultural and artistic revolution to match *la città nuova*: Italian poetry, Marinetti's included, continued to observe romantic lyric conventions, while the Italian art world still looked to its glorious classical and Renaissance past, suspicious of the "modernist" art movements making news in France and Germany.

Marinetti met this tension head on by publishing his manifesto in the leading Paris newspaper and, simultaneously, as a pamphlet sent out to a half dozen Italian newspapers that printed it. And, in keeping with Engels' demand for narrative, Marinetti created a framework that would make his "revolutionary" propositions palatable to his audience. Consider the opening:

> We had stayed up all night, my friends and I, under hanging mosque lamps with domes of filigreed brass, domes starred like our spirits, shrinking like them with the prisoned radiance of electric hearts. For hours we had trampled our atavistic ennui into rich oriental rugs, arguing up to the last confines of logic and blackening many reams of paper with our frenzied scribbling.
>
> An immense pride was buoying us up, because we felt ourselves alone at that hour, alone, awake, and on our feet, like proud beacons or forward sentries against an army of hostile stars glaring down at us from their celestial encampments. Alone with stokers feeding the hellish fires of great ships, alone with the black specters who grope in the red-hot bellies of locomotives launched down their crazy courses, alone with drunkards reeling like wounded birds along the city walls.[14]

Could anything be more late-Romantic than that second paragraph with its emphasis on the pride of the isolated protagonist, the metaphors of man as "proud beacon" or "forward sentry against an army of hostile stars, glaring down at us from their celestial encampments"? And what could be more kitschy than the image of those stokers "feeding the hellish fires of great ships," or the images of locomotives, with their "red-hot bellies" and "drunkards reeling like wounded birds along the city walls"?

But the larger picture is complicated by the images of "hanging mosque lamps," "domes of filigreed brass," and "rich oriental rugs" that compose Marinetti's décor. The exotic Eastern trappings (Marinetti grew up in Egypt and is describing his salon as it really was) give a fantastic cast to the imagery of locomotive and motorcar that follows. Indeed, the oriental rug becomes a kind of magic carpet, capable of carrying the group of young futurists into the same realm as those "sleek" planes, "whose propellers chatter in the wind." The radiance of the mosque lamps merges with the "electric hearts" of the new machines even as the "huge double-decker trams" outside are "ablaze with colored lights." Marinetti's is thus no realistic description of "good factory muck"; on the contrary, the modern metropolis becomes a utopian dream-space where the timeless pleasures of the East merge with everything that is forward-looking and revolutionary. Accordingly, even nature appears in a glamorous, artificial light. As the futurists rush out into the dawn, the narrator exclaims: "There's nothing to match the splendor of the sun's red sword, slashing for the first time through our millennial gloom!"[15] The phallic sun-sword quickly blends with the automobile's steering wheel, "a guillotine blade that threatened my stomach." Physical power, in this aggressive fantasy, is all: witness Boccioni's soon to be made sculpture *Unique Forms of Continuity in Space*, with its strange fusion of animal and machine, human and robot.

In the passage that follows, the specter of Death, substituting for the "ideal mistress" of romantic lyric, is "domesticated" in a sequence of animal images that carry the Introduction's longing for dehumanization to its hyperbolic limits. Death "gracefully" "holds out a paw," and "once in a while" makes "velvety caressing eyes at me from every puddle." The poet spins his car around "with a frenzy of a dog trying to bite its tail," the car, overturned in the ditch, is seen as a "big beached shark," charging ahead on its powerful fins. Animal matter fuses with "metallic waste" to create the setting wherein the actual manifesto can be performed:

O maternal ditch, almost full of muddy water! Fair factory drain! I gulped down your nourishing sludge; and I remembered the blessed black breast of my Sudanese nurse. . . . When I came up—torn, filthy, and stinking—from under the capsized car, I felt the white-hot iron of joy deliciously pass through my heart![16]

The narrative frame thus prepares us for the violence, power, energy, and sense of urgency of the manifesto itself. By the time the first proposition is put forward, Marinetti's audience was to have suspended its disbelief, especially since the pronouncements to follow are all uttered by a "We" rather than a more overtly egotistical "I": no longer is the individual in command.[17] Rather, the "we" are presented as representatives of the new masses, the factory workers and stokers, locomotive drivers and mechanics who constitute the new "workers of the world." Never mind that the workers of the world don't live among mosque lamps and oriental rugs and don't drive expensive automobiles or recall their Sudanese nurses, as does our poet. It seems, at least on the surface, that, in James Joyce's words, Here Comes Everybody.

And so we absorb the first two propositions: "1. We intend to sing the love of danger, the habit of energy and fearlessness," and "2. Courage, audacity and revolt will be essential elements of our poetry."[18] Who can quarrel with these prescriptions, designed to help Marinetti's readers move beyond lyric subjectivity and everyday discourse so as to participate in a new and meaningful project? The third proposition calls for the "feverish insomnia" we have just witnessed, together with the "racer's stride, the mortal leap, the punch and the slap." Marinetti's is a call to arms designed to awaken a listless, habit-bound populace from its long sleep. And so, in proprosition no. 4:

> We affirm that the world's magnificence has been enriched by a new beauty; the beauty of speed. A racing car whose hood is adorned with great pipes, like serpents of explosive breath—a roaring car that seems to ride on grapeshot—is more beautiful than the *Victory of Samothrace*.

Speed: half a century before the drug by that name came into use, the apotheosis of speed, never mind *toward what goal*, is celebrated by all the "fast" young men and women young enough to appreciate it.[19] More important: note that the "we" whose voice pronounces no. 4 has subtly become the coterie of right-minded artists who are Marinetti's acolytes. What, after all, does the stoker or engine driver know about the second-century B.C. marble statue at the top of the grand staircase in the Louvre? "*We* want to hymn man at the wheel," Marinetti declares in proposition no. 5, but it is not the man at the wheel who composes poetry or makes paintings. Never mind, as proposition no. 8 states: "Time and space died yesterday. We already live in the absolute, because we have created eternal, omnipresent speed."

The apocalyptic note of these lines—a mix of bombast and shrewdness, has already been calculated to put the audience into a frenzy. It is now the moment to introduce the notorious war clause:

We will glorify war—the world's only hygiene—militarism, patriotism, the destructive gesture of freedom-bringers (*le geste destructeur des anarchistes*), beautiful ideas worth dying for, and scorn for woman.

The Marinetti who wrote these words in 1908 considered himself an anarchist who wanted to rid Italy of the papacy and what was perceived to be the inertia and powerlessness of parliamentary democracy. The "destructive gesture" cited above refers specifically, so Berghaus tells us, to the "spectacular assassinations of Tsar Alexander II (1881) and King Umberto I of Savoy (1900) and the anarchist bomb attacks that shook Paris in 1892–1894"[20]— incidents that fascinated Marinetti when he was a young man studying fervent nationalism: an ardent irredentist, he was determined to bring the heavily Italian provinces "lost" to the Austrian-Hungarian empire—Trieste, Trentino, the Southern Tyrol—back into the fold of a proud Italia. As for the infamous "scorn for woman," with which the passage ends, later Marinetti documents make clear that the reference is to "scorn" for traditional bourgeois marriage arrangements, the conventional relationships between the sexes so beautifully satirized in the manifesto "Down with Tango and *Parsifal*."[21] Indeed, in an interview made shortly after the *Figaro* publication of the manifesto, Marinetti paid homage to the "magnificent elite of intellectual women" in Paris vis-à-vis their less enlightened Italian counterparts.

By 1911, however, Marinetti had come to feel "obliged" to "distinguish" Futurism from anarchism, dismissing the latter as the cowardly alternative to the "violent independence" of war.[22] Today, the drumbeating for Italy's grotesque Libyan War (1911), in which Marinetti served as war correspondent, makes painful reading. At the same time, his prescience about the "new" technology was remarkable. Consider the chapter in *Le Futurisme* called "Electrical War," in which Marinetti promulgates an "aesthetics of speed" that would "abolish the year, the day, and the hour" and "melt together day and night."[23] Here is the poet's vision of a *dielectric* future:

Through a network of metal cables, the double force of the Mediterranean and Adriatic seas climbs to the crest of the Apennines to be concentrated in great cages of iron and crystal, mighty accumulators, enormous nerve centers sited here and there along Italy's mountainous dorsal spine. Penetrating into every muscle, artery, and nerve of the peninsula, the energy of distant winds and the rebellions of the sea have been transformed by man's genius into many millions of kilowatts, spreading everywhere yet needing no wires, their fecundity governed by the control panels, like keyboards, throbbing under the fingers of the engineers. They live in high-tension rooms where 100,000 volts vibrate behind the plate-glass windows. They sit before switchboards, with dials to right and left, keyboards, regulators, and commutators, and everywhere the rich lucidity of polished levers. These men have finally won the joy of living behind walls of iron and glass. They have steel furniture, twenty times lighter and less expensive than ours. . . . They write in books of nickel no thicker than three centimeters, costing no more than eight francs, and still containing one hundred thousand pages.[24]

The Kindle, the cell phone, the word processor, the metal stack chair: all these and more are anticipated in "Electrical War." But what a World War, fought largely, not in the air like the Italian campaign in Tripoli of 1911, but in the trenches of Europe, would be like for those involved: this was clearly beyond Marinetti's imagination in 1909. Rather, his focus in this and related pre-War manifestos is on the need "to destroy the museums, libraries, academies of every kind" (proposition no. 10), as if the destruction of museums and destruction of human lives in war were the same thing. The rationale behind these demands is weak, but the rhetoric is so powerful that the "we" who listen are carried along by the manifesto's own energy and speed. And the crux of the issue comes in the final proposition (no. 11) of the first manifesto, which paves the way for the actual artworks made by Marinetti's fellow futurists, Boccioni and Balla, Carrà and Severini, Sant'Elia, and Russolo:

We will sing of great crowds excited by work, by pleasure, and by riot; we will sing of the multicolored, polyphonic tides of revolution in the modern capitals; we will sing of the vibrant nightly fervor of arsenals and shipyards blazing with violent electric moons; greedy railway stations that devour smoke-plumed serpents; factories hung on clouds by the crooked lines of their smoke; bridges that stride the rivers like giant gymnasts, flashing in the sun with a glitter of knives; adventurous steamers that sniff the horizon; deep-chested locomotives whose wheels paw the tracks like the hooves of enormous steel horses bridled by tubing; and the sleek flight of planes whose propellers chatter in the wind like banners and seem to cheer like an enthusiastic crowd.[25]

The imagery of this visionary passage has been anticipated from the first page of Marinetti's narrative: the radiance of electric hearts looks ahead to the "violent electric moons," the "splendor of the sun's red sword" to the bridges "flashing in the sun with a glitter of knives," and so on. "Violence and precision," in this context, also demand economy. Hyperbole works only when it is accompanied by speed. No wonder, then, that Marinetti's prescriptions were soon realized in specific paintings. Boccioni's *The City Rises*, for example, carries out the Marinettian program in uncanny ways. Here is the modern city seen as violent, colorful, frenzied, electrically charged space, in which vibrating forms dissolve and overlap. The great draft horse on the left surges forward, men are seen straining against it, while shafts of light dissolve solid shapes into fluid, flaming color strokes. At center right, a gigantic steed, whose collar metamorphoses into a blue propeller blade slashing the air, throws space into turmoil, while the factory chimneys and building scaffolds rise at a receding diagonal behind it. Here and in related Boccioni paintings like *The Street Enters the House* of 1911 are the "great crowds excited by work, by pleasure," the "multicolored, polyphonic tides" of agitated life in the modern capitals, the blazing electric lights, smoke, glitter of steel, and above all speed, soon to be abstracted by Balla in paintings like *Swift: Paths of Movement and Dynamic Sequence* and *The Vortices*.[26] And the bridge "flashing in the sun with a glitter of knives" surely inspired the shining knife-like girders of Joseph Stella's *Brooklyn Bridge*.

After the crescendo of its final numbered proposition, the manifesto turns more personal, more comic and burlesque. Questioning the necessity of museums and comparing them to cemeteries, Marinetti now bombards his captive audience with questions. Clowning playfully, he calls up the "gay incendiaries" who will "set fire to the library shelves" and "turn aside the canals to flood the museums." And Marinetti admits that his is a young person's sport: "The oldest of us is thirty: so we have at least a decade for finishing our work. When we are forty, other younger and stronger men will probably throw us in the wastebasket like useless manuscripts—we want it to happen!"[27]

Within the decade, Boccioni and Sant'Elia would be dead, killed in the Great War, and the Futurist *cénacle* of the 1910s would have lost its *raison d'être*. The call for speed and violence, for overturning the world, was to be answered in brutal and deadly ways the artists of the avant-guerre could never have anticipated. But then, as Marinetti declares at the end of his 1909 manifesto, "We don't want to understand." Art, in his view, must move beyond understanding, beyond rationality, to create its own superior mode of being. What makes the first futurist manifesto such a poignant document is thus its place on the cusp of an era it has largely misapprehended. The "great crowds excited by work, by pleasure" turn out to be the masses of soldiers dying in the trenches, and the desired "revolution" paves the way for the fascism of the 1920s.

Yet, a hundred years after the fact, the 1909 manifesto remains appealing in its utopian fervor, its audacity of hope. For Marinetti, as for his fellow futurists, art *matters* in a way all but inconceivable today. One must, the manifesto exhorts us, fight for art, even if the fight is dangerous and arduous. Vortex, as Pound was to put it, is *energy*. The "love of danger," the "habit of energy," the "beauty of speed": these make up a complex that gives the present moment its pungency and charm. And the audience, participating in the moment of declamation along with the poet, has no time to ask questions or draw inferences. The manifesto's dramatic, breathless "speedy" prose, embodying the very qualities it celebrates, becomes an end in itself.

As a rhetorical feat, the first manifesto is thus remarkable. It is lyrical, declamatory, and oracular without being in the least self-revelatory or intimate. Not that Marinetti did not possess an enormous ego, decry ego as he might. But in his manifestos and other writings, questions of individual psychology and personal emotion are consistently subordinated to the discourse's pathetic argument, its appeal to its audience to join his utopian movement, using question, exhortation, repetition, digression, enumeration, tropes, rhetorical figures, and sonic effects to draw the audience into the poet's radius of discourse:

> That one should make an annual pilgrimage, just as one goes to the graveyard on All Souls' Day—that I grant. That once a year one should leave a floral tribute beneath the *Gioconda*, I grant you that. . . . But I don't admit that our sorrows, our fragile courage, our morbid restlessness should be given a daily conducted tour through the museums. Why poison ourselves? Why rot?[28]

Marinetti claimed to have received more than ten thousand letters and articles in response to the publication of his manifesto in *Le Figaro*, and although much of this mail was negative, even angry and jeering, the response tells us a great deal about the power of early manifesto art. Within the year, the futurist painters, sculptors, architects, and musicians had adopted the model. *The Futurist Painting: Technical Manifesto*, composed in a single day by Boccioni and Russolo (although the signatures of Carrà, Balla, and Severini were also affixed to it), was launched in Marinetti's journal *Poesia* on February 11, 1910, and declaimed, a few weeks later, from the stage of the Teatro Chiarella in Turin to an audience of approximately three thousand artists, students, and factory workers. Addressed "TO THE YOUNG ARTISTS OF ITALY," it adopted the violent rhetoric of political manifestos. For example:

> In the eyes of other countries, Italy is still a land of the dead, a vast Pompeii white with sepulchres. But Italy is being reborn. Its political resurgence will be followed by a cultural resurgence. In the land inhabited by the illiterate peasant, schools will be set up; in the land where doing nothing in the sun (*nel paese del dolce far niente*) was the only available profession, millions of machines are already roaring.[29]

The roaring machines are not only a prominent manifesto subject; they also provide the manifesto writers with a new typographical format, a format drawn from the world of advertising posters and newspapers, which were soon to find their way into the literature and art of the period. Here the futurists were especially innovative. The pages of the futurist periodical *Lacerba* quickly became the site of experimentation with fonts, typefaces, nonlinear captions, onomatopoeic spelling, as in **STANTTTUFFI** (pistons) in the text by Carlo Carrà, or as in the pages of Marinetti's "The Music Hall," as printed in the London *Daily Mail* in November 1913. A typical page contains advertising slogans in large bold type ("**FUMEZ FUMEZ MANOLI FUMEZ MANOLI CIGARETTES**"; "**GIOCONDA ACQUA PURGATIVA ITALIANA**," with its lampoon on the *Mona Lisa*); the phonetic representation of screeching ambulance sirens ("**trrrr trrrr** sulla testa **trombeeee-beeebeeette** fiiiiiischi sirene d'autoambulanze + pompe elettriche"), and the burlesque cataloguing of erotic measurements ("donna in Camicia [50 m. + 120 altezza della casa = 170 m.]"). But, most important, the manifesto page substitutes white space or blanks for conventional punctuation so as to indicate an abrupt stop, a change of scene or image. The main effect is thus one of dislocation—of the abrupt "stop"/"go" momentum of heavy traffic.

Slovo Kak Takovóe

In "Electrical War" (1911), Marinetti, referring to the beauty of cannon fire, declares, "Let us applaud this lovely slap in the face of all the stupid cultivators of sepulchral little kitchen gardens."[30] A year later, in Moscow, appeared a modest pamphlet with the title *A Slap in the Face of Public Taste* (*Poschchéchina obshchestvennómu vkúsu*): *In Defense of Free Art, Verse, Prose, Essays*. The book opens with a manifesto by the same name, signed by David Burliuk, Alexander Kruchenykh, Vladimir Mayakovsky, and Velimir Khlebnikov.[31] Clearly prompted by the Italian futurists—Marinetti's first manifesto had been translated into Russian within a few months of its *Figaro* publication and his activities widely reported in Petersburg and Moscow—it contains in embryo the Russian version of futurist aesthetic:

> To the readers of our New First Unexpected.
> *We* alone are the *face* of *our* Time. Through us the horn of time blows in the art of the word.
> The past is too tight. The Academy and Pushkin are less intelligible than hieroglyphics.
> Throw Pushkin, Dostoevsky, Tolstoy, etc., etc. overboard from the Ship of Modernity.
> He who does not forget his *first* love will not recognize his last.

Who, trustingly, would turn his last love toward Balmont's perfumed lechery? Is this the reflection of today's virile soul?

Who, faintheartedly, would fear tearing from warrior Bryusov's black tuxedo the paper armorplate? Or does the dawn of unknown beauties shine from it?

Wash Your hands which have touched the filthy slime of the books written by those countless Leonid Andreyevs.

All those Maxim Gorkys, Kuprins, Bloks, Sologubs, Remizovs, Averchenkos, Chornys, Kuzmins, Bunins, etc. need only a dacha on the river. Such is the reward fate gives tailors.

From the heights of skyscrapers we gaze at their insignificance!

We *order* that the poets' rights be revered:

1. To enlarge the *scope* of the poet's vocabulary with arbitrary and derivative words (Word-novelty).
2. To feel an insurmountable hatred for the language existing before their time.
3. To push with horror off their proud brow the Wreath of cheap fame that you have made from bathhouse switches.
4. To stand on the rock of the word "we" amidst the sea of boos and outrage.

And if *for the time being* the filthy stigmas of Your "Common sense" and "good taste" are still present in our lines, these same lines for the first time already glimmer with the Summer Lightning of the New Coming Beauty of the Self-sufficient (self-centered) Word.

D. BURLIUK, ALEXANDER KRUCHENYKH, V. MAYAKOVSKY, VICTOR KHLEBNIKOV

There are many echoes of Marinetti's manifesto here, beginning with the collective "we": the aggression, bravado, contempt for the bourgeoisie, the claim to "make it new," and contempt for the past, the enumeration of propositions, and the heavy use of imperatives, questions, and infinitive phrases. *Violence and precision*: here again is the familiar formula.

But the difference between the two is profound. To begin with, the manifesto's mode of production is antithetical. Whereas Marinetti's manifesto went through many printings in many languages and did reach, at least in Italy, a mass audience, A Slap was printed in a limited letterpress edition of six hundred copies, its brownish cover (described by viewers as being the color of a fainted louse),[32] made of burlap and its gray and brown pages from wrapping paper. It was designed, not for the general public, but for the *literati* and artists of Moscow and Petersburg, who would appreciate its hand-made, one of a kind look. As such, despite its nod to technology in the declaration that "From the heights of the skyscrapers we gaze. . . ."—a bit of posturing since there were as yet no real skyscrapers in Moscow—the Russian futurist manifesto focuses on art rather than politics or culture. What is rejected, at least here, is not a way of life, but primarily Russian poetry from Pushkin to the present, the emphasis falling on twentieth-century Russian poets from the now forgotten Konstantin Balmont, to the symbolists Valerii Briusov and Alexandr Blok, to such realists as Leonid Andreev, Maxim Gorkii, and the satirist Sasha Chernyi.[33] For the Russian futurists, much more specifically than to their Italian counterparts, the anticipated revolution was to be a revolution of the arts, the great irony being that it was in Russia, not Italy, where the political revolution occurred.

But it is not just a matter of smaller scale. A *Slap in the Face of Public Taste* pictures poetry in quasi-mystical terms: "through us the horn of time blows in the art of the word." The horn of time meant nothing to the aggressively secular Marinetti, who had declared in the 1909 manifesto that "Time and space died yesterday"(no. 8) and announced in his "dielectric" manifesto that "We will soon arrive at the abolition of the year, the day, and the hour."[34] Indeed, the Russian futurists repeatedly refer to eternity, and the past they reject is not the past as such—only the immediate past of the nineteenth century and the scorned art culture of the present. One is reminded of Duchamp, who denounced the retinal art of Courbet and the impressionists but had a passion for Leonardo's *Notebooks*. Indeed, the issue, for Burliuk and his compatriots was less *speed* than *direction*: "He who does not forget his *first* love will not recognize his last." And that "last" was the specific call to forge a new *language*—the language of the self-sufficient word (*slovo kak takovóe*). Not iconic words-in-freedom spatially arranged on the page, but the word invented, charged with meaning, traced to its etymological roots.

The young Roman Jakobson—he was a sixteen-year old student in 1912 when the pamphlet appeared—declared that A *Slap in the Face of Public Taste* was "one of my very strongest artistic experiences." The poems of Khlebnikov, for example—A *Slap* included "Snake Trail" and "I and E"—"made a simply staggering impression on me."[35] Mayakovsky's "Night" and "Morning," David Burliuk's essay "Kubizm," where the formalist terms *sdvig* ("shift, dislocation") and *faktura* ("texture") are first introduced, and Khlebnikov's "A Sample of Neologisms," with its astonishingly fanciful etymological analysis of linguistic relationships—all these enchant the poet-critic. His disapproval is reserved for Kandinsky, four of whose little impressionistic sketches, later published in Germany as part of *Klänge*, were included in A *Slap*:

I didn't like Kandinsky at all; as a matter of fact, he later protested against having been included, declaring that while he was in favor of innovation, he was against scandals. I was already acquainted with his book *On the Spiritual in Art,* which seemed to be too closely linked to German art of the recent past and its foggy, abstract slogans. I was terribly proud of the manifesto *A Slap in the Face of Public Taste* itself.[36]

Nationalism, we see here, was as integral to Russian futurism as it was to its Italian counterpart—a nationalism similarly bellicose. Marinetti, visiting Moscow and Petersburg in January 1914, was dismissed by most of the Moscow and Petersburg poets and artists as a bombastic windbag, who tried to impose his false "Western" values on the Russian art scene.[37] But on the issue of Germany and impending war, there was agreement:

> The atmosphere in the Alpine Rose [café] was very friendly. When we were getting ready to leave there was a parting toast, and someone asked: "Will you come to visit us again soon?" Marinetti answered, "No, there will be a great war," and said that "we will be together with you against the Germans." I recall how [Natalia] Goncharova, quite strikingly, raised her glass and said: "To our meeting in Berlin!"[38]

That meeting, of course, never took place. Goncharova, one of the most brilliant of the futurist artists—and a great woman artist of the century—had declared in a 1913 catalogue preface, "I shake the dust from my feet and leave the West, considering its vulgarizing significance trivial and insignificant—my path is toward the source of all arts, the East. The art of my country is incomparably more profound and important than anything I know in the West."[39] But as a member of an ancient aristocratic family, Goncharova could not survive in post-revolutionary Russia. By 1918, she and her partner Larionov went into exile, first in Geneva, where Goncharova made designs for the Diaghilev ballet, and then to Paris where she remained the rest of her life. Whereas Marinetti's trajectory was from center (Paris) to periphery as he increasingly took up what he felt to be the great Italian cause, Goncharova's was from periphery to a center she had already rejected. The agon of Futurism was played out in this way.

Most of the Russian futurists, far from being aristocrats, came from peasant backgrounds in the distant provinces of the Russian empire. Kruchenykh and Malevich were born in the Ukraine, the former to a peasant, the latter to a foreman of a sugar factory in Kiev. In his memoir, Malevich recounts that he had never encountered an artist, until, in his twelfth year, three painters were brought from Petersburg to paint frescoes in the local church.[40] Mayakovsky was the son of a forest-ranger in Georgia, and Khlebnikov was born into the family of the Russian administrator of the Kalmyk nomads,

Mongolian Buddhists who inhabited the grassy steppes on the west bank of the Caspian Sea, some 1200 miles from Moscow. From these distant multi-ethnic locations, the poets converged on the rapidly industrializing cities of Moscow and Petersburg, attending art school or university and soon forming the vibrant cenacles of HylEa, Cubo-Futurism, and Suprematism. It was a moment of cataclysmic change. In *My Futurist Years*, Jakobson describes the impassioned all-night debates taking place among these rival groups—debates more violent and noisy than the *serate futuriste* of the Italians.

The great Russian manifesto of the period, one that marks the coming to an end, not the beginning of Futurism, is, to my mind, Malevich's *From Cubism and Futurism to Suprematism: the New Painterly Realism* (1915). On its first page we read:

> I have transformed myself *in the zero of form* and have fished myself out of the *rubbishy slough of academic art.*
> I have destroyed the ring of the horizon and got out of the circle of objects. . . .
> This accursed ring, by continually revealing novelty after novelty, leads the artist away from the *aim of destruction.*[41]

These cryptic sentences are at least as grandiose, outrageous, and apocalyptic as Marinetti's, although the artist's "I" replaces "we," and pronouncement replaces exhortation. Throughout the fifteen-page manifesto, the academy is, as for the Italian futurists, the central target of scorn: "And I say," the painter announces with Nietzschean fervor, "*That no torture chambers of the academies will withstand the days to come*" (120).[42] Indeed, Malevich's counterpart of Marinetti's despised Victory of Samothrace is the Venus de Milo, a statue dismissed as "a graphic example of decline. It is not a real woman, but a parody." Even Michelangelo's David is "a deformation: / His head and torso are modeled, as it were, from two incongruent forms. A fantastic head and a real torso." Naturalism fares no better: "the art of naturalism is the savage's idea, the aspiration to transmit what is seen, but not to create a new form."[43]

To counter academicism and the art of the past, Malevich once again invokes "the beauty of speed"[44] and the new technology:

> Can a man who always goes about in a cabriolet really understand the experiences and impressions of one who travels in an express or flies through the air?
> The academy is a moldy vault in which art is being flagellated.
> Gigantic wars, great inventions, conquest of the air, speed of travel, telephones, telegraphs, dreadnoughts are the realm of electricity.
> But our young artists paint Neros and half-naked Roman warriors.

Honor to the futurists who forbade the painting of female hams, the painting of portraits and guitars in the moonlight.[45]

If the call for "gigantic wars" and "speed of travel" recalls Marinetti—and World War I was already underway when Malevich wrote this passage coupling the conquest of the air with "gigantic wars"—there is a curious difference. The following is the telling passage:

> The new life of iron and the machine, the roar of motorcars, the brilliances of electric lights, the growling of propellers, have awakened the soul, which was suffocating in the catacombs of old reason and has emerged at the intersection of the paths of heaven and earth.
>   If all artists were to see the crossroads of these heavenly paths, if they were to comprehend these monstrous runways and intersections of our bodies with the clouds in the heavens, then they would not paint chrysanthemums.[46]

This passage begins as a near-echo of Marinetti's first Manifesto, with its celebration of roaring motorcars and brilliant electric lights. But Marinetti took the "growling of propellers" quite literally, whereas Malevich, who drove no motorcar and had never flown in an airplane when he wrote these words, moves rapidly from technology to the crossroads of heavenly paths. Runways? In 1915, Malevich had not yet seen one but he imagined it as the locus of intersection of our bodies with the clouds in the heavens (see his "Eight Red Rectangles").

And there's the rub. Russian Futurism—or Suprematism, as Malevich called its second, abstract phase—subsumed futurist technology, Marinetti's "dielectric" universe of kilowatts, cables, and switchboards—within an image of *flight* as the trajectory into a *zaum* (beyond-sense) realm beyond space, time, and gravity—the realm of the Fourth Dimension. For Marinetti, the airplane was the key icon of *ZANG TUUM TUUUM*, and of *Scraabbraang*—a world of exquisite noise and delirious motion; for Malevich, airplane and aviator were just means to an end—the conquest of outer space. For Marinetti, realism and impressionism had to be discarded, nature being the enemy of the New Technology. Malevich agreed that it was time to stop painting chrysanthemums, but believed that once one had given up putting "pieces of living nature on the hooks of [one's] walls," living forms could once again become a source of inspiration: "I have released all the birds from the eternal cage and flung open the gates to the animals in the zoological garden."[47]

In the same vein, Malevich's friend Khlebnikov, conceptualizing his own "city of the Futurians," created the following blueprint:

1. The idea is this: a container of molded glass, a mobile dwelling-module supplied with a door, with attachment couplings, mounted on wheels, with its inhabitant inside it. It is set on a train (special gauge with racks specially designed to hold such modules) or on a steamship, and inside, without ever leaving it, its inhabitant would travel to his destination. . . . And these units were able to be transported from one building to another. Thus was a great achievement attained: it was no longer the single individual who traveled, but his house on wheels, or more precisely, his booth capable of being attached to a flatrack on a train or to a steamship.

Just as a tree in winter lives in anticipation of leaves or needles, so these framework-buildings, these grillworks full of empty spaces, spread their arms like steel junipers and awaited their glass occupants. . . . Every city in the land, wherever a proprietor may decide to move in his glass cubicle, was required to offer a location in one of these framework-buildings for the mobile-dwelling-module. . . .

The number and row of the proprietor's unit was marked on the glass surface. He himself was able to sit quietly reading as they moved him into place. And in this way we created proprietors: (1) not on the basis of land ownership, but only on the right to a space in a framework-building; (2) not in any one particular city, but generally in any city in the country that takes part in this union for citizen exchange. And all this in order to serve the needs of a mobile population.[48]

Curiously, Khlebnikov's architectural conception is not so different from Sant'Elia's *Città nuova* sketches of 1914, in which large decentered buildings are designed to have airplane hangars on the roof and underground chambers through which trains and motorways could pass rapidly. Tubular external elevator shafts arise from a mysterious place below ground, ready to shoot their passengers up to the top in a complex network of levels and bridges, ramps and tunnels, made of metal filigree and solid concrete, the whole structure seemingly floating in the air in continuous circulation.[49]

In their utopian vision of an architecture designed to serve nothing so much as mobility, both vertical and horizontal, Sant'Elia and Khlebnikov were surely prophetic. But however appealing Khlebnikov's sketch above, the question he seems to have avoided is the economic one: who would have a right to a space in a given framework-building? Suppose X preferred Y's glass module to his own, or Z didn't want to move on to the next location? Or suppose someone wanted to be the possessor of two modules?

Khlebnikov conceived his "city of the Futurians" three years after the Revolution, a revolution in which he essentially believed, although the civil war that followed left him a victim of starvation. He died of gangrene poisoning two years later at the age of thirty-seven—the same age at which Boccioni died in the Great War. A century later, the futurist vision, especially in its remarkable Russian incarnation, remains, despite the events that overtook it, a dazzling tribute to the audacity of the human imagination. "Every city," wrote Khlebnikov, "had such a half-occupied iron framework waiting for glass occupants."[50] Yes, we see them everywhere we go.

Notes

1. Filippo Tommaso Marinetti, "We Abjure our Symbolist Masters, the Last Lovers of the Moon," *Le Futurisme* (1911), in Lawrence Rainey, Christine Poggi, Laura Whitman, eds., *Futurism: An Anthology* (New Haven: Yale University Press, 2009), 94. Subsequently cited as Rainey, *Anthology*.

2. Velimir Khlebnikov, "! Futurian," in Velimir Khlebnikov, *Collected Works*, Vol. 1, *Letters and Theoretical Writings*, trans. Paul Schmidt, ed. Charlotte Douglas (Cambridge: Harvard University Press, 1987), 260. Subsequently cited as Khlebnikov, *Collected Works*.

3. James Hall, "A Hundred Years at the Wheel (Futurism and its Lingering Afterburn)," *Times Literary Supplement*, July 31, 2009, 17; Adrian Searle, "Art Review: Futurism Falls Flat at Tate Modern," *The Guardian*, June 16, 2009; Rainey, *Anthology*, 47.

4. Filippo Tommaso Marinetti, *Let's Murder the Moonshine*, in Idem, *The Selected Writings of F.T. Marinetti*, ed. Robert Willard Flint (1971; Los Angeles: Sun & Moon Press, 1991), 51. All citations from the 1909 manifesto are taken from this edition (cited as Marinetti, *Selected Writings*). Flint's translation of this manifesto remains the best available. Berghaus's 2006 edition (cf. note 13) contains many more of Marinetti's writings than Flint's, and its scholarly apparatus is excellent, but the translations themselves, by Doug Thompson, are sometimes clumsy. For example, the opening line, "Nous avions veillé toute la nuit, mes amis et moi" is rendered by Thompson as "My friends and I had stayed up all night," which undercuts the anticipation of the appositional phrase. Rainey's translation in *Futurism: An Anthology* is similarly less idiomatic than Flint's. For the French version and its evolution, see Jean-Pierre A. de Villers, *Le Premier manifeste du futurisme, édition critique avec, en-fac-similé le manuscrit original de F.T. Marinetti* (Ottawa: Éditions de l'Université d'Ottawa, 1986), 110–13.

5. Guillaume Apollinaire, *Oeuvres en prose complètes* (Paris: Gallimard, 1993), 2: 6.

6. Ludwig Wittgenstein, *Tractatus Logico-Philosophicus*, no. 5.634.

7. E. M. Forster, *A Room with a View* (1908; New York: New Directions, 1922), 33.

8. Martin Puchner, *Poetry of the Revolution: Marx, Manifestos, and the Avant-Gardes* (Princeton: Princeton University Press, 2006), 20–22.

9. Filippo Tommaso Marinetti, letter to Gino Severini, September 1913, reproduced in *Archivi del futurismo*, ed. Maria Drudi Gambillo and Teresa Fiori, 2 vols. (Rome: De Luca, 1958–62), 1: 294–95; Marinetti to Henri Maassen, in Giovanni Lista, *Futurisme: Manifestes, documents, proclamations* (Lausanne: L'Age d'Homme, 1973), 18–19.

10. See Bonner Mitchell, ed., *Les Manifestes littéraires de la Belle Époque 1886–1914: Anthologie critique* (Paris: Editions Seghers, 1966), 103, my translation.

11. Giovanni Lista, ed., *Marinetti et le futurisme: Études, documents, iconographie, Cahiers des Avant-gardes* (Lausanne: L'Age d'Homme, 1977), 32–33. I discuss these early poems in *The Futurist Moment: Avant-Garde, Avant-Guerre, and the Language of Rupture* (1986; Chicago: University of Chicago Press, 2003), 83–84.

12. The coup in question at least partly depended on Marinetti's own personal wealth and contacts in Alexandria and Paris: see Rainey, *Anthology*, 5–6.

13. Günter Berghaus, "The Foundation of Futurism (1909)," in Filippo Tommaso Marinetti, *Critical Writings*. Edited by Günter Berghaus. New York: Farrar, Straus and Giroux, 2006, 9.

14. Marinetti, *Selected Writings*, 47.

15. Marinetti, *Selected Writings*, 48.

16. Marinetti, *Selected Writings*, 49.

17. According to De Villers, *Le Premier manifeste du futurisme*, 27, Marinetti originally opened the manifesto with the words, "J'avais veillé." The change to "Nous" ("We") is crucial, distinguishing Marinetti's futurist manifesto from the personal statement on the one hand, and the third-person discourse of the *Communist Manifesto* on the other.

18. Marinetti, *Selected Writings*, 49.

19. On *speed* as ruling myth of the period, see Jeffrey T. Schnapp, ed., *Speed Limits* (New York: Skira: The Wolfsonian, 2009). Schnapp's introduction provides excellent background on the cult of speed.

20. Berghaus in Marinetti, *Critical Writings*, 421.

21. For a discussion of *Down with Tango*, see my *Futurist Moment*, 107–9.

22. See "War, the Only Hygiene of the World," *Le Futurisme* (Paris, 1911), in Rainey, *Anthology*, 84–85. The book, originally published in French, was reissued in an expanded, more nationalist and militant collection in Italy in 1915: see Rainey, *Anthology*, 529.

23. "Electrical War" was also published in *Le Futurisme* (Paris, 1911); the book was reissued as a more militant and nationalist book in Italy in 1915: see Rainey, *Anthology*, 529–30. For the essay itself, 98–104.

24. Rainey, *Anthology*, 101–2.

25. Marinetti, *Selected Writings*, 50.

26. In a review-essay for *Artforum* (October 2009, 107–10) of various futurist exhibitions held in Italy in 2009, Maria Gough comments on the importance of the "incomparable Balla": "Thinking about Futurism in terms of its nascent abstraction, rather than its emphasis on the iconography of modernity—all those speeding automobiles and electric lights—defamiliarizes our object of study, affording it new plenitude and breadth."

27. Marinetti, *Selected Writings*, 51.

28. Marinetti, *Selected Writings*, 42.

29. Umbro Apollonio, ed., *Futurist Manifestos* (New York: Viking, 1973), 24–25.

30. Rainey, *Anthology*, 100.

31. The signatories of *A Slap* were members of a proto-futurist group called Hylaeia (in honor of the old Greek name of the Kherson province where Burliuk was vacationing in 1910). Later they took on the name "cubo-futurists," and then *budteliane*, a neologism coined by Khlebnikov, usually translated as "Futurians" but, more accurately, Harsha Ram notes, as "will-be-ists." See Harsha Ram, "Futurist Geographies: Uneven Modernities and the Struggle for Artistic Autonomy: Paris, Italy, Russia, 1909–1914," unpublished lecture, Yale University Futurism Symposium, 2009, forthcoming in *Global Modernities* (Oxford: Oxford University Press, 2012). For the manifesto itself, see Anna Lawton, ed., *Russian Futurism through its Manifestos, 1912–1928*, trans. Anna Lawton and Herbert Eagle (Ithaca, NY: Cornell University Press, 1988). Khlebnikov's first name was Victor; he changed it to Velimir when he moved to Petersburg in 1913.

32. Vladimir Markov, *Russian Futurism: A History* (Berkeley: University of California Press, 1968), 45.

33. See the Notes in Lawton, *Manifestos*, 306–7 for the identification of these poets.

34. Rainey, *Anthology*, 99.

35. Roman Jakobson, *My Futurist Years*, ed. Bengt Jangfeldt; trans. Stephen Rudy (New York: Marsilio, 1992), 13.

36. Jakobson, *My Futurist Years*, 13.

37. The story of Marinetti's visit to Russia in 1914 has been told many times; see, for example, Markov, *Russian Futurism*, 147–63. Khlebnikov was especially hostile to Marinetti, refusing to have anything to do with him and calling those Russian artists who did, "traitors."

38. Jakobson, *My Futurist Years*, 22.

39. Natalya Goncharova, "Preface to Catalogue of One-Man Exhibition, 1913," in John Bowlt, ed., *Russian Art of the Avant-Garde, Theory and Criticism 1902–1934* (New York: Viking, 1976), 57–58.

40. Kazimir Malevich, "Chapitres de l'Autobiographie de l'Artiste," in *Malévitch, 1878–1978, Actes du colloque international tenu au Centre Pompidou*, ed. Jean-Claude Marcadé (Paris: L'Age d'Homme, 1978), 157–59. For an English translation, see Kazimir Malevich and Alan Upchurch, "Chapters from the Autobiography of an Artist," *October* 34 (no. 102, Autumn 1985), 25–44.

41. Bowlt, *Russian Art*, 118.

42. Malevich, "Chapitres," 120.

43. Malevich, "Chapitres," 121.

44. Malevich, "Chapitres," 124.

45. Malevich, "Chapitres," 125.

46. Malevich, "Chapitres," 126.

47. Malevich, "Chapitres," 135.

48. Khlebnikov, "Ourselves and Our Buildings. Creators of Streetstreads. Proclamor" (1920), *Collected Works*, 350–51.

49. I discuss Sant'Elia's drawings more fully in the Introduction to the 2003 edition of *The Futurist Moment*, 19–21.

50. Khlebnikov, "Ourselves and Our Buildings," 351.

PART I

PRECURSORS

CHAPTER THREE

~

The Anthology *Poeti futuristi*

Poetry of Transition

DAVIDE PODAVINI

In 1912 the Anthology *Poeti futuristi* (Futurist Poets) was published for the Futurist Editions of *Poesia* in Milan.[1] A collection of ninety-three lyrical poems by thirteen authors, it opens with a plea by Marinetti to the Italian youth, followed by a description of the futurist framework and of the outcomes of futurist painting, and then by a study by Paolo Buzzi on the free verse. The thirteen authors are featured in alphabetical order, each of them with a different number of poems.[2] Among them are important Italian poets such as Govoni, Buzzi and Palazzeschi, as well as mere activists of the futurist movement like Armando Mazza, who had no real talent or poetic expertise. Nevertheless, in order to better understand this collection, it should be read as a whole and none of the authors should be considered individually. The thirteen poets were brought together neither casually nor to give birth to a diachronic sequence, but to illustrate futurism and its principles. Marinetti himself, the conceiver of the anthology, welcomed an organic and coherent reading of this work.

François Livi pointed out that in this collection of futurist poetry there are three thematic areas, which are contiguous but not really homogeneous among each other: an "intimate wing," with minimal and introspective themes, typical of crepuscularism; a vast "sober area," characterized by decadent themes; and an "avant-garde and experimentation area," capable of asserting a kind of poetry which is programmatically modern, thanks to its original and independent subjects and techniques. Therefore, according to Livi, the adjective *liberty*, typically ambiguous, may define all three of these areas, as there is no clear predominance of one above the others.[3] This chapter wants to consider how this "liberty" anthology fits into the futurist movement and how accurately it follows its literary rules. It is essential to keep in mind that Futurism, as an avant-garde movement clearly identified, suggested to all its members a radically innovative *corpus* of rules and *criteria*.

The publication of the anthology was preceded that same year by the *Manifesto tecnico della letteratura futurista* (Technical Manifesto of Futurist Literature) which appeared as a leaflet on May 11, 1912. It was the first manifesto, unlike previous series of proclamations, to dictate instructions and technical devices about futurist poetry. It seems that Marinetti wanted the appearance of the *Manifesto* to coincide with the publication of the anthology. His aim was to state the stylistic rules of the movement first, and then to supply a coherent and consistent example with the anthology. Strikingly, his principles were disregarded by almost all of the poets listed in the anthology and, paradoxically, also by the author himself. For instance, the third passage of the *Manifesto* states that "one must abolish the adjective, to allow the naked noun to preserve its original color." Yet the anthology is full of adjectives, which are often redundant. A clear example may be found in the five following verses by Mario Betuda:[4] "forza i tuoi remi *grondanti* / sull'acque *verdastre* e *pesanti* / e rema, rema a portarmi / nel *vasto* paese *divino* / del *mio dolce* nemico ed amico" ("force your *dripping* oars/ on *greenish heavy* waters / and row, row to take me / in the *wide divine* country / of my *sweet* enemy and friend"). This is very far from Marinetti's indications, who would not have agreed with the definition of the water as *heavy*, or of the enemy as *sweet*, in order to avoid, as Mengaldo defined it, the "psychic relation" between the subject and the object.[5]

Auro D'Alba's *Lirica comune* (Mutual Lyric Poetry) is another example where this "psychic relation" creates connections between the noun and the adjective, connections which are at once profound, qualifying and essential to understand the meaning of the lyrical poem: the adjective is often at the end of the verse and it rhymes with another adjective, and this to underline the semantic content.

> Stavano nel palazzo del sogno
> sin dai secoli *primitivi*,
> custodi di passi *furtivi*,
> di madrigali *corretti*,
> di *lucidi* corsaletti; . . .[6]

An additional strict forbiddance concerns the adverb. In the fourth passage of the *Manifesto*, it is defined as "an old belt buckle that holds two words together," and once again violations of the rule may be found. On the one hand the adverbs are not really recurring, but on the other hand the author himself makes occasional use of some conventional expressions, peculiar trait of decadent-symbolists (like *lugubremente*—bleakly).

The last explicit forbiddance is about punctuation. In the sixth passage, Marinetti states: "abolish even the punctuation. . . . To accentuate certain movements and indicate their directions, mathematical signs:+x:=>< and musical symbols will be used." The way of using punctuation changes with the author, yet punctuation marks are never completely absent and there are no traces of mathematical or musical symbols. Occasionally, there are long sentences without marks at all and others with a large number of them, so as to liven up the rhythm of the verse, like in Paolo Buzzi's verses:

> giungono lettere pallide cerulee! Sigillano,
> nelle linee flebili, il Mistero: sigillano,
> croste di cere d'oro e di sangue, l'anime di carta.[7]

After the analysis of the forbiddances listed in the *Manifesto tecnico*, the positive proposals should be considered, since they seem to have been better accepted by the poets of the anthology.

"Every noun should have its double" states the fifth rule of the *Manifesto* "that is, the noun should be followed, with no conjunction, by the noun to which it is related by analogy." This principle is part of the general theory of futurist analogy and it was well acknowledged, though not frequently used, by several poets of the anthology. For instance, *uomini ritmi* (men rythms) by Buzzi, *barca bicchiere* (boat glass) by Betuda and *treni-serpenti* (trains-snakes) by Marinetti. In the second passage, the *Manifesto* urges the use of the infinitive tense: "alone, the infinitive can provide a sense of the continuity of life and the elasticity of the intuition that perceives it." As usual, there are examples in the texts, but not many. One of them comes from Manzella-Frontini, who lists a series of infinitives in *Convalescenza* (Convalescence) "Only this way *to live*! / and *to see* men and things / as from a far-off mountainous shore, / *to move, to act, to grow* confused" ("Solo così *vivere*! / E *vedere* gli uomini e le cose / come su da un lontano montuoso lido, *muoversi, agire, confondersi, . . .*")[8] In the above verses, D'Annunzio's influence is evident and the next passage, taken from his work *Maia*, exemplifies the use of independent infinitives. As Mengaldo says, they appear as "optative and descriptive, linked in climax;" nevertheless "several infinitives depend on an initial finite verb form, but they stray from it with an ambiguous structure and become independent and implicitly descriptive."[9] After having clarified that the model was not a proper novelty, it is necessary to note that this case is not a regular occurrence throughout the anthology, mainly due to the fact that an additional rule of the *Manifesto* was not taken into account, the one which advises against the use of the first person in poetry. Its application turned far away from Marinetti's original idea (to be discussed later on). In the Italian language, the first person, as with every personal pronoun, implies its verb concordance.

As mentioned before, central to the *Manifesto* is the theory of the futurist analogy, the seventh rule stated by Marinetti. It declaims the necessity of "a more extensive chain of analogies. . . . An orchestral style at once polychromatic, polyphonic, and polymorphous can embrace the life of matter only by means of the most extensive analogies." This device is largely evident with all poets. In the following text, a passage from *Antenne* (Antennae) by Luciano Folgore, the analogical method involves the verb forms and becomes the semantic and structural base of verse construction:

> The pulleys creak,
> the diver anchors come up from the wires of the sea,
> the keels sway,
> and weave the voices of the command,
> a voiced web of shouts,
> a sail of huge words.[10]

Because of its total structural freedom, the futurist analogy is the best answer to two other devices declaimed by Marinetti, the free verse and the destruction of syntax, which are the subject of the first rule of the *Manifesto*. The free verse recurs steadily in all poems by means of different ways and styles, but there is no trace in the anthology of the destruction of syntax and its consequent concept of words-in-freedom. This will only occur in the "poema parolibero" (free-word poem) *Zang Tumb Tumb* written by Marinetti in 1914 and in the "tavole parolibere" (free-word tables) written by Buzzi for *L'ellisse e la spirale* (Ellipse and Spiral) in 1915.

Anyone who takes a bird's eye view of the anthology may note the avant-garde style based on the analogy, which was adopted by all poets, both in the use of the double nouns and of long analogical chains (often in the form of a nominal catalogue). Furthermore, there is a widespread and oblique renewal of some peculiar futurist themes, like speed and technological innovations of the beginning of the twentieth century. There are additional themes in the anthology. For instance, the futuristic "tendenza rurale-arcaica" (archaic, rural trend)[11] is a thread running through the entire work. There is however also a very large number of crepuscular subjects and devices. According to the previously mentioned classification suggested by Livi these themes may be traced back to the intimate wing of the anthology. Among the most important characteristics of crepuscular poetry is the linguistic clash between two vocabularies and the mix of two languages: solemn and prosaic. According to Vittorio Coletti, this feature is like a "posizione passiva" (passive position)[12] taken by crepuscular poets towards language. Because of their anonymous usage of the vocabulary, they seem to have no language as they combine, without thinking, the traditional and the common registers. In this way, they express a negative message: they deny both the traditional sender (the poet) and the traditional vehicle (the high, original, creative word). This mingling is present in the anthology with different modes and functions. A first example can be found in the lyrical poem *Notte* (Night) by Govoni. The passage below widely respects crepuscular linguistic devices:

> The lamps come up, wavering, at the corners of the streets,
> yellow blacklegs;
> they shine into a tabernacle
> on a plaster Holy Mother
> with Her flowers of coloured paper
> in a tomato-like can;
> at a window without stained glass
> a red carnation
> in a white chamber-pot.[13]

Also in the following verses, *Al porto di Amburgo* (In Hamburg's Harbor) by Paolo Buzzi, there is a quite evident dissonant lexical variety, where traditional and technical terms—referring to business and trade—are featured at once:

> The water is black and oiled
> just like the grease of a machine: it stammers, pitch paste,
> at the whirling of the steamer propeller.
> The foams exhale sulphur and coal fumes.[14]

This lexical mix does not represent a conscious uncritical attitude towards language nor is it intended to express a negative message, as previously mentioned. More likely, it is an osmotic passage from crepuscularism to futurism. The latter methodically refused traditional language, thus it started to embrace the new model in a superficial way.

It should be remembered that at the beginning of the twentieth century the persistence of traditional language was not surprising at all. Since Marinetti rejected everything that was linked to the past ("passatista"), readers shouldn't expect to find many archaisms and influences of Dante and D'Annunzio in a futurist anthology, yet the number of them is surprising. But also while combining solemn and prosaic in accordance with crepuscularism, the poets of the anthology introduced new futurist elements: technical terms, foreign words related to new technologies, to modern cities, construction sites, ports, etc. A clear example is found in *ciminiera colonna alta dell'opera potente* (smokestack high column of powerful work) by Folgore or in *docks dai muscoli d'acciaio* (iron-muscled docks) by Buzzi. In the latter poem, there is also an explicit reference (even though paradoxical) to the poet-craftsman (*poeta artiere*) who is also the main character of the famous poem *Il poeta* (The Poet), written by Carducci.

Another characteristic common with crepuscularism concerns landscapes. According to Coletti, there is a correspondence between the favorite crepuscular landscapes (parochial and suburban ones, with plenty of churches, bell towers, fountains, hospitals and graveyards) and the vocabulary used to describe them: "among the most common adjectives: *dolce* (sweet), *piccolo* (little), *triste* (sad), *bianco* (white), *buono* (good). The main verbs: *morire* (to die), *vedere* (to see), *piangere* (to cry), *amare* (to love); the leading adverb is *non più* ("no more," "no longer").[15] The source of these themes is often represented by the French and French-Belgian post-symbolist models (Jammes, Rodenbach, and Maeterlinck), already evoked by D'Annunzio. When glancing through the anthology, it is easy to find many of the above mentioned terms, which refer to parochial and suburban landscapes. The reader will often run into rural environments, gravediggers, churches and convents, which all belong to that aforesaid archaic trend. For instance, the poem *Cantico dei reclusi* (Canticle of the Confined Ones) by Buzzi is divided into seven sections entitled: *Dai monasteri* (From Monasteries), *Dai lupanari* (From Brothels), *Dalle caserme* (From Barracks), *Dagli ospedali* (From Hospitals), *Dalle prigioni* (From Prisons), *Dai manicomii* (From Asylums), *Dai cimiteri* (From Graveyards).

Analogies have been previously defined as the main devices in the anthology; they often occur as nominal lists. Also crepuscular poetry is rich in catalogues and their structure may be considered the most direct archetype of analogical catalogues, as in this stanza taken from the prototypical crepuscular poem *Signorina Felicita* (Mrs Felicita) by Gozzano:

> Beautiful, sad, inhabited building!
> Paunchy, outworn, twisted grids!
> Silence! Escape from the dead rooms!

> Smell of shadow!
> Smell of past!
> Smell of deserted abandonment!
> Deceased fairy tales of the transoms![16]

This short passage clearly shows that crepuscular catalogues do not try to define objects in specific ways. There is a constant exchange between man and nature and it seems that everything becomes humanized. Using once again Coletti's words, this phenomenon may be defined as "a kind of continuous anthropomorphism." Gian Luigi Beccaria perceived in this procedure the antechamber of futurist analogism.[17] He noticed that in the catalogues of humanized objects there is a first transition from crepuscular grayness to futurist eccentricity and subversion. Therefore, it can be stated that the "increasingly vast analogies" exalted by Marinetti, a fundamental note of futurist poetry, may find a structural and functional model in those coeval crepuscular catalogues, even if these analogies followed a principle which was original and independent within Futurism.

So far some of the devices transitioning from crepuscular into futurist poetry have been described. In order to better understand this exchange, the nature of the poems of the anthology needs to be explained more specifically. The aim is to point out the symbolist and decadent reminiscences only partially mentioned (they belong to the third thematic area classified by Livi that was already outlined at the beginning). In the end, the style of Corrado Govoni e Aldo Palazzeschi will be shortly analyzed. Because of their personal lives, these two poets best represent the blending of different structures and tunes.

Libero Altomare is the resonant pseudonym assumed by Remo Mannoni. He contributed to the futurist cause with some of his lyrical poems, such as *Canto futurista* (Futurist Chant) and *A un aviatore* (To an Aviator). On the contrary, in some other poems there is a clear reference to the crepuscular style. For instance, in *Le case parlano . . .* (Houses Talk . . .), as noted by Livi, the theme of the animated things is taken from Corazzini and it blends with the strong influence of Maeterlinck:[18]

> We are the closed greenhouses,
> we are the enervating aquariums,
> where anaemic jellyfish
> and rhachitic plants gasp
> while hate and lust
> embellish with a usurer's caution
> the secret walls with
> the cobweb of affection.[19]

This poem owes a debt to Maeterlinck (his collection *Serres chaudes* was published in 1889) and to his typical mysterious style. Moreover, it owes a lot to French-Belgian post-symbolist poetry which was previously mentioned. This kind of poetry molded crepuscular poets and the early works written by Govoni, as is evident throughout the anthology. With regard to the French style, it should be noted that Mario Betuda drew inspiration from symbolist poets, especially from Baudelaire. In the poem *Re Alcool* (King Alcohol), Betuda exalts oblivion and bewilderment caused by drunkenness: a direct parallelism to the poem *Le vin de l'assassin* by Baudelaire.

Within Futurism, Paolo Buzzi is considered one of the most literary, and at the same time, eclectic individuals. Born in Milan, he drew from the most recent trends in the Lombard cultural tradition, mainly the *Scapigliatura*, innovating them. The next short passage is taken from the poem *La donna dalla corazza d'acciaio* (The Woman in the Steel Armour) and it refers to the late style of the *Scapigliatura*:

> Cario closed her in a steel armour to be opened with a secret key.
> He kept the key in a box, in the innermost pocket over the heart.
> She suffered patiently in the summer heat Caliph Torquemada's supplice.
> The armour seemed to be lined with stings, burning against the nudity.[20]

The theme of the liberation from the tyrant is filtered by the love subject and refers to all of the devices of the Risorgimento retrieved by the *Scapigliatura*. In the passage above, one can find two more characteristics that are very typical: the Baroque realism and the taste for a deforming representation. These reflections introduce the presence of some traits of the *Scapigliatura* in the futurist movement. First of all, the poets of the *Scapigliatura* were among the first Italians to feel intolerant of convention regarding contemporary literature and middle-class morality. They also started to feel an impulse for refusal and rebellion which was revealing itself both in art and daily life. Thanks to the poets of the *Scapigliatura*, the conflict between artist and society first appeared in the Italian culture of the nineteenth century, which had already been fundamental for European Romanticism. Several different attitudes resulted from this conflict: rebellion and remonstrance against the middle-class, admiration for a dissipated life aiming at a complete refusal of morals and convention. The subversion of the poets of the *Scapigliatura* contributed to vitalizing the artistic debate, but it was not able to break off the previous themes and traditional language. It was a simple "connection between Romanticism and Decadentism."[21] On the contrary, the Futurist poets were able to get from that subversion an avant-garde potential which could not establish itself in the poetry of the *Scapigliatura*.

Enrico Cardile and Giuseppe Carrieri each presented only a single poem: *Ode alla Violenza* (Ode to Violence) the first, *Vittoria!* (Victory!) the second. The titles reveal the obedience of these two poets to the new themes, even if once again the influence of crepuscular poets and of D'Annunzio, both in style and structure, can be identified.

In some lyrical poems written by Enrico Cavacchioli, the same interest in futurist themes, for example in *Il siluro* (The Torpedo), *Sia maledetta la luna* (May the Moon Be Cursed) and *Fuga in aeroplano* (Escape Aboard an Air-plane) may be found, whereas, in other poems, the influence of the crepus-cular poetry is prevailing. In this regard, it may be noticed that in the poem *Tragedia di burattini* (Puppet Tragedy), there is a clear reference to *Dialogo di marionette* (Marionette Dialogue) written by Corazzini:

> Tied in a single bundle, in abandonment, rests
> in a bed of dust a bunch of puppets:
> used to playing in a childish theatre
> the basic tragedy of my youth.[22]

There are three lyrical poems written by Auro D'Alba and characterized by a deep influence of the *Scapigliatura*; among them *Il piccolo re* (The Little King) is peculiar because of the futurist celebration of electricity. Nevertheless, the subject is integrated in a completely crepuscular and symbolist context, as shown in the *incipit*:

> White electricity of new moon
> over the little parochial church:
> the hyperaemic lamps
> witches' yellow eyes—
> wait for the usual perjuries
> with the habitual calm. . . .
> The old Cinderella
> devotee of Saint Prassede—
> opens the book and watches over
> the monotonous waking.[23]

Once more, the futurist experience of Luciano Folgore follows a syncretic route. According to most critics, he has been the leading and the most talented poetic personality within the movement. He was able to blend the devilish atmospheres of the *Scapigliatura* with the vitalism of D'Annunzio as it is evident in his poem *Maia*. Moreover, Folgore is prone to a narrative trend which is typical of fairy tales and thanks to this style he makes an original use of the analogy. In all his works he is very insistent through burlesque, as demonstrated by the next passage taken from *Incendio nell'opificio* (Fire in the Factory):

> Howitzers of desperation,
> tins full of
> blazing petrol burst,
> screamed in the warehouses
> streams of spirit,
> lava flows sizzling in inflamed fats;
> the bitter
> columns of acids twisted,
> and, giddy lion,
> went up, with claws of burning blazes,
> the devilish coal.[24]

The three poems written by Gesualdo Manzella-Frontini belong to the decadent style. Even if they contain some futurist themes like violence and electricity, the poet seems to be more influenced by German expressionism. In this respect, it should be remembered that *Morgue*, written by Gottfried Benn, was published that same year, 1912, and that there are many other analogies between the collection of the poet from Mansfeld and poems such as *Sala anatomica* (Anatomy Room):

> The anatomy room blazed up
> by the last flames of a violet and crocus eventide.
> The tense torn corpses
> on the tables stained with blood and with clots.
> A spattering-eyed old man
> with a thin chest,
> and on the gluten of the fetid eye inconvenient flies
> Singing merrily.[25]

In the anthology there is only one poem by Armando Mazza, *A Venezia* (In Venice). It is a kind of uninspired translation of the manifesto published in 1910 by Marinetti, Boccioni, Carrà and Russolo, entitled *Contro Venezia passatista* (Against Past-Lover Venice). Mazza himself was quoted in that manifesto, not because of his poetic talent within Futurism, but rather because of his excellent skills as a boxer. Actually, it seems that a speech given by Marinetti at the Fenice theatre in Venice caused rage among the crowd and ended in a fight. According to some authors "Mazza's punches proved to be memorable." Indeed, he did not represent futurist poetry, but was a tough supporter of the general trend. He was among the few disciples who embraced Futurism completely. Consequently, his poem, devoid of any artistic talent, looks like a well-done piece of homework regarding the full rigor of a futurist theme.[26]

The anthology contains several poems written by the two outsiders: Govoni and Palazzeschi. Thanks to the complexity and quality of their works, they represent more than any of the others the overcoming of models in the liberty style that has been described so far. Corrado Govoni, during the time of his support of Futurism (support that will later be disavowed, or rather, rectified)[27] came from a symbolist period, namely through the models of Rodenbach and Maeterlinck, together with the influence of Pascoli and D'Annunzio and the thematic repertoire of crepuscularism. As noted by Gaetano Mariani,[28] Govoni made use of an expressive schematism: a recurrence of the same psychological or descriptive situations, a starting point creating infinite series of images. This procedure is related to the *Poema paradisiaco* (Heavenly Poem) by D'Annunzio (for instance, in the constant effects used to evoke parts of the day). Indeed, this poem also had a leading role for the forming of the crepuscular poets.

Moreover, the main characteristics of Govoni's style are the enumeration and a taste for analogy. Analogies are built with omnivorous nominal lists, full of details and imagination. Such a familiarity with analogies created a solid structural basis for the transition to Futurism. This change in perspective was favored by the differences between his poetry and the crepuscular style: his marked dynamism, color brightness, creations of "kaleidoscopes of appearances" (caleidoscopi di parvenze).[29] Govoni placed his unlimited talent at the disposal of the new taste, intensifying with creativity the analogical associations which were a sign of the modern technicalities.[30] He tried to abandon the previous thematic program (presenting that abundance of convents, parks, etc.), although he did not succeed completely. On the one hand, he strived to embrace futurist themes exalting the modern city, as proved by his poems in the anthology. On the other hand, his poetry was based on a spontaneous modernism with a rural sensitivity and an archaic ethos. His passion for country landscapes, silent and secluded corners, demonstrates the continuity of the crepuscular style. This is clearly evident in the following verses:

> A green ivy hope
> persists on an eave;
> a wisteria lays on the wall
> its lonely jolly grapes.

> In the evening, on the red tiles,
> paired as nuns
> doves go for their barefoot stroll,
> suffused with pallor;
> while on the dormers bookrests
> cats scrape the acrobatic
> music of the stars
> with their epileptic violins.[31]

In contrast, the French-Belgian symbolist influence plays a leading role when Govoni describes the modern city: he dwells on observing the corners of the lanes, the passing of beggars and spotless nuns. He also lingers under the windows of the hospitals. An example is given by the poem *Le capitali* (Capital Cities): Govoni's cities are shocking and inhospitable:

> And no ophthalmic lamps
> lengthen on the streets
> as yellow funerals
> of jaundice,
> but only white and dazzling ones.
> And mild slow rivers go
> under the bridges yoke
> like melt lead rivers
> with their odd abortions,
> with their sad suicides. . . .
> They pass under hospital windows.
> They see red flowers and white nuns
> and miserable sick people
> and wavering lovers on the bank
> and go crying in the sea.[32]

During his experience within the new movement, Govoni did not forget the main characteristics of his previous poetry, but rather tried to intensify them, giving rise to his best futurist performance.

Palazzeschi is a more complex figure. Before coming to Futurism, his poetry, yet partially influenced by crepuscularism, was fairly independent and original. He only assimilated crepuscular themes which were fairytale-like, childish and weird; drawing on themes such as old age, obsessive repetition of gestures, silent and still atmospheres, oneiric states and nonsense. This way, he disassociated from that side of the crepuscular poetry based on an "exhausted diction"[33] Palazzeschi created a totally impersonal world: there is a prevalence of the impersonal verb forms, no tragedy and almost no grammatical subjects. According to Mengaldo, this fact represents a silent but decisive innovation, the most radical Italian response to the old lyrical subjectivism. A similar opinion is given by Sanguineti, who states that the frequent anonymous collective noun *gente* (people) is the keyword of Palazzeschi's anti-subjectivism.[34]

Additional reflections on his "pre-futurist" period include vocabulary and meter. He covertly criticized traditional language and indeed, his lexicon was extremely common and humble. Palazzeschi's meter had a constant rhythm, from his first works leading to his experience within Futurism; trisyllabic foot with ictus on the second syllable, endlessly repeated. Actually, rhythm prevails over meaning, emptying any semantic content. This fact is related to the impressive mimic and theatrical aspects of his poetry. "Theatricality" characterizes Palazzeschi's work mainly in his *Poemi* (Poems) dated 1909, where a large number of dialogues and the transition from a weird and dreaming dimension to a comic and grotesque one may be found.

His lively and temporary support of Futurism, represented by his work *L'incendiario* (The Incendiary) written in 1910, took place without exact programs and precise poetry. Indeed, the manifesto *Il Controdolore* (The Counter-Pain) dated 1914 is clearly retrospective. This kind of support reveals that his avant-garde experience was very personalized and founded on a sort of interruption in culture and a clever "*naiveté*."[35] During his futurist period, Palazzeschi voiced an irreverent young ideology with his typical formal models. Dialogues and conflicting points of view are characterized by an insistent polyphony. He aligned with futurist themes through the anti-middle-class debate and its lively iconoclasm. He partially abolished the trisyllabic pattern in order to take up the free verse. However, he was able to adorn even the free verse with internal rhymes, false rhymes and a fragmented internal rhythm clearly derived from D'Annunzio. Furthermore, because of his particular use of the free verse, he did not linger over key futurist characteristics such as analogy and metaphor. Within the futurist style, he embraced only onomatopoeia and phonetic fragmentation. The most distinctive characteristics of his poetry are taste for grotesque, parody of traditional lyrical subjects, criticism of middle-class society and ideals. For instance, his poem *La fontana malata* (The Sick Fountain) is an obvious parody of *Pioggia nel pineto* (Rain in the Pinewood) by D'Annunzio:

> Silence,
> it doesn't throw
> anything anymore,
> silence,

> no sound is heard,
> no sound
> of any kind . . .
> What if . . .
> What if
> she's dead?
> How horrible!
> Oh, no!
> There she is again,
> she still
> coughs.
> Clof, clop, cloch,
> cloffete
> cloppete,
> clocchete,
> chchch . . . [36]

In addition to the parodic purpose, in this poem some of the characteristics previously described, such as the trisyllabic structure of the rhythm, may be found.

Among Palazzeschi's poems, *L'incendiario* may be defined as the best example of Futurism. Its allegorical figure fuelled the criticism of middle-class society. In the first part of the text, an anonymous and pressing crowd rails at the arsonist in order to make a mockery of him. Suddenly, the poet's voice stands out: he is the only one who praises the pyromaniac and he hushes everybody up:

> You're the Lord
> to whom I address,
> with all devotion
> in my heart,
> the sweetest prayer.
> To you, gentle creature,
> I come breathless, panting,
> I have crossed crags of thorns,
> I have climbed over high walls!
> I will free you![37]

It is no coincidence that later Palazzeschi recanted this poem, which does not appear in the collection *L'incendiario* published in 1913 (even though he kept the title, which is rather odd). Indeed, he could no more tolerate the futurist rhetorical mannerism present in this poem, to the detriment of his usual distorting and grotesque vein. According to Sanguineti,[38] this later re-fusal reflects a disagreement between Palazzeschi and the futurists about the sublime, "the big secret problem of the entire middle-class culture, namely of the whole romantic civilization." Sanguineti reckons that Foscolo was the last poet able to express an authentic sublime, a kind of sublime which was not bound to become a catastrophic literary machine, as it was in the style of Carducci or D'Annunzio. The critic describes Palazzeschi's poetry as a successful attempt to "reverse"; the poet knew that the sublime could become true only through a distorting stylization and a burlesque attitude. In Sanguineti's opinion *L'incendiario* is too straight to bear a reversed reading. On the contrary, futurist principles aimed to replace the traditional sublime with a new one, at the cost of destroying museums, libraries, etc. In the 1909 *Manifesto* they even stated that "a roaring motor car, which seems to run on machine-gun fire, is more beautiful than the Victory of Samothrace." Therefore, two very different views; but it is necessary to take a step forward and to point out that Palazzeschi's subversive style left more than a trace in futurist poetry; for instance, the burlesque invectives previously mentioned with reference to Folgore and Buzzi.

It is not by chance that we have mentioned D'Annunzio several times. Actually, he too played an important role in the poetry of the beginning of the twentieth century and had a remarkable influence over the entire age. Nevertheless, the regular presence of a certain kind of vocabulary in the anthology requires some further clarifications. We have already stressed the debts owed to the poem *Poema paradisiaco*, relevant also for its influence on crepuscular poetry, and we have even emphasized the linguistic heritage left by D'Annunzio, but it cannot be ignored that some terms clearly derived from the poet from Pescara do not depend on a sheer contamination. On the contrary, they reveal a well-considered use. For instance, the past participle *arborato*, described by Mengaldo as a very cultured past participle and clearly influenced by D'Annunzio.[39] In the anthology, it is used by Cavacchioli within an analogical structure.

Compound adjectives, such as *verdegiallo* (yellow-green) or *verdebiondo* (blonde-green), are another fruitful invention of D'Annunzio's. In the anthology, there are some similar adjectives, but more modern and burn-ing; for example, the *bifide lingue azzurroviola* (forked purple-blue tongues) of Libero Altomare. However, there are many more occurrences deriving from D'Annunzio: *lunghesso*, *schisto*, *muglio*, etc. From his work *Maia* dated 1903, Futurism took not only the vocabulary, but also his prepositional analogy, a very wise device. Moreover, in the first book of *Laudi*, written by D'Annunzio, it is easy to perceive a heroic vitalism, similar to the concept of superman which highly influenced certain elated futurist figures. Let's compare this passage taken from *Maia*:

> The Sun woke me up
> radiating my face.
> I saw through the wefts
> of my eyelids the splendour
> of my blood. . . .
> The buckets at dawn in the well
> overflowing with iced water
> with their silvery downpour
> kindled in my naked vigour
> the wholesome shiver
> of the morning cleansing
> covered with dew.[40]

with the poem *Nuotando nel Tevere* (Swimming in the Tiber River) by Altomare:

> Dawn, bowed to the river,
> jokes with the capricious whirls
> of the current,
> it winds with the grace of a snake.
> The steady still trees, of jade;
> the foliages still drip dew; . . .
> Here I am naked, arrogant, sincere;
> The veils of thought are torn for me
> of the thought which was drunk with dreams:
> the water is an opaque glass.[41]

It seems that Altomare, when writing these verses, kept D'Annunzio's work in mind. Indeed, several characteristics reflect D'Annunzio's poetry: certain recurring situations (dawn, awakening, the morning, vigorous nudity, water), the style in phonetics and rhymes and a flexible metrics but with the constant presence of hendecasyllables. There are no traces of free verse.

This essay highlights a number of models that have shaped the anthology *Poeti futuristi*, by means of an overall view of the complete text. Its style involves the main trends of the end of the nineteenth century and of the beginning of the twentieth century. These trends are overlapped and crossed within the words of the various poets. Most often, the devices defined by the *Manifesto tecnico* as avant-garde are derived from models of previous poetry. This fact is related to the most important characteristics of the anthology. The collection exemplifies the job done within the futurist workshop: a progression towards the avant-garde trying to leave the old models behind, yet exploiting them. This anthology does not contain the most significant and well-known outcomes of Futurism (such as the *tavole parolibere*), but there is a clear trace of the subsequent evolution. The texts in the anthology are precious witnesses of the origin of this new way.

Therefore, the anthology may be considered as the "thematization" of this poetry in progress. It is a kind of a poetry of transition. Consequently, according to a dialectic logic, the devices of the avant-garde and past models may be regarded as a whole. The authors of the anthology went their separate ways adopting very different styles: for instance, Palazzeschi evolved by means of a personalized manner, Altomare satirized his own previous works, Govoni disavowed his support of Futurism. They all exploited this early stage in order to achieve something else; actually, the poetry of the collection was considered purely instrumental, yet necessary, and thus abandoned.

Poeti futuristi is a case of poetry in progress, transitory, source of changes and a needed moment of transition. Poetry which was turned on and then abandoned by poets who were looking for evolution, but nevertheless it has its own nature. It sounds like a paradox because of its ambiguity between completeness and incompleteness, between examples of early avant-garde and of subsequent progress. Thus, it was bound to be left an orphan by its authors: prematurely, yet unavoidably.

Notes

1. Filippo Tommaso Marinetti, ed., *Poeti futuristi* (Milan: Edizioni Futuriste di "Poesia," 1912).

2. The authors present in the anthology are: Libero Altomare (fifteen poems); Mario Betuda (five poems); Paolo Buzzi (seventeen poems); Enrico Cardile (one poem); Giuseppe Carrieri (one poem); Enrico Cavacchioli (eleven poems); Auro d'Alba (three poems); Luciano Folgore (nine poems); Corrado Govoni (six poems); Gesualdo Manzella-Frontini (three poems); Filippo Tommaso Marinetti (ten poems); Armando Mazza (one poem); Aldo Palazzeschi (eleven poems).

3. François Livi, *Tra crepuscolarismo e futurismo: Govoni e Palazzeschi* (Milan: IPL, 1980), 68.

4. Marinetti, ed., *Poeti futuristi*, II 81–85; the passages taken from the anthology are indicated with the progressive number in which they appear in the section of the volume dedicated to each author and the indication of the listed verses.

5. Pier Vincenzo Mengaldo, *Storia della lingua italiana. Il Novecento* (Bologna: Il Mulino, 1994), 207.

6. "They stayed in the dream palace, / ever since the primordial ages, / keepers of covert paces, / of correct madrigals, / of shiny corselets." Marinetti, ed., *Poeti futuristi*, II 24–31.

7. "Here come pale cerulean letters! They seal, / in feeble lines, Mistery: they seal, / scabs of golden waxes and of blood, paper souls." Marinetti, ed., *Poeti futuristi*, VII 32–34.

8. Marinetti, ed., *Poeti futuristi*, I 26–33.

9. Pier Vincenzo Mengaldo, "Da d'Annunzio a Montale," in Id., *La tradizione del Novecento* (Milan: Feltrinelli, 1975), 43.

10. "Cigolano le carrucole, risalgono dai cavi del mare / le ancore palombare, / e ondeggian le carene, / e tessono le voci del comando, / un ordito sonoro di gridi, / una vela di gigantesche parole." Marinetti, ed., *Poeti futuristi*, VII 15–33.

11. Clelia Martignoni, "Corrado Govoni," in Cesare Segre and Carlo Ossola, eds., *Antologia della poesia italiana* (Turin: Einaudi/Gallimard, 1999), 788.

12. Vittorio Coletti, *Momenti del linguaggio poetico del Novecento* (Genoa: Il Melangolo, 1978), 53.

13. "Spuntano incerti ai canti delle vie / i fanali, gialli crumiri; / illuminano dentro un tabernacolo / una Madonna di stucco / coi suoi fiori di carta colorata / in un barattolo da pomodoro; / a una finestra senza vetriate un garofano rosso / in un bianco pitale." Marinetti, ed., *Poeti futuristi*, IV 56–64.

14. "L'acqua è negra e unta / come un grasso di macchina: ciangotta, pasta di pece, / al frullar dell'elica batteliera. / Le schiume esalano vapori di solfo e di carbone." Marinetti, ed., *Poeti futuristi*, XV 40–53.

15. Vittorio Coletti, *Storia dell'italiano letterario* (Turin: Einaudi, 1993), 410.

16. "Bell'edificio triste inabitato! / Grate panciute, logore, contorte! / Silenzio! / Fuga dalle stanze morte! / Odore d'ombra! Odore di passato! / Odore d'abbandono desolato! / Fiabe defunte delle sovrapporte!"

17. GianLuigi Beccaria, *Le forme della lontananza* (Milan: Garzanti, 1989).

18. Livi, *Tra crepuscolarismo*, 63.

19. "Siamo le serre chiuse, / siamo gli acquari snervanti, / dove meduse anemiche / e piante rachitiche boccheggiano / mentre l'odio e la lussuria / fregiano con usuraia cautela / le secrete pareti con / la ragnatela dell'affetto." Marinetti, ed., *Poeti futuristi*, XIII 18–25.

20. "Cario la chiuse in una corazza d'acciaio d'aprirsi con secreta chiave. / Egli tenea la chiave in un astuccio, nella più fonda tasca sovra il cuore. / Ella, paziente, pativa ne' solleoni il supplizio del Califfo Torquemada. / Parea, la corazza, foderata d'aculei roventi contro il nudo." Marinetti, ed., *Poeti futuristi*, IX 10–13.

21. Giuseppe Farinelli, *La scapigliatura* (Rome: Carocci, 2003).

22. "Legato in un solo fascio, in abbandono, riposa / in un letto di polvere un mazzo di burattini: / soliti a recitare in un teatro infantile / la tragedia elementare della mia giovinezza." Marinetti, ed., *Poeti futuristi*, II 1–4.

23. "Bianca elettricità di luna nuova / sulla chiesetta parrocchiale: / i fanali iperemici / occhi gialli di streghe— / attendono ai consueti spergiuri / con la calma abituale. . . . / la vecchia cenerentola / devota di Santa Prassede— / apre il libro e sorveglia / la monotona veglia." Marinetti, ed., *Poeti futuristi*, III 1–14.

24. "Scoppiavano, obici della disperazione, / le latte ricolme / di sfolgorante benzina, / urlavano nei magazzini / torrenti di spirito, / lave friggenti di grassi infiammati; / si torcevano le aspre / colonne degli acidi, / e, vertiginoso leone, / saliva, con artigli di ardenti vampate, / il demoniaco carbone." Marinetti, ed., *Poeti futuristi*, IV 43–53.

25. "La sala anatomica avvampata / dalle ultime fiamme di un vespro di viola e di croco. / I tesi cadaveri squarciati / su le tavole chiazzate di sangue e di grumi. / Un vecchio dall'occhio schizzante, / dal torace sottile, / e su la glutine dell'occhio fetente le mosche / importune a cantare liete." Marinetti, ed., *Poeti futuristi*, III 2–19.

26. Livi, *Tra crepuscolarismo*, 67.

27. In 1937, in the article "Revisione della poesia futurista" published in *Meridiano di Roma*, Govoni stated his futurist experience was amusing but incompatible with his real nature.

28. Gaetano Mariani, *Poesia e tecnica nella lirica del Novecento* (Padua: Liviana Editrice, 1958), 25–27.

29. Pier Vincenzo Mengaldo, *Poeti italiani del Novecento*. 5th ed. (Milan: Mondadori, 1994), 6.

30. Clelia Martignoni, "Corrado Govoni," in Segre and Ossola, *Antologia*, 788.

31. "Una verde speranza d'edera / s'ostina su una gronda; / un glicine dispone lungo un muro / la sua solitaria uva gioconda. / Alla sera, sui tegoli rossi, / a due a due come suore / fanno la loro scalza passeggiata / le colombe, soffuse di pallore; / mentre sopra i legii degli abbaini / i gatti scorticano l'acrobatica / musica delle stelle / con i loro epilettici violini." Marinetti, ed., *Poeti futuristi*, I 32–43.

32. "E non oftalmici fanali / s'allungan per le vie / simili a gialli funerali / d'itterizia, / ma soli bianchi a abbacinanti. / E fiumi docili e lenti vanno / sotto il giogo dei ponti / come fiumi di piombo liquefatto / coi loro strani aborti, / coi loro tristi suicidi. . . . / Passano sotto le finestre degli ospedali, / vedono i fiori rossi le suore bianche / e i poveri malati / e gli amanti indecisi sulla riva / e vanno a piangere al mare." Marinetti, ed., *Poeti futuristi*, III 99–107, 115–24, 128–32.

33. Mengaldo, *Poeti italiani del Novecento*, 49.

34. Edoardo Sanguineti, *Tra liberty e crepuscolarismo* (Milan: Mursia, 1977), 92–93.

35. Pier Vincenzo Mengaldo, *La tradizione del Novecento—Quarta serie* (Turin: Bollati Boringhieri, 2000).

36. "Si tace, / non getta / più nulla, / si tace, / non s'ode / romore / di sorta . . . / Che forse . . . / Che forse / sia morta? / Che orrore! / Ah, no! / Rieccola, ancora / tossisce. / Clof, clop, cloch, / cloffete / cloppete, / clocchete, / chchch . . . " Marinetti, ed., *Poeti futuristi*, II 25–42.

37. "Il Signore tu sei, / al quale rivolgo, / con tutta la devozione / del mio cuore, / la più soave orazione. / A te soave creatura, / giungo ansante, affannato, / ò traversato rupi di spine, / ò scavalcato alte mura! / Io ti libererò!" Marinetti, ed., *Poeti futuristi*, V 102–11.

38. Sanguineti, *Tra liberty e crepuscolarismo*, 85.

39. Mengaldo, "D'Annunzio e la lingua poetica del Novecento," in Id., *La tradizione del Novecento*, 196.

40. "Mi destò il Sole / raggiandomi la faccia. / Vidi per le trame / delle mie palpebre il fulgore / del mio sangue. . . . / Le secchie all'alba nel pozzo / traboccanti d'acqua ghiaccia / con lor croscio argentino / suscitaron nel mio vigore / nudo il brivido salubre / del lavacro mattutino / coperto di rugiada."

41. "L'alba, reclina sul fiume, / scherza con le volute capricciose / della corrente, / si snoda con la grazia di un serpente. / Li alberi fermi immobili, di giada; / le chiome ancora stillano rugiada; . . . / Eccomi nudo, protervo, sincero; / mi squarciano i veli del pensiero / ch'era ubbriaco di sogni: / l'acqua è di vetro opaco." Marinetti, ed., *Poeti futuristi*, XII 1–6, 14–17.

CHAPTER FOUR

~

Marinetti in France between Symbolism and Futurism

Vers et Prose *and* Les Guêpes

Eleonora Conti

Marinetti's poetic trajectory attests to a remarkable fidelity to all the elements that informed its diverse cultural background—Egypt and the Orient, Paris as a beacon of modernity and French Symbolism, and the influence of the three turn of the century guardian angels of Italian lyricism: Carducci, Pascoli and D'Annunzio, and Milan as a "modern" Italian city.[1] As such, Marinetti attempts to "pass over" all these experiences and models, and direct them to converge into the very creation of Futurism.[2] This is evidenced in his works, whether they be in Italian or French, pre-futurist or futurist. The poetic collaborations prior to the launch of Futurism demonstrate a coherence in Marinetti's approach that will never subside, even when he eventually adopts the iconoclastic tones typical of movement's manifestos. Paradoxically, what will remain uninterrupted is the relationship between the poetic works' own cultural roots and the project's overall determination to break with the past.

That being said, it is less surprising, but indeed for this reason particularly interesting, to analyze the Marinettian production both of that work, which straddled the threshold of Futurism, as well as the reactions that it gave rise to in France—in the nation as a whole, not only in Paris. In doing so, this essay will take into account both studies that by now are classic (primarily Heruli, Jannini, List, Livi, Mariani, Salaris) as well as first-hand, contemporary textual documentation. These significant excerpts, arguably, will orient the reader toward the specific horizon of expectation of Marinetti's presentations and works generated in France, the land to which he addressed his poetic work and that he saw as a privileged interlocutor for his politics of cultural mediation. And so, we will first focus on the translation by Marinetti of D'Annunzio, published in *Vers et Prose*; then, regarding Marinetti's reception in France, we will analyze the reception he was given in the Provençal journal *Les Guêpes*.

Marinetti and Paris: the Experience of *Vers et Prose* (1905–1912)

Since its founding in 1905, Marinetti participated in the Parisian magazine *Vers et Prose*, edited by Paul Fort. This journal represented, with its title evocative of Mallarmé, the French and international symbolist currents, and was in keeping with the approach that Marinetti impressed upon his own magazine *Poesia*, founded in Milan in the same year. The links between the two journals and between Marinetti and Paul Fort are numerous and deep, as is evidenced by the literary exchanges and the crossing of tributes. In regards to Marinetti's presence in the prestigious anthology that *Vers et Prose* would come to be, his collaboration was in two capacities: translator and a poet.

Before 1909 and the launch of Futurism, in fact, Marinetti placed his signature on several significant translations of poems by Carducci, Pascoli and D'Annunzio—that is, of the "three poetic crowns" representative of highbrow Italian tradition. By doing so, he makes a clear statement as to whom he considers the most representative authors with whose work he wants to promote Italian poetry to a French readership. Then, in 1912 and 1913, he participated as a poet himself with some texts that can be considered futurist.[3] Even while wearing the hat of "translator," Marinetti proved himself unequivocally as a poet, as his works emerged as authentic poetic adaptations. From these personalized revisions of the original texts, emerge, in fact, elements that blend into an original paste composed of Symbolism and the anticipations of Futurism. From this perspective, Marinetti's translations of the three poets, whom Futurism would only shortly thereafter brand as old fashioned, do not contradict his subsequent turn toward the avant-garde.

From Marinetti's translations published in *Vers et Prose*, in addition to measuring the relationship between Symbolism and Futurism, we can also reconstruct the cultural operation that Marinetti promoted in those years. In fact, let us not forget that he always aspired to act as mediator between Italy and France, following well-defined strategies. Therefore we cannot see as mere coincidence his choice of Carducci, Pascoli and D'Annunzio as Italian poets that should be valued in France. Recalling a categorization developed by François Livi, Carducci represented a kind of poetic model, the guarantor of a famous Italian tradition, worthy of appearing in a prestigious Parisian literary journal. D'Annunzio, on the other hand, represented a rather cumbersome poet, whom Marinetti sought to displace as mediator between France and Italy. Marinetti's desire to assume D'Annunzio's position was evidenced by his efforts to act as an apostle of French Symbolism within Italy, as well as by his own writing of symbolist poetry, in French, himself. Lastly, Pascoli, would finally be the great symbolist Italian poet Marinetti sought to spotlight on the French stage, once he had undermined the cumbersome and "immaginifico" D'Annunzio. Livi refers to Marinetti's not having fully succeeded in his threefold plan as an "incomplete mediation."[4]

But here we shall analyze the complex web of influences at Futurism's base, departing first from Marinetti's translations of the two D'Annunzian texts that appeared in French in *Vers et Prose*. In Italy, in 1903, Gabriele D'Annunzio had already published *Maia*, a long poem of over eight thousand verses, under the sub-heading of "Laus Vitae" which, together with the dedication "Alle pleiadi e ai fati" and "L'annunzio," composes the first book of *Laudi del cielo, della terra, del mare e degli eroi*, which is a work that marks a decisive break from his previous work. The poet transforms an autobiographical experience (i.e., a cruise in Greece) into:

> an initiating experience with an allegorical form, an immersion in nature and myth, with encounters that legitimize its own mission (as in that of the famous Ulysses) and with a sort of descent to the underworld (a grotesque representation of the squalor of modern cities and the horror of the crowd, evoked by an alienating classicistic language that tends to transfigure objects and people into mythological monsters) before the final ascent that definitively consecrated him as a champion, proudly self-conscious, of his status of an elect humanity designed to overcome the limitations of the human—the living symbol of the "Renaissance heroic."[5]

To represent D'Annunzio on two 1906 issues of *Vers et Prose*, Marinetti chose just two passages from *Maia* (the book referring not so much to the name of the Pleiades and to the correlating mythological figure of Hermes' mother—as he did to the subheading, "Laus Vitae," which evidently seemed more significant, allusive and more in line with his idea of poetry and his own temperament, and perhaps also less-classicist bent, in regards to the mythological figure of Maia). Marinetti's translation of these passages appeared in free verse with titles *Les villes terribles* and *Les émeutes* (see appendix).[6]

Marinetti's selection from *Maia* can be explained by his congeniality with epic poetry—in 1902 he had published *La conquête des étoiles* (The

Conquest of the Stars)—as well as by his affinity for certain themes and tones—the predilection for a heroic dimension, a maritime theme, the city and its crowds, diving into an infernal abyss in search of a new mission for the modern poet, the aestheticization of wartime experience. Also informing Marinetti's choice was his desire to present new work to the French public, as a proud ambassador in France of a poet worthy of being included in the important literary showcase founded by Paul Fort; who indeed in a few years would be crowned "the prince of poets."

The D'Annunzian thematics have more than one point of contact with those that run through even the most authentically futurist works, departing from the exuberance and from the desire to conquer the world with a new kind of epic and a new mythology—elements already evident in *Maia*. The poet from Pescara draws inspiration from the vitality of the ancient world. He imagines his Greek journey to be an endeavor to escape the prosaic present and an attempt to derive new energy from classical sources. Marinetti, on the other hand, appears to be oriented entirely towards modernity and is motivated by the desire to break with this past—even if that modernity is born from the absorption and assimilation of models already in place, rather than from a total break from them. Marinetti obviously had the need to "cross over" the poetry of D'Annunzio, Pascoli and Carducci, on his mission to found the new language of Futurism.

The first passage chosen by Marinetti for French anthologization corresponded to the long section titled "Le città terribili" (The Terrible Cities), which concludes poem XVI of *Maia*, that D'Annunzio places towards the end of his allegorical journey through ancient Greece: the poet posits a parallel between the song of destruction that rises from the battlefields of Greek soldiers to his contemporary, quotidian sphere: the one that rises from sprawling modern cities. The poet-prophet looks with disdain upon a landscape from which the god Pan is absent and which is populated by men constrained to the suffering of thankless work. The cities are represented by bright—at times expressionist—tones, and are selected in different moments of the day (vespers, sleep, dawn), as mentioned in the verses' *incipits*. In the case of *Maia*, the passage of time paces out the steps of a real leap into the infernal abyss of the city. The arrival at a highly symbolic dawn indicates a potential salvation from the world's disease by means of D'Annunzio's new poetry, of which the collection *Maia* constituted the first step toward renewal.[7]

In terms of French poetry, the theme of the city's relationship with the different times of the day, and in particular the battle with the evening, already belonged to the Baudelaire-Mallarmé tradition, which Marinetti certainly had in mind. Elvira Favretti refers to this when citing the poem

"Le soir et la ville," which appeared in *Anthologie Revue*, characterized by her as "bold couplings of the realistic and the spiritual" ("arditi accoppiamenti di qualità crudamente realistiche e di qualità dell'ordine spirituale").[8] And so, *Maia* leads the reader back through known territory. Beyond the approach defined by Baudelaire in his *Tableaux parisiens*, also evident is the influence of the Belgian poet Émile Verhaeren, who by scholars such as Brunella Eruli, Bruno Romani and Gaetano Mariani has been identified as one of Marinetti's principal sources of inspiration. In 1895 Verhaeren had published *Les villes tentaculaires*, a collection of poems celebrating the feverish convulsion of big cities packed with workers and idlers. This prosaic reality was celebrated in a robust and eloquent tone by a poet who a few years before this publication had turned to socialism and the workers' movement, conscious of changes that had happened in the modernizing world. This was a work to which his contemporaries and the avant-gardes looked upon with great interest, and indeed in their interest, became indebted to him for his concepts and imagery. Verhaeren's influence on Marinetti is so obvious that Michel Décaudin, speaking of *La ville charnelle*, defines Marinetti as "ce Verhaeren de sang latin" (that Verhaeren of Latin blood).[9] Gaetano Mariani has noted a number of other threads present, to a greater or lesser extent, in Marinetti's sources of inspiration—from Jules Laforgue's *Grande complainte de la ville de Paris*, to Paul Adam, to the Unanimism of Jules Romains, through to the aesthetics of speed and mechanical technology, implicit in the reality of the modern town, as theorized by Mario Morasso in the same years and through the articles about the glorification of war published by Enrico Corradini in *Il Regno*.[10]

As for the poetic path of Marinetti himself, Cescutti has eloquently demonstrated that the genesis of the Marinettian myth of the city and the metropolis reaches its height in *Destruction* (1904). It is here that urban space becomes a sort of Baudelairian "forêt de symboles" (forest of symbols) in which takes place the allegorical struggle between light and darkness, and between heaven and hell. It is here in which modern humanity, arisen from the depths of the ocean, wielding as weapons such mechanical devices forged by new technology and running through urban space in a fast rattling of trams and trains, that he expresses his own rebellion. The destruction of the archaic order is a necessary step toward the destination of a new world order, and not one without setbacks of nostalgia and tensions.[11] Finally, another motive evident in "Le città terribili," and present also in Verhaeren, is that of the sea, already dominant in the Marinettian *Conquête des étoiles*.

The second translated and anthologized text, called by Marinetti "Les Émeutes," is composed, rather, of two much shorter fragments and does not fully correspond to an episode of *Maia*, as does the other. Instead it is presented by the combination of two thematically related passages.[12] The text is woven together, inspired by the first poem, and as such is a continuation of that, in that it shows the phenomena of the new city of the masses. Urban riots, popular uprisings, and carnage are shown on the stage of the city, set against a backdrop of that restless passage from one century to the next. One thinks of the Milanese Bava Beccaris massacre in May 1898, which had inspired Marinetti to publish some quite briskly written pages in *La Revue Blanche* (1900).[13] The concept of insurrection caught Marinetti's attention so much that he took the liberty to rework the title of his translation to highlight the theme.

Translating or Adapting D'Annunzio

We said that rather than translations, Marinetti's French versions are adaptations. The first adaptation that immediately jumps off the page when contrasting the text to the D'Annunzian (and those of Pascoli and Carducci as well) originals, and that Marinetti did not fail to stress in the explanation at the end of the poem, is his choice of free verse. The original version of *Laus vitae* was in fact composed of stanzas of verse with varying degrees of prevalence of heptasyllabic and octosyllabic stanzas, marked by rhyme and assonance. It is true that the D'Annunzian prosody naturally tended toward a freedom much appreciated by Marinetti, if in a letter to D'Annunzio in those years, Marinetti praised his metrical style, claiming: "Vous êtes le premier verslibriste italien" (You are the first Italian poet of free verse),[14] which was a statement in keeping with the famous *Inchiesta internazionale sul verso libero* (International Inquiry Into Free Verse), that would be launched by *Poesia* in October 1905.

D'Annunzio himself had been involved in this inquiry, as is attested by the 1906 letters which appeared in concomitance with the translations by Marinetti's hand in *Vers et Prose*.

Thus, both thanks to the original text's theoretical positions in defense of free verse, as well as because Marinetti found it stimulating to adapt the verse to the French language, Marinetti freely adapted D'Annunzio's work. In doing so, he stretched it out, and rendered the verse more of a narrative by reconstructing syntactic links that D'Annunzio tended rather to assemble as a montage of images, separated only by commas. Furthermore, he manipulated the length of the stanzas, insisting—as we shall see—on the sound of the language, exploiting the musicality of the French to nearly brush against a phonic-symbolism that comes close to representing noise as experienced in the wild. Meanwhile, all these textual transformations were tendencies already present in D'Annunzio's poetry, but now they were forced to create new results.

Compared to the "Città terribili," translated as a whole by Marinetti, "Les émeutes" constitutes a free anthologization of two pieces given new names and then sewn together by Marinetti. Additionally, as opposed to "Città terribili," the translation is less faithful to the original. It is in fact even more pompous and emphatic than D'Annunzio's "Laus," thanks to the continuous use of apostrophes at the verses' outsets, styled as anaphora, and also for the many small dots that do not function as ellipses, but rather aim to create an atmosphere of suspension and almost an echo in the verses. Furthermore, Marinetti makes his mark in these verses with an abundance of emphatic exclamation points.

On the other hand the adaptation to French brings with it a simplification of the syntax and vocabulary; it is perhaps this textual transformation—from the refined and classicist, to the more colloquial—that is the most evident innovation in the adaptation. In this passage then, as in "Le città terribili," Marinetti shows his proclivity for a certain musicality in poetry which relies on alliterative phrases that lean toward onomatopoeia. This approach aims to champion the scopes of the avant-garde revolution by aggravating the music inherent to D'Annunzio's language, in order to incite it to break its grammar and liberate the energy of its words.[15] In this way it seems to exceed D'Annunzio's Parnassianism and musical extenuation, and to move towards a materiality that is colored with the sensuality of concreteness and movement. Let us compare D'Annunzio's orginal to Marinetti's adaptation, "Les émeutes":[16]

S'udiva tintinnare
l'acciaro nella bocca
degli inquieti cavalli,

Gli squilli, gli urli, il galoppo
il turbine duro che passa,
la vendemmia sotto l'ugne
ferrate, le carni calpeste,
i cranii fenduti, i cervelli
sgorganti, l'orrore consueto
della rivolta disfatta
e rotte sulle pietre grigie;[17]

Et le silence était rompu par les gourmettes
qui *tintinabulaient* sous les ganaches
des grands chevaux *sursautant d'inquiétude* . . .

> Puis ce fut le *tonnant brouhaha* de la lutte!
> *Tohu-bohu de cris* et de galops violents,
> et la tourbillonnante chevauchée sanguinaire,
> et le martellement des lourds sabots de fer,
> qui creusaient en passant leur vendange [éclarlante]
> de ventres défoncés et de crânes fendus,
> pêle-mêle aux gluants ruisselis des cervelles . . . [18]

This combines a taste for violent decomposition and for the bloody, that Mariani traces back to the influence of *Reflexions sur la violence* by Sorel (published in 1908, but already influential upon the younger generation's mentality) and that "now enclosed in purely aesthetic and literary desires, will transfer itself soon into a vitalizing human experience: war as the only hygiene of the world."[19] This is an eloquent passage displaying this aesthetic, from "Le città terribili" / "Les villes terribles":

> . . . rigurgito crasso
> delle cloache nell'ombra
> della divina Sera,
> tumulto della strada ingombra
> ove tutte le fami
> e le seti irrompono a gara
> d'avidità belluina[20]

> . . . glouglou fétides, hoquets gluants
> des cloaques voraces parmi l'ombre azurée
> d'un beau soir estatique;
> encombrement fumeux et brouhaha
> de la rue sombre où la cohue des appétits
> et de toutes les faims se rue à la curée
> s'entr'égorgeant avec l'avidité des bêtes fauves;[21]

Additionally, the tendency toward an exaggerated expressionism can be noted from these attempts at translation: in "Les villes terribles," Marinetti adds color where previously absent (*aurore blonde, bouche noire, bile verdâtre, ombre azurée*) to create chromatic contrasts more apparent when compared to the tonality suggested by D'Annunzio's original verse. Here is a passage in which chromaticism, violent decomposition, and sensuality combine to reproduce a vivid image that distills some of the central topoi of the pre-futurist Marinetti of those years. At dusk, the sun is shot to death against a maritime backdrop:

O la fièvre éclatante de ces villes terribles
quand le soleil agonisant
comme un monstre marin frappé par le trident
palpite sur la ligne extrême de la mer
et meurt parmi d'immense bouillonnements de sang
et de bile verdâtre . . . [22]

Marinetti adds adjectives at each verse's incipit ("gloria delle città terribili / gloire tragique, orrore delle città terribili /sublime horreur, febbre delle città terribili /fièvre éclatante, sonno delle città terribili /sommeil angoissant, alba delle città terribili /aube livide, aurore /aurore inattendue, aurore /aurore blonde"); he transforms images into complex chains of analogies configured in apposition. "espoir, ange, idéal" is an analogical condensation of the more archaic, musically extenauted and syntactically convoluted "speranza volante su ali recenti." That which happens along this line of analogically paired nouns is then theorized in the *Technical Manifesto of Futurist Literature* of 1912[23] and in the bold synesthesiae ("l'ivresse rouge des bacchantes," from the simpler "frenetiche come baccanti").

In the verses "tous entassés et morfondus, près de la bouche noire /de l'égout . . . ," the visual metaphor of "la bouche noire / de l'égout" around which the characters are crowded and languish ("entassés et morfondus") Marinetti's language is more powerful than D'Annunzio's simple image of "assopiti sopra la fogna." Here in fact Marinetti seems to play with sound to enhance the sense of the past participle "morfondus," which means "annoyed by a long wait." Indeed, "morfondus" to an Italian ear appears to be a lexical invention that plays on the idea of sleep, as it contains the root of the name of the god Morpheus [morph-] and in this way attaches itself therefore to D'Annunzio's "assopiti" while meaning something entirely different in French.

Also the next vibrant image, "la fenêtre clignotante d'un poète qui rêve" ("the flashing window of a dreaming poet") is a suggestive, eye-catching invention, and an expressive condensation of a more discursive and less surprising image, in the original Italian:

mentre s'amplia e s'arrossa
nei fumi la chiara finestra
del sapiente che indaga
e del poeta che sogna.[24]

cependant que flamboient dans la brume
la lucarne du savant penché sur son creuset
et la fenêtre clignotante d'un poète qui rêve![25]

This trend combined with the condensation united to the expressionism of the images and to a standardization of vocabulary to a level less courtly and archaic (aided by the French), finds, then, a modernizing opening in some elements that are true futurist foreshadowings:

> Gloria delle città
> terribili, quando a vespro
> s'arrestano le miriadi
> possenti dei cavalli
> che per tutto il giorno
> fremettero nelle vaste
> macchine mai stanchi,
> e s'accendono i bianchi
> globi come pendule lune
> tra le attonite file
> dei platani [. . .][26]

> C'est bien votre gloire tragique, ville terribile,
> quand la tombée du soir arrête tout à coup
> les puissantes myriades de *chevaux métalliques*
> qui, durant tout un jour, ont frémi de délire
> infatigable dans l'usine profonde.
> À l'heure où d'innombrables *lunes électriques*
> s'allument entre les files spectrales des platanes[27]

The reader will not miss the "chevaux métalliques" ("electric horses") and "lunes électriques" ("the electric moons") that are intentionally rhymed with each other, and that complete the modernization of a verse to emit the tone of a scene from a contemporary city (D'Annunzio, rather, had metered this verse based upon the rhythm of the proparoxytone words: accendono / pendule / attonite / platani (they light /pendulous/ astonished/plane trees). Similarly, the condensation of simile (i bianchi globi come pendule lune) (the white globes like pendulous moons) in proto-futurist metaphor (electric moons), decidedly in line with the modern frenzy of "usines" ("factories") so dear to Verhaeren, which is a word introduced freely by Marinetti in the previous verse, was employed to justify and complete the new framework.

In regards to the Marinettian lexicon, in respect to the original D'Annunzio, he prefers solid, concrete images to abstract concepts:

> ove tutte le fami
> e le seti irrompono a gara[28]
> où *la cohue des* appétits
> et de toutes les faims se rue à la curée[29]

Marinetti's lexical choices follow a coherence that will later be exercized by the poet upon his own texts. Several words that he employs in the translation-adaptation published in *Vers et Prose*, and that belong to a poetic lexicon akin to that of Symbolism and Decadentism return in *La ville charnelle* (1908). Take the examples of "empouacrées" and "ruisselis": "O rue étroite et tortueuse empouacrée d'ordure!" ("O Street narrow and winding, filthy of garbage!") (in "Les émeutes") / "sa tête empouacrée de sang et sa tignasse" ("his head dirty of blood and his mop") (in "Le voyageur mordu"—"The Bitten Traveler"). And again: "Pêle-mêle aux gluants ruisselis de cervelles . . ." ("Pell-mell slimy streams of brains . . . ") / "le ruisselis de pleurs et de jais bleus" ("the flow of tears and of blue jet") (in "Les benjohs du Désespoir et de l'Aventure"). Marinetti is not ashamed to resort to the preciousness of a *hapax* such as "ruisselis" to build his own original poetic universe.[30] While deep in admiration for the symbolic world, having already begun a Marinettian renewal of poetic language, thanks to the passage through and transcendence above D'Annunzio, a model is necessary and unavoidable. This transcendence can be seen as complete only two years later, with *La ville charnelle*.[31]

Marinetti and the French Province

But we come to the question of the reception of the work of Marinetti north of the Alps. As is known from *Fortuna del futurismo in Francia*,[32] an interesting chapter regarding this question concerns the relationship between the Italian movement and southern French literature. Marinetti had rather close ties to this region, so much so that he went on to devote two chapters of his memoirs to the area: "Poetesse attrici e poeti a Marsiglia" and "Il bosco di Provenza ove nasce il manifesto 'Uccidiamo il chiaro di luna.'" Jannini reminds us how, in particular, Marinetti admired and showcased the work of Frédéric Mistral in *Poesia*. To Marinetti, Mistral and his *félibres* movement stood for an original linguistic re-creation that had contributed greatly to the poetic tradition of the Occitan area.

According to Marcel Raymond, Southern literature had undergone a phase of revival at the start of the twentieth century, as evidenced by the emergence of numerous magazines in Southern centers—from Lyon to Toulouse to Valencia. Thus, the birth of Futurism (as publicized by Marinetti through the use of a massive leafleting, and total and partial membership requests directed at the leading French intellectuals and writers, in a highly charged manner not unlike that employed by modern media) incited quite a response in these magazines and provoked the reactions of many intellectuals, that were more or less linked with Marinetti and his Milanese magazine.

Indeed, the Toulouse magazine *Poésie* launched in the autumn of 1909 the *Manifesto del primitivismo*, not so much with the intention of founding a school of thought, as much as to take a stand against Futurism. This manifesto, signed by Marc Dhano, Georges Gaudion and Touny-Lérys, contested Marinetti point by point and reaffirmed traditional values, causing France's largest ever reaction to Futurism, as pointed out by Jannini. In general, the intellectuals who spoke their minds, even when they reaffirmed sympathy for Marinetti, were convinced that Futurism constituted a provocation, or even a "pitrerie" (a farce), a barbaric act that also contains something of the "odieux ridicule," or even declared themselves precursors of the Italian movement, having already returned to order: indeed this is mainly in regards to conservative and classicist intellectuals.

Significant in this vein is the Provençal magazine *Les Guêpes* (The Wasps, the title of the play by Aristophanes), founded by the *fantaisiste* poet Jean-Marc Bernard and his close friend Raoul Monier in Valence-Saint-Rambert-d'Albon (in the Drôme Provençale) in 1909.[33] It represents a living testimony to the vitality of Southern literature and debates regarding its main trends. The magazine *Les Guêpes* appeared monthly, adhering to a classicist and therefore anti-symbolist stance on the literary plane, and on the political plane conservative and even politically monarchist, while also supporting the catholicism of Charles Maurras. *Les Guêpes* consisted of short satirical notes and epigrams of "d'aiguillon prompt et cruel,"[34] which compiled, from the very first issue, an eloquent list of "ceux qui ne collaborent pas," that is to say the excluded, the declared enemies, those guilty of supporting literature compromised with free verse, with a languid, Nordic—rather than solidly classical and Mediterranean tone. As concluded by the founder Jean-Marc Bernard in the article "À propos du vers libre"[35] in 1910, this was a poetry that reduced verse to a bunch of "syllabes sauvages" ("savage syllables") that echo awkwardly known verses, satisfying only the ears of a bushman, "boschiman ou celles d'un jeanroyère."

The dig taken at Jean Royère is just one of many that targeted the supporter of neo-Symbolism and editor of the journal *La Phalange*. The myth of Mallarmé transforms itself for Royère, so sustain the *guêpes* in the tasty and ferocious rubric "Piqûres de guêpes," in an exhaustive imitation that lacked backbone and moral substance:

> Royère having rolled up his sleeve
> holds fast a chicken he would
> like to pluck.
> When the chicken asks in a flat voice:
> —Do you take me for Mallarmé?[36]

The magazine inserted itself in the line of symbolist and decadent discourse, and laid claim to a solid return to a tradition inspired by Greek and Latin classics. This need for solid classicism, since the last years of the nineteenth century, had produced a series of literary movements in France, such as *L'école romane* by Jean Moréas (1891) and *Naturisme* (1897) by Saint-Georges de Bouhélier. It dealt with reactions to the *impasse* in which Symbolism had reached—as noted Brunella Eruli—united by dissent regarding the poetic activity of Mallarmé, whose obscurity and silence had become symbolic of the difficulties which stirred the *fin de siècle* poetry.[37] The reaffirmation of the perennial value of Classicism and the conviction that "it was Romanticism that altered this principle both in conception and style, thereby disinheriting the French Muses from their rightful legacy,"[38] also reopens the controversy between the southern French literature and the "barbaric" literature of the North. This resulted in immediate antipathy for the Belgians—Verhaeren, Rodenbach, Maeterlinck, Möckel—who wanted to "conquer the French race" ("conquistare la razza francese").

With these departure points, it is easy to imagine what treatment would be reserved for Marinetti, director of *Poesia*, French symbolist poet, translator of Carducci, D'Annunzio and Pascoli into free verse, and, finally, a futurist. This is the same Marinetti, that in 1902—in contrast to the leading French intellectuals of the time (including Gide), all supporters of Victor Hugo—in the course of an investigation of *Ermitage* on his favorite poet had expressed the greatest enthusiasm for Mallarmé.[39] Certainly, when considering this position, one must take into account the Italian poet Marinetti's very different starting position as compared to his French contemporaries: while Mallarmé was experiencing an unfortunate moment in France for the reasons just mentioned, he was virtually unknown in Italy. In fact, Marinetti was one of his first proponents, through recitations of his works in the salons of Milan which he attended since his youth, and thanks to his translations, some of the first to have appeared in Italy.[40] This desire of Marinetti's, to insert himself at all costs into the French literary debates, is one of the targets of the "wasps":

> Regarding F.T. Marinetti:
>
> Admire this evil twist:
> Marinetti, the Milanese,
> being a bilin-
> gual poet, writes verse in French
> that he admires in Italian![41]

The controversy is not new. With his duality of cultural backgrounds—Italian and French (not to mention the added influence of his important

Egyptian roots)—Marinetti found himself in a particular position. Despite the extreme care to which he gave his literary advancements, and his particularly acute sensitivity in capturing the most vibrant literary trends, this in between position offered a vantage point that was simultaneously within and external to French literary society and that in any case implicated a shift in outlook that easily diverged into mockery. Marinetti himself returned several times to this point, to clarify the situation of his double background that put people on their guard about him in both France and Italy. His risk was of not being considered perfectly "settled" in one or the other country, and therefore to be regarded as an Italian-French poet in France and as a French-Italian poet in Italy. A few months after the fierce *piqûre de guêpe*, in the heat of the controversies following the launch of the first futurist *Manifesto*, and the presentation of *Roi Bombance* in Paris, he explained his complex cultural position in *L'Intransigéant*:

> I am called Italian. It's understood, yes, I am Italian, but I studied in Paris and completed my studies at the Sorbonne. I have various French diplomas that permit me to consider myself as belonging to a nation that I love.
>
> I have always thought, written and dreamed in French, and I am proud to have supported and spread the glory of French literature through conferences and the international journal *Poesia*.[42]

For the rest, it was almost impossible to ignore the multifaceted and tireless Italian author, especially in a 1909 full of bombastic and provocative events: April 3, just two months after the launch of Futurism in *Le Figaro*, performed to lukewarm reviews at the Théâtre de l'Oeuvre was the satirical tragedy in four acts (already published by Marinetti in 1904 for those of the *Mercure de France*) called *Le roi Bombance*. Although the newspapers discussed this at length, our *guêpes* did not ignore the opportunity to get another dig:

> She: "The Royal Feast! What a disaster!"

> He: "What do you want, this culinary work was begging to be roasted.[43]

It is significant to compare these quite bored reactions with those reported in numerous pages of self-promotion and self-publicity on the same work. By using the journal *Poesia* to laud the *Roi Bombance* as triumphant, Marinetti sought to impose himself on the Italian scene. By soliciting opinions from recognized poets and intellectuals in France, and by launching continuous surveys and going on to use the reactions of the French press to literally manipulate readers to his own advantage (as shown by the magazine's in-dexes),[44] he was most obviously seeking to obtain credentials to spend in Italy. But in the aftermath of Jules Romains' long letter of sarcastic support of Futurism sent to *Poesia*, Marinetti's practice was suspended, as the responses of the intellectual audience engaging in this journal's debate, in some cases, ended in overt hostility against Marinetti. The poet realized that the cold-ness and sarcasm aroused in France could actually achieve the opposite of his goal, and rather than garner support, it would obfuscate his position and credibility on the Italian literary scene. It is the journal *Les Guêpes*, in March 1909, that would publish in full this quite embarrassing answer, that begins:

> Let me first congratulate you on your initiative. The need for a new school has been keenly felt. It has been for more than six months that no circle at all has requested that I convert. And my neophyte's zeal was bored to be left without employment.[45]

Then up to December's *Notes* there is no mention whatsoever of the Italian futurist movement. Director Jean-Marc Bernard explains this silence in his own way:

> Futurism: If we have not judged it as fitting to annoy our readers about Futur-ism, this is because we have read in the manifesto of F. T. Marinetti (*Poesia*, February-March 1909) a very reassuring sentence: "The oldest among us is not yet thirty; so we have at least ten years in which to complete our task. When we reach forty, other, younger, and more courageous men will very likely toss us into the trash can, like useless manuscripts. . . . " Ten bad years to pass, we thought, and then it's over! But here's how inexhaustible, the director of *Poesia* has flooded the literary market with new futurist prospectuses where we read: "I feel my body twenty years younger! Ever more fragile, I always go back one step closer to the cradle. . . . I will return soon in the womb." If the futurists decide to be reborn at some point in the future, the game is over![46]

This comment, added to Romains' letter published in the journal, clearly indicates that the Italian movement was not taken seriously: it appeared after a sequence of movements and manifestos, and was in that way obscured in a sea of innovation. However, the attention conceded to Marinetti and his initiatives still indicated a strong not to be ignored vitality, and indeed despite all, Marinetti could not have been displeased with the attention given to him, an *ante litteram* publicity talent. Even Marinetti's great entre-preneurial spirit—one manifested in the tireless promotion of competitions and initiatives, and the funding of his own literary enterprises, and in his cultural mediation between France and Italy—soon became the butt of many jokes. And so, in March 1909, this issue came to be apostrophized in another anonymous tirade:

> King of the Franc and of the Lira
> girded with the laurel that you paid yourself.
> You believe yourself to be a carrier of the Lyre
> yet you are nothing but a carrier of cash.[47]

For the rest, a cutting and severe judgment by André Gide, in his Spring 1905 *Journal*, had branded Marinetti's explosive vitality with excessive superficiality and indifference:

> Tuesday . . . At two o'clock I receive a visit from a certain Marinetti, the director of a worthless artistic journal called *Poesia*. He is a very rich and very conceited idiot that has never shut his mouth.[48]

A bulky, omnipresent character, "the caffeine of Europe" in his work of cultural mediation between France and Italy and in the putting forth of himself as a bilingual poet, Marinetti lived in a situation common to many Italian intellectuals that gravitated to Paris. In the late nineteenth and early twentieth century, a trip to Paris meant "saut vital,"—to use Soffici's words, a bath of innovation—an experience which allowed to directly tap from the French language the most advanced instances of Symbolism and Decadentism. With the advance of the century, the foundation of Futurism for Marinetti, and the rise of fascism after the First World War, reversed the direction of movement of the "Italiens de Paris." At that point, the need increased to export the Italian language and literature abroad, and to promote and valorize it. This is an obvious move in the attitude of periodicals that mediated between the two countries. The direction reversed in the 1920s. Marinetti was precocious even in this: with the launch of the *Manifesto of Futurism* in 1909, he denied the symbolist masters, and sought to demonstrate how Italy was able to form its own avant-garde that could be exported abroad and that could renew the Italian language, literature and art, without indebtedness to the European avant-garde. When the defense of "Italianess" clashes with inflexible positions, such as those supported by *Les Guêpes*, the controversy heated. And so, if Marinetti's *Manifesti* proclaimed a desire to make a break by discontinuing the past in favor of a confident turn to a future full of promise, *Les Guêpes* did not lose any opportunity to laugh at this providential opportunity:

One wishes that as a sacrifice to the era that begins,
the past, present, everything be destroyed.
I perceive at least one immense advantage:
humanity will no longer have its conscience plagued
by the works of Marinetti.[49]

The frequency with which Marinetti is the subject of satirical epigrams in the journal is quite significant: if nothing else it shows how his goal of being the center of discussions and debates on French soil had been fully achieved. In any case, while Marinetti sought to export French poets to Italy, gathering them in the eclectic showcase of *Poesia*, he was accepted in France. Yet when he sought to posit himself as a leading player on the French scene, importing Italian innovation to France, he provoked a defensive reaction of which *Les Guêpes* serves as an eloquent example. And so was born the tendency to minimize Futurism's importance and influence in respect to the other European avant-garde movements (Cubism, Surrealism). It was only with the passage from the Milanese Futurism to the Florentine animated by the group of *Lacerba*, that France and Italy would develop a reciprocal understanding and respect.

Notes

1. Translation by Claudia M. Clemente.
2. This background is illustrated in Tatiana Cescutti, *Les origines mythiques du Futurisme. Marinetti poète symboliste (1902–1908)* (Paris: Presses Universitaires Paris-Sorbonne, 2009).
3. Filippo Tommaso Marinetti, "La bataille de Tripoli" (October 26, 1911), *Vers et Prose* (January–March 1912); Filippo Tommaso Marinetti, "Train de soldats malades. Mots en liberté," *Vers et Prose* (July–September 1913). This was found in *Vers et Prose*, archived in the Bibliothèque Nationale de France (BNF).
4. François Livi, "Pascoli e la rivista *Poesia* (1905–1909)," *Lettere Italiane* 3 (1985): 357–81; Idem, "Dal liberty al futurismo: la mediazione incompleta," in Idem, ed., *"Poesia" (1905–1909)* (Naples: Edizioni Scientifiche Italiane, 1992), 1–59; Idem, "Carducci et Pascoli dans *Vers et prose* de Paul Fort. Marinetti traducteur et médiateur," *Transalpina* (2007): 113–33 (please refer to the latter study for a larger picture of the underlying poetic prose in *Vers et prose*). Marinetti's oscillation between admiration and impatience with D'Annunzio is well documented by numerous speeches, notes, commentary that gradually appeared in the magazines of those years and collected in large part in a compilation that appeared in 1908 with the significant title of *Les dieux s'en vont, D'Annunzio reste*.
5. Hermann Grosser, *Il canone letterario, Tra Otto e Novecento*, vol. 5, (Milan: Principato, 2009), 488: "esperienza iniziatica dai contorni allegorici, un'immersione nella natura e nel mito, con incontri che legittimano la propria missione (come

quella del celeberrimo Ulisse) e con una sorta di discesa agli Inferni (una grottesca rappresentazione dello squallore delle città moderne e dell'orrore della folla, evocate mediante uno straniante linguaggio classicistico che tende a trasfigurare oggetti e persone in mostri mitologici) prima dell'ascesi finale che lo consacra definitivamente a campione, orgogliosamente consapevole di sé, di un'umanità eletta, destinata a superare i limiti dell'umano, simbolo vivente della "rinascenza eroica."

6. Gabriele D'Annunzio, "Les villes terribles," trans. Filippo Tommaso Marinetti, *Vers et Prose* V (March–May 1906): 80–83 and Gabriele D'Annunzio, "Les Émeutes," trans. Filippo Tommaso Marinetti, *Vers et Prose* VII (September–November 1906): 135–36. The edition consulted for the original text of *Maia* is Gabriele D'Annunzio, *Tutte le poesie*, ed. Gianni Oliva (Rome: Newton Compton, 1995). Translations in English, of both D'Annunzio's verse and Marinetti's adaptation, are by Claudia M. Clemente.

7. Assumpta Camps, "'Urbs inferna': dalla 'città infetta' alla 'città terribile' in *Maia, primo libro delle Laudi*," in Giorgio Bàrberi Squarotti and Carlo Ossola, eds., *Letteratura e industria. Il XX secolo* (Florence: Olschki, 2002), 2, 535–45.

8. Elvira Favretti, "Marinetti lettore e traduttore di Mallarmé," in Idem, *Il mito, l'avventura, la calda vita. Pascoli, Marinetti, Saba* (Alessandria: Edizioni dell'Orso, 1990), 69. The poem appears in *L'Anthologie Revue* 8 of year I.

9. Michel Décaudin, *La crise des valeurs symbolistes* (Geneva; Paris: Slatkine, 1981), 244.

10. Gaetano Mariani, *Il primo Marinetti* (Florence: Le Monnier, 1970), 62–74 and passim.

11. Tatiana Cescutti, "Destruction ou la genèse du mythe marinettien de la ville," in Idem, *Les origines mythiques*, 165–86.

12. The first fragment corresponds to the episode of "La strada"—"The Road" (canto XVIII, stanza IV)—while in the Laus Vitae the title "Il tumulto" (to which the Marinettian title corresponds, more or less, even if these turn to the plural) pertains to the two successive stanzas; the second fragment instead corresponds to the third stanza of the piece entitled "I ribelli" ("The rebels").

13. Filippo Tommaso Marinetti, "Les émeutes milanaises de mai 1898. Paysages et silhouettes," *La Revue Blanche* 173 (15 August 1900). Now reproduced in part by Mariani, *Il primo Marinetti*, 75–81.

14. Hand signed letter manuscript, not dated, on paper with a header of: "Poesia. Rassegna Internazionale," dating back to 1905–1906; reproduced in Livi, ed., *"Poesia" (1905–1909)*, 61–63.

15. A propensity for sonorous and words reduced to sound on the page, evident from the first poetic attempts in the Egyptian magazine *Le Papyrus*, as Pasquale-Anjel Jannini has demonstrated in the introduction to Filippo Tommaso Marinetti, *Scritti francesi* (Milan: Mondadori, 1983), 13.

16. Italics are ours.

17. D'Annunzio (trans.): "One could hear the jingling / of daggers in the mouths / of restless horses, . . . / The ringing, shouts, the gallop, / the hard whirlwind that passes, / the harvest under the nails / of iron, the trampled meat, / the cleft skulls, the brains / gushing out, the usual horror / of the revolt quelled / and defeats on the gray stones."

18. Marinetti (trans.): "And the silence was broken by the metal rings / jingling under the jaws / of the great horses balking from inquietude . . . / Then came the thundering noise of the fight! / The hubbub of shouting and violent gallops / and swirling bloody ride / and the pounding of heavy hooves of iron, / digging, passing their scarlet harvest / of smashed bellies and split skulls, / pell-mell slimy streams of brains . . . / And that's where I saw the immemorial horror / of these popular revolts in vain, / endlessly quelled, flat on the stone / and on the boiling hot asphalt of the street!"

19. Mariani, *Il primo Marinetti*, 25–26: "chiuso ora in un vagheggiamento puramente estetico-letterario, si trasferirà di lì a poco in una vitalizzante esperienza umana: la guerra sola igiene del mondo."

20. D'Annunzio (trans.): " . . . regurgitated bowels / of sewers in shadows / of the divine Evening, / the tumult of the clogged street / where all the cravings / and thirsts burst into race / against the beast of greed."

21. Marinetti (trans.): "gurgling fetid, slimy hiccups / of the voracious cesspools amid the azure shadow of a fine ecstatic evening; / smoky clutter and hoo-ha / of the dark street where the crowd of appetites / and all the hungers scramble for the spoils / slicing into each other's throats with the avidity of wild beasts."

22. "O striking fever of these terrible cities / when the sun, dying / like a sea monster struck by Neptune's trident, / pulses on the sea's edge / and dies in the midst of an immense effervescence of blood / and green bile. . . . "

23. "Every noun must have its double, that is, the noun has to be followed, without the use of conjunctions, by that noun to which it is linked by analogy. For example: man-torpedo boat, woman-bay, crowd-backwash, piazza-funnel, door-tap." (trans. Doug Thompson in Filippo Tommaso Marinetti, *Critical Writings*, ed. Günter Berghaus (New York: Farrar, Straus and Giroux, 2006), 108.

24. D'Annunzio: "and while it grows and reddens / in the smokes, the window is bright / of the scholar busy in his books / and the poet who dreams!"

25. Marinetti: "yet, that blaze in the haze: / the window of the scholar bent over his hearth / and the brilliant window of a poet who dreams!"

26. D'Annunzio (trans.): "Glory of the terrible cities / when at vespers / stop the myriad / powerful horses / that throughout the day / quivered tirelessly / in vast machines, / and when they light the white / globes like pendulous moons / among the astonished rows of plane trees. . . . "

27. Marinetti (trans.): "This is your tragic glory, terrible city / when at nightfall suddenly stop / the powerful myriads of metal horses / who, throughout the day, shuddered in delirium / tireless in the deep factory. / At a time when countless electric moons / illuminate the spectral lines of plane trees." Italics are ours.

28. D'Annunzio: ". . . here all the hungers / and thirsts burst into race."

29. Marinetti: ". . . where the crowd of appetites / and all the hungers scramble for the spoils."

30. "Ruisselis" is defined as hapax by the lexicon portal of the Centre National de Ressources Textuelles et Lexicales (CNRS, University of Nancy), as attested in Saint-Simon, *La Varende*, 1955: cnrtl.fr/définition/.

31. Cescutti documents and argues this in the chapter "La ville charnelle" regarding the instances of a "passage" through the poetry of D'Annunzio" (Cescutti, *Les origines*

mythiques, 295–336). It is interesting to remember the good reception *Vers et Prose* had for *La ville charnelle*: "*La ville charnelle* is a book about the most ardent type of love, the most vibrant passionate exaltation. One knows the lyric temperament of our illustrious and excellent comrade, Marinetti, whose entire life is oriented to Beauty incarnate and rhythms that are expressive, and sudden, like waves, violent." ("*La Ville Charnelle* est un livre de l'amour le plus ardent, de la plus vive exaltation passionnelle. On connaît le tempérament lyrique de notre illustre et excellent confrère Marinetti, dont la vie toute entière orientée vers la Beauté s'incarne en rythmes expressifs et, soudain, comme les vagues, violents.") "Notes," *Vers et Prose* XVI (1908): 1.

32. Pasquale-Anjel Jannini e.a., *La fortuna del futurismo in Francia* (Rome: Bulzoni, 1979).

33. As far as we know, the journal was in circulation from 1909 to 1913. The collection consulted is conserved in microfiche in the Bibliothèque Nationale de France in Paris (BNF). With regard to these rare documents it is relevant to point out the recently published information on the indexes from 1910–1912, including some images and texts from *Les Guêpes*, on the website of the Friends of Remy de Gourmont: www.remydegourmont.org/dialogue_amateurs/petitesrevues/guepes.htm, and regarding the indexes of numbers 2, 5, 6–34 of years 1909–1912 (with various texts) in the blog of Mikaël Lugan: petitesrevues.blogspot.com/p/liste-alphabetique-des-petites-revues.html (accessed September 18, 2011). The year 1909—that mostly interests us—only appears partially complete online.

34. Henri Clouard, "Préface" in Jean-Michel Bernard, *Œuvres complètes* (Paris: Le Divan, 1923), xv.

35. Jean-Michel Bernard, "À propos du vers libre," *Les Guêpes* (January 1910): 19–24. The page numbers and the month of publication are not always clearly extractable from the BNF microfiche. When possible they have been confronted with texts now available online or republished in other editions which are specified in the notes.

36. "Royère ayant troussé sa manche / tient un poulet qu'il veut plumer. / Lors le poulet d'une voix blanche. / —Tu me prends donc pour Mallarmé?" The text can be attributed to Alphonse Michet (probably a pseudonym), *Les Guêpes* (February 1909).

37. Brunella Eruli, "Preistoria francese del Futurismo," *Rivista di Letterature moderne e comparate* 23 (1970): 245–90. The citation is on page 252. Also the *Anthologie-Revue de France et d'Italie*, an Italian-French journal of mediation with its office in Milan, in which Marinetti makes his debut and which he would take as a model for his own journal *Poesia*, adheres to the program of naturism and dreams to fuse French Symbolism with the sources of the Latin genus: a given that one has to take into account in order to explain Marinettian cultural politics.

38. Jean Moréas, "Carta dei poeti romanici," *Le Figaro* (September 14, 1891).

39. Marinetti's answer to the inquiry is now in Eruli, "Preistoria francese," 262.

40. Stéphane Mallarmé, *Versi e prose*, trans. Filippo Tommaso Marinetti (Milan: Istituto Editoriale Italiano, 1916). It is the largest anthology translated until that moment: twenty-two poems and six texts in prose. The booklet is republished by Einaudi in 1987, with a note by Franco Fortini.

41. Jane Michet-Lys (probably a pseudonym), "Sur F. T. Marinetti," *Les Guêpes* (March 1909): "*Sur F.T. Marinetti*: // Admirez ce tour malin: / Marinetti, milanais, / Ètant poète bilin— / gue, écrit des vers en français / qu'il admire en italien!"

42. Filippo Tommaso Marinetti, "Les funerailles du Roi Bombance," *L'Intransigéant* 12 (April 1909), now in Eruli, "Preistoria francese," 245. "On m'a traité d'italien. C'est entendu je suis italien, mais j'ai fait mes études à Paris et je les ai achevées en Sorbonne. J'ai quelques diplômes bien français qui permettent de me considérer comme appartenant à une nation que j'aime. J'ai toujours pensé, écrit, rêvé en français et je suis fier d'avoir soutenu et répandu la gloire des lettres françaises par des conférences et par la revue internationale *Poesia*."

43. Anonymous, "Pour Marinetti," *Les Guêpes* (May 1909): "Elle: 'Le roi Bombance! Quel désastre!' / Lui: 'Que voulez-vous, il fallait un four pour cette pièce culinaire.'"

44. Livi, "*Poesia*" (*1905–1909*), 367–68.

45. "Laissez-moi d'abord vous féliciter de votre intiative. Le besoin d'une école nouvelle se faisait vivement sentir. Voilà plus de six mois qu'aucun cénacle n'avait sollicité ma conversion. Et mon zèle de néophyte s'ennuyait de rester ainsi sans emploi."

46. Jean-Marc Bernard, "Notes," *Les Guêpes*, (December 1909); available online petitesrevues.blogspot.com/2011/03/les-guepes-n10-decembre-1909.html (166–67). "Futurisme: Si nous n'avons pas jugé à propos d'ennuyer nos lecteurs au sujet du futurisme, c'est que nous avions lu dans le manifeste de F.T. Marinetti (*Poesia*, février-mars 1909) cette phrase très rassurante: 'Les plus âgés d'entre nous n'ont pas encore trente ans: nous avons donc au moins dix ans pour accomplir notre tâche. Quand nous aurons quarante ans, que de plus jeunes et plus vaillants que nous veuillent bien nous jeter dans un panier comme des manuscripts inutiles. . . . ' Dix, mauvaises années à passer, pensions-nous, et puis ce sera fini! Mais voici qu'infatigable, le directeur de *Poesia* inonde le marché littéraire de nouveaux prospectus futuristes où nous pouvons lire: 'Je sens mon corps de vingt ans qui rajeunit! Je reviens d'un pas toujours plus fragile vers mon berceau. . . . Je rentrerai bientôt dans le ventre de ma mère.' Si les futuristes se décident ainsi à renaître jusqu'à la Sainte Glinglin, ce n'est plus de jeu!"

47. "Roi du franc et de la lire / Ceint de laurier qu'il se paie / Tu crois être un porte-lyre: / Tu n'est qu'un porte-monnaie." Anonymous "À F. T. Marinetti," *Les Guêpes* (March 1909): 47. It can also be found in Eruli, "Preistoria francese," 247, note 4.

48. André Gide, *Journal* (*1899–1939*) (Paris: Gallimard, 1948), 152 (The comment dates to April/May 1905). Cited also in: Livi, "*Poesia*" (*1905–1909*), 14: "Mardi. . . . À 2 heures, visite d'un Marinetti, directeur d'une revue de camelote artistique du nom Poesia. C'est un sot très riche et très fat qui n'a jamais su se réduire au silence."

49. Raoul Monier, "Sur le Futurisme," *Les Guêpes* (1909); now in Bernard, *Œuvres complètes*, 298. "On veut qu'en sacrifice à l'ère qui commence, / du passé, du présent, tout soit anéanti. / J'y aperçois du moins un avantage immense: / l'humanité n'aura plus sur la conscience / les œuvres de Marinetti."

Appendix. D'Annunzio's Texts Translated by Marinetti

D'Annunzio, *Maia*, cap. XVI, "Le città terribili"	Clemente, trans. D'Annunzio, *Maia*, cap. XVI, "Le città terribili"	Marinetti, "Les villes terribiles," *Vers et prose*, tomo V, mars–avril	Clemente, trans. Marinetti, "The Terrible Cities," *Vers et prose*, tome V, March– April
Vesperi di primavera,	Vespers of spring,	Crépuscul du printemps,	Twilight of spring
crepuscoli d'estate,	twilights of summer,	crépuscul d'été.	twilight of summer,
prime piogge d'autunno	first autumn rains	premières pluies d'automne,	first autumn rains,
croscianti su l'immondizia	thundering on dusty	averses bruissantes sur l'immondice	showers rustling over powdery filth
polverosa che nera	garbage that, black,	poudreuse qui fermente sous les pas	that ferments in the footsteps of
fermenta sotto le suola	ferments under the soles	des mendiants;	beggars;
fendute onde si mostra	slicing it in waves revealing	pauvres semelles éclatées qui	poor soles that, burst open, reveal
il miserevole piede	the miserable foot	découvrez	a lamentable human foot like the root
umano come tòrta	human as a twisted	un lamentable pied humain pareil à	twisted, and bruised of a pain
radice di dolore	root of pain	la racine	violently uprooted;
divelta: rigurgito crasso	wrecked: regurgitated bowels	torse et meurtrie d'une douleur	gurgling fetid, slimy hiccups
delle cloache nell'ombra	of sewers in shadows	violemment arrachée;	of the voracious cesspools amid the
della divina Sera,	of the divine Evening,	glouglou fétides, hoquets gluants	azure shadow of a fine ecstatic
tumulto della strada ingombra	the tumult of the clogged street	des cloaques voraces parmi l'ombre	evening;
ove tutte le fami	where all the hungers	azurée	smoky clutter and hoo-ha
e le seti irrompono a gara	and thirsts burst into race	d'un beau soir extatique;	of the dark street where the crowd of
d'avidità belluina	against the beast of greed	encombrement fumeux et brouhaha	appetites
per la forza che impera	that rules by might	de la rue sombre où la cohue des	and all the hungers scramble for the
e partisce i beni col ferro,	and shares the goods with iron,	appétits	spoils
da voi sorgere io vidi	from you I saw rise	et de toutes les faims se rue à la	slicing into each other's throats with
non so quale orrida gloria.	I do not know what horrid glory.	curée	the avidity of wild beasts;
		s'entr'égorgeant avec l'avidité des	supreme law of the dominating force
Gloria delle città	Glory of the terrible cities	bêtes fauves;	it is here that the pittances are divided
terribili, quando a vespro	when at vespers	droit supreme de la force	by the knife's edge,
s'arrestano le miriadi	stop the myriad	dominatrice	it is from you, it is in you that I saw
possenti dei cavalli	powerful horses	et qui partage les pitances au	shine
che per tutto il giorno	that throughout the day	tranchant du couteau,	a sinister and terrifying glory.
fremettero nelle vaste	quivered tirelessly	c'est de vous, c'est en vous que j'ai	
macchine mai stanchi,	in vast machines,	vu resplendir	
		une gloire sinistre et terrifiante.	

e s'accendono i bianchi
globi come pendule lune
tra le attonite file
dei platani lungh'esse
le case mustruose
dalle cento e cento occhiaie,
e i carri su le rotaie
stridono carichi di scoria
umana scintillando
d'una luce più bella
che la luce degli astri,
e ne' cieli rossastri
grandeggiano solitarie
le cupo e le torri!

Orrore delle città
terribili, quando su le vie
arse cacono i larghi lembi
violacei della Sera
con un odor molle di morte,
e s'accendono su le porte
delle taverne i fanali
rossi che versano il sangue
luminoso al limitare
ove scoppierà la furente
rissa dopo l'ingiuria,
e i fuochi della lussuria
brillano negli occhi senili
della grigia larva che insegue
per l'ombra la vergine impube

and when they light the white
globes like pendulous moons
among the astonished rows
of plane trees lining
the monstrous houses
with hundreds and hundreds of
    orbits,
and the wagons on the rails
screech under loads of debris
of man sparkling
a most beautiful light
than the light of the stars,
and in the reddish skies
tower the solitary
domes and spires!

Horror of the terrible cities,
when on the streets
fall burnt pieces of large overhangs
violet from the Evening
with a soft smell of death,
and when they light above the doors
of taverns the lanterns
red that shed blood
luminous at the threshold
where will burst the furious
brawl after an insult,
and the fires of lust
twinkle in eyes of a senile

C'est bien là votre gloire tragique,
    ville terrible,
quand à la tombée du soir arrête
    tout à coup
les puissantes myriades de chevaux
    métalliques
qui, durant tout un jour, ont frémi
    de délire
infatigable dans l'usine profonde
À l'heure où d'innombrables lunes
    électriques
s'allument entre les files spectrales
    des platanes
tout le long des maisons devenues
    monstrueuses
les maisons aux cent yeux braqués
    sur l'invisible.
C'est bien là votre gloire tragique,
    ville terrible,
quand les chariots bondés d'une
    scorie humaine
font scintiller les rails d'un pur éclat
    de joie,
plus pur que la lumière immobile
    des astres,
cependant que l'orgueil solitaire des
    tours
et des cupoles s'amplifie dans le ciel
    rouge.

This is your tragic glory, terrible city
when at nightfall suddenly stop
the powerful myriads of metal horses
who, throughout the day, shuddered
    in delirium
tireless in the deep factory.
At a time when countless electric
    moons illuminate the spectral lines
    of plane trees
along the length of houses, they
    become monstrous
the houses with a hundred eyes fixed
    on the invisible.
This is your tragic glory, terrible town,
when the overcrowded trucks of
    human slag
make the rails glimmer in a pure burst
    of joy,
purer than the still starlight,
while that solitary pride of the towers
and the domes grow in the red sky.

Oh sublime horror of these terrible
    cities,
at a time when the tiles annealed by
    heat
amply let fall purple nests
dressed for evening, with a soft whiff
    of decay . . . .

(continued)

Appendix. (continued)

D'Annunzio, Maia, cap. XVI, "Le città terribili"	Clemente, trans. D'Annunzio, Maia, cap. XVI, "Le città terribili"	Marinetti, "Les villes terribiles," Vers et prose, tomo V, mars–avril	Clemente, trans. Marinetti, "The Terrible Cities," Vers et prose, tome V, March–April

con nel passo malfermo
l'indizio del morbo dorsale,
e il bardassa tra per le scale
già buie il soldato che ride,
e la libidine incide
l'enorme priàpo sul muro!
	gray skeleton that chases
	in shadow the pubescent virgin
	with unsteady step in
	quest of the dorsal disease
	and that lout between the stairs
	already dark the soldier laughs,
	and lust affects the enormous
	Priapus on the wall!
		O la sublime horreur de ces villes
		  terribles,
		à l'heure où sur les dalles recuites
		  de chaleur
		défaillent amplement les pans
		  violets
		de la robe du soir, avec un relent
		  mou
		de pourriture...
		à l'heure louche où sur la porte des
		  tavernes
		s'allument les lanternes qui versent
		  tout leur sang
		lumineux sur le seuil...
			at a lecherous time when the tavern
			  doors
			light up the lanterns that pay all their
			  blood
			light on the threshold . . . .
			the threshold where the brawl will
			  soon erupt
			frightening, the violent blast of an
			  insult.
			Here, the sneaky flash of lust
			sharpens
			the eyes of a little old man

Febbre delle città
terribili, quando il sole
come un mostro colpito
dal tridente marino
palpita ai limiti delle acque
in una immensità di sangue
e di bile moribondo,
e nel duolo del ciel profondo
la gran piaga persiste
livida di cancrena,
e s'ode la sirena
del vascello che giunge
caldo di più caldi mari,
e s'accendono i fari
su l'alte scogliere,
e le ciurme straniere
si precipitano all'orgia
frenetiche come baccanti,
e il porto suona di canti
di scherni di sfide di colpi
di crapula e d'oro!
	Fever of terrible cities,
	when the sun
	as if a monster, hit
	by Neptune's Trident,
	throbs at the the water's limits
	in an immensity of blood
	and bile, dying,
	and in the grief of the deep sky
	the great plague persists
	livid with gangrene,
	and we hear the siren
	of the vessel which arrives
	hot from warmer seas,
	and lighthouse are lit
	on the high cliffs,
	and foreign crews
	rush to the orgy
	frenetic as Bacchantes,
	and the port sounds of songs
	of taunts and dares to strike,
	of debauchery and of gold!
		sur le seuil où bientôt éclatera la
		  rixe
		effrayante, au violent boute-feu
		  d'une injure.
		Voici, l'éclair sournois de la luxure
		  aiguise
		les yeux d'un petit vieux
		tâtonnant acharné aux trousses
		  d'une pucelle.
		Ses genoux las tremblotent et sa tête
		  tressaille!
		en révélant le mal subtil qui le
		  tenaille!
		Voici, le proxénète entraîne vers le
		  noir
			groping fiercely, hot on the heels of
			  a virgin.
			His knees tremble and head quivers!
			revealing the subtle evil pincer!
			Here, the pimp leads to the black
			of the stairs, a heavy soldier guffaws
			  in laughter,
			yet but a cad expresses the baseness
			of his nature, and blackens the wall
			with an enormous phallus.
			
			O striking fever of these terrible cities
			when the sun, dying
			like a sea monster struck by Neptune's
			  trident,
			pulses on the sea's edge

Slumber of the terrible
cities, when from the slothful
river (where decomposes,
between the slime and filth,
the pulp of suicides,
phosphorescent as
the slime of dead jellyfish
on salty shores)
surge the array of skeletons
the fog as it falls silent
with a thousand tender tentacles
that brush against each and every
door
and palpitate the poor and the
insane,
the thief and the vain Venus,
the bitter mouthed drunk,
the orphan with his deformed bones
nodding off over the sewer,
and while it grows and reddens
in the smokes, the window is bright
of the scholar busy in his books
and the poet who dreams!

Dawn in the terrible
cities, dawn which rings
with a thousand trumpets of copper
on the opaque silence of rooftops
calling the sleeping into battle,
the first dart of the Sun is launched

and dies in the midst of an immense
effervescence of blood and green
bile . . . .
at a time when the aching flesh of sky
the vast solar wound expands,
purulent
and streaked with gangrene ... while
the echoes
resound of far jerky sobs
of a distant ship's siren! ...
Ship, the sail of which still smells of
burning
aromatic scents of a tropical sea,
to be guided by the beacons lit
on the high cliffs! ... Oh frenetic
bands
of foreign seafarers who you kick en
masse
with red bacchanalian intoxication,
this is the seedy bar where your
obscene songs
beat out in time to lightning flashes of
daggers
and the clear clinking of your evil
gold.

Oh agonizing sleep of these terrible
cities,
when the river drowsy with lassitude
and of shadow

de l'escalier, un lourd soldat qui
s'esclaffe de rire,
cependant qu'un goujat esprime
tout son rut
en charbonnant sur la muraille un
phallus colossal.

O la fièvre éclatante de ces villes
terribles
quand le soleil agonisant
comme un monstre marin frappé
par le trident
palpite sur la ligne extrême de la
mer
et meurt parmi d'immense
bouillonnements de sang
et de bile verdâtre...
à l'heure où sur la chair endolorie
du ciel
la vaste plaie solaire s'élargit
purulente
et striée de gangrènes...tandis que
les échos
répercutent au loin les sanglots
saccadés
d'une lointaine sirène de navire!...
Navire dont la voile fleure encore
le brûlant
parfum aromatique d'une mer
tropicale,

Sonno delle città
terribili, quando dal fiume
accidioso (ove vi si stempra
tra la melma e il pattume
la polpa dei suicidi
fosforescente come
su i salsi lidi il viscidume
delle meduse morte)
sorgono le larve diffuse
della caligine tacente
con mille tentacoli molli
che sfiorano tutte le porte
e palpano i miseri e i folli,
il ladro e la venere vaga,
l'ebro dalla bocca amara
l'orfano dall'ossa contorte
assopiti sopra la fogna,
mentre s'amplia e s'arrossa
nei fumi la chiara finestra
del sapiente che indaga
e del poeta che sogna!

Alba delle città
terribili, aurora che squilla
con mille trombe di rame
sul silenzio opaco dei tetti
chiamando i dormenti a battaglia,
primo dardo che il Sole scaglia
a fiedere le sfere d'oro
su le cupole ancor notturne
e le cime ardue dei camini

(continued)

Appendix. *(continued)*

D'Annunzio, *Maia*, cap. XVI, "Le città terribili"	Clemente, trans. D'Annunzio, *Maia*, cap. XVI, "Le città terribili"	Marinetti, "Les villes terribles," *Vers et prose*, tomo V, mars–avril	Clemente, trans. Marinetti, "The Terrible Cities," *Vers et prose*, tome V, March–April
emuli delle torri e le bianche statue degli archi trionfali,	to wound the spheres of gold onto the domes, still in their night,	c'est pour guider tes pas que s'allument les phares	goes dissolving in funeral, amid its fetid mud
Speranza volante su ali recenti come i fiori nati sotto le rugiade celesti,	the arduous chimney tops imitators of the towers and the white statues of triumphal arches,	sur les hautes falaises!... O bandes frénétiques	the large bloated corpses of suicides, of which the pulp is as sticky and phosphorous
passo degli artefici desti all'opere sonoro come	Hope, flying and winged, recent as the flowers born	de marins étrangers qui vous ruez en masse	as jellyfish on the sand of beaches! . . .
scalpitìo d'esercito grande, rombo che si spande dai mossi congegni pel vitreo duomo,	beneath celestial dewdrops, a step of the awake creators toward the sonorous works	avec l'ivresse rouge des bacchantes, voilà le bouge ouvert où vos chansons obscènes	at the silent hour, exasperated by the river, the ghost children loom through the fog
oh Alba, oh risveglio dell'Uomo eletto al dominio del Mondo!	as the pawing of a massive army, a roar that expands from quakes, dissects the glassy dome, oh Dawn! oh awakening of the Human elected to the domain of the World!	rythmeront les éclairs foudrayants du poignard et le clair tintement de votre or crapuleux!	and go pressing their countless moist tentacles against the doors, caressing the destitute, the fools and thieves,
		O sommeil angoissant de ces villes terribles, quand le fleuve engourdi de lassitude et d'ombre	the street-walking Venus, the drunkard of the bitter laugh, the gaunt and stunted orphan,
		va dissolvant funèbrement parmi sa boue fétide	all piled up, dejected, near the black mouth
		les grands cadavres boursouflés de suicides, dont la pulpe est gluante et phosphoreuse	of the sewer...yet, that blaze in the haze: the window of the scholar bent over his hearth
		ainsi que les méduses sur le sable des plages!	and the brilliant window of a poet who dreams!
		à l'heure où du silence exaspéré du fleuve	Livid dawn of these terrible cities! . . . Unexpected dawn that suddenly sings your fiery trumpets of glittering copper

s'élèvent les fantômes enfantés par
    la brume
et qui s'en vont poussant leurs
    innombrables
tentacules fluides contre toutes les
    portes,
palpant les miséreux, les foux et les
    voleurs,
la Vénus des trottoirs, l'ivrogne au
    rire amer,
l'orphelin décharné et rachitique,
tous entassés et morfondus, près de
    la bouche noire
de l'égout... cependant que
    flamboient dans la brume
la lucarne du savant penché sur son
    creuset
et la fenêtre clignotante d'un poète
    qui rêve!
Aube livide de ces villes terribles!....
Aurore inattendue qui fais soudain
    chanter
tes fougueuses trompettes de cuivre
    étincelant
sur le silence opaque des toits
    accumulés
pour appeler tous les dormants à la
    bataille!
Oh la première flèche que le soleil
    décoche

on the opaque silence of the roofs
    accumulated
to call all the sleeping ones into
    battle!
Oh the first arrow the sun shot
against the dazzling curve of gold
    spheres
on the domes still embedded in
    darkness!
Rays, arrows launched against the
    chimneys
that would rise higher than the turrets
and the white statues of triumphal
    arches!
Hope, perfect angel, that flies in the
    sky
on radiant new and springtime of
    your nascent wings
such flowers fed a divine dew! . . .
Shuffling sound of workers on their
    way
to their daily work, you evoke the
    enormous
resounding roar of an army on the
    verge of battle!
Oh long buzz that permeates the
    space
of the great belfry of louvered
    blackened dome!

(continued)

Appendix. *(continued)*

D'Annunzio, *Maià*, cap. XVI, "Le città terribili"	Clemente, trans. D'Annunzio, *Maià*, cap. XVI, "Le città terribili"	Marinetti, "Les villes terribiles," *Vers et prose*, tomo V, mars–avril	Clemente, trans. Marinetti, "The Terrible Cities," *Vers et prose*, tome V, March– April
		contre la courbe éblouissante des sphères d'or	Blonde Aurora, dazzling revival of Man
		sur les coupoles encore noyées dans l'ombre!	elected to the supreme Empire of the World!
		Rayons, flèches lancées contre les cheminées	
		qui voudraient s'élever plus haut que les tourelles	
		et les blanches statues des arches triomphales!	
		Espoir, ange idéal, qui voles dans le ciel	
		sur l'éclat neuf et printanier de tes ailes naissantes	
		telles des fleurs nourries d'une rosée divine! . . .	
		Piétinement sonore des ouvriers en marche	
		vers le travail quotidien, vous évoquez l'énorme	
		fracas retentissant d'une armée qui s'ébranle!	
		O long bourdonnement que répand dans l'espace	
		le grand beffroi du dome aux abat-sons noircis!	
		Aurore blonde, éblouissante réveil de l'Homme	
		élu pour le suprême Empire du Monde! . . .	

CHAPTER FIVE

~

Futurist Roots in Palermo

Federico De Maria between
Anti-Classicism and Anti-Marinettism

LAURA GRECO

At the turn of the twentieth century Sicily became, if only for a limited period of time, an important literary center for the diffusion of futurist ideas:[1] "Sicily itself appears to be a metaphor of the new, because in those years it was a melting pot of innovative ideas and experience in the fields of arts, the land itself was penetrated by Futurism."[2] In the 1890s, the Sicilian capital had participated prominently in the Italian economic, industrial, social and cultural renaissance, having preceded Milan, Turin and Venice in organizing the National Exhibition in 1891–1892.[3] In this context full of cultural creativity, futurist avant-garde found fertile ground, particularly in Palermo itself. Although the cultural renaissance extended over the entire island and involved a vast group of scholars with an open mind for innovation, Marinetti's search for people and places to be involved in his ambitious project of cultural innovation brought the futurist leader to focus mainly on the city of Palermo.

In this Palermo, it was Federico De Maria who played a central role in this climate of literary palingenesis.[4] Initially, De Maria's exaltation of progress was full of utopian expectations. Like Verga, he first had to experiment with the evils of modernity in order to then be able to critique it. European travels lent him an awareness of how his island home was relatively undeveloped, in terms of social and economic development, and of the great gulf that separated it from the more developed North. It is understandable that the initial enthusiasm Sicilian artists demonstrated for cultural innovation was seen as a means of forgetting a limited and backward past. It is precisely for this reason that Futurism received wide approval in Sicily.

Up until the first few years of the twentieth century, De Maria put himself in the spotlight by arguing against all academia and all forms of art which did not mirror their time. In one of his early lyric poems, *La vita dolorosa*[5] ("The Painful Life"), published in *La Boheme* May 16, 1900, he says "I challenge men, the world and the future" ("gli uomini, il mondo e l'avvenire io sfido"). The proud and audacious manner in which he declared his challenge seems to already have anticipated the futurist approach. The philo-*Scapigliatura* atmosphere breathed during those "bohemian" years facilitated De Maria's assimilation of avant-garde themes and voices, enabling him to move easily in the context of Futurism both regionally and nationally, which led up to the drafting of the Marinetti *Manifesto* in 1909.[6]

In 1901 the writer laid down his literary propositions in *Il fabbro* (The Blacksmith):

> I want to open
> to men the roads to the future
> and I prepare myself to close the past.
> . . .
> Oh custodian of old rubbish,
> the altars erected to your false gods
> will be overthrown by our truth!
> In the future life; and art is life
> and future.[7]

Il fabbro and *La canzone nuova* (The New Song)[8] represent well this early phase of his poetry marked by the poet's incessant attack on classicism. In *Il fabbro*, De Maria illustrates his ceaseless commitment to his role of poet, identifying himself with the blacksmith, "I am the blacksmith" ("Io sono il fabbro"); the determination of his own propositions are expressed by the blacksmith's determination to hammer the anvil. In the same way the poet carries out his work:

> And strikes and strikes the anvil
> terribly, it never has a moment's rest,
> and forges the most important, powerful
> and magnificent work: the will.[9]

Aspiring to pave the way to the future of art for the whole of humanity by abolishing all stereotypes belonging to an obsolete dimension, De Maria erects himself as a new Prometheus, and as hero assigns the flaming torch to the progress of man renewing his mythical assimilation with God followed by the possession of fire. So we see in his lyric poem *Ai nemici miei* (To my enemies), which immediately precedes *Il fabbro*:

> I am the God
> of youth, I am
> Prometheus who advances solemnly with the flaming torch
> In his fist: . . .
> I will break down the doors
> to the prison where shines
> enclosed: Truth, the purest gem! [10]

In the "holy" battle, De Maria invoked the alliance between "the children of art and of the new and eternal thought" ("Figli dell'arte e del pensiero / nuovo ed eterno"), because together they could bring down "the false god" ("falso nume") and consecrate the altars of "new deities" ("nuove deità").[11] The same proposition was to be reaffirmed in the later rebellious proclamation of the *frondisti* (rebels). "The false and lying gods have been adored for long enough, it is time to overthrow them" ("Gli dei falsi e bugiardi sono stati adorati abbastanza, è tempo di rovesciarli").[12] Here we see him use explicit metaphor to attack the empty forms adopted by the classicists.

The marked distinction between blacksmith and goldsmith—"I now disdain that occupation which one day I adored / that of a goldsmith" ("ora io disdegno quel che un dì bramai / lavoro di niello")[13]—develops a new attack on classic art. The activity of the goldsmith is carried out for the few capable of possessing his precious work product; it is therefore the symbol of an elite art, of which only a minority of scholars can comprehend the metric-rhetoric whims and references to tradition.

La canzone nuova (1905) follows this declaration of his poetics, and posits a critical comparison between the poems of the classicists, who, at the beginning of a new epoch, stubbornly stick to academic poems, and those of emerging poets, of whom De Maria is a spokesman. This is continued by an invective against the "poets of the century" ("poeti del secolo"), viewing the followers of Carducci "the singers of fogs and cypresses" ("cantori delle nebbie e di cipressi") as truly "decadent" as they are authors of a necrotic poetry; this is suggested by his description of them as "shriveled" ("incartapecoriti") referring to "Petrarchan, idyllic, humanist" ("petrarcheschi, idilliaci, umanisti"), the simile made comparing pre-futurists to "mummies," as well as by the subsequent reference to the centenarian Aristarchus. The author attacked both the content—

"You who never write a verse . . . without a blue swan, or two whitepeacocks, without heavenly visions, without pure white whinnying horses" ("voi che non fate un verso . . . /mai senza un cigno azzurro o due paoni/ bianchi, senza celesti visioni, / senza cavalle candide annitrenti")—and the form: the metaphor that compares a sonnet to a curse word communicates how violently the poet abhorred the purists' *labor limae*.[14]

By the way, in 1905, following a visit to Palermo, Massimo Bontempelli dedicated a sonnet[15] to the iconoclast De Maria, calling him an "adversary of classical rubbish,"[16] which inevitably generated a heated debate. In typical style of the old *tenzone* competitions between poets, the Sicilian replied with a sonnet in turn[17] that deftly repeated Bontempelli's sonnet's rhyme and that declared a predilection for the ancient free-style poem. De Maria's essay "Prima esegesi del metro libero"[18] ("First exegesis of free meter") had already explained this preference, arguing that rhythm and meter need not be preordained, but should rather be coordinated with the poem's content.

The writer of *La Canzone nuova* presents himself provocatively as "a good peasant" ("un buon villano") crowned "with pungent flowers of the field" ("d'acri fiori / di campo"); this crowning is reminiscent of classic laurel crowns, but is described here in striking contrast, as something common. His face "tanned" ("arso") by the southern summer sun, is counterposed to the white pallor of the "sons of the byzantine Parnassus / chlorotic poets of winter" ("figli del Parnaso bizantino, / clorotici poeti degli inverni"). De Maria's poetry is like his skin, tanned and rough, because it takes its lifeblood from the time and space that generated it, distant from artificial, academic manners. It is down to earth poetry, metaphorically represented by vermilion flowers and rays of the sun, counterposed to the moon's pallor and the pale light of stars, which only reflects that of the sun and is therefore artificial and weak like the classicists' poetry.[19] The poet's vitality sings out in a simile:

> like a strong tree and the heat
> in the fields of dry rivers flowed,
> I blossom here and drink in large gulps
> the infinite breath of nature.[20]

This comparison reveals how the strength of De Maria's poetry is drawn from the relationship between man and that which surrounds him. The tree has long roots deep under ground, but lives and enjoys that which is above the soil, stretching its branches ever higher. De Maria sought to teach this lesson to the classicists, telling them "the things sung by no-one," "a song never sung!" ("le cose da nessun cantate," "una canzone non cantata mai!").[21] From the Petrarchan song, he only takes the naming.

The relationship between Palermo and Futurism produced its most significant results in the first years of the twentieth century. This was when De Maria conceived the idea of founding the literary weekly *La Fronda* (The Rebel). Of the three seasons of Sicilian Futurism, the first,[22] exclusively literary, was centered on this magazine. The term "fronda" ("rebel") comes from the wave of agitation that shook France in the seventeenth century and emphasizes the anticipatory anti-past Illuminism of the magazine writers. The widely used expression "vento di fronda" ("wind of rebellion") is the title of a column in the magazine. An identical anti-traditionalist meaning is attributed to the motto on the banner head which is actually an expression from Chateaubriand, "Les dieux s'en vont" ("The Gods Go"), taken by Marinetti in 1908 for his volume *Les dieux s'en vont, D'Annunzio reste* (The Gods Go, D'Annunzio remains).[23] The *La Fronda* writers state in their program:

> We have a strong desire to see and to demonstrate that it is true that Italy is not going to produce neo-classicists and neo-romantics for eternity. [. . .] From the beginning our work will be demolition, the space is already full and we must first knock down in order to then rebuild. The false and lying gods have been adored enough, now it is time to overthrow them.[24]

The first issue's program, "Il perché di una cosa inutile" ("The why of a useless thing"), anticipates, complete with ironic title, how De Maria will respond to attacks regarding the journal's very existence, given the fact that so many literary journals already exist. De Maria argues that "a magazine that has finally the courage to rise up against public opinion" ("un giornale che abbia finalmente il coraggio di insorgere contro l'opinione pubblica"), can be the unique tool in the hands of the young rebels to try and knock down "the enormous monstrous conservatism" ("l'enorme mostruoso conservatorismo"). The main target is once again "academia, old fashioned ideas" ("l'accademia, la precettistica"):

> For us, the only great art is that which mirrors life aimed towards the future. . . . We therefore want the maker of art to be today's man, son of the last two centuries, blazing with a wonderful light, brother of those who have brought steam to humanity, electric machines, wireless telegraph, the radio and thousands of bright promises for the future. . . .
>   Is it possible that the poets of Italy and across the Latin countries are so bad that they must rummage about among the ashes of tradition? These traditions

must be thrown into the sea along with the glories of the past, when they no longer have any use but to obstruct us instead of acting as beacons to a free path.

Or we would better oust all of those who do not know how to put anything in front of their eyes other than the past, the past, this eternal past!

Boring and blind people who don't know how to draw the best teachings out of their lifeless doctrine and haven't noticed that the dust, shed from the volumes they harbor, falls all over them.[25]

The first part of the piece is aimed at indicating the way forward to the contemporary artist, using terms of guidance such as "life . . . , future . . . , today . . . , light . . . , upcoming . . ." ("vita . . . , futuro . . . , oggi . . . , luce . . . , avvenire . . ."), the second half on the other hand presents all the negative terms, "ashes of death . . . , tradition . . . , past . . . , obstruct us . . . , boring . . . , lifeless . . . , dust . . ." ("morte ceneri . . . , tradizione . . . , passato . . . , incepparci . . . , noiosa . . . , inerte . . . , polvere . . ."), reaching a climax in the final repetition, "the past, the past, this eternal past!" ("il passato, il passato, quest'eterno passato!") underlining the bankruptcy of the twentieth century poet, by now deprived of strength by the centuries old slavery that has tied them to the tyrannical tradition. A useful illustration of this is in the juxtaposition between "obstruct us" and "free path" ("incepparci" e "libero cammino").

On November 5, 1907, in the daily paper *L'Ora*, De Maria continues the unfinished discussion, stating audaciously:

> What has art been down the ages, throughout the lives of peoples, if not the spiritual physiognomy of every age, the moral story of every people? . . . We no longer walk with the steps of evolution but one can say that we proceed from revolution to revolution.
>
> All this is largely due to the means of production, exchange, transport, from steam to electricity.
>
> Our age is eminently mechanical: the machine has changed our life and also had a great effect on our sentiment and ideals. . . .
>
> The three tendencies: pastist, presentist, and futurist, meet everywhere, where they fuse, where they separate. The last, heralded by Walt Whitman, is beginning to have its own art.
>
> For now look at this new art, more than anywhere else in architecture . . . ; look at the great mechanical monuments; the enormous factories, . . . thirty floor buildings built on steel frames, unprecedented harbors towards the ocean, towers that touch the sky, buildings . . . that have the beauty of strength and rational utility.
>
> Destruction, rebuilding. Ancient man disappears, ancient societies disappear.[26]

Even a cursory reading will pick up the similarity in themes and tones to the later, and more famous, *Futurist Manifesto*:

We declare that the magnificence of the world is enriched by a new beauty, the beauty of speed. A racing car with its horn adorned with large tubes like a serpent with explosive breath . . . a machine that roars, that seems to run on grape shot, is more beautiful than the Victory of Samothrace. . . . We want to destroy museums, libraries, all kinds of academy. . . . We will sing the praises of the vibrant nocturnal fervor of dockyards and building sites lit up by violent electric moons; greedy stations devouring smoking serpents; factories hanging at the clouds with the contorted threads of their smoke; bridges that straddle rivers like giant gymnasts, flashing in the sunlight with their sparkling knife-like beams; the adventurous steam ships that break up the horizon, the wide breasted locomotives pawing the ground with their wheels like enormous steel horses bridled with tubes, and the slithering flight of the airplanes with their propeller blowing in the wind like a flag that seems to applaud like a crazy crowd. . . . we want to rid this country of the fetid gangrene of professors, archaeologists, guides, antiquarians. . . . we no longer wish to hear of the past, we young and strong futurists! . . . Burn down the library shelves! . . . demolish, demolish without pity the venerated cities.[27]

"Estetica della macchina" (Aesthetics of the machine), preface to *Antologia dei nuovi poeti futuristi* (Anthology of new Futurist poets)[28] in 1925, takes up the language and concepts already expressed by De Maria in his essay "Estetica della meccanica" (Aesthetics of Mechanics); similarly, compositions such as *Saffica pagana* (Pagan Sapphic), *Inno al sole* (Anthem to the Sun), *La canzone della vela* (The song of the Sail), *Gli abissi azzurri* (The Blue Abysses), *Il volo* (The flight), *Al vento* (To the Wind), *La vecchia casa*[29] (The Old House), all sing the praises of modern twentieth-century inventions. *Interludio classico* (Classical Interlude), which includes most of these essays, starting from provocatively classical forms, is the collection that most closely represents pre-futurist tastes, already evident in some of his early works.

While the conservatives had reproached De Maria "for treating our glorious metric tradition with such presumptuous indifference" ("di trattare con presuntuosa indifferenza le nostre gloriose tradizioni metriche"),[30] *Interludio classico* opens with an argument from the author *A le persone classiche* (To all classical scholars), to "elected theory / of custodianship of the traditions" ("eletta teoria/ di custodi de le tradizioni") with which he prepared for "literary dispute" ("tenzonar"):[31]

> I humbly publish a few studies of verses.
> . . . hoping that at least this time the literary bureaucracy will treat me benignly.
> I am sure that it will not look at what I say, or attempt to find out why I say it, it will at least be satisfied, turning over these few pages, that they are symmetrical.[32]

The return to classic meter of the Italian poetic tradition—the sonnet, the ballad, the epic poem, the madrigal—and, in a lesser way to the Greco-Roman tradition of the dithyramb, the Sapphic, the hymn—came to be associated with choices informed by the poetic content or by polemics with the very meter about which they served as vehicles,[33] or by strictly 1900s choices that would highlight their anachronistic nature.[34] By comparing the poetic structure and content, attention was placed on the necessity for a formal renewal in a contemporary key.

In returning to classical meter and in the placing of it on the realistic level of an exalted modernity, De Maria's attention was brought to the Carduccian barbarian model and his "modern classicism," as it has been defined by Luperini.[35] Nevertheless while finding the foundations for the revival of meter in the *Odi barbare* (Barbaric Odes), De Maria disdained to imitate them, convinced as he was of the value of every autonomous poetic expression and against the irrelevance of mimetic action.[36] Following through with his anti-traditionalist polemics, De Maria's collection of work privileged, above the "barbaric" form, the metric structures of Italian and Romance classicism.

His harsh criticism moved to the sonnet in *La canzone nuova* and the *querelle* developed for that reason between Bontempelli and De Maria was now enriched by a new detail, considering the prevalence inside the collection of that "serene artifice" ("sereno artifizio") where the poet tried to compress the "tempestuous wave of passion" ("tempestosa onda di Passione"), the "impetus inside the strophe limited / in this instant of elevation" ("impeto, dentro la strofe costretto / in quest'istante d'elevazione").[37]

In *Saffica pagana* the choice of a formal structure suggested by the title is probably dictated by the intention to compete with his friend Bontempelli who had chosen the same meter for five parts of his *Odi siciliane*, (Sicilian Odes)[38] on the model of the *Odi barbare* and Carducci's Sapphic poems.[39]

A twentieth-century poet, according to De Maria could not portray handmaidens in white tunics. They could instead turn for inspiration to twentieth century portraits of women in their dresses "of cashmere with their little red hats with a veil that slightly shades the eyes" ("di casimirro, con la capotine / rossa, col velo che annebbia un poco / gli occhi").[40] If the twentieth century is dressed in modern clothes like its women,[41] so must poetry adapt, in its content, and consequently its structure. And so the passerby, as much as the son, that the poet imagines he can generate with her, free of the "dusty archaeological soul in the breast, / and that knows how to live, rejoicing / in his life" ("polverosa / anima archeologica nel seno, / e che sapesse vivere, esultando/ della sua vita"),[42] are metaphors for poetry that should focus upon the present and the future. The pre-futurist echoes—the dust on the volumes in the library and archaeology—are noteworthy, as they will become two of the futurists' favorite targets. These are also two key concepts of their literature, that rival with the enthusiasm for their own era.

De Maria loves to strike the readers with his conceptual leaps, the first stanzas of the *Inno al sole* (Hymn to the Sun) seem to be the traditional description of a dawn, but already in the second stanza an element appears that breaks with it "the high and ferrous factory / from the chimney top / smokes" ("l'opificio alto e ferrigno/ dal comignolo / fuma") still more strident if you consider that usually the hymn was used to praise God and the Virgin Mary. To that norm De Maria added his triple anaphor of the interjection "Ave."[43]

Ascending to new divinities and connoting the trees of the new age, the factories and modern machinery become the subjects of much avant-garde art. And if the futurists stated in 1909 "we will sing . . . adventurous steam ships that break the horizon" ("canteremo . . . i piroscafi avventurosi che fiutano l'orizzonte"), De Maria showed a certain precursive spirit in his *La canzone della vela* (The Song of the Sail). In this poem De Maria limits himself to rhymes that follow the pattern ABC ABC C DEED FF, and to the organization of the stanza in *fronte*, key and *sirma* following the Petrarchan module. We can see from the content of the first four stanzas which praise the beauty of the pure white sail, that this gives the illusion of being a canonical song, the most solemn form in the Italian tradition of the lyric poem. Even the final verse, in which the poet turns to the song itself, brings us back to the same matrix. This conviction is then broken by the adverse conjunction "ma" ("but") and the concessive phrase "also if" ("pur se") half way down the fourth verse that introduces a first rapid comparison between sail boats and modern steam boats:

> Beautiful still, if you forbid yourself
> the dead calm and the great sail hangs inert
> along the sheets, ahead of the steaming
> scorn of your giant
> emulator, that, roaring in the open
> immensity against the green sphinx,
> strong, sure, fast pushes itself.[44]

The main theme of this lyric poem is speed and the frenetic pace of human life, amply demonstrated by the use of terms that return to that semantic field, for example "rapid," "speed," "faster and more courageous" ("rapido," "velocità," "più ratta e più gagliarda,"), strident due to the use of antithesis, in the expression "Beautiful but late," "slow/ beauty," "the wind that blows you / long and late," "calm" ("Bella ma tarda," "lenta/ bellezza," "il soffio che t'avventa/ lungi e tardo," "serena").[45] Notice the divergence between the "great flight" ("gran volo") of the sail as the north-westerly wind that blows it—this metaphor is anticipated by the image of the "wing" ("ala")—and the real flights of man, having a rapidity hyperbolically associated to that of thought.[46]

Once again using hyperbole in the essay *Il volo* (The Flight) the sensation of gliding is associated with the sensation felt when traveling by train.[47] The sensorial association is punctuated by the exclamation "And you fly, you fly!" ("E si vola, si vola!") and also by the repetition of the adverb "Here it is" ("Ecco"), highlighting the swift sequence of images that flow from the window and to which the poet must immediately say goodbye. It is also there in the adjective "rapid" ("rapido") referring through the use of hypallage to "telegraph poles along / the railway track" ("pali telegrafici lungo / la strada ferrata") and in the verb "to sparkle" ("balena"), and finally in the comparison between traveling in a cart "slow, slow" ("lento, lento") as well as from the ascendant climax that ends the essay with the image of the sky towards which the train seems to be extending.[48]

It was some time later before the futurists were to claim "the magnificence of the world is enriched by a new beauty, the beauty of speed" ("la magnificenza del mondo si è arricchita di una bellezza nuova: la bellezza della velocità"). The poet's enthusiasm for the technological advances of his age is clear in *Gli abissi azzurri* (*The Blue Abysses*). The apostrophe to Neptune "old," "ridiculous," "deity / plodding of ancient times" ("vecchio," "ridicolo," "nume / arrembaticcio degli antichi tempi"), conjures images of not only a cultural, but also a historical and technological past, which evolves into an exhortation where the poet invites the God of the sea to visit on a submarine "the deep lowest depths / the mister of the profound voids / the liquid atmosphere never traveled / by the sun, new countries and new climates, / populated by a thousand unknown beings" ("i profondi ceruli imi, / il mister dei voraginosi vuoti, / la liquida atmosfera mai percorsa / dal sol, nuovi paesi e nuovi climi, / popolati di mille esseri ignoti").[49] De Maria now introduces the theme of man's victory over nature, not such a terrifying notion as in the past. The argument has already been referred to in *La canzone della vela*, where the anastrophe "prisoner / man curtailed also the raging / thunderbolt" ("prigioniero / l'uomo ridusse pure il furibondo/ fulmine"), aims to foreshadow the prominence of the term "prisoner" ("prigioniero"), complement to the sentence's object "raging / thunderbolt" ("furibondo / fulmine").[50] This construction highlights how the twentieth century has subjugated natural phenomena and can now use them for its own pleasure.

The regression of these natural forces coincides with the evolution of man, whose physical and intellectual capacities are rendered powerful by modern technology. In *Gli abissi azzurri* the poet describes the "lynx eyes" ("occhi lincei") that enable exploration under unknown seas, until now, to the same Neptune, "God / deposed . . . ," "vanquishable god," ("Dio / spodestato," "vincibile signore,") his dominions have no more secrets for the "conqueror of the worlds" ("vincitor di mondi") from the "chariot . . . of iron" ("cocchio . . . di ferro"). The author exalts, as a "sun of modern genius," ("sol del genio modern") the lamp that the "powerful boat / . . . / carries in front . . . , that hurls / —to split open the great night—thousands of darts / of light" ("battello portentoso / . . . / reca in fronte . . . , che scaglia / —a squarciar la gran notte—mille strali / di luce"),[51] evoking once more the "violent electric moons" ("violente lune elettriche") in the manifesto *Uccidiamo il chiaro di luna* (*Let's Kill Off the Moonlight*).[52]

In the lyric poem *Al vento* (To the Wind) De Maria writes of the triumph over wind power exploited by man "until the remote day / in which the . . . first brother / . . . / in the excavated fur . . . / pulled up the first sail on the shapeless ship." ("fin dal giorno remoto / in cui il . . . primo fratello / . . . / nell'abete scavato . . . / impennò su l'informe nave la prima vela").[53] The description of the fury of the wind to which the writer dedicates more than a third of the lyric poem starts from the deliberate intention to point out the value of human enterprise. The poet describes the stages of continuous, ascending progress, beginning with the invention of the windmill and then moving on to the hot air balloon. In doing so, he expresses the prophetic hope to soon see the skies furrowed with a "powerful airplane" ("aereo portento"),[54] which is in fact praised in a later, 1910 lyric poem, *Aeroplano di Latham*, "For the first human flight in the storm" ("Pel primo volo umano nella tempesta").[55]

Compared to these new means of transport the sail boat is singly reduced to "a nice motif / pictorial, on the live / blue-green of the sea" ("un bel motivo / pittorico, tra il vivo / glauco del mare"),[56] an antiquated object, only beautiful to look at, and in *Gli abissi azzurri*, the carcass of a ship on the bottom of the ocean is used as a symbol of the coffin of unrealized dreams of conquest. In this case, however, De Maria shows a certain reverence, a kind of religious respect for a past that has sacrificed itself for a good future. The multiple failures that human history has produced represent the fundamental basis for subsequent conquests. De Maria adds to his gallery of metaphors in *La vecchia casa*. The collapse of the old building under the strikes of pickaxes are evoked by an alliterated C—"the old house collapses / unroofed" ("la vecchia casa crolla /

scoperchiata")—here the poet celebrates death in a poem totally free of nostalgia as he considers the bulky decadence of the building:

> Remain
> always anonymous for us,
> with your useless weight
> of your past, of your
> pale distant memories,
> it is better than to leave you
> longer, other than to occupy space
> of blue and infertile
> soil . . . ,
> now you are broken, decrepit, wrecked
> it is better than to prop up your shattered
> obesity with supports
> and strengthen your crumbling walls,
> it is better that you fall to pieces,
> oh old and useless house.[57]

The concept of death, announced by the metaphor of the cadaver—"The old
house . . . /is a monstrous cadaver tortured by enormous wounds" ("La vecchia casa . . . / è un mostruoso cadavere straziato da enormi ferite")—returns
with the association between the destruction and agony of the building in
which the soul "slowly, slowly breathes its last" ("s'è esalata a poco a poco)
in a slow intermediate stage in which it prepares to become "the tomb / of
the past" ("la tomba / del passato").[58] But it is no longer about a grave around
which the poet invokes the light of a "victorious funeral pyre" ("rogo di vittoria"),[59] as we saw previously, where the sunken boat rose up almost to a
sacred altar, a symbol of the congenital human attraction for discovery. In
this instance the tomb represented by the house is knocked down and then
transformed into a new world. The building raised to the ground leaves space
for factories, for "a new cloak / for galliard life" ("nuovo mantello/ a vita
gagliarda"), for bridges, docks and railways.[60] Death therefore generates new
life, and it is nature that imposes this eternal cycle of becoming.

These verses clearly had an effect on Marinetti, unconsciously called
South by his African origins,[61] but clearly flattered by the attention paid him
by the "frondisti." The column *Vento di fronda*, brought news from Paris of
the first night of Marinetti's play *Le roi Bombance* and of its forthcoming publication in Italian.[62] The success that Marinetti had among the young Sicilians including the founder of *La Fronda* who in his review of Marinetti's play
praised its revolutionary spirit, induced the Milanese intellectual to forge

bonds of friendship and culture with the islanders, that was consolidated by an intense exchange of letters with De Maria. The birth of this relationship promised to be advantageous for both interlocutors. On the one hand it responded to Marinetti's need to spread his new cultural creed through the creation of outreach centers in the South. On the other hand it met the need of the young Sicilians to spread their fame nationwide.

Marinetti, wanting to relate to the birth of the new movement, said to De Maria even before Lucini "the next issue of *Poesia* . . . will be highly important and will contain exceptional things" ("Il prossimo numero di *Poesia* . . . sarà importantissimo e conterrà cose eccezionali"). After having given news of the "Turin storm" ("bufera torinese") that had given him "the opportunity to spit once again on the ugly face of the imbecilic public" ("fornito l'occasione di sputare una volta di più sul grugno del pubblico imbecille"), sure of his friend's approval he continues: "we are both armed and decided to fight to the end for our ideal" ("siamo ambedue armati e decisi a lottare ad oltranza per il nostro ideale").[63] It is worth showing here for its unquestionable testimonial value, the letter, which immediately followed on February 5, 1909:

> I send you the Futurist manifesto in which . . . we have summarized all our scattered aspirations both destructive and innovative.
>
> I beg you . . . to start a bold and daring campaign in all the Sicilian newspapers with which you are able to collaborate, given the universal imbecility.
>
> What is necessary is that you publish it wherever you can in large and small papers, enabling and stirring up debate, arguments, protests and comments so that we travel in the middle of an uproar of shouts—I hope—and insults.
>
> Forward, dear friend!
>
> I will create an enormous clamor around Futurism, with thousands and thousands of manuscripts and blurbs who will naturally put you among the first Futurists.[64]

In effect, De Maria, together with Marinetti, Buzzi, Cavacchioli, was one of the first four authors to sign their names to the manifesto. The letter presented to him remains unique on several counts. The use of the possessive in the first person plural, "our," highlights the amalgam nature of the text, having been drawn from various sources and comprising heterogeneous elements that Marinetti cleverly manages to marry together and synthesize. The letter is also an acknowledgment of De Maria's important role; it recognizes that the fundamentals upon which Futurism is based are comprised of the group's communal convictions. On the other hand, the possessive adjective indirectly calls for the emergence of a solid team spirit, which is essential for effectively conducting an extensive advertising campaign. De Maria's reply was not as enthusiastic, a sign of his subsequent distancing from Futurism and an indication that he was not comfortable with the newborn movement, along with other intellectuals not only from the South including Lucini, Prezzolini, Papini, Soffici, Palazzeschi, Cardile.[65]

The motives for De Maria's divorce from Marinetti need to be explained. The Sicilian writer laid claim with his gesture of deserter, to the authorship of many Futurist statements, recognized by scholars such as Pedrina, Biondo-lillo and Ruta.[66] For De Marchis however it was about unfounded announce-ments of Futurism because the 1909 Manifesto "was intentionally constituted as an act of foundation of a brand new movement where Marinetti imposed the name and the poetry to give to a real and proper organisation."[67] What De Maria was missing was the ability to organize and unify the multiple echoes of his poetry by imposing himself as leader of the literary renaissance. Nevertheless in 1945 the ex-writer of *La Fronda* wrote *Contributo alla storia delle origini del futurismo e del novecentismo* ("Contribution to the History of the Origins of Futurism and Twentieth-Century Art") where he confirms the role of his poetry as a forerunner of Futurism.[68]

Another reason for the split can be found in his lack of understanding of the futurist radicalism with its breaking of rules of syntax, words-in-freedom poems and the graphic games loved by the Milanese group and praised in the 1912 *Manifesto tecnico della letteratura futurista* (*Technical Manifesto of Futurist Literature*) and in the 1913 *Distruzione della sintassi* (*Destruction of Syntax*). De Maria had no intention of canceling all the "rules" of art, the innovative character of his work, his openness to modernity, never lose sight of measure. The affirmation that "art brings brakes and laws, even when it is the artist himself who puts on this brake and imposes this law" ("l'arte comporta freno e legge, anche quando questo freno e questa legge è l'artista stesso a crearseli e imporseli"),[69] can significantly be taken as a manifesto of De Maria's poetry and it makes one think of the passage from *L'Estetica della meccanica* to the *Estetica crociana*. An important point here is that the fall in the enthusiasm of Palermo's futurists coincided with the end of the economic well being in the city. Avant-garde theories could not penetrate the mainstream socio-cultural fabric of the Sicilians, who were only at first, intoxicated by the exuberance of innovation.

Federico De Maria confirmed his distance from Marinetti in two articles, *Storia passata di una cosa futura* ("Past History of a Future Thing") and *Vol-garizzazione della cosa abominevole* ("The Vulgarization of an Abominable Thing"), published in *L'Ora* on 14 and 19 July 1910. In the first article[70] he deals with an extended historical *excursus* into considering the assumption that "All men, some more, some less have always held out a large part of themselves in thinking about the future" ("Tutti gli uomini, qual più qual meno hanno teso sempre gran parte di sé nel pensiero del futuro"):

> I am interested in demonstrating . . . that humanity in its totality and of individual men, have always had an innate tendency towards the future, and that it has been this that has created progress and civilization. From day to day he has always met his primitive needs, new desires, he has felt new desires, he has been obsessed with new ideals. . . . This tension in man and in society has however always existed, the idea of renewal for improvement, renunciation of past objects because they are now inadequate to meet new needs.[71]

Subsequent to this premise the analysis of the natural consequences for which art tends to follow a parallel evolutionary vocation:

> Due to a justifiable reaction, another thing happens, art which at first always operated without the artist ever discussing his actions and intentions, gradually began to show signs of reasoning, not wanting to be dominated by criticism from on high. And this was not enough: criticism with its air of pedantic instructor, wanted to retrain art, this eternal restless maiden, within the limits assigned it by the past. . . . Due to this conflict therefore art sharpened its hatred of the past. At first this took place in the form of rebellious words, murmured in a low voice, without much courage. This was backed up by manifest activity—but the criticism, discussing, never accepted them, never allowed the art to be performed, carried out. Now armies of equal sizes were needed, they had to shout more loudly, discuss.[72]

In 1905 the statement above was the main purpose for creating *La Fronda*. Reconstructing approximately the historical and cultural stages that brought about the birth of Futurism, De Maria set out his attachment to the substrata of progressive ideals, existing in man from his origins, from which those specifically futurist ideals would be developed. A critique of Marinetti, which is central to his subsequent article, had already come to light, although covertly in the recognition in the Milanese poet of one single priority, that of creating a poetry of violence. Apart from that the *Manifesto* only united "the common ideas of many young people" ("idee comuni a molti giovani").

In his second article touching on the various points of the *Manifesto* the writer proposed "to carry out a vulgarization of Futurism, to unmask it in public, to show what it truly is, in order to discuss it as calmly as possible" ("di fare un volgarizzamento del futurismo, per svelarlo al pubblico quale esso è veramente, per discuterlo con la massima serenità"). At the same time he clarified his reasons to refute not Futurism, with which he shared the basic principles, but rather Marinettism—the personal method imposed by Marinetti on a common project in search of new ideas:

> It is about eighteen months since someone rose up to shout out a new word, a word which intended to mean a world of unusual things, it was greeted by the misoneists, those haters of change, as mad, grotesque, absurd.
>
> The word—already spoken in my previous article—was *Futurism* and the person who waved it as a revolutionary banner was called Marinetti.
>
> The French-Italian poet used that terrible word to proclaim the unnamed thing that has always been in the heart of men of every age, at least of men of action. He only invented a name responding to the form taken on by the universal sentiment of his personality. . . .
>
> Marinetti with his explosive nature and volcanic temperament not just as an artist but also as a man, has expressed his feelings about the future in violent and aggressive terms. What should be the pronouncement of an idea has instead been given the character of the poet, a passionate rattling of images. The Futurist Manifesto is more than a critical and polemic program, it is also a lyric poem, an expression of a state of mind, a subjective work.
>
> Any critic, historian or journalist could have written what in substance Marinetti wanted to say without causing such a sensation, on the contrary gathering approval and consensus, at least among young people, who also have—with few exceptions—crucified Futurism. It would have been enough not to use such a pompous style with so many resounding, apolitical symbols, an excessively personal style. Marinetti the poet always wants to impose the tone of his poetry onto every form of communication, private correspondence and conversation. Those who have read or listened to the manifesto have taken the content too literally, they have stopped to look at the cover and that excessive exterior has distracted them.
>
> Marinetti rather than come up with concepts has given us intuition—following B. Croce's terminology—and they express not an absolute truth but a relative sentiment. Admitting that the love for the future could be baptized as *Futurism*, Futurism thus proclaimed was a lyrical commotion coming from Marinetti alone, not even the others who had given their signatures (among those here at the foot of the page) all felt it precisely as he did.
>
> So what does Futurism want? That which certainly is desired, I repeat, by all men who are concerned with the continuing progress of society, with slight formal rather than substantial differences.[73]

From De Maria's brief reference to Croce, the influence of *Estetica come scienza dell'espressione e linguistica generale* (Aesthetics as the Science of Expression and General Linguistics) can easily be heard here. This work by Benedetto Croce was edited in Palermo in 1902 by Sandron. It is highly probable that his closeness to Croce's aesthetic constituted another reason for distancing himself from Marinetti's ideas.

De Maria's Futurism, while developing a polemical position to the past, placed at the center of his reflection the theme of man's leaning towards the other man-brother, the result of the synthesis between the past and the present. De Maria was firmly convinced of the need for the new to engage with the old and believed in the necessity to recognize a relationship of derivation between the modern and traditional artist. "We want . . . that he who makes art is a man of today, son of these last two centuries blazing with wonderful light" ("Vogliamo . . . che chi fa arte sia uomo d'oggi, figlio di questi due ultimi secoli ardenti di luce meravigliosa").[74]

This would have obviously excluded the literal reference to the fathers. It would have been useful to offer a mirror image of these rather than collecting higher results, to transform in every way with a new rhythm into an art adhering to the present. It is clear that De Maria was not criticizing a love of the future, one of the most primitive and instinctive of humanity. In this sense Marinetti had no advantage of priority, but he criticized the form with which the *Manifesto* was expressed, here the sentiment was only expressed as a relative interpretation coinciding with Marinetti's own destructive spirit. Flora distinguishes Marinettism, which he defines as "a whim," "a formula" ("un capriccio," "una formula"), from Futurism which coincides with a "spiritual atmosphere" ("un'atmosfera spirituale").[75]

De Maria's articles were followed by a letter from Marinetti on July 29, 1910, the longest of the correspondence:

> I have ascertained that with a great profusion of intelligence and critical acumen, you have not managed to demonstrate that the word *Futurism* is a bad word. Fundamentally this is the only thing that separates us. And excuse me infinitively if I state this to you. If you do not like the word *Futurism* that simply means that you are still a misoneist.[76]

The disappointment felt by Marinetti as a result of De Maria's distancing from him and taking a more moderate position, did not however induce him to break their bonds of friendship, this was confirmed for example when Marinetti attended De Maria's wedding as his witness in Palermo in 1911. He also oversaw the publication of De Maria's collection of poems *La leggenda della vita* (The Legend of Life) by *Poesia*.

De Maria's refutation of the more extreme results of Futurism also demonstrated his opposition to the ties to certain forms of expression which all schools of art bring with them, however avant-garde and contemporary they are. The youthful baggage carried forward by the poet against the canons of classicism subsequently took on greater dimensions. De Maria totally shares the opinion of Enrico Cardile who said "it is no longer possible . . . to stay with Marinetti's futurist poets . . . because Marinetti, elected pope of the Tuscan-Lombard set, now sold his futurist recipes all over the world with the same dogmatic authority of the popes of the old system."[77] This conviction was reaffirmed by Benedetto Migliore in the article *Dai fischi di Milano agli applausi di Palermo* (From the Whistles of Milan to the Applause of Palermo): "if they want to destroy the prejudices of the past, they are in their turn victim of a new prejudice and the new constraints of a school."[78]

The risk that Futurism could stagnate inside its "method" alarmed many of it supporters who gradually began to distance themselves from it. Luciano Folgore parodied his own first futurist writings, as an instrument of renewal is vital for every avant-garde movement.[79] Similarly Ruggero Vasari, a futurist from Messina, also employed a poetic system in his work. In the same years in which De Maria declared the collapse of any form of progressivist illusion referring to A *l'uomo di domani* (To the man of tomorrow)—"I see you in your peace / made of war, splitter / of the atom," "this world . . . moves towards / with the annihilation / of the individual, to leveling / of every character, to make everything a perfect / common place, of every aspect / different from monotony / of a precise mechanical series / without top and without bottom" ("Ti vedo nella tua pace / fatta di guerra, disintegratore / dell'atomo," "questo mondo . . . s'avvia / all'annientamento / dell'individuo, al livellamento / d'ogni carattere, a far d'ogni cosa un perfetto / luogo comune, d'ogni aspetto / diverso la monotonia / d'una serie precisa meccanica, / senza vette e senza fondo").[80] Vasari, after the publication of *L'angoscia delle macchine*[81] (The Anguish of the Machine), nearly the introduction of a new creative phase, emblematically represented by the play *Raun*,[82] stated as follows in a letter to his friend Guglielmo Jannelli:

> Now is the time to finish with programmatic art! . . . I go beyond Futurism because while on the one hand I praise the machine (Cambronne, how praise is to show you are alive!) on the other it horrifies me! And why? Because mechanization destroys the spirit! When the spirit is dead, man is also dead or stays automated without life, without desires, without joy. . . . What would Marinetti have demanded? That I finish *Raun* with four rhetorical words as is his habit and said: "Oh marvelous machine, slippery creature, I am totally in thrall to your sinuous gears, I want to drink your torrid heart, savoring it like a sweet!" Oh for goodness sake. . . . [83]

The parallels drawn here further clarify that, although the thread that tied De Maria to the futurists was considerably strong as we can see from particular insistences, for example, "on the man of the new century" ("sull 'uomo del secolo nuovo'"), on the "sun of modern genius" ("sole del genio moderno"), "on the icons of the car, train, ship, airplane" ("sulle icone della macchina, del treno, della nave, dell'aereo"),[84] he evidently went beyond them, growing consistently in his own ongoing artistic evolution.

Notes

1. Translation by Claudia M. Clemente.

2. "La Sicilia stessa appare come metafora del nuovo, perché essa è in quegli anni un crogiolo di esperienze innovative nel campo delle arti, terra essa stessa di penetrazione futurista." Lia Fava Guzzetta, "Marinetti, Pirandello. Il fuoco, la Sicilia," in Idem, *Tra simbolismo e futurismo. Verso sud* (Pesaro: Metauro, 2009), 21.

3. Anna M. Ruta, *Il Futurismo in Sicilia. Per una storia dell'avanguardia letteraria* (Marina di Patti: Pungitopo, 1990), 20–23.

4. Federico De Maria was born in Palermo on July 21, 1883. His main vocation, manifested precociously, was for literature. At the age of fourteen he won a narrative competition, thanks to the Sicilian journal *La Bohème*, with his first publication, *La leggenda del Giamma*; at eighteen he was already a confirmed conference-attendee (he remains renowned for his contribution in celebration of the centenary commemoration of Victor Hugo); at twenty he published his first poetry collection, *Voci* (Palermo-Rome: Sandron), 1903.

5. Federico De Maria, "La vita dolorosa," *La Bohème* 7 (May 16, 1900).

6. In De Maria the passage from a post-*Scapigliatura* phase to a pre-futurist or a futurist one came in an extremely gradual manner. See on this evolution Francesco Flora, *Dal Romanticismo al Futurismo* (Milan: Mondadori, 1925), 67.

7. "Io voglio aprire / agli uomini le vie dell'avvenire / e a chiudere il passato mi preparo. . . . / Oh custodi del vecchiume,/ gli altari eretti al vostro falso nume / il nostro vero li rovescerà! / Nell'avvenir la vita; e l'arte è vita / e avvenire." Federico De Maria, *Il fabbro*, first in *Arte Nuova*, November 1901; then in De Maria, *Voci* 9, 18–20, 34–38.

8. Federico De Maria, *La canzone nuova*, in Idem, *Canzoni rosse* (Palermo-Rome: Sandron, 1905), 9.

9. "E batte e batte e batte orribilmente / il maglio che riposo mai non ha, / e foggia il primo e pure il più possente / magnifico lavor: la volontà"; De Maria, *Il Fabbro*, vv. 1; 21–24. The comprehensive image recalls the similarity between the smith and the poet set out by Carducci in *Congedo* (Farewell).

10. "Io sono il Dio / di giovinezza, io sono / Prometeo che incede con la fiaccola / in pugno: . . . / . . . infrangerò le porte / del carcere ove splende / chiusa,

la Verità, gemma purissima!" De Maria, *Ai nemici miei*, in Idem, *Voci*, 8, vv. 10; 8–18. The Promethean motif would then be exploited at large by the futurists: "Il futurismo . . . da una parte, voleva, con romantico impeto prometeico, dar l'assalto al firmamento e intronizzare al posto di dio morto l'uomo deificato; dall'altro, con ardore, frenesia, entusiasmo, si tuffava negli aspetti più esterni, effimeri, e vistosi della civiltà tecnologica . . . . ("Futurism . . . on the one hand, sought to (with a romantic Promethean surge) assault the heavens and enthrone in the place of a 'dead god,' instead that of a deified man, and, on the other hand, with ardor, hustle, enthusiasm, plunge in the most outer, ephemeral, and showy aspects of technologi-cal civilization. . . . ") Luciano De Maria, *F. T. Marinetti. Teoria e invenzione del futurismo* (Milan: Mondadori, 1968), xxix.

11. De Maria, *Il fabbro*, vv. 32, 29–30, 35–36.

12. Federico De Maria, in *La Fronda* 1 (25–5–1905).

13. De Maria, *Il fabbro*, vv. 9–10.

14. De Maria, *La canzone nuova*, vv. 1, 2, 5, 10, 9, 10, 15, 5–8.

15. Massimo Bontempelli, *A Federico De Maria*, in Francesco Biondolillo, *Di un poeta e delle origini della poesia contemporanea* (Palermo: Palumbo, 1951). These liter-ary exhortations are irrevocably tied nonetheless to Classicism, Bontempelli being, after all, the future promoter of literature of "the Twentieth Century," and "Magical Realism."

16. Massimo Bontempelli, letter of July 21, 1910, in Anna M. Ruta, "Lettere di Massimo Bontempelli a Federico De Maria," in *L'Illuminista* (Rome: Ponte Sisto, 2005), 297–321. The correspondence of Bontempelli to De Maria has been preserved by the De Maria Foundation, in the "Biblioteca Comunale di Palermo" (52 Qq–D 501 nn.1–17/ 52 Qq D n.2020).

17. De Maria, *A Massimo Bontempelli*, in Biondolillo, *Di un poeta*, 30–31.

18. De Maria, *Prima esegesi del metro libero*, conference held at Palermo's "Circolo di Cultura" in October 1906. Then in Federico De Maria, introduction to *La Ritor-nata* (Catania: S.E.M.), 1932.

19. De Maria, *La canzone nuova*, vv. 17–19.

20. " . . . come un albero forte a la calura / nei campi dai fiumi aridi percorsi, / io qui fiorisco e bevo a larghi sorsi / l'infinito respir della natura." De Maria, *La canzone nuova*, vv. 41–44.

21. De Maria, *La canzone nuova*, vv. 52, 56.

22. The first stage of Sicilian Futurism took place in Palermo from 1905 to 1913, year of the fiasco of Marinetti's first *Elettricità* at the Teatro Politeama.

23. Filippo T. Marinetti, *Les dieux s'en vont, D'Annunzio reste* (Paris: Sansot, 1908).

24. "Abbiamo vivo desiderio di vedere e di mostrare se è vero che l'Italia non sia buona a produrre eternamente che neoclassici e neoromantici. . . . Da principio l'opera nostra sarà di demolizione: lo spazio è ormai ingombro e bisogna prima abbat-tere per ben riedificare. Gli dei falsi e bugiardi sono stati adorati abbastanza, è tempo di rovesciarli." De Maria, Proclama of *La Fronda* 1 (25–5–1905).

25. "Per noi insomma è arte grande solo quella che rispecchia la vita mirando al futuro. . . . Vogliamo quindi che chi fa arte sia uomo d'oggi, figlio di questi due ultimi secoli ardenti di luce meravigliosa, fratello di coloro che hanno dato all'umanità il vapore, le macchine elettriche, il telegrafo senza fili, il radio e mille fulgide promesse per l'avvenire. . . . Possibile che i poeti d'Italia e di tutta la latinità ora non siano buoni che a frugare rimestando tra le morte ceneri della tradizione? Siano allora buttate a mare queste tradizioni e queste glorie del passato, quando non servono che ad incepparci invece di esserci fari in un libero cammino. O diamo meglio uno sgambetto a tutti coloro i quali non sanno metterci d'innanzi agli occhi che il passato, il passato, quest'eterno passato! Gente noiosa e talpesca che non sa trarre gli ammaestramenti migliori dalla sua inerte dottrina e non s'accorge che la polvere, spazzata dai volumi che cura, ricade tutta addosso a lei." De Maria, "Il perché di una cosa inutile." *La Fronda* 1 (25–5–1905).

26. "Che cosa è stata l'arte attraverso le ère, attraverso la vita dei popoli se non la fisionomia spirituale d'ogni epoca, la storia morale di ogni popolo? . . . Noi non cam-miniamo più coi passi dell'evoluzione ma si può dire che procediamo di rivoluzione in rivoluzione. Tutto ciò è dovuto massimamente ai mezzi di produzione, di scambio, di trasporto: al vapore e all'elettricità. L'età nostra è eminentemente meccanica: la macchina ha mutato la nostra vita e in gran parte i nostri sentimenti e gli ideali. . . . Le tre tendenze: passatista, presentista ed avvenirista, si incontrano ovunque, ove fuse, ove separate. L'ultima, cui fu araldo Walt Whitman, comincia ad avere la sua arte. Per ora guardatela quest'arte nuova, più che in ogni altro nell'architettura . . . ; guardate i grandi monumenti meccanici; le fabbriche gigantesche, . . . i palazzi a trenta piani dalle ossature d'acciaio, i porti inauditi sull'oceano, le torri che toc-cano le nuvole, edifizi . . . che hanno la bellezza della forza e dell'utilità razionale. Dissoluzione, rielaborazione. L'antico uomo si dissolve, si dissolvono le antiche società." De Maria, "Estetica della meccanica e del capriccio," partially in *La Fronda* (25–5–1905); integrated into *L'Ora* (5–11–1907). The essay was then included in De Maria, introduction to *La Ritornata*.

27. "Noi affermiamo che la magnificenza del mondo si è arricchita di una bellezza nuova: la bellezza della velocità. Un'automobile da corsa con il suo cofano adorno di grossi tubi simili a serpenti dall'alito esplosivo . . . un'automobile ruggente, che sem-bra correre sulla mitraglia, è più bello della Vittoria di Samotracia. . . . Noi vogliamo distruggere i musei, le biblioteche, le accademie di ogni specie. . . . Canteremo il vibrante fervore notturno degli arsenali e dei cantieri incendiati da violente lune elettriche; le stazioni ingorde divoratrici di serpi che fumano; le officine appese alle nuvole pei contorti fili dei loro fumi; i ponti simili a ginnasti giganti che scavalcano i fiumi, balenanti al sole con un luccichio di coltelli; i piroscafi avventurosi che fiutano l'orizzonte, le locomotive dall'ampio petto, che scalpitano sulle rotaie, come enormi cavalli d'acciaio imbrigliati di tubi, e il volo scivolante degli aeroplani, la cui elica garrisce al vento come una bandiera e sembra applaudire come una folla entusiasta. . . . vogliamo liberare questo paese dalla fetida cancrena di professori, d'archeologi, di ciceroni, d'antiquari. . . . noi non vogliamo più saperne, del passato, noi giovani e

forti futuristi! Date fuoco agli scaffali delle biblioteche! . . . demolite, demolite senza pietà le città venerate!" Filippo Tommaso Marinetti, "Il Manifesto del Futurismo," in *I Manifesti del Futurismo* (Florence: Lacerba, 1914).

28. Filippo Tommaso Marinetti, "Estetica della macchina," in *Antologia dei nuovi poeti futuristi* (Rome: Edizioni Futuriste di "Poesia," 1925).

29. De Maria, *Saffica pagana, Inno al sole, La canzone della vela, Gli abissi azzurri* in Idem, *Interludio Classico* (Rome: La Voce Letteraria, 1907); Idem, *Il volo*, in *Canzoni Rosse*; Idem, *Al vento, La vecchia casa*, in Idem, *La Leggenda della vita* (Milan: Edizioni Futuriste di "Poesia," 1909).

30. De Maria, *A le persone classiche*, in Idem, *Interludio classico*, 5.

31. De Maria, *La sosta*, in Idem, *Interludio classico*, 8.

32. ". . . io pubblico pochi studi di versi—umilmente. . . . sperando che almeno questa volta la burocrazia letteraria vorrà essermi benigna. E, poi che son sicuro che essa non guarderà a quel che dico né si curerà di sapere perché lo dico, resterà almeno soddisfatta, sfogliando queste poche paginette, della lor simmetria." De Maria, *A le persone classiche*, 5.

33. De Maria, *Ditirambo del metro libero*, in Idem, *Interludio classico*, 30; Idem, *La Canzone nuova*, in Idem, *Canzoni rosse*, 9.

34. De Maria, *Saffica pagana, Canzone della vela, Inno al sole*, in Idem, *Interludio classico*, 15, 23, 27.

35. Romano Luperini e.a., *La scrittura e l'interpretazione* (Palermo: Palumbo, 1997), vol. XII, 81.

36. De Maria, *Prima esegesi del metro libero*.

37. De Maria, *La passione*, in Idem, *Interludio classico*, 10, vv. 3–6.

38. Massimo Bontempelli, *Odi siciliane* (Palermo: Sandron, 1906).

39. Giosuè Carducci, *Odi Barbare* (Bologna: Zanichelli, 1877).

40. De Maria, *Saffica pagana*, vv. 18–20.

41. De Maria in *La vecchia casa* (vv. 45–49) affirms: "we will build smokestacks / factories animated by the roars / of enormous mechanical spools / that weave a new robe / a vigorous life" ("fabbricheremo fumanti/ opifici animati da la romba/ de le macchine- enormi spole/ che tessono un nuovo mantello/ a la vita gagliarda").

42. De Maria, *Saffica Pagana*, vv. 29–32.

43. De Maria, *Inno al Sole*, vv. 10–12, 43, 49, 55.

44. "Bella pur, se ti vieti / la bonaccia il gran volo e pendi inerte / lungo le scotte, innanzi alla fumante / beffa del tuo gigante / emulo, che, rugghiando, nelle aperte / immensità contro la verde Sfinge, / forte securo rapido si spinge." De Maria, *La canzone della vela*, vv. 53, 78, 82; 46; 48–52.

45. De Maria, *La canzone della vela*, vv. 52–53, 56, 60–64, 77–78.

46. De Maria, *La canzone della vela*, vv. 47; 4.

47. The metric choice of the couplet renders the train's motion not only rhythmically, but also visually. In fact, it seems to portray the platforms through which it slides, or the out-of-focus landscapes rushing past as the wagons run on the rails.

48. De Maria, *Il volo*, vv. 35, 50; 9, 17, 32, 36–37; 41–42; 47.

49. De Maria, *Gli abissi azzurri*, vv. 1, 37; 1; 7–8; 26–30.

50. De Maria, *La canzone della Vela*, vv. 53–55. The value of man's victory over lightning is, among other things, stressed by the prominent position of the adjective "furious" ("furibondo") in the enbjambment. The poet specifies humanity has competed with a *Fury*, succeeding, at last, in dominating it.

51. De Maria, *Gli abissi azzurri*, vv. 9; 12–14; 17; 31–36.

52. Filippo Tommaso Marinetti, *Uccidiamo il chiaro di luna* (Milan: Edizioni Futuriste di "Poesia," 1911).

53. De Maria, *Al vento*, vv. 49–56. The lyric in question, as in the one that follows, *La vecchia casa*, is tied to De Maria's production phase just after what has been examined here, that is however contemporary to the publication to the first Futurist Manifesto. Incidentally, a collection that includes both works was published in the edizioni futuriste di "Poesia."

54. De Maria, *Al vento*, v. 84.

55. De Maria, *Aeroplano di Latham*, in Idem, *Estate di San Martino* (Palermo: Trimalchi, 1935).

56. De Maria, *La canzone della vela*, vv. 61–63.

57. De Maria, *La vecchia casa*, vv. 1–2; 25–39.

58. De Maria, *La vecchia casa*, vv. 4; 11; 49–50.

59. De Maria, *Gli abissi azzurri*, v. 90.

60. De Maria, *La vecchia casa*, vv. 48–49.

61. Giorgio Guzzetta, "L'Africa come una 'pesante ferita aperta': per una ricerca sull'infanzia egiziana di Marinetti e la sua identità nazionale," in Guzzetta, *Tra simbolismo e futurismo*, 129–43.

62. Federico De Maria, "Le roi Bombance," *Vento di Fronda* in *La Fronda* 12 (10–8–1905) e 16 (7–9–1905).

63. Filippo Tommaso Marinetti, letter V (1908–1909), in Anna M. Ruta, "Ancora sul carteggio Marinetti-De Maria," in *Nuovi quaderni del meridione* 97–98 (1987): 138.

64. "Ti mando il manifesto del futurismo nel quale . . . abbiamo riassunto tutte le nostre sparpagliate aspirazioni demolitrici ed innovatrici. Ti prego . . . di cominciare in tutti i giornali di Sicilia, ove tu puoi collaborare, una campagna audace ed abile, data l'imbecillità universale. Quello che è necessario, è che tu lo faccia pubblicare dovunque, in grossi e piccoli giornali, permettendo e aizzando polemiche, proteste, e commenti, poiché viaggeremo in mezzo ad un frastuono di urli—spero—e d'insulti. Avanti, caro amico! Farò il più grande fragore intorno al Futurismo, con migliaia e migliaia di manoscritti e soffietti, che naturalmente mettono te fra i primi futuristi." Marinetti, letter VI (5–2–1909), in Ruta, "Ancora sul carteggio," 141. Unlike other letters in the exchange, of which the lack of the postal envelopes makes dating them difficult (dating can only be derived in most cases from the context of events mentioned in the text), in this case the exact date has been confirmed by Biondolillo, *Di un poeta*, 27.

65. See Gian P. Lucini, "Come ho sorpassato il Futurismo," *La Voce* 15 (10–4–1913); Enrico Cardile, "Io e il Futurismo," in *Determinazioni*, I (Palermo: Trimalchi, 1915), 45–78.

66. Francesco Pedrina, *Il poeta precursore* (Palermo: Palumbo, 1954), 2–3; Biondolillo, *Di un poeta*, 27; Anna M. Ruta, "Federico De Maria, un precursore non

riconosciuto," preface to Federico De Maria, *Passeggiate sentimentali in Tripolitania* (Palermo: L'Epos, 2004).

67. ". . . si costituisce intenzionalmente come atto di fondazione di un nuovissimo movimento, cui Marinetti impone il nome e la poetica e cui darà una vera e propria organizzazione"; Giorgio De Marchis, "Il Futurismo è tutto da ripensare," *Alfabeta* 113 (1989): 34.

68. Federico De Maria, "Contributo alla storia delle origini del Futurismo e del Novecentismo," *Accademia* 7–8 (1945): 3–8. De Maria published the article following the death of Marinetti, intending to carry out a survey of his own poetic trajectory.

69. De Maria, *Prima esegesi del metro libero*, 8.

70. De Maria, "Storia passata di una cosa futura," *L'Ora* (14–7–1910).

71. "A me interessa dimostrare . . . che l'umanità nel suo complesso e gli uomini, individualmente presi, hanno sempre avuto questa innata tendenza all'avvenire, e che è stato ciò a fare il progresso e la civiltà. Di giorno in giorno ha avuto sempre, soddisfatti i bisogni primitivi, nuovi desideri, ha sentito nuovi desideri, è stato assillato da nuovi ideali. . . . Questa tensione negli uomini e nella società, dunque è sempre esistita: rinnovare per migliorare, rinnegare le cose passate perché inadeguate alle necessità nuove."

72. "Per una giustificabile reazione, accade un altro fatto: che l'arte, la quale prima operava sempre senza discutere mai le proprie azioni e intenzioni, prese a poco a poco a manifestarle ragionandoci su, non volendo lasciarsi sopraffare dalla critica altezzosa. Né bastava: la critica con la sua aria da pedante istitutrice, voleva infrenare l'arte, quest'eterna irrequieta fanciulla, nei limiti assegnatile dal passato. . . . Per questo conflitto, dunque, l'arte prese a inasprirsi contro il passato. E furono da prima sorde parole di ribellione, mormorate a bassa voce, ancora senza troppo coraggio. Ci furono degli atti palesi—ma la critica, discutendo, non li accettò non li lasciò compiere. Occorreva contrapporre armi eguali, gridare più forte discutere."

73. "Diciotto mesi or sono, circa, sorse uno a gridare una parola nuova, la quale pareva volesse significare un mondo di cose insolite e, dicevano i misoneisti, pazzesche, grottesche, assurde. La parola—dissi già nel mio precedente articolo—era futurismo e chi la sventolava come un orifiamma rivoluzionario si chiamava Marinetti. Il poeta franco-italiano, con quella parola terribile altro non faceva che proclamare la innominata cosa che è stata in ogni tempo nel cuore degli uomini, per lo meno degli uomini d'azione. Egli inventava soltanto un nome rispondente a la forma assunta da quel sentimento universale nella sua personalità. . . . Marinetti, natura esplosiva, indole vulcanica non solo come artista ma anche come uomo, ha espresso il suo sentimento del futuro in forma violenta e aggressiva. Quello che doveva essere un pronunciamento di idee, è stato invece, dato il carattere del poeta, un crepitare appassionato di immagini. Il manifesto del futurismo, più che un programma critico e polemico, è una lirica, espressione di uno stato d'animo, opera soggettiva. Qualunque critico o storiografo o giornalista avrebbe potuto dire ciò che in sostanza volle dire Marinetti senza suscitare tanto scalpore, riscotendo—invece—l'approvazione e il consenso, per lo meno, dei giovani, i quali pure hanno—fatta eccezione di pochi—crocifigiato il futurismo. Sarebbe bastato non adoperare uno stile ampolloso, tutto a simboli, roboante, apocalittico, eccessivamente personale qual è

quello di Marinetti, poeta, che vuole sempre, anche nella corrispondenza privata, anche nella conversazione, imporre i toni della sua poesia. Quanti hanno letto o ascoltato il manifesto si sono troppo attenuti alla lettera, si sono fermati a guardare l'involucro e quell'eccessività esteriore li ha distratti. Quelli di Marinetti, dunque, più che concetti erano intuizioni—secondo la terminologia di B. Croce—ed esprimevano non già una verità assoluta ma un sentimento relativo. Ammettendo anche che l'amore pel futuro possa essere battezzato futurismo, il futurismo così bandito era una commozione lirica del solo Marinetti, ma nemmeno gli altri che vi avevano apposto le loro firme (tra cui quella qui in calce) lo sentivano in tutto e precisamente come lui. In sostanza che cosa vuole il futurismo? Quello che certamente vogliono, io ripeto, gli uomini tutti che si preoccupano del progresso continuo della società, con lievissime differenze più formali che sostanziali." De Maria, "Volgarizzazione della cosa abominevole," *L'Ora* (19–7–1910).

74. De Maria, "Il perché di una cosa inutile," 1.

75. Flora, *Dal romanticismo*, 69.

76. "Ho constatato che con una grande profusione di ingegno e di acume critico, non sei riuscito a dimostrare che la parola futurismo è una brutta parola. Questa è, in fondo, l'unica cosa che ci separa. E scusami infinitamente se te lo dichiaro. Se la parola futurismo non ti piace, è semplicemente perché sei ancora misoneista." Marinetti, letter IX, in Ruta, "Ancora sul carteggio," 145.

77. ". . . non è più possibile . . . rimanere coi poeti futuristi marinettiani . . . perché Marinetti, eletto pontefice della combriccola tosco-lombarda, spaccia ora a tutto il mondo le sue ricette futuriste con la stessa autorità dogmatica dei pontefici del vecchio sistema passatista." Cardile, "Io e il Futurismo," 45–78.

78. ". . . se essi vogliono distruggere i pregiudizi del passato sono alla loro volta vittime di un nuovo pregiudizio e di un nuovo vincolo di scuola." Benedetto Migliore, "Dai fischi di Milano agli applausi di Palermo," *Giornale di Sicilia* (28–4–11).

79. See Luciano Folgore, *Poeti controluce. Parodie* (Foligno: Campitelli, 1922); Idem, *Poeti allo specchio. Parodie* (Foligno: Campitelli, 1926).

80. De Maria, A L'uomo di domani, in Idem, *Estate di San Martino* (Palermo: Trimalchi, 1935), 79, vv. 8–18.

81. Ruggero Vasari, "L'angoscia delle macchine," *Der Sturm* I (1925).

82. Ruggero Vasari, *Raun* (Milan: La Lanterna, 1932).

83. "È ora di finirla con l'arte programmatica! . . . Io vado al di là del futurismo perché mentre da un lato esalto la macchina (Cambronne, come l'esalto e la faccio vivere!) dall'altro ne provo orrore! E perché? Perché la meccanizzazione distrugge lo spirito! Quando lo spirito è morto, anche l'uomo è morto o resta l'automa senza vita, senza desideri, senza gioie, . . . Cosa avrebbe preteso Marinetti? Che io finissi *Raun* con quattro paroloni rettorici come sua abitudine, e dicessi: "Oh, macchina meravigliosa anguillante creatura, io sono tutto preso nei tuoi ingranaggi nervi e voglio bere il tuo cuore torrido, assaporandolo come una caramella!" Ma insomma . . ." Ruggero Vasari, letter to G. Jannelli, 14–2–1931, in Ruggero Vasari, *L'angoscia delle macchine (e altre sintesi futuriste)*, ed. Maria E. Versari (Palermo: Duepunti Edizioni, 2009).

84. Ruta, *Federico De Maria*, 26.

CHAPTER SIX

~

The Statistical Sublime

Jeffrey T. Schnapp

I begin with (anything but) a coincidence.[1] On the one side: Friedrich Schlegel's 1797 *Fragmente zur Litteratur und Poesie* with its characteristic notations of everything from the absolute novel to Goethe's essence to *Das poetische Ideal*. On the other: Alfio Berretta's 1916 words-in-freedom *Autoequazione* where the self is equated with the square root of, more or less, the square root of the *I* multiplied by the fraction formed by *lei* over *lui* to the second power, equated with *K* squared—K being the standard variable for kinetic energy in physics—plus *K* times ten plus *lei*, all of which yields a grand total of zero (see figure 6.1).[2]

One needn't be a mathematical genius to recognize that Berretta's self-equation makes sense only in a domain where mathematical notation has been invaded and invalidated by poetic play. Berretta's self-identical self is a logical hall of mirrors. The square root of the square root of an I whose kinetic energy is multiplied thanks to an erotic triangle involving a *him* on the bottom and a *her* on top equivalent to zero . . . is *zero*. Even if the series of nested square roots were to extend to infinity, the outcome would be the same: the square root of zero is zero. Not zero, more or less, but *exactly zero*.

The case of Schlegel is the richer of the two and summons up the dream, anticipated in the universal language schemes of the prior century but exceeded in ways that point forward to Futurism, of a language that transcends or subtends time and space. Abbreviations abound in Schlegel's *Fragmente* and are typically Greek, as per the notational conventions of period science. They are flanked by eccentric usages of +, −, the fraction 1/o, and the broken

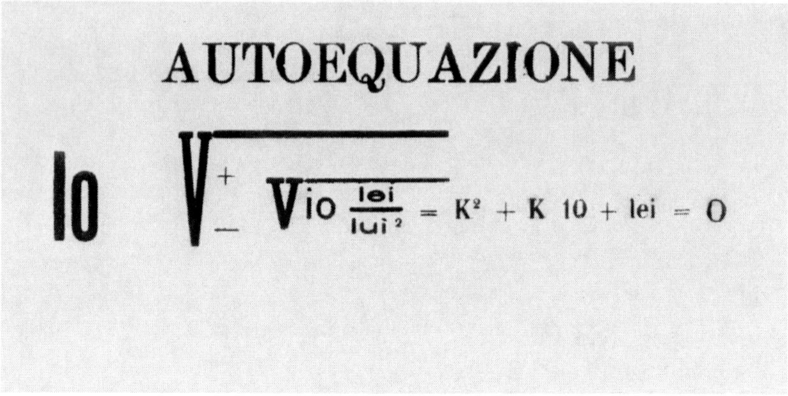

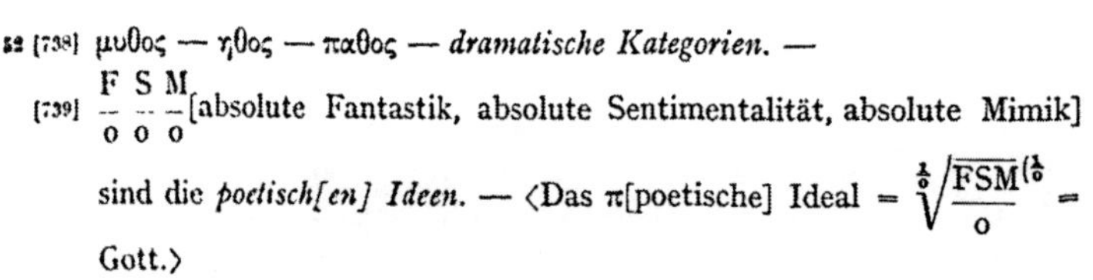

AUTOEQUAZIONE

$$\text{Io} \quad \sqrt[{}^+_-]{\sqrt{\text{io} \frac{\text{lei}}{\text{lui}^2}}} = K^2 + K\ 10 + \text{lei} = O$$

8. 52 [738] μῦθος — ἦθος — πάθος — *dramatische Kategorien.* —

[739] $\frac{F}{o} \frac{S}{o} \frac{M}{o}$ [absolute Fantastik, absolute Sentimentalität, absolute Mimik]

sind die *poetisch[en] Ideen.* — ⟨Das π[poetische] Ideal = $\sqrt[\frac{1}{o}]{\frac{FSM^{(\frac{1}{o}}}{o}}$ =

Gott.⟩

Figure 6.1.   Alfio Berretta, *Autoequazione*, Words-in-Freedom Poem 1916.

Friedrich Schlegel, fragment 739 from *Fragmente zur Litteratur und Poesie* (1797), cited from Ernst Behler, ed., *Kritische Friedrich Schlegel Ausgabe*, vol. 16, (Paderborn: F. Schöningh; Zurich: Thomas, 1958–), 148.

fraction /o standing respectively for positive, negative, infinite, and absolute, as well as by variants such as Δ/o = *absolute Drama* and Π/o = *absolute Poetry*. The square root of the self makes a solo appearance in the *Fragmente* as the marker of essence: "The Poem is a higher and deeper self that detaches itself from the self = √ the I."[3] And then there is the celebrated equation from Fragment 734 where Schlegel synthesizes a broader argument regarding the novel as a poetic ideal. Bred from the comingling of absolute fantasy (F/o), sentimentality (S/o), and mimicry (M/o), the novel alone can achieve totality and, as such, alone can express God. Here metaphysics bursts the dam of the mathematically sensical, for to divide by zero is not to divide at all.

However great the distance in time and spirit separating Schlegel's romantic idealism from Berretta's futurist mirthmaking, both appropriations of mathematical logic are animated by a belief that mathematics occupies a privileged place within the hierarchy of creations of the human mind. In the words of Oswald Spengler, "mathematics . . . is a science of the most rigorous kind, like logic but more comprehensive and fuller; it is a true art, along with sculpture and music, needing the guidance of inspiration and developing under great conventions of form; it is, lastly, a metaphysic of the highest rank, as Plato and above all Leibniz show us."[4] And it is the privileged status of mathematics that drives both Schlegel and Berretta to unbalance what Kant had dubbed *the mathematical sublime*: in other words, to seek to exceed the bounds of reason by means of a playful misuse of reason's most powerful tool—the logic of numbers.[5]

In the *Critique of Judgment*, the mathematical sublime is that experience of overwhelming vastness caused by finite objects that appear so vertiginously large as to defy human abilities to imaginatively comprehend them: a form of displeasure that gives rise to a compensatory pleasure when reason reasserts itself over and against the imagination's feverish workings by recognizing the transcendental character of suprasensible laws.[6] Kant's examples are spatial (pyramids and mountains). But what if the literal realm of numbers were itself to become the source of vertigo and shock? And what if, rather than prompting the return of reason, this numerical vertigo were to breed ever renewable dislocations between reason and imagination, logic and sensation, seriousness and play? Such is the domain that I'd like to examine here under the title of *the statistical sublime*. The enumeration of assemblies of statistical persons, data arrays cut and pasted into words-in-freedom tableaux, gargantuan inventories, chains of magic or random numbers and their prismatic interrelations, notational systems that compress the finite but seemingly infinite into nonsensical equations: this is the quantitative terrain mined by Futurism and transmitted as a legacy to subsequent avant-gardes that I will be surveying here.

Numbers have, of course, always been integral to another higher language for the expression of thought, namely poetry, from the quantitative metrics of ancient verse to Dante's definition of poetry as *numeri regolati* and beyond. Likewise, it goes without saying that golden and other ideal ratios have underwritten compositional norms in architecture, music, and the visual arts since remote antiquity. Yet it is only in the twentieth century that numbers and mathematical notation stride out onto the catwalk of cultural communication whether to star in on-stage recitations of random sequences (Balla's *Sconcertazione di stati d'animo*), to perform as typographical characters (Cangiullo's *Alfabeto a sorpresa*; the ciphers in El Lissitzky's children's books), or to explore new modes of expressivity (Khlebnikov), reference (Marinetti, Soffici), and hyperbole (Mayakovsky, Marinetti). Global Futurism plays a decisive role in this shift, claiming from the outset that it will sing the statistical battlefields of modern war, the city's number-studded landscapes, and a world of human multitudes navigating a sea of that newest product of the contemporary social sciences: statistics regarding demographics, production, consumption, and mobility. And these worlds of number are closely allied with and indeed animated by, on the one side, mathematics as associated with contemporary technics and, on the other, statistical hype of the sort extending from commercial advertising to political propaganda.

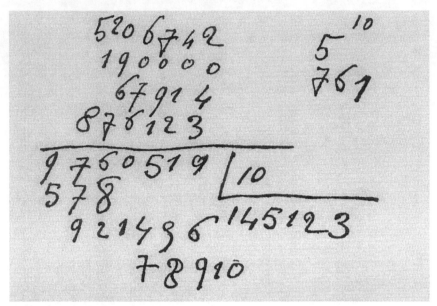

Figure 6.2. Tzara's 1916 *Manifeste de Monsieur Antipyrene,* read at first Dada soirée at Zunfthaus zur Waag in Zurich on July 14, 1916; printed in *Littérature* 2.13 (May 1920): 17.

Futurism's staging of number and mathematical notation is at once celebratory of this integer-rich environment and subversive to the degree that its playful embrace of number readily spills over into expressions of the nonsensical and the comic (like this example from Tzara's 1916 *Manifeste de Monsieur Antipyrene,* see figure 6.2).

But, as romantic precedent suggests, the purely quantitative is but the visible horizon of a deeper set of *qualitative* aspirations. Behind many a Man in Black taunting a Man in White with the command *111.111.011 I forbid you to laugh,* behind many an embrace of "the marvelous mathematical and geometrical elements that constitute the objects of our age" (Boccioni), behind many a celebration of math's "abstract simplicity of anonymous gearworks," there hover magic formulae, integers of esoteric inspiration (*numeri innamorati*), dreams of an absolute, intuitive, interior, lyrical mathematics, drives towards *qualitative* dimensions like those that provide the title for one of Marinetti's final contributions to the manifesto genre: *La matematica futurista immaginativa qualitativa* (1941).

In this attempt at an overall mapping of futurist mathematical practice, I provide little more than snapshots of five domains:

- *mathematics renotated* = what futurism does with notational conventions borrowed from mathematics

- *hyperbolic math* = large integers as intensifiers and persuaders
- *inventorying sensations* = fictions of cataloging and itemization
- *choral singularities* = synecdoches of number or how finite data sets are telescoped into seemingly infinite data arrays and vice versa
- *magic formulae* = numbers as expressions of the higher, lower, primordial or absolute.

Mathematics Renotated

Marinetti's attitude towards mathematical notation evolves during the movement's initial years. It debuts with paeans to semiotic economy as, for instance, in his response to objections to the *Technical Manifesto of Futurist Literature* where "the abstract aridity of mathematical signs . . . used to render quantitative relations" averts "the dangerous mania for wasting time in all the crannies of the sentence, in the minute labors of the mosaic maker, the jeweler, or the shoeshine boy." Here, telegraphic concision prevails over all other aims much as in subsequent experiments with compact messaging. The futurist leader was evangelical on the subject:

> In letters and postcards (best to use the latter because they impose brevity and synthesis), I advise you to make frequent use of numerical (+ − × =) notations of feelings qua sensations. Usefulness of writing in words-in-freedom *to all friends*. Spread the word. Address the problem that traditional letters have become ridiculous.[7]

By the time of the *Destruction of Syntax* manifesto, the emphasis has shifted from texting to the regulation of stylistic speed. But the true turning point comes one year later, in 1914, with the publication of the *Geometrical and Mechanical Splendor* manifesto in which considerations of *expression*, not just synthesis, inform an overall theorization of the notion of "numerical sensibility." Marinetti writes:

> I create true theorems or lyrical equations, introducing numbers which I've intuitively chosen and placed within the very center of a word; with a certain quantity of + − × +, I can give the thicknesses, the mass, the volumes of things which words otherwise have to express. The arrangement + − + − + + ×, for example, serves to render the changes and accelerations in the speed of an automobile. The arrangement + + + + + serves to render the clustering of equal sensations.

Here Futurism's *duce* is fully aligned with the thought of Spengler for whom, "in the last analysis, the number language of mathematics and the grammar of a tongue are structurally alike."[8] So just as the futurist revolution in poetic language has freed the word from the constraints of syntax, punctuation, and typographical predictability, now it will carry out an emancipation of number from logic, thereby giving rise to verbal-mathematical hybrids—*true* theorems and *lyrical* equations—and to new use scenarios for mathematical signs. The result is that notation will still retain some familiar semantic attributes—the + sign = addition or increase; the − sign = subtraction or decrease—but deviant ones arise as well: "the × sign," for instance, will be used "to indicate interrogative pauses of thought." More importantly, no longer limited to coupling numbers, mathematical signs can now be shaped into free-floating, atmospheric clusters that inflect a manifold of other visual-verbal elements, much like verbs in the infinitive simultaneously interconnect multiple subjects and predicates.

One example will have to stand in for an array of poetic and pictorial experiments with hybrid notational systems extending from the 1910s into the late 1930s: Marinetti's *montagne + vallate + strade × Joffre*, first published in 1915 but later included in the 1919 *Les mots en liberté futuriste* under the alternate title *Après la Marne, Joffre visita le front en auto* (see figure 6.3).

Here in the bottom left hand corner, the square root of the noun *Prussiens*—equated with war noises accompanied by strings of sensations, interrogative pauses, and equivalencies, all said to equal zero—serves as the springboard for a sequence of integral sign S's that string together an entire typographical tableau. The integral sign S, devised by Leibniz, is the standard sign for *summation* and here the summations form a spiral roadway that leads the reader's eye through a circuit of polyvalent M's = *montagne* = *mon ami* (Male) and *ma petite* (Female) = *mort aux Boches*, with other letters similarly multiple in their declensions: V = *vallate* = *victoire* = *vive la France* = *verbalisation* = *vitesse* = *virer vir volant*. Criss-crossing the circuit are figures composed of +, −, x, and = signs, each shaping a local set of meanings. The circuit rises, rotates to the right, and then falls, in keeping the physical principles alluded to by the ascending lightness (*léger*) and descending heaviness (*lourd*) signs inserted into the top right corner.

The cluster splitting BEL-LE, alternately assignable to *Belle France* or *Ma petite*, for example, suggests a block of affirmative sensations haunted by a minor doubt. Likewise, the vertical lines of plus signs plunging down through *Mon Amiiii* and flanked by a flock of swallow-like curly brackets (braces) suggest affirmation and acceleration towards *MaAA AAapetite*. But as one traverses *MaAA AAapetite* following the line of signs running diagonally between the upper right hand M and the lower MN, the driver's momentum

Figure 6.3. **Filippo Tommaso Marinetti's** *Montagne + vallate + strade x Joffre,* **first published in 1915 but later included in** *Les mots en liberté futuristes* **(Milan: Edizioni Futuriste di Poesia, 1919), under the alternate title** *Après la Marne, Joffre visita le front en auto.*

oscillates between accelerations and decelerations. Repeated × signs mark pauses in thought as victory nears so as to mark the slowness of Joffre's reconquest of *la belle France* at the Battle of the Marne.

The bracketed zone in the lower right hand corner serves as a synoptic table with respect to the composition as a whole, with fragments of road noise run through cyclical variations (*angolò angolì angolà angolin*), all summed up in a final refrain of *rarumà viar viar viar*, with its clear allusions to a semantic node conjoining themes of virility (*vir*), speed (*vite*), steering (*volant*), curve (*virage*), and roadway (*via*).[9]

Hyperbolic Math

To set mathematical notation free from the constraints of logical syntax is also to cut numbers free from representational obligations and limits. It is to open numbers up to the sorts of operations of quotation, decontextualization, and contamination that are routinely carried out in the visual and verbal realms by the early avant-gardes. The most familiar version of this procedure involves the collage-based practice of inserting product, newsprint, or place numbers into works, much as in Boccioni's 1913 *Scarpetta di società + orina* a walk down a London street is rendered as a row of building numbers gradually diminishing in scale (see figure 6.4).

Figure 6.4. Umberto Boccioni, "Scarpetta di società + orina," *Lacerba* (November 15, 1913).

But more telling as regards the effort to wed signs of precision and finitude to intimations of the infinite and absolute that I am here referring to as the statistical sublime, are four other rhetorics of number and it is to these that I would now like to turn:

- the additive use of zeros
- recourse to arithmetic and geometric series
- pseudo-inventories
- the cutting and pasting of apparently boundless data arrays.

The additive use of zeros as a form of statistical hyperbole is a defining feature of the futurist engagement with numbers from the time of Marinetti's first words-in-freedom poem, *Battaglia Peso + odore*, where the scale and scope of the theater of battle is conveyed by loosely hinged equations involving three thousand flags, two thousand arms, twenty thousand feet, ten thousand eyes, four thousand meters/battalions/boilers, and so on and so forth. As in subsequent instances, the figure stakes out a claim to precision even as it drops implicit or even explicit hints that the sequence of zeros could be infinitely prolonged. Little does it matter whether the exact number is sixty thousand, one million, 150 million, or an infinitesimally small fraction: the zero functions as an intensifier and persuader, as well as a marker of overwhelming scale.[10] It is an instrument governed not by a referent but by the intuition of a poet/artist endowed with a numerical sensibility and improvisatory skills.

An important variant on the hyperbolic zero is the no less hyperbolic use of arithmetic and geometric progressions: crescendos and diminuendos, composed of potentially infinite integer sequences, that enact a principle that is perhaps best described as *numerical dynamism*. Rather than functioning as stable markers that point to stable referents, futurist numbers are live feeds. They are generative and endowed with a natural tendency to *cascade*: to extend themselves in the mode of contraction or, more typically, expansion.

Inventorying Sensations

Mock inventories proliferate within the futurist fold, repurposing accounting conventions, statistical tools, and templates devised by state bureaucracies for the inventorying of manifold sensations, perceptions, and phenomena.

In the case of Guglielmo Jannelli's *Ufficiale d'ispezione*, an actual army inspection form is reworked into a words-in-freedom field report filed from the WWI front, with the full apparatus of army titles, footnotes, form numbers, and passwords left intact, even as the blanks are filled in with lyrical responses to non-lyrical requests like that found at the top of column 2: state the hour of your inspection (see figure 6.5).

Jannelli's horizontal response is a proper *12:30 at night*, but their vertical accompaniment abandons external description for something at once more elusive and allusive: *surprise visit reciprocal overheard algebraic painted telemetric frozen.* In the left hand column, a nonsensical equation describes the condition of the guard station as the inspector encountered it upon his arrival: heat absorbed by stone walls + weight of sleeping howitzers = 102 tons, × the weight of (30.6) × 216.945 sleeping grenades = 38906 kilos. The patrol's field battery, in turn, weighs in at a nimble 752 grams of red lead. In short, the

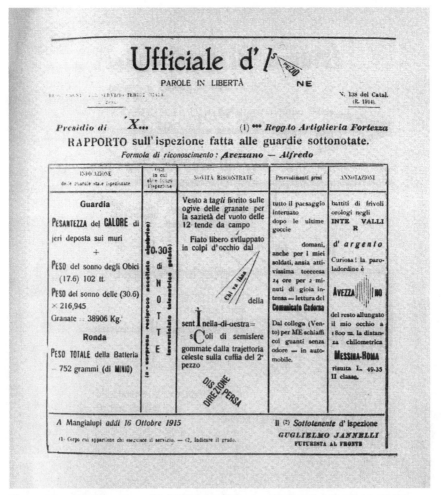

Figure 6.5.   Guglielmo Jannelli, "Ufficiale d'ispezione," *La Balza* (April 10, 1915).

same mix of gravity and levity present throughout a typographical composition that registers anxious waiting and bouts of boredom but concludes with a comic doubling: the 1,800 meter vista surrounding the outpost is mirrored by the 1800 kilometers supposedly separating Messina from Rome, quantified as 49.35 lire—the price of a one-way second class rail ticket.

Jannelli's sly reworking of military reporting conventions is radicalized in the *Contrabbando di guerra* section of Marinetti's *Zang Tumb Tumb* where the templates of a cargo manifest become devices for structuring an account of a ship being loaded in and departing the port of Rotterdam, one thousand miles from the Balkan battlefront (see figure 6.6).

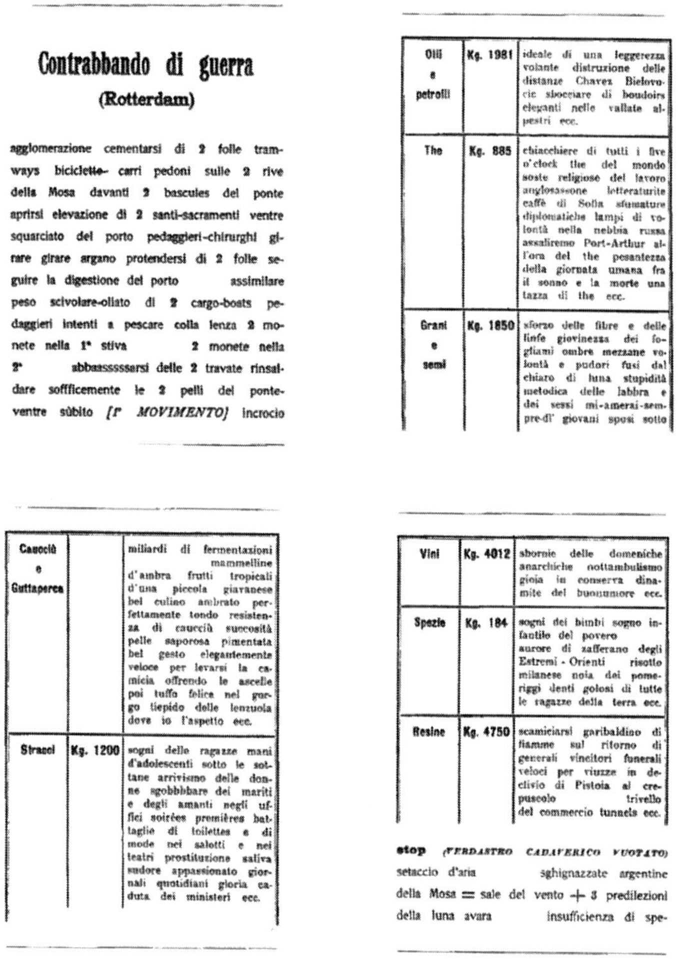

Contrabbando di guerra
(Rotterdam)

agglomerazione cementarsi di 2 folle tramways biciclette- carri pedoni sulle 2 rive della Mosa davanti 2 bascules del ponte aprirsi elevazione di 2 santi-sacramenti ventre squarciato del porto pedaggieri-chirurghi girare girare argano protendersi di 2 folle seguire la digestione del porto assimilare peso scivolare-oliato di 2 cargo-boats pedaggieri intenti a pescare colla lenza 2 monete nella 1ª stiva 2 monete nella 2ª abbaasssssarsi delle 2 travate rinsaldare soffficemente le 2 pelli del ponte-ventre sùbito [1° MOVIMENTO] incrocio

Olii e petrolii	Kg. 1981	ideale di una leggerezza volante distruzione delle distanze Chavez Bielovocic sbocciare di boudoirs eleganti nelle vallate alpestri ecc.
The	Kg. 885	chiacchiere di tutti i five o'clock the del mondo soste religiose del lavoro anglosassone letteraturite caffè di Sofia sfumature diplomatiche lampi di violontà nella nebbia russa assaliremo Port-Arthur all'ora del the pesantezza della giornata umana fra il sonno e la morte una tazza di the ecc.
Grani e semi	Kg. 1850	sforzo delle fibre e delle linfe giovinezza dei fogliami ombre mezzane volontà e pudori fasi dal chiaro di luna stupidità metodica delle labbra e dei sessi mi-amerai-sempre-dì giovani sposi sotto

Cauociù e Guttaperca	miliardi di fermentazioni mammelline d'ambra frutti tropicali d'una piccola giavanese bel culino ambrato perfettamente tondo resistenza di cauociù succosità pelle saporosa pimentata bel gesto elegantemente veloce per levarsi la camicia offrendo le ascelle poi tuffa felice nel gorgo tiepido delle lenzuola dove io l'aspetto ecc.
Stracci	Kg. 1200	sogni delle ragazze mani d'adolescenti sotto le sottane arrivismo delle donne sgobbbbare dei mariti e degli amanti negli uffici soirées premières battaglie di toilettes e di mode nei salotti e nei teatri prostituzioni saliva sudore appassionato giornali quotidiani gloria caduta dei ministeri ecc.

Vini	Kg. 4012	sbornie delle domeniche anarchiche nottambulismo gioia in conserva dinamite del buonumore ecc.
Spezie	Kg. 184	sogni dei bimbi sogno infantile del povero aurore di zafferano degli Estremi - Orienti risotto milanese noia del pomeriggi denti golosi di tutte le ragazze della terra ecc.
Resine	Kg. 4750	scamiciarsi garibaldino di fiamme sul ritorno di generali vincitori funerali veloci per viuzze in declivio di Pistoia al crepuscolo trivello del commercio tunnels ecc.

stop (VERDASTRO CADAVERICO VUOTATO)
setaccio d'aria sghignazzate argentine
della Mosa ≡ sale del vento + 3 predilezioni
della luna avara insufficienza di spe-

Figure 6.6. *Contrabbando di guerra* section of Filippo Tommaso Marinetti, *Zang Tumb Tumb* (Milan: Edizioni Futuriste di Poesia, 1914).

The action unfolds like a telegram divided into morse code letter sequences followed by stops. Suspended between two stops, as if an external document collaged into the telegram, is a five page cargo manifest listing the quantities of raw materials taken on board. The left column lists the quantities by weight; the right column "completes" the manifest, freighting the inventory with information belonging to wildly diverse orders of description from the molecular to the cosmological. *1981 kilos of oil and petroleum* destined for the Balkan front are thus described by two pioneering transalpine flights: "the ideal of weightless flight // abolition of distances // Chavez Bielovucic // opening of elegant boudoirs in Alpine valleys etc." *885 kilos of tea* are glossed as "chit chats of all the world's five o'clock teas // religious Anglo-Saxon breaks from work // the disease of literaturitis // cafés in Sofia // diplomatic nuances // flashes of will power in the Russian fog etc." The list goes on to inventory another half dozen items with each entry ending in *et caetera*. The implication is clear: even a simple quantitative itemization of this kind has embedded within it a web of potential connections, associations, and data sets so vast, unstable, and complex that it defies standardized modes of accounting. The chorus of *et caeterae* celebrates the poet's emancipation from any and all concepts of enumeration that would chain statistics to the analysis and description of stable and finite phenomena.

Choral Singularities

Foremost among the futurist strategies for recontextualizing and recoding number sets is a practice that was already prefigured in *montagne + vallate + strade × Joffre*: the insertion of fragments of numerical fields into typographical or visual compositions. The technique reaches maturity in one of *Les Mots en liberté futuristes*'s typographical high points: *Une Assemblée tumultueuse*, a composition subtitled *sensibilité numérique* (see figure 6.7).

Here the *assembly* consists in a cut-and-paste *assemblage* that evokes a mass rally dated 1918 in the upper right hand corner: the year of the end of World War I and of the beginning of the postwar uprising against the peace of Versailles. That the rally's tumult ticks to the standardized rhythms of industrial era clocks is indicated by the presence of dials on the upper right and by a drummer in the lower left. That it enfolds the poet himself can be ascertained by piecing together zig-zagging fragments of signage: *ma anch'io del cento per 100* ("me too, I'm in 100 percent").

These details do little more than confirm what the overall composition communicates by pitting numbers against numbers, cutouts against cutouts, lists against lists. Namely, that the war is never really over. The extended

Figure 6.7.   Filippo Tommaso Marinetti, "Une Assemblée tumultueuse," from *Les mots en liberté futuristes* (Milan: Edizioni Futuriste di Poesia, 1919).

arcs at the center trace the trajectories of artillery shells and bombs, as confirmed by Marinetti's preparatory collages. They mimic the shape of military dirigibles that are firing and being fired upon. The chunks of data that the poet has cut up and reassembled have been freed from mnemonic functions and cut loose from obligations to instrumental reason. They consist in multilingual word lists from telegraph coding books, arithmetic tables, financial balance sheets, all pressed together so as to suggest that the poet's summation-assemblage captures but a single sublime moment within a vortex of ever shifting registers and surging data streams.

The assembler of the elements that swirl across the page stands both inside and outside the vortex. A statistical person like the two or five or fifty thousand assembled, he also figures as a transcendental principle: as the *IO* that drives the blimp forward; as the divine maker who cuts and pastes; as the 1 that surges forth in the upper right hand corner as if haranguing the crowd from atop a balcony, alongside another number 1, perhaps the mass leader (see figure 6.8)?

Figure 6.8. Marietta Angelini, "Ritratto di Marinetti," *Vela latina* (1916); Jean Pasquali, Antonio Galeazzi, and Luigi Colombo, *1+1+1=1, Dinamite. Poesie Proletarie, Rosso + Nero* (Turin: Istituto di Cultura Proletaria, 1922).

Here a choral fiction arises that leaves traces throughout futurist artifacts. The one and many are revealed as potentially reversible numbers: reversible when the exponentially multiplied futurist subject constitutes an oceanic mass that is, in turn, reshaped into a collective singularity, whether by war or revolution. 1 + 1 + 1 thus comes to equal 1: little does it matter whether the equation is typeset in red or black. "The world of numbers," writes Vladimir Tatlin in *The Initiative Individual in the Creativity of the Collective*, "as the nearest to the architectonics of art, gives us: 1) confirmation of the existence of the inventor; 2) a complete organic connection of the individual with the collective numeral."[11]

Magic Formulae

In the passage just cited, Tatlin goes on to cite from Velimir Khlebnikov, the most forceful Russian proponent of the view that numbers have the attributes of personhood: "In a series of natural numbers, prime numbers, indivisible and non-recurring, are scattered. Each of these numbers carries with it its new numerical world. From this it follows that among numbers too there are inventors." The notion recurs in *The Scythian Headress: A Mysterium*, in which a "sea of phantoms" made up of irrational numbers leads the speaker to declare himself the square root of a *minus individual* and then to call upon "people to find the square roots of themselves and of minus-individuals."[12] In his bold theoretical writings with their mathematized theories of word creation, futurian conceptions of history, tables of destiny, and trigonometric laws, Khlebnikov even inserts a mathematical theorem qua self-portrait:

> The equations of the soul: I was born on October 28, 1885 + 3^8 + 3^8 = November 3, 1921; at the Red Star in Baku I predicted the Soviet Government, December 17, 1920 = $2 \times 3^8 - 317$; I was elected a President of Planet Earth on $3^8 + 3^8 - 3^7 - 48$ = December 20, 1915 (from birth) or $2 \times 3^8 - 3^7 - 48$. On the day of the battle of Tsushima I conceived of the idea of overthrowing the state by means of an idea; on the day of the surrender of Przemysl I entered the domain of chemistry.[13]

Though eccentric in some respects, Khlebnikov remains close to the futurist mainstream. Indeed, when compared with Marinetti's late embrace of a pataphysical mathematics, carried out in collaboration with the mathematician and student of both quantum mechanics and diffusion patterns of infectious diseases, Marcello Puma, a mathematics "hostile to symmetry, entirely launched toward the discontinuous and exceptional, that invites each person make his own subjective calculus of probabilities," Klebnikov's efforts to determine numerical patterns of predictive value might seem almost positivistic.[14]

In short, emancipated from humdrum tasks of applied mathematics, suspended in an interstitial realm between metaphysics and interiority/intuition/individual sensibility, between imagination and play, numbers find themselves free to resume some of their traditional speculative functions, whether symbolic, philosophical, and/or magical. The spectrum of such functions is wide within the futurist fold. From Marinetti's superstitious devotion to the number eleven, to Carrà's mediumistic words-in-freedom divagations, to the psychism of Settimelli, Ginna, and Corra founded on their conviction that "art is a cerebral secretion that can be measured with precision," to Giacomo Balla's and Benedetta Marinetti's flirtations, respectively, with theosophy and spiritism, qualitative math always trumps the merely quantitative. Hence in Balla's *Numeri innamorati*, the lone survivor of a number of studies of numerical sequences, a Fibonacci sequence is interrupted by the intrusion of the number 4 (see figure 6.9).

Personified much like Khlebnikov's inventor-integers, the four is attracted to the five, a prime number, literally "kissing" it—opposites attract—even as

Figure 6.9.   Giacomo Balla, *Numeri innamorati*, 1920, oil on canvas, Museo di Arte Moderna e Contemporanea di Trento e Rovereto.

it appears aligned with a far closer numerical peer, the 8, so as to imply the existence of an alternate arithmetic sequence (4, 8, 16, 32 . . .) extending beyond the picture plane to the left and to the right. The tension between the two poles of attraction pulls the 5 out of alignment and skews the entire spatial grid. Benedetta's *Il grande X* is, in a sense, more simple: it depicts a quite literal east-west hyperbola whose force pulls the edges of the painting's frame inward towards the center (C). But in so doing, it renders visible something that, mathematically speaking, can only occur in infinity: the two parabolas kiss right at the point where a radio tower broadcasts mysterious cosmic vibrations.

No more ambitious nor symptomatic compendium of these and other futurist stagings of number and notation exists than Paolo Buzzi's *L'ellisse e la spirale* and with this extravagant *film + parole in libertà* I conclude (see figure 6.10).

Buzzi's novel recounts the high symbolist saga of Naxar, the orphic composer who, abdicating a freshly inherited imperial throne, escapes high into the azure in an aircraft. The sky in question is none other than the Mallarmeian *azur* where Naxar undergoes a process of radical rarefaction. The tale of his transformation into an immaterial being is divided into three sections of

Figure 6.10. Paolo Buzzi, *L'ellisse e la spirale—Film + Parole in libertà* (Milan: Edizioni Futuriste di Poesia, 1915), title page and portrait of author.

twelve chapters each. The first section is framed by subtitles that provide *altitudes*; the second by subtitles in the form of *equations* derived from calculus, physics, and chemistry; the third by subtitles bearing astrophysical *locations*.[15] Buzzi dresses up everything in *L'ellisse e la spirale* in garish mathematical garb (see figure 6.11).

Figure 6.11. **Twelve examples of the pseudo-equations that accompany titles from Paolo Buzzi, *L'ellisse e la spirale—Film + Parole in libertà* (Milan: Edizioni Futuriste di Poesia, 1915).**

But to what end? Do the trappings of exactitude shape the novel's depths or hover instead like vaporous clouds?

Some examples: Section One announces itself as made up of 3533 meters and, indeed, chapters 1–12 are accompanied by subtitles that indicate altitudes which, added together, come out to 4057 or 3533 + 524: 524 being the altitude assigned to chapter 7, *La flotta aerea*. The numerical coincidence seems deliberate, but leaves no trace within the narrative itself.

Then there is the question of the section divisions, marked by pages on which a single equation appears in isolation. Section Two thus opens with a two-part equation, sensical in part. Its left side will recur in the section's first chapter (ch. 13) *I motori della polizia*, and is the quadratic formula, here graphable as a parabola that meets the x axis in one of two possible ways. The right side is a mangled version of the correctly notated formula that appears in the last chapter of the second section (ch. 24) *La cavalcata nazionale*, describing the relationship between two circles A and R. A nonsensical plus sign joins them together. The equation is meaningful to the degree that it enframes all of section two, even if it does so with a typographical inversion on the far right that inadvertently repeats the "error" deliberately committed by Schlegel, Berretta, and Marinetti: namely, division by zero.

Section Three begins with another full page equation: this one equating *delta*—a standard variable for height above the horizon line—with a set of degrees, minutes, and seconds, followed by a second figure—a celestial location, or so it would appear, close to that of the Big Dipper (at a 55 degree declination). Other celestial addresses follow, some intelligible, most not.

Amidst these external framing devices, promiscuous crossbreedings of the mathematically sensical and nonsensical proliferate, setting off sometimes dazzling, sometimes distracting sparks. Real math makes a cameo appearance: the law of tangents, iterated derivatives, and calculations of angular momentum. But always in the company of typographical inversions, notational errors, interventions that seem to gleefully shred the rules of logic even as they set out to mimic them. The novel ends with a triumphal sequence of nineteen words-in-freedom tables, the last of which is a sound bit of geometry: a classic r = theta logarithmic spiral, with theta standing for the plane angle that determines the tightness with which a spiral is wound (see figure 6.12).

In summation, Buzzi's manual of futurist mathematics lays bare at once the richness and the vacuity of a world of unencumbered experimentalism—Futurism's own distinctive world—spiraling outward towards the wholesale embrace of irrationality and spiraling inward toward acritical faith in the status of the artist as demiurge of the era of industry.

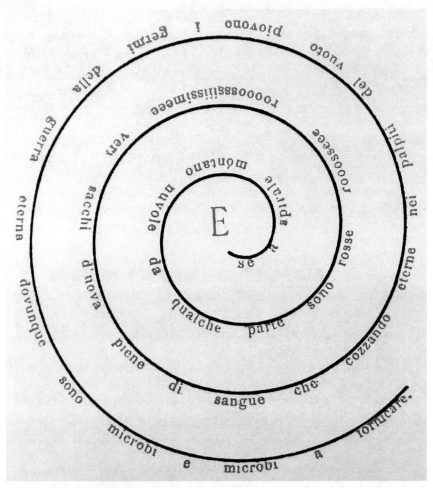

Figure 6.12. Final spiral from Paolo Buzzi, *L'ellisse e la spirale—Film + Parole in libertà* (Milan: Edizioni Futuriste di Poesia, 1915), 345.

Notes

1. A sincere thanks to Daniel Kane, Alejandro Perdomo, and Peter Galison for help in deciphering Buzzi's mathematics are due; I would also like to thank Renata Piccinetti for her expert help in navigating the Buzzi archive in Milan.

2. Alfio Berretta's (1897–1977) futurist phase was limited to the years of WWI. He was the founding editor of the review *La Scalata*, one of the few direct bridges between Futurism and Dada. He later went on to become a highly successful journalist and author of romance novels.

3. "Das Gedicht ist ein höheres oder tieferes Ich, das sich aus dem Ich ablöst = √ Ich." (1802) *Zur Poetik und Äesthetik*, fragmente von 1802–1812.

4. Oswald Spengler, *The Decline of the West*, trans. Charles Francis Atkinson (London: George Allen and Unwin, 1918), 56.

5. Burke's *artificial infinite* seems closely related.

6. "The feeling of the sublime is, therefore, at once a feeling of displeasure, arising from the inadequacy of imagination in the aesthetic estimation of magnitude to attain to its estimation by reason, and simultaneously awakened pleasure, arising from this very judgment of the inadequacy of the greatest faculty of sense being in accord with the ideas of reason, so far as the effort to attain to these is for us a law. It is, in other words, for us a law (of reason), which goes to make us what we are, that we should esteem as small in comparison with ideas of reason everything which for us is great in nature as an object of sense; and that which makes us alive to the feeling of this supersensible side of our being harmonizes with that law." Kant, *Critique of Judgment*, part 1, sect. 1, bk. 1, p. 2 (SS. 27).

7. Letter from Marinetti to Paolo Buzzi, dated December 9, 1915, reproduced in Paolo Buzzi, *Futurismo: scritti, carteggi, testimonianze*, ed. Mario Morini and Giampaolo Pignatari, I Quaderni del Palazzo Sormani 7, Ripartizione Cultura e Spettacolo (Milan: Palazzo Sormani, 1983), vol. 3, 462.

8. Spengler, *The Decline of the West*, 57.

9. It is worth noting that this example was cited by Russolo in his *The Art of Noises* as an example of "the great efficacy and intensity of expression attained through the use of consonants."

10. A case in point is Paolo Buzzi's posthumously published *Conflagrazione, epopea parolibera* (Florence: Il Fauno, 1963), whose frequent recourse to war statistics are all built upon powers of ten.

11. Vladimir Tatlin, "The Initiative Individual in the Creativity of the Collective," Larissa Alekseevna Zhadova, *Tatlin* (New York: Rizzoli, 1988), 257. Tatlin goes on to quote Khlebnikov at length: "There is no error in Khlebnikov's example. 1) 'In a series of natural numbers, prime numbers, indivisible and non-recurring, are scattered. Each of these numbers carries with it its new numerical world. From this it follows that among numbers too there are inventors.' 2) 'If we take the principle of addition, and add one more to a thousand individuals, the arrival and departure of this individual will be unnoticed. If we take the principle of multiplication, then a positive singular multiplied by a thousand makes the entire thousand positive. A negative singular multiplied by a thousand makes the whole thousand negative. From this it follows that there exists a complete organic connection between the individual and the collective numeral.'"

12. Velimir Khlebnikov, *Collected Works*, ed. Charlotte Douglas, trans. Paul Schmidt (Cambridge: Harvard University Press, 1987), vol. 2, 94.

13. Khlebnikov, *Collected Works*, vol. 1, 402.

14. The publication history of the manifesto is complex. The final version was published in *Autori e Scrittori* 6.6 (June 1941) and bears the full title of "Calcolo

poetico delle battaglie—La matematica futurista immaginativa qualitativa," without mention of the collaboration of Puma or Pino Masnata. But a prior edition,
"La matematica futurista—Manifesto," *Gazzetta del Popolo* (Feb. 2, 1940), lists all
three authors. Marinetti's publications on mathematics extend back to "Quarta
dimensione di matematici e artisti," published in *Gazzetta del Popolo* (Nov. 30,
1928) and "Superare la matematica. Verso la quarta dimensione," *Oggi e Domani*
1.7 (June 2, 1930).

15. The critic Lionello Fiumi wrote in *La Diana* 3.25 (March 1916): "Nell'*Ellisse
e la Spirale* (1915), 'film + parole in libertà', l'istinto scientifico e numerico raggiunge
la esasperazione e le formule del calcolo intonano il 'metraggio pellicolare della
fantasia,' 'alle sue progressive trascendenze enarmoniche.' È un romanzo d'eccezione
nel più lato senso della parola. La letteratura italiana non possiede nulla di eguale."
Cited from Buzzi, *Futurismo*, vol. 4, 462. He later adds: "Nel complesso, *L'Ellisse e la
Spirale*: un ammalinante sforzo di cerebrismo che contratto in una tensione nervosa
per trecentocinquanta pagine sconcerta ma incatena, spossa ma soggioga" (464).

~

CHAPTER SEVEN

Mapping Futurism

Performance in Rome and Across Italy, 1909–1915 with a Coda on Interwar Calabria

PATRICIA GABORIK

When Filippo Tommaso Marinetti's play *La donna è mobile* (the Italian version of his *Poupées électriques*) opened on January 15, 1909, the audience didn't much care for it.[1] When they started to whistle—as is the Italian way to express discontent with a show—after the second act, Marinetti climbed onto the stage, absorbed the jeers, and thanked the crowd for "this whistling, which does me great honor." This incited total uproar, for it wasn't normal behavior in the theatre. "Not all of the nuts are in the nuthouse," declared the reviewer from *Il Lavoro*, while the one from the *Gazzetta del Popolo* reported that "What we saw last night was not a performance, but a battle, pandemonium, chaos." In other words, on this night, Marinetti created a new sort of relationship with the public—the type of provocation that would become synonymous with his movement. The *Foundation and Manifesto of Futurism* sat at home on his desk, awaiting its moment to step into the spotlight. This night, at the Teatro Alfieri, Marinetti set the stage for its appearance.[2]

All of this happened in neither of the founding cities of futurist legend—Milan or Paris—but in Turin. As such, it highlights two of the key issues I will address here: the centrality of live performance to the futurist project and the extent to which the movement immediately relied on a far and wide diffusion across Italy. It was not, as tends to be perceived, a movement that spread from Milan (where Marinetti lived), to Florence (where the *Lacerba* group finally allied itself to Marinetti's), to Rome ("città passatista," or "passeist city," *par excellence*), and finally to the provinces (when it wasn't so of the future any-more). Rather, Italian Futurism, from the very start, relied on the participation of writers and artists from all over Italy and a broad dissemination of their works across the country.

In order to bring these points into stark relief, I will literally map the movement's expansion up until the Great War. The events signaled on the maps are those which, due to their live nature, can all be grouped under the umbrella of "performance" and include lectures, demonstrations, confer-ences, concerts, poetry readings, plays, and the legendary *serate*, which were essentially shows comprised of all of the above. I provide total numbers of these events instead of a breakdown by type, first, for legibility's sake, and, second, because part of the futurists' genius was in blurring boundaries: when they threw flyers against La Scala's "passeism" at the premiere of Strauss' *Rosenkavelier*, was it a simple act of hooliganism or a performance in its own right? Were their poetry declamations at interventionist demonstrations (for, as is well known, the futurists were fervent supporters of Italy's entrance into World War I) political acts or also street shows-cum-publicity stunts? I have tried to be as comprehensive as possible in documenting official futurist events—those organized by and/or with the participation of Marinetti and those closest to him—that surely took place. However, available informa-tion is spotty at best and contradictory at worst. To document with absolute certainty would require extensive archival research, an undertaking beyond the scope of this essay.[3]

I have not included art exhibitions in my total numbers except where otherwise indicated. This serves to highlight the relative importance of per-formance; while paintings and sculptures (in addition to manifestos) live on as futurist relics, the number of live performances far surpassed the number of art exhibitions held up until Italy entered the war in 1915: there were at least 115 performance events but fewer than twenty art exhibits. This is not to suggest that performance was "more important" than manifestos or works of art, but to recall the fact that if the futurists aimed not just to perceive but to experience, not just to represent but to "reconstruct" the universe, then live performance—which absorbed these other forms while it promoted them, which was phantasmagoric, ephemeral and interactive with the masses in ways these others were not—naturally became the force driving their move-ment's dissemination.[4]

Yet I must acknowledge that drawing a sharp line between exhibit and performance is also difficult because, as is well known, *serate* could include the presentations of new futurist paintings. At the same time, performances (such as poetry declamations or lectures on Futurism) could be held in conjunction with art shows: not infrequently, such happenings inaugurated the exhibits. This means that performance and art were in any case inherently linked, and mutually promotional—one could serve as a vehicle for the other—but also that the number of performance events is actually higher than I have recorded here, as specific information on what happened at exhibitions is not always readily available and therefore surely some exhibit-related events have been excluded from my count.[5]

Let us turn to the maps.

In 1909, black dots indicate where the year's three live events took place: Turin, La Spezia, and Trieste (figure 7.1). The year is notable for Milan's absence. The city is of undeniable importance, as Marinetti lived there and

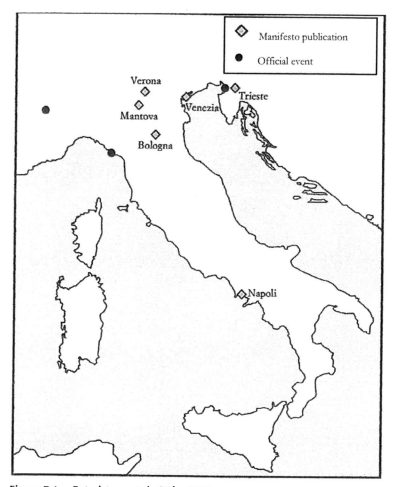

Figure 7.1.   Futurist events in Italy, 1909.

published *Poesia*—and under its auspices many futurist works—from his home office until he relocated to Rome in 1925. However, Futurism's public debuts, live and in print, happened elsewhere. In addition to Turin and Paris, La Spezia and Trieste were the select hosts of futurist events. With performances comprised of theatre in the strictest sense and public appearances of a more political nature (like Marinetti's delivery of *Trieste nostra bella polveriera*, a speech celebrating the city's centrality to the irredentist cause), 1909 would lay the groundwork for an ever-expanding futurist program of provocation, of many types, from many launching pads.

Thanks to the front-page publication of the *Founding and Manifesto* in *Le Figaro* on February 20, 1909, Paris is the other city credited with Futurism's launching. But, as is by now well known, the manifesto appeared in the papers of Italian cities before the Parisian unveiling. (Milan does not figure among them; it appeared after the fact, in *Poesia*.) On the map, the miniature press indicates the cities whose newspapers published the *Manifesto* before the Parisian debut. It could be read in its entirety on February 5th in Bologna (*The Gazzetta dell'Emilia*), on the 6th in *Il Pugnolo* and the 14th in *La Tavola Rotonda* (Naples), in the *Gazzetta di Mantova* on the 9th, and in *L'Arena*'s (Verona) issue of the 9th–10th. Other papers (*Il Mattino* of Naples, Trieste's *Il Piccolo della Sera*, and the *Gazzetta di Venezia*) carried articles explaining, or, in the last case, satirizing the text and reproducing large portions of it.[6] Even in the first year, then, when Futurism's existence was tied almost exclusively to its presence in print, numerous Italian cities were involved in the movement's launching. Naples, for one, took great interest in Marinetti's doings, reporting copiously on the *Donna è mobile* scandal and reproducing the manifesto in three papers. This city, along with Rome, would later become a futurist hub.

The infamous *serate futuriste* began in 1910, with Trieste again receiving the honor of primacy, hosting the first on January 12; Milan comes onto the map now, holding the second on February 15 (figure 7.2). In 1910–1911, about one-half of the thirty performance events were *serate*, these more than doubling the number of art exhibitions the futurists participated in, all but one of which were in Milan (figure 7.3).

Usually Marinetti emceed the evenings, held in large municipal theatres rented and packed to the rafters, with the shockingly aggressive and derisory posture we have become acquainted with through his manifestos: "I've had enough of the femininity of the crowd and the weakness of their collective virginity."[7] Marinetti and cohort (which then included Aldo Palazesschi, Armando Mazza, and poets from the Roman futurist circle Libero Altomare and Giuseppe Carrieri) declaimed poems and manifestos and, once painters and

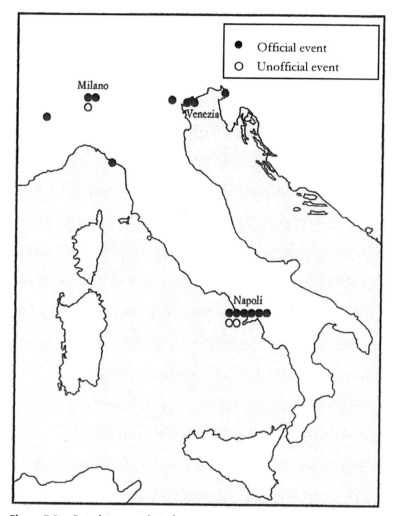

Figure 7.2. Futurist events in Italy, 1910.

musicians began to produce, displayed art and played music. What's more, the *serate* were often announced with sprees through the city streets, where the group threw flyers from their cars or otherwise kicked up dust in making their arrival known. Frequently, the evenings concluded with triumphant parades and brawls (perhaps with the same naysayers who had pelted them with vegetables during the show) in the *piazze*. All of these hijinks were of course part of the act, gestures of rebellion against the traditions of the bourgeois theatre that the futurists so despised.

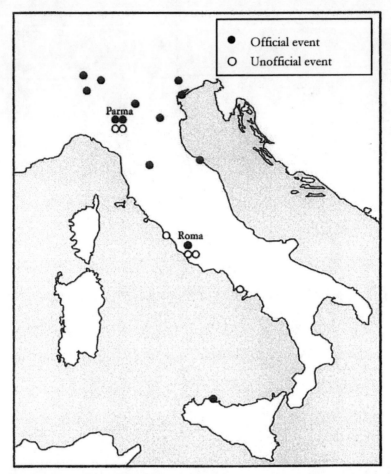

Figure 7.3. Futurist events in Italy, 1911.

As the map indicates, almost nothing happened—in Italy—in 1912 (figure 7.4). This was a year of systematic attempts to gain recognition abroad, the first exhibition of the futurist painters (which began in Paris and traveled to several other cities like Budapest, London, and Zurich) being the centerpiece of this endeavor. Generally speaking, we might observe that, outside of Italy, it was art rather than performance that led the futurist charge: across Europe, exhibits far outnumbered known performance events, with the exception of Paris and London (bearing in mind, however, the aforementioned caveat that many art exhibits were also accompanied with some performance events).

In 1913, the futurists returned to Italy with a force (figure 7.5). With plays and *serata* tours, some nineteen cities from Catania to Turin saw the

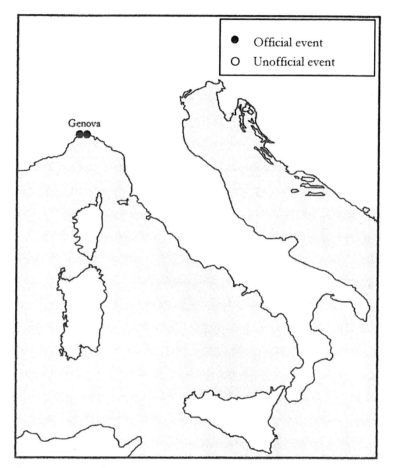

Figure 7.4.   Futurist events in Italy, 1912.

futurists in action. In addition, unofficial futurist events proliferated; these were not organized by the core group centered around Marinetti but by local admirers, some of whom were also in contact with the "real" futurists. Luciano Folgore and Anton Giulio Bragaglia, Roman futurists, agreed for instance to participate in a *serata* tour organized by an Umbrian enthusiast. This string of evenings is indicated on the map with white dots; there is uncertainty that all the performances took place, but the plans for a rather extensive round of two tours stopping in the eight central Italian towns is noteworthy nonetheless.[8]

All of this adds up to mean that 1913 saw a marked diffusion of Futurism across the country. However, this is when the trouble started: there was great

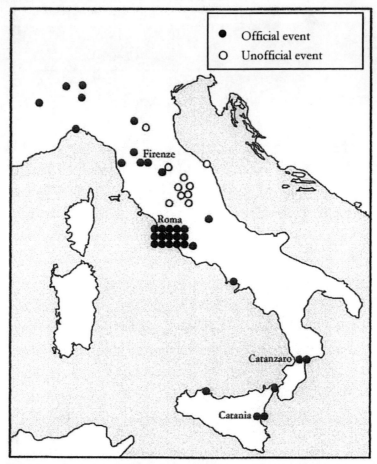

Figure 7.5. Futurist events in Italy, 1913.

tumult surrounding the hallmark *serate*, which actually gained too much momentum for Marinetti's taste, as the street brawls got increasingly dangerous and, what's more, audiences had become so accustomed to the boisterous rituals that they went ready for battle. The futurists were frustrated by the crowds that were so agitated from the very start that the performers failed to even make themselves heard from the stage. After what came to be known as "the Battle of Florence"—held at the Teatro Verdi on December 12, when yet another overly raucous evening ended through police intervention—Marinetti sought a change that would minimize the chaos. "Futurism doesn't need a lot of fuss right now, but rather direct communication with the few truly futurist spirits a city has," he wrote to Sicilian companion Guglielmo Jannelli, saying that the Florence *serata* was "sufficiently detrimental."[9]

Therefore, as the 1914 map shows, the futurists began to pull back the reins (figure 7.6). On the one hand we see that the group held events in fewer cities; on the other, we might notice that the movement's work intensified, concentrating efforts on those "few truly futurist spirits." Their strategy for doing so was to open two permanent futurist galleries, run by collector Giuseppe Sprovieri, in Rome in December of 1913 and Naples in May of 1914 (a third planned for Palermo never opened due to the war).[10] These were smaller, more manageable sites that allowed the people truly interested in Futurism as a movement—not as an excuse for public misbehaviour—to see what its adherents were up to. In other words, the futurists changed their battle plan. They were no longer on a recruitment blitz; out-of-hand crowds

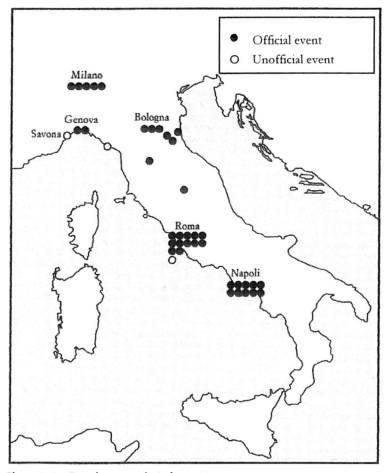

Figure 7.6.   Futurist events in Italy, 1914.

were more likely to impede than advance the charge. Now, focus fell on the establishment of Rome and Naples as the major centers of activity.

The typical gallery performance was much like a *serata*, with poetry and manifesto declamation and the playing of music. In addition to having art permanently on display, the galleries offered an intimate space for staging new theatrical experiments such as Francesco Cangiullo's celebrated *Piedi-grotta*, a paean to the Neapolitan festival of the same name. They were thus a proving grounds for the principles laid out in the 1913 *Variety Theatre Manifesto* and fertile soil for the extensive development of forms such as the *Teatro sintetico* (which in fact had its first tours during the war, in 1915 and 1916) and *Teatro della sorpresa* a few years later. In the "futurist cities" chronology below, I give titles of some key works presented, but it should be remembered that performances were often comprised of multiple stagings, declamations, etc.

The years 1914 and 1915 on the maps (figure 7.7 and figure 7.8) and on the diagram (figure 7.9) show a peak in 1913–1914 and a seeming drop in 1915 (unsurprising, given the futurists' mobilization for war). However, if their testimonies are true, the number and variety of activities in the galleries in late 1913 and 1914 was astounding. Alongside the continual art displays, there was at least one show per week, usually the *serata*-like events described above. In Naples, Cangiullo reported, the public demanded two to three per week, though later research indicates that financial troubles and a desire to funnel resources to Rome meant that activity in Naples quickly waned.[11] Sundays were typical event days in the thriving Roman space. I have only counted specifically documented performances, which means that the actual number of events, until Italy's entrance into the war when Sprovieri closed the galleries until 1918, is possibly much higher than what is reported here. Even without these unknowns, however, from 1913 on, events in Rome and Naples far outnumbered those in Milan or any other city.

There were also interventionist demonstrations in Bologna, Milan, and Rome in 1914–1915, some organized and others only participated in by the futurists (the latter of which are not counted here). Marinetti and crew found themselves arrested a few times (September 1914 in Milan, February and April 1915 in Rome, in this last oft-noted instance with Benito Musso-lini). One other unofficial futurist event merits special mention: the Roman release of the film *Mondo Baldoria* (with a clear reference to the Italian title of Marinetti's *Roi Bombance, Re Baldoria*). The film was publicized as the "primo soggetto futurista in cinematografia" (essentially, the first futurist screenplay), containing futurist music, photos, and placards and even a clip in which Marinetti and others appeared. The futurist ringleader rejected it

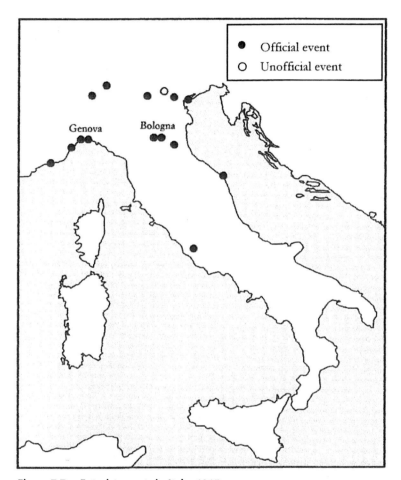

Figure 7.7. Futurist events in Italy, 1915.

outright because its director Aldo Molinari was not a member of the group, but there is little doubt that the event went down as a futurist one, and when Marinetti published an absolute pan of it in the newspaper, it certainly only increased the chatter about Futurism in a city overtaken by it.[12]

Roma passatista?

Rome's vitality at this point in Futurism's development is an issue that merits special comment. As noted above, Futurism is commonly imagined as a Milanese movement, the product and exaltation of that city's relative industrial advancement and, more generally, its modernity. In turn, the

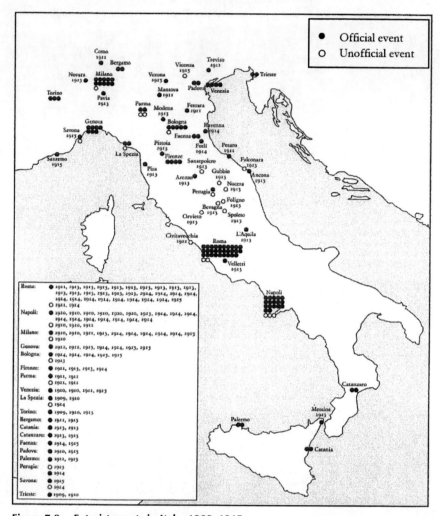

Figure 7.8. Futurist events in Italy, 1909–1915.

idea that Rome was a non-participant in the movement's first hour is wide-spread. Much has been made of the city's belated arrival on the scene; until 1913, it held only one lecture by star painter-sculptor Umberto Boccioni (in 1911) and thus far fewer events than Milan or Naples. The supposedly delayed adoption of Futurism has been offered as proof that the invective in the 1910 manifesto *Contro Roma passatista* was founded—that Rome "lay rotting in the leprosy of its ruins."[13] Though it is reported that Rome essentially replaced Milan as Futurism's headquarters after Marinetti relocated to his wife Benedetta's city in 1925, the image of Rome the latecomer,

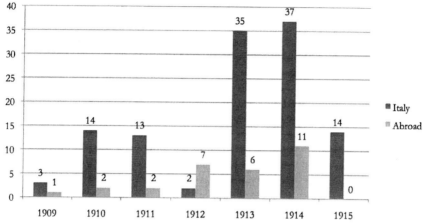

Figure 7.9. Futurist Events in Italy and Abroad, 1909–1915.

Roma *passatista*, despite observations to the contrary by Italian scholars Claudia Salaris and Enrico Crispolti, persists.[14]

However, this tardiness is highly exaggerated. Not only did Rome become Futurism's most vibrant and active city already in 1913, but it was also the home of several figures who stood arm in arm with Marinetti as he got the movement on its feet. Remo Mannoni, who re-baptized himself Libero Altomare upon his adhesion to the futurist group, was in contact with Marinetti since 1908; he received an enthusiastic welcome to the fold and saw his poem "Apocalisse" printed in the watershed February-March issue of *Poesia*. In 1910, Altomare introduced Marinetti to Boccioni, who had lived in Rome from 1901–1905. Moreover, it was at Boccioni's 1911 lecture in Rome that Giacomo Balla met Marinetti. The poet Folgore (Omero Vecchi in his non-futurist days—the Romans were especially fond of showing their exuberance with new, electro-charged names) became a futurist in April 1909, and Giuseppe Carrieri, a young Calabrese in Rome to study law, was another who spread the word in the early days when Futurism was a literary and not yet an art movement. Finally, there were the brothers Bragaglia. Though Anton Giulio only officially broke into the group in 1912, with his brother Arturo he had been experimenting with *fotodinamismo* since at least mid-1911 and by fall of that year gave talks and exhibitions on this new photography. (Bragaglia's activities, researched comprehensively, would add pegs to the futurist map, for he is known to have presented his work in Lazio, Campania, Abruzzo, and le Marche.)

The Città Futuriste timeline below shows just how active the capital city was from 1913 on and also offers a comparison to the two other most active centers, Naples and Milan. Though my analysis principally covers the years up until the outbreak of war, it is also valuable to point out that the Roman futurists' dedication during the war was arguably instrumental in the move- ment's survival. Not only did they continue to create, but, as Crispolti has observed, their international outlook lent tremendous vitality to ongoing experiments.[15] I would add that this can be said both of the futurists and of those who came into contact with them, the best example of which is the collaboration between the futurists and Serge Diaghilev's Ballets Russes, an alliance in the making as early as 1914 when Stravinsky attended a futurist concert in London. Diaghilev, the dancers, choreographer Léonide Massine, scenographers Larionov and Goncharova and collaborators Jean Cocteau and Pablo Picasso spent months in Rome prior to the April 1917 debut of *Feu d'artifice*, a ballet without dancers composed by Stravinsky and designed by Balla. The encounter—which resulted in a new aesthetic for the Diaghi- lev company—revolutionized modern dance.[16] Thanks to the efforts upheld by the futurists in Rome throughout the dark days of the war, the movement not only continued to thrive, but contributed in fundamental ways to the development of performance culture not only in Italy and Europe but beyond their borders as well.

Futurist performance and exhibits reached nearly forty Italian and twenty foreign cities in the very first years (1909–1915) (see table 7.1), while broad distribution of their publications, widespread press coverage, and the enthusiastic efforts of sympathizers ensured that the movement made its mark even in places the futurists did not visit. As we have seen, several cities built Futurism from its very start, but it is true that the expan- sion was nonetheless strikingly profuse in later phases, that is, through the 1930s. If activities in the inter-war period have been deemed less explosive, there was nonetheless no lack of innovation, nor of impassioned adherents. In many of the provinces, like le Marche or Puglia, for instance, Futurism seems to have lived on mainly in press reports about activities elsewhere. In other areas, like Sicily, new publications abounded. Sicily's poets had participated in the movement from the earliest days, and this would sug- gest that early fulguration could and often did lead to ongoing productivity. Elsewhere still, fond memories of the pre-war glory days ensured an active carrying on of the futurist flag. Liguria, for instance, maintained a calendar full of activities from 1909 until Marinetti's death in 1944, in part because he and Benedetta had spent much time there.[17]

Table 7.1. The Futurist Cities: Milan, Rome, Naples, 1909–1915.

Date	Milan	Rome	Naples
1909	—	—	—
1910			
15 February	S, serata		
19 March	E, collective with works by Boccioni, Bonzagni, Carrà		
20 April			S, serata (Benedetto Croce in attendance)
22 April			S, Marinetti speaks
23 April			S, Marinetti speaks
24 April			S, mini-serata for students
26 June			S, Marinetti speaks
27 June			S, reading of Palazzeschi's poems
29 or 30 July	S, Marinetti speaks		
24 August	E, collective with works by Boccioni, Bonzagni, Carrà		
October	S, Trial against Marinetti for indecency		
20 December	E, collective, with works by Boccioni, Bonzagni, Carrà, and Russolo		
1911			
27 February	S, protest against "passatismo" at La Scala during Strauss' *Rosenkavalier*		
30 April	E, collective, with works by Boccioni, Carrà, and Russolo		
29 May		S, Boccioni speaks	
19 November			C, music by Pratella

(continued)

Table 7.1. (*continued*)

Date	Milan	Rome	Naples
12 December	E, collective, with Boccioni, Carrà, and Russolo		
1912	—	—	—
1913			
11 February		E, *Prima esposizione di Pittura futurista*	
12 February	S, Marinetti speaks		
21 February		S + C, serata with concert	
26 February		S, Boccioni speaks	
27 February		S, Marinetti speaks, poetry readings, Valentine Saint-Point dances	
9 March		S + C, serata with concert	
21 March		S, futurist banquet	
24 March		S + E, exhibition of Bragaglia's *fotodinamiche* inaugurated by Marinetti speech	
26 March		S, Marinetti speaks, poetry reading	
27 March		S, reception for futurists	
18 April		S, Marinetti speaks, poetry readings. In the same week, there was another similar event at the Circolo Marchigiano di Roma	
24 April		S, conference by Bragaglia	
? April		S, Marinetti poetry reading	
? April		E, "Fu Balla": display and auction of Balla's "passeist" works	
11 October	C, *intonarumori*		
5 November			S, serata with Marinetti's *Elettricità*

Date	Milan	Rome	Naples
6 December		The Futurist Gallery Sprovieri opens E, Boccioni	
14 December		S, readings by Marinetti	
28 December		S, readings by Boccioni	
29 December		S, readings by Auro D'Alba	
1914			
12 Janaury		C, Pratella, *Inno alla vita*	
16 January	S, serata with Marinetti's *Elettricità*		
28 January		S, reading by Marinetti	
1 February		S, reading by Marinetti	
11 February		E, paintings	
15 February		S, film *Mondo Baldoria*	
? February		E, futurist collective	
8 March		S, Folgore, *Negli hangars del futurismo*	
15 March		S, *Hangars* and readings of Paolo Buzzi's poetry	
19 March		S, *Zang Tumb Tumb* reading	
29 March		S, Cangiullo's *Piedigrotta*	
5 April		S, Cangiullo's *Piedigrotta*	
13 April		S + E, Futurist International Exposition of Painters and Sculptors, inaugurated by Marinetti, and shows including *Funeral of a Passeist Critic* (Benedetto Croce)	
21 April	C, *intonarumori*		
26 April		S, Grande Convegno Futurista	

(continued)

Table 7.1. *(continued)*

Date	Milan	Rome	Naples
3? May			Futurist Gallery opens, inaugurated with poetry readings by Marinetti
12 May			S, *Piedigrotta*
14 May			S + E, Futurist painting exhibition opens with show
17 May			S, *Serata in onore di Yvonne*
24 May			S, *Piedigrotta*
27 May			S, serata, works by Cangiullo
31 May			S, *Yvonne*
4 June			S, *Piedigrotta*
6 June			S, poetry readings
7 June			S, *Hangars*
9 June			S, poetry readings
11 July	P + E, Marinetti and Sant'Elia launch the *La città nuova*		
15 September	P, Interventionist demonstrations during a Puccini show at La Scala		
16 September	P, Interventionist demonstrations at the Galleria Vittorio Emanuele		
29 November	S, launching of *In quest'anno futurista*		
9 December		P, Interventionist demonstrations at the University	
11 December		P, Interventionist demonstrations at the University	

Date	Milan	Rome	Naples
1915			
28 April	S, poetry reading		
15 December		S + E, readings by Marinetti (on military leave) at the inauguration of *Fu Balla* and *Balla futurista*	

E = Art exhibit
P = Political protest action
C = Concert
S = Show, which includes plays, *serate*, lectures, conferences, and readings of poetry, manifestos, etc.

Futurism in Calabria

Here I spotlight the southern region of Calabria (see "Calabria futurista" below) as an example of the movement's spreading throughout the provinces from the 1910s all the way through the early 1940s. For Claudia Salaris, Calabria saw a relatively "scant diffusion of the movement,"[18] and it is an interesting case for this very reason: even a little activity meant quite a lot happening, as the variety of events included lectures and exhibits, publication of journals and books, and even the foundation of futurist circles. Also noteworthy is the fascist government's support of futurist activities—and the blurring of the boundary between futurist and fascist events. The continued innovation in futurist art and performance throughout this period meant that, despite the arguments of those who would have us believe that fascism killed any and all creativity, the futurists never ceased their attempts to create the "nuova spr[i]tualità plastica" (new plastic spirituality)[19] of the world they lived in (see figure 7.10).

Calabria throws into stark relief the issue that has motivated this research: there is something to be learned in the places we least expect. Perhaps the greatest challenge to mapping Futurism is the variation in the level of investigation conducted in and about Italy's territories. I consulted many dozens of general histories and studies focused on particular cities or regions. Nearly every region has attempted to claim Futurism as its own, but these endeavors have been unequal in depth and scope. Of course, research begets research, so some regions, like Liguria and Sicily, appear important both because they in fact were and because they have been better studied; the converse is true for regions like the Abruzzo. In such cases, however, it is uncertain whether absence of evidence is actually evidence of absence or simply a signal that there is more work to be done.

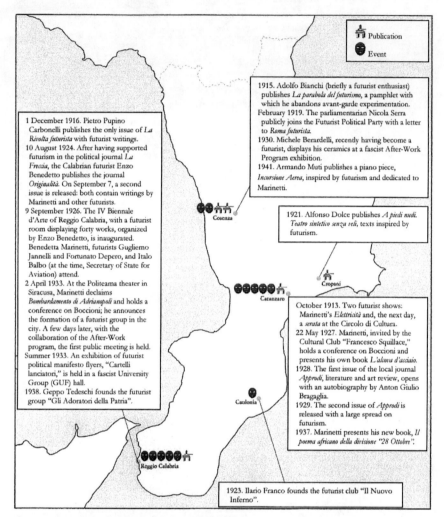

Figure 7.10.   Futurism in Calabria, 1909–1944.

Mapping Futurism for the Future

My focus on the performance event here highlights my conviction that we can better understand Futurism if we reckon with the live events that were the driving force behind the movement's dissemination. Once we realize how many there were, where they took place, and who participated, we suddenly begin to shed a little more light on numerous names (of poems, of plays, of participants) that have been overshadowed by the usual ones. For example, the data on Rome presented here is sufficient enough reason to stop depicting Futurism as simply the product of a Mad Milanese Millionaire and finally get serious about analyzing the movement as the fruit of indefatigable toil by a large group of passionate intellectuals and artists from all over Italy. In this essay, it was important to focus on Futurism's "heroic" years, to show that such key premises anchoring Futurism research—even those about the period we know best—need to be revisited. But the ideal would have been to conduct this same sort of research on the 1920s and 1930s as well. When it comes to performance, for example, we already know quite a bit about the *serate* (necessarily covered here because of the time frame), but not as much about the synthetic theatre, theatre of surprise, or Enrico Prampolini's pantomime theatre, which came into being over the course of the following decade. To map all of this later activity would mean to reveal more unsung heroes of time and place, and hopefully in turn to readjust our critical lens on Futurism's later years as well. Though much has been left untouched here, I think the research is comprehensive enough to provide a new basis for discussion; disappointment over any exclusions will, I hope, motivate further consideration of the questions, cities, and personalities as yet insufficiently explored.

Notes

1. Thanks go the Italian publishing house Einaudi for permission to publish this essay, a shorter version of that commissioned for the third volume of the *Atlante della letteratura italiana*, edited by Sergio Luzzatto and Gabriele Pedullà, to be released in September 2012. The original Italian version, "Lo spettacolo futurista," far more detailed, may be consulted there. The graphics used here are those elaborated by Einaudi, modified for the English-language text. Unless otherwise indicated, all translations throughout the essay are my own.

2. For accounts of the premier of *La donna è mobile* and its reception in the press, see Giovanni Antonucci, *Cronache del teatro futurista* (Rome: Abete, 1975) 35–41; Günter Berghaus, *Italian Futurist Theatre, 1909–1944* (Oxford: Clarendon Press, 1998), 32–35; Matteo D'Ambrosio, *Nuove verità crudeli: Origini e primi sviluppi del futurismo a Napoli* (Naples: Guida, 1990) 43–47; and Jeffrey T. Schnapp, introduction to Filippo Tommaso Marinetti, *Teatro* (Milan: Mondadori, 2004), xiv–xviii.

3. The research for this essay required the consultation of several dozens of sources, not all of which can be included here. I have elected to include the publications that offer the most comprehensive and/or accurate information available, as well as those that were particularly helpful in addressing specific aspects of the paper, such as the focus on Rome and Calabria. Given the focus of this essay, many of the sources cited here pertain to futurist performance, but dozens of exhibition catalogues, biographies, and other such sources were also consulted.

4. In addition to those already named, sources particularly concerned with futurist performance include Simona Bertini, *Marinetti e le eroiche serate* (Novara: Interlinea, 2002); Paolo Fossati, *La realtà attrezzata*. *Scena e spettacolo dei futuristi* (Turin: Einaudi, 1977); Lia Lapini, *Il teatro futurista italiano* (Milan: Mursia, 1977); Claudia Salaris, *Storia del futurismo* (Rome: Editori Riuniti, 1985); and Anna Caterina Toni, ed., *I luoghi del futurismo (1909–1944)* (Rome: Multigrafica, 1986).

5. I thank Günter Berghaus for the reflections he offered on this matter at the conference from which this volume stems, *Futurisms: Precursors, Protagonists, Legacies*, University of Utrecht, December 1–3, 2009, as well as for the clarity he offered in particular cases of conflicting data. A helpful source for tracking exhibitions is Enrico Crispolti, ed., *Nuovi archivi del futurismo* (Rome: De Luca CNR, 2010).

6. Christine Poggi, *Inventing Futurism: The Art and Politics of Artificial Optimism* (Princeton: Princeton University Press, 2009), 4–5.

7. From the manifesto "La declamazione dinamica e sinottica," of March 11, 1916. Filippo Tommaso Marinetti, *Teoria e invenzione del futurismo* (Milan: Mondadori, 1968), 105–6.

8. For Bragaglia and Futurism, see Anton Giulio Bragaglia, *Fotodinamismo futurista* (Turin: Einaudi, 1980); Giovanni Lista, *Cinema e fotografia futurista* (Milan: Skira, 2001); Mario Verdone, *I fratelli Bragaglia* (Rome: Lucarini, 1991); *Anton Giulio Bragalia* (Rome: Centro Sperimentale di Cinematografia, 1965); and Giuliana Scimé, ed., *Il laboratorio dei Bragaglia 1911/1932* (Ravenna: Agenzia Editoriale coop. r.l., 1986). For additional information on the unofficial Umbria Tour, see Claudia Salaris, *Luciano Folgore e le avanguardie* (Scandicci: La Nuova Italia, 1997) and the essay by Massimo Duranti in Toni, *I luoghi del futurismo*.

9. From a letter dated January 6, 1914, reprinted in Giuseppe Miligi, *Prefuturismo e primo futurismo in Sicilia* (Messina: Sicania 1989), 294–95.

10. Regarding futurist activity in Naples and Palermo, see Enrico Crispolti, ed., *Futurismo e Meridione* (Naples: Electa, 1996); Miligi, *Prefuturismo*; Anna Maria Ruta, *Il futurismo in Sicilia* (Marina di Patti: Silvana, 1991); Matteo D'Ambrosio, *Futurismo a Napoli* (Naples: Liguori, 1995); Idem, *Nuove verità crudeli*, and Ugo Piscopo, *Futurismo a Napoli 1915–1928* (Naples: Tullio Pironti, 1981).

11. Francesco Cangiullo, *Le serate futuriste: romanzo storico vissuto* (Naples: Editrice Tirrena, 1930), 146.

12. Lista, *Cinema e fotografia*, 31–37.

13. Marinetti, *Teoria e invenzione*, 246.

14. Principal sources on Roman futurist activity include Claudia Salaris, *La Roma delle avanguardie. Dal futurismo all'underground* (Rome: Editori Riuniti, 1999) and *Luciano Folgore*; Giovanni Antonucci e.a., *Il futurismo e Roma* (Rome: Istituto di Studi Romani, 1978); Lista, *Cinema e fotografia*; Giovanni Lista, Paolo Baldacci, and Livia Velani, eds., *Balla. La modernità futurista* (Milan: Skira, 2008); Enrico Crispolti, ed., *Casa Balla e il futurismo a Roma* (Rome: Istituto Poligrafico e Zecca dello Stato, 1989); and Elisabetta Mondello, *Roma futurista* (Milan: Franco Angeli, 1990).

15. See Crispolti, "Pittura, scultura, architettura e ambientazioni futuriste a Roma (appunti)" in Antonucci, *Il futurismo a Roma*, 47–69 and "Posizione e luoghi, e tempi del futurismo italiano" in Toni, *I luoghi del futurismo*, 11–20.

16. Regarding the collaboration between the Italian futurists and the Ballets Russes, see Patricia Gaborik and Andrea Harris, "From Italy and Russia to France and the U.S.: 'Fascist Futurism' and Balanchine's 'American' Ballet" in Mike Sell, ed., *Avant-Garde Performance and Material Exchange: Vectors of the Radical* (London: Palgrave, 2011), 23–40; Lynn Garafola, *Diaghilev's Ballets Russes* (Cambridge, MA: Da Capo Press, 1998); and Valerian Sveltov, "The Diaghileff Ballet in Paris," *The Dancing Times* (December 1929).

17. On Genova and the Liguria region, see Franco Ragazzi, ed., *Liguria futurista* (Milan: Mazzotta, 1997) and Idem, ed., *Marinetti e il futurismo in Liguria* (Genoa: De Ferrari, 2006).

18. Salaris, *Storia*, 149. For additional information on Futurism in Calabria, see Vittorio Cappelli and Luciano Caruso, eds., *Calabria futurista* (Soveria Mannelli: Rubbettino, 1997 and 2009); Franco Magro, *Catanzaro vento futurista* (Soveria Mannelli: Calabria Letteraria, 2004); Luigi Tallarico, *Il futurismo e la Calabria* (Reggio Calabria: Iiriti, 2003).

19. The "new plastic spirituality." From the *Manifesto della aeropittura*, Marinetti, *Teoria e invenzione*, 171.

PART II

~

PROTAGONISTS

~

Time and Space in the Writings of Marinetti, Palazzeschi, the Group of *L'Italia futurista,* and Other Futurist Writers

Beatrice Sica

In this chapter I explore the relationship between Futurism and time in creative writing.[1] In the first part I deal with Marinetti's claims on time as found in the *Foundation and Manifesto of Futurism* (1909), the *Technical Manifesto of Futurist Literature* (1912), and *Destruction of Syntax—Imagination without Strings—Words-in-Freedom* (1913).[2] In the second part I consider time both as a theme and a technical writing issue in various pieces by different futurist authors. This is also an opportunity to present a selection of texts—some of which have not been translated into English before—on the subject, a sort of chrestomathy of Futurism on time. In the end I argue that despite Marinetti's one-sided theoretical prescriptions for creating a new, swift literature, the practice of futurist writers was multifaceted and allowed for different writing and reading speeds. Indeed, Marinetti, far from imposing a style, was able to promote a varied range of creative production and with his passionate calls brought together different writers in the name of literary playfulness and experimentation.

Time and Space Died Yesterday

The foundational manifesto of Futurism (*Fondazione e manifesto del futurismo*) makes a very clear and radical point, among others: "Time and space died yesterday."[3] The claim appears amidst other assertions only in the eighth of Marinetti's eleven points; however, it certainly sounded of primary importance and struck contemporary readers. Twenty years later Massimo Bontempelli, founding Italian magic realism with the aim of surpassing Futurism, could open the first editorial of his new journal 900 with this call: "The most urgent and clear task of the twentieth century will be that of building a new time and space."[4] These latter categories, still recalled by Bontempelli, were precisely those that Marinetti had pronounced dead in 1909. His diagnosis of the death of time and space, however, must have sounded not only radical, but also puzzling, in that it was accompanied by the prescription for a cure: the future. Indeed, the movement that chose to baptize itself in the name of *Futuro* was being born precisely when, as it declared, time and space had just died. If time and space died yesterday, does it make any sense to speak about tomorrow? And yet it was not just a paradox for paradox's sake; Marinetti was not ironical—on the contrary, he was very serious. With his radical, puzzling, serious provocation he warned the readers of the French newspaper *Le Figaro* that his own was not an "–ism" like the many that had been proliferating in the previous decades in the arts, especially in France: the stakes in the new Italian movement were very high and they must not be underestimated.

By calling themselves futurists, Marinetti and his followers openly included time in the colors of their regiment. However, their engagement with the future was not limited to a generic praise of the time to come and the singing of modernity with its then-most-obvious attributes, such as speed, dynamism, electricity, and the machine. Those were flags that could help people identify the newly born movement, while also providing its members with fresh myths to feed their spirit in the battle against the past. But Marinetti knew well that a new engagement with time—was this latter really dead or alive—had to have more far-reaching implications than a simple praise of cars and airplanes. Above all, he was well aware that, like any others, futurist authors and their works were subject to the same natural law that governs all marketable goods in a capitalist system: that is, they were perishable. In the bourgeois world driven by profit, art could not offer eternal values anymore, unless it detached itself from society and tried to survive with the illusion of inhabiting a superior, self-sufficient cosmos. Marinetti deeply felt that in a market-driven world, art was as perishable as any other commodity. Thus, writers who were young and whose works were new in the first decades of the twentieth century would soon become, already in the early 1920s, old and outdated. However, instead of lamenting the cruel fate of authors and works in the modern era, Marinetti declared that the futurists, in fact, desired such a fate, they truly wanted to be outdated and be considered useless one day; in other words, they were ready to be killed and to die:

> The oldest among us are thirty; so we have at least a decade for finishing our work. When we reach forty, others who are younger and stronger will throw us into the wastebasket, like useless manuscripts. —We want it to happen!
> They will come against us, our successors, will come from far away, from every direction, . . . extending their hooked, predatory claws. . . . [5]

Wishing to become useless and outdated and to be ready to be killed, however, did not mean that the futurists passively accepted their destiny as modern authors: instead of succumbing unresistingly to the fatal laws of modernity, Marinetti and his followers planned to turn these laws to their own advantage; the day they expected to be discarded, they would light a fire with their own books, warming their hands by the flames of their own writings, and then would fly again by means of new, more powerful images:

> But we won't be there . . . They'll find us, at last—one winter's night—in the open country, beneath a sad roof drummed by a monotonous rain. They'll see us crouched beside our trembling airplanes and in the act of warming our hands by the poor little fire that our books of today will give out flaming beneath the flight of our images. [6]

Newer literary images would be born, able to fly like airplanes; one could say that the images are, in fact, the airplanes themselves. In Marinetti's metaphorical system, modernity is embodied by the machine, which brings both the ruin and the salvation of literature: the leader of Futurism writes that he stretches out on his car "like a corpse on its bier"[7] and almost dies in a car accident, but he immediately resurges, ready to dictate the eleven points of his foundational manifesto.[8] Then, as we have just seen, he predicts the time to come for futurist writers and books: he and his peers will crouch beside their planes, ready to fly with new images over the small fire of their old works. The metaphorical play between literature and the machine is clear. Later, in the *Technical Manifesto of Futurist Literature* (*Manifesto tecnico della letteratura futurista*), it is on an aircraft that Marinetti realizes "the ridiculous inanity of the old syntax . . . inherited from Homer"[9] and feels "a furious need to liberate words;"[10] it is the airplane itself, actually, that, like a new god in the sky of modernity, dictates to Marinetti the commandments for the new literature.[11]

Speed and Simultaneity

Stephen Kern has analyzed the relationship of intellectuals and artists with the categories of time and space in the late nineteenth and early twentieth century. As far as the concept of the present is concerned, he writes:

> The ability to experience many distant events at the same time . . . was part of a major change in the experience of the present. Thinking on the subject was divided over two basic issues: whether the present is a sequence of single local events or a simultaneity of multiple distant events, and whether the present is an infinitesimal slice of time between past and future or of more extended duration. The latter debate was limited largely to philosophers, but the issue of sequence versus simultaneity was expressed by numerous artists, poets, and novelists. . . . [12]

The futurists were no exception and were among those who addressed these issues most explicitly. They considered either the—faster and faster—taking place of events in one location or various events taking place simultaneously in different locations. In *Destruction of Syntax—Imagination without Strings—Words-in-Freedom* (*Distruzione della sintassi. Immaginazione senza fili. Parole in libertà*) Marinetti explains that Futurism was based on the new sensibility brought to humans by the very recent technological and scientific discoveries,[13] and praises "Acceleration of life which today has a swift pace. Physical, intellectual, and sentimental equilibration on the tightrope of speed stretched between contrary magnetisms. Multiple and simultaneous states of mind within the same individual."[14] For the futurists, the increase of speed and simultaneity were the two main issues to address if they wanted to establish a new relationship with time. Here, as my analysis is limited to literary texts, I will concentrate on speed rather than on simultaneity. In point of fact, literature is by its nature perceived more as a sequence—of sounds, words, and images—; it is something that, like music, one experiences primarily in time, and which can therefore render the sense of a faster or slower succession—of sounds, words, images, or events—in a more evident and perspicuous way. Simultaneity, on the contrary, concerns and appears mainly in that which, by its nature, deals with spatial representation: for example in paintings, or in what Marinetti called *radia*.[15] The futurists experimented even with more "spatial" literary forms, such as *tavole parolibere*, where the process of reading takes place like in a picture, on a surface that shows its parts all at once, without a direction for the eye to follow, as happens in a poem. However, *tavole parolibere*, which some consider more a form of visual art than pieces of literature,[16] will not be considered here, as they would require a different kind of analysis.

When he pronounces time and space dead, Marinetti also adds something about speed: "Time and space died yesterday. We already live in the absolute, because we have already created eternal, omnipresent speed."[17] It is well known, and certainly it was to Marinetti as well, that speed is the quotient of space over time. I do not think that Marinetti bothered too much about calculations and formulas—although, as I will show later, he occasionally liked to play with them, particularly with those related to speed. What interests us here is his description of speed, which incorporates precisely its components— time and space—through the adjectives "eternal" and "omnipresent." "Eternal" means everlasting, having an infinite duration. "Omnipresent" means ubiquitous, being everywhere. Marinetti transfers the qualities of an infinite time and an infinite space directly into their quotient, speed. Eventually, his emphasis on the "eternal" and "omnipresent"—that is, unlimited in every aspect—speed reflects the unbounded nature of the futurist revolution.

If the world goes faster and faster and the futurists want to keep pace with it, they need to break any limitations that make them go slow. In the realm of creative writing, this means to create a literature that, in its turn, can go faster and faster. It is no surprise, then, that references to speed and the problem of a faster pacing are the most recurrent in Marinetti's literary manifestos. All his prescriptions go in the same direction: to technically reduce the time, both of reading and writing. Thus, adjectives must be abolished, because "the adjective . . . presupposes a pause, a meditation" that makes it "inconceivable within our dynamic vision."[18] The same can be said of adverbs: an adverb is, in Marinetti's words, just an "old clamp which joins one word to another."[19]

> Adjectives and adverbs . . . indicate the pace—light or heavy, slow or rapid—of the noun as it moves along in the sentence. They are, from time to time, the walking stick or the crutches of the noun. Their length and their weight regulate the pace of the style, which, as a result, is always under their guardianship, and they thus prevent it from emulating the flight of the imagination.[20]

Conjunctions such as *like*, *as*, and *similar to*, which one finds in comparisons, must also be abolished, in that they are not in line with "the speed of air travel" and the new "perception through analogy" that "is becoming even more natural for human beings."[21] Even punctuation must be suppressed, so that the discourse can proceed "without the absurd pauses of commas and periods."[22] In their place, Marinetti suggests using mathematical signs, such as $+ - \times : = > <$, "to render quantitative relations by epitomizing a longer explanation, without any filler, and avoiding the dangerous mania for wasting time in all the crannies of the sentence."[23] In sum, "What we have to guard against, in reality, is a fatal time-wasting."[24]

In *Destruction of Syntax—Imagination without Strings—Words-in-Freedom* Marinetti reasserts the need for a "need for laconicism [that] responds . . . to the laws of speed."[25] He writes: "Dread of slowness, minutiae, analyses, and detailed explanations. Love of speed, abbreviation, and synopsis. 'Quick, give me the whole thing *in two words!*'"[26] While in the technical manifesto he calls for verbs in the infinitive because they free literature from the "I" and psychology, here he touches on their effect on speed: with no indication of tenses, "The verb in the infinitive, by its very nature, disallows the existence of the sentence and prevents the style from coming to a halt and sitting down at any specific point."[27] He also rejects again qualifying adjectives, which presuppose "a halt in intuition":[28]

> What is necessary is to use the adjective as little as possible and in a manner that is absolutely different from how it has been used hitherto. The adjective should be viewed as a railway signal or traffic signal of style, serving to regulate the impetus, the slowing down, and the stops in the flow of the analogies. What I call a semaphoric adjective . . . is an adjective separated from its noun and isolated in parentheses, which turns into a sort of absolute noun, vaster and more powerful than a noun proper.[29]

Once verbs are employed in the infinitive form and adjectives are isolated from nouns and used in a pure, highly concentrated figuration, writers will be able to "render the analogical ground of life, telegraphically, which is to say with the same economical rapidity that the telegraph imposes on reporters and war correspondents in their summary reports."[30] In sum, it is clear in which direction Marinetti pushes writers. Futurism calls for speed. Slowness, time-wasting, retards, pauses, stops, arrests: to all these perils, Marinetti responds by urging writers to go faster. The new literature must change its tempo: now it must be *presto*; no, even more: *prestissimo*.

Words-in-Freedom and Freedom in Words

With prescriptions as radical as those illustrated above, Marinetti must have appeared a one-of-a-kind liberator: the moment he invited writers to free themselves from the prison of syntax and grammar, he imposed counter-rules that sounded, in fact, like a new grammar, precisely a counter-grammar. How much freedom could one find in words-in-freedom? Could writers really let their imagination and inspiration flow freely and make poetry "be a continuous stream of new images,"[31] as he hoped, if they had to worry so much about speed, verbs in the infinitive form, adjectives isolated in parenthesis or suppressed altogether? And finally, what remained of literature, once it was stripped of tensed verbs, adverbs, adjectives, punctuation and filled with mathematical or musical signs?

Not all futurist writers felt at ease with words-in-freedom; to some, the new rules seemed a cage they did not want to enter, and Marinetti a dictator they did not want to follow that far. Palazzeschi, for example, called him "the czar of words-in-freedom," a definition the founder of Futurism did not really agree with.[32] In fact, Marinetti was not interested in imposing his technical rules as much as he wanted to shake the edifice of Literature. Those rules were means, not ends. Even they, alone, would not work if platitudes and rhetorical clichés were not removed from writing. In *Destruction of Syntax—Imagination without Strings—Words-in-Freedom* he wrote: "There is no need . . . to worry too much about these latter aspects. But at all costs we must avoid rhetoric and commonplaces expressed telegraphically."[33] He made clear several times in his literary manifestos that he was neither categorical nor systematic in his indications. For example, in the *Technical Manifesto of Futurist Literature* he wrote:

> In all this, there is nothing absolute, nothing systematic. Genius experiences impetuous flurries and muddy torrents. Sometimes it demands slow analyses and explanations. No one can renovate his own sensibility all at once. Dead cells are mixed together with the live ones. Art is the need to destroy and scatter oneself, a great watering can of heroism that drowns the world. And don't forget: microbes are necessary for the health of the stomach and the intestines. Just so there is also a species of microbes that are necessary for the health of art—art, this extension of the forest of our veins that flows beyond the body and extends into the infinity of space and time.[34]

Thus Marinetti opened a space—and a time—for literary experiments as they had never been made before in Italy. Many responded to his call; feeling now authorized to be free, they experimented with new poetic forms and ways of writing without worrying too much about models and perhaps sometimes even about results: they could even go slow, if they wanted; what was important was that they moved and lived, launching their vitality into the infinite.

One of the most obvious ways for futurist poets to address time was to sing the novelty of the futurist movement and visualize the abandoning of old traditions in terms of destruction and renovation, just as Marinetti did in the very first part of his launching manifesto, where he fictionalized the "foundation" of the movement. "Apocalisse" ("Apocalypse," 1912) by Libero Altomare follows precisely that model. It represents the explosion of the new vital energies of Futurism as an apocalypse: the new centuries are "strangled at birth" and the futurists move in the universe as "Freebooters of time."[35] Even Auro d'Alba's "Orchestra lirica" ("Lyric Orchestra," 1915) is quite Marinetti-like in its approach and style. Following Marinetti's technical indications, d'Alba adopts words-in-freedom to express the swift rhythm of Futurism. He starts by these very words: "In a single night in a single hour in a single moment / freeing oneself from the past" and depicts the futurists as "indomitable pirates" and "revolutionary precursors."[36]

Another way in which futurists addressed time, more attuned to the modern ear, was through depicting the swift rhythm of modern life. The metropolis provided them with the most appropriate scenery, and cars, locomotives, and airplanes featured among their most favorite objects. Within this general pattern, which soon became quite predictable, one finds some personal interpretations. In "Crocicchio plastic veloce di donne" ("Swift Plastic Crossroads of Women," 1925) Escodamè describes a busy crossroad of an unspecified city. A "Traffic police chief black Minos with helmet whistle red+white club most terrible"—a Dantesque figure, but modernized—directs the traffic of the damned of the modern city. The poet sees women of different sorts, until one of them makes the traffic stop by crossing the street very slowly. Her words remind again of Dante's Inferno, of the same Canto V in which Minos is, and where the infernal blast drives the carnal sinners "here and there, down and up";[37] in Escodamè, however, it is the woman's scent, not the infernal blast, that spreads "here there in front in back." Eventually the overall scene looks like a middle way between Dante's sonnet "So gentle and so honest appears"[38] and Walther Ruttmann's movie Berlin, Symphony of a Great City.[39] Escodamè's woman character passes on the street like Beatrice, but, whereas in Dante, as the lady passes, "every tongue, trembling, becomes mute," in Escodamè it is the cars, instead, that stop and become silent. Moreover, this modern Beatrice is not as "clothed in humility" as in Dante; on the contrary, she seems very self-conscious and uses all her seductive arts to charm her Minos and stop the traffic.[40] When the traffic stops in the poem, the verses also stop in their turn with a blank line; then the chaos of bodies, machines, and sounds resumes, in a way that reminds of the scene in Ruttmann's movie which shows an old officer holding a child's hand and helping him cross the street—a short pause in the incessant movement of the city. Indeed, even though there are clear references to Dante in terms of both language and situation, what prevails from the very beginning in Escodamè is the sense of a swift passing and a chaotic accumulation, as cinematic montage would show particularly well. The same juxtaposition of disparate elements Escodamè's poem conveys through words-in-freedom, free verses, and onomatopoeias:

Traffic police chief black Minos with helmet whistle red+white club most terrible
    don't mess with him   STOP GO
        STOP GO   columns vehicles marching
. . .
"here there in front in back I offer warm scents through this fine fashionable crepe
    Well balanced, I strut   narrow skirt narrow pavement what if it
    buckles?   This way that way
very slowly   while I charm the police"   the traffic has stopped!
But now it resumes . . .
Swift zigzag swerving turning passing nimbly among the real and phony vehicles
STOP GO   STOP GO
            puUTTTputt   puUTTTputt   driiiiiiiin
            diiiing-a-ling "liiiiiiiife"[41]

Halts like the one to which the traffic is brought in Escodamè's "Swift Plastic Crossroads of Women" are not as common in futurist poetry. Luciano Folgore writes "Città ferma" ("Still city," 1914), but there the reason for the city's inactivity is clear: a general strike; moreover, behind the bored yawn of the men of today one sees action and war tomorrow: "Perhaps tomorrow / storms of machine gun fires / thunderbolts of bayonets / dreadful songs of cannons."[42] At any rate, when they feature in a poem, such halts or still images mostly serve to emphasize the movement that precedes and follows. More often, futurist poetry describes a continued swift movement or a progressive acceleration. Escodamè also wrote "Veloci in pioggia" ("Fast in [the] Rain," 1925),[43] in which he describes a nocturnal race on a straight stretch with a Lancia Lambda limousine, one of the most innovative cars on the market in those years.[44] The momentum gathered in futurist races is very often sexualized: Escodamè, running in a cold night under a pelting rain, finds a "feminine intimacy in this warm traveling alcove" that is his Lancia Lambda. Alternatively, the desired woman and futurist muse is mechanized, as in the last verses of Alberto Vianello's "luci fischi spilli anidride carbonica" ("Lights Whistles Pins Carbon Dioxide," 1925): "I am not speaking / I am trembling / you are speed / machine creator of syllables / grinder / thus I want you machine / and our children will be / precision devices."[45] If such a parallel between the woman and the machine ever sounded innovative and unheard of in the early twentieth century, when it was supposed, in the futurist view, to contrast the sentimentality of bourgeois love, the same cannot be said today, after the flood of car advertising that plays exactly on the same association and which has been proposed for decades and decades thereafter.[46] At any rate, there were also futurist poets who addressed the string of speed–woman–creativity in a more interesting way; Alfredo Trimarco, for example, wrote an "Inaugurazione della giornata veloce" ("Inauguration of the Swift Day," 1937):[47]

> Dawn. / The sun / has opened / its golden shutters. / Constructed on a stage / of sunsets and sunrises, / in the moving pictures / of my colorful / days, / my lyrical locomotives / race / to infinity. / Locomotives: / blue arrows / shot / from the brain's / golden bow / theatrical stage / of dream. / Women / dressed in silk and sun: / poetry machines; / Luna Park / . . . / sword-skyscrapers / . . . / formidable airships / loaded / with pure oxygen / and starry pinwheels; / mad propellers / of joy-space, / gems and daisies / of my brain. / Go, / all of you, / run around the world / through the golden forests / of the universe![48]

Here Trimarco deploys a series of imaginative analogies quite in the manner of Corrado Govoni, who is recalled in the very title of the poem (see Govoni's collection *Inauguration of the Spring*).

Watches and Clocks

Among the primary objects that inhabit futurist texts, watches and clocks are particularly relevant here, as they measure time. The relationship with them varies from author to author and it would be difficult to point out a general tendency; of course, the reason why they feature so prominently in futurist writings is precisely that they measure time in an exact and inexorable fashion and embody mechanical precision. This fact leads to different reactions. Remo Chiti, for example, in "Dio orologio" ("Clock God," 1917), tells the reader that he adores his watch for its metallic brightness, which gives him the sense of a sentimental neatness: as life and literature appear to him full of sentimentality, he turns to the watch to experience the world in a more authentic way and see things not through the lenses of literary long-winded passages but with a purity similar to that of his metal device:

> I have a little God in front of me: the *clock*: stiff, impeccable, selfish; no resemblance to a creature, no human substance; I adore it; it marks time with utmost sentimental neatness! Just like that, then: to have the formidable purity of metal. I know it: the shared exasperation for the nagging, indolent epilogue

of all passions calls for this fixed and consoling chastity. . . . Life is not lined with sentiments: it is smeared with them.[49]

Clocks tell the hours and the minutes. Their inexorable measuring of time provokes, as said, different reactions. Nelson Morpurgo in "Conversazioni notturne" ("Nocturnal Conversations," 1920) observes things around him and feels detached from the general flow of life: "the night advances," "a cricket sings," "two plants plaints,"

The moon smiles in the violet sky
I do not   I am ecstatic watching the clock's hands continuing to
revolve undisturbed[50]

Sometimes there are many clocks, which do not tell exactly the same hour. Loris Catrizzi in "Stradaseragennaio" ("Streetnightjanuary," 1925):

4 electric clocks:	6:46
2 » »:	6:42
other » »:	from 6:30 to 6:55[51]

Does this mean that not even electric clocks are reliable and scientifically impeccable? Catrizzi does not clarify. In any case, whatever hour clocks may tell, there are poets who fantasize about stopping or even killing them. In "Vorrei" ("I'd like," 1925) Farfa wishes he could stop all watches in the world and enjoy the spectacle as a king:

I'd Like

to transmit with the imagination
a charge that would stop
all the clocks
and see suddenly immobile
this multiple, idiotic speed,
immobilized the billows of humanity,
and enjoy a show worthy of a king
who has ordered his subjects
to get off all airplanes trains cars
trucks trolleys carts and carriages
palaces villas and houses
and, bewildered
by the loss of the notion of time,
ask every stock-still pedestrian
self-statued on the street
pardon me what's the tiiiiiiiiime[52]

Farfa's is an unconventional and anarchic joke against the foundational myths of Futurism, the fixation for the machine and speed ("multiple, idiotic speed"[53]). In this playful fantasy he imagines to stop all clocks in the world and make people get off from planes, trains, and cars or come out of their palaces, villas, and houses. If this could really happen, they, not knowing the time, would be dismayed and ask any pedestrian on the street for it. With his playfulness, Farfa tells us about a time that has lost, in fact, its significance: people just move blindly in the world using various kinds of transportation, but what is their notion of time passing? The ultimate function of clocks, in this blind universe, is not really to measure events, helping people to make sense of their lives; on the contrary, clocks only serve to direct the traffic of a multitude of persons unaware of themselves. Playing the cheeky boy, Farfa uses his irony against the myths of modernity and Futurism, so as to rediscover, at least for a second, at least in his imagination, a more authentic sense of reality.

Unlike Farfa's, Palazzeschi's fantasy with "L'orologio" ("The Clock," 1910) is a very personal one, in the sense that it stages a sinister encounter between the poet-narrator and the old clock in his bedroom: just the two of them, one on one.

> For a long, long time / the clock hasn't ticked. / I used to watch it with a sneer, / plotting to put an end / to that evil box of cheer, / a very sorry end. // . . . / On that vile clock / I hurled all my wrath, / I threw against it / all that crossed my path. / Insults, spit, filth, / shoes, inkwells! / And it stopped. / It stopped at six o'clock. // At first I felt / that I was free from it, / that it wasn't ticking anymore, / that it had stopped dead. / But the next day / that time came, / I looked at it, / and from its fierce immobility / I understood: / that would be the time, / inexorably! / Would I, every day / at that time, have to die? / . . . / In my despair / I rushed to the clock, / and gutted it! / I threw it all out, its hands, / its sharp / hellish gear, / I scattered it all about. / Now all that is left to see / is a face pierced through, / and a piece of chain / still hanging / with a wheel attached. / Shreds of the filthy belly / I had disemboweled. // . . . / No! I'll build a tower on a mountain, / make it the tallest in the world, / on top of all your minutes / I'll stack all of its bricks, / and climb it in my own time, / the time I've chosen. / I'll stop to hear the ticking / of all the clocks in the world, / useless, vile hearts, / and will call out: clock, look, here I jump! / And feign the move. / Ha! I heard a click! / It was you, you already marked the time, / you thought that was it! / Hahahahahaha! / No, that wasn't it, / it's a time I know! / Now I'm the one in charge, / I'm the one who'll tell you the time, Time! / I'll find in my throat, / dig up from my belly, / the most hysterical, most obscene laughs, / the most indecent jokes, / the shrillest scoffing outpour / and keep you waiting / five minutes more.[54]

This is clearly a very personal way to develop the theme of the clock. Palazzeschi stages a poetic "I" who recites his long monologue and has an exclusive, stifling relationship with his device; ideally, we imagine him at the very center of the stage, talking to his silent clock, which becomes a mirror reflecting the protagonist's difficult relationship with the world. Through this persona, Palazzeschi, far from representing a collective subject or a futurist type, represents only himself. His persona is at the opposite poles of Marinetti's model as proposed, for example, in the futurist *serate* (evenings): while the founder of Futurism came on stage speaking for a group ("we, the futurists") and "served as an object the audience could react *against*,"[55] Palazzeschi imagined a poetic "I" alone, who, instead, reacts against the crowd, but not directly, rather in a figurative and metaphorical way. There is no crowd here; only a clock: by destroying it and conquering the power to decide about his own destiny, the protagonist defines his identity and establishes his position against the external world. In sum, Palazzeschi's poem "The Clock" does not sing the futurist conquest of time at all, but rather stages the author's difficult search for identity.[56]

Palazzeschi, who never admitted openly his homosexuality, took part in the futurist *serate*, but apparently had a feeble voice that was not the most effective for reciting the poems in front of a riotous crowd.[57] And yet, even if he was never completely into these kinds of performances, it was thanks to Marinetti and the model of futurist evenings that Palazzeschi found his way to express the hidden and blocked contents of his first, pre-futurist collections of poems, such as *Cavalli bianchi* (*White Horses*, 1905) or *Lanterna* (*Lantern*, 1907).[58] Before "freeing himself from his liberator,"[59] the Florentine poet could find in him and his movement a particularly suitable common ground; and vice versa, of course.[60] "The Clock" featured prominently in the futurist *serate*, even when his author was not physically present.[61]

Glimpses and Knives

Within the futurist movement, a more philosophical, so to speak, reflection on time was conducted by the group of *L'Italia futurista*, to which even Remo Chiti, quoted above, belonged. This group was formed, among others, by the brothers Bruno Corra and Arnaldo Ginna and the latter's wife Maria Ginanni, who were all interested in theosophy, esotericism, and oriental studies. Instead of singing speed and the machine through words-in-freedom, these writers addressed perceptions of the human mind and developed a kind of writing influenced by spiritualism and occultism. In "La piazza del tempo" ("The Square of Time," 1917), for example, Maria Ginanni imagines a metaphysical space close to her villa—a space that strikingly reminds one of Palazzeschi's pre-futurist poems—where she waits for "an instant of absolute truth."[62] Indeed, this is what these poets mostly search for: moments of truth, illuminations in time, liberation from time. They try to overcome the human limits. So writes Corra in "Per l'onnipotenza" ("For the Sake of Omnipotence," 1915):

> I thought about it. Past and future are but two infinites emptying themselves into one another through the present. The present allows time to go from the future to the past, to move, flow, live. It is the heart and pivotal point of time. I examined the present, this instantaneous atmosphere in which an event lives its glowing moment and then becomes that which was. I will exploit the relation between the event and the present moment, I will avail myself of the precipitous movement of an event from the immensity of the future to the immensity of the past through the indisputable smallness of a *current moment*. I have noticed how this fleeting and yet lively and tenacious present moment is extremely concerned with predicting events, so as to get ready to let them pass easily. . . . *We will then only need to catch the present off guard; conjure up all of a sudden, right in front of a current moment, an event shaped in the most bizarre and unpredictable manner.* The instant will be cloven by the event smashing through it, and time will cease to live. . . . Perhaps the intellectual powers, now freed of time, will immediately give us that omnipotence *that has become a right of our all-too-proud life*.[63]

In order to kill the present, which represents time's core in his analysis, Corra intends to act in the strangest and most unpredictable way, and starts looking for the most extreme action. Unpredictability is the key to unblock time's mechanism: against the chain of events, which flows by pivoting on the present, Corra proposes himself to find something that is not supposed to be part of that chain, and which will therefore allow him to be released from time's eternal flow. Writers of *L'Italia futurista* share with other futurists the same concern with time; but instead of searching for poetic forms that reflect speed, they prefer to reflect upon the past, the present, the future, and eternity. One does not find too many cars and airplanes in their writings; rather, one sees glimpses of omnipotence[64] and mediumistic forces in place.

One last and most interesting example in this group is Bontempelli's opening poem for his volume *Il Purosangue. L'ubriaco* (*The Thoroughbred. The Drunk*, 1919) which came out in a series directed by Maria Ginanni.[65] Its interest is also to be seen prospectively: a few years later, Bontempelli would write on 900 those words that I have quoted at the very beginning, a call for reconstructing time and space in their eternity[66] so as to surpass Futurism. Before that, in the years 1916–1919, during and after World War I, Bontempelli, almost and over forty—he was born in 1878—joined Futurism. Regarding his personal literary carrier up to then, it was quite a late and odd membership: when Marinetti had founded Futurism, Bontempelli had kept writing in a classicist manner, publishing books of poetry that bore titles such as *Settenari e sonetti* (*Seven-syllable lines and sonnets*, 1910) and *Odi* (*Odes*, 1910).[67] After the First World War, the avant-garde must have seemed to him the only way to find a mode of writing more attuned to the changes brought by the war and its unprecedented destructions. In this spirit he joined Futurism, attracted not by machines and words-in-freedom—too radical, this latter, for a former classicist—but rather by the idea of stopping time, killing eternity, playing with the infinite, exploring new worlds. Here are his free verses "Isola" ("Island," dated 1916, published in 1919):[68]

> I
> I want to give man a knife / to cut off Eternity. // This eternity that has worn him out. // And then a new one starts / he bears that one as well / but he must have learned at last // that even Eternity / is as mortal as he is. // he crushes it in his turn / makes Time his toy / knead again with his hands / the motionless ideas that are in heaven / he blows out the Creator's light. // Surely man will have fun, / when he has a knife / to cut Eternity.

> II
> Time has stopped all of a sudden, / all of it, around me, as far as the sea. // Beyond the horizon all around / the crystal of motionless Time / wraps the whole globe // reaches up to me up to the shore / because I am on an island, always, / wherever I go, I remain on the Island // and up up into heaven / where no airplanes can reach / no eagles / no thoughts // because up above God's head / all around time has stopped / time / rhythm / the infinite. // Only my thought spins dizzily / only my thought is / rhythm / time / life / world / Eternity.[69]

Knowing Bontempelli's later developments, one realizes that the moment he joins Futurism, he also sees the end of this encounter. When one reads about the new eternity that he foresees—one to be borne like the old one, but knowing this time that not even eternity is eternal—one cannot but be reminded of Bontempelli's later founding of magic realism. In a few years, he will invite writers to build time and space anew and precisely to play with them as magicians do.[70] Writers will make time and space their toys (as in v. 10), having a new awareness of their (own) mortality.

Calculations and Movements

Futurist writers also addressed time, space, speed, and eternity in numbers. They did not follow, however, the strict rules of science, but applied them playfully. Marinetti for example evoked science ironically—certainly not rigorously—in "Problem: how to can a space X in a time X," the second section of his *Spagna veloce e toro futurista* (*Swift Spain and Futurist Toro*, 1931), where he played with the formula of average speed. The title wrongly uses the same variable X to denote different entities (space and time); but it is, in fact, the text that offers the best of Marinetti's qualities in terms of "imaginative futurist mathematics."[71] The narrator is heading to Madrid for a conference on Futurism, when he must stop due to engine failure. This unpredicted fact cannot but make changes to his scheduled trip, which he visualizes as a can or box he holds in his hands: "Abrupt, forced stop. / Immediately, the time and space I kept bundled up tight between my hands tear through the wrapping."[72] The unplanned engine failure becomes the pretext for poetic variations on the formula of speed; starting from that image of the can, Marinetti fantasizes about compressing all sorts of different things into it:

> Irritating immobility of the automobile before the precipitant problem to be solved: I must fit the 400 kilometers that separate me from Madrid into the 4-hour box that separates me from the 9:00 o'clock hour already standing there waiting for my lecture on Futurism in the world.
> In the same box I also must fit those 5 red clay villages and those precious flowing waters, feverish silver mounted in the brown plain.
> . . .
> I must, I must shove into the tiny 1-minute box the 3 kilometers that separate me from the indispensable fuel in the next village!
> . . .
> strrrain, strrrain to fit the 23 kilometers that separate us from Alcañiz into this other 5-minute box. The burning thumbs of the 4 tires press down.[73]

Of course, in line with Marinetti's futurist view, the machine has a great part in avoiding the "crime of delay:" "The engine participates in the / violent arithmetic calculation."[74]

Even Palazzeschi plays with mathematics, but in a different way. Reading the tombstones in his "La fiera dei morti" ("Fair of the dead,"1910), he points out how farcical human destinies can be, because the accounts of life often don't balance.[75] Palazzeschi also plays with speed, traveling, going for a walk: in sum, with different kinds of movements. However, whereas Marinetti and most of the other futurists tended to compress time and space, like in Marinetti's speed can, and to reduce the line of time to a dot, Palazzeschi enjoyed doing the opposite, stretching time and space like rubber bands. In "Le carovane" ("Caravans," 1910) we do not find fast cars running on the street, but an endless procession of everything—hands, feet, eyes, trees, houses, castles, ships, men, women—passing by the poet's house:

> Today I see before me
> the longest
> unending road,
> packed with caravans.
> Long and dusty road
> extending into infinity
> right in front of my house.
> At the window of my bedroom
> I stand and watch
> all that coming and going,
> all that puffing, that standing around.
> Stalled, wandering, flying
> caravans lost
> on the road here before me.[76]

There is no beginning and no end to this procession: the poetic "I" just watches this infinite long line of things that fade away in the distance, just like the words and sounds do on the written page:

> But what's all this passing through,
> all this travelling, this stopping for a bit? . . .
> All these caravans caravans caravans. . . .
> *vans vans vans vans vans.* . . .
> *ans ans ans ans ans.* . . .
> *sssssssssssssssssssss.* . . .
> *s . . . s . . . s . . . s . . . s . . .*[77]

Finally, Palazzeschi offered with "La passeggiata" ("Promenade," 1913) an example of slow narrative at a constant speed with almost no verbs. The text has only two verbs, "to go," and "to head back," which constitute the frame of the poem. The rest is what the eye records and reports impersonally verse after verse: signs, advertisements, street numbers, whatever one finds written while passing on a street.

> "Shall we go?"
> "Let's go."
>
> To the art of embroidery,
> trimming workshop,
> orders, supplies.

> Purtaré sisters,
> to the city of Paris,
> nouveauté.
> Benedetto Paradiso,
> new owner after Michele Salvato,
> historical pharmacy,
> laboratory founded in the year 1783.
> Important announcement to the ladies!
> facial beauty!
> Silky skin,
> brand-new, unbeatable soap.
> Precision watches.
> 43.
> Millionaire lottery.
> . . .
> "Shall we head back?"
> "Let's head back."
> . . . . [78]

The action is not described as such, but remains implicit, being only suggested by the variations in signs and advertisements that the eye records. It is as if, instead of a body, an eye went for a walk. The speed of this poem is that of the imagined feet stepping forward, or of the eye reading the signs-verses. It can vary, but it is not high, as this is a promenade, not a run. Even more importantly, one should technically speak of velocity here, not speed, as the text constantly indicates the direction of the walk. Indeed, if we borrowed the terms from physics—where speed is a scalar quantity indicating how fast an object moves, while velocity is a vector quantity indicating speed together with the direction of travel—we could say that, unlike Marinetti's cans, which embody the speed of his story as a scalar quantity, referring to how fast his car moves, Palazzeschi's signs-verses, which are direction-aware, visualize the velocity of the poem, telling the speed (of the feet, or the eye) and also keeping track of direction. Of course, we are dealing here with literature, not science. But the recourse to these terms as applied in physics can help us describe in just another way the difference between Palazzeschi's and other futurists' writings.

The Last Stop

The aim of this essay was not to constitute an exhaustive survey of the relationship between Futurism and time in writing. However, I hope it gives an idea of the variety of modes of such a relationship. Notwithstanding Marinetti's prescriptive counter-grammar of words-in-freedom, which urged writers to abolish all those elements in a sentence that "imply a pause, a moment of contemplation," futurist writers did not simply submit to "the laws of speed," praising the machines and trying themselves to go faster and faster in their poems; they engaged with time and speed in various ways, having recourse to various means for "emulating the flight of the imagination." Thus, it would be unfair to label the *tempo* of futurist creative writings only as *presto* or *prestissimo*, which are the ones Marinetti kept insisting on in his manifestos. It is true that most futurists, following his guidelines, experimented primarily with *mosso*, *accelerando*, and *precipitando*, but, as I showed, there was also room for writers who played their pieces in slower modes, such as *andante moderato*, *largo*, or even *larghissimo*. What all authors shared in their concern with time was, certainly, the need to shake, strike, or even kill time, that is the need to hit it in some ways and rebel against it. Corra trying to catch a glimpse of omnipotence, Palazzeschi smashing his clock to pieces, Bontempelli offering a knife to humans for killing Eternity, all show the effort to digest their "thickened present," to use Stephen Kern's definition.[79]

Furthermore, in their attempts to come to terms with the new technological time as perceived since the late nineteenth century, the futurists were generally very playful. Although this is not always apparent and Marinetti stressed the need for violence, not playfulness, to make sure he would really shake the edifice of literature and be taken seriously, the background—if not even the foreground—for all these experiments with time was marked by high spirits. This is what the leader of Futurism undeniably provided underneath his rhetoric of war and literary prescriptions. Each writer engaged with the "thickened present" and the "high spirits" differently and in different times. Farfa pursued his career of "millionaire of imagination"[80] into the 1930s and 1940s; Palazzeschi found in Futurism a way to free himself by releasing his personas and amusingly provoking his readers, but did not follow his literary liberator beyond World War I; Bontempelli joined the movement late, after the Great War, but only to leave it after a few years: it was the last stop for his poetry (he would not write any more verses thereafter), before he started his magic realism, in which he made time his toy—there, finally, for real. Futurism was a great and far-reaching breeding ground for writers and artists, in which they could experiment freely with all categories and media in a mood that, if generally *allegro*, was not always *spensierato*.

Notes

1. I first addressed this topic in Italian in my "Il futurismo e il tempo," in Elisabetta Graziosi, ed., *Il tempo e la poesia. Un quadro novecentesco* (Bologna: CLUEB, 2008), 57–85. The present essay is not a translation of that study, but reformulates,

updates, and expands it. For reasons of space I do not treat all quotations from that article with the new ones presented here: the two essays should ultimately be seen as complementary.

2. I have relied on three translations of Marinetti's manifestos: by Robert Willard Flint, in Umbro Apollonio, ed., *Futurist Manifestos* (London: Thames and Hudson, 1973); by Doug Thompson, in Filippo Tommaso Marinetti, *Critical Writings*, ed. Günter Berghaus (New York: Farrar, Straus and Giroux, 2006); and by Lawrence Rainey, in Lawrence Rainey e.a., eds., *Futurism: An Anthology* (New Haven; London: Yale University Press, 2009). The titles with which Marinetti's manifestos have been translated into English slightly vary; for each individual quotation I have chosen to use what I consider the best rendering in English; all modifications are signaled. Translations will be cited as Flint, *Manifestos*, Thompson, *Critical Writings*, and Rainey, *Anthology*.

3. Flint, *Manifestos*, 22, Thompson, *Critical Writings*, 14, and Rainey, *Anthology*, 51.

4. Massimo Bontempelli, "Justification," 900 1 (1926), 7; my translation. It is worth noting that, just as Marinetti made the first big launch of his manifesto in French in the newspaper *Le Figaro*, so Bontempelli published the Italian journal 900 in French, until, after the fourth issue, the fascist regime imposed the Italian language.

5. Here I rely on Flint, *Manifestos*, 23, Thompson, *Critical Writings*, 16, and Rainey, *Anthology*, 53.

6. Here I quote Flint, *Manifestos*, 23, Thompson, *Critical Writings*, 16, and Rainey, *Anthology*, 53, with minor modifications.

7. Flint, *Manifestos*, 20 and Thompson, *Critical Writings*, 12. Rainey, *Anthology*, 49 has "coffin" instead of "bier."

8. See Flint, *Manifestos*, 20–21, Thompson, *Critical Writings*, 12–13, and Rainey, *Anthology*, 50–51.

9. Rainey, *Anthology*, 119.

10. Thompson, *Critical Writings*, 107.

11. "This is what the swirling propeller told me, as I sped along at two hundred meters above the powerful chimney stacks of Milan. And the propeller went even further" (here I rely on Thompson, *Critical Writings*, 107 and Rainey, *Anthology*, 119).

12. Stephen Kern, *The Culture of Time and Space 1880–1918* (Cambridge: Harvard University Press, 1983), 67–68.

13. "Futurism is based on the complete renewal of human sensibility that has occurred as an effect of science's major discoveries. Those people who today make use of the telegraph, the telephone, the gramophone, the train, the bicycle, the motorcycle, the automobile, the ocean liner, the dirigible, the airplane, the cinema, the great newspaper (the synthesis of a day in the world's life), do not realize that these various means of communication, transportation and information have a decisive influence on their psyches." Here I rely on Rainey, *Anthology*, 143 and Flint, *Manifestos*, 96.

14. Here I rely on Flint, *Manifestos*, 96, Thompson, *Critical Writings*, 121, and Rainey, *Anthology*, 144.

15. See Marinetti's and Pino Masnata's "The Radia: Futurist Manifesto" (1933): "Radia abolishes: space . . . [and] time . . . Radia will be . . . An art without time or space without yesterday or tomorrow[.] The possibility of picking up transmissions from stations in different time zones merged together and the lack of light destroy the hours the day the night . . . Syntheses of infinite simultaneous actions" (Rainey, *Anthology*, 293–94).

16. Alberto Viviani considers *tavole parolibere* "the nodal point, brought to its extreme consequences, of a research that eventually led to and placated itself in its natural channel, that of painting." See his "Testo introduttivo," in Paolo Buzzi, *Conflagrazione: epopea parolibera*, with an introductory critical study by Alberto Viviani and an explanatory note by Emilio Guicciardi (Florence: Il Fauno, 1963), 14; my translation.

17. Flint, *Manifestos*, 22.

18. Rainey, *Anthology*, 120.

19. Thompson, *Critical Writings*, 107–8.

20. Here I quote Thompson, *Critical Writings*, 116 and Rainey, *Anthology*, 126–27, with minor modifications.

21. Thompson, *Critical Writings*, 108.

22. Thompson, *Critical Writings*, 108 and Rainey, *Anthology*, 120.

23. Rainey, *Anthology*, 127.

24. Thompson, *Critical Writings*, 109.

25. Rainey, *Anthology*, 145–46.

26. Here I rely on Thompson, *Critical Writings*, 122 and Rainey, *Anthology*, 145.

27. Here I rely on Thompson, *Critical Writings*, 127 and Rainey, *Anthology*, 149.

28. Rainey, *Anthology*, 148.

29. Here I quote Rainey, *Anthology*, 148 and Thompson, *Critical Writings*, 126, with minor modifications.

30. Here I rely on Thompson, 123 and Rainey, *Anthology*, 145.

31. Thompson, *Critical Writings*, 109.

32. See Marinetti's letter to Palazzeschi on 27th January 1914: "You must have noticed from the newspapers (of which I am sending you a bunch) that Marinetti, whom you have denounced as *the czar of words-in-freedom*, admires you, loves you, and glorifies you in all respects." (Filippo Tommaso Marinetti and Aldo Palazzeschi, *Carteggio. Con un'Appendice di altre lettere a Palazzeschi*, ed. Paolo Prestigiacomo, foreword by Luciano de Maria (Milan: Mondadori, 1978), 90; my translation.

33. Here I rely on Thompson, *Critical Writings*, 124 and Rainey, *Anthology*, 146.

34. Here I rely on Thompson, *Critical Writings*, 113 and Rainey, *Anthology*, 124. See also Marinetti in *Destruction of Syntax—Imagination without Strings—Words-in-Freedom*: "When I speak of destroying the canals of syntax, I am being neither peremptory nor systematic. In the words-in-freedom of my unchained lyricism, there will still be traces here and there of regular syntax and even of true, logical periods. This inequality in concision and freedom is inevitable and natural" (Rainey, *Anthology*, 146). À propos of the suppression of the qualifying adjective: "None of this is

categorical. I speak of a tendency" (Flint, *Manifestos*, 103), and the verb in the infinitive: "Here, too, my pronouncements are not categorical" (Flint, *Manifestos*, 103 and Rainey, *Anthology*, 148).

35. My translation. See Glauco Viazzi, ed., *I poeti del futurismo 1909–1944* (Milan: Longanesi, 1978), 206, vv. 1, 29–30. Subsequently cited as Viazzi, *I poeti*.

36. Italian text with facing English translation in Willard Bohn, ed., *Italian Futurist Poetry*, trans. Willard Bohn (Toronto: University of Toronto Press, 2005), 50–51, vv. 1–2, 46. In this edition, "evolutionary" is clearly a typo; see the text in Italian: "rivoluzionari." Subsequently cited as Bohn, *Futurist Poetry*. All quotations from this book are reprinted with permission of the publisher.

37. Dante, *The Inferno*, ed. Robert Hollander, trans. Robert and Jean Hollander (New York: Anchor Books, 2002), 93, v. 43.

38. Dante, *Vita Nuova*, trans. Dino Cervigni and Edward Vasta (Notre Dame: University of Notre Dame Press, 1995), 111–12.

39. The movie dates back to 1927, two years after the publication of Escodamè's poem. My mentioning of it here intends only to remind that the theme of the metropolis as a place of speed and traffic was common in those years in different medias and was often emphasized, as I point out later in my text, by showing the contrast between the continued flux of cars and buses and a very short interruption provoked by someone—usually a boy, or a woman, that is a subject perceived as "weak"—crossing the street.

40. Dante, *Vita Nuova*, 111–12.

41. Bohn, *Futurist Poetry*, 163, with modifications by Marella Feltrin-Morris and myself.

42. My translation. One sees why the poem, first published in Luciano Folgore, *Ponti sull'Oceano* (Milan: Edizioni Futuriste di Poesia, 1914), could easily feature in Mario Carli and Giuseppe Attilio Fanelli, eds., *Antologia degli scrittori fascisti* (Florence: Bemporad, 1931), 314–16; here vv. 80–89.

43. Bohn, *Futurist Poetry*, 165 translates the title as *Speeding in the Rain*.

44. See Franco Amatori, "Lancia 1906–1969," in *Storia della Lancia: impresa, tecnologie, mercati: 1906–1969* (Milan: Fabbri, 1992), 38–40.

45. Bohn, *Futurist Poetry*, 181.

46. If this sounds unfair, see a more detailed discussion of Vianello's entire poem in Willard Bohn, *The Other Futurism: Futurist Activity in Venice, Padua, and Verona* (Toronto: University of Toronto Press, 2004), 31–34.

47. Bohn, *Futurist Poetry*, 135 translates the title as "Dawn of a Swift Day." However, this title does not show Trimarco's clear reference to Corrado Govoni's collection *Inauguration of the Spring* (*Inaugurazione della primavera*, 1915).

48. Bohn, *Futurist Poetry*, 135 and 137, with modifications by Marella Feltrin-Morris. These are the vv. 1–23, 29, 35–47. For reasons of space this poem, like others quoted later, is printed with slashes to indicate line breaks.

49. See Viazzi, *I poeti*, 366. Translation by Marella Feltrin-Morris. Viazzi signals that the text was published in *Antologia degli scrittori fascisti*, 136–38, with the title "Steel" ("L'acciaio"), but does not seem to be aware of the first actual print in *L'Italia futurista* 2:6 (1917).

50. Bohn, *Futurist Poetry*, 127, vv. 1–3.

51. Bohn, *Futurist Poetry*, 151.

52. See *I nuovi poeti futuristi* (Rome: Edizioni Futuriste di Poesia, 1925), 126. Translation by Marella Feltrin-Morris.

53. The text underwent a curious change: when it was reprinted in Farfa, *Noi, miliardario della fantasia* (Milan: La Prora, 1933), it did not contain the adjective "idiotic."

54. See Aldo Palazzeschi, *Tutte le poesie*, ed. Adele Dei (Milan: Mondadori, 2002), 265–69. These are the vv. 11–16, 29–49, 59–72, 108–33. Translation by Marella Feltrin-Morris.

55. Günter Berghaus, *Theater, Performance, and the Historical Avant-garde* (New York: Palgrave Macmillan, 2005), 102.

56. See Glauco Viazzi's "Aldo Palazzeschi" in Viazzi, *I poeti*, 148: "The impossibility to declare one's own identity also implies a continuous search for it: this is the case of [Palazzeschi's] 'I'-narrator in front of the mirror . . . ; or else [Palazzeschi's] 'I'-narrator and the clock: if stopped, the clock, by interrupting the time's flow, would allow him to stop, and therefore to affirm, an identity as well." My translation.

57. See Giacinto Spagnoletti, *Palazzeschi* (Milan: Longanesi, 1971), 110–12.

58. Marinetti made one most insightful comment on this poem. See Marinetti, "Il poeta futurista Aldo Palazzeschi," in *Teoria e invenzione futurista*, edited by Luciano de Maria (Milan: Mondadori, 1983), 63: "Palazzeschi was the first and the only one to offer, precisely in 'The Clock,' the cry of human liberty; he tragically synthesized in an absolutely new lyrical and dramatic form the feverish and extreme anxiety of the *Self* striving to break its iron cage of determinism or fatality." My translation.

59. Paolo Febbraro, "Saba e Palazzeschi. Pagine di epistolario," in Idem, *Saba, Umberto* (Rome: Alberto Gaffi, 2008), 84. My translation. On Palazzeschi's different emotions towards Marinetti, see 81–85.

60. See again Marinetti, "Il poeta futurista Aldo Palazzeschi," 62–63: "Let us explain ourselves, then, on the precise meaning of this word. '*Futurism*' means above all '*originality*,' that is original inspiration, supported by and developed through a will and a mania for originality. '*Futurist movement*' means untiring, organized, systematic encouragement of the creative originality, even if this latter seems crazy. It is not, therefore, a distorting influence exerted on the free spirit of a poet, but rather an anti-traditional, anti-cultural, unconventional atmosphere, in which this spirit was able to dare and felt understood and loved, whereas [before] it was lonely, typical, indigestible for everybody, mocked by critics and ignored by the public. | Here is what binds the great poet Aldo Palazzeschi to Futurism—which [yes, it] is a school, if you like it, but one in which one is taught how to rebel and be original and independent." My translation.

61. See Spagnoletti, *Palazzeschi*, 123.

62. See Viazzi, *I poeti*, 370. My translation.

63. See Viazzi, *I poeti*, 332–33. Translation by Marella Feltrin-Morris.

64. See Bruno Corra's "Glimpse" ("Spiraglio," dated 1913, published 1914) and "Futurist Glimpse ("Spiraglio futurista," 1916) in Viazzi, *I poeti*, 331 and 337 respectively.

65. Massimo Bontempelli, *Il Purosangue. L'Ubriaco* (Milan: Facchi Editore, 1919); a new edition came out as *Il Purosangue* (Milan: Edizioni La Prora, 1933).

66. This is how the opening of "Justification" quoted at note 4 continues: "After restoring them [= time and space] in their eternity, immobility and coldness, we will take care to put them back in the place they had lost, within the three dimensions of the infinite, outside man" (p. 7). My translation.

67. Massimo Bontempelli, *Settenari e sonetti* (Ancona: G. Puccini e figli, 1910) and *Odi* (Modena: Formiggini, 1910). Later Bontempelli officially disowned them along with other volumes of his classicist period.

68. I rely on Massimo Bontempelli, *Opere scelte*, ed. Luigi Baldacci (Milan: Mondadori, 1978), 899–900. As Baldacci points out (p. 963), "Isola" as such appears only in the 1933 edition. In the 1919 edition, the first part (I) constituted the opening poem for the entire collection, whereas the second part (II) appeared as the fourth section of another piece entitled *Giochi* ("Games"). This does not affect my discourse, as both parts were already present in the 1919 volume; only, they were arranged differently and did not constitute one single piece entitled *Isola*, as it is the case in 1933.

69. Translation by Marella-Feltrin Morris and myself.

70. See Bontempelli, "Justification," 8–9: "For, if the art of the twentieth century succeeds in this effort of building anew and perfect an external world outside man, it will be to finally master it, and also to turn its laws upside down as one likes. Now, the art of mastering nature, it's magic. Here are explained, then, certain magic characters and vague desires, which one sees dawning in this 'atmosphere in formation' that 900 claims to represent and favor." My translation.

71. See "Qualitative Imaginative Futurist Mathematics" (1941) by Filippo Tommaso Marinetti with Marcello Puma and Pino Masnata, in which *Swift Spain and Futurist Toro* is also recalled (see Rainey, *Anthology*, 298).

72. See Viazzi, *I poeti*, 89. This passage and the following ones quoted from this work by Marinetti have been translated into English by Marella Feltrin-Morris.

73. See Viazzi, *I poeti*, 89–90.

74. See Viazzi, *I poeti*, 90.

75. See Palazzeschi, *Tutte le poesie*, 193–99, in particular the vv. 113–36. Even this poem, together with the above-mentioned "The Clock," was successfully read by Marinetti during the *serate* (see Spagnoletti, *Palazzeschi*, 131).

76. See Palazzeschi, *Tutte le poesie*, 221–22. These are the vv. 1–14. Translation by Nicholas Benson, available online at intranslation.brooklynrail.org/italian/poems-by-aldo-palazzeschi.

77. See the previous note. These are the vv. 45–51.

78. See Palazzeschi, *Tutte le poesie*, 295–98. These are the vv. 1–19, 127–29. Translation by Marella Feltrin-Morris.

79. See Kern, *The Culture of Time and Space*, 88.

80. "We the millionaire of imagination" is the title of one of Farfa's collections of poems: see note 52.

~

CHAPTER NINE

The Great War in the Words-in-Freedom Style of an Atypical Futurist

Conflagrazione *by Paolo Buzzi*

MONICA BIASIOLO

In the fields,
as a child, I adored whipping
the grass and cutting off buttercups' heads.
Free malleolus at each ankle-side, this was my desire,
a *Mercury* was I, with my own feet longing eternally to fly.
Sublime visions full of blood
Felt upon my head. I was inside *the Myth of Mars.*
My soul was full of such vermilion visions.
My father inflamed my scarlet dreams
with his fantastic stories of war about Garibaldi and his men.[1]

War, why are we drowning now in peace?
Sitting in the comfortable leather of my peaceful armchair
I feel the hate. These verses, which I write now
and I feel, oh!—oft—horrible in the screeching,
are part of homicidal greed which is going away, patriotic,
and no garland of glory can crown them.[2]

With these words Paolo Buzzi (who would later be defined by Marinetti as "one of the first advocates and protagonists of Futurism because, together with him [Marinetti], he was the protagonist of a turning point")[3] introduces one of his poems in his poetry collection *Aeroplani* (Airplanes) in 1908. But in spite of its title, "Inno alla guerra" (Hymn to War), it begins with a rather idyllic image—a child playing in the fields—instead of with a bloodthirsty one. Its first verbal predicate would have been far from a tribute to war were it not for the two infinitive verbs that specify the child's favorite pastime, whipping the grass and cutting off flower heads. These add a sinister and violent stress to the child's image and character. Because of the context they are used in, deliberate mythological (Mercury and Mars, vv. 5 and 7) and historical references (the stories his father told him about Garibaldi and his soldiers, v. 10) underline the longing for brutality and ferocity the first person narrator affirms to have had since his childhood. Throughout the poem the enthusiasm of the writer-protagonist gains force step by step until the underlying reasons for his ardor are disclosed: hatred and a desire for blood.[4] To allow for complete comprehension of such rancor and greed and the understanding of their causes, it is necessary to mention the historical context in which these and the other verses of the poem were created and how they are to be interpreted.

In 1908 the First World War has not broken out yet, but many of the threads that will lead to the conflict already exist. One example is the problem of the unredeemed Italian lands that still belong to the Austro-Hungarian Empire. Despite the military alliance between Austria-Hungary and Italy (which also Germany takes part in) the general discontent is very strong. The violent confrontations that took place in Innsbruck in 1903 and the hostile demonstrations in Trento and Trieste are both symptoms of and significant reactions to the political situation. Things get worse with the Bosnian crisis, when Austria refuses to give Italy the unredeemed territories it promised in exchange for official recognition of its annexation of Bosnia-Herzegovina, as previously agreed upon in the Triple Alliance treaties with Austria-Hungary.

At this time more than ever the war—"the most beautiful futurist poem that has ever appeared until now"[5]—is considered the only realistic solution. Marinetti's collage *Irredentismo* (Irredentism) is dated 1914,[6] but the aspirations for the recapture of the unredeemed lands are also perceivable through other events: in December of the same year. Balla, Marinetti himself, and Depero participate in an interventionist demonstration organized by the University of Rome, during which Cangiullo puts on the "Antineutral Dress."[7] But how could these events be narrated? Many European and non-European artists and writers have used their art to protest against the conflict. Names such as Remarque, Hemingway, Barbusse, Ungaretti with his collection of poems *Allegria di naufragi* (*The Joy*)[8] as well as Dix and Kirchner, are but a few of those who attempted to depict the Great War; they are the first that come to mind when searching for literary works or paintings on the subject.[9] However, the futurist artists, first of all Marinetti, came up with contributions of similar importance.

Lesser known than the works of these artists, if known at all[10] is *Conflagrazione. Epopea parolibera* (Conflagration. A Free-Word Epic) by Paolo Buzzi,[11] one of the most interesting works ever produced within the field of Futurism and one which actually exceeds it. The lack of its critical reception is caused by the delay of the publication of his volume[12] and its scanty number of copies. This essay will try to analyze this text by reconstructing its history.

According to the foreword written at its publication by Emilio Guicciardi, Buzzi would have liked to see *Conflagrazione* printed in better times for Italy and the world, but the work remained unedited in accordance with the writer's will.[13] Maybe as an expression of his disillusionment following the enthusiasm he and most people had felt at the beginning of the war but which gradually diminished during the course of events, Buzzi would write in his novel *Il soldato ignoto* (The Unknown Soldier): "Oh, if the poor woman [Buzzi probably refers here to Risca, the female protagonist] could see now where the so-called 'hygiene of the world' has led to!"[14] *Conflagrazione* would therefore be published posthumously, at the initiative of the author's widow.[15]

Mario Morini attests to the fact that Buzzi did not hide his work but on the contrary continued to proudly show it to his closest friends many years after its realization. Recalling the last period of his friend's life, he states:

> One day—maybe in May—Paolo led us to an attic room in his villa and wanted to show us some dusty packages of manuscripts and newspaper bundles. Between them there was a kind of war diary from 1915–1918, consisting of sheets to which newspaper cuttings had been glued. The aim had been to create a daily synthesis of war events from all over the world following the then-futurist syntax. It was entitled Conflagrations. That kind of child's play (as which it could appear at first sight), those conjunctions of lines, that criss-cross of titles in "bold characters," of red and blue scribbles, could not in the end have been an empty effort when the history we experienced and endured was still able to move us, despite the fact that so many years had passed since then.[16]

Despite the existence of a few books about the writer[17] and a collection of his papers in the Sormani Library in Milan, in which some of Buzzi's unpublished works are stored[18]—information on this *œuvre* is amazingly scarce. *Conflagrazione*, composed between 1914 and 1918, is not Buzzi's first work. His literary achievements already included numerous publications. It was also not—at least for eager followers of his work—the first to have been published containing *parole in libertà*. In fact, the use of this futurist writing technique had already been applied by Buzzi in *L'Ellisse e la Spirale. Film + parole in libertà* (1915) (The Ellipse and the Spiral. Film + Words-in-Freedom),[19] a novel that in this respect partially overlaps with *Conflagrazione*. But there are two fundamental aspects that distinguish the then-unedited work from all previously published ones. Its novelty does not lie in the use of *papier collé* but in the continued development of the words-in-freedom technique (*paroliberismo*) and in the massive and consequential application of handwriting. The *paroliberismo* does not require a narrative sequence anymore, but displays—using some words from Marinetti referring to this approach in general—"the simultaneous polyexpression of the world."[20] The style must be incisive and assertive, even if the writer gives up translating his feelings or thoughts into typographical signs. For this reason Buzzi has to reorganize the space of the page, choosing the most successful methods and procedures to express the content, the specific language of forms and colors which he is going to employ, the depth of the lines, their connection, freedom and intersection, and its visual and auditory impact:

> The "free words" aim to orchestrate colours, noises and sounds, to combine standard language with dialect, mathematical and geometrical formulas with their mechanical and numerical splendor (see my novel the *Ellipse and the Spiral*), musical signs, old, deformed or new words, cries of animals and of engines.[21]

The volume is divided into five parts, or, as Buzzi would define the structure of his works at its beginning,[22] into four years, which is the timeline from 1914 to 1918. Each section contains a different number of plates: 77 tables from 1914, 107 in the following section, and 45 dated 1916, while 23 are included in the section 1917. Only fifteen plates form the last narrative segment, totalling 267 plates. Some of these contain newspaper clippings, while most of the others are handwritten.[23] Originally, there seems to have been an even much higher number, which is suggested by an irregularity in the chronology of some dates that cannot be found in other passages.[24] Nowadays only three of the original plates remain preserved—all of them were displayed in spring 2009 by the Sormani Library on the occasion of an exhibition dedicated to Paolo Buzzi and held in the Lodovico Isolabella collection.[25]

Content and structure of the work are both summarized in its title, *Conflagrazione. Epopea parolibera*, in which "conflagrazione" clearly refers to the outbreak of the war but also indicates the technique used, that of words-in-freedom. The *paroliberismo* does not impose a grammatical scheme, rules of punctuation, the mere horizontal or vertical ordering of words, or the types of characters being used.[26] The words are not static units. They are allowed to move, to interact, to cross. They are free, as Buzzi underlines in the subtitle.

Their combination forms a synthesis that means a new approach to writing and an emancipation from the constraints of tradition. This emancipation is first documented by the combination of the substantive "epopea" ("epic") with the adjective "parolibera" connecting the narration of war and the aforementioned futurist practice of *paroliberismo* in a way that—at least partially—was also realized by Marinetti, for example in *Zang Tumb Tumb*,[27] a work on the siege of Adrianopolis during the First Balkan War. Buzzi's words are conflagrated words that show the reader not only the destruction and the devastation that has penetrated (and at that time was still penetrating human existence: the ear-splitting sounds of artillery rounds firing nearby or exploding bombs), but a syntactic outbreak, too. The word *epopea* was also selected for a specific reason, as Buzzi states:

> Today poetry is not really music, but a roar. War is noise. . . . And with the war as noise the whole futurist program inevitably establishes itself in its fullness and its significance. [. . .] And I will sing the *Conflagration*, this terrible epic of the present, a little different from Homer, the only epic poet standing behind us (Virgil, Tasso, Victor Hugo, d'Annunzio are imitators of Homer) and whom we surpass and erase, we futurists, the ones who are worthy to live in the age of the airplane.[28]

Buzzi believed Homer was the only real poet that nevertheless had to be surpassed, and with him Buzzi shared a literary theme: war. But while the legendary ancient Greek poet recounts in the *Iliad* only the final year of the Trojan War, Buzzi writes about the complete First World War. He also does not depict it by following the rules of the antique poem (or better, by following the established metric systems or rhetorical devices) even if the facts and events that are described still remain heroic and memorable. Rather, these incidents are expressed in a way analogous to that used by Ungaretti, namely in a lapidary, synthetic fashion that reduces the phrase or the image to the bare essentials. Like the poet of *Allegria di naufragi*, Buzzi creates poetical fragments, silent spaces modulating the narration. Even if his work can be seen as analogous to that of Ungaretti on this point, it differs in focalization. They are connected by the fact that some of the tables show the rawness that can also be found in Ungaretti's verses. But Buzzi's pages mostly concentrate on events, not on their protagonists or first-hand experiences from the front line. His chronicle of the war, like that of Ungaretti, is meant to be immediate, concise, and disillusioned:

> Although I have sung of the epic and extraordinary figure of Garibaldi in ottava rima (a rhyming stanza that always delected the Italian music instinct)

I have attempted, in this way, to render the [First] World War [in]to free-word compositions. The work will be entitled *Conflagration*: the electrical notation, the aviatory and submarinal throbbing, the graphic thrill, the screeching cry, the suggestiveness of the capitals of newspaper headlines, and the lapidary simplicity of reports from the General Staff are principal elements of the anti-rhetorical new epic that finally attempts to break away from Homer.[29]

Conflagrazione was partially created at the same time as *Guerrapittura* (1915) (Warpainting) by Carlo Carrà,[30] with whom Buzzi shared a pro-war enthusi-asm as well as the use of *papier collé*. But while Carrà clearly prefers printed characters, as in *Cielo di guerra* (Sky of War),[31] the artist of *Conflagrazione* introduces more liberty to his words-in-freedom plates and new instruments by using the technique of handwriting. Buzzi, who readopts some aspects of his *epopea* in the still completely unpublished *Il soldato ignoto*,[32] also shows a slight preference for geometrical forms. They differ, though, from the ones used by his friend, who plays with vanishing points that make the paper look like geometrical works. But Buzzi's pages, because of less regularity in their structure and composition and the less placid visual impact created, show a new development when compared to those of his "Dum-Dum della Grande Guerra" (Dum-Dum of the Great War)[33] written at a time which partly overlaps with the period when he was writing *Conflagrazione*. These ele-ments of *Conflagrazione* confirm the uniqueness of this work, although Buzzi published with *La luminaria azzurra. Romanzo dal fronte interno* (The Azure Lamp. Novel from the Internal Front) in 1917 a kind of additional national epos, which once more thematizes the war.[34]

The term "epopea," which demonstrates some eloquence, does not completely account for the complexity of the work. Far from passing under any pre-existing literary label (as it certainly is a war diary containing the characteristics of this genre, for example the date) it is a chronicle—if not a history book—in the sense that Buzzi uses news from the press mixed with information contained in letters received from friends who were at the front, which together form his main source of knowledge of the war. The technique of the registration of the daily events is no new element in Buzzi's work, either. Already in "L'incendio" (The Fire) (1890–1892), "Le giovanissime" (The Earliest Ones) (1893–1895) and "Romanze" (Romances) (1901–1907), where Buzzi uses a structure like in a "Gidian book,"[35] "poetry becomes the expression of a particular fragment of life."[36]

Buzzi is not part of the *lost generation* of young people caught in the "ec-stasy of emotion"[37] that would eventually kill them. When Buzzi began to write *Conflagrazione* he was already forty, and worked as first secretary at the administrative division of the province of Milan, "the Bastille of bread" as he called it referring to the sense of imprisonment it gave him.[38] Although he had applied for a place at the front, a situation in which many of his friends were living at that time, his requests for a transfer were rejected.[39] The experience he had of the war therefore differs both from that of Ungaretti—who was stationed at the front—and also from that of Remarque, whose recollection of war was made long after the events it addresses. Forced to remain in his office, Buzzi was still living the war in a more indirect way as the messages of killed and wounded friends or acquaintances began to arrive more frequently as the war went on. Marinetti and Russolo—who were both volunteers—Sironi, Funi, and other friends were wounded, while Sant'Elia and Carlo Erba were killed. The enthusiasm that accompanied the first calls to the front transformed into fear and fright.

The announcement of the imminent war and the German ultimatum to Russia and France was reported by Buzzi, who in 1908 had extolled the war in a poem dedicated to Marinetti,[40] narrating the hatred felt towards the enemy and celebrating a kind of mysticism of blood—thus stressing the biblical value of sacrificial blood on the one hand[41] and a certain stylistic affinity to expressionism on the other[42]—in the color of the blood that will soon be spilled everywhere. Red, the color of tragedy, in fact covers most of the first plate that is dated August 2, 1914, and is otherwise composed of the headlines spreading the news.[43] But it is used as part of the chronicle of events, rather than as a rhetoric element. The futurists frequently made use of red.[44] In the propaganda postcard *La Bandiera Futurista* (The Futurist Flag) the color is the background of "march, not to rot":[45] "Red overruns and inflames the passatist Green and White."[46] Comparing and supplementing the interpretation of its use with Buzzi's statements in the keynote article "I giovani poeti e la guerra" published on December 1, 1916, in number 11 of *L'Italia futurista*, the poet seems to be far from intending a denunciation.

> Today Poetry is War, our victorious Great War against Austria and for the shifting of the Central Empires, antipoetic professors of every barbaric deed. [. . .] It was Futurism that marked the irruption of war into arts and militarized the artists that were to renew Italy.[47]

The position he assumes here, however, seems to give way to quite a contrary expression, at least in the artistic poetry production of the following year, when Buzzi in "Canzone dei bersaglieri" (Song of the Bersaglieri) (published in number 23 of the same journal)[48] depicts the abrupt and cruel end of the soldier who has gone to war. This theme is not mentioned at all in the plates of *Conflagrazione* of July 1917, where the poet gives information instead about the Russian prisoners on the first day of the new offensive beyond the Russian threat in Galicia and Kerensky's political power.[49]

An interesting starting-point when defining the position taken by Buzzi with respect to military events is his correspondence with Palazzeschi. One of the letters shows signs of Buzzi's concern for the high price that Italy will have to pay in Cyrenaica for the annexation of Libya, an act that is defined as an "act of bravery."[50] Buzzi's position is also expressed in his article "Il futurismo dopo la guerra," in which he summarizes the past experience with a hint of irony:

> *Futurism* therefore does not belie its typical characteristic as an armed and versatile group, which was also put into evidence by its couragious participation in the most recent major political event, especially as it finished with a nice *payment in body-counts*. Consistent with the irredentistic principles of the prewar period, its place could not have been any different from what it was.[51]

Both as a sign of the intense concentration of tragedy and an accusation against the enemy, a page is dedicated to Cesare Battisti, who had been captured by the Austrian forces, charged with high treason, and hanged on July 12, 1916.[52] A similar event was registered by Buzzi on the plate in memory of his friend Roberto Sarfatti,[53] who had voluntarily joined the army (he had become lance corporal of the sixth regiment of the Alpine soldiers) and was killed in action on January 28, 1918, in the second assault on the recapture of Val Bella, Col del Rosso, Col d'Echele and Case Ruggi.[54] Buzzi composed it one month after Sarfatti's death and recorded the events, including the name of the young man and information about his premature death. He also stressed both the adjective "over-alive" ("stravivo") and the substantive indicating the loss of the loved one.

Even excluding the title plate[55] and the ones in which red is used for painting the Italian flag[56]—which stands as a symbol for the recapture of those parts of Italy that previously had fallen under the Austrian administration—the color appears on about fifteen pages. The greater part of these accounts treats massacres and deaths like the Battle of the Marne[57] or the victory in the artillery assault of Argonne.[58] For the Marne as well as for the Vistula and the Isonzo, scenes of especially bloody massacres, the predominant color shown is azure.[59] This color also symbolizes the tragedies that have taken place on sea, like the sinking of the cruiser *Hampshire* near the Orkney Islands, which took the life of H. Herbert Kitchener, Secretary of State for War at the time.

As far as 1915 is concerned—the year of the Treaty of London and of the Italian entry into the war—it is important to focus attention on other parts of Buzzi's correspondence that have survived. In a letter dated September 25, 1915, and sent to Cangiullo[60] some previous events are registered in the section dedicated to war themes:[61] "Conversation. Injured Bersaglieri Monte Nero collection of Austrian shrapnels."[62] The name of this theatre of war is repeated in the pages of *Conflagrazione*, but in one concerning June 1915,[63] not September. The first map is inserted into a plate on August 4, 1914, and is centered on the town of Liège. It is not only given a central position, but the name of Liège is also repeated in the four diagonal lines emanating from it, this time followed by a question mark that represents the uncertainty of the situation.[64] The drawing techniques Buzzi employed do not always remain constant. In the images, the motive of inserting a graphical representation of the then-current theatre of war is combined with cuttings of press headlines or handwritten letters, whereas the position of the map and shape of the map snippet vary. This is best demonstrated by using some examples like "The raging battles on the Carpathians. Austro-German counterattacks on the Latorcza,"[65] in which the map is split into three parts with added shadows that partly surround headlines inserted into the shape of explosion fumes. The main headlines are distributed in the form of a semi-ellipsoid; the rest is ordered vertically, in spite of the difference in position and the interspersion of three parts of a map of the central region of the Carpathian Mountains, between the Dukla and the Uzsok Pass, as the captions indicate. The map is laid crosswise, from the left to the right side of the page. Every element has a bordered line, with a blackened area where two arcs meet at the perimeter.

In other places a map is substituted by extracts of articles such as in the one from January 1st to the 5th, 1916, where the text is a part of the speech given by German emperor Wilhelm II: here a summary of the previous year's achievements is presented and the conscientiousness that will lead Germany to its greatness is underlined.[66] The page serves as a reflection of the overall situation at that time: the titles announce the counterattack of the Russian army in Galicia and the progress of the Bulgarian and German troops towards Greece. To the lower right: parts of a column of a daily paper can be seen, whose title tells of a child massacre. Another page, this time from 21 until 28 February 1917, resumes the amounts of the allied and neutral naval forces that have been destroyed by the enemies as a result of the naval blockade of Germany.[67] In distinct contrast to the map of the Carpathian Mountains, where the *papier collé* reproducing the geographical territories under discussion is divided into three parts, this plate presents a superposition of images. This makes the whole illustration at first sight seem to be cut, even if it is only divided by the words "violated by three thousand ships every day" ("violato da tre mila navi ogni giorno") that are glued over it.

In other cases[68] the center of the page is formed by pieces of poetry. The first one narrates the events of November and December of 1917, that is, the great counterattack of the Italians at the rivers Grappa and Piave which followed the defeat of Caporetto. The second celebrates the unconditional surrender of Austria and the entry of Italian troops into Trento and Trieste. The city's particular "soul" had already been depicted by the Triestine Scipio Slataper.[69] The name of Slataper is not cited by Buzzi, who mentions another name from the literary panorama instead, that of D'Annunzio.[70] Buzzi's reference to D'Annunzio is about the audacious enterprise in October 1917, known as the *impresa di Cattaro*.[71] On that occasion he appeared as an aircraft captain during the air raid over the gulf of the same name, which was one of the most important naval strongholds employed by Austria-Hungary at the time. Some of these pieces of words-in-freedom poetry are to be counted as the most significant uses of *papier collé* by Buzzi who, as already described, incorporates it in his own graphical way, one which is also to be considered from the phono-symbolic point of view. Even as Buzzi partly denounces the war, his enchantment with it prevails. This seems to be confirmed by a letter dated 1919 (when his work was already finished) and addressed to some of his friends, in which the poet expresses his pride of authorship with respect to the "Ode ad Asinari di Bernezzo" (Ode to Asinari di Bernezzo).[72]

Is there a detectable change of route or an attenuation of Buzzi's position under the "graphic and plastic and tactile signs of my fantasy and my impressionability"[73] (as the poet defines his handwriting for the plates of his "unpublished sensibilitic epic of the modern Great War")[74] to be observed if we compare them with the verses of "Inno alla guerra"? Certainly we can recognize a change: there is a different type of emphasis in the pages of *Conflagrazione*. This is less visionary even if it is more visual, less pitiless even if it is more awful. An analysis of Buzzi's methods of documentation is even more interesting if we also consider the use of mathematical signs and numbers, the application of which Marinetti had already welcomed in point 6 of the *Manifesto tecnico della letteratura futurista* (*Technical Manifesto of Futurist Literature*).[75] Buzzi makes frequent use of this to indicate distances, military movements, the number of injured people or dead soldiers as well as the quantity of the lost or purchased weapons. The "love of precision and concentrated brevity"[76] that Marinetti wrote about in *Lo splendore geometrico e meccanico e la sensibilità numerica* (Geometric and Mechanical Splendor and the Numerical Sensibility), referring to the mathematical notation, recurs in Buzzi, too. A number, at least in this example of Buzzi's work, holds a concrete significance: there is no mathematical theory or metaphysics, and no mathematical series like the one from Balla's *Numeri innamorati* (Numbers in Love).[77]

Even if similar to Marinetti's *Zang Tumb Tumb* in the use of martial vocabulary, which is marked by words like "shrapnel,"[78] Buzzi exceeds him in the quality of graphic processes he adopts. Particularly remarkable in this respect can also be the plate entitled *Un attimo della mia giornata a Palazzo Monforte* (A Moment of My Day at Palazzo Monforte) published on October 1, 1916, in number 7 of *L'Italia futurista*,[79] where Buzzi seems structurally and semantically to recall, but contemporaneously to redefine the Manifesto *Sintesi futurista della guerra* (Futurist Synthesis of the War) of the *Direzione* of the Futurist Movement signed in September 1914 by Marinetti, Boccioni, Carrà, Russolo, and Piatti.[80] Buzzi is well aware of his contribution to this debate, as we can read in his letter dated September 26, 1919, when he expresses his admiration for D'Annunzio: "I think I have always had a *prime* position in Futurism. Even Marinetti was aesthetically unable to reach the audacitiy of the 'free words' of *Conflagration*, my poem about the Great War."[81]

Some reviewers of Buzzi's work described his graphic processes as being similar to those of automatic writing or as an automatic transcription of the unconscious that also was used by the surrealists.[82] Buzzi himself recognizes this relationship: "In my prose poem 'The Ellipse and the Spiral' (Ed. 1915) and particularly in the unpublished *Conflagrazione* (Epic Poem. War 1914–1918) I gave the highest contribution of passion to substantial and formal graphic processes, which need in fact to be considered pure effluxes of psychic automatism with the aim of conveying the real working of thoughts through the most refined distillation of the word and the more than perfect drafting of the verbal sign, to finally realize a more convulsive, arcane beauty."[83] Buzzi looks at surrealism with interest because of "the disturbing so-called electrocuted equation of the verb, the probability calculations able to create the Great Voice of the Soul and the Universe from the minimal line and even—as Carlo Bo would say—from the blank on blank."[84]

Among the great number of plates included in Buzzi's book, one seems to be missing: the illustration dedicated to the German capitulation on November 11, 1918, when the armistice was signed with the Entente Powers. The verb "seems" is used here although chances are high that this one was never painted, and that the artist stopped his recordings of history exactly at the moment when the hostilities between Italy and Austria-Hungary ended. Buzzi would continue his experiment with words-in-freedom—though not taken to the limits he had reached in *Conflagrazione*—in *Popolo, canta così!* (People, sing like this!).[85] The poet, forced to confront himself in the following period with another war, the Second World War,[86] would explicitly declare the absurd tragic nature of the event. The unpublished work "L'umana tragedia" (The Human Tragedy) dated 1941–1945 remains clear evidence of Buzzi's sentiments against the martyrdom of his homeland.[87]

Notes

1. The choice of this adjective is not to be underestimated because through it Buzzi plays here, as in the previous verses, with the use of red. The "Garibaldini," the young volunteers that followed Garibaldi and fought at his side, were in fact also called "Redshirts" ("Camicie rosse") or "Red coats" ("Giubbe rosse"), their most recognizeable feature.

2. "Nei prati, / bimbo, adoravo fustigare / l'erbe e tagliare la testa ai ranuncoli. / Liberi malleoli volevo, / ero un Mercurio che anelava eterno, de' piedi, volare. / Sere divine di sangue / mi dilagavano sopra la testa. Stavo nel Mito di Marte. / L'anima mi s'abbeverò di quel vermiglio. / Mio padre accendeva i miei sogni scarlatti / co' suoi racconti magnifici di guerra tutti garibaldini. // Guerra, perché ci anneghittiamo ormai nella Pace? / Seduto sul cuoio della mia poltrona pacifica, / io odio. Questi versi ch'io scrivo / e sento, ahi!—spesso— orribili nello stridore, / sono della libidine omicidiaria che se ne va, patriottica, / e che nessuna ghirlanda di gloria incorona." Paolo Buzzi, "Inno alla guerra," in Idem, Aeroplani. Canti alati col II Proclama futurista di F.T. Marinetti, with a foreword by Giampaolo Pignatari (Milan: Lampi di Stampa, 2009), 29 (The italics are mine). The period in which the poems of the collection were composed partially overlaps with that of the formulation of the Manifesto of Futurism by which it seems to be strongly influenced. As far as the temporal crossing is concerned see Giampaolo Pignatari, "Per una chiarificazione della genesi del futurismo in Paolo Buzzi," in Paolo Buzzi, Futurismo: scritti, carteggi, testimonianze, ed. Mario Morini and Giampaolo Pignatari, I Quaderni di Palazzo Sormani 7 (Milan: Palazzo Sormani, 1983), 1: xxxvii.

3. ". . . fra i primi assertori e protagonisti del futurismo, perché protagonista al suo [di Marinetti, M.B.] fianco, del cambiamento.") Pignatari, "Per una chiarificazione," xxxix.

4. For an in-depth examination of the content of this work I refer to Pignatari's remarks in Buzzi, Futurismo, xxvi–xxvii.

5. ". . . il più bel poema futurista apparso finora." Filippo Tommaso Marinetti, "1915. In quest'anno futurista," in Idem, Opere, ed. Luciano De Maria (Milan: Mondadori, 1968), 286. Also published with the title "In quest'anno futurista," L'Italia futurista, no. 15 (May 1917) and no. 18 (June 1917).

6. Filippo Tommaso Marinetti, Irredentismo. Ink, pastel and paper collage, 1914. Lugano, Private Collection, in Enrico Crispolti and Franco Sborgi, eds., Futurismo: I grandi temi (1909–1944) (Milan: Mazzotta, 1998), 247.

7. On this episode see Ernestina Pellegrini's comments in Filippo Tommaso Marinetti and Francesco Cangiullo, *Lettere (1910–1943)*, ed. Ernestina Pellegrini (Florence: Vallecchi, 1989), 17.

8. Giuseppe Ungaretti, *Allegria di naufragi* (Florence: Vallecchi, 1919).

9. For a survey about the theme see *La Grande Guerra degli artisti: Propaganda e iconografia bellica in Italia negli anni della prima guerra mondiale*, ed. Nadia Marchioni (Florence: Pagliai Polistampa, 2005).

10. The work was published in a limited edition. Fifteen copies are signed by the poet's wife Maria Buzzi.

11. Paolo Buzzi, *Conflagrazione: Epopea parolibera*, with a critical introduction by Alberto Viviani and an explanatory note by Emilio Guicciardi (Florence: Il Fauno, 1963).

12. Pignatari, "Per una chiarificazione," xi–xii.

13. Emilio Guicciardi in Buzzi, *Conflagrazione*, 23–24. In 1933 Buzzi writes about his volume: "Aside from the burning free-word compositions of the *Ellipse and the Spiral*, I have written a poem, *Conflagration*, which has never seen the light of day, but which in those days (the postwar period) would not be unworthy to figure in an edition of Dinamo-Azari, with one of those bindings held together by two aluminium bolts that make the volume look like the mouth of a squeezing machine." ("A parte le tavole parolibere arroventate di *Ellisse e la Spirale*, io ho scritto un poema *Conflagrazione* che non ha mai visto la luce ma che, ai suoi tempi [il dopoguerra] non sarebbe stato indegno di figurare in una edizione Dinamo-Azari, con una di quelle rilegature bullonate che facevano somigliare il volume allo sportello di una macchina sotto-pressione.") Quoted in Luciano Caruso, "'Ebbrezza trionfale' nel futurismo," in Claudio Parmiggiani, ed., *Alfabeto in sogno: Dal carme figurato alla poesia concreta* (Milan: Mazzotta, 2002), 301. There is no doubt that Buzzi alludes here to the *Libro bullonato* (*Depero futurista*) realized by Fortunato Depero and issued by the publishing house Dinamo-Azari in 1927. Depero's work is bound with a punched cover and a clasp made of two aluminium bolts. The failed publication of *Conflagrazione* is probably due also to difficulties related to the printing process.

14. "Oh, se-ora-la poveretta [Buzzi probably refers here to Risca, the female protagonist], avesse potuto vedere dove conduce la cosiddetta 'igiene del mondo'!" Paolo Buzzi, "Il soldato ignoto," unedited typescript (1921), 93. The typescript is held at the Fondo Buzzi (MSS Buzzi 29/2), Milan: Centro Stendhaliano.

15. Guicciardi in Buzzi, *Conflagrazione*, 24.

16. "Un giorno—forse era il mese di maggio—Paolo ci condusse in una stanza sotto tetto nella sua villa, e volle mostrarci alcuni pacchi polverosi di manoscritti e di giornali. Tra questi una specie di diario della guerra 1915–1918 costituito da fogli sui quali erano stati incollati ritagli di stampa a comporre una sintesi quotidiana degli avvenimenti bellici di tutto il mondo, esposti secondo le sintassi futuriste di allora. Recava per titolo: Conflagrazioni. Quella specie di gioco da bambini, come poteva apparire a un esame superficiale, quelle congiunzioni di linee, quell'intersecarsi di titoli in 'grassetto,' di segnacci rosso-blu, non risultavano poi tanto vacui, se infine la

storia vissuta e sofferta anche in quel modo era riuscita a commuoverci malgrado la cenere degli anni calatavi sopra." Mario Morini, "Ultimi anni," (Last Years) in Maria Buzzi, ed., *Omaggio a Paolo Buzzi*, with a foreword by Francesco Flora (Turin: Tipi dell'Impronta, 1958), 85. Emilio Guicciardi, another of Buzzi's friends, also writes about this episode in 1963 (in Buzzi, *Conflagrazione*, 24).

17. For a detailed bibliography on Buzzi's work, see Maria Buzzi, ed., *Bibliografia generale di Paolo Buzzi*, with a foreword by Lino Montagna and a speech transcription by Emilio Guicciardi (Turin: Tipi dell'Impronta, 1959).

18. Some information about Buzzi's archive folders can be found under "Fondo Paolo Buzzi," accessed July 19, 2009, mssormani.comune.milano.it/sub_manoscritti/Fondi/fondo_buzzi.htm.

19. Paolo Buzzi, *L'Ellisse e la Spirale. Film + Parole in libertà* (Milan: Edizioni Futuriste di *Poesia*, 1915). A more precise date for the writing of this work can be reconstructed using Buzzi's published correspondence. In a letter sent from Milan to Luciano Folgore on November 27, 1914, Buzzi notes: "I am thinking about a volume with Words-in-Freedom. We will talk about it" ("Sto pensando un volume di parole in libertà. Ne parleremo"), in Buzzi, *Futurismo*, 3: 280.

20. ". . . la poliespressione simultanea del mondo." Filippo Tommaso Marinetti, "La tecnica della nuova poesia," in Idem, *Opere*, 182.

21. "Le parole in libertà vogliono orchestrare i colori, i rumori e i suoni, combinare i materiali della lingua e dei dialetti, le formule aritmetiche e geometriche col loro splendore meccanico e numerico (veggasi il mio romanzo l'*Ellisse e la Spirale*), i segni musicali, le parole vecchie, deformate o nuove, i gridi degli animali e dei motori." Paolo Buzzi, "Il Futurismo dopo la guerra," *Il Mondo*, no. 5 (February 1920). Reprinted in Buzzi, *Futurismo*, 1: 61.

22. Buzzi, *Conflagrazione* (first page after the explanatory note).

23. After the first five plates, which make repeated use of press cuttings, Buzzi seems to give up this technique in order to almost exclusively employ the handwriting. The greater part of the following plates is indeed characterized as pages, in which the graphic handwriting of the author prevails. Alberto Viviani, "'Conflagrazione.' Le tavole parolibere di Paolo Buzzi (Florence, April 24, 1963)," in Buzzi, *Conflagrazione*, 16.

24. On the dates, see Guicciardi in Buzzi, *Conflagrazione*, 23.

25. The exhibition opened on March 17, 2009, and hosted two sections: *La mia Anima è musicale. Immagini sonore nell'opera di Paolo Buzzi futurista dalle raccolte della Biblioteca Centrale*, by Giampaolo Pignatari; and *Conflagrazione. La vertigine polifonica della guerra nelle opere della collezione Lodovico Isolabella*, by Luigi Sansone.

26. The word *conflagrazione* is also used by Marinetti, who on July 8, 1917, publishes an article on "Il Futurismo e la Conflagrazione" in *L'Italia futurista* (no. 21): "The conflagration was already to be found to its full extent in the first *Manifesto of Futurism* (published in Paris in *Le Figaro* on February 20, 1909), which appeared to be contradictory and crazy while being simply prophetical." ("La conflagrazione era già tutto contenuta nel primo *Manifesto del Futurismo* [pubblicato in *Le Figaro*

di Parigi il 20 febbraio 1909] che sembrò contradditorio e pazzesco, mentre era semplicemente profetico.")

27. Filippo Tommaso Marinetti, *Zang Tumb Tumb* (Milan: Edizioni Futuriste di *Poesia*, 1914).

28. "Oggi la Poesia non è tanto musica, quanto rombo. La guerra è rumore. . . . E colla guerra-rumore, tutto il programma futurista fatalmente si afferma nella sua pienezza e nel suo significato. . . . E la *Conflagrazione*, questa epopea terribile del presente, io la canterò, un po' diversamente da Omero, l'unico poeta epico che abbiamo dietro di noi (Virgilio, Tasso, Victor Hugo, d'Annunzio sono sempre Omero) e che noi sorpassiamo e cancelliamo, noi futuristi, degni di vivere al tempo dell'aeroplano." Paolo Buzzi, "Le parole in libertà," in Buzzi, *Futurismo*, 1: 55, 57. The passages quoted here are to be found in Paolo Buzzi, "I giovani poeti e la guerra," *L'Italia futurista*, no. 11 (December 1916).

29. "Pur avendo cantato la figura epica e romanzesca di Garibaldi in ottava rima (forma canora sempre diletta all'istinto musicale italiano) io ho, così, tentato di rendere la grande guerra mondiale in tavole parolibere. *Conflagrazione* sarà il titolo dell'opera: la notazione elettrica, il respiro aviatorio e sottomarino, il brivido grafico, l'urlo strillonico, la suggestività dei titoli maiuscoli di prima pagina dei giornali e la semplicità lapidaria dei bollettini dello Stato Maggiore, sono elementi precipui della nuova Epopea antiretorica, che vuole finalmente emanciparsi da Omero." Paolo Buzzi, "Il Futurismo dopo la guerra," in Buzzi, *Futurismo*, 1: 61.

30. The work wants, as indicated by the subtitle, to embrace the whole spectrum of *Futurismo politico, dinamismo plastico, disegni guerreschi* and *parole in libertà*. Carlo Carrà, *Guerrapittura: Futurismo politico, dinamismo plastico, 12 disegni guerreschi, parole in libertà* (Milan: Edizioni Futuriste di *Poesia*, 1915).

31. Carlo Carrà, *Cielo di guerra*. Ink, pencil and paper collage, 1914–1915, in Carrà, *Guerrapittura*, 21.

32. *Il soldato ignoto* is a work in prose going back to the beginning of the 1920s, see Buzzi, *Futurismo*, 4: 528. Daniela Bon of the Sormany Library kindly responded to my queries about this work (e-mail September 7, 2009).

33. The plates belonging to "Dum-Dum della Grande Guerra" (in total 19) are dated between 1915 and 1918. The unedited work has partially been published in Buzzi, *Futurismo*, 2: 225–26. For previous publications of the edited plates see also Buzzi, *Futurismo*, 4: 527.

34. In the dedication to his friend Armando Mazza Buzzi defines the work as follows: "it is an undoubtedly futurist attempt to write a novel about the internal front, that is, anti-cowardly and anti-charming, certainly necessary" ("è un tentativo di romanzo, indubbiamente futurista, cioè antivigliacco ed antigrazioso certo necessario del fronte interno"). In the copy of the work held in the Sormani Library in Milan and quoted by Barbara Stagnitti in a page of Buzzi's correspondence with Ada Negri, the poet defines his book in the dedication to Ugo Casalis written on the title-page as a "rifting bomb, which was ripped apart by the acephalous and amoebic, Italian censorship" ("squarcio bombardesco squarciato dalla censura d'Italia acefala ed ameba");

Ada Negri and Paolo Buzzi, *Diorami lombardi: Carteggio (1896–1944)*, ed. Barbara Stagnitti (Milan: Il Poligrafo, 2008), 72; Paolo Buzzi, *La luminaria azzurra: Romanzo dal fronte interno* (Florence: Vallecchi, 1917).

35. ". . . libro gidiano." Pignatari, "Per una chiarificazione," xiii. The documentary touch as characteristic sign of Buzzi's work has also been recognized by Emilio Guicciardi, "Paolo Buzzi milanese," in Buzi, *Bibliografia generale*, 17.

36. ". . . la poesia . . . diventa l'espressione di un particolare frammento di vita." Pignatari, "Per una chiarificazione," xiii.

37. The reference is to the concept of "Rausch des Gefühls,"coined by Ernst Toller, "Eine Jugend in Deutschland," in Idem, *Prosa, Briefe, Dramen, Gedichte*, with a foreword by Kurt Hiller (Reinbek: Rowohlt, 1961), 60.

38. ". . . la Bastiglia del pane." This image is used as the title of the "Dodicesima Sinfonia" in Paolo Buzzi, *Poema dei quarantanni* (Milan: Edizioni Futuriste di *Poesia*, 1922), 239.

39. Guicciardi, "Paolo Buzzi milanese," 32.

40. Here the verses of "Inno alla guerra" are referenced that are partially quoted in the opening page of this contribution. The inscription at the beginning of the volume is: "A F.T. Marinetti / principe dei guerrieri / con animo grato fraterno"; Buzzi, "Inno alla guerra" [27]. A second inscription preceding these lines contains the words: "To the Triestine Flag, which we shall win back" ("Alla bandiera di Trieste che riconquisteremo") [25].

41. In addition to these biblical references it is worth mentioning the ones directed towards chemistry that mainly appear in the lexical choice made for the composition of the ninth and eleventh stanzas. Buzzi, "Inno alla guerra," 33–34. The use of this particular language seems to be influenced by the progression of research of those years as well as what would soon happen in the war, namely the employment of chemical substances.

42. See Pignatari, foreword to Buzzi, *Aeroplani*, xxvii.

43. Buzzi, *Conflagrazione*, 29.

44. The use of the red color reoccurs in Carlo Carrà's cover for the book *Per la coscienza della nuova Italia* published by Francesco Penazzo in 1914 and in the leaflet entitled "Sintesi della guerra mondiale," in which it is used as a background for the list of lands that are named as those fighting for freedom and against barbarity. Francesco Penazzo, *Per la coscienza della nuova Italia* (Milan: Bertarelli, 1914). Claudia Salaris, *Storia del futurismo: Libri, giornali, manifesti*, 2nd ed. (Rome: Editori Riuniti, 1992), 74, 79.

45. ". . . marciare non marcire." Salaris, *Storia del futurismo*, 75.

46. ". . . il Rosso invade e accende il Verde e il Bianco passatisti." Filippo Tommaso Marinetti, Futurist Postcard, Type-Cangiullo, Futurist Movement directed by Marinetti, Corso Venezia, 61, Milan, in Salaris, *Storia del futurismo*, fig. 76.

47. "Oggi la Poesia è la Guerra, la nostra grande guerra vittoriosa contro l'Austria e per lo strangolamento degli Imperi Centrali, professori antipoetici d'ogni barbarie.

. . . Fu il futurismo che segnò l'irruzione della guerra nell'arte e militarizzò gli artisti novatori d'Italia." Buzzi, "I giovani poeti e la guerra."

48. Paolo Buzzi, "Canzone dei Bersaglieri," *L'Italia futurista*, no. 23 (July 22, 1917). Reprinted in Buzzi, *Futurismo*, 2: 236.

49. Buzzi, *Conflagrazione*, 281–82.

50. ". . . atto di coraggio." Paolo Buzzi to Aldo Palazzeschi [location not indicated], February 1, 1912, in Filippo Tommaso Marinetti and Aldo Palazzeschi, *Carteggio, con un'appendice di altre lettere a Palazzeschi*, introductory note by Luciano De Maria, ed. Paolo Prestigiacomo (Milan: Mondadori, 1978), 98 [Appendix]. Buzzi will later explain the significance war holds for him and the other futurists in the article "I tempi di *Poesia*" printed in *La Fiera Letteraria* on May 6, 1928. This article also contains a concise and essential view of the enthusiasm that contemporary youth showed in respect to the Libyan war, the reactions to the assassination in Sarajevo and the interventionism that prevailed at those times.

51. "Il *Futurismo* non smentirà, dunque, la sua tipica caratteristica, di fascio armato ed elastico, della quale anche la coraggiosa partecipazione all'ultima grande vicenda politica fu una chiara prova, finita se non altro, con dei simpatici *pagamenti di persona*. Coerente ai principi irredentistici dell'anteguerra, il suo posto non poteva essere che quello che fu." Paolo Buzzi, "Il Futurismo dopo la guerra," in Buzzi, *Futurismo*, 1: 63.

52. Buzzi, *Conflagrazione*, 247. The plate recalls one of the heading titles of the *Corriere della Sera* of July 20, 1916 ("Battisti fu impiccato morente") being a synthesis of the information about the event.

53. Buzzi, *Conflagrazione*, 294.

54. Buzzi also narrates about the young man in a passage of his *Poema dei quarantanni* (48).

55. Buzzi, *Conflagrazione*, 25.

56. Buzzi, *Conflagrazione*, 157, 180, 237, 250, 302, 307.

57. Buzzi, *Conflagrazione*, 58.

58. Buzzi, *Conflagrazione*, 112.

59. Buzzi, *Conflagrazione*, 90, 179, 301. Azure is also the color Buzzi uses for announcing the declaration of imminent victory by the French general Joffre. The poet presents Joffre's political personality following the method used by Alfredo Panzini in his sentimental war diary. Confront the illustration at page 59 of *Conflagrazione* with Alfredo Panzini, *Diario sentimentale della guerra: Dal luglio 1914 al maggio 1915* (Milan: Mondadori, 1923), 80.

60. The chance to find more references to the Great War in the correspondence between Buzzi and Cangiullo is very limited given the fact that only a small part of the letters has survived the war. Cangiullo refers to this loss in a message to Maria Carloni Buzzi written on Easter Sunday of 1957. Buzzi, *Futurismo*, 3: 266.

61. The synthetic module of futurist letters that consisted of a tabular divided into seven spaces dedicated to the same number of themes (Futurism, war, pleasures,

news, women, travels and greetings) and concluded with the caption "total," resuming the overall mood of the moment of writing, had been created by Cangiullo. Cf. Buzzi, *Futurismo*, 3: 266.

62. "Conversazione. Bersaglieri feriti Monte Nero raccolta shrapnels austriaci." Paolo Buzzi to Francesco Cangiullo [location not indicated], September 25, 1915, in Buzzi, *Futurismo*, 3: 261.

63. Buzzi, *Conflagrazione*, 161.

64. Buzzi, *Conflagrazione*, 31.

65. "I furibondi combattimenti nei Carpazi. Contrattacchi autro-tedeschi sul Latorcza." Buzzi, *Conflagrazione*, 143. See also John J. White, *Literary Futurism: Aspects of the First Avant-Garde* (Oxford: Clarendon Press, 1990), 134–35.

66. Buzzi, *Conflagrazione*, 219.

67. Buzzi, *Conflagrazione*, 271.

68. Buzzi, *Conflagrazione*, 289, 307.

69. The question of Trieste is also handled in the first section of Carlo Carrà's *Guerrapittura* (*Guerra nell'Adriatico*, 11). It was in this same town that Marinetti had given his patriotic speech entitled "Il mare tricolore. Esordio patriottico," published on April 1908 in *Poesia*.

70. D'Annunzio is present in Buzzi's work in the form of quotations of some of his verses. Concerning these citations see Pignatari, "Per una chiarificazione," xxi–xxiii.

71. Buzzi, *Conflagrazione*, 286. See also Alfredo Bonadeo, *D'Annunzio and the Great War* (Madison-Teaneck: Fairleigh Dickinson University Press, 1995), 108–9.

72. Buzzi, *Poema dei quarantanni*, 236–38. Buzzi's consent to war as well as his belief in it are also declared in an article written in 1928 and dedicated to the period spent as journalist for the journal *Poesia*. Paolo Buzzi, "I tempi di *Poesia*," *La Fiera Letteraria*, May 6, 1928. General Vittorio Asinari di Bernezzo had been forced to retire for voicing anti-Austrian sentiments during a feast with officers.

73. ". . . segni grafici e plastici e tattilici della mia fantasia e della mia impressionabilità." Paolo Buzzi, "Il Futurismo nel panorama della mia spiritualità," in Buzzi, *Futurismo*, 1: 19. This text is the script of a lecture held by Buzzi on April 5, 1930.

74. "Epopea sensibilistica inedita della grande guerra moderna." Buzzi, *Futurismo*, 18–19.

75. See point 6 of the *Manifesto tecnico della letteratura futurista* and the letter sent by Marinetti to Buzzi on September 12, [1]915, in Buzzi, *Futurismo*, 3: 295.

76. ". . . amore della precisione e della brevità essenziale." See point 9 of *Lo splendore geometrico e meccanico e la sensibilità numerica* (in *Manifesti del Futurismo*, 135).

77. Giacomo Balla, *Numeri innamorati*. Oil on canvas, ca. 1924. Mart, VAF-Stiftung, Rovereto. Balla adopts here Fibonacci's famous sequence of numbers, in which each number represents the sum of the two numbers preceding it. The only variation made by Balla concerns the presence of the number four not contained in the original sequence.

78. This vocabulary is also used in part of the correspondence.

79. Paolo Buzzi, "Un attimo della mia giornata a Palazzo Monforte," *L'Italia futurista*, no. 7 (October 1, 1916). Reprinted in Buzzi, *Futurismo*, 2: 229.

80. *Sintesi futurista della guerra*, 1914. Signed by Marinetti, Boccioni, Carrà, Russolo and Piatti. Reprinted in *Manifesti del Futurismo*, [148]–[149].

81. ". . . credo di avere sempre una posizione di *primissimo ordine* nel Futurismo. Esteticamente, alle audacie parolibere di *Conflagrazione*, il mio Poema sulla grande guerra, non è arrivato neppure Marinetti." Paolo Buzzi to his friends, Milan, 26 September 1919, in Buzzi, *Futurismo*, 3: 250. Similar words are also used by Buzzi at the end of a letter addressed to Castrense Civello and dated 8 December 1954. Ibid., 259.

82. As far as the relationship between Buzzi and surrealism is concerned see for example Günter Berghaus, "Futurism, Dada, and Surrealism: Some Cross-Fertilizations Among The Historical Avant-Garde," in Idem, ed., *International Futurism in Arts and Literature* (Berlin: De Gruyter, 2000), 302. Paolo Buzzi, "Nota del traduttore," in Marcel Nadeau, ed., *Antologia del surrealismo*, trans. and with an introductory note by Paolo Buzzi (Rome: Macchia, 1948), 7. See also Paolo Buzzi, *Novecento letterario* (Rome: Edizioni del Grifone, 1948).

83. "Nel mio Poema in prosa 'L'Ellisse e la Spirale' (ed. 1915) e soprattutto nell'inedita *Conflagrazione* (Epopea parolibera guerra 1914–1918) diedi il massimo contributo di passione a processi grafici, sostanziali e formali, da considerarsi appunto pure emanazioni d'automatismo psichico volte a rendere il funzionamento reale del pensiero a mezzo la distillazione più raffinata possibile della parola e la più che perfetta stesura del segno verbale, ai fini realizzatori d'una più convulsiva arcana bellezza." Buzzi, "Nota del traduttore," 7.

84. ". . . le sconcertanti così dette equazioni folgorative del verbo, i calcoli di probabilità atti a trarre dalla minima linea e magari—direbbe Carlo Bo—dallo stesso bianco su bianco la grande Voce dell'anima e dell'universo." Buzzi, "Nota del traduttore," 7.

85. Paolo Buzzi, *Popolo, canta così! Canzoni d'arti e mestieri del popolo italiano* (Milan: Facchi, 1920).

86. In 1939 Buzzi moves to Perledo on Lake Como. From there many of his letters to Ada Negri are sent. See here Negri and Buzzi, *Diorami lombardi*, 151 ff.

87. Paolo Buzzi, *L'umana tragedia. Poema salmodico (1941–1945)* in Fondo Buzzi (MSS Buzzi 22), Centro Stendhaliano, Milan. On other works in which this theme is prefigured see Guicciardi, "Paolo Buzzi milanese," 26–27.

~

CHAPTER TEN

How to Become a Woman of the Future

Una donna con tre anime—Un ventre di donna

SILVIA CONTARINI

In the years 1916–1918, while Italy was at war and many women joined the avant-garde movement, a passionate debate on the feminine question of gender, that sought to pit men and women against each other, was unleashed in the columns of *L'Italia futurista*.[1] This long and harsh debate is well known.[2] In summary: at first, men responded with critically misogynistic tones and language, accusing women of being stupid, frivolous, and the source of all evil. Some women futurists reacted. Let us particularly recall the work of Rosa Rosà,[3] who developed the concept of the "woman of beyond-tomorrow" (donna del postdomani), and addressed the core issues of the feminine condition and sexual identity. Similarly relevant is the work of Enif Robert,[4] who highlights a fundamental contradiction in male futurists: despite the slogans of the avant-garde movement, rejection of the past, transformation of the present and outlook toward the future, the futurists prove conservative when it comes to any change regarding the position of woman in society.

In this context of conflict, the publication of the Marinettian "manual" *Come si seducono le donne* (How to Seduce Women) is seen as a provocation to which Rosa Rosà and Enif Robert reacted through their fiction, by publishing two novels in which they describe two different ways to become a woman of the future. The confrontation thus moves from the theoretical plane of the debate to one of literary creation and imagination, becoming a platform for the exchange of world views, and ideas about the women and men of the future. After a brief consideration of Marinetti's book, which will facilitate the understanding of the role it played, I will analyze these two (feminine) futurist novels, both astonishing for their formal modernity and important thanks to the issues they raise and for the solutions they envisage.

How to Seduce Women

Come si seducono le donne is a manual on the art of seduction; light and vulgar, intentionally provocative, in which Marinetti describes his manly exploits and gives advice to men on the best seductive techniques. At base, it aims to amuse, and raise the morale of soldiers on the battle front. It appeared in the fall of 1917 after an intense promotional campaign in the pages of *L'Italia futurista* that presented it as the solution to "the problem of women." But what is the problem? What is the solution?

In the preface entitled "intimo Marinetti," Bruno Corra and Emilio Settimelli—two major figures of the Florentine Futurism—praise the irresistible charm and vigor of their leader, reaffirming his reputation as *Latin lover*. They also reinforce a conception of the erotic heroism, which closely links masculinity and war. Above all, they present the multiplicity and mechanicity of the Marinettian adventures as the implicit paradigm of male-female relationships—relationships in which the woman consistently is seen as playing the passive role.

This tone-setting preface precedes eleven short chapters, of which the most famous, "The Manual of the Perfect Seducer" ("Manuale del perfetto seduttore") contains a list of twenty-two "very instructive moral maxims full of indulgence and devoid of bitterness" ("massime morali piene d'indulgenza, prive d'acredine e molto istruttive").[5] I quote the last one, by way of an example: "The brain is a superfluous engine, quite unfit for women's bodies that have the uterus as their natural motor" ("Il cervello è un motore aggiunto e inadatto al chassis della donna che ha per motore naturale l'utero").[6]

The "problem of women" is presented as the following: instead of accepting their uterine nature, they claim to also have a brain. In the eight chapters entitled "La donna e" (la varietà, la strategia, la guerra, la velocità-pericolo, il coraggio, la gelosia, la complicazione, il futurista—variety, strategy, war, dangerous velocity, courage, jealousy, complication, the futurist), Marinetti describes in an anecdotal and amusing way a number of cases in which he is the protagonist-seducer, preying upon females of all sorts, in places as diverse as the traditional lounge or the more futuristic train carriage.

In the last two chapters, "Women, you prefer the Glorious Mutilated" and "The Futurist Bomber's Salute to the Italian Woman" ("Donne, preferite i gloriosi mutilati" and "Saluto di un bombardiere futurista alla donna italiana"), the registry changes. Marinetti addresses women in order to encourage them to love their fatherland and to support the soldiers. These two chapters, so different from the rest of the manual, had previously been published in *L'Italia futurista*, in June and November 1916, though this is not indicated in the manual.

The second edition of *Come si seducono le donne*, dated 1918, contains an appendix *Polemics Surrounding This Book* (Polemiche sul presente libro), which brings together articles written by Enif Robert, Rosa Rosà, Shara Marini and Volt; Marinetti declares to have selected these articles to offer a platform to the controversies it raised, saying they are "selected from the survey on the 'feminine problem' that has appeared in *Italia futurista*" ("scelte dall'inchiesta sul 'problema femminile' svolta sull'*Italia futurista*").[7] Since these articles are not dated, the unwary reader is kept ignorant about the fact that they were published before the first edition of the manual. In reality, while *Come si seducono le donne* is published in the thick of the gender debate, it is not its cause.

A certain unclarity, most probably intentional, on the editing dates of the manual is also to be noted. In a new edition of 1920 entitled *How to seduce women . . . and betray men . . .* (Come si seducono le donne . . . e si tradiscono gli uomini . . .) which includes significant changes and important additions,[8] Marinetti states that he wrote this book while in hospital in Udine, in May 1917, while in his note to the editions of 1917 and 1918 he claimed having dictated this manual to Corra in September 1916 and then having corrected the proofs in Udine. By advancing the date of editing from 1917 to 1916, Marinetti could have made one believe that it was indeed that very manual that had sparked the controversy on the issue of women, which is not the case. His manual, however, seems designed as a way of intrusion into an ongoing debate, with a specific purpose of depleting it of certain ideas that he does not like, redirecting it towards his own themes and offering his "solutions."

As long as one discusses the art of seduction, one departs from the fundamental reflection on the prerogatives of the new woman. Maxim number 20: "To understand a beautiful woman's conversation, you have to listen to her with your nose" ("Per capire bene la conversazione d'una donna bella, bisogna ascoltarla col naso").[9] With this kind of provocation, Marinetti obviously aims to give rise to a scandal, aiming to hijack the attempts of emancipation that futurist women are expressing, so that the woman remains in her natural state as a passive object of seduction.

A Woman with Three Souls

To this reductionist and merely sexual view of the woman proposed by Marinetti and shared by the many men who appreciate his futurist manual, Rosa Rosà posits a bold vision, daring to ascribe the woman a multiplication of souls. After her articles in *L'Italia futurista* she published the novel *Una donna con tre anime*[10] in 1918. The protagonist Giorgina Rossi— the surname could not be more common and banal—is a "dusty" woman, the prototype of small ordinary people attached to the worries of a dull everyday life. In the absence of her husband (let us underline this), thanks to extraordinary energy and elements in the air, she suddenly undergoes three successive mutations. This transformation calls for two initial remarks.

The first: nothing in Giorgina's life as a housewife or in her personality predisposes her to change; this means that any woman could, just like her, change and take on new personalities—the evolution of women, even if it is personal and intimate, is intended to be common and collective. The second: the capacity for renewal does not depend—as is the case for the Marinettian hero Mafarka—on the mere effort of will, but depends rather, in this case, on the benefits of science combined with imagination. While the man owes the realization of a radical change to his own determination, the woman surrenders the possibility of her change to the invention of new worlds, and the upheavals of the present universe.

Let us examine the three evolutionary phases of Giorgina Rossi. The first one affects her physical size and appearance. The chemicals she inhales cause an increase in her expressive power and vitality. It is her femininity, therefore her sensuality, that is being exalted and pushes her out of the confined space of her house in order to mingle with the crowd that fills the streets.[11] The gray housewife becomes a charming woman; she walks through the city, agile, laughing and sure of herself, attracting the lust of men. The types of women who receive her admiration, presented as the first alternative to the kind of old-fashioned woman she used to be, are elegant ones getting into a car, or the tarts that excite the desire of men. These are conventional female role models, consistent with futuristic orthodoxy.

The narrator explains, however, that Giorgina can admire these luxurious women because she has been rid of all moral criteria: every moralistic criterion has vanished from her soul. She had really experienced an erosion of the bourgeois mentality. She felt internally authorized to do whatsoever she pleased.[12] Her first transformation is marked by a loss of inhibitions and the acquisition of a taste for transgression. She concludes her story, logically, in a seduction scene in an illegal casino, where Giorgina is the active protagonist.

The first stage of the new woman is thus sexual liberation and the acquisition of awareness about her own desire.

The second change concerns the mind and freedom of speech. Giorgina becomes an experienced and informed speaker who wants to convey the word of the new science. Many ideas crowd her mind simultaneously, which is a multiplication that requires mastery of new means of expression, speed and ability to synthesize. She recites with determination in front of the crowd who boos her and throws carrots at her. This is normal: just like the futurist heroes or the protagonists of the "evenings," she has become a spokesperson for the world of the future; her prescient words can only elicit hostile reactions. Let us note that this intellectual change in Giorgina is accompanied by a physical change later on: the erotic body marking a resplendent womanhood, gives way to more masculine physical traits:

> Her physical appearance had changed one more time. The good and modest wife of Umberto Rossi was gone, the magnetically sexual and amoral woman of the previous night was also gone. Her features had become energetic and hard. Her gestures were violent, sharply angled and precise. Her voice cutting and determined.[13]

The last phase of the change affects the sphere of artistic creation and manifests itself in writing: poetry is the ultimate, highest stage of transformation of the present world into the world of the future and, therefore, of the present woman into the woman of the future. In fact, the latter is not really a woman any more, but a being without flesh, who expresses her quest for liberation from materiality in lyrical-conceptual zest.

Giorgina Rossi, transformed in this way, writes a letter—from this point on in the first person—in which she expresses her desire to fly away from earthly shackles, to other temporal and spatial dimensions. She says that the most advanced individual will be multiple; different personalities can finally coexist in the same person. This letter-testament is the last act of the new woman before the old Giorgina Rossi finds herself restored to her dismal domestic condition as a housewife. Her story ends, not the book.

In the last chapter, it is the author who takes the floor to expose both his ideas about the relationship between "pre-cognizance" ("precoscienza") and reality, and his concept of the woman of "beyond tomorrow" ("postdomani"). She specifies that the three souls of Giorgina Rossi, without excluding each other, are components of what will be a woman's life in the future.

She sums them up as follows: the first soul will contain the spirit of adventure, the multiple erotic experience, and the devaluation of love. The second, more evolved, will consist of features forming a "more masculine than feminine" woman, and then, will come the soul of a woman interested in understanding the mysteries of the universe. Rosà stresses that this superior type of woman cannot be realized in the present. So, it is in an even more distant future that the third soul will be able to manifest itself: the new woman will flourish then in a dimension of unreality, due to her mystical efforts.

Since it proposes a form of liberation of women, this novel can be read as a double utopia: futurist and feminist.[14] Its limit is obvious: in her hypothetical elaboration of a new model of a woman, Rosà offers a science-fiction scenario that immerses the implementation of the new woman in a dimension of unreality, reducing its scope considerably. Moreover, the final therapeutic treatment to which scientists and her husband submit Giorgina, that poor woman who had to bear the weight of three souls in spite of her own will, indicates that in her present day, this transformative and liberating experience can only fail. While waiting for the time and the scientific discoveries to do their work, Giorgina returns to her daily life as a housewife. The day when the woman has more than one soul has not yet come.

This acceptance of the impossibility of a real and immediate evolution may seem in contrast to Rosa Rosà's articles, in which she said that concrete changes were in fact happening. However, when reading them more carefully, these articles show that Rosà based her forecast of changes on an external event—the war—in the hope that it would cause major upheavals. So, it is *hope* that animates it, a hope behind which the doubt remains that women did not at that time yet have the means to achieve their ambitions of metamorphosis. In this perspective, the motifs of flight, madness and dream that Rosa uses in her novel to allow her heroine to "rise" up to men, although futurist *topoi*, can also be interpreted as moments a character may escape from the restrictions of a mediocre daily life. These are dreams of change that can be read as an expression of a housewife's frustration, who has no other way out of her dull life but of fantasizing about adventures she will never live.

That being said, this futurist-feminist novel contains interesting insights. In particular, applying the principles of futurist simultaneity and compenetration allows for women to admit the coexistence of several different personalities and to work around, or even to resolve, the contradiction between several models of women. By appropriating male characteristics, without sacrificing the sexual specificity of the feminine, the new woman imagined by Rosa Rosà can juxtapose three souls, three facets of a personality. In other words, the refusal of some feminine values adapts to an assumed femininity, and the preservation of a female sensuality is compatible with male intellectual qualities. Something that male futurists, of which Marinetti comes to mind, continue to refute.

Rosà agrees with the futuristic men on one thing: love does not deserve to be given importance. With one difference. For her, feelings are a source of weakness especially for women, as they are the foundation of her submission to man. This implies among other things, the assertion of sexual freedom. This theme, however, is barely touched by Rosà, who was without a doubt infuriated by the erotic fixation of the male futurists; indeed rather than engage in the discourse at that level, she preferred to imagine and theorize the development of cerebral and spiritual qualities of women, seeking to draw the evolution of their "souls."[15]

A Woman's Womb

Enif Robert also imagined the transformation of a woman into a futurist female in a novel published in 1919, *Un ventre di donna: romanzo chirurgico* (A Woman's Womb: a Surgical Novel). It is true that this novel is jointly signed with her name and that of Marinetti's,[16] but a closer look reveals that most of the texts are by Robert, interspersed with a few letters of Marinetti's.[17]

In her preface, *Coraggio + Verità* (Courage + Truth), Robert explicitly places the novel in the framework of the debate on women held in *L'Italia Futurista*.[18] Herein is a literary extension and thus a response to the two works already published, *Come si seducono le donne* by Marinetti and *Una donna con tre anime* by Rosa Rosà. In the preface, Robert reviews all that the futurist woman should not be: neither rebel nor pretty, nor sentimental, of course, but also not detached from reality, or enclosed in an aesthetic dimension, spiritual or dreamy, as are the women of *L'Italia futurista*. Enif Robert mentions the "scrittrici *azzurre*" (blue women writers) and the "dreams" of Rosa Rosà as examples one should *not* follow. The futuristic woman, she says, must have the courage to tell real life, the stark truth of everyday life, in all its coarseness. This is what she does by telling of a dramatic event in her life: a serious illness.

A woman's womb is at a first glance the chronicle of a real disease experienced by Enif Robert,[19] but throughout it a transformation more metaphorical of the protagonist of *Un ventre di donna* is developed, who says, from the first pages, that she feels "so little a woman" because she is more attracted by art than by love.[20] The disease in question also affects her body in its most deeply feminine part: the reproductive organs. This gives rise to a reflection on gender identity and the status of women that is the starting point of her mutation process. This is the main plot of the novel.

Marinetti's letters, that enter the plot at a certain moment, assimilate this mutation process in a symbolic battle. Marinetti, from the front, wrote to Robert: "That which happens today to your womb is profoundly symbolic. In fact, your womb is like that of the earth, that has an immense surgical wound today in the trenches," and again: "At base, I am in the same situation as you. You, confined to your bed; I in a muddy trench."[21]

The disease of the one is set in a parallel with the war of the other, intimate battles are paralleled with the battles in the trenches.[22] This merger establishes an analogy of situation and resources. Whether one fights against an enemy within or against an external enemy, the futurist ways to achieve victory—courage and commitment—are no different: However, it should be noted that the forms of struggle remain essentially either feminine or masculine: the woman leads the fight in the confined space of the chamber and within the private sphere, the man faces the battle in the field of political, social and pub-lic confrontation; the woman suffers passively and individually, the man is in a collective and exhilarating action. This difference is highlighted at the outset; at the first signs of her infection, the narrator exclaims: "How disgusting it is to be a suffering uterus, while all the men are at war!"[23]

Let us return to the process of change and its different phases. Despite the terrible suffering, the protagonist tries to understand what is happening within her and around her. She is intrigued by the complexity of her own womanhood, as revealed to her through this experience. The disease which affects her stomach and which the official—and manly—science cannot heal because it is unable to understand its origin, makes her realize that a woman cannot be reduced to her genitals, that a woman does not only have female attributes. A body, even a very feminine one, may go together with a male spirit, contrary to the maxims of the Marinettian manual. This is the helpless conclusion her doctor draws after having visited her: "you strike me as a too virile brain in a far too feminine body."[24]

These words are perceived as a compliment by the patient, who is proud to possess a man's cerebralness and in this way overcome her female status. However, this merging of conflicting powers—feminine sensuality and intel-lectual virility—has its price: the severity of the infection requires a complete removal of reproductive organs. At the insistence of the patient, the surgeon, who is reluctant to deprive her of her prerogatives as a reproductive woman, will be obliged to operate.

The narrator does not hide her instinctive distrust in this surgeon; indeed he only acquiesces and removes her infected organs when her life is in mortal danger. The surgeon—a repository of ancient knowledge—is, like the entire official science that insists on thinking "Tota mulier in utero," unsuited to new realities. That's why doctors cannot find solutions to her problems, which are, she says, the problems of the new woman. Could the futuristic doctrine provide an answer? Futurism becomes the new science, even the new religion of the protagonist: in her hospital bed, she declares herself an atheist, refuses the comfort of a priest and waves the futuristic books *Sam Dunn è morto* and *Zang Tumb Tumb*.[25]

It is at this point in the story that Enif Robert's diary turns into correspondence with Marinetti. In the middle of the book, in chapter eight, entitled "Il ventre della terra ha un'immensa ferita chirurgica di trincee" ("The Earth's Womb has an Immense Surgical Wound of Trenches"), Marinetti encourages his friend with a story about his life in the trenches; he establishes thus a first analogy between wounds and scars, real and symbolic. In another letter, he is convinced he can heal the sick woman with a "futurist cure," based on the principle of desire. He then details his advice in a "Therapeutic manual of Desire-Imagination" ("Manuale terapeutico del desiderio-immaginazione").[26] However, the cure proposed by Marinetti did not produce the desired effect. The patient decided to channel her effort of will in another form of therapy: writing. If writing contributes to her awareness, literary creativity becomes a moment of affirmation of her new personality and plays an essential role in the transition to a higher dimension, to that of the *artist*:

> For some time I have had the idea that to write my surgical musings via *words in freedom*. . . . I sense that my occupation of futurist literature would be a distraction for the too gloomy thought of my illness. . . . What purpose? Here it is: the most absurd, the most difficult, the most distant: that of becoming . . . a futurist writer! I will write immediately, bringing together all the scraps of my poor will, a volume of *words in freedom*, entitled "Surgical feelings" and I will send it to Marinetti. Am getting straight to work.[27]

The results are free-word poems entitled "Sensazioni chirurgiche" ("Surgical Sensations,") followed by a "Conversazione tra il sole e il mio ventre" ("Conversation between the Sun and my Womb"). The inclusion of these literary creations in the body of an autobiographical or correspondence story points out that *Un ventre di donna*, a book about the quest for the female identity, a history of the transformation of a conventional woman into an artist and a female futurist, is also a literary work.

Some realistic elements placed at the beginning of the sixteenth and final chapter would suggest we are about to read a happy ending: the healing of the protagonist. There is, rather, an unexpected and disconcerting epilogue that surprises the reader. The story told in the first person by the patient suddenly stops (in ellipsis at the end of chapter 15) and now gives way to the story of a certain princess De Ruderis. This character is suffering from a stomach illness unknown to science, the main causes of which seem to have been the delivery of too many babies and the wearing of tight corsets too often.

Renowned scientists conferring at a congress concede defeat when it comes to diagnosing and treating her pain. The prince De Ruderis, an aristocrat whose name emphasizes the attachment to the past, requests that no one actually touch the body of his wife, despite her own repeated requests to undergo an operation. And then comes the twist: a brave *Ardito* futuristically stabs the prince; the young woman is finally freed—from the old husband and from the past—and can now undergo an operation on her midriff. She also shows how she has the strength and courage of futurist women. In the last scene we see her on the balcony: naked, beautiful and resolute.

This final triumph, so different from the rest of the novel, provides a key to understanding the whole. If the disease is allegorical, healing is as well. The protagonist Enif Robert, unlike the princess, fails to reach to the end of the process of healing / transformation / liberation. However, by a very successful *mise en abyme*, Enif Robert, the author, confesses to an imaginary character that she takes up the path to liberation and transformation into a female futurist.

With this novel, Robert suggests on the one hand that the evolution of women is a long and painful process, and on the other, that the new female identity is forged by striking a balance between male and female prerogatives, between body, mind and spirit. She imagines thus the combination of a body that preserves a feminine sensuality, not necessarily predestined to procreation, with a virilized mind that allows the woman to fulfill herself in the process of creation.

Note that the process of change also frees itself of formal aspects. This "surgical novel" is indeed characterized by a succession of genres and registers. Very accurate in this regard, is the formal analysis of Barbara Zecchi on the evolution of the literary genre:[28] Robert's original text in diary form (which is commonly accepted as a feminine genre in its intimacy) gives way to the letter exchange with Marinetti (mixed genre) and finally leads to fiction (masculine genre); besides, the narrative moves from first to third person. The evolution of the literary genre accompanies thus the evolution of *gender*, the transition of feminine to masculine, and with it, the emancipation of the protagonist.

Conclusion

Come si seducono le donne, Una donna con tre anime and *Un ventre di donna*: these three literary texts published in the space of two years can be considered the summit of reflection and conclusion to Futurism's debate regarding the *new woman*. At the same time, they also mark the end to the utopian advent of the woman irrevocably back to the female, sending her back to her uterine essence, fixing the roles between the sexes. Marinetti is consistent of the future.

We have seen how Marinetti, with his entirely sexual solution to what he calls the problem of women, hijacks the debate and tries to end the involvement of futurist women in developing new models. Under the guise of jokes and provocation, his manual of seduction brings the woman from start to finish: the male conquers and the female is prey. Rosà and Robert answer in their own respective ways, but the similarities are many. Their two, atypical, novels are both artistic and theoretical responses to this Marinettian intrusion. On the literary level, it is necessary to emphasize their formal modernity: Rosa Rosà and Enif Robert—who spend time articulating their questions of how to become female artists—are without question worthy of the title of "artist" in their own right. On the theoretical side, we must emphasize the modernity of their thoughts on gender issues, especially the distinction that the one and the other operate between gender and the definition of the prerogatives of the gender. If they do not clearly define sexual identity of the woman of the future, obviously they exceed the essentialist view (woman = uterus = female = nature) and therefore claim for women qualities that are not necessarily feminine.

Rosà and Robert are not close to each other, yet, their vision is close: the woman has to change but cannot do that but by her own will; the change process will be long, the new woman is not for now; this process will involve giving up some female attributes (e.g., the womb) in order to acquire certain masculine ones (e.g., the soul); the new model of a woman will merge qualities of the two genders. Certainly, Robert and Rosà's limitations are obvious: they fail to transcend their circumstances to band together with other female authors/artists in order to formulate and posit a common approach. Instead, by nature of the circumstances that limit them, their vision of women is rooted in the idealization of the male and virile model. But the failure of the new woman does not primarily have to do with these authors' weaknesses or limitations.

It is striking to conclude, beyond the dreamy and utopian aspects of their vision, that they are very lucid and fully aware of the fact that time and society of their moment were not ready to accept any adjustment to the status of women. Their fellow futurists, as hopefully demonstrated here in this essay, were resistant to the concept of altering woman's status within the system, as well. These two women writers, who joined the futurist movement around

1915, convince us that, more than feminism, it is in fact *Futurism*—a movement of rupture—that would allow them to change their status in 1919, in the wake of World War I. The two novels, *Una donna con tre anime* and *Un ventre di donna* are these authors' final gestures before conceding any futile attempt to change, and before abandoning Futurism at all.

Notes

1. Translation by Claudia M. Clemente.

2. Many points developed in this essay are also covered in my book *La femme futuriste: Mythes, modèles et représentations de la femme dans la théorie et la littérature futuristes* (Nanterre: Presses Universitaires de Paris 10, 2006), particularly in its chapter "L'Italia futurista: la polémique" (204–13).

3. Her birth name is Edith von Haynau Arnaldi; Rosa Rosà published four articles in: *L'Italia futurista*: "Le donne del posdomani," 18 (June 17, 1917); "Risposta a Jean-Jacques," 20 (July 1, 1917); "Le donne cambiano, finalmente . . . ," 27 (August 26, 1917); "Le donne del posdomani (II)," 30 (October 7, 1917).

4. Enif Robert, "Una parola serena," *L'Italia futurista* 30 (July 7, 1917); "Come si seducono le donne, Lettera aperta a Marinetti," *L'Italia futurista* 36 (December 31, 1917).

5. Filippo Tommaso Marinetti, *Come si seducono le donne* (Florence: Edizioni da Centomila Copie, 1917), 66.

6. Marinetti, *Come si seducono*, 69.

7. Marinetti, *Come si seducono*, 159.

8. Filippo Tommaso Marinetti, *Come si seducono le donne . . . e si tradiscono gli uomini* (Milan: Sonzogno, 1920).

9. Marinetti, *Come si seducono le donne*, 69.

10. Rosa Rosà, *Una donna con tre anime* (Milan: Studio Editoriale Lombardo, 1918). New edition *Non c'è che te! Una donna con tre anime e altre novelle* (Milan: Facchi, 1919). Now in: Claudia Salaris, *Rosa Rosà. Una donna con tre anime: romanzo futurista* (Milan: Edizioni delle Donne, 1982), from which these citations come.

11. Rosa Rosà was without a doubt influenced by her friend Bruno Corra, and his novel *Sam Dunn è morto* (Milan: Edizioni Futuriste di "Poesia," 1917); 2nd edition, *Sam Dunn è morto: romanzo sintetico futurista, con sei illustrazioni di Rosa Rosà* (Milan: Studio Editoriale Lombardo, 1917), that had already imagined a fictional situation in which the unleashing of a strange and extraordinary energy effected people and towns: the streets of Paris were lit up raucously, with contagious, mad laughter. The motif of contagious folly is picked up again in Rosa Rosà's novella *La sarabanda*, where the madness that breaks out turns into a homicidal frenzy.

12. "Ogni criterio morale è svanito dal suo spirito. Era avvenuto in lei veramente uno sgretolamento della coscienza borghese. Essa si sentiva internamente autorizzata tutto cio che le piaceva." Rosà, *Una donna con tre anime*, 54.

13. Rosà, *Una donna con tre anime*, 59.

14. Cf. Lucia Re, "Scrittura della metamorfosi e metamorfosi della scrittura: Rosa Rosà e il futurismo," in *Les femmes écrivains en Italie (1870–1920): ordre et libertés, Chroniques Italiennes*, 39–40 (1994), 311–27.

15. Gian Battista Nazzaro observes rightly that Rosà, Ginanni and the other female futurists of the *pattuglia azzurra* privilege an aesthetic approach informed by the feminine unconscious, and, finally, they are more interested by creativity than by treating social and political themes. Nazzaro, however, replicating and propagating the male hegemonic approach, neglects the interest in female emancipation and liberation clearly manifested by the female authors in their writing, which is of course in itself a social and political theme. Gian Battista Nazzaro, *Introduzione al futurismo* (Naples: Guida, 1984), 152.

16. Filippo Tommaso Marinetti, Enif Robert, *Un ventre di donna: romanzo chirurgico* (Milan: Facchi, 1919). The preface dates to March 1918. The recounted events take place in 1915–1916.

17. On the correspondence and the personal relationship between Marinetti and Robert, see Filippo Tommaso Marinetti, *Taccuini 1915–1921*, ed. Alberto Bertoni, introduction by Renzo De Felice and Ezio Raimondi (Bologna: Il Mulino, 1987), 71 and 552.

18. The preface begins with this phrase: "We have not yet understood well, it seems, what 'Donna Futurista' actually means," "Non abbiamo ancora ben compreso, mi sembra, ciò che vuol dire DONNA FUTURISTA," Marinetti, Robert, *Un ventre di donna*, XI.

19. This could justify an autobiographical reading, as proposed by Barbara Meazzi, "Enif Robert & Filippo Tommaso Marinetti: *Un ventre di donna* e l'autobiografia futurista," which was presented at the AIPI 2006 conference in Ascoli Piceno (www .infoaipi.org/attion.asp).

20. "I think that I would have been a weak painter and weak poet, had I been born a man. Love is not enough for me. In this moment, I actually don't quite feel fully female" ("Io penso che sarei stata un poco pittore e un poco poeta, se fossi nata uomo. L'amore non mi basta. Mi sento veramente, in questo momento, poco donna"); Marinetti, Robert, *Un ventre di donna*, 4.

21. "Ciò che accade oggi al vostro ventre è profondamente simbolico. Infatti, il vostro ventre somiglia a quello della terra, che ha oggi un'immensa ferito chirurgica di trincee." "In fondo, io sono nella vostra stessa situazione. Voi inchiodata in un letto; io in una trincea fangosa." Marinetti, Robert, *Un ventre di donna*, 113 and 171.

22. On this point, see my article "Guerre maschili / guerre femminili: corpi e corpus futuristi in azione / trasformazione," in Federico Luisetti and Luca Somigli, eds., *A Century of Futurism: 1909–2009*, in *Annali d'Italianistica* 27 (2009), 125–38.

23. "Che schifo, essere un utero sofferente, mentre tutti gli uomini si battono!" Marinetti, Robert, *Un ventre di donna*, 25.

24. ". . . lei mi sembra un cervello troppo virile in un corpo troppo femminile." Marinetti, Robert, *Un ventre di donna*, 97.

25. These are works by Corra, *Sam Dunn è morto*, and by Filippo Tommaso Marinetti, *Zang Tumb Tumb* (Edizioni Futuriste di "Poesia," 1914).

26. Marinetti, Robert, *Un ventre di donna*, 160.

27. "Ho da tempo l'idea di scrivere in parole in libertà le mie sensazione chirurgiche. . . . Sento che è un diversivo al pensiero troppo tetro del mio male l'occuparmi di letteratura futurista. . . . Quale scopo? Eccolo: il più assurdo, il più difficile, il più lontano, quello di diventare . . . una scrittrice futurista! Scriverò subito, riunendo tutti i rottami della mia povera volonta, un volume di parole in libertà, intitolato 'Sensazioni chirurgiche' e lo manderò a Marinetti. Subito al lavoro." Marinetti, Robert, *Un ventre di donna*, 109 and 134.

28. Barbara Zecchi, "Il corpo femminile tra scrittura e volo. Enif Robert e Biancamaria Frabotta: settant'anni verso il tempo delle donne," *Italica* 4 (1992), 505–18.

CHAPTER ELEVEN

~

Love, Politics, and an Explosive Future

Volt's La fine del mondo

KYLE HALL

Vincenzo Fani Ciotti, generally known by his futurist pseudonym "Volt," has occupied an ambiguous position in the history of Italian culture throughout the twentieth century and into the twenty-first. Although never completely forgotten by scholars of Futurism and fascism, the extent and indeed variety of his publications, from his futurist debut in 1916 to his death in 1927, is oftentimes overlooked. A telling quote can be found in Enrico Crispolti's *Storia e critica del futurismo*: "The futurist fascist groups in February of 1919 were around twenty, one in Rome (which included among its more significant adherents Balla, Carli, Volt, Giuseppe Bottai, Auro d'Alba, Gino Galli, Remo Chiti). . . ."[1] "Significant," yes: but the reader searching the index for more information would find that this is the only reference to Volt in the entire book. So it is perhaps not surprising that one of Volt's most fascinating works, a novel published in 1921 entitled *La fine del mondo* [*The End of the World*], would be forgotten for students of Italian literature, languishing as only a first edition before finally being republished in 2003 thanks to the efforts of Gianfranco de Turris, one of Italy's premier science fiction scholars.

That Volt chose to write a science fiction novel (*ante litteram*, considering that the term did not exist in English or Italian at the time) now proves fortuitous in that it led De Turris to rediscover it. And indeed, this feature alone can render the novel noteworthy, as one of the very early examples of an organic science fiction novel written in Italian.[2] But the novel is also an intriguing window on the nature of the relationship between Futurism and fascism during the years following the Armistice in 1918 and prior to the March on Rome in 1922.[3] The continuity of thought that exists between this work and the political treatises that Volt published under both futurist and fascist auspices are striking in revealing the shifting relationship between the two (at times competing and at times collaborating) camps. More accurately described as a political theorist, Volt shifted his medium and overlapped art and politics, as he first repackaged political writings into a more popular form and then later retained vestiges from *La fine del mondo* in his political treatises.

Our knowledge of Volt's life comes mainly from the few sources that dedicate substantial thought to his writings, and there is clearly work yet to be undertaken in this area.[4] Born in Viterbo to an aristocratic family, Volt demonstrates throughout his life a predilection for the political right. His first publication, *Per la scuola media* [*Regarding Middle Schools*], came out in 1907 when he was only nineteen years old. The years leading up to the outbreak of World War I saw his involvement in the nationalist movements that were trying to precipitate intervention, but he was not a participant in the war itself, likely due his continuous struggle with tuberculosis. His involvement with the futurists began with his meeting Marinetti in 1916 at Viareggio, soon followed by an edition of *parole in libertà* [words-in-freedom] entitled *Archi voltaici* (*Voltaic Arcs*). It is this volume that supplies the pseudonym that he will use for the rest of his life, including his fascist publications. While *Archi voltaici* did not break particularly new ground, it has been justly called one of the "most beautiful examples of futurist typography."[5]

In addition to its striking layouts, particularly those of the four fold-out compositions, the collection is also notable in that it reveals some characteristic aspects of Volt's privileged background, a background that will color his worldview and his writings no matter the format. Settings for various poems include hotels, a lawyer's office, and an "Eighteenth-century villa."[6] In one poem, a group of young women play amorous games with their suitors: "this young man is playing footsies / is it a sin to not draw back my foot? / I shall confess as soon as I return to my lodgings."[7] This sort of playfully aristocratic and proper tone is found throughout the collection, although it is generally a subtle trace rather than a driving force, a trace that nonetheless made him stand out a bit in the futurist crowd which tended more to the left. But typical futurist principles are just as prevalent, for example with psychology derided as being "masturbation of the soul" and Romain Rolland criticized as the premier author for all the "CONSUMPTIVES and TUBERCULOSIS SUFFERERS of the world."[8] The judgment of psychology is directly in line with earlier futurist writings, such as in Marinetti's "The Variety Theater" where, when one considers psychology, "both the reality and the word are foul."[9] As a whole, *Archi voltaici* shows that while innovation may have been difficult for Volt considering his late entrance into the futurist movement, the poetics of the movement were still fully functioning despite the effects of the war. But as mentioned above, his real value as a futurist comes in demonstrating *in nuce* the political and artistic shifts that occur in the wake of the war.

From its inception, Futurism contained an inherent political element, through which art was able to be understood both in reference to itself and to the political world in which it emerged. This can be seen directly through the many manifestos and equally clearly in artistic productions. A few weeks after the publication in *Le Figaro* of the *Futurist Manifesto*, there came the publication of the first *Futurist Political Manifesto*, produced in response to the coming general elections.[10] Günter Berghaus has shown that even prior to the formation of Futurism as an artistic movement, Marinetti's own life was heavily tinged by political thought and writing, and it is no surprise that such thought would continue to be evident in Futurism's development.[11] The early years of Futurism saw its members at the front lines of the interventionist movement, a view that came out strongly in the works produced by Boccioni, Carrà, and others.[12] Coming out of the experiences of interventionism and the war, Futurism takes on an even more direct political engagement, including the establishment in 1918 of the Futurist Political Party and its alliance with Mussolini's *Fasci* during the elections in November of that same year.[13] Emilio Gentile points out that this early stage after the war sees Volt moving along as both a futurist and a fascist, for the simple reason that he saw both organizations as fundamentally motivated by the same desires and goals.[14] As time went on, however, Volt clearly became more invested in the fascist cause. The 1920s, until Volt's death in 1927, would be characterized by occasional futurist writings, but with much more thought dedicated to articulating and arguing the fascist position.

In the midst of the political shifts prior to the March on Rome, *La fine del mondo* was published. Therein however lies a small bibliographic problem that should be addressed, as was done by De Turris in the introduction to the 2003 edition.[15] While we know that there is a first edition published by Modernissima in 1921, there are also several sources that claim the existence of a 1919 edition. One of these in particular, Giancarlo Scriboni's *Tra nazionalismo e futurismo*, is important as it is the result of Scriboni's work in the Fani Ciotti family archives, and one of the only academic works that attempts to engage Volt's political thought on a significant level. But while Scriboni's bibliography points to an edition published in Bologna, the other work that attests to a 1919 edition, Ezio Godoli's *Il dizionario del futurismo*, claims that the work was published in Rocca San Casciano. Ultimately, however, there are no extant copies that have been found carrying a date of 1919. In support of the primacy of the 1921 publication date there are the bibliographic entries offered by Claudia Salaris in the *Bibliografia del futurismo 1909–1944* and Pablo Echaurren in *Futurcollezionismo*. Combined with the fact that the Modernissima publication carries the indication of being a "first edition" (which, to cite a ready example, it did not do with its 1921 republication of D'Annunzio's *Il fuoco*, published first by Treves in 1900), it seems that 1921 is to be taken as the accurate date, unless further evidence can be offered in favor of an earlier edition. Of course, this is the publication date as opposed to the date of composition, an argument that will be returned to in the concluding section of this essay.

Before considering the work itself, I would like to look at Volt's decision to write a novel and then the decision by Modernissima to publish it. In terms of futurist products, the choice of writing a novel already places this work in a rather restricted group. While there are several famous examples of futurist novels, chief among them Marinetti's *Mafarka il futurista* (*Mafarka the Futurist*) and Palazzeschi's *Il codice di Perelà* (*The Code of Perelà*), for the most part literary Futurism is remembered for its poetic productions, namely the words-in-freedom. In fact, the general lack of attention paid to the prose productions of futurists has enabled critics to question the very existence of a "futurist narrative."[16] Yet works, including *La fine del mondo*, continue to emerge that suggest that their number may be greater than is generally assumed. Alessandro Masi's edited 1995 volume *Zig Zag: Il romanzo futurista* (*Zig Zag: The Futurist Novel*) republished a number of prose works, by authors including Corra, Ginna, Soffici, and Benedetta; but it remains the case that futurist prose is neglected in most studies (and it is worth again noting that Volt's novel was rediscovered not by a scholar of Futurism, but by an expert on science fiction).

That said, Volt's novel will immediately strike the reader as occupying a particular position even within the restricted circle of examples that exist. He incorporates fictionalized elements in his writing, but without including any metaphysical or esoteric content that was popular in other futurist novels.[17] Although De Turris sees some political connections with Julius Evola, a figure oftentimes associated with the mystical elements of the fascist regime,[18] if one is looking at poetics there is little that could be considered mysterious or spiritual about *La fine del mondo*, in direct opposition to what can be found in other futurist novels such as Corra's *Sam Dunn è morto* (*Sam Dunn is Dead*).[19] Volt instead remains solidly tied to the reality that surrounds him, expanding upon it and utilizing fictional precepts to do so, but without escaping into the realm of the invisible or the oniric. Volt's novel is not to be restricted as either futurist, fascist, or science fiction; it is part of and also distinct from each of these categories. Including *La fine del mondo* within these corpora reveals the variety that exists under certain cultural umbrellas that, while useful for conceptual purposes, should still be complicated to avoid the trap of reductionism.

A brief aside as to the publisher for this novel that had few real precedents in Italian culture at the time. Despite a relatively brief life, Modernissima proved to be an important source of literature in Italy from its founding in 1919 through the early 1930s.[20] Unfortunately, as was already seen with Volt's works and their related sources, information is rather scarce, as even such facts as its date of birth are subject to errors in the brief profiles of the house that are available.[21] There were two distinct parts to its life, however, which are readily seen by perusing its catalogue. The latter part of its run, directed by Gian Dàuli from 1924, saw a turn toward translations of foreign books, including Thornton Wilder's *The Bridge of San Luis Rey*, Thomas Mann's *The Magic Mountain*, and a large part of Jack London's oeuvre. During the early years of its life, however, Modernissima published original works by authors ranging from the futurists, including Marinetti's *Lussuria velocità* [*Lust Speed*] in 1921, to Tullio Murri, whose *Galera* (*Prison*), first published in 1920, depicted the world of sexual violence that accompanied prison life. Overall it is an eclectic collection, making Modernissima a rather natural home for an early science fiction novel.

The publisher declared that its purpose was to produce "excellent novels, Italian and foreign, which are not only the usual narratives that have by now bored the public, but that instead represent unique and vital artistic expression, expressions of a new vocabulary, true and proper works of art."[22] Volt's novel would certainly seem to fit into the category of not being "the usual narratives." At the same time, the political bent of Volt's book also fits within Modernissima's willingness to take part in public debate, another fact revealed by the house's early publications. From the previously mentioned *Galera* to the biographical series *Gli uomini del giorno* [*The Men of the Day*], which profiled important political and cultural figures, Modernissima was politically involved without necessarily being politically motivated. Both of these features, political involvement and a desire to publish unique artistic works, are on display in *La fine del mondo*. If nothing else, Volt's novel illustrates the willingness of the publisher to engage works that may seem out of place in many catalogues; one could have only wished for their confidence to be rewarded with a few more copies sold.[23]

The End of the World: Political Science (Fiction)?

La fine del mondo, as is the case with many works of fiction, straddles a line between fantasy and reality. Fiction gives the author free reign within the world of his creation: in the words of Thomas Pavel, the reader must exercise "tolerance" with the fictional text.[24] That said, despite the presence of fantastical elements, Volt goes out of his way to create a fictional work that mirrors readily recognizable reality. His characters are related to real-world counterparts, a fictional future is put forward as a logical conclusion to actual historical events, and the emotional side of his writing deals with everyday and, at least for the Western tradition, eternal questions relating to life and love. Although it retains a distinct and obvious link to the reality in which it was written, *La fine del mondo* also presents some more complicated variations on these themes, including the rapport between private relationships and public life, the nature of sacrifice, and the psychology of action. All of these themes are explored through an entertaining tale of the future, a blend of escapism and politics.

The novel opens on the outskirts of Rome, where the reader finds an exiled pope and his followers. An apocalyptic tone, which is generally lacking from the rest of the narrative, is distinctly brought out in the pope's opening words: "Woe to you—thundered the venerable old man, with his index finger pointed toward the city of the seven hills—woe to you, Rome! But what am I saying, Rome? Woe to you, Babylon! And so the prophecy of our forebears has come true."[25] But as happens with many apocalyptic declarations, these warnings are ignored within the city walls. The pope's words function in creating a certain sense of expectation in the reader, but they are immediately left behind as the narration transfers itself to the events going on in Rome. The rest of this opening chapter, functioning as a prologue to the rest of the novel, gives the reader the journalistic answers: who, what, when, where, why. To transmit this information, there is the presence of a seemingly omniscient third person narrator, a narratological expedient that, it must be noted, takes away much of the novel's possible suspense.

The following chapters focus on various characters that are soon introduced, but the narrator that brings the reader through all of these turns acts as a matter-of-fact guide that decidedly reduces any apprehension on the part of the reader (this lack of suspense is even more apparent if one thinks of other early science fiction works, such as H. G. Wells's *The Time Machine*, where the first person narration contributes greatly to apprehension and a certain amount of trial and error associated with the Time Traveller's various hypotheses, eventual realizations, and the emotions associated with each).

But the narrator does serve to quickly bring the reader up to speed: we are in Rome, in the year 2247, a time in which Italy had not only taken its place as the "greatest power" of Europe after the "last world war" (a prescient use of the qualifier "last" if ever there was one), but it also housed the capital of the United States of Europe, which answered only to the world congress located in Washington, D.C.[26] The pope's exile is also explained, as he was kicked out of the city after the last revolution, which then availed itself of St. Peter's Basilica for use as the seat of the European Parliament. This exile would seem to fit well with the futurist desire for a true anti-clericalism in society, a critical part of Marinetti's founding manifesto of the Futurist Political Party.[27]

Ironically, the pope's new home outside the city places him directly across from the "*Compagnia transeterica*," the "Transetheric Group" that constructs and prepares the spaceships ("*eteronavi*") that have been used for over half a century to explore the rest of the galaxy. It is this company that is at the heart of the battle over interstellar conquest that forms the crisis of the novel. In articulating the papal camp and the "transetheric" camp, separated literally by the Aniene River and figuratively by the contrast between dynamism and inaction, the prologue presents both apocalypse and rebirth prior to the reader entering properly into the narrative.

This entrance focuses on the novel's protagonist, the space explorer and now parliamentary representative Paolo Fonte.[28] But the strong Paolo who would be a perfect futurist representative, with his ardent nature and willing bellicosity as are demonstrated by his space travels and position on intergalactic colonization, is also immediately revealed as a broken Paolo, wracked with health problems and unable to fulfil what he sees as his destiny of leading the expedition back to Jupiter. Jupiter, as will be explained in the following chapter through a scientific discourse/recap given at the Collegio Romano, has been found to be the most welcoming planet for human colonization, despite the presence of a strange race referred to as "The Lemurs."[29] The description of his illness as well as the recommended rest on the French Riviera reveal, in a direct parallel with Volt's own life, that Paolo is struck by tuberculosis, the same disease that would finally kill Volt in 1927, at the age of thirty-nine. This chapter, like the prologue before it, introduces two distinct factors to the story: Paolo's professional life in all its dynamism and his personal life that revolves around his lover, Marinette.

Marinette strikes the reader for a number of reasons. The first is the clear link between the names of Marinette and Marinetti. Indeed, there is no shortage of contemporary figures that appear in the novel: as has been noted by Domenico Cammarota, the reader finds stand-ins for Bruno Corra, Arnaldo Ginna, Emilio Settimelli, and Gilbert Clavel.[30] These minor figures in the novel are joined by more central ones: there is Marinetti's stand-in, Tomaso El-Barka, founder of the "Dynamic Party," the "Partito dinamico," as well as the leader of the European Parliament, Abramo Lattes, whose real-world counterpart is found in Rome's former mayor, Ernesto Nathan. However, none of this explains the reasons behind the choice of "Marinette" as the name of Paolo's lover, nor is there any indication given in the text of why Volt would choose this name. What is sure about Marinette is that she is a figure caught between tradition and independence. She is a sensual presence without being a caricature of futurist ideals. Indeed, she is in some ways shown to be a conservative figure, in no way fulfilling the maxims that Volt will give with the 1920 *Manifesto della moda femminile futurista* (*Manifesto of Futurist Women's Fashion*). Ideally the futurist woman will wear asymmetrical designs, "zig zag decolletés" and "sleeves, each different from the other."[31] But Marinette does none of this,[32] opting for rich furs and a general elegance, gaining Paolo's attention upon their first meeting by stretching her legs, "baring them as high as her calf," surely a less than scandalous occurrence.[33] However, she is distinctly constrained by the manner in which she must earn her living. She is, to put it discreetly, a "kept woman," a principle complaint about women put forward by Volt in the pages of *Roma futurista* in 1919.[34] Yet she is also portrayed as intelligent, capable of fending for herself, and faithful in her own way. Paolo's love for her is never condemned, be it from a futurist point of view or not, and even the difficulties that invade their relationship are felt by the reader as indicating the strength of their bond. The reader sees her as a positive figure, able to contain within herself both independence and sentiment. The depth of her love is revealed in the novel's final pages, which will be discussed below, but it is quite clear throughout that Marinette is a decent and respectable companion for Paolo.

But this is a popular novel,[35] and Marinette is also available as a possible titillation for the reader, a feature that is not out-of-place even in other futurist novels such as Corra's *L'isola dei baci* (*The Island of Kisses*).[36] Volt remains relatively discreet but he does include several scenes that could just as easily be found in some of the novels written around the same time by bestselling authors such as Guido da Verona or Liala. It is worth quoting from one of these at length to demonstrate the variety of material that Volt utilized in an effort to create a novel that could appeal to an array of different readers. At the close of the first chapter, Marinette comes in after Paolo has heard from the doctor that he would be unable to survive an intergalactic trip, with the flesh being an ultimate comfort to both:

But he loved perversely playing with her desire. His aware hands explored every sinew of her feminine body, indulging in those places where her flesh prickled under the joy of his caress. His lover's flesh expanded under his caress, like the corolla of an opening flower. Her breath came more quickly. Every so often, a sigh escaped her lips.

A caress, this one bolder than the others, caused her to throw herself against him impetuously. "Take me!" she hissed, in a commanding tone. And her hands wound themselves around his neck, as if a vise.[37]

"Desire," "caress," "sigh," here we find lexicon and sentence structure that work together to give an unobtrusive yet easily recognizable sense of eroticism to what is a novel steeped in both (pseudo) science and politics. It is noteworthy that this love scene is directly followed by an extended scientific and historical explanation of the world of 2247, continuing in many ways the prologue in quickly revealing to the reader the universe that Volt has created. This intertwining of different stories is immediately evident. Volt does not remain with a single thread for too long, as he tries to inject variety into his tale. He even recognizes during this scientific speech that some listeners may be bored: "Manifest signs of inattention began to be seen in the audience. Evidently, the speaker was boring them."[38] By blending the fantastic and the political, history and love interest, Volt attempts to convey a political message while yet retaining the attention of the reader looking to be entertained. The uniform valence found in political essays or provocative manifestos is abandoned for a more readily pleasing sense of variety.

In terms of science, Volt reveals a certain sophistication in his story, utilizing some known precepts with some fictional ones, in the service of a larger political allegory on the beneficial effects of colonization and consequent cultural advancement. Though the action of the novel takes place entirely on Earth, Volt uses several detailed passages to explain the methods through which intergalactic travel has been achieved by this time. In the early twentieth century the primary obstacle to space travel was understood to be the gravitational force exerted by the Earth.[39] This same problem is present in the novel. To solve it, Volt describes the alchemical creation of a certain foreign element, called *piombide*, which essentially replicates an element contained in a different part of the solar system.[40] As such, it is attracted by the forces of that other source, pulling it away from the Earth's gravitation and allowing for a ship to be taken along with it.[41] By finding various combinations of these types of elements, space travel has been perfected by combining these elements in the proper amounts so as to properly aim a vessel at the desired target.[42] This may well be a blend of medieval alchemy and poor science to the twenty-first century reader, but it is certainly no less far-fetched than other early science fiction works (or indeed even later science fiction).

While he evidently had some scientific concepts that he was willing to use, it must be remembered that Volt did not feel any real need to represent faithfully the affairs of our solar system. While Jupiter had not yet been discovered to be a gaseous planet (this will take place around 1930), it was known that its atmosphere, temperature, and general "state of things" was "very dissimilar to that affecting our own globe."[43] So when Volt writes that "the planet that offers the most favorable conditions for the development of our species is without a doubt Jupiter, [. . .] its temperature is not notably different than our own, [. . .] Jupiter's landscape largely resembles earthly panoramas," it is not at all in line with what was then scientifically established.[44] Beyond just Jupiter, Venus is described in the novel as housing a race much like our own, but with an atmosphere that "has strangely inebriating properties," to the point that it is bottled and its use has substituted for that of opium and morphine. Mars is also inhabited by a strange race called the "Amorfozoi," although "Mars hasn't revealed to us anything else of note at this point."[45] Indeed, Volt gives life to many of the planets heretofore explored in our solar system, a fact presented with no sense of awe or strangeness.

Space exploration provides the opportunity for the thinly veiled political allegory to arise. Just as there would be no real shock at finding inhabitants on an island in the middle of the Pacific Ocean, interstellar inhabitants are merely practical situations to be dealt with accordingly. The standard questions of colonization are raised with regard to the Lemurs, about whom "a whole branch of literature has blossomed."[46] Are they intelligent? Do they display what would be considered "civilized" behavior? Are they man or beast, do they possess souls to be converted? For Paolo, however, all of these questions are superfluous; he rather spends his time describing the most efficient way of killing the Lemurs. His motivation is quite simple: there is a need for mankind to expand for reasons of both environment and politics. The Earth is constantly changing to be less hospitable to mankind and the presence of a single world government has restricted the possibilities for human cultural development. Keeping these necessities in mind, "The existence of the Lemurs is incompatible with the diffusion of the human race on Jupiter. If we wish to colonize Jupiter, it will be necessary to methodically exterminate the Lemurs."[47] This advocation of what will be referred to again a few pages later as a "methodical extermination" is an eerie precursor of what will later come to be termed "genocide," a word that is not coined in English until 1944, and also entering into the Italian language around this time.[48]

Despite our current reactions to such language, however, there is nothing in the book to suggest that the reader should take a moral stand against Paolo, who throughout is nothing but a consummate hero, if also a bit tortured by his current personal and professional situations. His argument before the Parliament for just such a colonizing effort is framed not as a hygienic war, to use Marinetti's famous wording, but as humanity's surest safety valve, war as "the safety valve of humanity."[49] This is the exact phrase that Volt used several years earlier in the unpublished *Teoria sociologica della guerra* (*Sociological Theory of War*): "War represents the safety valve that prevents individual passions from gushing out within the breast of the collective state."[50] This argument can seem, in a political setting, to be entirely bombastic particularly when considered in light of the casualties seen during the war. But Paolo's speech, like the book as a whole, while containing some radical ideas, has its radicalism muted for a variety of reasons. First, there is nothing truly new about them, even for Volt himself.

These are ideas that have been part of the Italian cultural landscape for over a decade. Further, the form of the narration is so matter-of-fact that it removes the dynamism that could be seen with, for example, Marinetti's *Mafarka the futurist* or even Volt's own *Voltaic Arcs*. Finally, the introspective look that the reader has of Paolo, with all of his doubts, regrets, and wholly recognizable emotions, has already given the reader the impression that he is a thoughtful and admirable person. He is neither bombastic nor disturbing: and this is exactly the point, as Volt seeks to rework a political message, one that he himself had already developed even in terms of lexicon, through a different and more readily gratifying medium.

Following Paolo's speech to Parliament, the novel rapidly approaches its climax. This is achieved by running through the various viewpoints of the narration, merging public and private, political and scientific until all of these considerations are brought together in Paolo's final heroic gesture: taking a bomb into a meeting of Parliament and blowing up the ancient basilica in order to effect a political revolution that will allow for the mission to Jupiter to go forward. His reasoning in taking on a suicide mission is clear: due to his inability to lead or even participate in the colonizing project, and the political necessity and even validity of such an act (since, in this world, revolutions are always licit *post factum*),[51] he volunteers: "He among us who will be least useful to our cause in the future must sacrifice himself. And this, without a doubt, is me. My illness does not allow me to accomplish long-term suffering. But I feel perfectly capable of making a singular violent action, once and for all."[52] He seems here to be a perfect futurist hero, destroying a building and, with it, a passeist political body that both represent a failed system. That this brings with it a self-sacrifice only emphasizes the necessity and justice of such an action. Nonetheless, Paolo is not a perfect Mafarkian subject: he distinctly feels pangs of regret and sadness, particularly when considering Marinette. His decision to sacrifice himself is also linked to her well-being; he sees it as a way of releasing her, continuing a thought process that runs throughout the novel. As he kisses Marinette for what he knows to be the last time, he goes to make a futurist gesture while romanticized thoughts run through his mind:

> Paolo put into that kiss his farewell to life. Ah, life! Women's smiles, the blue of the sky! Man's turmoil, the thrill of victory, never again! Farewell to fleeting jubilation and to his long burning sadness. But life had been beautiful, notwithstanding his pain. Oh, to live yet another few years, with all of the humiliation, with all of the suffering, but to live! A year, a month, a week, content with a caress from his lady and a spot under the golden sun![53]

Paolo is resolute if saddened by his coming end. It is, however, wholly necessary and recognized as such by both Paolo and the reader. The only real twist that Volt utilizes was in some ways necessitated as well by the need to have no loose ends at the end of the story: Marinette will color the end of the novel not with a futurist sacrifice, but with a more Shakespearean one. She follows Paolo on his final mission, stalking him through the streets as he goes to the Basilica. She pushes through the crowds, hoping that Paolo will leave the bomb and escape prior to its going off, but those hopes are quickly dashed: as Paolo approaches Abramo Lattes at the center of the basilica and activates the bomb, both he and Lattes are evidently hit by bullets fired by Lattes's bodyguards. Marinette collapses on Paolo's body, where she remains when the residents of Rome "saw the cupola rise up, dance in the sky like an eggshell, and fall in a rain of wreckage behind the columns of the crumbling façade."[54] Her death is not in the service of any ideal above that of love: while Paolo was completing a mission and through that mission also resolving a personal matter, Marinette is rejecting in and of itself a life without her partner. Paolo may never have understood the depths of her commitment to him, but Volt concedes him an instant of recognition prior to his death: "Paolo's expression changed. He recognized her."[55] But the moment of realization is also the moment of destruction, liberating though it may be. Following the cupola's dance into the sky, the novel quickly concludes with a brief epilogue that mirrors the prologue. Volt again focuses on the pope, who prays with his head to the ground as the great intergalactic fleet takes off in pursuit of the "conquest of Jupiter."[56] The world has not ended, but the revolution has taken hold.

Into the Beyond, Beyond Futurism

The attraction that this book holds is centered on its story and the manner in which politics is repackaged in a literary form. At the same time, Volt's novel is certainly to be critiqued from a literary standpoint. His skills at constructing a political argument in essay form were evident in many different forums, from *Roma futurista* to the 1924 collection of essays published as part of a series examining "*I problemi del Fascismo*" ("The Issues of Fascism"), entitled "*Programma della destra fascista*" ("Program for the Fascist Right"). But the straightforward manner with which these arguments were constructed becomes a fault when applied to a more literary form. The language used in the novel is stunted, demonstrating no sense of experimentation. The general poetics are not only unremarkable but also at times even trite, and the innovative layouts that Futurism was known for are entirely lacking, even when allowing for the more generally restrictive nature of prose. As mentioned earlier, the use of the omniscient narrator removes much of the possible suspense from the novel, as the reader is informed as to rather than intrigued by the course of events. These structural and narratological issues that weigh *La fine del mondo* down are unfortunate, yet the story still stands out.

The idea of transforming the various struggles against internationalism, passeist cultural norms, and the parliamentary system, as they were being experienced in the post-war period, into a story of the world 200 years in the future was plainly a strategic because entertaining move. There was a surfeit of avenues available for the development and distribution of political ideas during this time, and Volt was active in many of them. At the same time, the audience for such a book would seem to be different than those that may pick up, a few years later, his essays on the fascist right. In wondering about the audience, it could be helpful to think as well about what is not included in *La fine del mondo*. The political side of the story focuses on the mistaken nature of internationalist arguments, specifically as they were beginning to develop not through socialist channels, but rather through Woodrow Wilson's Fourteen Points.[57] The novel leaves aside all of the economic questions that plagued Europe at this time, questions that Volt would point to as fundamental in the *Programma della destra fascista*, questions that were clearly on display during the violent upheavals that characterized the years 1919–20. In fact, Volt specifically denies the economic basis for revolution in *La fine del mondo* from the very beginning, pointing to scientific developments that allowed for the feeding of the populace despite Earth's growing inhospitality as a result of various environmental changes.[58] The people who come forward to support the Jupiter mission and Paolo's Partito Dinamico are driven not by complex economic or philosophical arguments, but rather by the emotional desire to unite against an outside enemy, the Lemurs. They heed Paolo's call to create a "national consciousness for humanity" based on the confrontation with the "other."[59] The book seeks an emotional response rather than a reasoned argument, hoping that its audience will acquiesce to this wish.

In considering the purpose of this novel, we should also note the distinction between Marinetti's famous statement on war as hygiene and Volt's formulation of war as the "safety valve" of humanity. It may seem as if there is little difference between the two, but in fact there is a vast difference, centered on the question of "for whom is war a safety valve?" Unlike Marinetti or Mussolini, who both came out of a leftist political background, Volt was consistently oriented on the right. He did not see the masses as individuals, but rather merely as members of social groups and states.[60] Without a properly administered hierarchy both within the nation and internationally, the people can only be seen as a jumbled mass of potential, to be molded in the interests of the nation. Likewise, their violent potential should be utilized within a system, be it for its preservation or for its overturning. War is not hygienic, but it is a safety valve; a safety valve that should be utilized by the hierarchical command to preserve and advance the nation.

With this said, just as any economic basis is ignored, war is not actually depicted in La fine del mondo; instead the story is about the hierarchy that is first overturned and then recreated, with the people being effective only in their willingness to follow as a group the leaders of the Partito Dinamico. There is a brief moment of violence, the climax in which St. Peter's is destroyed, but this is nothing more than an aberration. Volt is not for a continual revolution, and in fact the swift return to order that is seen in the novel is prescient, in that it will be the same return to order that he sees following the March on Rome: speaking of that seizure of power in Programma della destra fascista, he will say that "The march on Rome was not a revolution in the liberal or 1848 sense of the word. It was instead a legal revolution in the highest sense of the word. Fascism violated only that minimum of formal law that was necessary in order to reestablish the empire of natural rights."[61] That sense of legality in the novel will, of course, include an eventual extermination of another race on a far-away planet, but this extermination is protected by legal precepts. The point of blowing up the Parliament is in order to reformulate the law and act within it, as the Partito Dinamico's actions would be ratified by the world congress. Again, Volt will recycle this idea in his later justification of the actual events surrounding the illegalities of fascism. After the brief "revolution" of October 1922, "It will be within the law, rather than against the law, that other necessary reforms will be undertaken to consolidate the new regime, including a possible constitutional reform."[62]

The links between *La fine del mondo* and Volt's *Programma della destra fascista*, the earlier although unpublished *Teoria sociologica della guerra* and other works published in various journals from roughly 1917 to 1924 are quite evident when reading them all together as part of a single oeuvre, even to the point that in *Programma della destra fascista* Volt makes a remark that "the day in which we encounter the inhabitants of Mars, humanity will acquire, through the possibility of interplanetary conflict, something similar to a national consciousness."[63] Of course, the implication here is that until that day, nations must continue to cultivate a sense of antagonism here on Earth. But despite the similarities and continuities that can be found among Volt's various formats and writings, *La fine del mondo* is very much so bounded in time, in that the political shifts referenced earlier would not allow for the work to be composed during each of those eight years equally. The direct praise for the "National Futurist Party" and the Partito Dinamico, particularly Tomaso El-Barka, likely constrains the composition of the work to the time period running from the foundation of the Futurist Political Party in December of 1918 to the electoral defeat of November 1919. Marinetti's subsequent retreat from direct political involvement and Volt's disillusionment with this move as noted by Berghaus in "The Futurist Political Party" would seem to preclude such heady praise for El-Barka as is found in the novel, a man who is literally shown as a fighter, unwilling to retreat from political action.[64]

We know that at the time of its publication in 1921, Volt had turned away from Futurism as any sort of political movement and fully invested himself in the fascist cause, not only as a follower but also as a developer. Yet this change is not to be found in the text of the novel, but rather in the brief dedication found at the beginning of the work: "To Benito Mussolini, I offer this bloody vision."[65] This dedication likely functioned as a small personal *mea culpa* on Volt's part, but also as an indication to the reader that despite what is about to be read, the characters contained within are superseded by the character referred to in the dedication. Volt would continue to publish as a "futurist" after 1919, and in fact the two manifestos for which he is generally remembered, on feminine fashion and the futurist house, were both published in 1920. But politically, there was little possibility for Volt, an aristocratic elitist, to return to the fold of Marinetti's "anarchic individualism" of "Al di là del comunismo" ("Beyond Communism").[66] Instead he would follow Mussolini, working to create a properly bellicose yet conservative fascism that could be considered clean of socialist vestiges.

Simply reading Volt is not to gain a wholly new perspective on the true nature of Futurism or fascism, nor the relationship between the two groups. Nor should he be incorporated into either a futurist, fascist, or even science fiction canon merely because he had the fortune of being rediscovered in the early twenty-first century. But it would be a mistake to continue overlooking his writings, as they enhance our understanding of the actual relationship between art and politics that existed during these crucial years. He straddled the lines between two critical movements, prescient in describing quite precisely the very near future of fascism while continuing to participate in the artistic development of Futurism. He can also be seen as a safeguard against the reduction of either Futurism to Marinetti or fascism to Mussolini. He reveals the discontinuities that existed within both groups, functioning against the desire to separate Futurism and fascism as a way to rehabilitate the artistic movement as well as against the desire to combine the two in order to condemn political actions. Volt never quite fit in perfectly with either side, just as *La fine del mondo* does not fit neatly into any one category. But by studying his writings and the ways that he manipulated form while retaining content will result in a clearer picture of what went on during these years, even if that clearer picture may reveal itself to be a fractured one.

Notes

1. "I Fasci futuristi nel febbraio 1919 erano una ventina, a Roma (fra gli aderenti più significativi Balla, Carli, Volt, Giuseppe Bottai, Auro d'Alba, Gino Galli, Remo Chiti) . . . " Enrico Crispolti, *La storia e critica del futurismo* (Rome: Laterza, 1986), 202. Unless otherwise noted, all translations are my own.

2. Some of these others are even well known, such as the stories by Emilio Salgari that come out at the beginning of the twentieth century. Translations of foreign works were also becoming common during these same years with authors such as H. G. Wells and Jules Verne. But these were still very specialized examples that were not yet codified in any meaningful way. For a thorough and concise examination of the early history of the genre in Italy, see Gianfranco de Turris, *Le aeronavi dei Savoia* (Milan: Editrice Nord, 2001), iii–xxiii. For specific aspects of Volt's novel that differ from other early science fiction works, see De Turris's introduction to Volt, *La fine del mondo* (Florence: Vallecchi, 2003), 11–12.

3. The most thorough and informative look at this relationship is provided by Günter Berghaus, *Futurism and Politics* (Providence: Berghahn Books, 1996), a work that will be referred to often during this discussion.

4. See particularly De Turris's introduction in Volt, *La fine del mondo*, 5–21, which contains the most accurate of the available information; also see Giancarlo Scriboni,

Tra nazionalismo e futurismo: testimonianze inedite di Volt (Venice: Marsilio, 1980) and Marcello Carriero, *Volt: futurista* (Viterbo: Sette Città, 2006).

5. Carriero, *Volt futurista*, 35. This opinion was borne out as well when in 1995 the Florentine publisher S.P.E.S. reproduced a number of key futurist works in a *Dossier futurista*, in which Volt's *Archi voltaici* is the most prominent example of *parole in libertà*.

6. Volt, *Archi voltaici* (Milan: Edizioni Futuriste di Poesia, 1916), 9; 23; 55.

7. Volt, *Archi voltaici*, 23: "questo ragazzotto fa il piedino / faccio peccato a non ritirare il mio? / me ne confesserò appena ritornata in pensionato."

8. Volt, *Archi voltaici*, 52: "onanismo dello spirito"; Volt, *Archi voltaici*, 48: "TISICI e TUBERCOLITICI di tutto il mondo."

9. Filippo Tommaso Marinetti, *Critical Writings*, ed. Günter Berghaus (New York: Farrar, Straus, and Giroux, 2006), 186.

10. Marinetti, *Critical Writings*, 49–50.

11. Günter Berghaus, *The Genesis of Futurism* (Leeds: Society for Italian Studies, 1995).

12. Carrà's 1915 *Guerra pittura* is a perfect example of the merging of art and politics, using as its subtitle "*futurismo politico, dinamismo plastico.*"

13. Günter Berghaus, "The Futurist Political Party," in Sascha Bru and Gunter Martens, eds., *The Invention of Politics in the European Avant-garde* (New York: Rodopi, 2006), 153–77.

14. Emilio Gentile, *Futuristi in politica* (Rome: Laterza, 2009), 91.

15. Volt, *La fine del mondo*, 9–11.

16. Luciano de Maria, cited in Alessandro Masi, *Zig Zag: Il romanzo futurista* (Milan: Saggiatore, 1995), 6: "Esiste una narrativa futurista? Una narrativa d'avanguardia, intendo, diversificata dagli schemi romanzeschi del tempo e accomunata da requisiti indelebilmente propri."

17. Masi, *Zig Zag*, 10; 16–17.

18. Volt, *La fine del mondo*, 19.

19. Masi, *Zig Zag*, 17.

20. Modernissima also saw a brief rebirth under Gian Dàuli in the 1940s; but this did not prove to be a particularly lengthy nor noteworthy reappearance.

21. Just to cite one example, in a book that focuses directly on minor publishing houses between the two wars, Ada Gigli Marchetti and Luisa Finocchi eds., *Stampa e piccola editoria tra le due guerre* (Milan: Franco Angeli, 1997), 203, Modernissima is dated to 1920. But there are extant copies of books that show clear evidence that Modernissima was publishing in January of 1919, as is seen with the first edition of the profile of Mussolini under the series *Gli uomini del giorno*.

22. Adele Scarpari, "Le carte Gian Dauli nella Biblioteca Civica Bertoliana di Vicenza," *La fabbrica del libro. Bollettino di storia dell'editoria in Italia*, VIII (2002), n. 2, 51–54. Accessed September 14, 2009, online at www.fondazionemondadori.it/cms/file_download/475: "ottimi romanzi italiani e stranieri, i quali non sono le solite

narrazioni che hanno ormai tediato il pubblico, ma rappresentino invece realizzazioni artistiche singolari e vitali, espressioni di una parola nuova, vere e proprie opere d'arte" (51).

23. As De Turris notes in his introduction, *La fine del mondo* also carried an indication that there would be two more novels by Volt to be published by Modernissima, which in reality never appeared: *Un pazzo nel ristorante, novelle* and *Popolonia, romanzo* (10).

24. Thomas Pavel, *Fictional Worlds* (Cambridge: Harvard University Press, 1986), 16.

25. "Guai a te—tuonava il vegliardo con l'indice della mano teso verso la città dei sette colli—guai a te, o Roma! Ma che dico Roma? Guai a te, Babilonia! Poiché la profezia dei padri nostri si è avverata," Volt, *La fine del mondo*, 27.

26. Volt, *La fine del mondo*, 92, 29.

27. Marinetti, *Critical Writings*, 272.

28. In terms of studies of Volt and particularly this novel, it is interesting to note that in a recent exhibition on Volt held in his hometown of Viterbo, which was conserved as Carriero's *Volt: futurista*, there are repeated references to this character as "Paolo Forte" in the two brief pages that center on *La fine del mondo* (77); what's more, the book also refers to a "guerra galattica" that does not in any way describe accurately the action of the novel.

29. "I Lemuri"; a possible nod to Wells's *The Time Machine*, where the Time Traveller at one point refers to the subterranean Morlocks as "Lemurs." See H. G. Wells, *Four Complete Novels* (New York: Fall River Press, 1994), 44.

30. Domenico Cammarota, *Futurismo: bibliografia di 500 scrittori italiani* (Milan: Skira, 2006), 194.

31. Included in Volt, *La fine del mondo*, 171.

32. Just as Marinette does not conform to Volt's manifesto on women's fashion, nor does the city of Rome display any of the features advocated for futurist architecture in *La casa futurista*, both manifestos being written around this same time and published in 1920. On this point see also De Turris's introduction to *La fine del mondo*,14.

33. "Scoprendosele fino all'altezza del polpaccio," Volt, *La fine del mondo*, 73.

34. Carriero, *Volt: futurista*, 48.

35. In defining the work as a "popular" novel I am referring to the formulation put forward by Umberto Eco in his *Il superuomo di massa* (Milan: Bompiani, 2005), 7–26: the popular novel is not problematic in terms of its plot structure, as it will in the end provide the reader with a true catharsis.

36. Masi, *Zig Zag*, 22.

37. "Ma egli amava temporeggiare col suo desiderio, perversamente. Le sue mani conscie esploravano tutte le sinuosità del corpo femminile, indugiandosi là dove le carni più rabbrividivano sotto il piacere della carezza. La carne dell'amante si dilatava, si espandeva sotto la carezza, come la corolla di un fiore che si apra. Il suo respiro si faceva più frequente. Di tanto in tanto, un gemito sommesso usciva dalle

sue labbra. Una carezza più audace delle altre la gettò tutta contro di lui, impetuosamente.—Prends-moi!—sibilò, imperiosa. E gli avvinghiò le mani dietro il collo, come una morsa." Volt, *La fine del mondo*, 38.

38. "Segni manifesti di disattenzione cominciavano a notarsi nell'uditorio. Evidentemente, il conferenziere annoiava." Volt, *La fine del mondo*, 45.

39. Hermann Noordung, *The Problem of Space Travel*, NASA History Series, accessed October 15, 2009, www.hq.nasa.gov/office/pao/History/SP-4026/contents.html.

40. A word of Volt's own creation, without any effective translation, although it does contain the root word for the element "piombo," "lead."

41. In his introduction, De Turris notes that an antigravitational solution has some precedents in other science fiction works by authors including H. G. Wells and Anton Ettore Zuliani; Volt, *La fine del mondo*, 12.

42. Volt, *La fine del mondo*, 44–45.

43. All scientific information on Jupiter is culled from the entry "Jupiter" in the 1911 Encyclopedia Brittanica, accessed October 27, 2009, encyclopedia.jrank.org/JUN_KHA/JUPITER.html.

44. "il pianeta che offre condizioni di vita più favorevoli allo sviluppo della nostra specie è senza dubbio il pianeta Giove [. . .] la sua temperatura non differisce notevolmente dalla nostra [. . .] Il paessaggio di Giove riproduce in grande i panorami terrestri." Volt, *La fine del mondo*, 44.

45. Volt, *La fine del mondo*, 46, 47.

46. Volt, *La fine del mondo*, 48.

47. "L'esistenza dei Lemuri è incompatibile con la diffusione della specie umana sul pianeta Giove. Se vogliamo colonizzare Giove ci occorre sterminare metodicamente la razza dei Lemuri." Volt, *La fine del mondo*, 55.

48. Volt, *La fine del mondo*, 57. From the Oxford English Dictionary: "1944 R. Lemkin, *Axis Rule in Occupied Europe*, ix. 79. By 'genocide' we mean the destruction of a nation or of an ethnic group."

49. ". . . la valvola di sicurezza dell'umanità." Volt, *La fine del mondo*, 96.

50. "La guerra rappresenta come la valvola di sicurezza che impedisce il prorompere delle passioni individuali nel seno della collettività statale." Volt, *La fine del mondo*, 159.

51. During the planning of the attack, the narrator is precise: "Ma poi, il Congresso non sarebbe intervenuto, se avessero fatto la rivoluzione a tempo. Non si era mai verificato che il Congresso rifiutasse di ratificare una rivoluzione, a fatti compiuti." Volt, *La fine del mondo*, 124.

52. "Si deve sacrificare colui di noi che potrà essere meno utile alla nostra causa per l'avvenire. E questi sono senza dubbio io. La mia malattia non mi consente di compiere un travaglio continuato. Ma mi sento perfettamente in grado di fare, una volta per tutte, uno sforzo violento." Volt, *La fine del mondo*, 124–25.

53. "Paolo dava in quel bacio il suo addio alla vita. Oh vita! sorriso di donne, azzurro di cieli! tumulto di uomini, ebbrezza di vittorie, non più! Addio alle brevi esultanze ed al suo lungo cocente dolore. Ma era pur bella la vita, malgrado il suo dolore.

Oh, vivere ancora qualche anno, a costo di tutte le umiliazioni, di tutte le sofferenze, ma vivere! Un anno solo, un mese, una settimana, contentandosi di una carezza della sua donna e di un posticino sotto il sole d'oro!" Volt, *La fine del mondo*, 128.

54. ". . . videro il «cupolone» sollevarsi, balzare nel cielo, come un guscio d'uovo, e ricadere in pioggia di rottami dietro le colonne dell'alta facciata crollante." Volt, *La fine del mondo*, 133.

55. "Il volto di Paolo si trasfigurò. L'aveva riconosciuta." Volt, *La fine del mondo*, 132.

56. Volt, *La fine del mondo*, 138.

57. Volt, *La fine del mondo*, 92.

58. Volt, *La fine del mondo*, 30.

59. Volt, *La fine del mondo*, 93.

60. Volt, *Programma della destra fascista* (Florence: Soc. An. Editrice "La Voce," 1924), 128.

61. Volt, *Programma della destra fascista*, 144 (italics in original): "La marcia su Roma non fu una rivoluzione nel senso liberale e quarantottesco della parola. Fu invece una rivoluzione *legalitaria* nel senso più alto della parola. Il fascismo violò solo quel *minimum* di diritto formale che era necessario violare per ristabilire l'impero del diritto naturale."

62. Volt, *Programma della destra fascista*, 144: "Nella legge e non contro la legge saranno compiute tutte le altre riforme che si mostreranno necessarie al consolidamento del nuovo regime, compresa una possibile riforma costituzionale."

63. Volt, *Programma della destra fascista*, 58: "il giorno che noi venissimo a contatto con gli abitanti di Marte, l'umanità acquisterebbe, con l'eventualità di un conflitto interplanetario, qualcosa di simile a una coscienza nazionale."

64. Berghaus, "The Futurist Political Party," 176; Volt, *La fine del mondo*, 63; 101.

65. Volt, *La fine del mondo*, 27: "A Benito Mussolini offro questa visione sanguigna."

66. Marinetti, *Critical Writings*, 339.

CHAPTER TWELVE

~

Auto-Commentary in Ardengo Soffici's *BÏF§ZF+18*
Simultaneità e chimismi lirici

Dirk Vanden Berghe

Ardengo Soffici's major artistic-literary productivity is situated between his return in 1907 from a long stay in Paris and the end of World War I.[1] During his Parisian years, Soffici witnessed the crisis of the symbolist cultural expressions. Like many other artists settled in the French capital and with whom he became acquainted—Picasso and Apollinaire, to name but two—he was aware that an aesthetic, figurative and literary canon was being destroyed: by then reality demanded to be expressed in its concreteness, and at the same time in its confused and vital force. Soffici's imagination was dominated by a substantial realism that was incompatible with the idealism so typical of symbolist art.

His return to Tuscany signalled the author's rapprochement to the idea of natural concreteness (in subsequent years he would indicate it as "italianità,") and the consequent refusal of any idealistic component of symbolism. As an active collaborator to Prezzolini's *La Voce* from 1908 onward with remarkable essays on the recent developments in French art, Soffici embraced the trend towards autobiography, typical for so many writers in the circle around Prezzolini's journal. This is particularly clear in his project for a work entitled *Vita*, of which only the pages relating to the years 1879–1896 were completed. But Soffici also acknowledged the autobiographic nature of other works produced in these years: the unfinished novel *La famiglia Turchi* (which can be dated around 1908), the short portrait *Ignoto toscano* (1909), and his second novel *Lemmonio Boreo* (1912).[2]

Generally speaking, we can say that in Soffici's entire literary production the works of an autobiographic nature (diaries and memoirs) largely prevail on the more imaginative ones. On works of fiction like the novel, the novella and the drama, the author took a quietly provocative position, first in his *Giornale di bordo* of 1913, and later—in the 1930s and 1950s—reasserting these opinions precedently expressed in avant-garde circles.[3] Unsurprisingly, then, Soffici soon abandoned his novelistic aspirations, leaving unfinished both *La famiglia Turchi* and *Lemmonio Boreo*. The second was initially conceived as a saga, such that the already published chapters represented only a limited part of the whole project.

Soffici's first long narrative works, however, certainly were no literary failures. In the unachieved writings of 1908, the reader is struck by the clear and attentive descriptions of reality in its different manifestations, from the most idyllic to the most abject (in the latter Soffici reaches a remarkably expressive style). This realism was not at all meant to be mimetic: it was such that the *romantic* memory of secret correspondence was to be preserved, but its principle of unity however could not be of any metaphysical order. In Soffici's view the task of the artist consists in being a guide to the mysteries of the world, in turning the perception of these mysteries into an authentic dynamic fabric of rhythms and colors. Soffici's predilection for the autobiographic genres has been dictated by the effort to get out of literature as a conscious fiction. Much more congenial to the lyrical temperament than long narratives are his ample poetical-fragmentistic production, particularly the *Giornale di bordo* from 1913, and the futurist collection *BÏF§ZF+18. Simultaneità e Chimismi lirici* from 1915.[4]

For Soffici the attempts to achieve a major literary directness through the autobiographic genre did not mean a falling back on a spontaneous style, deprived of cultural references. Recent scholarship has underlined that what traditionally is considered Soffici's *virginity*—his allegedly direct inspiration from nature—is not simply the outcome of a particular "gift" (as Renato Serra called it),[5] but rather the product of his work, or even of his choice of genre. As a better historical knowledge of his work gradually has imposed itself, it has been proved that Soffici's "gifted" natural poetical talents were to a large degree inspired by a very active literary memory. Amongst the narrative points of reference the most conspicuous are those to Alfieri, Cellini, Boccaccio and Sacchetti, besides Carlyle, Rolland and Unamuno; amongst the poetical are the major French symbolists, as well as the Parisian avantgarde of the early twentieth century (Apollinaire, Cendrars).[6] Between these, Rimbaud was the most effective catalyst for the definition of the aesthetics which would guide Soffici throughout his entire career as a man of letters.

The foundation of the periodical *Lacerba* in 1913 in collaboration with his close friend Giovanni Papini, meant for Soffici the final release from the didactical-divulgative commitments which had engaged him in Prezzolini's *La Voce*. With the new periodical, mainly dedicated to avant-garde literature, he wanted to hold on to his convictions about the absolute and intrinsic cognitive value of the artistic activity. In Prezzolini's opinion, strongly influenced by Croce's aesthetics, art was one of the different activities of the spirit, whilst for Soffici it was *the* activity of the spirit. It should be pointed out that the brief collaboration of *Lacerba* with the futurist group around Marinetti (between 1914 and 1915) ended, very significantly, because of the evident irreconcilability on two opposed aesthetical visions. Soffici, Papini and Palazzeschi considered art to be an activity of a subjective and spiritualistic nature; but Marinetti and his followers considered it of an objective and materialistic nature. For Soffici, the discriminating point in art remains the persistence of the lirical "I" as center where all the sensations aggregate, in contrast to its total abolition in favor of the objectivity of the *matter* as professed by Marinetti. Consequently, Soffici made an attempt (paradoxical but explicit) to endorse the understanding of Futurism first of all with the draft of his theoretical articles which in 1920 would constitute the *Primi principi di un'estetica futurista* (First Principles of a Futurist Aesthetics).[7]

The Auto-Commentary of
BÏF§ZF+18. Simultaneità e chimismi lirici

Between 1909 and 1921, Soffici undertook an epistolary correspondence with Benedetto Croce, which was rather intermittent and linked to a variety of occasions.[8] That correspondence would then be halted in 1921 with a number of clarifications, on the part of Soffici, relative to its own futuristic activities: it is in that context that the author wrote the annotated version of his own poetry collection published a few years before. In a letter to Soffici on March 1, 1921, Croce expressed the desire to procure documentation about the futurist avant-garde. Among the documents which the philosopher stated he wished to receive for his library were the first edition of *BÏF§ZF+18. Simultaneità e chimismi lirici* (*BÏF§ZF+18. Simultaneity and Lyrical Chemistries*).[9] Soffici did not hesitate to respond to Croce's request, and sent him the book in its folio format published in 1915, together with *Primi principi di un'estetica futurista* and a copy of the second edition of the poetry collection. In the text of this second edition (as he would have done in a not very dissimilar way in 1938), he added punctuation by hand, along with more than 60 different types of explanatory notes.[10] If we now compare

Soffici's annotated copy of 1921 with the third edition of *Simultaneità e chimismi lirici*, included in the collection of *Marsia e Apollo*, 1938, what is striking is the absolute overabundance of punctuation added seventeen years before the new edition; what stands out above all is the usage of the comma, which was far more moderate in 1938.[11]

But let us turn to the characteristics of Soffici's exegis about his own text. Given the circumstances of its composition, it should be seen as an epi-text[12] of an entirely private nature, which responds to a specific number of functions.[13] Soffici's annotations in the margins of his own text, first of all perform a "genetic" clarification: the poet informs the reader about the different occasions of the poetic compositions.[14] In this addition to the text, the author has employed an "agonistic" principle,[15] which functioned to guide readers away from receiving the texts as inconsistent, hermetic or even ungrammatical (particularly by virtue of the texts' lack of punctuation). Indeed, this was the objection that could easily have been made by a reader such as Croce, known for his critical stance in regards to contemporary literature. Soffici's intention to employ the annotated commentary in order to avoid a polemical reaction in the philosopher, is articulated in his article "Croce e il futurismo" ("Croce and Futurism") published in 1954 in the *Nuovo Corriere della Sera*:

> In this way I made Croce understand:
>
> 1) that one only needs to add punctuation to restore order to the written grammar of the various parts of the poetic discourse;
> 2) that all which could be seen as obscure and hermetic was, after all, very clear;
> 3) that each image and expression, apparently arbitrary, irreverent, bizarre, rambling, and even charlatanesque, instead had its legitimate foundation in specific references to examples, models, data (in some cases even of scholarly research and scientific thought, other than those actually observed), in documents and monuments of the most genuine and authentic classical nature.[16]

If, as Cesare Segre emphasized in a 1992 article, a commentary addended to a text serves as a "thermometer of the difficulties of communication,"[17] in this case it has not been a presumed historical or geographic distance that gauges the ensemble of glosses. This is in contrast to what usually happens in the case of classical or foreign texts, in which cases an addended commentary could bridge the considerable distance between different cultural or chronological standpoints—although for some, limited aspects, the geographic distance between the environments in which the author and the receiver of the auto-commentary operate, could have had its relevance. Rather, the cultural distance between Soffici's futurist activities and Croce's more conventional literary interests impeded Croce's immediate appreciation of the texts. To phrase it in Segre's words again, a part of Soffici's "cultural encyclopedia" was unknown to Croce, the former author embracing the acquisitions gained by the contemporary French avant-garde, together with the popular and local traditions of his native Tuscany.

Apart from the "metalinguistic" function of the auto-commentary (the textual layer meant to clarify phrases or verses) one is struck by the number of Soffici's autobiographical references. The poet posits himself, therefore, as his own "testimonial instance," and as a reputable commentator on the text's allusions to the external world.[18] About half of the notes belong to this category:[19]

> this twilight resigned in slippers (Poetry, § 1): *The poet had abandoned poetry in order to give himself to the most common and prosaic disciplines.*[20]

> La Ville t'offre still every morning / the bouquet flowered at Square de Cluny (Rainbow, vv. 33–34): *The poet lived then on the B[oulevar]d. S[ain]t-Michel by the Cluny Museum.*[21]

> these fields (*Rainbow, v. 36*): *Poggio to Caiano.*[22]

> The cod that experiments Nirvana flowers in tomatoes in blue churns (*Morning, v. 16*): *In Tuscany, dried cod fish is softened in round water churns; in this process a ripe tomato is placed above each fish.*[23]

> (My hair is sinister) (*Morning, v. 24*): *The poet who in passing sees his reflection in the mirror, later makes this remark to himself regarding his own ill-combed hair.*[24]

We can say that it is a kind of commentary totally in keeping with his 1913 poetic autobiography, *Giornale di bordo*, in which he proclaimed that the "books of the future" would be "collections of lyrical effusions, autobiographies, epistolary compilations, and volumes composed of psychological musings."[25] At the same time, Soffici's exaltation of the role of the first person pronoun "I" was a clear stand-off against Marinetti's concept of the "I" that is to say, this emphasis on the first person subject was in itself a rejection of a fundamental tenet of Marinetti's approach since the movement's founding Manifesto that called for the programmatic elimination of every sort of subjectivity in art.

However, as we have mentioned, in regards to the specific artistic decisions/choices, Soffici used the glosses, either by paraphrasing or by reformulating entirely:

> silences the spleens (*Poesia, § 2*): *Heals the tedium*[26]

> of many withdrawns before the body to the body with bitter metaphysics (ibid.): *Of all the renunciations before the fight with the hard reality of ordinary life.*[27]

that we are never dead (*Poesia*, § 3): *we have never ceased to be poets.*[28]

idol scattered of sun, musical pyrotechnics in a rut (*Apollo*, p. 85): *An allusion to the solar myth and music of Apollo.*[29]

verdure of eternity (ibid.): *The laurel.*[30]

For us premature tomorrow in league with life-genesis of a new world (ibid.): *For us, these shows argue for a new aesthetics and poetry.*[31]

A "metatextual" function of the auto-commentary[32] can be revealed, above all, in its reformulations of the considerations of futurist poetics that had already appeared in the *Primi principi di un'estetica futurista* (*First Principles of a Futurist Aesthetic*). This essay by Soffici, was posted to Croce in 1921 together with the collection *Simultaneità e chimismi lirici,* and Soffici had already recommended its reading to the philosopher.[33]

Rather instructive in this regard is the comprehensive commentary of the section *Simultaneità*. Here we find an authentic declaration of the poetics, which reconsiders the position on the same argument articulated in the *Primi principi*; for the other poems however, we could look to the 1911 essay on Arthur Rimbaud.[34] It is also significant that, while illustrating the type of "moment-drive" ("occasione-spinta") which generated the collection *Simultaneità*, the author-commentator did not renounce the call to use actual, lived experience as credible and authentic testimony:

Simultaneity
Comment about the title
The poet assumes that the phenomena of life-circumstances are not reflected in his spirit according to a logical order of succession, but whirlingly, tumultuously intersecting each other, breaking down the categories of space and time and so impressing the enthusiastic soul in a pacing of release and velocity. Generating unexpected jumbles, unexpected analogies and contrasts, stimulating fantasy with images of far-off things and with dissociated thoughts, but that the musical flow of the verb, propagating itself to infinity, will approach and link in a live, simultaneous togetherness. The experience seems to justify this poetic conception. It often happens in life that seeing a thing, and talking with someone, that thousands and thousands of images present themselves to the spirit, cross the mind, are called up from far away places and other times, prompted by a fact that is happening around us or by an observation that we make in the moment in which one looks or talks. This assumption explains the title of this part of the book, and presides over the poetic approach adopted in it.[35]

Along with the information relative to their choices of expression, the most consistent part of the glosses of the auto-commentary regards the clarifications Soffici makes about the theoretical principles that respond to "simultaneity" and "chemistries." For example:

> *Still Life*: Description of a "futurist" painting by its author entitled: "decomposition of the plans of a kerosene lamp." Trying to translate the chromatic harmony of the picture into words.[36]

> *Buffet Station*: Attempt to merge painting and poetry. Joke like that of Rabelais who built cups, bowls, jars, etc. by means of print.[37]

> *Walk*: Sensations and images suggested by the invention of urban industrialism for the countryside. The advertisements, the mechanisms that violate nature as it was understood by traditional poets, and that create a new aesthetic of the artificial.[38]

But, as we see, often the extra-textual and directly autobiographical aspects directly overlap with these expressions of the poetics. Remaining untouched are any explanations regarding the linguistic-stylistic registers, the rhetorical procedures, and of author's readings that might have informed the conception of the work (i.e. the work's intertextuality). In short, the "meta-locutionary" function, by which the author introduces his workshop to the reader, is under-represented in Soffici's commentary; in this way, the author is conforming to an approach shared by many twentieth century auto-commentaries.

Yet upon a close reading of the collection one immediately discerns Soffici's distinctly metaphorical language, marked in particular by the frequency of metaphors constructed as prepositional phrases, for example "rest of emeralds" (riposo di smeraldi), "pistil of fire" (pistillo di fuoco), "arches of gold" (portici d'oro), "commas of platinum" (virgole di platino) and "caravan of amarillo" (carovane d'amarillo) encompassed in this scope of "lyrical chemistries" (see *Lume a petrolio* and *Bicchier d'acqua*), "the bridge of fire and gems" (il ponte di fuoco e di gemme), "my blue lips of crystal" (le mie labbre azzurre di cristallo) in the "simultaneità" (*Arcobaleno* and *Specchio*).

A good deal of obsessive, coloristic underlining accompanies this construction of metaphors in Soffici's 1913–1915 verse and prose. In this respect, Arthur Rimbaud's influence on Soffici's work is apparent. In Soffici's eyes, the specific nature of Rimbaud's art would have been found in the revival of the "transfiguration and transposition of natural psychological characteristics" together with "the 'glorification of rhythm and color.'"[39] On what is in effect a Rimbaudian model—"herbages of acier" (Mystique), "dômes of

Emeraude" and "verges de rubis" (*Fleurs*), or even "de diamants diligence" (*Villes*).[40] Soffici may have coined many poetic pieces with the intention of expresssing a special "coloring that is at once material, emotional and spiritual," that, as he wrote to Giovanni Papini in 1908, was much loved by him in modern French poetry.[41] Of course, the prepositional metaphorical construction was very common in late and post-symbolist poetry, but in the meantime, Soffici had declared that his interest in French poetry from Baudelaire onwards, was fundamentally based in its chromatics.

Moreover, Soffici's anti-narrative, descriptive, and lyric writing that came about during the futurist period was inspired by strong links to visual experience;[42] this was also the case in his literary criticism. An example of this would be his 1911 essay on Rimbaud that recalled in its vocabulary, style, and approach, his thoughts on modern art.[43] The Rimbaudian intertextuality and an adherance to the contemporary French poetry tradition, in this case to Apollinaire,[44] is very evident in "Simultaneità." And so, for that part of the collection, one is tempted to think that Soffici had intended really to allude to the sources of his poetry. If the auto-commentary does not treat Soffici's textual references, it is true that for the author of *BÏF§ZF+18*; other aspects had become more highly prioritized. As we have already mentioned, the new great work was the collaboration in a new life-project, dedicated to an Italy, to be recognized and respected better than before.[45] France, considered too indifferent to Italy in the years directly after the war, was losing its appeal for Soffici, who would have been further motivated by the wish for cultural autarchy in order to produce the ideal design. The removal of any sympathy with contemporary French culture would inform a text as cynical as the 1934 *Ritratto delle cose di Francia* (Portrait of French Things).

One could certainly say that Soffici's auto-commentary was a first manifestation, even if private, of the author's subsequent return to order. Among what are perhaps less unsuccessful (but in reality anything but innovative) poetic results of this new phase, emerged a hendecasyllabic blank verse text of blatantly Leopardian-Foscolian style: l'*Elegia dell'Ambra*. If Soffici now felt entitled to intervene in such a loose way on his own prewar poems, his stance could be seen as stemming from the fact that in his eyes Futurism had been motivated by the desire to infuse an inherently Italian character to the peninsula's necessary cultural innovations. For him of great importance was the effort to rejuvenate an inherently Italian literary and artistic world by not adhering to proposals with a clearly foreign origin, as had happened many times in the past, and as had, perhaps at even greater speed, in the years that had followed the unification of Italy. To Soffici, Futurism would have ideally laid the groundwork for a new life—one connoted by the movement's cheerfulness and enthusiasm. That being said, for Soffici, at some point the avant-garde would necessarily lose its function as a producer of truly, pure art itself.[46]

It should not be forgotten that in his literary and artistic activities since 1908, Soffici's approach was aimed at developing the elements of his native Tuscany, which were to him the most authentic material for expression. In particular, he was very aware of the components of popular art and the colloquial vernacular. He highlighted, with more attention than before, the human qualities and courage of the many Italians who had been forced by the historic circumstances of the First World War to become simple soldiers. It is those very values that would be posited as the foundation for an Italy that he wished more modern, mature and conscious after the victory. In that light, the *Primi principi di un'estetica futurista* was a first step towards the actualization of a new life;[47] literature remained a mere support for the all-encompassing work: a new Italy.

It is precisely the *Principi* that predicted the end of art: in the *Tutto-arte* section the author described a vision "of the human world conceived, itself, as a work of art—which is to say of a world where art, in as much as it is an individual product, no longer has reason to exist. This is simply because expression, which is its base, has passed from pertaining only to personal works, conceived in the common acts of life; the feeling was reflected in sentiment and action: Lyricism, in one word, has become the law and harmonic rule for the existence of all."[48] And so, a vision of human life could emerge: "not as the unfolding of disordered, arbitrary, disordered actions, but rather as a *representation*—very similar to that of theater, where everyone does their part according to a principle of art—and an *aesthetics*. And every human action, not as the *natural* explanation of a vital energy, but rather as a part—*a pose*."[49]

As Soffici's major concerns after the First World War addressed a new project about Italian life and society, rather than wide-reaching literary projects, one can better understand why, in 1921, Soffici would have viewed his futurist work through a different lens, and, would have had no difficulty in neutralizing even the most anti-conformist components, regarded at that point to be functionless and obsolete.

Notes

1. Translation by Claudia M. Clemente.

2. Ardengo Soffici, *Ignoto toscano* (Florence: Seeber, 1909); Idem, *Lemmonio Boreo* (Florence: Libreria della Voce, 1912); both were republished in Ardengo Soffici,

Opere (Florence: Vallecchi, 1959), II, 1–23 and 25–320. *La famiglia Turchi* and *Vita* have been published in Dirk Vanden Berghe, *Ardengo Soffici dal romanzo al "puro lirismo"* (Florence: Olschki, 1997), II, 13–130 and 131–60.

3. Ardengo Soffici, *Giornale di bordo* (Florence: Libreria della Voce, 1915); republished in Soffici, *Opere*, IV, 1–197.

4. Ardengo Soffici, *BÏF§ZF+18. Simultaneità e Chimismi lirici* (Florence: Libreria della Voce, 1915) (enlarged edition Florence: Vallecchi, 1919); revised editions in Ardengo Soffici, *Marsia e Apollo* (Florence: Vallecchi, 1938), 35–81, and in Soffici, *Opere*, IV, 687–829.

5. Renato Serra, *Le lettere*, ed. Umberto Pirotti (Ravenna: Longo, 1989), 90.

6. For further reading about Soffici's reference authors, see Mario Richter, *La formazione francese di Ardengo Soffici* (Prato: Pentalinea, 2000); Idem, "Riflessi apollinairiani in Italia," in *Apollinaire. Il rinnovamento della scrittura poetica all'inizio del Novecento* (Bologna: Il Mulino, 1990), 331–70; Eraldo Bellini, *Studi su Ardengo Soffici* (Milan: Vita e Pensiero, 1987); Vanden Berghe, *Ardengo Soffici*.

7. Ardengo Soffici, *Primi principi di una estetica futurista* (Florence: Vallecchi, 1920); republished in vol. I of Soffici, *Opere*. A more comprehensive outline of the writer's career can be found in Dirk Vanden Berghe, "Ardengo Soffici," in Gaetana Marrone, Paolo Puppa and Luca Somigli, eds., *Encyclopedia of Italian Literary Studies* (New York: Routledge, 2007), 2, 1171–74.

8. Dirk Vanden Berghe, "Il carteggio tra Benedetto Croce e Ardengo Soffici (1909–1921)," *Bulletin de l'Institut Historique Belge de Rome/Bulletin van het Belgisch Historisch Instituut te Rome* 60 (1990): 123–60.

9. Croce had written to Soffici: "Dear Signor Soffici, I was saying to my friend Casati, who is here, that now, Futurism over, I regret not having some documents of the recent past in my library: in particular, your *Chimismi*. I saw the album, but do not own it. Casati suggested that I write about this to you, as perhaps you will be able to send me a copy. Do see if that is possible." ("Caro Sig.r Soffici, dicevo all'amico Casati, che è qui, che ora, finito il futurismo, io rimpiango di non avere nella mia biblioteca alcuni documenti di quel recente passato: e in particolare i Suoi Chimismi. Vidi quell'album, ma non lo posseggo. Il Casati mi suggerisce di scriverne a Lei, che forse potrà mandarmene una copia. Veda se la cosa è possibile.") The letter was published by Soffici himself, in Ardengo Soffici, "Croce e il futurismo," *Nuovo Corriere della Sera*, August 25, 1954; later in Soffici, *Opere*, IV, 399–403 (with a few revisions), and one can read it now in Vanden Berghe, "Il carteggio," 156. For Croce in regards to Futurism, see his: *Pensieri sull'arte dell'avvenire*, in particular "Il futurismo come cosa estranea all'arte," *La Critica* 16 (1918): 383–84.

10. The notes addended by the author are published as an integrated text in Dirk Vanden Berghe, "L'autocommento inedito di Soffici a 'Simultaneità e chimismi lirici,'" *Studi sofficiani* 5 (1999): 75–86.

11. The introduction of punctuation re-establishes an important principle of traditional syntactic organization. And the punctuation was missing altogether in *Chimismi lirici* texts; Soffici's text which neared Marinetti's suggestions the most, even if

from the point of syntactic life they did not reach the extreme outcomes suggested in the *Technical Manifesto of Futurist Literature* (in Soffici are present: adjectives, adverbs, nouns, noun pairs, verbs if not in the infinitive then often impersonal); the *Simultaneità*, which also lacked punctuation, was marked from the beginning with noun phrases and paratactic syntax. In addition, since 1938, the calli-grammatic and figurative aspects of the section *Chimismi lirici* would eventually disappear even if in the fourth edition, Soffici would recover two "figurative" components to accompany the conventional transcription of a part of the text contained (*Station Buffet* and *Typography*). As for the few linguistic variants and metrics, which do not reveal a specific corrective strategy, it is to be noted that until the 1919 edition it is possible to observe a moderate increase in the multilingual inserts, above all in the section *Simultaneità*: a fact that also corresponds to Soffici's precise poetics, for which the polyglottism was an integral part of 'simultaneity' in art (and these, in turn, arose from "influence of the 'speed' on the artistic vision," as one reads in *Primi principi di un'estetica futurista*, 730–31). For these aspects, see Mariarosa Giacon, "Simbolismo, *avant-garde* e plurilinguismo in *Simultaneità. Chimismi lirici* di Ardengo Soffici," in Lorenzo Renzi, ed., *Poetica e stile* (Padua: Liviana, 1976), 107–49.

12. The concept was evolved by Gérard Genette, *Seuils* (Paris: Éditions du Seuil, 1987), 341–70.

13. For the definition of these functions, we can draw upon categories highlighted by recent theoretical work on the praxis of 20th-century auto-commentary: Enrico Testa, "Dal nominativo al dativo. Poesia e autocommenti novecenteschi," in Monica Berisso, Simona Morando and Paolo Zublena, eds., *L'autocommento* (Alessandria: Edizioni dell'Orso, 2004), 47–58; Stefano Prandi, "Problemi dell'autocommento novecentesco," in Massimo Gezzi and Thomas Stein, eds., *L'autocommento nella poesia del Novecento: Italia e Svizzera italiana* (Pisa: Pacini, 2010), 5–24; Filippo Secchieri, "Luoghi e modi dell'autocommento," in Gezzi and Stein, eds., *L'autocommento*, 91–105. Gianfranco Folena's comments remain valid in the *Premessa* to the volume Gianfelice Peron, ed., *L'autocommento* (Padova: Esedra Editrice, 1994), 1–10.

14. Enrico Testa, "Dal nominativo al dativo. Poesia e autocommenti novecenteschi," in Gezzi and Stein, eds., *L'autocommento*, 54.

15. Testa, "Dal nominativo al dativo," 55.

16. "Davo così a divedere a Croce: 1) che bastava mettere la punteggiatura allo scritto per ristabilire l'ordine grammaticale dei membri del discorso poetico; 2) che tutto quanto potesse sembrare oscuro ed ermetico era, insomma, assai chiaro; 3) che ogni immagine ed espressione, in apparenza arbitraria, impertinente, cervellotica, sconclusionata, e magari ciarlatanesca, aveva invece il suo fondamento legittimo in certi richiami e riferimenti ad esempi, modelli, dati (in taluni casi anche di erudizione e scientifici; oltre che di realtà osservate sul vivo), in documenti e monumenti della più genuina e autentica classicità."

17. Cesare Segre, *Per una definizione del commento ai testi*, in Ottavio Besomi and Carlo Caruso, eds., *Il commento ai testi* (Basel: Birkhäuser Verlag, 1992), 4.

18. Prandi, "Problemi dell'autocomento novecentesco," 19–20.

19. For all the citations of the auto-commentary, see Vanden Berghe, "L'autocommento inedito di Soffic," 81–86. The notes are in italics.

20. ". . . questo crepuscolo rassegnato in pantofole (*Poesia*, § 1): *Il poeta aveva abbandonato la poesia per darsi a discipline più comuni e prosaiche.*"

21. "La Ville t'offre ancora ogni mattina / il bouquet fiorito dello Square de Cluny (*Arcobaleno*, vv. 33–34): *Il poeta abitava allora sul B[oulevar]d. S[ain]t.-Michel presso il Museo di Cluny.*"

22. ". . . queste campagne (*Arcobaleno*, v. 36): *Poggio a Caiano.*"

23. "Il baccalà che sperimenta il Nirvana fiorito di pomodori nelle zangole azzurre (*Mattina*, v. 16): *In Toscana si mette a rinvenire il baccalà in zangole tonde con acqua, e sopra ogni pesce un pomodoro maturo.*"

24. "(I miei capelli sono sinistri) (*Mattina*, v. 24): *Il poeta che si è mirato nello specchio passando, fa più tardi tra sé quest'osservazione sui propri capelli mal pettinati.*"

25. "Libri dell'avvenire" le "raccolte di pure effusioni liriche, autobiografie, epistolari e volumi di osservazioni psicologiche." Ardengo Soffici, *Giornale di bordo*, in Soffici, *Opere*, IV, 125.

26. ". . . tacita gli spleens (*Poesia*, § 2): *Guarisce il tedio.*"

27. ". . . di tante ritirate prima del corpo a corpo con le metafisiche acerbe (*ibid*): *Di tante rinunzie prima della lotta con la realtà dura della vita ordinaria.*"

28. ". . . che non siamo mai morti (*Poesia*, § 3): *che non abbiamo mai cessati di essere poeti.*"

29. ". . . idolo sparpagliato di sole, pirotecnica musicale in fregola (*Apollo*, p. 85): *Allusione al mito solare e musicale di Apollo.*"

30. ". . . verzure d'eternità (*ibid.*): *Il lauro.*"

31. "Per noi domani prematuro in combutta di vita genesi di un mondo nuovo (*ibid.*): *Per noi questi spettacoli sono argomento di una nuova estetica e poesia.*"

32. Prandi, "Problemi dell'autocommento novecentesco," 21.

33. Vanden Berghe, "Il carteggio," 158.

34. At the time of *Arthur Rimbaud*'s composition (1909–1910) one could not suspect Soffici of having sympathies for the avant-garde movement just created by Marinetti, while in the first poème and prose of the *Illuminations* (*Après le déluge*) he found the example of a simultaneous representation of reality. Further, as has been well noted by Edoardo Sanguineti, in many passages of the monograph *Arthur Rimbaud*, Soffici really reached to the "definition of his own ideal writing" ("definizione della propria scrittura ideale"), Edoardo Sanguineti, "Poetica e poesia di Soffici," in Idem, *Tra liberty e crepuscolarismo* (Milan: Mursia, 1961), 144.

35. "*Simultaneità*, Commento al titolo. Il poeta suppone che i fenomeni della vita circostante non si riflettono nel suo spirito secondo un ordine di successione logica, ma turbinosamente, in tumulto intersecandosi fra loro, rompendo le categorie dello spazio e del tempo e perciò impressionando l'anima entusiasta con ritmo libero e veloce. Generando accozzi imprevisti, analogie e contrasti impensati, stimolando la fantasia con immagini di cose lontane fra loro e con pensieri dissociati, ma che il flusso musicale del verbo, propagandosi all'infinito, ravvicinerà e collegherà in un in-

sieme vivo e simultaneo. L'esperienza sembra giustificare questa concezione poetica. Avviene spesso nella vita che vedendo una cosa, e parlando con qualcuno, mille idee e mille immagini si presentano allo spirito, traversando la mente, richiamate di lontano e a altre epoche, da un fatto che avviene intorno a noi o da un'osservazione che facciamo nel momento in cui si guarda o si parla. Questa supposizione spiega il titolo di quest parte del libro, e presiede alla maniera poetica adottata in essa."

36. "*Natura morta*: Descrizione di un dipinto "futurista" dell'autore intitolato: "scomposizione dei piani di un lume a petrolio." Tentativo di tradurre in parole l'armonia cromatica del quadro."

37. "*Buffet di stazione*: Tentativo di fusione di pittura e poesia. Scherzo come quelli di Rabelais che costruiva con i mezzi della tipografia tazze, coppe, anfore, ecc." Yet here should be mentioned a drawing of a coffee cup in perspective, attached to the auto-commentary to explain the calligram of *Buffet di stazione*. It is therefore a comment that is figurative, and *restorative* compared to how it appears in the text and the collection.

38. "*Passeggiata*: Sensazioni ed immagini suggerite dall'invenzione dell'industrialismo cittadino per le campagne. Le réclames, i meccanismi che violano la natura come era compresa dai poeti della tradizione, e generano una nuova estetica dell'artificiale."

39. Soffici, *Arthur Rimbaud*, in Idem, *Opere*, I, 193.

40. Jean-Arthur Rimbaud, *Illuminations*, in Idem, *Œuvres* (Paris: Mercure de France, 1898), 3, 5, 14 (in the years 1909–1910, Soffici had employed the revised edition of 1898, as one gathers from a footnote in Soffici, *Arthur Rimbaud*, 68). For a more recent reference edition, see Jean-Arthur Rimbaud, *Œuvres complètes*, ed. Antoine Adam (Paris: Gallimard, 1972), 139, 141, 136.

41. Giovanni Papini, Ardengo Soffici, *Carteggio*, I, ed. Mario Richter (Rome-Fiesole: Edizioni di Storia e Letteratura-Fondazione Primo Conti, 1991), 307–8.

42. One needs only think of *Natura morta*, a "futuristic painting of the author" as noted in the auto-commentary.

43. Relevant to this is my essay "Soffici tra critica e poesia: descrizioni pittoriche e 'immagini chiaramente colorite,'" in Marcello Ciccuto and Alexandra Zingone, eds., *Letteratura italiana del '900 e arte figurativa* (Lucca: Mauro Baroni, 1998), 211–24.

44. See Mario Richter, *La formazione francese di Ardengo Soffici* (Prato: Pentalinea, 2000); Idem, "Riflessi apollinairiani in Italia," in Idem, *Apollinaire. Il rinnovamento della scrittura poetica all'inizio del Novecento* (Bologna: Il Mulino, 1990), 331–70. Further information can be found in Vanden Berghe, *Ardengo Soffici*, I, 116–23.

45. For these aspects, also see: Mario Richter, "Il conflitto visto da Papini e da Soffici" in Idem, *Papini e Soffici. Mezzo secolo di vita italiana (1903–1957)* (Florence: Le Lettere, 2005), 129–61. Citation, translated in text: "del mondo umano concepito esso stesso come opera d'arte; che è come dire di un mondo dove l'arte, in quanto prodotto individuale, non ha più ragione di essere, unicamente perché l'espressione, che è la sua base è passata, dalle opere particolari, negli atti comuni della vita; la sensazione si è tradotta in sentimento e azione: il Lirismo, in una parola, è divenuto la legge e la regola armonica dell'esistenza di tutti."

46. Citation from the chapter "*Tutto-arte* di *Primi principi di un'estetica futurista*," in Soffici, *Opere*, I, 720 and 724.

47. Richter, "Il conflitto visto da Papini e da Soffici," 149.

48. ". . . porrò qui mo' d'intermezzo una visione del mondo umano concepito esso stesso come opera d'arte; che è come dire di un mondo dove l'arte, in quanto prodotto individuale, non ha più ragione di essere, unicamente perché l'espressione, che è la sua base, è passata, dalle opere particolari, negli atti comuni della vita; la sensazione si è tradotta in sentimento ed azione: il Lirismo, in una parola, è divenuto la legge e la regola armonica dell'esistenza di tutti." Soffici, *Opere*, I, 720.

49. Soffici, *Opere*, I, 720. Citation translated in the text: "non più come lo svolgersi di azioni disordinate, arbitrarie, incomposte, ma invece come una *rappresentazione*— molto simile a quella del teatro, dove ognuno fa la sua parte secondo un principio d'arte- un'*estetica*. E ogni azione umana, non come l'esplicazione *naturale* di una energia vitale, ma come una parte—*una posa*." And Soffici concluded: "having every civilized people absorbed bit by bit and placed in the principles of art, in act, it would have been possible to establish that men are destined to become, with time, artists each and every one; and that artistic expression, strictly spoken, was able to reveal itself in the end to be useless, and therefore stop" ("avendo ogni popolo civilizzato assorbito a poco a poco e posto in atto i principî delle arti, sarebbe stato possibile stabilire che gli uomini sono destinati a divenire, col tempo, tutti artisti; e che l'espressione artistica propriamente detta poteva rivelarsi alla fine inutile e quindi cessare").

CHAPTER THIRTEEN

~

Luciano Folgore's Self-Parody

End or Renewal of Futurism?

STEFANO MAGNI

At the outset of his career in the first decade of the twentieth century, Luciano Folgore (pseudonym for Omero Vecchi) published several collections of poems in futurist circles.[1] The avant-garde approach is already evident in the titles *Il canto dei motori* (The Song of the Engines), 1912; *Ponti sull'Oceano. Versi liberi (Lirismo sintetico) e parole in libertà* (Bridges Over the Ocean. Free verses (Synthetic Lyricism) and Words-in-Freedom), 1914; *Città veloce* (Speeding City), 1919.[2] In these titles appear futurist myths about speed, engines, and the power of words. There also appears the reference to Marinetti's words-in-freedom, the futurist technique of literary composition which involved the elimination of syntax, the abolition of adverbs, adjectives and punctuation, the infinitive and the use of the analogy to suggest an intuition or observation.[3] These titles preconceived the search for graphic heterogeneity, with a mixture of characteristics and formats that aimed, as a whole, to render the dynamism of modern life.

After this first phase, Folgore radically changed his artistic perspective and dedicated many years to revisions and parodies. In works such as *Poeti controluce. Parodie* (Backlit Poets. Parodies), 1922; *Poeti allo specchio. Parodie* (Poets in the Mirror. Parodies), 1926; *Novellieri allo specchio* (Novelists in the Mirror), 1935,[4] the author had infused his revisions with a lot of irony, and with a ludic purpose, not only many recent and contemporary Italian authors, but the futurist authors themselves. Folgore's dichotomous career raises questions about the continuity in his writing and about the connection between futurism

247

and the author's parodic phase. These questions seem especially relevant, since Folgore himself states that during the second part of their career authors should know how to caricature their first artistic phase.[5]

From Futurism to the Parodies: Folgore's Artistic Evolution

Folgore's artistic career showed a remarkable evolution, departing from a first moment in which the author adheres to Futurism, to a later moment in which he distances himself from the avant-garde in order to write parodies. Yet, if we analyze his futurist collaborations, we soon realize that from the outset these were not without a certain amount of intellectual independence. Of course, the Roman author had fervently upheld the artistic ideas of the avant-garde; indeed, Folgore had celebrated Marinetti and Futurism on several occasions, had networked in the futurist circles—dedicating his early works to them— and had actively participated in the group's social life, regularly spending time with the group's members and often taking part in the movement's debates. At a poetic level, however, while still defining itself in the wake of Marinetti's *parole in libertà*, he proposed an alternative solution, that was at once more flexible and less stylistically aggressive, a *lirismo sintetico*, a poetic approach characterized by a noun phrase—but not rigorous—and free of Marinettian excesses.

Folgore's poetry, in fact, even while choosing colors and futuristic themes, exhibits choices that are less radical than those adopted by the movement's master. An excerpt from the poem "La cellula" (The cell) contained in the collection *Canto dei motori* (Song of engines), exemplifies these characteristics. In exception to the nominal structure of the sentence, this poem contains two conjugated verbs, "they seek" and "they ascend" ("cercan" e "ascendon") while other aspects of the poem clearly display a Futurist affinity, for example, thematics, tone, and the vocabulary ("vagoni, stazioni, rapidi, aeroplani, hangars"—"wagons, stations, fast planes, hangars"):

> Tomorrow, no more *wagons*, no more *stations*
> but *rapid* and far
> in rapacious circles,
> acute *airplanes*,
> that *seek* azure ports,
> and *ascend* in rebellious flight
> to *hangars* of the stars.[6]

If these early works already denote a poetic individuality that was different from the avant-garde circle, we can also consider that work which by most critics is regarded as his last futurist work—preceding his parodic turn—*Città veloce* (1919), as connoted by an unusual versification. Hidden by an aggressive title, in fact, is a quite *crepuscolar* sensibility. Images of the city appear in all the poems of this collection, but this does not necessarily go hand in hand with the cult of modernity. Rather, here emerges an urban spirit that exhibits moments such as that of a melancholic gaze left to rest on the wooden wheels of the cars at night, as in the poem "Notte di carrozze" (Night of Carriages). This particular poem is prototypical for its wavering between futurist tones—such as "uncini di elettricità viola" ("hooks of violet electricity"), or "cavalli di fumo" ("smoke horses")—and *crepuscular* notes—expressions such as / "pioggia di mezzanotte" ("Midnight rain"), "Piazza di solitudine" ("square of solitude"), "soltanto un lampione rimane" ("only a lamppost remains")—where "inerzia mondiale" ("worldly inertia") and "on the parallel (the latitude) of worldly inertia" ("sul parallelo dell'inerzia mondiale"), assume an almost parodic worth in respect to the avant-garde myth of *velocity*. Because of this obscure and troubled spirit, Mengaldo speaks of "intimate melancholy" "malinconia intimista":[7]

> Midnight Rain
>
> an archipelago of cars for hire
> stationed in mud.
> Square of solitude
> with four hooks of violet electricity
> at center.
> Black umbrellas at the Northern corner
> struggle against the darkness with edges of transparent drops.
> Smoke horses,
> Reddish headlights that face forward
> always.
> A cab driver in slumber.
> So goes the night.
> Longitudinally.
> On the parallel of worldly inertia.[8]

This would be precisely the work that marks the turning point of Folgore's poetics and the moment of his distancing from the avant-garde. Following this, from 1922 on, the Roman author devotes himself to parody, to which critics gave little attention. He writes only imitating and devoting himself first to poetic works and then later to those in prose. Rigorous in his approach, the parodist chooses to anonymize the authors he parodies chronologically and geographically, as he only reworks the writing of modern, contemporary Italian authors. He explains, programmatically, in the preface of *Poeti controluce*:

> In this first book, save an occasional exception, justified by the need to render this collection homogeneous, I have grouped lyric poetry from 1870 to 1900. In the second volume I will publish the parodies of poets from 1900 to 1922; the work as a whole will reflect these authors as if in a convex mirror, comically, inauthentically the internal and external elements of the poetry of the New Italy.[9]

Folgore's affirmation refers to poetic works, but the same discourse is valid for the *Novellieri allo specchio* (Storytellers in the Mirror) from 1935, in which, without making it explicit, he imposes the same temporal and geographic parameters.

In these poetic texts, the mimetic process is uniform: in almost the entirety of cases, the author carries out the same operation, mimicking the style of a writer without parodying the contents of one particular text. Only in one case does Folgore actualize a textual parody, (that is to say, a textual parody, according to Genette's definition). In this case, the text in question is D'Annunzio's *La pioggia nel pineto* (The Rain in the Pinewood) that becomes in Folgore's work *La pioggia sul cappello* (The Rain on the Hat). With an eye to lowering the tone in respect to that of the original, Folgore substitutes the walk taken by two divine characters with that of a simple citizen, devastated by a storm: "but I hear on my hat / of straw / of twenty-five drachmas / the crashing drop" ("ma odo sul mio cappello / di paglia, / da venti dracme e cinquanta / la gocciola che si schianta").[10] For the rest he composes several pastiches that refer back to various characteristic hallmarks of the selected author. For example, for its brevity and for the effectiveness of the parody's comic aim, we can consider here the *L'importo sepolto* (Buried Interest), which refers in its title to Ungaretti's first collection of poems (*Porto sepolto*), but that in its actual execution does not actively rewrite any particular Ungarettian text:

> Today is Saturday
> tomorrow
> will be
> Sunday
> then, Monday;
> it's always like this
> and not from yesterday.
> I said it.

> Now
> I'm going
> to bed
> willingly,
> because
> I am tired
> of these
> big thoughts.[11]

Folgore employs the same procedure in prose. As in the other texts, in the preface to *Novellieri allo specchio* he presents the lists of the authors who will be parodied in his work: "D'Annunzio, Pirandello, Deledda, Marinetti, Panzini, Zuccoli, Gotta, Rosso di S. Secondo, Sarfatti, Moretti, Vivanti, Milanesi, Brocchi, F. M. Martini, Beltramelli, Ada Negri, Bontempelli, Da Verona." The mimetic operation is analogous and uniform: in every case he imitates the style of one particular author, without parodying the contents of an identifiable original piece, but always indicating in the title of the remade text, who is the victim. The text gives all the elements necessary to appreciate the parody; the reader already knows the hypotext (that is, the original), and is thus able to understand the parodist's subtleties:

> The ideal reader of the parody, the target reader would be one that knows the referenced work well, and comes to it seriously and with enthusiasm, reading it with gratification. An inadequate reader would not be able to understand the parodic message in its entirety as he would not have the tools with which to interpret the references of the meta-text.[12]

The parody obtains the desired result if the reader possesses sufficient knowledge of the author(s) being parodied. These are mostly chosen from the contemporary and successful authors. In the adaptation of Bontempelli, for example, Folgore refers to the story "*La donna che non vidi mai, parodia di Massimo Bontempelli*" ("*The woman I never saw*, parody of Massimo Bontempelli").[13] The title evokes the ambiances and unusual and marvelous titles by that author from Como, such as *La donna dei miei sogni* (The Woman of My Dreams), a novella from 1925, or *Il figlio di due madri* (The Son of Two Mothers), a novel from 1929; and the rewriting forms an estranging and fantastic pastiche of Bontempelli's magical realism, that is, of the poetic that creates a fantastic and surreal perception of the everyday.

The rewritten texts are ironic and irreverent, and that holds a certain importance when the targeted author is an exponent of the futurist nucleus. Among these, in fact, appears Marinetti, whom Folgore counterfeits in his

La zuffa tropicale (The Tropical Riot).[14] In this story, the Roman parodist picks up the linguistic verve, and literary and cultural mythology, of the main representative of Futurism, as well as the exotic element, that relates to the author's Egyptian childhood,[15] which is an element that shines above all in his prose.[16] In order to understand the type of operation that was carried out, we will here briefly present and analyze the text. The story recounts the complicated romantic encounter between the character "Marinetti" and a young African woman, who is described as markedly savage. The idyll is interrupted by the intervention of two men, one characterized as Maghrebi and the other as originally from the deepest Africa—of which the former is the African woman's husband. Marinetti engages in a fight with these men, metrically scanned onomapoetically to the violent sound in the purest futurist style. Here transcribed is a short extract which highlights several key words that support the hypothesis, in that they gather in them the exoticism, the myth of progress and of war[17]—introduced by the technicism of the most common caliber of Italian cannons ("pezzi da 75 rigati")—as well as by words-in-freedom poetics, enriched by the futurist movement leader's onomapoetic language:

> *The* young *mulatto woman* of the purple socks and of the *ipecac* eyes was buffed and oiled like *the internal combustion engine of a car at a race's starting line.* Her elastic flesh, on which my kisses bounce like rubber balls, smelled of that typical tropical aroma reminiscent of *camel* and early fruit of date wood. . . . I took as much air as I could in my reinforced concrete thorax and launched a quick flurry of blows accompanied by appropriate onomatopoeitic utterings. "*Papapapaaa-ciak.*" *Tumult. Surprise.* My opponents stopped. I took advantage of the opportunity to create an original pugilistic and footbalistic poem. "*Zung-Tumb;*" two formidable punches on the skull of the Negroes. "Plaff" a swift kick in the shins of Mohammed. A "cian" here, a "pak" there, a "crak" above, a "Splane" below: hail of *humorous slap* on noses, mouths, and the eyes of the enemies. "*Taratatatazin rataratatazac*": rapid machine gun rounds, accurate, calibrated. The orchestral accompaniment was astonishing the Negroes. I felt inside the bombarded lungs, mortar fire, *cannon balls from 75 caliber aperture cannons.* . . . the negroes recoil . . . Also this time *the words-in-freedom* had won. I went outside and looked at the sky. *Not even a star. If they had taken flight* old-fashionedly on the ways of the infinite enthusiastically carried-away by my *futuristic and humorous* outburst of my terrific *genius in compressed air.*[18]

Note that in the end, more than the rivalry in love, the victory of the words-in-freedom over traditionalism counts: "Also this time *the words-in-freedom* had won." Marinetti's true battle is that of the literary avant-garde versus tradition. Folgore's parody departs therefore from Marinettian themes, then goes on to treat the linguistic sounds, and ultimately arrives at its model's poetics.

The Folgorian reading of Marinetti carries a subtext not necessarily shared by other parodies in the collection, as it addresses the main representative of Futurism—a movement which Folgore himself had joined in the first phase of his career. This begs the question as to the author's position during the years of his parodies. On the one hand we know that, when in 1915 the group suffered a fracture and Papini, Soffici and Palazzeschi distanced themselves from Marinetti, Folgore, albeit diplomatically, also took his distance from Futurism's "despotic leader."[19] But whether the parody of the undisputed leader of the movement would have been due to this reason seems rather difficult to affirm, also because the futurist parodies do not end at Marinetti. In *Poeti allo specchio* Folgore imitates the same Palazzeschi and then goes on to treat other futurist authors.[20]

Beyond the personal disagreements, it seems more interesting to question the relationship that the parodist had with the avant-garde and with his past in that moment when he chooses an autonomous artistic path that lays outside the dominant artistic circles and currents. We will consider this issue by offering some reflections on poetics, beginning with the question of what value to give the term "humor" that appears in the above quoted extract, inflected in two senses and that, in interviews, Folgore associated to the idea of parody.[21] Based on this nexus, one may wonder what would be the bond that he perceives between the comic element, and the avant-garde (and it follows, consequently, between the parody and the avant-garde) to see if his second artistic phase would truly be an inversion of the first or in reality, rather a second facet.

Two Distinct Phases?

To answer this question, at first we shall investigate the notions of "comedy" and "parody" in relation to the author's personal chronology. If in 1919 Folgore published *Città veloce*, the text that, according to Mengaldo, marks his distancing from Futurism,[22] it is also true that in the same year he sent a book of fiction to press. This narrative work is *Crepapelle*, a humorous short story collection. This work is introduced by a "Futurist measurement" ("Misurazione futurista")[23] of the text by Marinetti, in which the spokesperson of Italian Futurism writes a few pages explaining how the text is exemplary of futurist literature. His essay begins with the phrase "Luciano Folgore's *Crepapelle* is a typically futurist work" ("*Crepapelle* di Luciano Folgore è un'opera tipicamente futurista"). Six points follow this statement, supported by numerous examples from the text. In this way Marinetti explains how *Crepapelle* belongs to the avant-garde, insisting that it is in fact the comic—as it appears in its various forms such as humor, and irony—that element which renders this book a futurist text, as it is capable of introducing literary innovation. Also apparent from reading these arguments is Marinetti's standpoint about the irreverent power of humor to debunk the status quo as an essential element of Futurism: he sees it as an essential tool with which to mock the tradition with irreverence. In fact, in *Crepapelle* one finds:

A strange and totally new mix of laughs and flaps of wings, of *lyricism* and humor

and then:
A very successful, fast, synthetic attempt at designing a landscape,
Ironification of the rustic landscape and city
a construction of *humor* with inappropriate materials: sadness, nostalgia and moral
   depression, disgrace, and every day tragedy
a construction of *humor* of the *absurd*, in unreality and madness
the brilliant intuition about a special way of seeing and judging human facts on
   behalf of all small animals, especially birds.[24]

The year 1919 does not mark the final divorce from Futurism. In this year, Folgore sent two printed works to press—one in verse that would mark the author's weakening ties to Futurism, and one in prose which shows the author's most ardent and convinced futurist spirit. The internal chronology of Folgore's works cannot therefore be represented as a uniform, straight path, but is rather subject to question. Additionally, a careful analysis of the other element that is key to determining Folgore's inherent change in production—the practice of rewriting, the parody—shows that in reality mimetic writing as a practice traverses Folgore's work in a transverse way, as it had already appeared earlier on in his career. Based on the analysis of these two parameters (chronology and innovation) let us consider Folgore's artistic evolution.

From 1922, Folgore enters into his comparative work with the authors; it is in 1926 in particular, in *Poeti allo specchio*, that he carries out a parody of a good number of futurist authors: Marinetti, Papini, Lucini, Gozzano, Buzzi, Govoni, Palazzeschi, and himself. Folgore treats these authors with an intentionally irreverent parody. To explain this concept, let us now look to the textual rewriting of Govoni, the author whom the parodist mocks with an endless repertoire of images and—citing Mengaldo—"formal sloppiness" ("la trasandatezza formale").[25]

Colourings of autumn. Parody of Corrado Govoni, former Futurist
No more mornings of virgin beeswax
diluted in the polenta of the sun,
with wind with a pickled scent
and violets that smell
of municipal security guards.[26]

One notes at first that Folgore refers to several everyday images typical of the parodied author, only to go on to pointedly and irreverently distort them. For example, in the textual instance cited here, the reference to the violets is likely a parodic, tonal lowering of the verses "a most acute smell of hay / a most acute smell of violets" ("un odore acutissimo di fieno / un odore acutissimo di viole") from the Romagnole poet's poem "Tre stracci ad asciugare" (Three rags to dry).[27] The effect is decisively, and even quite tackily, comical. In regards to this, critics have defined Folgore's parodies according to different values, referring to them as grand stylistic elegies, but they notice at times that his rewritings adopt quite vulgar overtones.[28]

But inherent to the act of rewriting, that is, intrinsic to the act of imitating a style or an author, in fact, was something already present in his futurist work. In the 1912 *Il Canto dei motori*, the futurist collection that came about internally to futurist circles and that was dedicated to "F. T. Marinetti, and the triumph of Futurism" ("A F.T. Marinetti e al trionfo del futurismo"),[29] many pieces are written "in homage" to several authors—and reproduce stylistic traits of the relevant authors—among whom is included Govoni and others who would be parodied in the 1920s.[30] It is therefore interesting to investigate the line between homage and parody, especially if we consider Almansi and Fink's famous definition of "the false consecrating" ("falso consacrante"),[31] according to which, parody would be the expression of admiration that celebrates style, and consecrates a text as its role model.

In 1912, in *Il Canto dei motori*, Folgore publishes "Sul fiume azzurro" (On the Yangtze River), dedicating it to Corrado Govoni. In the text, he elaborates freely on Govoni's verse:

They mourn the talc lanterns
the yellowish tears of light;
the sailing junk leads us
on the wave that glides in silence,
infinite wave of oil,
that widens toward the mouth of the sea.

> The boatmen groan
> a song of the ancient land of tea,
> and rhythm on the oar the words,
> suffocated by the heat while sailing
> hanging limply from the tree.[32]

In this case as well Folgore imitates the model to obtain a parodic note. The lines ending with "luce" and "conduce" "le lacrime giallastre della luce; / la giunca veleggiando ci conduce") unequivocally reproduce the style of rhyming poetry characteristic of Govoni. In the line "a song of the ancient land of tea" ("una canzoncina antica del paese del tè") one reads a sonorous and cultural reference to the strong rhyme of "musmè—netzkè" of the *Ventagli giapponesi*,[33] in which, as explained by Sanguineti, tea is at the center of the image.[34] In these verses written "in the manner of . . ." you may note an intrinsic irony. In particular, "la vela floscia" ("the limp sail") of the last verse seems to be a comic parody of Govoni's "vecchie vele tignose" ("mangy old sails").[35] In his 1981 definition of parody, Giovanni Sinicropi states that the switching of just one single element is sufficient to achieve parody and that, conversely, a parody based on a large number of transmutations carries, for the most part, a trivial effect.[36] Even without this result, mimesis, writing as a "leech" ("sanguisughe"),[37] seems to be a trait typical of Folgore's style. In the second phase, in *Poeti controluce* and *Poeti allo specchio*, he adds both trivializing and irreverent effect, even if we can affirm that Folgore, at base, has always found a source of inspiration in rewriting and textual imitation.

The difference between the two Folgore experiences is in the finality of the text, which is in one case, in the authorial intention, "a white parody" (using Jameson's definition)[38] and in the second case, a way to laugh at, deride, in a manner that goes beyond the parodic, to that of satire, of the selected author. The crucial point is that Folgore often choses to laugh at the same futurist authors, and in the last poem of *Poeti allo specchio*, even at himself. On the one hand, therefore, we could read this irreverent laughter as a distancing from the avant-garde, and as a parody of the styles to which he himself had subscribed. According to the author, otherwise, humor, parody (associated concepts according to Folgore), the comic cannot function within the avant-garde and the humorist—therefore, from Folgore's perspective, the parodist—like the popular poet, remains tied more than any other to tradition. The comic element would lose its irreverent value to become, a turning in on itself, in a state of Freudian narcissism.[39] In choosing to make his readers laugh, Folgore deliberately moves away from the avant-garde perspective.

The Dialogue with Futurism and the Avant-Gardes

Moving on to the parodies, Folgore's attempt is perhaps only to renew himself, as he had done with Futurism in its early stages. Novelty—the introduction of a metamorphosis in one's own career—could be read as a moment of rebirth, necessary to prevent the repetition of stale styles, according to the widely diffused idea of modernity propagated by Sartre:[40] modernity as permanent revolution. Folgore aligns himself in this way in that advanced trench mentioned by Antonio Saccone to describe, with a futurist metaphor, the need to overcome the legacy of Futurism to implement the major project of modernity.[41] Further, Folgore realized that it would be foolish to perpetuate the past. He suggests the parody *Ritratto dal di dentro* (*Portrait from Within*) that has as its main hypotext Palazzeschi's poem "Chi sono?" (Who am I?) In this poem, one of the Tuscan author's most famous, the poet wonders about his identity, without finding an answer:

> Am I a poet?
> No, of course.
> It does not write a word, strangely,
> the pen of my soul:
> "Madness."
> So therefore I am a painter?
> Not even
> . . . A musician then?
> Not even . . .
> Who am I?
> The acrobat of my soul.[42]

In *Ritratto dal di dentro*, Folgore proceeds according to an analogous structure. He proposes several possible statutes of his being, only to renounce them in the subsequent verse:

> *Portrait from Within.* Parody of Aldo Palazzeschi
> . . .
> A simpleton? Maybe!
> I would resemble a lot
> of crepuscular poets!
> A sacristan? No:
> it would touch me every morning
> having a crutch for the beguines.
> Instead I feel . . .

> A futurist? Not even:
> I would have to redo the whistle
> of the train
> and the verse of the plunger
> and it would be very funny,
> or rather, very dumb
> if I were to get myself to whistle
> myself.[43]

As we can deduce from the last two stanzas, Folgore believes it would be funny to continue to imitate, to "do the verse" of one's selves. Implicitly, this idea leads to the aim of permanent innovation, and also introduces an ironic look on the artistic extravagance of the futurist avant-garde. We find this concept supported elsewhere in the work of the Roman writer, for example in the novella "Il padrone della fortuna" (The Master of Fortune),[44] and in the collection of humorous short stories entitled *Mia cugina la luna* (My Cousin the Moon), published by Folgore in 1926. Here the author inserts himself as a character in the story. In the fictional piece, he, a writer that has been futurist, is incompetent in the whole area of the *future*, when confronted with an anonymous man who has found a formula to win the lottery, and then control the future. For this reason, the interlocutor is defined as "more futurist" than Folgore, because one does not need to sing about the engines and modernity to be competent in the actual matter of modernity. In addition to supporting this strongly self-critical thesis, the story is also quite auto-ironic, as it sheds a discrediting light on futurist literature, as an experience of beginners, "as a presumptuous boy" ("come un fanciullo presuntuoso") who has perhaps not known how to attack bourgeois society as he would have liked.[45] In the skit, the "Master of Fortune" character addresses the protagonist:

Excuse me, but do not think I make fun of Your thoughts. I was laughing at that book that rests on your knees. Reread the title "Song of the engines," *keep in mind the name "Luciano Folgore" and above all the adjective that follows it: Futurist. And afterwards reason with me.* I found it opportune to warn you/him that I had written that volume of poems fifteen years before and that I had to buy it again, used, from a bookstand at the Campo de Fiori. I wanted to remove from circulation its too laudatory dedication to a young critic who now works as a grocer. . . But let's leave this bit of genealogical definition and go back to you, a poet of an almost ridiculous ingenuousness . . . Let me explain. *You sang the motors as a presumptuous boy.* You were thrilled by the propeller / cylinder, pulley and pin only by virtue of their sound and believed to grasp the essence by means of this totally external knowledge. *Then you proclaimed yourself prophet* of your own motion *and pretended you knew how to see into the future. What did you read in the future? Zero. I'm more Futurist than you are.*[46]

Through its ironic manner, this piece predicts a boost to the renewal process that also manifests itself when, at the end of the second and last volume of parodies of poets, in the poem *Contro me stesso* (Against myself), Folgore parodies himself. Tracing back the fifty years of poetry that he has imitated, the author closes the poem with: "I was annoyed by me" ("mi sono scocciato di me"):

> *Against myself*. Parody of Luciano Folgore
>
> The terra cotta pot
> that cooked, into parody,
> fifty years of poetry.
> . . .
> *Patùnfete*
> *Cràcchete*
> *Preè*
> I was annoyed by me.[47]

The *mi sono scocciato di me* is located in an ambivalent position, as it is placed after some futurist onomatopoeia with which he seals his membership in the movement, while at the same time declaring the ephemeral creative resource that pervades him. The final couplet, a double novenary, makes an end to his previous onomatopoetic futurist phase (*Patùnfete / Cracchete / Preè*), and perhaps, on the contrary, also to the author's present role as a parodist, actually in the name of a return to Futurism. Was Folgore tired of himself in the name of a return to words-in-freedom (*Patùnfete / Cracchete / Preè*), or was he dried out by the parodies and hypothesizes a return to the futurist onomatopoeia? In reality, the verses seem to refute both past experiences. Basically, one can read this verse as a poetic manifesto dedicated to the eternal renewal that symbolically seals and perhaps rejects the two experiences he had gone through.

But what should be stressed, and what creates continuity in this line of reasoning is, once again, the need for an analysis of the term "comic." The sign of renewal, the rebirth of Folgore, occurs in fact via an auto-ironic phrase: "I was annoyed by me." The comic runs through all Folgore's work, from the futurist experience of *Crepapelle* to the parodies, and to the announcement of having overcome the same. This detail covers an important aspect, in that the interest in comic forms was born together with the twentieth century itself, and manifested on a philosophical level as well as in artistic expression. Between the nineteenth and twentieth centuries, laughter acquired significance in parallel to the crisis of rationality: modernity, at least in the Baudelairian sense of the word, was born in fact as a result of the crisis of science and traditional philosophy. As is widely known, philosophy and art are of interest to the comic. In *Jenseits von Gut und Böse. Vorspiel einer Philosophie der Zukunft* (1886), Nietzsche proposed that philosophers be classified according to their ability to laugh, adding that "real" truth must be accompanied by laughter.[48]

That the new century was born in the sign of the laugh, can be seen in the study of Bergson, *Le rire* (1900),[49] Freud's *Der Witz und seine Beziehung zum Unbewußten* (1905),[50] and, in Italy, in Pirandello's famous text on humor (1908).[51] In 1918, in *L'Esprit Nouveau et les poètes*, Apollinaire considers that laughter is a resource capable of developing occasional, unexpected poetry.[52] Laughter, in the sense of hilarity, but also in the sense of derision and satire, is among the favorite weapons of the futurists. Among the most outstanding works of avant-garde poetry, think of Palazzeschi's *E lasciatemi divertire* (And Let me Have Fun!). In his manifesto, *Il controdolore* (The Painkiller), published by *Lacerba* in 1914, the Tuscan author calls the reader "to enter in the light of laughter" ("entrare nella luce della risata")[53] as if in a state of grace. Comedy earns its place in literature as well as in theater,[54] and influences the other avant-gardes, such as dadaism and surrealism.[55]

The work, which immediately follows the poetic parodies, is profoundly involved with the avant-garde and the comic. Between 1924 and 1926 Folgore published two collections of short stories, *Nuda ma dipinta* (Nude but Painted)[56] and the aforementioned *Mia cugina la luna* (My Cousin the Moon). These works are fully avant-garde, making full use of the vanguard's streams of fantasy and surrealist humor. In fact, in these collections we witness extravagant and improbable stories, in which the element of surreal humor and the comic are bound together happily and with consistency. In the preface, Folgore also reports a theory of humor, that it would be expedient to seek the truth: "Humor is the art of turning inside out the clothing of appearance, all of a sudden, to show the lining of the truth" ("L'umorismo è l'arte di rovesciare all'improvviso l'abito della apparenza per mettere in luce la fodera della verità").[57] This definition is added to that proposed by the author in 1917 in the journal *Avanscoperta*, for the grotesque.[58] And, not coincidentally, according to Folgore, the grotesque approaches the traditional concept of humor in many respects. In addition to demonstrating that the comic is central to his artistic interest, Folgore seems to argue, in the vein of Nietzsche, that it is through the laugh and surreal, "through laughter," that we can come to the truth. The search for truth is indeed the focus of the first short story collection *Nuda ma dipinta*, in which three people already in the opening section, search for the truth in order to color it, indeed intending, therefore, to distort it:

> Three. And we all wanted to *color the truth.* . . . it was searched for from house to house, from shop to shop, from street corner to street corner, leaving behind an invisible web around the city, hoping to find at last the desired thing therein.[59]

In the author's own words, the purpose of the collection is to paint life, "that if we would not color it with love, irony, lyricism, it would be too sad to live in its gray nakedness" ("che se non la colorassimo di amore, di ironia, di lirismo sarebbe troppo triste viverla nella sua grigia nudità").[60] Life, truth, but also the artwork are sought, but also colored with humor and parodic deformation. These tools are employed in the exploration of new artistic possibilities, and a new perception of art and life.

While he devoted himself to the futurist parodies, and at the same time made a clear announcement about his distancing from the avant-garde, he put into practice an ambivalent process. In giving himself up to the act of rewriting, he inherited the avant-garde gusto for comedy, for irreverence and for renewal; in this way, he identified Futurism's ephemeral side.[61] Folgore's concept of the feeling of turning in on oneself would not therefore be a rejection of the vanguard that, intrinsically and implicitly, cannot endure and remain the same, if not by debasing itself by adapting to a more vulgar form. In changing style, in fact, the author innovates, renews and nourishes a Futurism that is self-parody, reproduced serially. The futurist predicts progress in life as well as in the arts. In this project, then, springs the fountain of modernity's riches. And it is there that the *sensibility* theorized by the futurists is situated, as discussed by Serge Milan in the essay "The 'Futurist Sensibility': An Anti-philosophy for the Age of Technology." As stated in this study, it has to do with a form of attention to modernity and cultural evolution, valid for both the futurists and for the avant-garde movements of the period, such as surrealism.[62]

Parodying Marinetti, Soffici and himself, Folgore laughs at his past and his conformity in its form of repetition. By its very nature, the only way to remain on the edge of the avant-garde is reinvention; this becomes a way to enter the European vanguard climate and the way to keep the futurist spirit alive. Here, therefore, now seen in a new light, is the sharp dichotomy between futurist experience and parody traditionally read into Folgore's work by critics.

Notes

1. Translation by Claudia M. Clemente.

2. Luciano Folgore, *Il canto dei motori* (Milan: Edizioni Futuriste di "Poesia," 1912); Idem, *Città veloce. Lirismo sintetico 1915–1918* (Rome: La Voce, 1919).

3. Filippo Tommaso Marinetti, "Distruzione della sintassi. Immaginazione senza fili. Parole in libertà," May 11, 1913, in Luciano De Maria, ed., *Marinetti e i futuristi* (Milan: Garzanti, 1994), 100–11. In 1922, Marinetti turns to the argument, proclaiming the stylistic victory of "Parole in libertà." Cit. from Marinetti, "Lo stile paro libero," 1922, in Filippo Tommaso Marinetti, *Teoria e invenzione futurista*, ed. Luciano De Maria (Milan: Mondadori, 1983), 923: "From our *words-in-freedom* is born the new synthetic Italian style, fast, simultaneous, incisive, the new style absolutely liberated from all the classical frills and trappings, capable of integrally explaining our soul of the super fast winners of Vittorio Veneto. Destruction of the period's stairways, drapes and festoons. Short sentences without verb. Punctuation employed only to evade the equivocal. Some words isolated between two periods, as, in this way they transform in environment or atmosphere." ("Dalle nostre parole in libertà nasce il nuovo stile italiano sintetico, veloce, simultaneo, incisivo, il nuovo stile liberato assolutamente da tutti i fronzoli e paludamenti classici, capace di esprimere integralmente la nostra anima di ultra-veloci vincitori di Vittorio Veneto. Distruzione del periodo a scalini, drappeggi e festoni. Frasi brevi senza verbo. La punteggiatura impiegata soltanto per evitare l'equivoco. Alcune parole isolate fra due punti perché si trasformino in ambiente o atmosfera.")

4. Folgore, *Poeti controluce* (Foligno: Campitelli, 1922); *Poeti allo specchio* (Foligno: Campitelli, 1926); *Novellieri allo specchio* (Milan: Ceschina, 1935).

5. Folgore, "S," in *Avanscoperta* 2 (25 February 1917); republished with the title "Bibita" ("Drink") in Folgore, *Crepapelle* (Rome: Ugoletti, 1919), 77. According to the author, writers prefer to avoid change, out of fear of losing their public.

6. Folgore, *La cellula*, in *Il canto dei motori*, 13. "Domani non più *vagoni*, non più *stazioni*, / ma *rapidi* e lontani / in cerchi rapaci, / gli acuti *aeroplani*, / che *cercan* porti d'azzurro, / e *ascendon* con volo ribelle / agli *hangars* delle stelle." Italics are ours.

7. Pier Vincenzo Mengaldo, *Poeti italiani del Novecento* (Milan: Mondadori, 1978), 238.

8. Folgore, *Notte di carrozze*, in Folgore, *Città Veloce. Lirismo sintetico 1915–1918* (Rome: La Voce, 1919), 28–29. "Pioggia di Mezzanotte. / Un arcipelago di vetture da nolo / staziona nel fango. / *Piazza di solitudine* / con quattro uncini di elettricità viola / nel centro. / Gli ombrelli di nero nell'angolo nord / sforzano il buio con orli di gocciole chiare. / *Cavalli di fumo.* / Fanali rossastri che guardano in avanti / sempre. / *Un vetturino in dormiveglia.* / Così la notte./ Longitudinalmente. / *Sul parallelo dell'inerzia mondiale.*"

9. Folgore, *Poeti controluce*, preface. "In questo mio primo libro, salvo qualche eccezione, giustificata del resto dalla necessità di dare un carattere omogeneo alla raccolta, ho raggruppato i lirici dal 1870 al 1900. Nel secondo volume pubblicherò

le parodie dei poeti dal 1900 al 1922 e l'opera completa sarà come uno specchio convesso in cui si rifletteranno, comicamente contraffatti, i lineamenti esterni e interni della poesia della nuova Italia." The parodied poets are in *Poeti controluce*: Carducci, Pascoli, Rapisardi, Stecchetti, Graf, Pascarella, D'annunzio, Marradi, De Bosis, Aganoor, Pompilj, Orsini, Cena Orvieto, Cesareo, Trilussa, Giorgieri-Contri, Bertacchi, Chiesa, Pastonchi, Benelli; in *Poeti allo specchio*: Marinetti, Papini, G. P. Lucini, Gozzano, Soffici, Aleramo, Da Verona, Guglielminetti, Buzzi, Térésah, Govoni, Onofri, Corazzini, Negri, Zucca, Ungaretti, F.M. Martini, Moscardelli, Palazzeschi, A. S. Novaro, Moretti, Folgore.

10. Folgore, "La pioggia sul cappello. Parodia di Gabriele D'Annunzio," in Folgore, *Poeti controluce*, 41–48.

11. Folgore, "L'importo sepolto. Parodia di Giuseppe Ungaretti," in Folgore, *Poeti allo specchio*, 79–82. "Oggi è sabato, / domani / sarà / domenica / poi, lunedì; / sempre così / e non da ieri. / L'ho detto. / Ora / me ne vado / a letto / volentieri, / perché / sono stanco / di questi / grandi pensieri."

12. Giusi Baldissone, "Il canto della distanza," in Giorgio Barberi Squarotti e.a., eds., *Lo specchio che deforma: le immagini della parodia* (Turin: Tirrena, 1998), 11. "Il lettore prediletto della parodia stessa è un lettore bersaglio, uno che conosce bene l'Opera referente e vi si è calato con serietà ed entusiasmo, ricevendone gratificazione. Il lettore inadeguato non può capire fino in fondo il messaggio parodico perché non ha gli strumenti per interpretare i rimandi del meta-testo."

13. Folgore, *Novellieri allo specchio*, 177.

14. Folgore, "*La zuffa tropicale*, parodia di F.T. Marinetti," in Idem, *Novellieri allo specchio*, 39–46.

15. Marinetti remained in Egypt until the age of seventeen.

16. Marinetti, *Mafarka le futuriste. Roman africain* (Paris: Sansot, 1909). Written in French, the novel takes place in Africa; the first chapter is called "The viol des négresses" (The Rape of Black Women), where we find images of the African woman as an object of desire, as in the Folgorian parody. The Marinettian exoticism is also present in other works. The main characters of *Gli indomabili* (The Indomitables) (Milan: Edizioni Futuriste di "Poesia," 1922) act between oasis and dunes, and even if you do not perceive precise geographical references, the context is clearly African. In this regard, in the preface of *L'alcova d'acciaio* (The Alcove of Steel), the 1921 novel that chronicles the last stages of the First World War "from the containment of the last Austrian offensive in June 1918 to the Italian counter-offensive, which in late October and early November put an end to the conflict," Marinetti, 1921 (Milan: Serra e Riva, 1985), xii. ("dal contenimento dell'ultima offensiva austriaca nel giugno 1918 alla controffensiva italiana, che tra la fine di ottobre e i primi di novembre pose fine al conflitto") Alfredo Giuliani notes that Marinetti's exotic childhood and adolescence mark more strongly than one might think all his production and, in this same novel, one can find culturally "African" influences relative to the youth of the writer (*Ibid*, ix–xvii). In addition to this, the view onto the exotic is connoted by a note of nationalism that does not escape the parodist.

17. Remember this about the strong futuristic propaganda in favor of the First World War and the warlike proclamations contained in speeches, articles, poems such as those of Papini, 1914, or Fernando Agnoletti, "Canto per Trento e Trieste, in Firenze," in *Lacerba* (1 November 1914): 297.

18. Folgore, "*La zuffa tropicale*," in Folgore, *Novellieri allo specchio*, 39–46. Italics are ours. "*La mulatta* dalle calze viola e dagli occhi di *ipecacuana* giovane era lucida e oliata come *il motore a scoppio di una automobile pronta alla corsa*. La sua carne elastica, su cui i miei baci rimbalzano simili a palle di gomma, odorava di quel caratteristico aroma tropicale che sa di *cammello* e di dattero primaticcio. . . . Trassi quanta più aria potevo nel mio torace di cemento armato e lanciai una rapida folata di schiaffi accompagnandola con adeguate onomatopee. "*Papapapaaa-ciak.*" *Tumulto. Sorpresa. Sosta dei miei avversari.* Ne approfittai per creare sulla loro carcassa una originale poesia pugilistica e calcistica. "*Zung-Tumb*"; due formidabili cazzotti sul cranio dei negri. "Plaff" una fulminea pedata negli stinchi di Mohammed. "Cian" di qua, "pak" di là, "crak" di su, "splan" di giù: gragnola di *ceffoni umoristici* su nasi, bocche, occhi nemici. "Taratatatazin rataratatazac": mitragliatrice di colpi rapidi, precisi, calibrati. L'accompagnamento orchestrale sbalordiva i negri. Mi sentivo dentro i polmoni bombarde, mortai, *pezzi da 75 rigati*. . . . I negri rincularono. . . Anche questa volta *le parole in libertà* avevano vinto. Uscii all'aperto e guardai il cielo. *Neppure una stella. Se l'erano date a gambe* passatisticamente sulle vie dell'infinito travolte dalla foga *futuristica e umoristica* del mio spaventoso *genio ad aria compressa*."

19. Gian Pietro Lucini, letter to Folgore of July 1912, cit. in Claudia Salaris, *Luciano Folgore e le avanguardie* (Florence: La Nuova Italia, 1997), 239, and Giovanni Papini, "Futurismo e Marinettismo," in *Lacerba* 3 (14 February 1915).

20. Among these there is still Marinetti. The text is entitled "*La mareggiata frenetica (Parodia di* F.T. Marinetti *futurista*)" (The frenetic storm [Parody of F. T. Marinetti Futurist]), in Folgore, *Poeti allo specchio*, 7–10. The poem, in many places, is more a parody of the character Marinetti than of his poetics: "I feel full of hailproof cannons/ of sick revolvers, of misunderstood genius / And I want to mangle the Triton's metatarsus / And palpate the great sympathy of the sirens / swaying in the boulevards of the Atlantis. / It's time for the impetus of fireworks, the orthographic leap, / I am pregnant with Futurism, I am purple in labor / for the Titanic's birth, and with the golden sword / of the sun I will do a caesarean section on my pregnant monstrous belly/ and I will give birth to 200,000 copies /of incendiary posters" ("Mi sento pieno di cannoni grandinifughi / Di rivoltelle ammalate, di genio incompreso / E ho voglia di maciullare il metatarso ai tritoni / E di tattileggiare il gran simpatico delle sirene / Scutrettoleggianti nei boulevards dell'Atlantide. / È l'ora dell'impeto pirotecnico, del balzo ortografico, / sono incinto di futurismo, ho le doglie purpuree / del parto titanico, e con la sciabola d'oro / del sole farò il taglio cesareo alla mia gravidanza / mostruosa e partorirò 200.000 copie / di manifesti incendiari").

21. U. Pacillo, "Pensieri sull'umorismo," in *Noi: rivista d'arte futurista* (December 16, 1934).

22. Mengaldo, *Poeti italiani*, 5.

23. This element helps one understand that the collaboration between the two intellectuals was still productive after the rifts of 1915.

24. The list of Marinetti's arguments is sustained by many examples with which he explains every category. "Una stranissima e assolutamente nuova miscela di risate e colpi d'ala, di *umorismo* e lirismo" and further "un riuscitissimo tentativo di paesaggismo veloce e sintetico," "un *'ironizzazione* del paesaggio e della città," "una costruzione di *umorismo* con materiali inadatti; tristezza, nostalgia, depressione morale, disgrazie, tragicità giornaliera," "una costruzione di *umorismo* nell'*assurdo*, nell'*irreale* e nella pazzia," "L'intuizione geniale del modo speciale di vedere e giudicare i fatti umani da parte di tutti i piccoli animali, specialmente degli uccelli."

25. Mengaldo, *Poeti italiani*, 5.

26. Folgore, *Poeti allo specchio*, "*Colorazioni d'autunno. Parodia di* Corrado Govoni *già futurista //* Non più mattine di cera vergine / stemperate nella polenta del sole, / col vento che sa di sott'aceti / e le viole che odorano / di guardia di pubblica sicurezza."

27. Corrado Govoni, *Tre stracci ad asciugare*, in *Armonia in grigio et in silenzio: Poema* (Florence: Francesco Lumachi, 1904).

28. Luigi Russo praised Folgore for his fine aesthetic. With the publication of *Poeti controluce*, he noted that rendering Folgore's parodies precious is their strength of critical penetration; the parodies do not stop at the level of content, but touch style, with attention to formal research (Russo, "Luciano Folgore. Poeti controluce," 1922). According to Emilio Cecchi, however, the Roman author hesitates between high and low parody, since he uses both the "popular caricature" and "vulgar" or, on the contrary, an "aristocratic and superior" register. See Emilio Cecchi [Il Tarlo], "Libri nuovi e usati," in *La tribuna* (October 1922).

29. Folgore, *Il Canto dei motori* is presented as an almost programmatic example of Futurist art. The work is dedicated to Marinetti and the last poem, "Futurismo Hurrà!," assuming, in part, the character of a program or a poster proclaiming the success of the movement.

30. This is regarding "Sul fiume azzurro" of Govoni and "Le antenne" of Palazzeschi. The entire section of *Velocità* is dedicated to F. T. Marinetti (twelve poems), in the section *Canti futuristi* the part *Canto degli hangars* is in homage to Paolo Buzzi. The poem *Alla patria* (To the fatherland), finally, is dedicated to Gian Pietro Lucini, civil poet.

31. Guido Almansi and Guido Fink, *Quasi come. Parodia come letteratura, letteratura come parodia* (Milan: Bompiani, 1976), 137–236. The definition of the two critics refers to post-war authors, read in a postmodern perspective. They believe it is difficult to separate contemporary authors whose intentions are playful from those who aim to pay homage to a model. That's why they speak of "false consecration": that is, an admiration that celebrates a certain style to consecrate it as a paradigm. Even if Almansi and Fink's definition was proposed in a very different cultural context from that in which Folgore operated, in many ways it can apply to the Roman parodist. However, there are differences between a Folgorian textual rewriting and a postmodern one, and these reside particularly in the ultimate

value of the copy. For Folgore it has to do with the text as a fundamentally comic instrument, while for postmodern writers the text is the only creative resource when faced with a creative void and the impossibility of not handling, copying, counterfeiting, or imitating the past.

32. "Piangono le lanterne di talco / le lacrime giallastre della luce; / la giunca veleggiando ci conduce / sul flutto che scivola in silenzio, / onda infinita d'olio, / verso la foce che s'allarga al mare. // I battellieri gemono / una canzona antica del paese del tè, / e ritmano sul remo le parole, / mentre la vela soffocata dall'afa / pende floscia dall'albero."

33. Govoni, "Ventagli giapponesi," in Govoni, Le fiale (Florence: Lumachi, 1903): "On a liminal sits a musmè / quilting insects onto a screen / and of a rare chalcedony: / close, between the lacquers and the netzkè, is red on the polished floor / in a yellow vase a peony" ("Sul liminare siede una musmè / trapuntando d'insetti un paravento / e d'una qualche rara calcedonia: / vicino, tra le lacche ed i netzkè, rosseggia sul polito pavimento, / in un vaso giallastro una peonia").

34. Edoardo Sanguineti, Il chierico organico. Scritture intellettuali, ed. Erminio Risso (Milan: Feltrinelli, 2000), 290: "But if we look at the exoticism of language, and objects, it will carry a lot more effect, so to speak—in the 1903 Govoni of the vials, with its Japanistic aspects and his Fans, a musmè (a musma) marries well in rhyme with the netzkè, in a Paesaggio (Landscape), and with the simple the (tea) in an Interno (Interior)" ("Ma se guardiamo all'esotismo linguistico, e cosale, farà molto più effetto, tanto per dire, il Govoni del 1903 delle fiale, con le giapponeserie dei suoi Ventagli, dove una musmè si sposa in rima con i netzkè, in un Paesaggio, e con il semplice the in un Interno").

35. Govoni, "I tetti," in Idem, Poesie elettriche (Milan: Edizioni Futuriste di "Poesia," 1911): "Mangy old sails / tanned by the sun and by intemperance / dry in a canal without exit" ("Vecchie vele tignose / conciate dal sole e dall'intemperie, / in secca in un canale senza uscita").

36. Giovanni Sinicropi, "La struttura della parodia," Strumenti critici (June 1981): 245: "[An] alteration, implemented by means of commutation of the homological correspondence between the functional elements of a text and that of a pretext on which the model is constructed, which has resulted in the subversion of the relationship of solidarity that binds the elements of the model itself." ("[Un'] alterazione, attuata mediante commutazione, della corrispondenza omologica fra gli elementi funzionali di un testo e quelli di un modello pretestuale sul quale si costruisce, che ha come risultato il sovvertimento della relazione di solidarietà che lega gli elementi del modello stesso.")

37. Justifying their idea of "false consecration" Almansi and Fink wrote: "Men of letters, of course, are noble leeches, and how they could survive without the daily ration of blood? Defending the sanctity of a text means to ensure death, sentencing it to a dusty shelf in the library. Defending plagiary means to ensure the text instead of a metempsychotic life. Culture exists because literary minds produce forgeries" (Almansi and Fink, Quasi come, viii). ("I letterati, è chiaro, sono nobili sanguisughe:

e come potrebbero sopravvivere senza la razione quotidiana di sangue? Difendere la sacralità di un testo significa assicurarne la morte, condannarlo a un polveroso scaffale di biblioteca. Difendere il plagio significa invece assicurare al testo una metempsicotica vita. La cultura esiste perché i letterati sono falsari.")

38. Fredric Jameson, "Postmodernism, or the cultural Logic of the Capitalism," *New Left Review* 146 (1984). As we already pointed out about the reference to the criticism of Almansi and Fink, the use of an expression coined in the 1990s in reference to postmodern literature is made in this article not without theoretical reflection. In particular, we hold that the definition of "white parody" helps explain the different parodic levels implemented by Folgore. The long disquisitions on the postmodern, on the other hand, have shown that this trend has picked up on literary techniques of the past. The reference to these critics can therefore develop a reflection on the closeness/distance of postmodernism in respect to Folgore, that, even if not entirely relevant, can certainly be productive.

39. Pacillo, "Pensieri sull'umorismo": "[Humor] in as much as parody, therefore that which relates to the front line of comedy [. . . cannot] have vanguard functions at least in its aims." ("[l'umorismo] in quanto parodia, quindi ciò che riguarda il primo piano comico, [. . . non può] avere almeno come scopo funzioni di avanguardia.")

40. Referring to these thinkers, we do not intend to intimate that Folgore is in the same stream.

41. Antonio Saccone, *"La trincea avanzata" e "la città dei conquistatori." Futurismo e modernità* (Naples: Liguori, 2000).

42. Aldo Palazzeschi, *Chi sono?*, in Palazzeschi, *Poesie 1904–1909* (Florence: Vallecchi, 1925). "Son forse un poeta? / No, certo. / Non scrive che una parola, ben strana, / la penna dell'anima mia: / 'follia'. / Son dunque un pittore? / Neanche / . . . Un musico allora? / Nemmeno . . . / Chi sono? / Il saltimbanco dell'anima mia."

43. Folgore, "Ritratto dal di dentro. *Parodia di* Aldo Palazzeschi," in Folgore, *Poeti allo specchio*, 93–95. "Un grullo? Magari! / Assomiglierei a tanti / poeti crepuscolari! / Un sacrestano? No: / mi toccherebbe tutte le mattine / prendere la cotta per le beghine. / Invece io mi sento . . . / Un futurista? Nemmeno: / dovrei rifare il fischio / del treno / e il verso dello stantuffo / e sarebbe molto buffo, / o per dir meglio, assai fesso / ch'io mi mettessi a fischiare / me stesso."

44. Folgore, *Mia cugina la luna* (Rome: Edizioni d'Arte Fauno, 1926), 27–32.

45. See in this regard Lawrence Rainey, ed., *Marinetti and the Italian Futurists.* Special issue of *Modernism/Modernity* 3 (September 1994): 195–220.

46. Folgore, *Mia cugina*, 29–30. Bolds are ours. "Scusi sa, ma non creda ch'io mi burli dei suoi pensieri. Ridevo di quel libro che tiene sulle ginocchia. Rilegga il titolo 'Canto dei motori,' *tenga presente il nome dell'autore 'Luciano Folgore' e soprattutto l'aggettivo che lo segue: futurista. Indi ragioni con me.* Trovai opportuno avvertirlo che quel volume di versi l'avevo scritto io quindici anni prima e che m'era toccato ricomprarmelo usato sopra una bancarella di Campo di Fiori per togliere dalla circolazione una mia dedica troppo elogiativa per un giovane critico dell'epoca che ora fa il droghiere. . . . Ma lasciamo da parte questa etichetta anagrafica e torniamo

a lei, che è un poeta di una ingenuità quasi ridicola. . . . Mi spiego. *Lei ha cantato i motori come un fanciullo presuntuoso.* Si è entusiasmato dell'elica, / del cilindro, della puleggia e del perno soltanto in virtù del loro suono ed ha creduto di afferrare l'essenza mediante questa conoscenza tutta esteriore. *Poi si è proclamato profeta di motu proprio e ha ritenuto di saper leggere nel futuro. Che cosa ha letto nell'avvenire? Zero. Io sono più futurista di lei.*"

47. Folgore, *Poeti allo specchio*, 106. "Contro me stesso. *Parodia di* Luciano Folgore // La pentola di terracotta / c'ha cucinato in parodia / cinquant'anni di poesia. / . . . / *Patùnfete / Kràcchete / Preè /* Mi sono scocciato di me."

48. Friedrich Nietzsche, *Così parlò Zarathustra*, 1885 (Bari-Rome: Laterza, 1985), 85: "And for us every truth would be false, if not accompanied by laughter."

49. Henri Bergson, *Le rire*, 1900 (Paris: Presses Universitaires de France, 1993).

50. Sigmund Freud, *Il motto di spirito e la sua relazione con l'inconscio*, 1905, in Idem, *Opere*, ed. Cesare Musatti (Turin: Bollati & Boringhieri, 1989).

51. Luigi Pirandello, *L'umorismo*, 1908 (Milan: Mondadori, 1986).

52. Guillaume Apollinaire, "L'Esprit Nouveau et les poètes," (1918), in Vol. III of *Œuvres Complètes*, ed. Michel Décaudin and Pierre Faucheux (Paris: André Balland et Jacques Lecat, 1966), 900–10. The comic is part of everyday life, as is heroism, and must find its place in poetry. In particular, see 905–06: "*Surprise is the grand, new motivation.* It is by surprise, by the important place that the new spirit distinguishes itself from all artistic and literary movements that preceded it . . . Today, even the ridiculous is pursued, we seek to seize hold of it, and it has its place in poetry, because it is part of life as well as the heroism and all that once fed the enthusiasm of poets." ("*La surprise est le grand ressort nouveau.* C'est par la surprise, par la place importante qu'il fait à la surprise que l'esprit nouveau se distingue de tous les mouvements artistiques et littéraires qui l'ont précédé . . . Aujourd'hui, le ridicule même est poursuivi, on cherche à s'en emparer et il a sa place dans la poésie, parce qu'il fait partie de la vie au même titre que l'héroïsme et tout ce qui nourrissait jadis l'enthousiasme des poètes.")

53. Palazzeschi, "Il controdolore," *Lacerba* (29 December1913).

54. Cf. the "teatro sintetico" that picks up the comic and variety theater tradition.

55. André Breton, *Anthologie de l'humour noir*, 1939 (Paris: Soc. nouvelle des éd. Pauvert, 1985).

56. Folgore, *Nuda ma dipinta* (Foligno: Campitelli, 1924).

57. Folgore, *Mia cugina la luna*, preface.

58. Folgore proposes two types of grotesque: "There are two types of the grotesque. That of ignorance and that of intelligence. The first, characteristic of the barbarian peoples, is born of the artist's imperiousness and from the coarseness of his sensitivity (primitive and infantile art). The second is a result of a transcendence, and is a product of a particular deformation regulated by refined and original temperaments (modern art caricature). Both objectively considered, they pique our curiosity, but while in the first we only look for a bit of something that makes sense, in the second we study the architecture of intelligence." ("Vi sono due specie di grottesco. Il

grottesco dell'ignoranza e il grottesco dell'intelligenza. Il primo, caratteristico dei popoli barbari, nasce dall'imperizia dell'artista e dalla rozzezza della sua sensibilità (arte negra e infantile), il secondo è il frutto di un superamento, è il prodotto di una deformazione particolare regolata da temperamenti raffinati e originali (arte caricaturale moderna). Tutti e due considerati obbiettivamente, interessano la nostra curiosità, ma mentre nel primo ricerchiamo soltanto qualche linea di sensibilità, nel secondo studiamo architetture d'intelligenza"). See Folgore, "S." Claudia Salaris uses humor to relate the grotesque to Folgore, and traces both back to the thread of Italian magic and the notion of the *meraviglioso*. This deals with a sur-real, rather than "the surreal" as developed in Italy. Salaris inserts Folgore's parodies into this tradition. See Salaris, *Luciano Folgore*, 75.

59. Folgore, "Tre a colorare la verità," in *Nuda ma dipinta*, 13–18. Italics are ours. "Tre. E tutti volevamo *colorare la verità*. [. . .] si cercava da casa a casa, da bottega a bottega, da cantonata a cantonata e si lasciava una ragnatela invisibile per la città, sperando di trovarci finalmente dentro la cosa desiderata."

60. Folgore, *Nuda ma dipinta*, preface.

61. Following this perspective, Elda Maria Bertelli in 1922 situates Folgore's parodies in the iconoclastic spirit of Futurism, citing as precursor the text of Enrico Cavacchioli, *Le ranocchie turchine* (Milan: Edizioni Futuriste di "Poesia," 1909), a book that scratched a light satire on several true literary authorities, such as D'Annunzio and Pascoli. Cit. in Claudia Salaris, *Luciano Folgore*, 341.

62. Serge Milan, "The 'Futurist Sensibility': An Anti-philosophy for the Age of Technology," in *Futurism and the technological Imagination*, ed. Günter Berghaus (Amsterdam; New York: Rodopi, 2009), 63–76.

CHAPTER FOURTEEN

~

Fortunato Depero's *Radio-Lyrics*

FRANCESCA BRAVI

Already in a 1916 text titled "*onomalingua*" Fortunato Depero describes the essential elements of the language that only much later, in 1934, would inspire his *Liriche radiofoniche* (*Radio-Lyrics*), the collection of poems in which Depero programmatically describes the characteristics of his radio-poetry. The word *onomalingua* refers to both the concept of onomatopoeia from which it is derived and important features of Futurism on the other. The futurists exalted the quality of the sound of a text, which was vigorously presented to theatre audiences through "dynamic declamation." It is the universal language that both the natural elements and the artificial ones use for which no translators are needed. Depero invented this form of abstract verbalization through which literature is able to speak the language of nature and technique, thereby constituting a sort of manifesto.

> The "onomalingua" is derived from onomatopoeia, from "rumorismo," from the brutality of futurist words-in-freedom. It's the language of natural forces: wind, rain, sea, river, brook, etc . . . , of the noisy artificial man-made beings: bicycles, tramcars, trains, cars and all kind of machines; it's the ensemble of all the emotions and sensations that are expressed with a more rudimentary and more effective language. Depero created and declaimed these original compositions before enthusiastic and before adverse crowds. In the monologues of clowns and comic variety actors we notice some typical hints to the "onomalingua," which will be developed in the future, and are the most

271

successful stage language, particularly with the more amusing exaggerations. With onomalingua it is possible to speak and effectively to agree with the elements of the world, with animals and with machines. Onomalingua is a poetical language of universal understanding, and no translators are needed.[1]

In its visual representation the word *onomalingua* occupies the centre of the page and it is placed oblique from down left to up right. A sort of subhead in capital letters is constituted by the words "creazione Depero—1916" and starting from the inferior part of the "g," "verbalizzazione astratta" (abstract verbalization). These words are in bold. The left part of the page is empty, while the space on the right under the title *onomalingua* contains the description of what *onomalingua* is. In this text some words are highlighted. These are the group of words referring to nature—"vento" (wind), "pioggia" (rain), "mare" (sea), "fiume" (river), "ruscello" (brook), etc.—which are written in a bigger and wider way and are separated by a special character, the interpunct. The other group of words which are particularly emphasized are the ones belonging to the world of machines ("Biciclette, tram, treni, automobili e tutte le machine," bicycles, tram, cars, and all the machines). These words are in bold and the font is higher although narrower. The two ways of modifying the font can depict graphically what they stand for: wide, natural landscapes and intricate, narrow mechanisms.

Onomalingua is the language of natural forces ("i prodotti sfolgoranti di madre natura," the blazing products of mother nature) and of the machines created by men ("prodotti artificiali di sapienti forze umane," the artificial products of learned artificial forces). It is the language through which communication between all the elements of the universe, animals and machines is possible. Nevertheless it is not to be confounded with the "parole in libertà,"[2] even if the futurist words-in-freedom play an important part in its development. They were an elaborate polemical explosion opposed to a specific existing way of doing poetry. Depero on the contrary shaped this language in a very impulsive but natural way. Carlo Belli describes his way of reciting this sound poetry. It required the whole body. Sometimes Belli did not have the strength to look at Depero while he was performing his onomalinguistic poetry because his eyes and his lips moved strangely, his mouth created very weird, onomatopoetic sounds mixed with words of logical meaning:

> I can still hear his extraordinary versatile voice while he was pronouncing Ambla no-òffa èmbla caramba/pendulous nostrils/matercòlostro . . . I did not have always the strength to look at him when he was flooding into those nursery rhymes of sounds: according to fat or dry sounds, his lips were bending to

express a violent contempt, his face cleared in an unexpected lighting, or his eyes got fierce ringing of tar.[3]

It is easy to understand that in this kind of expressiveness the sound owns a very special sort of physicality ("la grassezza o l'asciuttezza dei suoni," fat or dry sounds) and through its body it becomes word and significance. These characteristics confer to this form of expression the quality of both prose and poetry. It is therefore the perfect language for both nature and machines. The world Depero describes in his texts does not know any fracture between opposite poles, because it binds them in a single body in which the acoustic element plays the most important cohesive part.

This idea of a common language between nature and machines is at the core of the texts that were collected almost twenty years later in the *Liriche radiofoniche*. Both natural and artificial beings are sung in those texts, which at the same time represent an important step forward in the development of his idea of *onomalingua*.

The Voice of the Aerial: *La voce dell'antenna*

"Tinn tinn tinn tinn/peee peee peee peee/S. O. S. 35 nord 4.7 ovest"[4]: Here it is, the voice of the aerial (*La voce dell'antenna*), which is diffusing like a gushing fountain ("zampillando," gushing). In this way Fortunato Depero praises aerials, the devices through which radio waves are sent or received and which allowed his *Liriche radiofoniche* to be broadcast. A landscape opens to his eyes which is made of vast blooming fields building up the colorful pieces of land of imaginary tapestry, like the real ones that can be admired in the Depero house (*Casa d'arte futurista*) in Rovereto. In those landscapes the aerials stand out from the ground like mechanical and luminous pistils ("pistilli meccanici, di luce, fuggenti dalla terra").[5]

On the book-cover of the 1934 edition published by Morreale in Milan, the radio is depicted metonymically in the form of a stylized aerial. Depero designed it himself; previous sketches and drawings are evidence of it.[6] From the aerial in form of a square-edged pyramid irradiate circular sound waves. Those shapes are repeated in alternating colors (black and red) and suggest the idea of their movement towards the listener. Both the lines and the alternating colors red and black suggest, not only the idea of the movement of the soundwaves, but they also remind of the strength of metallic structures (black) and of energy (red). But red can also stand for the fire, as Depero compared aerials to matches and called them high matches of sound ("alti fiammiferi del suono"). In the final version of the cover the shape of the aerial is repeated twice: once as vertical and as horizontal form supported from the semicircular waves. This gives the impression that the aerial has really dropped off the ground and the soundwaves are lifting it up ("Dalle loro punte estreme partono le acustiche membrane delle onde di Hertz: tinn tinn tinn tinn/pee pee pee pee/ espandersi—circoli—onde—timbri . . .").[7] Depero transforms in this way sound data into visual multimedia. The aerial is personified and can thus become something more than a medium. "Io, antenna, con le mie ossa puntute, geometriche ed incrociate; piantata su di un cuscino duro di cemento armato, sono la sentinella dello spazio."[8] The aerial has a voice (*La voce dell'antenna*) and it conveys through signals images and sounds that Depero articulates in a peculiar language that moves from the idea of "abstract verbalization," which he had elaborated some years earlier. He now enriches it and pushes it to its limits.

Radio-Lyrics

Exactly in the same way as in *onomalingua* both the natural and mechanical beings are unified in the same language. The texts we find in the collection *Liriche radiofoniche* testify to the presence of these two poles. It is made up of twenty-two poems. Some of the texts are focused on nature with titles like *Pioggia, Il vento, Il gallo* (Rain, the Wind, the Rooster) and others portray the world of the city and of the machines in poems such as *La voce dell'antenna, La febbre del telegrafo, Broadway, Brindisi all'Hôtel Fifth Avenue* (The Voice of the Aerial, The Fever of the Telegraph, Broadway, Toast at the Hôtel Fifth Avenue). Thus what seems most important and peculiar is that both spheres are combined and fused in unusual references as the poem *Neve-città* (Snow-Town) shows. Nature and mechanics speak the same vibrating language, made of overwhelming, dazing sounds and fluorescent, luminous colors.

Even if in some fundamental elements this language recalls what Marinetti had produced only one year before, in 1933, with *La radia*,[9] the quality of Depero's writing instantly shows its autonomy and originality. The radio is not a theatre, a cinema or a book. In Marinetti's view those mass media did not have a good influence on works of art. In the radio, on the contrary, space and time do not exist, neither the unit of action nor characters or the public, considered as judging mass. It is obviously on the trail of this kind of re-evaluation of the radiophonic medium that Depero's literary attempt of the *Liriche radiofoniche* has to be seen. Those poems contain many different atmospheres that were meant to be sent vibrating through the radio ("trasmessi per radio, vibranti nello spazio," broadcast through the radio, vibrating in the space) and by doing so they were able to reach a lot of people.

Depero explains the title of his collection of poems *Liriche radiofoniche* in an introductory text to the first edition of 1934. He defines the texts as "radiophonic" because some of them were expressively created for transmissions on the radio and other ones for their peculiar elements that remind of this medium.

> I defined those poems as "radiophonic" because some of them were expressly created for radio-broadcast and because the others also contain the essential elements demanded by radio-broadcast.[10]

In the introduction Depero precisely lists the characteristics of his radiophonic lyrics. They do not have the characteristics we usually expect from poems in their various metrical forms, but they undoubtedly have poetical quality which is based on precise rhetorical means. They are made of easy understandable elements such as brevity, variety, contemporaneity, simultaneity, lyricism both poetic and acustic, onomatopoeia and synesthesia.

> Easily understandable elements such as:
> brevity of time
> concise variety of images
> contemporary subject
> simultaneous and playful style
> poetical lyricism fused with phonic lyricism of *rumorismo*;
> onomatopoeia: imitative and interpretative;
> nonsense language; cheering up songs and voices; surprising state of mind.
> Colorful and concise expressions broken from life, daily beating, changeable;
>   with aspects, tragedies, materials and fast relentless mechanisms.[11]

The "transmission" seems to be its most important element. It is the moment in which the energy flows, the vibration goes from the source of the human voice through the mechanics and in the end reaches the listeners and builds that magic of "simultaneità coraggiosa" ("courageous simultaneity"). Depero's *Liriche radiofoniche* must be read aloud and performed in a certain way just like their author wanted. It is a pity not to have any sort of recording of Depero broadcasting them himself.

The poems of *Liriche radiofoniche* meant to interest and delight the listeners and contrast the traditional broadcasting programs or theatrical pieces that were "ordinary" and "insignificant" to Depero.

> These radio-lyrics are interesting, they cheer up. They are more effective than the usual and useless broadcasts of known music, of the ordinary usual literary

talk and of the meaningless theatre quarrellings that are good until they stay closed in a book or framed in a theatre scene. But they are broadcast in the radio, vibrating through the space, they lose their whole meaning and every logical consistency.[12]

A very important role is played in this kind of poetry by the listener; he is involved in the poetical process, in its vibrating energy. The transmission of the vibrations does not crash into an empty and indifferent space, but is meant to reach the listeners. To Depero those poems are like the sound waves that transmit them, they have to change themselves into a vibrating, synthetic and synesthetic vision for the listeners and in the end the listener himself has to shine like a bright neon.

> The listener is not uniquely gathered in a silent and romantic living room, but he is everywhere: on the road, in a bar, on a plane, on ship decks, in a thousand different atmospheres.
> [. . .] It has to vibrate on the reality which surrounds the listener like a LU-MINOUS NEON; like an appearance, a landscape and a cosmic media vision.[13]

The *Liriche radiofoniche* are not simply onomatopoetic poems. They are generated by a voice transmitted through the aerials to a listener and they are made of words and images that have the characteristics of monochrome tonality. They show metropolitan automatons and at the same time the colorful, sunny and rough world that Depero knew from Trentino Alto-Adige where he was born and that he had discovered again by his comeback after the years in Rome, Paris and New York between 1913 and 1949. The radio is able to serve like a megaphone for those landscapes he had collected in the big cities and also for those he knew from his childhood and he is able to melt them together creating something new.

If we look at the texts on the page, they look more like prose than like poetry. But Depero chooses the word *liriche* for his texts on purpose, because he is aware of their poetical value. Furthermore, they have something in their lay-out which turns them into poetical sound. Depero was able to unify in his poetry nature and the machine by using their language and was also able to transform their sound in visual signs. His poetry always moves on the small edge where opposites meet and melt. He was a magic and original poetical tightrope walker.

An Example: *Puledro innamorato*

The general characteristics of this collection of poems have been shown, but an example[14] will certainly point out better the peculiar qualities of the poetic-radiophonic language of Depero's texts. In *Puledro innamorato* the listener experiences the crazy and quivering running of a young horse. The scene with which everything begins is rather static. A whinny breaks it. It is impossible not to refer to a painting by Fortunato Depero, *Nitrito in velocità* (Speedy whinny) of 1922.[15] In this painting Depero is able to recreate the rapidity of the movement of a running horse through the visual regularity given by repetition of geometrical forms of its outline and the use of different shadows of grey. The horse is in the middle of the painting but at the same time the observer has the impression that the horse is moving out of it. Another visual detail near the muzzle is very important, because it generates the whinnying. As a result the observer does not only see a fast running horse, but he hears its whinnying. This painting is very interesting if put in relation to the poem *Puledro innamorato* at least partially. The poem is of course more complex and articulated.

At first Depero describes the scene of a farmyard by pointing his attention on different details listed one after the other and separated from commas. Those details connect to different senses: the hearing is dominant at first and later in the poem, for example in the description of the sound made by the water or by the hens. The sight is also important in the description of the dizziness of the air or the red tongue of a cat and its tail of a peculiar black shining blue. The sense of smell is also represented sometimes in a synesthetic and metaphorical relation to the other senses, for example the smell of the heat or the stink of the fertilizer. The farmyard seems to be a really peaceful place and Depero portrays it in the heat of a summer day, gurgling water and chatting hens are to be heard, a cat licks his tail.

> Farmyard:
> gurgling water, chatter, dust of gold in the air, scent of heat, stink of fertilizer, gossip of hens and red tongue of a cat that is leaking and polishing its black tail sprinkled with celestial down.[16]

A foal brakes into this scene: it wants to go out and run. From this point on the scene is dominated by the strength and the impatient desire of the animal. The animal needs some more oats before this can happen. He perfectly knows what he wants—"Voglio lanciarmi per la verde immensità della prateria" (I want to ride at full sleep in the green immensity of the prairie); "Voglio scappare dalla pelle" (I want to escape from my skin).[17] The horse explodes in its crazy galloping. Its movement has a clear destination. The young horse wants to reach a young mare. It wants to run after her and love her: "Adhering my nostrils to her straight neck. Plunging my smoking muzzle in her black mane of blood willows in the wind."[18] The horse is then exhausted from the galloping and from the ecstasy of love and looks for a place where it can have a rest. It lays down and dreams ("At last I lay down exhausted, I fall asleep and dream. . . .").[19] The five dots used by Depero mark the edge between real world and dream. In the dream the horse continues its ride but the landscape does not consist in grass, water and ground. The horse is riding from cloud to cloud on mobile carpets, grass of silk and it meets colorful mares ("On mobile carpets, through grass of silk, through gentle bruches woods, through transparent mares with curls of light and loving whynnings").[20] A breeze awakens him from his dream and he comes back to the real world where everything seems to go on almost unspectacularly.

The scene is described almost only by the sounds that are heard. The words are listed and separated this time by a long dash. This sequence presents voices, slamming doors, a hammer, a rooster, chains and the water of the fountain ("Raw, rumbling: the doors slam—the hammer beats—the rooster shouts—the chain screeches—the bolt squeaks—the boy howls [. . .] The fountain boringly gurgles and rustles").[21] This moment of apparent peace is suddenly broken just like it happened before. The foal starts its run again and gallops to the place where the dreamed mare is waiting. The wild movement of the horse is accompanied throughout the poem by the onomatopoetic sound of its whinnying and by a sensation of immense joy ("birri-birri cirrrrri/birri-birri cirrrrri," "birri birri birri/come sono felice!," "birri birri birri/e via di corsa," "birri birri birri/che spasimo, che felicità"). Those lines are also printed in bold and they become through this graphic quality louder in their acoustic one.

I will try to emphasize below some of the most important poetical elements of this text. These show the peculiar characteristics of the radiophonic writing of Fortunato Depero.

The very rich acoustic component is created through: direct ("birri-birri cirri") and indirect onomatopoeia ("Squicchera e squaccola la fontana") and also through anaphora ("Desidero allargare . . . ," "Desidero aprire . . . ," "Desidero mostrare . . . ," "Mi accarezza. Mi parla. Mi liscia e mi pettina").

Brevity, succinctness, simultaneity refer to the typical elements of radio-telegraphy and are made through ellipsis (of the verb "Ancora una manciata d'avena" another handful of oats) or the use of double or triple nouns or verb constructions ("erba-acqua-terra," "aprire-uscire-saltare").

The visual component can be found in the reference to colors ("Rincorrere la cavallina ora bianca, ora rosa, ora bigia, pura, ardente," chase after the mare which is now white, now pink, now grey, pure, burning). The landscape seems to be dipped into a thick mist. In the whole text there are many allusions to some sort of dust that restricts the view: "pulviscolo" (dust),

"Nuvoloni di polvere" (big clouds of dust), "di nube in nube" (from clod to cloud), "coltre di nube viaggiante" (blanket of traveling cloud).

It is also possible to find many procedures that are typical film techniques, for example the change in the perspective in scene at the beginning of *Puledro innamorato* creates a superimposition of the poetic self and the young horse. Furthermore the change from static to dynamic scene is accomplished by using nouns and the elision of verbs for the static sequences ("gorgoglio d'acqua, chiacchierio"), while verbs are the fundamental vehicle for movement ("Balzo, scatto, mi raddrizzo, fischio, cincischio, rischio e frr frr frrremo nel galoppo"). This effect is also created graphically with particular marks. Velocity is also established in the written text through punctuation marks (especially points, commas, dashes and dots) that are able to open or close the scene and to change rapidly from one sequence to the other. The acoustic quality is not only conveyed through the pauses connected with the punctuation marks or through the rhythm they create, but also using font in bold.

Finally there is what has been defined as the work's "componente fiabesco surrea" (surreal and fairy tale-like component), referring to an oneiric dimension in the texts.[22] In the poem *Puledro innamorato* the young horse is exhausted from running, it falls asleep and dreams. In the dream the golden atmosphere described at first changes then into silver and a series of landscapes follow silently one another like huge settings of gauze ("panorami silenziosi che rotolano come immensi scenari di Garza,") just like Depero did in his wonderful and unique tapestry or clothes.

In this text and in the other ones of the collection *Liriche radiofoniche* Fortunato Depero creates a marvelous mixture of reality and fantasy. Similes and analogies clearly show it. Natural elements magically transform and obtain human characteristics. All the elements of the landscape are personified and alive. They are not dead parts of a background scenery but living beings. In the same way for example a machine, a train, receives through a metaphor natural qualities and is called the big iron snake ("il gran serpente di ferro"). These are some of the rhetorical components that convey to Depero's texts their poetical character, this vibrating energy which passes through all the *Liriche radiofoniche* and is the peculiarity of radiophonic poetry: "The characteristic of radio-lyrics has to be spatial, keen, sonorous, unexpected, magical."[23]

Notes

1. "È derivata dall'onomatopea, dal rumorismo, dalla brutalità delle parole in libertà, futuriste. È il linguaggio delle forze naturali: vento, pioggia, mare, fiume, ruscello, ecc.,

degli esseri artificiali rumoreggianti creati dagli uomini: Biciclette, tram, treni, automobili e tutte le macchine. È l'assieme delle emozioni e delle sensazioni espresso con il linguaggio più rudimentale e più efficace. Depero creò e declamò queste sue originali composizioni davanti a folle entusiaste ed ostili. Nei monologhi dei clowns e dei comici di varietà vi sono tipici accenni all'onomalingua che avranno futuri sviluppi, costituendo la lingua più indovinata per la scena e specialmente per le esagerazioni esilaranti. Con l'onomalingua si può parlare ed intendersi efficacemente con gli elementi dell'universo, con gli animali e con le macchine. L'onomalingua è un linguaggio poetico di comprensione universale per il quale non sono necessari traduttori." Fortunato Depero, *Pestavo anch'io sul palcoscenico dei ribelli. Antologia degli scritti letterari* (Trento: L'Editore, 1992).

2. "Parole in libertà: intuizione di poesia pura, morte dell'impressionismo, cioè: separazione, crollo formidabile del ponte-legame fra poesia e prosa finora stupidamente confuse." (Words-in-freedom: intuition of pure poetry, death of impressionism, that is: separation, powerful collapse of the bridge between poetry and prose that were until now confused.) Guglielmo Jannelli, "Vocale-ambiente in libertà," *La Balza*, Messina, April 10, 1915.

3. "Sento ancora la sua voce straordinariamente mobile quando mi scandiva: Ambla no-òffa èmbla carèmba/narici pèndule/matercòlostro . . . Non avevo sempre la forza di guardarlo nel momento in cui irrompeva in queste filastrocche sonore: secondo l'intensità, la grassezza o l'asciuttezza dei suoni, le sue labbra si piegavano ad esprimere uno sprezzo violento, il suo volto si schiariva in un'improvvisa illuminazione, oppure i suoi occhi diventavano feroci squilli di catrame." Carlo Belli, "Memoria di Depero," in *Fortunato Depero 1892–1960* (Bassano del Grappa: Museo Civico, 1970), also on www.ulu-late.com/poesiavisuale/capitolo14.htm.

4. Fortunato Depero, *Liriche radiofoniche* (Milan: Editore Morreale, 1934), 24.

5. "Le antenne metalliche delle radio-stazioni scattano da questi tappeti vasti ed intricati, come alti pistilli meccanici, di luce, fuggenti dalla terra," Depero, *Liriche radiofoniche*, 23.

6. A sketch for the cover of the *Liriche radiofoniche*, shown at the exhibition *Futurismi*, Aosta, November 28, 2008–April 26, 2009, is available at gallery.panorama .it/gallery/100_anni_di_futurismo_in_mostra_ad_aosta/142233_fortunato_depero_ liriche_radiofoniche.html.

7. "From their extreme tops come off the acoustic membrane of the Hertz waves: tinn tinn tinn tinn/pee pee pee pee/ expanding—circles—waves—timbre. . . " Depero, *Liriche radiofoniche*, 24.

8. "It's me, the aerial, with my pointed bones, geometric and crisscross; planted in a hard pillow of reinforced concrete, I am the guard of the space." Depero, *Liriche radiofoniche*, 26.

9. "Aspettando l'invenzione del teletattilismo del teleprofumo e del telesapore noi futuristi perfezioniamo la radiofonia destinata a centuplicare il genio creatore della razza italiana abolire l'antico strazio nostalgico delle lontananze e imporre dovunque le parole in libertà come suo logico e naturale modo di esprimersi," Filippo Tommaso Marinetti, *La radia*, in *Gazzetta del Popolo*, 1933, accessed at: www.kunstradio .at/2002A/27_01_02/laradia-it.html.

10. "Ho definito queste liriche 'radiofoniche' perché alcune di esse furono create espressamente per radio-trasmissioni e perché le altre contengono pure gli elementi necessari che le radio-trasmissioni esigono." Depero, *Liriche radiofoniche*, 7–8.

11. "Elementi facilmente comprensibili quali: /Brevità di tempo. / Varietà concisa di immagini. / Soggetto contemporaneo. / Stile simultaneo e giocondo. / Lirismo poetico fuso con il lirismo fonico, sonoro e rumorista; / onomatopee: imitative e interpretative; / linguaggi inventati; canti e voci rallegranti; stati d'animo a sorpresa. / Espressioni colorate e sintetiche strappate dalla vita, quotidianamente pulsante, mutevole; con aspetti, drammi, materie e macchinismi velocemente inesorabili." Depero, *Liriche radiofoniche*, 7–8.

12. "Queste liriche radiofoniche interessano, rallegrano. Sono più efficaci delle solite ed inutili trasmissioni di musica conosciuta, delle banali chiacchiere letterarie abituali e dei bisticci insignificanti teatrali, che vanno bene finché rimangono chiuse in un libro o incorniciati su di una scena teatrale. Ma trasmessi per radio, vibranti nello spazio, perdono ogni loro significato ed ogni loro consistenza logica." Depero, *Liriche radiofoniche*, 7–8.

13. "L'ascoltatore non è più unicamente raccolto in un salotto silenzioso e romantico, ma si trova ovunque: per strada, nei caffè, in aeroplano, sui ponti di una nave, in mille atmosfere diverse. . . . Sulla realtà che circonda l'ascoltatore deve vibrare come un NEON LUMINOSO; come una apparizione, un paesaggio ed una visione cosmica medianica." Depero, *Liriche radiofoniche*, 7–8.

14. Depero, *Liriche radiofoniche*, 45–48.

15. The original painting is at the Galleria d'Arte Moderna in Genoa. Depero, *Liriche radiofoniche*, 50.

16. "Cortile: / gorgoglio d'acqua, chiacchierio, pulviscolo d'oro nell'aria, odor di caldo, tanfo di concime, pettegolezzi di galline e lingua rossa d'un gatto che si lecca e liscia la coda nerissima cosparsa di peluria celeste." Depero, *Liriche radiofoniche*, 45.

17. Depero, *Liriche radiofoniche*, 45–46.

18. "Aderire le mie narici al suo collo diritto. Tuffare il mio muso fumante nella sua criniera di salici sanguigni al vento." Depero, *Liriche radiofoniche*, 46.

19. "Infine esausto mi sdraio, mi addormento e sogno. . . ." Depero, *Liriche radio-foniche*, 47.

20. ". . . su tappeti mobili, fra erbe di seta, fra boschi di spazzole gentili, fra caval-line trasparenti con riccioli di luce e dai nitriti innamorati." Depero, *Liriche radio-foniche*, 47.

21. ". . . crude, rumoreggianti: le porte sbattono—il martello picchia—il gallo grida—la catena stride—il catenaccio cigola—il garzone ulula . . . squicchera e squac-cola la fontana noiosamente." Depero, *Liriche radiofoniche*, 48.

22. Antonio Lucio Giannone, "La poesia 'radiofonica' di Depero," in Depero, *Liriche radiofoniche*, xlviii–lv.

23. ". . . il carattere della lirica radiofonica deve essere spaziale, volitivo, sonoro, inaspettato, magico." Depero, *Liriche radiofoniche*, 8.

~

CHAPTER FIFTEEN

A Vitalist Art

Filippo Tommaso Marinetti's sintesi radiofoniche

FEDERICO LUISETTI

Filippo Tommaso Marinetti's 1933 *sintesi radiofoniche* (radio syntheses)[1] are five short experimental radio compositions that date back to Marinetti's late futurist period and coincide with his *Manifesto futurista della radio*, also known as *La radia*.[2] Compared to other radio performances by Marinetti, including his radio drama *Violetta e gli aeroplani* (1932),[3] the *sintesi radiofoniche* present the significant advantage of being abstract and programmatic, thus revealing Marinetti's unconventional approach to technology.[4] According to Arndt Niebisch, what is at stake with the futurist use of the "radia" is not an aesthetic innovation but a new relation with the "nervous system of the listeners:" "the radio *sintesi* do not unfold a complicated narrative, but adopt an absolutely minimalistic aesthetic based on alternating sounds, noises, and silence . . . what Marinetti tries to affect with his radio *sintesi* is not the critical mind of the audience but the nervous system of the listeners."[5] Taking up an idea by Wolf Kittler, Niebisch relates the symbolic function of traditional art to communication noise, which presupposes a hermeneutical decoding by the receivers, and Marinetti's medial practices to a signal technology channeled directly, as in Artaud's theatre of cruelty, to the sensorial apparatus: "'Signal' in opposition to 'symbol' is a semiotic category that requires no interpretation, but provokes reflexes."[6]

As declared in *La radia*, Marinetti's engagement with radio transmission aims explicitly at creating unprecedented medial topologies and modalities of reception: "A new Art that begins where theatre cinema and narration leave off. . . . Immense enlargement of space. . . . A pure organism of radiophonic sensations. . . . An art without time or space without yesterday or tomorrow. . . . The elimination of the concept or the esteem of the audience which has always had a deforming and worsening influence even on the book."[7] The replacement of the standard substantive "radio" with the playful neologism "radia" suggests a disjunction between the ordinary social use of technology and artistic sabotage. While the radio is a normalized communication device, "la radia" requires a distortion of aesthetic categories and experiential habits:

> La radia abolishes 1. space or any required scenery in the theater including the Futurist synthetic theater (action unfolding against a fixed or constant scene) and film (actions unfolding against extremely rapid and highly variable simultaneous and always realistic scenes) 2. time 3. unity of action 4. The dramatic character 5. the audience understood as a mass self-appointed judge systematically hostile and servile always misoneist always retrograde.[8]

Following Friedrich Kittler's ground-breaking inquiries into the history of media connectivity,[9] Timothy Campbell has rescued the notion of the "wireless" from the "gray zone between telegraphy and humble genealogies of early radio,"[10] outlining the impact on literary structures of Marinetti's appropriation of the logic of communication media. Although Campbell's analyses concentrate exclusively on Marinetti's literary manifestos and *parole in libertà*, his description of the emerging practices of "wireless writing" grasps indirectly the medial context of Marinetti's radio experimentations. Beginning in the late 1920s, a fundamental mutation in medial interconnectivity reframes, together with the nature of radio broadcasting, the relation of speaker and listener, the exchange of inscription technologies and sound, the hierarchy of archival traces and spoken language: "Once the frequencies in voice transmissions and technological storage converged, sounds could be cut and mixed in montage, resulting in important temporal effects, especially in the field of time manipulation."[11] From this moment "wireless writing" becomes a matter of frequency modulation, of machinic couplings and spacing, of bodily interfacing.[12]

The *sintesi radiofoniche* and the manifesto *La radia* followed in the footsteps of a heated debate, taking place in the late 1920s and early 1930s, on the impact of radio broadcasting and new communication technologies on traditional aesthetic practices such as theatre and literary recitations.[13] In his commentaries on Bertolt Brecht, Walter Benjamin has highlighted the technological implications of Brecht's epic theatre—"The forms of epic theatre correspond to the new technical forms—cinema and radio. Epic theatre corresponds to the modern level of technology"—and underlined the fundamental changes in the nature of aesthetic perception introduced by Brecht's method of interruption, capturing the "moment when the mass begins to differentiate itself in discussion and responsible decisions . . . the moment the false and deceptive totality called 'audience' begins to disintegrate."[14]

Like Marinetti's "radia," epic theatre is "a new art" that implies unusual space-time relations and a transformed attitude by the audience. Yet, unlike Marinetti's vitalist language of "radio sensations," Brecht's interruptions and *Verfremdungseffekt* are predicated in the context of a pedagogical and human-ist Marxist *episteme*, which explains Benjamin's well known condemnation of Marinetti's futurist sensibility.[15]

As in Brecht's epic theatre, the central feature of the *sintesi* is the interplay of acoustical fragments and interruptions, intervals and boundaries. This is the logic of Marinetti's "radia," which corresponds to the non-representational fu-turist use of the media: the language of the *sintesi* does not presuppose symbols and rhetorical articulations of meaning but a defamiliarizing practice of con-nectivity, deferred movements and setting-in-relation of multiple elements; a landscape of signals and *stimulai*, processes of fusion and spacing of expressive materials. Most importantly, the *sintesi*'s alternation of intervals and interrup-tions points to a continuous field of intensity, a vitalist logic of condensation and expansion. Between the acoustical intervals and the interruptions that both separate and connect the multiple segments of the *sintesi* there is not a difference of nature but a difference in degree, which can be intensified or weakened, accelerated to the point of absolute variation or suspended in the stillness of repetition. Beyond the appearance of an unsurpassable heteroge-neity of elemental acoustic substances and irrational interruptions, we can observe the emergence of a subtle aesthetics of the interstitial, a technological production of new perceptual intervals.

Stati intermomentali

In order to understand the centrality assigned to intervals and interruptions by Marinetti, we need to go back to the debate surrounding the temporal experience of presence that was unfolding at the beginning of the twentieth century. According to Henri Bergson, a key influence on Marinetti and the avant-gardes at large, behind the illusory instantaneousness of the present lays the reality of "duration," of "elastic" blocks of temporal segments. These unities comprise a temporal span; they last, because they are tensed up be-tween the immanent polarities of the virtual and the actual, the powerless past and the active present. These blocks of duration are thin yet dense, since they continuously frustrate the presence-to-itself of the instantaneous and non-dimensional present. Whereas the Euclidean spatial habits of human reason and perception have privileged "representation"—that is a mimetic reproduction of presence, based on the illusion of an a-temporal relationship with the thing represented—Bergson concentrates on the infra-representational intervals, questioning the spaceless non-dimensionality of interruptions: "In the living mobility of things, the understanding is bent on marking real and virtual stations. It notes departures and arrivals. It is more than human to grasp what is happening in the interval."[16]

Following this Bergsonian notion of interval, Anton Giulio Bragaglia bases his *Fotodinamismo*, a pioneering technique of avant-garde photography, on the concept of *stati intermomentali* [inter-momental states]. According to Bragaglia, the aim of photography is to reveal the non-representational nature of the intervals that constitute everyday gestures, dispelling the illusion of the instantaneity of snap-shot photography.[17] Marcel Duchamp's notion of *infra-mince* [infra-thin] is another modulation of the Bergsonian aesthetics of intervals. In his posthumous notes to the *Large Glass*, Duchamp attacks in a Bergsonian language the instantaneity of present: " = in each fraction of duration (?) all / future and antecedent fractions are reproduced—All these past and future fractions / thus coexist in a present which is / really no longer what one usually calls / the instant present, but a sort of / present of multiple extensions—."[18] While the visuality of traditional art is inextricably linked to the myth of an "instant present"—the present of production and reception of images, of interpretation and communication of meanings, of the marketing and taste of artworks—Duchamp's absorption of the Bergsonian logics of infra-representational intervals transforms artworks into non-artistic works of "multiple extensions;" "infra-thin" objects, works that do not belong to representation and that occupy the paradoxical spatiality of duration. This is the nature of the "ready-mades:" they are aporetic "things," which dwell in the perceptual and conceptual "thinness" of non-representational intervals.

For contextualizing Marinetti's construction of sound intervals it is useful to take into account also the developments taking place in the field of experimental physiology. By relying on technical devices such as the "chronoscope" illustrated in Wilhelm Wundt's *Principles of Physiological Psychology* (1874), psychophysiological experiments aimed at measuring "physiological time," the physiological interval between stimulus and reaction that questioned the instantaneity of perception and thought. Symbolist writers, painters, and composers such as Debussy and Janáček were fascinated by the experiential territory revealed by the discovery of the non-instantaneousness of perceptual mechanisms. What was happening during these short, and yet dense, intervals?

Janáček emphasized that when one tone or chord passes to another, the first does not instantaneously cease to be, but lingers both in memory and physiologically as the fibers in the cochlea continue to vibrate for the briefest moment after the second tone has begun to sound. Janáček believed this moment lasted about 1/10 of a second. Hence, it became important to attend to the particular quality of that moment *between* two sounds in order to grasp the quality of the connection. For the idea of the actual psychophysiological coexistence of tones, Janáček cited Hermann von Helmholtz's classic text *On the Sensations of Tone.* At other times, he referred to Wundt's and others' findings that a rather long delay subsisted between the disposition of attending to one object and the disposition of attending to another. . . . The general point to be drawn from all of this is that Janáček's fascination for the *in-betweenness* of certain events amounted to a fairly coherent and all-encompassing aesthetics of the interstitial, which took stock of available musical materials and found that the perhaps most interesting and vital were specifically those which were most easily and often overlooked: the moment, virtual or actual, *between* two apparently contiguous tones; the delicate relation of one millisecond to another in a barely apperceived phonemic succession. . . . As a composer, Janáček did not miss opportunities to exploit a sense of being in-between, of opening up gaps in a temporal fabric, so that one never quite settles comfortably into a forward flow while listening to his music.[19]

In his captivating reconstruction of musical modernism, Benjamin Steege mentions also Russolo's *intonarumori* as an example of interstitial art, in which "the apparent stability and unity of everyday aural experience would be productively fractured by a kind of listening available to what he calls 'futurist ears.'" Marinetti's *sintesi radiofoniche* are yet another example of this subtle art on the in-between.

Interruptions

Marinetti's first *sintesi radiofonica, An Acoustical Landscape,* is made of three blocks of sounds: a fire's crackling, a water's lapping, and the whistle of a blackbird:

An Acoustical Landscape
The whistle of a blackbird envious of the fire's crackle ended up putting out
     the water's
whispery gossip
10 seconds of lapping.

1 second of crackling.
8 seconds of lapping.
1 second of crackling.
5 seconds of lapping.
1 second of crackling.
19 seconds of lapping.
1 second of crackling.
25 seconds of lapping.
1 second of crackling.
35 seconds of lapping.
6 seconds of blackbird whistling.[20]

The crackling lasts constantly for 1 second while the lapping follows a dramatic *crescendo* and *decrescendo* (10, 8, 5, 19, 25, 35 seconds), ended up by the abrupt whistle of the blackbird. This *sintesi* presents the basic elements of Marinetti's radio language: although the three sounds can be erroneously interpreted as heterogeneous materials, separated by differences of kind, they function as differences in degree of emotional intensity. In order to achieve this effect, Marinetti transforms the lapping into a repetitive interruption, the five 1 second segments. These interruptions are at the same time connectors and modulators of the degree of intensity of the lapping. Instead of a flow of punctiform heterogeneous materials, we are now experiencing an assemblage of acoustical repetitions and variations.

In the second *sintesi*, *Drama of distances*, the alternating occurrences of soundscapes from distant geographical regions and environments—the military, entertainment, everyday urban or rural life, religion—are assembled without distinct interrupting intervals, following a strict rule of repetitive unities of eleven seconds:

Drama of distances
11 seconds a military march in Rome.
11 seconds a tango being danced in Santos.
11 seconds of Japanese religious music being played in Tokyo.
11 seconds of a lively rustic dance in the Varese countryside.
11 seconds of a boxing match in New York.
11 seconds of street noise in Milan.
11 seconds of a Neapolitan love song sung in the Copacabana Hotel in Rio de Janeiro.[21]

In this circumstance, the communal element is the medium of radio itself, the flowing continuum of radio waves. Radio broadcasting "immensifies space," but it does so artificially, by coupling and modulating differences.

What is at stake is the logic of intermediality, the power of connectivity of radio transmission.

In the third *sintesi*, *Silences speak among themselves*, the medial constructivism of Marinetti becomes overtly complex and the distinction between intervals and interruptions is blurred: is silence interrupting sounds of vice versa?

> *Silences speak among themselves*
> 15 seconds of pure silence.
> A flute's do re mi.
> 8 seconds of pure silence.
> A flute's do re mi.
> 29 seconds of pure silence.
> A piano's sol.
> A trumpet's do.
> 40 seconds of pure silence.
> A trumpet's do.
> An infant's wah wah.
> 11 seconds of pure silence.
> An eleven year old girl's stupefied ooooh.[22]

Since the blocks of silence and the musical and human sounds vary according to a *crescendo* and *decrescendo* of time patterns—15, 8, 29, 40, 11 seconds of "pure silences"—it becomes increasingly difficult to distinguish between repetitions and variations, modulations and qualitatively different segments of musical instruments. Given the abstraction of silences and the singular concreteness of human voices, it is also impossible to establish differences of kind between forms and contents, structural and thematic elements. What is clear is that we need to grasp the differences in degree of the emotional life-space constructed by the "radia." A paradoxical reversal takes place: silence is not the empty background filled in by the fullness of media communication. Quite the opposite is true: the apparently triumphal efficacy of inter-connected global networks rests on the fragile foundation of virtual silences, of silences that "speak among themselves," penetrating and overcoming the barriers of human and technological communication.[23]

The *Battle of Rhythms* intensifies the exchanges between interruptions and intervals, silences and sounds:

Battle of Rhythms
A prudent and patient slowness expressed by means of the tap tap tap of water drops
first cut off then killed off by
A flying elasticity composed of arpeggios of piano notes first cut off then killed off
by

A loud ringing of an electric doorbell first cut off and then killed off by
A three minute long silence first cut off and then killed off by
A toiling key in lock tat rum ta trac followed by
A one minute long silence.[24]

Here, each acoustical segment is first "cut off" and then "killed off" by the following segment. What this means is that each block functions initially as an interruption, and then as a dense interval. Furthermore, an acoustical segment can be "slow" or "elastic," "loud," or "silent"— the tap tap of water, the arpeggios of piano, the three minutes of silence[25]—thus showing a variety of intertwined spatial and temporal characteristics. Not only is there no difference of kind between interruptions and intervals, silences and sounds. Also quality and quantity, time and space are technologically coupled, assembled by the machinic performance of the "radia" and addressed to the listeners as a mysterious field of pulsations.

The fifth *sintesi*, *Building a Silence*, reveals the foundations of Marinetti's topological constructivism:

Building a Silence
1) Build a wall on the left with a drum roll (one half minute)
2) Build a wall on the right with trumpeting—shouting—auto tram a squealing of capital (one half minute)
3) Build a floor with the gurgling of water in pipes (one half minute)
4) Build a ceiling terrace with the chip chip chip of sparrows and swallows (20 seconds).[26]

Here Marinetti avoids any distinction between intervals and interruptions. Since their difference is in degree, intervals and interruptions are hinges, devices for folding and shaping space-time phenomena. Consequently, each acoustical material—drum rolls, auto tram squealing, gurgling water, bird's chip chips—is used as a joint, a turning point for building the ideal "infra-thin" artificial environment: silence.[27]

Entre-deux

The *sintesi* are sound collages, constructivist montages, assemblages of silences and acoustical *objects trouvés* infused with a modernist sensibility for unmediated conceptual structures and *readymade* materials. As such, they follow a minimalist cubist aesthetics and pave the way for John Cage's radio music and *musique informelle*.[28] Yet, because of their primary concern with the articulation of interstices and cuts, they also belong to a more specific lineage of avant-garde experimentalism that, from Bertolt Brecht to Jean-Luc Godard, has emphasized the use of gaps and interruptions: "the interrupting of action is one of the principal concerns of epic theatre. . . . often its main function is not to illustrate or advance the action but, on the contrary, to interrupt it: not only the action of others, but also the action of one's own. It is the retarding quality of these interruptions and the episodic quality of this framing of action which allows gestural theatre to become epic theatre."[29]

In Gilles Deleuze's ontology of "irrational cuts"—which is based on Godard's cinema theory, in its turn directly influenced by Brecht's *Verfremdungseffekt*—Benjamin's uncovering of Brecht's interruptions is radicalized, becoming the central device for reconstructing the logic of modern cinema. Like Marinetti, Deleuze is immune to Brecht's marxist humanism and pedagogical tenets and develops his conception of the "in-between," the *entre-deux*, on a purely vitalist terrain. In his two-volume study on cinema, Deleuze's arguments culminate in the theorization of a "method of irrational cuts," that generates an "interstice between images." In the cinema of Rohmer, Dryer, Bresson, and Godard,

> the question is no longer that of the association or attraction of images. What counts is on the contrary the interstice between images, between two images. . . . Given one image, another image has to be chosen which will induce an interstice between the two. This is not an operation of association, but of differentiation. . . . As physicists say: given one potential, another one has to be chosen, not any whatever, but in such a way that the difference of potential is established between the two, which will be productive of a third or of something new.[30]

This example of interstitial differentiation, the difference of potential between two images, which produces an interstice between the two, can guide us toward the key intuition of Deleuze. What matters for Deleuze is a peculiar movement: not a locomotion but a process of becoming, a power of transformation whose driving force is localized in the "transcendental field:" "What is a transcendental field? It is distinct from experience in that it neither refers to an object nor belongs to a subject (empirical representation). It therefore appears as a pure a-subjective current of consciousness, an impersonal prereflexive consciousness, a qualitative duration of consciousness without self. . . . The transcendental field is defined by a plane of immanence, and the plane of immanence by a life."[31] In the transcendental field, life is "a life," events take place at "absolute speed" in an "empty time," in the nonrepresentational duration of a non-human interval: "This indefinite life does not itself have moments, however close together they might be, but only meantime (*des entre-temps*), between-moments."[32]

At least apparently, Deleuze follows Marinetti in developing a refined logic of the in-between, conceived as an organum for vitalist art practices. And yet, Deleuze separates sharply interruptions from intervals, attributing to cuts and ruptures the task of relating the finite and the transcendental fields, the actual and the virtual. Because of this architectural function, interruptions for Deleuze are not intervals, and they are not mutually exchangeable. They join and disconnect segments by cutting and penetrating the empirical plane. However, their power originates from an intensive field that we must not confuse with everyday perceptual experience. Interruptions for Deleuze are in-betweens understood as a pure power of differentiation of the transcendental field.

As a result, Deleuze's descriptions of the in-between presuppose a topology of interruptions, incompatible with Marinetti's exchanges of cuts and intervals. Deleuze's logics of "irrational cuts" is a method for intersecting immanence and transcendence, absolute life and relative movements: the pure, void intensive Outside and the impure territory of worldly phenomena. A line of escape, not an interval:

> The in-between is not an average, a centrism, a moderation. It is an absolute velocity. . . . We call absolute the speed of a movement between two points, in between them, which traces a line of escape. . . . Such a movement does not take place from one location to another. It happens between two degrees, as in a potential difference. It is a difference in intensity which produces a phenomenon, letting him escape, expelling it, into space. . . . Speed means belonging to a becoming, something different from a development or an evolution.[33]

The Deleuzian in-between is an autonomous and incommensurable cut, not coordinated with the beginnings and ends of other blocs of life; not exchangeable with intervals. This is, according to Deleuze, the logic of avant-garde art and cinema: "The modern image initiates the reign of 'incommensurables' or irrational cuts: this is to say that the cut no longer forms part of one or the other image, of one or the other sequence that it separates and divides. . . . The interval is set free, the interstice becomes irreducible and stands on its own."[34] The transcendental non-dimensionality of the Deleuzian in-between requires a theology of the Outside, an ontological Void that sustains all the operations of irrational cutting:

> Because of the method of the BETWEEN: "between two actions, between two affections, between two perceptions, between two visual images, between two sound images, between the sound and the visual" . . . the whole undergoes a mutation . . . The whole thus merges with what Blanchot calls the "force of

dispersal of the Outside," or "the vertigo of spacing": that void which is no longer a motor-part of the image, and which the image would cross in order to continue, but is the radical calling into question of the image.[35]

We may try to imagine how Deleuze would have approached Marinetti's *sintesi radiofoniche*: their "primitive" interruptions, their use of raw sounds and unpredictable cuts, would have been understood as the evidence of an irrational interstitial power, the trace of an absolute freedom of becoming, the signal of a line of flight leading to the superior life of the machinic intervals, the life of a "spiritual automaton."

And yet, the density of Marinetti's silences—which are never a void and never do produce a "vertigo of spacing"—and the thick dimensionality of the *sintesi*'s cuts—with their constant exchange of intervals and interruptions— suggest that, contrary to the Deleuzian in-betweens, Marinetti's intervals *do* "form part of one, or the other, sequence that they separate and divide." For this reason, in order to approach the *sintesi*'s nature, we must reach a vitalist and yet post-Deleuzian conception of the in-between, envisioning a topology of intervals syntonized with Marinetti's non-transcendental geometry of interruptions. That is, we need to elaborate a truly vitalist critique, able to decipher the language spoken by the "radia."[36] Unfortunately, we are still quite far from this objective. What we have instead are a few hermetic objects, such as Marinetti's *sintesi*, which encourage a yet to be articulated theory of their puzzling artistic life.

Notes

1. The scores for the *sintesi radiofoniche* have been originally published in the journal *Autori e scrittori* (August 1941), then in Filippo Tommaso Marinetti, *Teatro*, ed. Jeffrey T. Schnapp, vol. 2 (Milan: Mondadori, 2004): 629–37, and recently translated into English by Jeffrey T. Schnapp, "Radio Syntheses. Introduction and Translation by Jeffrey T. Schnapp," *Modernism / modernity* 16, 2 (2009): 415–20. The *sintesi radiofoniche* have never been broadcast by Marinetti; a 1978 recording by composer Daniele Lombardi is included in the cd *Musica Futurista: The Art of Noises 1909–1935*, LTM Recordings (2006). The audio files of this recording are also available on line: www.futurismo.altervista.org/audio.htm. For information on other performances of the *sintesi radiofoniche* see Margaret Fisher, "Futurism and Radio," in Günter Berghaus, ed., *Futurism and Technological Imagination* (Amsterdam; New York: Rodopi , 2009), 245.

2. The *Manifesto futurista della radio*, co-authored with Pino Masnata, has been published on September 22, 1933, in the Italian newspaper *Gazzetta del popolo*. The manifesto appeared as *Manifesto della radio* in *Futurismo* (1 October 1933) and as

La radia, Manifesto futurista dell'ottobre 1933 in *Autori e scrittori* (August 1941). It is now available in Marinetti, *Teatro*, vol. 2, 769–74; English trans. *The Radia. Futurist Manifesto*, in Lawrence Rainey, Christine Poggi, Laura Wittman, eds., *Futurism. An Anthology* (New Haven: Yale University Press, 2009), 292–95, subsequently cited as Rainey, *Anthology*. The manifesto was followed in 1935 by a forty-four-page unpublished exegesis by Pino Masnata. Translated excerpts from this exegesis will appear in *Modernism / modernity* 19, 1. On this gloss see Margaret Fisher, "New Information Regarding the Futurist Radio Manifesto," published in March 2011 in *Italogramma*, the on-line journal of Italian studies of the Italian Institute, Faculty of Letters, Università Eötvös Loránd in Budapest.

3. See Marinetti, *Teatro*, vol. 2, 638–56. For a history of Italian radio aesthetics, see Angela Ida De Benedictis, *Radiodramma e arte radiofonica. Storia e funzioni della musica per radio in Italia* (Turin: EDT, 2005).

4. "Marinetti's experiments with recorded sound begin in 1914 with a series of recordings of poetic recitations carried out in a London recording studio. His interest in the medium of radio dates back to Futurism's beginnings but starts carrying over into the realm of practice in the mid to late 1920s. During his 1926 tour of South America, Marinetti makes repeated appearances on Brazilian and Argentine radio stations. These are followed by sixteen years of active collaboration with the Italian national radio (the EIAR), founded in 1928, which involve everything from declaiming aeropoems, to serving as a live action commentator of major events like the August 1932 return from the United States of Italo Balbo's flying squadron, to hosting a regularly broadcast radio bulletin on the activities of the futurist movement," Schnapp, "Radio Syntheses," 415. On Marinetti's and the futurists' engagement with radio, see Fisher, "Futurism and Radio," 229–62.

5. Arndt Niebisch, "Cruel Media. On F.T. Marinetti's Media Aesthetics," *Annali d'Italianistica* 27 (2009), *A Century of Futurism: 1909–2009*, ed. Federico Luisetti and Luca Somigli, 343–44.

6. Niebisch, "Cruel Media," 344.

7. Rainey, *Anthology*, 294–95.

8. Rainey, *Anthology*, 293–94.

9. See Friedrich A. Kittler, *Discourse Networks, 1800/1900*, trans. Michael Metteer (Stanford: Stanford University Press, 1990) and *Gramophone, Film, Typewriter*, trans. Geoffrey Winthrop-Young and Michael Wutz (Stanford: Stanford University Press, 1999).

10. Timothy C. Campbell, *Wireless Writing in the Age of Marconi* (Minneapolis: University of Minnesota Press, 2005), x.

11. Campbell, *Wireless Writing*, xii.

12. Timothy Campbell calls the attention on Marinetti's literary "simulation of wireless functions" and the deficiencies of his "translation of sense data into their written analogue," Campbell, *Wireless Writing*, 91. In my essay I approach directly Marinetti's medial logic, abandoning the privileges of the literary field.

13. See for instance Bertolt Brecht, "The Radio as an Apparatus of Communication" (1932), in John Willett, ed., *Brecht on Theatre. The Development of an Aesthetic* (New York: Hill and Wang, 1964), 51–53.

14. Walter Benjamin, *What is Epic Theatre* [*First version*], in *Understanding Brecht*, trans. Anna Bostock (London: Verso, 1983), 6, 10. On Brecht's epic theatre see Fredric Jameson, *Brecht and Method* (London; New York: Verso, 1998).

15. See Walter Benjamin, "The Work of Art in the Age of Mechanical Reproduction," in *Illuminations*, trans. Harry Zohn (New York: Schocken Books, 1969), 241–42.

16. Henri Bergson, *Introduction to Metaphysics*, trans. Thomas Ernest Hulme (New York: Putnam, 1912), 77.

17. Anton Giulio Bragaglia, *Fotodinamismo futurista* (Turin: Einaudi, 1970). On Bergsonian intervals in Bragaglia's *Fotodinamismo* see Federico Luisetti, *Una vita. Pensiero selvaggio e filosofia dell'intensità* (Milan: Mimesis, 2011), 119–38. In *Fotodinamismo futurista* (34) Bragaglia quotes the previous passage on intervals from Bergson's *Introduction to Metaphysics*.

18. Marcel Duchamp, *Notes*, ed. and trans. Paul Matisse (Boston: G.K. Hall, 1983), 135 n.

19. Benjamin Steege, "Musical Modernism and the Culture of Experiment," unpublished essay; read at *100 Years of Futurism: Sounds, Science, and Literature: An Interdisciplinary Colloquium*, University of North Carolina at Greensboro, February 20–21, 2009. Courtesy of the author.

20. Schnapp, "Radio Syntheses," 416.

21. Schnapp, "Radio Syntheses," 417.

22. Schnapp, "Radio Syntheses," 418.

23. The role played by silences in Marinetti's radio *sintesi* trails from Enzo Ferrieri's 1931 manifesto, *Radio as a Creative Force*. Ferrieri, artistic director for Italian radio from 1929, "introduced the seminal idea that the source of radio's true, paradoxical power derives from silences;"see Margaret Fisher, "New Information."

24. Schnapp, "Radio Syntheses," 419.

25. On this three minute silence, see De Benedictis, *Radiodramma e arte radiofonica*, 66.

26. Schnapp, "Radio Syntheses," 420.

27. For the role of silence as the minimal, "keyed-in unit of spacing," "necessary for one sound to be joined to another," see Campbell's pages on Sergi's measuring of the gap between unities of excitation, *Wireless Writing in the Age of Marconi*, 70–72.

28. See Schnapp, "Introduzione" to Marinetti, *Teatro*, vol. 1, XLII.

29. Benjamin, *What is Epic Theatre*, 3–4. On the structural affinities between Brecht's epic theatre and Marinetti's theatrical techniques see Elena Coda, "Teatro di straniamento in Marinetti e Brecht," *Carte Italiane: A Journal of Italian Studies* 13 (1993–1994): 1–15.

30. Gilles Deleuze, *Cinema 2. The Time-Image*, trans. Hugh Tomlinson and Robert Galeta (Minneapolis: University of Minnesota Press, 1989), 179–80.

31. Gilles Deleuze, *Immanence: A Life . . .* , trans. Nick Millett, *Theory Culture Society* 14, 3 (1997): 4.

32. Deleuze, *Immanence: A Life . . .* , 5.

33. Gilles Deleuze and Claire Parnet, *Dialogues* (New York: Columbia University Press, 1989), 37, 39.

34. Deleuze, *Cinema 2*, 277.

35. Deleuze, *Cinema 2*, 180.

36. Given the hegemony of transcendental paradigms in Western thought and aesthetics, a vitalist critique may benefit more by looking Eastward, for instance at Chinese thought and art, where the "subtle," the suspended complexity of virtual and yet real experiences, of immanent gaps between the present and the absent, has been for centuries at the center of philosophical and artistic practices: "There are various angles from which the subtle becomes accessible to experience. In aesthetics, for example, there is the exquisite flavor of the barely perceptible, whether in sound or image, in the transitional stage between silence and sonority in music or between emptiness and fullness in painting, when the sonic or pictorial realization is barely evident or on the verge of vanishing. . . . All Chinese practices derive from this." François Jullien, *Vital Nourishment. Departing from Happiness* (New York: Zone Books, 2007), 25.

PART III

LEGACIES

~

CHAPTER SIXTEEN

The End of an Avant-Garde?

*Filippo Tommaso Marinetti and Futurism
in World War I and its Aftermath*

WALTER L. ADAMSON

The question I want to pursue in this essay is: when does Italian Futurism end as an avant-garde, and how should we understand that ending? To some degree, the answer depends on our understanding of the larger questions of how any avant-garde movement ends and how we know generally when such an ending has occurred. Yet I will argue that Marinetti's Futurism has a particularly full itinerary as an avant-garde and that its ending is particularly instructive for us as we try to understand the legacy of all the historical avant-gardes including Vorticism, Dada, De Stijl, Bauhaus, Purism, and Surrealism as well as Futurism.

Let me begin my pursuit of this question with a story. When Marinetti arrived in Buenos Aires on the evening of Monday, June 7, 1926, the press was alive with reports that the Brazilians had booed him off the stage as a "fascist" and that, in at least some instances during his just concluded visit there, he had been unable to speak. Not surprisingly then, in his first conversation with the Argentine press on June 8, Marinetti denied that he was a fascist and declared that his mission was not political but purely artistic.[1] This was very likely untrue: the most plausible explanation for why he had come to Argentina was that he was trying to ingratiate himself with Mussolini by playing the role of Italian cultural ambassador, but of course this mission had to be denied in order for it to have any possibility of success. In any case, his political objective demanded a cultural strategy. And in his many performances over the next three weeks—at universities, in theatres, at the Colosseum—he made the usual spectacle of himself, dressing in outlandish costumes such as red pajamas to impersonate the Devil, haranguing *passatisti* such as Giovanni Papini, championing synthetic theatre and theatre of surprise, claiming to have been a great soccer player, and hosting "semi-futurist" art exhibitions.

Yet, while Marinetti's reception in Argentina seems to have been more dignified than the one he received in Brazil, press reports suggest that it was quite cool. Jorge Luis Borges, then a twenty-six-year-old poet and editor of the avant-garde review *Proa*, suggested in an interview with *Crítica* that Marinetti had played an important role in undermining the symbolist and decadentist movements, but that "his books have little value—they are Italian simulacra of Whitman, Kipling and perhaps Jules Romains, any one of whom is superior to him."[2] Borges expressed indifference regarding the importance of the visit for the Argentine avant-garde community—"there will be banquets with a store of epitaphs, conferences with many ticket booths and deliberately manufactured high expectations"—but the visit will have no impact ("none") on Argentine culture.[3] Similarly, the painter Emilio Pettoruti, who had spent time in Italy with Marinetti and declared himself "a personal friend," and whose work was central to the "semi-futurist" art exhibitions Marinetti's visit had spawned, limited his praise to polite formulas ("Marinetti . . . is a man of disconcerting, childlike ingenuity") and defended him against the charge of being fascist.[4] Yet nowhere in a long interview did he give any indication that he still thought of Marinetti as having fresh ideas about art or continuing relevance to avant-garde efforts to merge art and life. In short, both Borges and Pettoruti treated Marinetti as an historical relic—a blast from the past—a man who once played a significant cultural role but one that was now played out.

Interestingly, however, if we go back to the 1909 founding manifesto, we can see that Marinetti anticipated this result. The manifesto is at once a birth announcement—we are "forward sentinels facing an army of enemy stars"—and an obituary.[5] That is, it already envisions a time in which "our successors . . . will throw us in the wastebasket like useless manuscripts—we want it to happen!"[6] Not only will Futurism necessarily die, but its death is precisely the point: avant-gardes, Marinetti quite clearly understands, must produce their own obsolescence, for that is precisely what makes them successful as avant-gardes.

On Avant-Gardes

Let me try to contextualize this point by providing a somewhat schematic mini-account of what avant-gardes are and what they do. Here I am indebted first and foremost to the American philosopher, Richard Rorty. Rorty argued that the great tradition of Western metaphysics stretching from Plato to Kant had effectively ended with Hegel who, though offering his own pantheistic idealism as a kind of final metaphysics, also, and more importantly, presented a vivid portrayal of the historicity of existence through his *Phenomenology*.[7] For Rorty, Hegel was the first philosopher to understand intellectual history as (in effect) a series of altered vocabularies, altered via "avant-garde" innovation.[8] Hegel criticized his predecessors not in the sense that their views were false but that their languages were obsolete. He thereby inaugurated what Rorty called the "ironist" philosophical tradition that continues with Nietzsche, Heidegger, and Derrida, one that sees philosophy as a literary genre. Because this tradition understands itself in relation to its predecessors rather than in relation to truth, the point of the enterprise is that each philosopher is trying to artfully overcome his predecessor by producing what Rorty called a new "final vocabulary" (final not in the sense of static or fixed but in the sense that what it expresses is "as far as one can go with language"). The philosopher's hope is that this vocabulary cannot be "*aufgehoben*"—cannot be redescribed in ways that will make that philosopher just another link in a chain of tradition.

Within this understanding of the philosophical enterprise, first self-consciously articulated by Nietzsche in his youthful essay, *On the Uses and Disadvantages of History for Life*, the fundamental value becomes individual and collective "self-creation." As Nietzsche puts the point there: "the thought of being mere epigones, which can often be a painful thought, is also capable of evoking great effects and grand hopes for the future in both an individual and in a nation, provided we regard ourselves as the heirs and successors of the astonishing powers of antiquity and see in this our honor and our spur."[9] Historical cultures, for Nietzsche, present the "painful thought" that you or I might merely be an "epigone"—"a copy or a replica," as Harold Bloom would later put it—yet, in Nietzsche's view, if we make inspired, creative use of history, we can triumph over it by fashioning new metaphors that cast us as uniquely interesting, fully autonomous self-creations.[10] That is, in Rorty's words, we can "get out from under inherited contingencies and make . . . [our] own contingencies." From this perspective, the "perfect life will be one which closes in the assurance that the last of his [the individual's] final vocabularies, at least really was wholly his."[11]

Yet, in an important sense, the final vocabulary never arrives for Rorty's ironist. Ironists are people who are always questioning their present vocabularies, and yet they also know that arguments in the present vocabulary cannot put an end to their doubts and that no vocabulary gets us "closer to reality" than alternative ones. Vocabularies are like a set of tools that open the world in a certain way. If we are living actively and creatively—if our lives are in motion—then we are likely to get tired of our present tool set, think up some new metaphors, and revise our vocabulary accordingly, or even invent a new one. Hence for the ironist, a vocabulary is always under construction.

In my view, avant-gardists are aesthetic ironists, and they proceed much in the way that Rorty's post-Hegelian philosophers do. They begin by articulating a vocabulary— hopefully an innovative, even original one dedicated to self-creation and aimed at overcoming the "anxiety of influence." This vocabulary will be very much under constant construction, yet it will operate as a kind of launching pad from which a desirable cultural trajectory can be brought into view. As Giordano Bruno Guerri says about Marinetti's Futurism: "it was for thirty-five years a building *in fieri*, a model to be continually reshaped with new intentions and adaptations to the times."[12] Presented first in a founding manifesto, an avant-garde vocabulary will be supplemented and amended by subsequent manifestos (in Marinetti's case, with a vengeance). Such manifestos are the cardinal avant-garde practice. However, an avant-garde like Futurism will not be satisfied with this lone practice. Rather it will also continually seek to identify additional "practices" through which it can foist its vocabulary on the culture in question and, indeed, remake the culture in its image. These practices will reflect the particular avant-garde's understanding regarding the relationship of artist, audience, the public sphere in which they are jointly situated, the work of art, and the presentation, staging, or performance of that work.

Does this general picture suggest anything about when the work of such an avant-garde will be completed? At this stage let me just venture an analogy with what the distinguished psychoanalyst Jonathan Lear says about when the work of a psychoanalyst is completed. He argues that we must distinguish between being an analyst and doing an analysis. Being an analyst is more than just doing something (like being a newspaper reader); it is an identity, a "who we are." And that "who we are" is never fixed: to be an analyst one must always be in the process of becoming an analyst. If you have arrived, then you have ceased to be an analyst. Being an analyst is "re-creative repetition."[13] On the other hand, doing an analysis involves a finite, personal relationship. It comes to an end in one of two ways: betrayal and termination. Betrayal means that in some way the implicit rules and limits of the relationship have been violated (e.g., the analysand is no longer trying to work things through). As in a love relationship that has been betrayed, the analyst will likely try to interpret what happened as something other than a betrayal. But, Lear writes, "there comes a point where one's ability honestly to understand an event in another light runs out."[14] Termination is a more natural end: either the therapy has resulted in a "getting better," perhaps even a "cure," or one party or the other has simply decided to bring the therapy to conclusion. The analysand therefore no longer needs or wants the analyst and the latter must "let go" in the way a parent must when a child reaches maturity. One might say that the relationship represented a project which has now either been realized or simply abandoned.

Similarly, I would suggest, to understand when Futurism ended as an avant-garde, we will need to distinguish between the identity of Marinetti and other futurists as avant-gardists, on the one hand, and—on the other—the futurist movement as a vocabulary, set of practices, and changing set of participants intersecting with Italian society in concrete historical circumstances. I will also suggest that Lear's notions of "betrayal" and "termination," appropriately reformulated for the avant-garde context, are helpful in understanding the sense in which Futurism is or is not an avant-garde during its various phases of development. So let us now turn to a reflection on the historical development of Futurism from its founding in 1909 through the heart of the fascist period, commenting upon its turns—and thus on its potential "endings" as an avant-garde—from the point of view of Futurism's historiography.

On Futurism's Itinerary

Anyone who reads much in Marinetti is likely to be aware of the anxiety of influence he suffered. Consider the following paragraph written in 1922: "I am not the equal of anyone. New type. Inimitable model. Don't you copy me. Plagiaristic clouds! Enough! I know all your shapes. I have catalogued them all. Originality! Fantasy!"[15] Less obvious perhaps is the idea that Marinetti's self-proclaimed avant-gardism and inimitability can be located in a Nietzschean tradition. Yet the point has been persuasively argued by Luca Somigli who shows that, despite Marinetti's own denials, he not only drew upon Nietzsche's concept of "life" but used it as the rhetorical structure of the founding manifesto.[16] And indeed, just before the manifesto pictures his car as landing in a "maternal ditch," its driver shouts, "Let's leave wisdom behind as one does a horrible shell." Later in the text, "wisdom" is parsed as "the eternal and useless admiration of the past."[17] The only real difference between this argument and Nietzsche's is that while the latter concedes the usefulness of some careful "monumental," "antiquarian," and "critical" appropriations of the past, Marinetti discards it as altogether useless.

The manifesto develops the initial futurist vocabulary for which it has become (in)famous: "love of danger," "war, sole hygiene of the world," "scorn for woman," "beauty of struggle," "destroy museums," and the like. Somewhat less well understood is the mode through which Marinetti hoped his vocabulary would become implanted in mass culture and thereby seize the masses as a revolutionary force. Whether or not he was fully conscious of it in this way, I am among those who believe that Marinetti deployed his vocabulary as a Sorelian myth.[18]

In his *Reflections on Violence*, which appeared in 1908 and which Marinetti very likely read, Sorel conceived "myth" in a very different way from our everyday usage. To develop his notion of myth, Sorel drew upon Bergson's notion of intuition, which points us to a "self" that knows in time as lived duration, that lives, as it were, internal to the world. When this self intuits, it literally enters into the object. The contrast term is intellect, which views the world from the outside, inspects it, dissects it, analyzes it, describes it. Hence myth for Sorel is "not a description of the world but a determination to act," which projects a powerful image—like the "general strike" or "class war"—as a way of "entering" the social world and revolutionizing it.[19] In contrast, the form of political thought which develops myths in the everyday sense (descriptions or at least models of what is coming or what ought to be) Sorel called a "utopia." Myths, for Sorel, lead people who have made them their own, into action, action that is likely to be truly revolutionary; utopias are more rationalistic, more about systematic programs, and they encourage reform not revolution.

In my view, early Futurism is a myth in this sense: it wants to provoke violent change—in a word, war—and it deploys its vocabulary as well as modes of communication based on simultaneity and the destruction of syntax through words-in-freedom [*parole in libertà*] to stimulate desire for a new world, one that has been cleansed of all residues from the past and acculturated into a receptivity toward modern technology. Because he understood that the futurist myth could not simply be imposed top-down, however, Marinetti was not satisfied merely to articulate a myth; he also needed to perform it in a context in which the masses might make it their own. The main venue he invented for performance was of course the *serata* or futurist evening, which enacted the myth of the coming great war as the pelting of on-stage poets by the organic refuse that the audience has brought as ammunition. Similar mythic enactments were bound up with the demonstrations of the 1914–1915 intervention campaign.

Yet once Italy enters the war in the spring of 1915, matters begin to change—and rather quickly. For once the war has arrived as an Italian reality, Futurism's original myth has, arguably, been realized. The war is no longer a mythic projection into the future but a present reality. And this has enormous consequences in itself: for if the founding myth has been realized, the rationale for the movement no longer exists. In addition, of course, the war would soon change the futurist movement in more direct, material ways. Some important futurists like Boccioni and the architect Sant'Elia died in it; others like Carrà and Soffici were stimulated by the war to adopt more culturally conservative and/or more populist orientations. Marinetti, when he was not at the front, focused his energies on a circle of young futurist enthusiasts in Florence, one that was completely different from his older prewar circle based in Milan. Indeed, not only was it younger and Tuscan, but it included a number of important female participants, a fact that seems to have reflected a recognition of the intensified need to cultivate a female audience for Futurism during wartime. Ultimately, through this circle, Marinetti sought to reinvigorate the movement, but no longer in terms of a revolutionary myth of violence and war. Instead, *L'Italia futurista* mostly devoted its early issues to literature, and then, in later ones, took stock of the effects of the war. In this latter connection, it hosted an important debate about the social role of women in wartime and postwar Italian society. Finally, in its concluding issue of February 11, 1918, the journal published Marinetti's *Manifesto del partito futurista italiano*.[20] Over the next two years, Marinetti entered an intensely political phase in which he sought to organize a futurist party and entered into strategic alliances with militant ex-combatants such as the *arditi* as well as Mussolini's *fasci di combattimento*. He also wrote key political texts such as *Democrazia futurista* (1919) and *Al di là del comunismo* (1920). The futurist utopia had arrived.

Given this transformation, it should not be surprising that there exists an important historiographical tradition on Futurism which holds that it ends as an avant-garde around 1916. Consider, for example, the views of Maurizio Calvesi, as formulated in the late 1960s and early 1970s.[21] Calvesi argued that Futurism was an "integrated proposal for cultural renewal" based on an "absolutely new and revolutionary formula, a tendency toward direct confrontation, and a stress on the continuity between art and life."[22] By an integrated proposal, Calvesi meant that Futurism should be understood as a social movement fusing culture and politics, rather than as an essentially aesthetic movement seeking to impact public life or as an essentially political movement making use of aesthetic means. Moreover, Calvesi argued strongly that Marinetti was the undeniable creator and central promoter of the futurist social movement, and that any effort to marginalize his role by treating Futurism as a multiplicity with many competing centers was untenable. Calvesi understood perfectly well why many commentators found the political dimensions of Marinetti's early views unpalatable, yet he argued that it was useless to try to purify the movement by, for example, treating Umberto Boccioni as its creative center (conveniently the painter's death in 1916 meant that he could not be linked with fascism), since there were "many elements, even external and objective ones, that demonstrate the perfect solidarity of Boccioni (it is enough to read his correspondence) with Marinetti."[23] Indeed, the startling innovativeness of the futurist social movement grew directly from some key Marinetti insights: that the modern structure of communication had implicit within it the possibility of a totalizing concept of modernity; that artistic-literary production and the production of goods under capitalism were strongly interconnected; that modernity implied a "civilization of images" and that artists should work to develop the visual element within poetry and, more generally, in the presentation of print; and that in the context of this economic-cultural-communicative convergence, artists could and ought to learn to engage popular crowds.[24]

This picture of Futurism relies almost entirely on images drawn from what have come to be called the "heroic years" (1909–1916). While Calvesi makes occasional reference to concrete futurist projects developed later, such as the aeropainting of the 1930s, his work contains no sustained historical analysis of the development of the movement after 1916. Hence, intended or unintended as it may be, the implication of his work is that everything that happened within the futurist orbit after 1916 was a kind of "non-re-creative" repetition—a mere referencing of the vocabulary, practices, and ideals already available. Thus while Calvesi, so far as I can determine, did not explicitly discuss the question of when Futurism's avant-garde status may have ended, the inevitable implication of his work is that it did not extend beyond the heroic years.

There are many features of Calvesi's argument with which I find myself in full agreement. Certainly I concur that the Futurism of the heroic years is an integrated social movement, although I would want to complicate the point in at least two ways. First, it is quite clear that Marinetti was the driving force behind the integrated culture-politics, and that many of the futurist painters, for example, participated in what they regarded as the movement's more explicitly political aspects with some reluctance. Secondly, in 1920, at the height of his "utopian" period, Marinetti co-published a manifesto which quite clearly sets out in separate lists what it means to be a "futurist in life," a "futurist in politics," and a "futurist in art."[25] And there are indications that these separations were formulated as early as 1910 and thus are not simply a function of the shift from Futurism as myth to Futurism as utopia.[26] I also agree with Calvesi's insistence on Futurism's "Marinetti-centrism," to use a phrase later introduced by Enrico

Crispolti, whose own view of the movement is quite the opposite.[27] Yet it is certainly also true that as we proceed into the later war years and postwar period, and especially after Futurism's break with fascism in early 1920, there is much more "multiplicity" (to use another of Crispolti's favorite terms) in the movement than during its heroic phase.

To understand what gets left behind as Futurism shifts from the mythic orientation of the heroic years to the more programmatic, utopian vocabulary of the late war years, we need to consider two additional points. First, while Marx famously wrote that in capitalist societies "all that is solid melts into air," the society he championed aimed to resolidify the modern world by eradicating hierarchies and strengthening social ties around stable values of community and equality. In contrast, the young Marinetti welcomed the entropy and dizzying pace of modern life. He celebrated speed, simultaneity, crowds and noise, took pleasure in being booed, and dreamed of fast cars and sleek airplanes. There were also ways in which even the young Marinetti held firm to traditional values connected with fixity and stability, as his commitment to the Italian nation reminds us, yet the degree to which his early mythic vision separated itself from structure remains remarkable. When his vocabulary gets redeployed in a more utopian orientation, however, a more structured view of the world is an inevitable byproduct. Second, and related, in developing a party program Marinetti necessarily moved away from a rhetoric of images and slogans to a more pragmatic logic of means and ends in support of concrete policy objectives. To compare even his expressly political manifestos from the prewar period with the 1918 program is to be immediately struck by this stylistic shift.

Should any of these considerations incline us toward the view that, by the late war years, either Marinetti or Futurism generally has abandoned an avant-garde perspective or adopted a relationship with the Italian public sphere that is either less avant-garde or not avant-garde at all? I want to argue against any such conclusion regarding "avant-garde perspective" but to suggest that the avant-garde nature of the relationship between Futurism and its public did weaken somewhat. To return to Lear's notions, I would suggest that "betrayal" occurs when the original avant-garde vocabulary is explicitly contradicted or repudiated and that a "termination" occurs either when that vocabulary is abandoned or ceases to be "re-creatively repeated," or when social practices integrated with that vocabulary (for example, in the case of Futurism, the *serata*) are terminated. (Another form of avant-garde ending is a simple surrender of movement autonomy, which may be judged either a betrayal or a termination, depending on circumstances and motivations). In my view, the move from a mythic to a utopian basis for Futurism involved no betrayal—the vocabulary is neither contradicted nor repudiated but simply supplemented and amended, a process that, as already suggested, goes on all the time in any case. Nor do I think that Futurism lost its autonomy as an integrated social movement with this shift. Yet I would suggest that the shift did entail a weakening of integrated social practices since the *serata* was almost completely abandoned and the futurist political party never found any comparably powerful mode of interacting with the broad public.[28] Indeed, as Marinetti's party manifesto made quite clear, "the futurist political party that we are founding today, and that we will organize after the war is over, will be entirely separate from the futurist art movement. . . . All Italians can belong to the futurist political party, men and women of all classes and all ages, even if they are entirely lacking in artistic and literary concepts."[29]

How, then, should we understand the nature of what I am calling Futurism's utopian phase? In my view, the fullest exploration of this phase is to be found in the work of Emilio Gentile, and a brief summation of some of his analysis will help to answer our question.[30] Although Gentile believes that what he calls "political Futurism" can be traced back into the political manifestos of the prewar era, he sees the specific origins of the mentality that produced the concept of a futurist political party in the summer of 1917, above all in an article written by one of the central figures in *L'Italia futurista*, Emilio Settimelli. In the article, Settimelli argued that "art is only part of the futurist program—the most developed part, but certainly not the most important."[31] Futurism is "not to be confused with a kind of supermanism and absolutist aristocracy. Nothing could be further from the truth. Futurism is *democracy*. . . . We recognize all the rights of the working and productive classes and our program is in the front line of '*the economic defense and education of the proletariat*.' Our nationalism is anti-traditionalist and *eminently democratic*."[32]

Certainly the "democratic" accent in this rhetorical shift is important and helps us to understand the nature of the break between the futurist generation of Umberto Boccioni and Carlo Carrà and that of Settimelli and Mario Carli. Yet the shift was not merely generational. One is reminded of a similar shift away from elitism and towards a respect for the "*popolo*" undergone by Ardengo Soffici at roughly the same moment.[33] In any case, the democratic tenor of futurist rhetoric in this period is certainly reflected in the socio-political debates in the last half year of *L'Italia futurista*, in its successor journal, *Roma futurista*, which began (significantly enough) on 20 September 1918, and, of course, in Marinetti's party program. As Gentile points out, the manifesto itself registered a democratic, even leftist turn in at least three ways: in its suggested social and institutional reforms, in its omission of violent and anti-socialist rhetoric, and in its concomitant up-grading of anti-Vatican and anticlerical rhetoric.[34] Moreover, at this point the futurists were overwhelmingly republican, even if Settimelli and Carli would revert to monarchism in the 1920s.

Gentile's argument is that this intensified "political Futurism"—what I am calling the utopian phase of the movement—begins to fade after Marinetti's disappointing two weeks at Fiume in September 1919 and then comes to a decisive halt after the November elections, which were disastrous for the fu-turists as well as for their fascist allies. This ending is registered in the abrupt reorientation of *Roma futurista* from a political to an aesthetic journal early in February 1920 and is merely affirmed by the formal break between the futurists and the fascists at the Second Fascist Congress in May (rather than originating there, as many historians had earlier suggested). Then, during the summer, Marinetti writes *Al di là del comunismo*, which proclaims that "hu-manity is moving toward anarchic individualism, the goal and dream of every strong spirit," in contrast to communism, which embodies a "bureaucratic cancer."[35] Gentile takes this declaration to represent a break with the "mod-ernist nationalism" that had always undergirded Marinetti's futurist politics and thus, for all practical purposes, the end of his political life. "In the fascist regime, Marinetti and the futurists wearing black shirts continued to express themselves as rebellious innovators, but they delegated to the Duce and to the fascist party the creation of the new Italian in the totalitarian laboratory in which conformism became religious dogma."[36] Hence, in Gentile's view, the story of political Futurism ends in 1920.

While Gentile's account is very valuable for its narrative of futurist politics, 1917–1920, it seems to me inappropriately contextualized as well as misleading in the way it ends the story. First of all, I would reject his premise that we can simply divide "artistic Futurism" from "political Futurism" and treat them as parallel stories that begin in 1909 and then run alongside one another until 1920 when the latter ends and the former continues by itself. Rather I have been suggesting that we should see Futurism as an integrated social movement which moves from a mythic phase in which Futurism func-tions as the harbinger of an alternative form of capitalist mass culture into a utopian phase in which it transmutes into an alternative party politics cou-pled with a supportive aesthetics. In this latter utopian phase, the integration of the movement weakens but does not dissolve. And I would now further suggest that, after a few years of utopian reflection and reorientation—uto-pian in the usual sense quite different from the Sorelian one—Marinetti in 1923 leads the movement into a final phase in which it styles itself the aesthetic basis for a spiritualized mass culture of fascism.

Secondly, I would suggest that if we move beyond Gentile's rather narrow focus on the internal mechanics of futurist politics and bring into view the wider picture of Marinetti's biography, we get a rather different picture of what is happening to him in 1920. As Claudia Salaris has shown, Marinetti established a love relationship with Benedetta Cappa in the fall of 1919—at precisely the same time, then, that he was undergoing a political disillusionment. And, together with Benedetta, Marinetti underwent a personal and intellectual reorientation over the next three years in which he embraced many ideals he had earlier scorned such as "love and friendship," rejected a concept of life based on "materialist appetites," developed new spiritualist ideas such as *tattilismo* (tactilism), and moved his personal life in a "return to order" direction that encompassed marriage, children, and an active family life including religious practices such as baptism and communion.[37] From this perspective, what Gentile takes as Marinetti's shift away from nationalist politics toward "anarchic individualism" in the summer of 1920 is better understood as part of a spiritual transformation that will move him precisely in the opposite direction: toward an embrace of a spiritualized understanding of fascism. Similarly, Marinetti's 1928 decision to accept Mussolini's invitation to join the Italian Academy should be understood not as a mere tactical maneuver nor as resulting from some enduring contradiction between his aesthetics and politics, but as a natural result of his new more spiritual and conservative approach to life. In short, Marinetti's reorientation in the early 1920s puts us in a position to see that his impending accommodation with the regime was also in many ways a convergence.

Finally, I would suggest that Gentile is too extreme in his "Marinetti-centric" approach to Futurism, which comes very close to being a Marinetti-exclusive approach. From the broader perspective of Futurism, what happens in the early 1920s is less the termination of political Futurism than its fragmentation. Thus, we get a left-wing Futurism—led in Turin by Benedetta's brother, Arturo Cappa, and involving important independent artists like Ivo Pannaggi and Vinicio Paladini—while in Rome we find the more conservative, regime-loyalist Futurism of Settimelli, Carli, and the circle around their journal, *L'Impero*.

Thus, I would argue that while Gentile is certainly correct to maintain that Marinetti and futurists loyal to him subordinated themselves to Mussolini and fascism in and after 1923 by accepting the role of being its aesthetic arm rather than an autonomous social movement, they nonetheless continued to pursue a futurist cultural politics. What Gentile calls their posturings as "rebellious innovators" must be seen, at least in part, as a political effort to push fascism in directions amenable to a futurist movement which continued to hold congresses, to publish journals, and to seek generally to have a public voice and to make a public impact. Marinetti's voyage to South America in 1926, with which we began, must be seen in this light. In the 1930s, Marinetti turned most of his attention to Italy, and certainly promoted fascist imperialism with speeches at rallies and with service in the army both during the Ethiopian campaign and at the Russian front in World War II. Yet, as Marja Härmänmaa has shown, Marinetti developed his own concept of the "new man" in the 1930s, which included a commitment to fascism but went well beyond it with a rhetoric of hyper-individualism, a continued commitment to a Sorelian project of overcoming decadence, and unabated Nietzschean anxieties about being perceived as a mere epigone.[38] He also promoted "aeropainting" and other forms of "aero-art" which were certainly of propagandistic value for the regime. Yet my own view is that aeropainting cannot be reduced to propaganda, and there continued to be, in the 1930s, an active futurist movement independent of fascist politics, even if it was one that risked parody of its own early "heroic" period by pursuing a more commercial and populist orientation. Futurist *case d'arte* emerged, which sold posters, ceramics, clothes, cookbooks and related items to a public that, it seems, was eager to buy them. As such, it may even have functioned as a kind of cultural alternative to the regime, although in no sense an explicitly anti-fascist one.[39]

How Futurism Ended as an Avant-Garde and Why the Ending Matters

Still, it will doubtless come as no surprise when I now argue that Borges and Pettoruti were right to assert that the Futurism they had before them was no longer avant-garde. The important point is to try to understand why this was the case—in terms that can be adapted to other avant-gardes. I would suggest that there are three reasons why Futurism should be seen as having died as an avant-garde in 1923. First of all, an avant-garde comes to an end ("terminates") when it either loses its identity as an avant-garde or continues to have one but with a sense of having "arrived," hence without the "re-creative repetition" of its founding vocabulary that I earlier suggested is essential to being an avant-gardist. Guerri may be right that Futurism continued to think of itself as "*in fieri*." Certainly manifestos continued to be produced, exhibitions held, and journals published. Yet when Marinetti and other futurists declare that they want Futurism to become an art of state, there is an unmistakable air of an arrival, of a journey having ceased, even if the goal remains unachieved (as was in fact the case).[40] To put the point another way, what is painfully absent from Futurism after 1923 is a "return" in Foucault's sense of the word—a revisiting of the original vocabulary in order to disrupt mere nostalgic repetitions of it and to revitalize current work.[41]

Second, an avant-garde comes to an end when its vocabulary and practices are "betrayed," which is to say, contradicted or repudiated. Obviously, Marinetti's decision to join the Italian Academy contradicted on a practical level his heroic-period repudiation of "museums, libraries, academies of any sort."[42] Yet Marinetti went much further in his new-found fondness for *passatismo* than simply joining the Academy. As scholars recently have shown, he actively engaged in the work of the Academy by writing articles celebrating important Italians of the past, and he lowered Futurism to the level of publicitarian support for regime projects such as the draining of the Agro Pontino marshes.[43] In general, one might say with Giovanni Lista that the Futurism of the fascist-regime years "does not struggle against the museum but for the museum. Its battle is not one of contestation and opposition but of integration."[44]

Finally, an avant-garde comes to an end when its vocabulary and practices are "terminated" in the sense that it is no longer autonomous or self-determining but has become an appendage of something larger which exercises control over it. Surely this is the decisive point: lacking self-determination, an avant-garde is no longer credible. But how are we to understand this outcome? In one sense, Marinetti in 1923 suffered a failure of nerve: he self-consciously decided to seek shelter under the protective wing of the regime. In a larger and more important sense, however, the totalitarian aspirations and rapidly emerging police-state in Italy (soon to be confirmed by the murder of Giacomo Matteotti in 1924) certainly encouraged this decision. Far from being a bee buzzing in the ear of the fascist state, Futurism would prove to be a faithful sheepdog in the African and Mediterranean pastures through which Mussolini's military machine, such as it was, would seek to roam. No doubt, had Futurism chosen to play the role of the bee in an aggressive manner, it would have run the risk of being summarily swatted and destroyed. Arguably, sustained avant-gardism is possible only in liberal political cultures in which a wide swath is given to public expression, and Italian fascism, however anemic in comparison with Nazi Germany and Stalinist Russia, was certainly not one of those. Nonetheless, there were Italian intellectuals during the fascist regime who played critical roles—typically, but not always, from exile—and I would argue that Marinetti might have made fascist-regime Futurism more the buzzing bee than it was.

Thus, as we reflect on Futurism's legacy, I would suggest that we ought to consider the counter-factual question of how Futurism might have adapted to the role of a buzzing bee or "disconcerting" force, to recall Pettoruti's word, even in a rather inhospitable political environment. Futurism, as we have seen, went through two avant-garde phases. Mythic Futurism was avant-garde in the way its integrated cultural-political performance signaled a spectacularly "revolutionized" vision of modernity. Utopian Futurism was avant-garde because of its creative project of reshaping mythic Futurism into a concrete political ("reformist") program for Italy and leading an alliance of similarly minded groups (*arditi*, *fasci di combattimento*) in an actual electoral campaign. In both these phases or modes, Futurism was avant-garde in the traditional sense of imagining itself on the margin, apart from the center or mainstream, indeed in organized opposition to it. However, the second of these phases—precisely by representing a fundamentally new project—suggests a third possible response (beyond "betrayal" and "termination") that an avant-garde may make when it senses that its founding vocabulary is collapsing: that of creative "transformation." In this "transformation" scenario, "termination" is followed by a creative renewal in which an avant-garde vocabulary is fundamentally revised or even created anew. I would now suggest that Futurism faced another crisis situation in 1923 to which it might have responded with a "transformation" (as it did in 1916), although this transformation would have been not to another form of cultural or political "opposition" but rather to an "immanent" role within the fascist regime—that of the disconcerting, disturbing, contestatory, provocative, iconoclastic element within the mainstream. In this role, an avant-garde functions to keep the system "open" by contesting its "meanings" and "practices," thereby keeping it from becoming complacent, unreflective, corrupt, humdrum, standardized, or otherwise static and safe. With a nod to Adorno, I would call this role "immanently critical" or simply "immanent avant-gardism." This is the kind of role that, for example, Walter Gropius chose to play in 1918 as he sought to transform a now exhausted prewar German expressionism into a Bauhaus movement committed to an immanent critique of art-industry relations in Weimar Germany.

Like Settimelli's characterization of Futurism as "democratic" in 1917, immanent avant-gardism is democratic, yet not simply because—indeed, not primarily because—it is committed to democratic ideals such as equal rights for all or respect for common people. Immanent avant-gardism is democratic because it understands that democracy is always a work in progress. In the terms set forth by Jacques Derrida in a late work, immanent avant-gardism represents and seeks to perform the "singularity" that keeps the system open, that prevents "closure." Immanent avant-gardism understands that democracy is an ideal that is never achieved in practice but is a telos: democracy implies what Derrida calls a "democracy to come."[45] Immanent avant-gardism therefore can certainly incorporate utopian elements—albeit of the sort Marinetti played with in the early 1920s (like "tactilism") rather than of the intellectualist and programmatic sort he developed, 1918–1920—but its main thrust will be critical. Immanent avant-gardism implies skepticism regarding any notion of a finished ideal and a stress on the human-all-too-human. Immanent avant-gardism understands that the things ordinary people take for granted often contain hidden complexities of which they are not aware, that the most basic questions are always unanswerable, and that we must therefore learn to live with those questions even as we may wish to have them resolved.

Had Marinetti and the futurists cast an immanent role for Futurism under fascism, then, they would not have accepted but would have sought to undermine the cult of the Duce and other modes of fixing the meaning of the regime. They would have insisted that fascism remain the open, fluid "doctrine in action" that it constantly proclaimed itself to be rather than the ossified regime it actually became. They would therefore have worked more vigorously against the intransigent, "squadrista" types such as Roberto Farinacci and Achille Starace, and they would simultaneously have promoted a positive image of the "new man" who could not be reduced to the innocuous and often ridiculous image of the futurist as the person whose utopian aspirations are limited to those that can be satisfied by futurist cookbooks. And, in performing this role, they would have anticipated the role that avant-gardes must necessarily perform in late capitalist cultures if they are to continue to have a role in a decentered political world in which center/margin or mainstream/opposition models no longer correspond to historical realities.

Thus, as I see it, the most important legacy of Futurism lies in its trajectory which, to my mind, is suggestive of a "natural" trajectory for avant-gardism in general. No doubt Futurism was strongest in its mythic-heroic period, yet it operated then as an oppositional force that, paradoxically, was bound to be fatally undermined to the degree that its ideals were realized. It then made perfect sense to jettison the mythic structure in favor of a pragmatic logic of means and ends, which is what Futurism did during its subsequent utopian phase. In this phase, the futurist movement weakened especially in terms of its ability to attract and interact with a broad public, and during the fascist-regime phase it arguably weakened in this respect still further. Perhaps it then died a natural death, as Marinetti had initially predicted it would. Yet if there was, as I believe, unrealized potential in this final phase, then it is precisely that aspect of Futurism that is most worthy of further scholarly attention today. The problem for avant-gardes after World War II and for those seeking to operate in contemporary, liberal-democratic cultures is how to be "critical" without either falling off into an unrealizable stance as an "opposition" or "betraying" themselves by becoming fully "integrated" movements whose messages simply "circulate" without any disconcerting, practical effect.[46]

Notes

1. The present account of Marinetti's visit to Argentina is based on a reading of *Crítica*, a Buenos Aires daily, from May 15 through July 1, 1926. For a fuller account based on this same source, see Sylvia Saítta, *Regueros de Tinta: El Diario "Crítica" en la Década de 1920* (Buenos Aires: Editorial Sudamericana, 1998), 164–73.

2. Jorge Luis Borges, "Marinetti Fue una Medida Profilactica," *Crítica* (May 20, 1926): 5. The original reads: "Pienso que sus libros valen muy poco. Son simulacros italianos de Whitman, de Kipling, tal vez de Jules Romains. Cualquiera de esos tres le sobra." Unless otherwise indicated all translations in this paper are my own. For my usage of the concept of "avant-garde," see my *Embattled Avant-gardes: Modernism's Resistance to Commodity Culture in Europe* (Berkeley: University of California Press, 2007), 17–18.

3. "Habrá banquetes con su reserva de epitafios; habrá conferencias con abundancia de boleterías y de premeditatos aspavientos." In answer to the question, "Que influencia ejercerá Marinetti en la literatura argentina," Borges' answer was: "Ninguna." Borges, "Marinetti Fue una Medida Profilactica": 5.

4. Emilio Pettoruti, "Marinetti es un Hombre de una Ingenuidad Infantil que Desconcierta," *Crítica* (May 28, 1926): 5.

5. Filippo Tommaso Marinetti, "Fondazione e Manifesto del Futurismo" (1909), in *Teoria e invenzione futurista*, ed. Luciano De Maria (Milan: Mondadori, 1968), 7 (hereafter abbreviated TIF)—". . . come sentinelle avanzate, di fronte all'esercito delle stelle nemiche."

6. TIF, 13. "Nostri successori . . . ci gettino pure nel cestino, come manoscritti inutili. Noi lo desideriamo!"

7. Richard Rorty, *Contingency, Irony, and Solidarity* (Cambridge: Cambridge University Press, 1989).

8. Although Rorty is not directly concerned in this book with avant-gardes, he uses the word at least twice in connection with his argument; see Rorty, *Contingency*, 48 and 56.

9. Friedrich Nietzsche, *Untimely Meditations*, ed. D. Breazeale, trans. R. J. Hollingdale (Cambridge: Cambridge University Press, 1997), 103.

10. Harold Bloom, *The Anxiety of Influence: A Theory of Poetry* (London: Oxford University Press, 1973), 80.

11. Rorty, *Contingency*, 97, emphasis deleted.

12. Giordano Bruno Guerri, *Filippo Tommaso Marinetti: Invenzioni, avventure e passioni di un rivoluzionario* (Milan: Mondadori, 2009), 90—". . . come fu per trentacinque

anni—un edificio *in fieri*, un modello da plasmare di continuo con nuove intuizioni e adattamenti ai tempi."

13. Jonathan Lear, *Therapeutic Action: An Earnest Plea for Irony* (New York: Other Press, 2003), 32.

14. Lear, *Therapeutic* Action, 55.

15. "Ad ogni uomo, ogni giorno, un mestiere diverso! Inegualismo e Artecrazia" (1922), in TIF, 551. "Non sono l'eguale di nessuno. Tipo nuovo. Modello inimitabile. Non copiatemi, voi. Nuvole plagiarie! Basta! conosco tutte le vostre forme. Sono tutte da me catalogate. Originalità! Fantasia!"

16. Luca Somigli, *Legitimizing the Artist: Manifesto Writing and European Modernism 1885–1915* (Toronto: University of Toronto Press, 2003), 104–14, 248n26.

17. "Fondazione e Manifesto del Futurismo," TIF, 9. "Usciamo dalla saggezza come da un orribile guscio . . . questa eterna et inutile ammirazione del passato."

18. See, among others, Luciano De Maria, "Introduzione," in TIF, lvii–lix; Robert S. Dombroski, *L'esistenza ubbidiente: Letterati italiani sotto il fascismo* (Naples: Guida, 1984), 43–45; and Cinzia Sartini Blum, *The Other Modernism: F.T. Marinetti's Futurist Fiction of Power* (Berkeley: University of California Press, 1996), viii, 16. However, these scholars tend to see Futurism as myth extending into the postwar period whereas I see it as effectively ending with its "realization" in the war.

19. Georges Sorel, *Reflections on Violence*, trans. T. E. Hulme and J. Roth (New York: Collier, 1961), 50.

20. For a fuller discussion of *L'Italia futurista*, see my *Embattled Avant-gardes*, 102–4, and *Avant-garde Florence: From Modernism to Fascism* (Cambridge: Harvard University Press, 1993), 219–24. See also Luciano Caruso, ed., *L'Italia futurista* (Florence: SPES, 1992), which includes an anastatic reproduction and index of the journal's entire print run.

21. Maurizio Calvesi, *Le due avanguardie*, 2 vols. [Vol. 1, *Studi sul Futurismo*] (Milan: Lerici, 1966); *Il Futurismo* (Milan: Fabbri, 1970); and *Il Futurismo: La fusione della vita nell'arte* (Milan: Fabbri, 1977).

22. Calvesi, *Le due avanguardie*, 1:47—"proposta integrale di rinnovamento della cultura . . . realizzando così, con una formula del tutto nuova e rivoluzionaria, una tendenza all'incontro diretto e alla continuazione tra arte e vita."

23. Calvesi, *Le due avanguardie*, 1:6—"troppi elementi, anche esterni e oggettivi, stanno a dimostrare la perfetta solidarietà di Boccioni (e basta legger il suo epistolario) con il Marinetti."

24. Calvesi, "Attraverso Marinetti," a preface to Claudia Salaris, *Filippo Tommaso Marinetti* (Scandicci: La Nuova Italia, 1988), 31—"civiltà delle immagini."

25. Filippo Tommaso Marinetti, Emilio Settimelli, Mario Carli, *Che cos'è il Futurismo: Nozioni elementari* (Milan: Direzione del movimento futurista, 1920).

26. See Filippo Tommaso Marinetti, *Critical Writings*, ed. Günter Berghaus, trans. D. Thompson (New York: Farrar, Straus, and Giroux, 2006), 369.

27. Enrico Crispolti, *Storia e critica del Futurismo* (Rome and Bari: Laterza, 1986), xv—"marinetticentrismo."

28. Emilio Gentile suggests that Marinetti asserted a continuity between the *serate*, the interventionist demonstrations, and the *squadrismo* of the early postwar years, and that he was right to do so. Yet *squadrismo* was never a specifically futurist practice and the role of the futurists in it was minimal, even if highly celebrated by them. See Gentile, *"La nostra sfida alle stelle": Futuristi in politica* (Rome: Laterza, 2009), 95.

29. "Manifesto del partito futurista italiano" (1918), in TIF, 158. "Il partito politico futurista che noi fondiamo oggi, e che organizzeremo dopo la guerra, sarà nettamente distinto dal movimento artistico futurista. . . . Potranno aderire al partito futurista tutti gli italiani, uomini e donne d'ogni classe e d'ogni età, anche se negati a qualsiasi concetto artistico e letterario."

30. Gentile, *"La nostra sfida alle stelle"* and "Il Futurismo e la politica: Dal nazionalismo modernista al fascismo (1909–1920)," in Renzo de Felice, ed., *Futurismo, cultura e politica* (Turin: Fondazione Giovanni Agnelli, 1988), 105–59.

31. Emilio Settimelli, "Il massacro dei Pancioni," *L'Italia futurista* 2, 26 (12 August 1917): 1–2. "L'arte non è che una parte del programma futurista. Sarà la più sviluppata, ma non è certo la più importante."

32. Settimelli, "Il massacro dei Pancioni," "Si confonde il Futurismo con una specie di superomismo e di aristocrazia assolutista. Niente di più falso. Il Futurismo è *democratico*. . . . Riconosciamo tutti i diritti alle classi lavoratrici e produttrici e nel nostro programma è in prima linea '*la difesa economica e l'educazione del proletariato.*' Il nostro nazionalismo è antitradizionale ed *eminentemente democratico.*"

33. Ardengo Soffici, "Principî di un'estetica futurista," *La Raccolta* (15 August–15 October 1918), 95–98. See also the discussion in my "Soffici and the Religion of Art," in Matthew Affron and Mark Antliff, eds., *Fascist Visions: Art and Ideology in France and Italy* (Princeton: Princeton University Press, 1997), 59–60.

34. Gentile, *"La nostra sfida alle stelle,"* 53.

35. *Al di là del comunismo* (1920), in TIF, 473, and Gentile, *"La nostra sfida alle stelle,"* 125. "L'umanità cammina verso l'individualismo anarchico, mèta e sogno d'ogni spirito forte. . . . Il comunismo è l'esasperazione [l'espressione] del cancro burocratico."

36. Gentile, *"La nostra sfida alle stelle,"* 128. "Nel regime fascista, Marinetti e i futuristi in camicia nera continuarono ad avere atteggiamenti da ribelli novatori, ma delegarono al duce e al partito fascista la creazione dell'italiano nuovo nel laboratorio totalitario dove il conformismo era dogma di messa."

37. "Il tattilismo" (1921), TIF, 161 ("l'amore e l'amicizia"; "gli appetiti materiali"); Claudia Salaris, *Marinetti: Arte e vita futurista* (Rome: Editori Riuniti, 1997), 212–53.

38. Marja Härmänmaa, *Un patriota che sfidò la decadenza: F. T. Marinetti e l'idea dell'uomo nuovo fascista, 1929–1944* (Helsinki: Academia Scientiarum Fennica, 2000).

39. For more on the futurist cultural politics of the 1930s, see Claudia Salaris, *Artecrazia: L'avanguardia futurista negli anni del fascismo* (Florence: La Nuova Italia, 1992) and my *Embattled Avant-gardes*, 247 48.

40. One of the documents that most clearly exemplifies this sense of arrival is Fillia, "Rapporto tra Futurismo e fascismo" (1930), now in Luciano Caruso, ed.,

Manifesti, proclami, interventi e documenti teorici del Futurismo, 1909–1944, 4 vols. (Florence: Coedizioni SPES-Salimbeni, 1990), vol. 2, document 196.

41. Michel Foucault, "What is an Author?" in *Language, Counter-memory, Practice: Selected Essays and Interviews*, ed. Donald F. Bouchard, trans. Donald F. Bouchard and Sherry Simon (Ithaca: Cornell University Press, 1977), 131–36. See also Hal Foster, *The Return of the Real: The Avant-garde at the End of the Century* (Cambridge, MA: MIT Press, 1996), 1–4.

42. "Fondazione e Manifesto del Futurismo," in TIF, 11 ("i musei, le biblioteche, le accademie d'ogni specie").

43. Matteo D'Ambrosio, *Le "Commemorazioni in Avanti" di F.T. Marinetti* (Naples: Liguori, 1999) and Massimiliano Vittori, ed., *Futurismo e Agro Pontino* (Latina: Novecento, 2000). See also Härmänmaa, *Un patriota che sfidò la decadenza*, 152–60.

44. Giovanni Lista, *Arte e politica: Il futurismo di sinistra in Italia* (Milan: Multhipla, 1980), 19.

45. Jacques Derrida, *The Politics of Friendship*, trans. George Collins (London: Verso, 1997), 22, 104.

46. The latter alternative is the nightmare described in Paul Mann, *The Theory-Death of the Avant-garde* (Bloomington: Indiana University Press, 1991) and *Masocriticism* (Albany: State University of New York Press, 1999).

~

CHAPTER SEVENTEEN

Futurism and the Politics of the Ugly

Theory, History, and Actuality

SASCHA BRU

The Mock Turtle went on. "We had the best of educations . . . Reeling and Writing, of course, to begin with, and then the different branches of Arithmetic—Ambition, Distraction, Uglification, and Derision."

"I never heard of Uglification," Alice ventured to say. "What is it?"

The Gryphon lifted up both its paws in surprise. "Never heard of ugli-fying!" it exclaimed. "You know what to beautify is, I suppose?"

"Yes," said Alice, doubtfully: "it means—to—make—anything—prettier."

"Well, then," the Gryphon went on, "if you don't know what to uglify is, you are a simpleton."

—Lewis Carroll, *The Adventures of Alice in Wonderland* (1865)

Modern art and literature have always been drawn to the ugly. Few studies so forcibly bring out that Italian Futurism marked a pivotal turning point in this respect as Karl Vossler's *Italienische Literatur der Gegenwart* (1914). An admirer of Benedetto Croce and teacher of Erich Auerbach, Vossler concluded his book with a mere four pages on Futurism. Like many of his contemporaries he was quick to highlight Futurism's deviatory poetic. After a book-length survey of Italian literature since Romanticism, he claimed that with Futurism the bond between literature and life had been completely cut.[1] Futurism, Vossler averred, brought nothing but perennial noise and a grotesque, monstrous laughter, beyond good and evil, and immersed in solipsism. As evidence he cited Aldo Palazzeschi's *Il Controdolore* (1913) at some length (mentioning neither author nor title).[2] Palazzeschi's provocative manifesto, Vossler stressed, encouraged readers to laugh heartily in the face of deformity, disease, famine, poverty, old age, natural disaster and death—without grounding the necessity thereof. Briefly mocking Futurism's activities in the plastic arts as well, Vossler may have had Umberto Boccioni's *Antigrazioso* (1912) in mind. He also referred to Marinetti's 1912 *Manifesto tecnico*, highlighting its poetic of substantivization, its promotion of the infinitive and of numerical symbols, and its plea to do away with syntax. Such hollow poetic exploits, Vossler claimed, left not much intact of Futurism's imperialist, pan-Italian "Grossenwahn," and, by extension, of its intent to unite art and life.[3] For the futurists, busy "burying the one old art," were in fact the sign of a deeper crisis in contemporary Italian literature, according to Vossler. While all other fields in Italy were rapidly advancing, Futurism embodied a standstill in literature. Closing his book on Italian literary history on this bleak note, Vossler might have realized that a more optimistic final paragraph was needed. He concluded: "But is it a problem if in the language of the heart an interval occurs? I for my part am even convinced it is a positive thing. In order for the heart to say something sincere, it often needs to be silent for a while." Adding insult to injury, Vossler thus depicted Futurism as a "pause" in Italian literary history, as a moment upon which literature got put on hold so that it could recharge itself and eventually rearticulate itself with "life."[4]

Vossler's assessment of Futurism, perhaps more than any other diatribe against the movement launched at this point, raises a number of pivotal questions. How, for instance, could or can "literature" be "paused"? Clearly, Vossler did not consider Futurism to be art or literature. Why? An admirer of Croce,[5] Vossler's first and most obvious reason to condemn Futurism might have been the movement's outward despising of Croce. Croce was both a central figure in Italian artistic debate and, as a philosopher influenced by Hegel, a known Germanophile. As a result, Marinetti and his followers seized every opportunity to attack Croce in public.[6] Yet so did Vossler's *Italienische Literatur* on closer inspection. For this book too, especially in its treatment of Futurism, was not fully in accord with Croce's aesthetic. Whether Vossler misinterpreted Crocean aesthetics or not is unimportant. Relevant is that when his book is read alongside Croce's aesthetics, a fundamental disagreement between both critics emerges on the nature of the ugly.

All the examples from Futurism Vossler drew on brought out its repulsive, distorted, nauseating and disgusting nature. This suggests that to Vossler Futurism was not art or literature because of its deliberate promotion of the ugly. He saw but ugliness in the movement's exploits and for this reason was unable to qualify them as literary or aesthetic. Vossler, admittedly, did not mention the term "ugly" in his book, but he could easily have done so. Quoting Marinetti's 1912 technical manifesto, for example, he must have paused at the outcry: "Let us courageously make ugly things in literature, and let's kill solemness everywhere."[7] By implying that the ugly forms and contents of Futurism did not deserve to be treated as literature, Vossler closely followed Hegel in a direction Croce refused to. In his writings on aesthetics, Hegel always had been quite unambiguous when dealing with the ugly: avoid it, soften it if needs be, but know that the ugly has no place in art, which is the realm of beauty. Whence his famous claim that there is no room in art for the Devil.

By contrast, Croce's *Estetica* (1902)—and this is all too often forgotten—marked what is perhaps best considered the emergence of an aesthetic theory that stood firmly in line with the foregrounding of the ugly so characteristic of the modernist avant-gardes at large. Indeed, it has often been argued that with the advent of the modernist avant-gardes the beautiful and the sublime made room for the ugly. As Clement Greenberg, trailblazer of the avant-garde, once remarked: "all profoundly original art looks ugly at first."[8] Breaching audiences' and readers' expectations, and going against the aesthetic norm, Greenberg claimed, the novelty of all avant-gardes is at par with their ugliness. This is why the modernist avant-gardes were quite consistently rejected in their own time as "dissonant, obscure, scandalous, immoral, subversive, and generally 'antisocial.'"[9] A (misogynous) "cult of ugliness"[10] took root in nearly all (continental) avant-gardes.[11] Rightly so, it has often been observed (as Vossler did as well in *Italienische Literatur*) that the avant-gardes thereby extended certain features of (Post-)Symbolism and Decadentism. Yet, as will become apparent, Italian Futurism went much further than any preceding modernist movement. Moreover, it was also in Italy, with Croce's *Estetica*, that the first systematized theory of (and apology for) the ugly emerged. To bring out the innovative nature of both Futurism's and Croce's aesthetic, a brief survey is warranted first of the history of the ugly in modern literature and aesthetics.

Croce's *Estetica*: A Futurist Theory of the Ugly

Up and until Croce, the ugly in modern aesthetics had been defined as those forms, topics and practices which, at a certain point in history, challenge what counts as art and literature. The ugly thus always had been depicted as broadening the domain of beauty within a specific historical constellation. Some of the founding texts of modern art and literature already dealt with the ugly. No doubt the most famous of these is Friedrich Schlegel's *Über das Studium der griechischen Poesie* (1795). Espousing a view typical of Jena Romanticism,[12] Schlegel claimed that art only became truly modern with authors like himself, writers who also paid attention to the ugly. As Schlegel had it, beauty had always been the norm, with neither the sublime nor the interesting marking its true counterpart, but the ugly, that which simply was not treated or seen as art. A modern artist, self-conscious of his practice, was therefore also to plunge head-first into the ugly, to explore it, and to consider whether advances in art could also be made by bringing aspects of the ugly into the realm of beauty.[13] Hans-Robert Jauss has pointed out that Schlegel should be considered one of the founders of modern art and literature,[14] because with Schlegel the insight emerged that the entire dynamic of change in modern aesthetics could well be summarized by an endless exploration of the ugly. True change in modern art always occurs by bringing into art ugly contents and forms that at a certain point in time are not considered as part of art. This is, for example, why the symbolists' turn to the city and everyday metropolitan life in poetry was received as both distasteful and groundbreaking. This is also why today Marcel Duchamp's simplest ready-mades are still being remembered by a wider audience.

What Schlegel's study of (pre)modern poetry did for German Romanticism, Victor Hugo's long introduction to his play *Cromwell* (1827) did for French Romanticism. Art portrays nature, Hugo argued, and because nature on occasion is also ugly, its more seedy aspects too were to be the subject of writing. As Schlegel before, however, Hugo made beauty turn full circle: here too the ugly and the grotesque were in the end to add luster to, or to expand, the domain of beauty.[15] This tendency to subjugate the ugly to beauty was also characteristic of Karl Rozenkranz's famous *Ästhetik des Hässlichen* (1853), a study that deeply influenced many French symbolists, most notably Charles Baudelaire. A student of Hegel, Rozenkranz was the first to systematically think about the ugly in all its forms. Distinguishing various such forms (in nature, in thought, and in art), he paid ample attention to the grotesque and to caricature. Yet for Rozenkranz too it was the *beauty* of the ugly in art, the way in which seemingly ugly phenomena could be made to bear on beauty that really mattered.[16] An affluent reader of Rozenkranz, Baudelaire in turn looked to *beautify* the ugly. The title of his most famous book of poetry is obviously telling in this respect: *Les fleurs du mal*. Thematically introducing in poetry aspects of everyday life that before had no place there—extreme poverty, subjects dying, carcasses, etc.—Baudelaire further praised Goya's portrayal of ugly, monstrous figures, because of their imaginative power. Goya's monsters did not exist in reality, and Baudelaire thereby seconded Hugo's earlier observation that the introduction of the ugly into the realm of beauty could also considerably expand that realm's imaginative horizon.[17]

Although it is impossible to do full justice here to Croce's dense and rich *Estetica come scienza dell'espressione e linguistica generale* (1902), its treatment of the ugly is worth highlighting, since it quite radically broke with previous approaches to the issue. Croce's treatise took stock of the history of the ugly in modern aesthetics, and claimed, quite simply, that everyone before him had looked at it the wrong way. Chapters X and XI of his study are entirely devoted to the ugly, and his post-Hegelian view of it can be summarized thus:

(i)   the aesthetic aspect of the spirit (*Geist*) is fundamental to all other spiritual activities. For to express itself as stimuli fall upon it, the spirit must first impose a form on them, and precisely this is aesthetic activity. Thus, even the most modest of linguistic utterances is in essence aesthetic. Whenever the spirit *expresses* itself and gives form to the world surrounding it, it engages in aesthetic activity. Put still differently, language, as the first manifestation of the spirit, *is* the aesthetic.

(ii) Art, and literature in particular, is to be considered one of the most vital aspects of human existence, yet in the broadest of terms all human expressions (even those in science) are aesthetic. What distinguishes the poet's words from others' is their *form*. A poet is a subject who engages primarily in aesthetic activity, from which all other human activities take their cue. These other activities are the logical (the conceptualization of the world), the economical (the regulation of desires and wantings) and the ethical (the differentiation of good and evil). None of these other activities are relevant in defining art. When a subject regards a work of art or reads a poem, all of these activities are of course brought into play. But what ultimately defines a work of art is the moment of its creation, the moment upon which the poet intuitively expresses his idea or mood in a particular form.

(iii) By consequence, the contents of a work of art is always secondary. Content emerges only after aesthetic activity, when conceptual or logical activity (interpretation) takes off. As a result, it does not matter which feeling, object or stimulus an artistic subject wishes to express. Whether that object is commonly considered beautiful or ugly is irrelevant too. There is in fact no distinction between the beautiful and the ugly. By nature, expression *simpliciter* and the aesthetic always coincide.

Croce's idealist aesthetic fundamentally broke with previous attempts to domesticate the ugly. To begin with it clearly implied that predecessors had been mistaken when they coupled the ugly to moral and ethical matters entailed by works of art. Likewise, it was a mistake to think of the ugliness/

beauty opposition in terms of feelings of pleasure and displeasure. All of these aspects come *after* the aesthetic activity, and do not define the work of art as such. The aim (and quintessence) of any creative work, rather, is imitation, reproduction, or expression of the idea or mood dominant in the creator's mind. So what of it if that idea is ugly? To be good art, it needs only accurate form or expression. It is ugly in the aesthetic sense only if it is poor expression.

That Vossler in his *Italienische Literatur* did not fully adhere to Croce's aesthetic will be clear now. Perhaps himself still intuitively responding to Futurism, Vossler's assessment of Futurism seems above all to have been grounded in deep feelings of displeasure. As a result, he was able to see only ugliness in Futurism, and, going against Croce, concluded that literature had thereby momentarily been put on hold, leading to a devastating crisis in Italian literature. From a Crocean perspective no such crisis could be discerned, however. At best, Futurism could be blamed for presenting bad, inaccurate forms. Vossler's difficulty to bring home Futurism's aesthetic later resurfaced in a letter to Marinetti: "Indeed, I gather that in Futurism there is something which is already gone, already dead or born dead, and this is particularly its ironical and playful humor in relation to reality, something completely outdated which we find as such in the romantics, particularly the German ones." Now putting Futurism on a par with modern literature since (German) Romanticism, he added: "I wouldn't exclude that some day I might write an article with an interpretation of Futurism."[18] That day never came, however, but Vossler's change of heart suggests that perhaps he had come to realize that Futurism and Croce were less removed from one another than public debate made it out to be.

Indeed, given the centrality of the ugly in the modernist avant-gardes at large, it would be no exaggeration to state that Croce's aesthetic theory came as a timely approach to the ugly. Placing full responsibility in the hands of sovereign, creative subjects, his work in a way liberated artists and writers from bothering with an issue that had been troubling writers for at least a century. Croce's trans-historical or general stance *vis-à-vis* (the ugly in) art came particularly close to Futurism's iconoclastic, presentist poetic. That the futurists did not publicly draw on Croce as a supporter is therefore highly ironic. For soon after the publication of Croce's *Estetica*, they began to flesh out Croce's aesthetic in their artistic and literary practices. In this process, the liberation of intuition, and the stress on the aesthetic act for its own sake, were but a few aspects that would forcibly re-emerge. The questions raised by Vossler's *Italienische Literatur*, in short, uncover the story of a missed opportunity to arrive at a fruitful dialogue. Marinetti's manifestos, for instance, never put forth a distinctly futurist theory of the ugly—although Futurism's aesthetic practices do allow us to reconstruct such a theory, as we will presently see. Hence, Crocean aesthetics may well have boiled down to the theory of the ugly lacking in Marinetti's writings.

All of this is not to say of course that Croce's idealist aesthetic would be useful to describe historical changes in modern art. To this aim the romanticist paradigm that emerged with Schlegel proves much more fruitful. It can indeed be argued that the dynamic of modern art and literature is largely governed by the introduction of ever different "foreign," "inaesthetic" objects, topics and motifs—in general, ugly contents—and ugly forms and modes of report. This in turn is not to suggest that the ugly would be a stable aesthetic category. It is in fact always historically and culturally contingent. Aiming to define art in general, none of this was Croce's concern. It should be ours, however, if we want to assess the importance of Futurism with regards to the modern tradition of the ugly. Did Futurism introduce true ugliness into art in its own time? And, if so, did this fundamentally change art and literature thereafter?

Futurism's "Beautification" of Politics

Like their modern predecessors, futurists to an extent continued to work with the opposition between the ugly and beauty, trying to domesticate the former within the latter. In his manifestos Marinetti rhetorically did away with all traditions except with that of the ugly. Like Schlegel, he appears to have believed that for (futurist) art to present a considerable advance, it had to introduce certain forms and contents that so far had not been assigned a place in art. In his *Discorso futurista ai veneziani* (1910), for example, he warned: "Citizens of Venice, slaves of the past, do not cry out against the alleged ugliness of locomotives, of tramways and of automobiles, from which we are able to extract, by flashes of genius, the great futurist aesthetic!"[19] Thus firmly inscribing Futurism into a distinctly modern tradition, and explicitly "uglifying" art, Marinetti's efforts at first sight presented little more than a radicalization of Aestheticism's championing of modern technological advances, violence and war.

And yet, there was some truth to his claim in the *Manifesto tecnico* that a wedge could be driven between literature from Homer onward, and Futurism proper. As can be deduced from my all too brief survey of the ugly in literary aesthetics, before Futurism the ugly had been mainly introduced into literature on a *noumenal* level—that is, as an idea, motif or form for *contemplation*. Futurism went one step further by extending this process to the *phenomenal* level as well—that is, to the domain of aesthetic *action*. In so doing it not only broadened (performative) writing to include the performance of texts.

As Marinetti exclaimed in a speech first given in 1910: "We glorify at the same time patriotism, war—the world's only hygiene—destructive actions by libertarians, and beautiful ideas to die for, gloriously opposed to ugly ideas people live for."[20] To Marinetti, then, the ugly too was to be found perhaps first and foremost on the level of aesthetic practices, not on the level of reflection or aesthetic ideas. Hence, Futurism also considerably broadened the range of the ugly itself. For with the radicalization of previous tendencies in Aestheticism there also came a casting outward of those tendencies, and this is most typically illustrated by Futurism's "art-action" program, its introduction of various practices that were arguably not considered part and parcel of (Italian) art and literature at the time. It is not my intention here to recall all such futurist (performance) practices.[21] Rather, I would like to isolate one such form of "art-action" to the end of sketching out the legacy and lasting actuality of Futurism when it comes to the ugly: its transgressive treatment of politics *as* art, which culminated in the erection of the Futurist Political Party (hereafter FPP) in 1919.

Futurism and Politics

Much has been made of the ties between Futurism and politics, but I know of no critic who has read these ties in light of the modern debate on the nature of the ugly.[22] That Croce was no admirer of Futurism's political "excursions" is an understatement. In 1924 he stressed that the seeds of fascism had been able to grow in Futurism. The movement's determination to go down on the streets, to impose its desires and moods on others, to shut others with dissenting views up if needs be: all of these practices foreshadowed fascist politics, according to Croce.[23] Yet Croce did not define these practices as distinctly aesthetic. Rather, he differentiated Futurism's political actions from its artistic and literary exploits. A decade later, Walter Benjamin did exactly the opposite when he asserted that the futurists had dangerously embarked on an "aestheticization of politics."[24] Yet, whereas Croce put the stress on Futurism's public actions, Benjamin in turn restricted his scope to Futurism's texts and artworks, placing the movement within a post-Nietzschean and anarchist tradition that glorified *beaux gestes libertaires*, and depicted the social masses as a malleable, aesthetic object. Only when Croce and Benjamin are read in tandem, by consequence, does the real change entailed by Futurism's exploits show itself: it was perhaps the first artistic movement with roots in literature to introduce *practical* politics into the realm of art.

The synergy of Futurism and politics up to and until the instauration of the FPP in 1919 has been documented extensively.[25] Ferruccio Vecchi, one of the *Arditi* working closely together with Marinetti since the end of the Great War, observed that until the abysmal failure of the FPP in the 1919 elections Marinetti turned to practical politics as an object of aesthetic play.[26] Indications thereof first surfaced in the year Marinetti's founding manifesto was published in *Le Figaro*. In 1909 he issued the first political manifesto of Futurism. With this short text addressing "Elettori futuristi" Marinetti launched his movement in the public sphere as a political force, and gave rise to rumors that he would one day stand in elections. Throughout the following decade numerous manifestos, street actions and performances continued to boost such rumors. Yet Marinetti simultaneously remained vague about what Futurism exactly proposed in practical political terms.

This changed in early 1918, when he published the *Manifesto del partito futurista italiano* in the final issue of *L'Italia futurista*. Here, Marinetti laid out a design for a new state, announcing a veritable constitutional turn-over to be followed by a series of measures that would radically break with Italian traditions in all domains of society. A performative act, the manifesto launched the FPP at a time when no such party existed yet. Although Marinetti thereafter on occasion distinguished the futurists' actions in politics from those in art, just before the 1919 elections he left little doubt about their unison. *Democrazia futurista. Dinamismo politica* (1919), for instance, opened with a preface entitled "Un movimento artistico crea un Partito Politico." In all pamphlets and manifestos to appear from here on the same message was time and again repeated, Marinetti meanwhile painstakingly (and only partially successfully) trying to get his FPP off the ground. Ultimately, artists would come to power if the FPP won the elections, because the whole of "life" was an art form.[27] Whence his proposal to foster the aesthetic sensibility of as many (young) people as possible, whom he characterized as a suppressed proletariat of geniuses. For if life is an art-form, everyone is an artist. In the projected futurist state, therefore, everyone would in addition become a (potential) politician.

In brief, Marinetti regarded politics not as something distinct from art, but as art, as an ugly object that had to find a place within art as well. In so doing he created a sort of *readymade politics*. Citing elements from constitutional and civil law in his manifestos, addressing audiences in speeches that at least in part copied conventional forms of political address, he re-inscribed those elements and forms into novel constellations, holding them before the electorate as a deforming mirror. By trying to put his ideas into practice, moreover, he embarked on what would soon turn out to be an impossible endeavor in liberal democracies: to expand the boundaries of the socially differentiated field of art so that art also came to include the field of politics. Marinetti's pre-election writings and actions, as so often, mainly abolished what was. Only if and when the FPP would have seized power, would the real work have begun. Perhaps luckily, this real "beautification" of politics never came about.

Clearly, an idealist aesthetic akin to Croce's informed the entire endeavor. As intuitive "aesthetic activity" to Croce grounded all other human activity, Croce's view basically entailed that everyone was a poet as well—although the term "aesthetic" in Croce of course covered a much wider terrain than that of art alone. Typical too, especially of the years shortly before the 1919 elections, is that Marinetti no longer bothered to label his political-*cum*-aesthetic project "ugly." Partially grounding the necessity of the FPP's success in "objective" social and political data (unemployment rates, evidence of social unrest, etc.) it was above all the artists' intuition that warranted (and allegedly guaranteed) the FPP's success. The distinction between beauty/ugliness thus ceased to be pertinent as well.

An enormous amount of critical work, whether apologetic or condemning, has situated Futurism within its specifically Italian political culture in order to explain why, from the outset, politics and art were fused in the "great book of Futurism," as Marinetti would later call it in *Gli Indomabili* (1922).[28] But despite the baffling stock of work on Futurism and politics, it would seem that the "ugliness" of politics *as art* to this very day continues to trouble audiences. Indeed, what makes Futurism's aesthetic-*cum*-political experimentation so pertinent to modern art and literature is precisely that it continues to question what counts as art and what not. None of the great exhibitions on Futurism, for example, have ventured to incorporate the process leading up to the FPP into Futurism's aesthetic project. Whether we turn to the exhibition held at MoMA in 1961,[29] to the most comprehensive Futurism show so far organized by Pontus Hulten in the Palazzo Grassi in Venice,[30] or, even more recently, to the exhibition *Le futurisme à Paris* at the Centre Pompidou,[31] curators as a rule tend to exclude this most radical aspect of the movement, and relegate it to the margins as non-art. In this sense, Futurism is certainly no isolated instance. Many examples could be given of writers and artists who later on in the twentieth century set up projects similar to that of the futurists, while not being taken all that seriously as writers or artists.[32]

Post-Futurism: Jeder Mensch ein Politiker

Debates continue to be waged as to whether Futurism's attempted "beautification" of politics went hand in glove with the foundation of fascist politics—despite the fact that it has long been shown that there was a strong left wing within Futurism as well.[33] Futurism's wide array of positions on the political palette can be explained precisely by reading them against the backdrop of an aesthetic that introduced practical politics as a building block of art. For such an aesthetic has no predefined political "color." To illustrate this, it suffices to move a bit further into twentieth-century art, and to look at certain artists whose work would probably be unthinkable without the rupture of sorts brought about by Futurism.

Futurism's "beautification" of politics not only presented a break when read against the background of foregoing discussions about the ugly. It also made possible later practices in twentieth-century art and literature. The attraction of practical politics as an ugly aspect of everyday life to be domesticated in art indeed marks a great deal of twentieth-century art. Of all the avatars of the neo-avant-garde, Joseph Beuys is perhaps particularly worth mentioning in this context, as he is arguably not frequently associated with Italian Futurism.[34] Known among others for his further exploration of the ugly, and for his love-hate relationship with Duchamp, Beuys criticized the latter's readymades for only implying, and not spelling out, that all men are artists.[35] As if recalling Marinetti, Beuys therefore time and again repeated that the "most important thing, for someone looking at my objects, is my fundamental thesis: EACH MAN IS AN ARTIST. There is my contribution to the 'history of art.'"[36] That same thesis also rested at the heart of his concept of "social sculpture," Beuys' conviction that people could come to change themselves and society only from within the aesthetic realm, by looking at the social as a work of art.[37] Beuys developed this concept slowly and in phases. In 1971 he launched a performance, an event of "art-action" of his own, entitled *So kann die Parteien-Diktatur überwunden werden* (This is How to Surpass Party Dictatorship). In essence a deforestation protest involving the sweeping of a forest floor and painting white crosses and rings on all trees slated to be felled, the title of Beuys' performance was curious, to say the least. Why sweep a forest if you are against political parties? In response to this query, Beuys a year later launched his *Organisation für direkte Demokratie durch Volksabstimmung* (Organization for Direct Democracy through Plebiscite). The basic idea underlying this organization was simple: political power had to be taken out of the hands of political parties, which tended to serve their own interests, and people, especially those who have no right to speak in official politics, had to be engaged in democratic politics directly by means of referenda. Thus, following the launch of his *Organisation für direkte Demokratie*, Beuys organized a marathon of debate lasting one hundred days during the fifth Documenta in Kassel. Sidestepping the downtrodden paths of party-politics, Beuys gathered environmental, peace, ethnic, women's, civil rights, and spiritual movements, all drawing up designs for a better future and devising concrete initiatives to be taken within practical politics.[38]

As had been the case with Marinetti, Beuys too was tempted to go out and test the barriers of the artistic institution to the point of collapse. In 1976 he first became an independent candidate for the German Bundestag and three years later, under the auspices of the Green Party, became a candidate for the European Parliament. Although Beuys did play a role in founding the Green Party, he never went as far as to erect his own artistic party. Moreover, just as he accused Duchamp for not making explicit that each man was an artist, Beuys in turn could be accused of not having said that, as an artist by nature, each man is a politician too. Giving countless lectures on his views of politics in the 1980s, Beuys indeed was hesitant to reiterate what Futurism had made explicit before. And yet, the example of Beuys—and no doubt many others could be added here—illustrates how practical politics throughout the foregoing century kept cropping up as an ugly phenomenon to be conquered for art. Curiously, it would appear that artists here very often began from scratch, frequently suffering from forms of memory loss as well by not referring to Italian Futurism. But as will be clear now, Beuys' and others' actions testing the boundaries between art and politics after Futurism justly deserve to be called exactly that: *post*-futurist.

The Eclipse of the Ugly, or, the End of Art?

While a comprehensive and scholarly study of the ugly in Western aesthetics still has to be written, Umberto Eco's recent *Storia dell bruttezza* (History of Ugliness, 2007) comes perhaps the closest to it. Locating "the triumph of the ugly" in the modernist avant-gardes as well, the final chapter of Eco's book, "Il brutto oggi" (Ugliness Today), suggests that today we may well be witnessing the eclipse of ugliness' aesthetic distinctness, as the ugly has pervaded and come to fashion popular culture and everyday life at large.[39] When Eco contrasts two images of heavily pierced, goggle-eyed grotesques from a sixteenth-century painting by Hieronymus Bosch with a 1998 photograph of a punk, his point seems to be well-made. Yet, is it correct? If it were indeed true that there is no ugliness left for contemporary writers and artists to "beautify," then this comes with far-reaching ramifications, especially when viewed from within the paradigm of the ugly launched with Romanticism. Within that paradigm progress in art would then no longer be conceivable.

If so, we would now be dealing with the negative cliché found in Vossler's *Italienische Literatur*. Vossler unearthed only ugliness in Futurism and because of that failed to regard it as art. When we recall Vossler's indebtedness to Hegel there was a profundity to his words not yet highlighted. For Vossler's claim that Futurism put (Italian) literature on hold also could be taken literally; his concluding remarks—"dass es gut ist" (that it's good)—signaling no more than an afterthought covering up the seriousness of his diagnosis. Vossler's analysis of Futurism, after all, figured within a book-length study of modern Italian literature from Romanticism onward. As is well-known, to Hegel Romanticism marked both the perfection and end-point of literature as an expressive form. Literature (the highest of all art forms), for Hegel, had reached its expressive limit; its spirit or *Geist*, had been exhausted in Romanticism as literature made full-circle in attaining complete awareness of itself *as literature*.[40] It is this very process of growing self-awareness that Vossler too charted in his *Italienische Literatur*. Starting out with the "harmonious" work of Manzoni and Leopardi, which could still depict a world in which individual and community coincided, his literary history ended with the triumph of individualism, fragmentation, and social disintegration. Hence, like György Lukács would do somewhat later with Expressionism, Vossler might in part also have projected a teleological Hegelian narrative of which Futurism was the logical conclusion. Similarly, Eco's alleged "end of the ugly" could be interpreted as a sign of a much deeper crisis, coinciding at worst with the end of art, when the latter is defined as the realm of beauty. Such wholesale claims, naturally, always beg caution, yet Futurism would appear to offer a way of testing them. If, indeed, practical politics is one of the most ugly, seemingly inaesthetic, if not outright dangerous, facets of modern life art can harbor, is there work of recent years to suggest that the ugly *as such* has lost its pivotal role in art?

Perhaps. Artist groups like the Yes Men, for example, suggest that we may well have reached a point where the boundaries have evaporated between the realm of beauty and its "negative," as Theodor Adorno called the ugly in *Ästhetische Theorie*.[41] The Yes Men, composed of performance artists and designers Andy Bichlbaum and Mike Bonanno, have gained somewhat of a cult-status in the United States. Their actions cover a wide range of areas, and appear to have brought the tradition launched by Marinetti, the foregrounding of practical politics as ugly, to its logical conclusion. For, unlike their predecessors, the Yes Men no longer engage in discussions about their or others' identity *as artists*. Nor do they claim, as Beuys could have dubbed Marinetti, that everyone is a politician. Instead, their work shows that within art, subjects can take up whatever role as social *agent* they desire— the distinction between the ugly/beauty as a result also fully collapsing, since there is in fact nothing distinguishing the inside of the realm of beauty from the outside. Their list of exploits is rather long.[42] Perhaps most famously, after having set up a fake website on which Yes Men members figured as Dow Chemical representatives, one of the Yes Men in 2004 appeared on a live news program of the BBC in the guise of a high-level executive from Dow Chemical. This was timed to coincide with the twentieth anniversary of a major chemical leak in Bhopal, India, that killed nearly 4,000 people and became one of the largest industrial disasters in history. During the interview the fake Dow executive announced (falsely of course) to a worldwide television audience that Dow would take full responsibility for the accident by liquidating a major division of the company and spending the gained twelve million dollars on compensating victims and cleaning up the still toxic site. Although a hoax, Dow Chemical's stock value that same day plunged a billion dollars. In such and other actions that have involved the mass distribution of spoof newspapers, and the design (and alleged mass production) of "Survivalballs," which Mike Bonanno on CNN described as outlandish inflatable garments that would allow wearers to survive any environmental catastrophe, the Yes Men have posed as spoof businessmen, politicians, industrialists, and media moguls.

At first sight, this duo brings little more than hoaxes or pranks. Yet it might also be argued that they present the logical conclusion to the tradition first launched by Marinetti. The Yes Men cite verbatim. They do no longer pretend to be artists. Their art is truly readymade, and theirs is an affirmative or "uncreative" aesthetic politics. Luckily perhaps, the politicized aesthetic of the Yes Men to date does not define the center of artistic practice. It may in fact never do so. For as Hugo already observed almost two centuries ago: beauty by definition is finite; ugliness will always be infinite. Only when "life" itself will have stopped evolving, when man stops to invent and create, will progress in art and literature as well have become unthinkable. At least from a Crocean perspective, this prospect seems highly unlikely. The era of Post-Futurism may indeed not be over yet.

Notes

1. Karl Vossler, *Italienische Literatur der Gegenwart von der Romantik zum Futurismus* (Heidelberg: Carl Winter Universitätsverlag, 1914), 121–22.
2. Vossler must have taken note of Palazzeschi's qualms with *Marinettismo* and his gradual move away from Futurism by the time *Italienische Literatur* came out. Whence probably his choice not to name Palazzeschi (or his manifesto).
3. Vossler, *Italienische Literatur*, 123.
4. ". . . die eine alte Kunst zu Grabe tragen. . . . Aber was schadet es, wenn in der Sprache des Herzens eine Pause eintritt? Ich glaube sogar, dass es gut ist. Damit

das Herz etwas Aufrichtiges sage, muss es oft lange schweigen." Vossler, *Italienische Literatur*, 123–24.

5. In fact, Vossler's *Italienische Literatur* concluded with an epilogue entitled "Erneuerung der Ästhetik und literarischen Kritik—Benedetto Croce" (Innovation of Aesthetics and Literary Critique—Benedetto Croce). Coming right after his assessment of Futurism the epilogue's intended message must have been crystal-clear: Croce was the answer to the crisis Futurism had brought about.

6. Private encounters between Croce and individual futurists, by contrast, often proved rather amicable. Carrà, for example, recalled a sympathetic conversation with Croce at Naples in 1911. See: Carlo Carrà, *La mia vita* (Rome: Longanesi, 1943), 148.

7. "Facciamo coraggiosamente il 'brutto' in letteratura, e uccidiamo dovunque la sollennità." Filippo Tommaso Marinetti, *Teoria e invenzione futurista*, ed. Luciano De Maria (Milan: Mondadori, 20013), 53. In his recent edition of Marinetti's *Critical Writings*, Günter Berghaus appends a note to these words from Marinetti's *Manifesto tecnico*, claiming that Marinetti might have had Karl Rozenkranz's *Ästhetik des Hässlichen* in mind when he wrote them. (Filippo Tommaso Marinetti, *Critical Writings*, ed. Günter Berghaus [New York: Farrar, Straus and Giroux, 2006], 446, note 9.) Although Marinetti, as far as I know, never actually mentioned Rozenkranz, Berghaus' assertion is hard to rebut considering the role Rozenkranz's book played throughout (Post-)Symbolism. Yet as I hope to show it is not excluded that Marinetti here also referred to Croce's *Estetica* (1902).

8. Clement Greenberg, "Review of Exhibitions of Mondrian, Kandinsky and Pollock; of the Annual Exhibition of American Abstract Artists; and of the Exhibition *European Artists in America*" (1945), in Idem, *The Collected Essays and Criticism*, Vol. 2 (Chicago: University of Chicago Press, 1986), 14–18, here 17.

9. Fredric Jameson, *Postmodernism, or, the Cultural Logic of Late Capitalism* (Durham: Duke University Press, 1993), 78.

10. Lesley Higgins, *The Modernist Cult of Ugliness. Aesthetic and Gender Politics* (New York: Palgrave Macmillan, 2002). As Higgins shows, ugliness in the modernist avant-gardes was quite consistently a manly affair. Pitted against soft, female prettiness, the ugly in the modernist avant-gardes, with few exceptions, is always presented as a hard and male perspective.

11. For a good study of the ugly in expressionist writing, see Christoph Eykman, *Die Funktion des Hässlichen in der Lyrik Georg Heyms, Georg Trakls und Gottfried Benns: zur Krise der Wirklichkeitserfahrung im deutschen Expressionismus* (Bonn: Bouvier, 1985). Few writers make the ugly in Surrealism stand out as well as Georges Bataille. For the role of the ugly in Dada, consult: Hanne Bergius, *Das Lachen DADAs. Die Berliner Dadaisten und ihre Aktionen* (Anabas: Giessen, 1989).

12. Now generally considered to have been one of Europe's first self-conscious avant-garde movements; see Philippe Lacoue-Labarte and Jean-Luc Nancy, *L'Absolu littéraire: théorie de la literature du romantisme* (Paris: Seuil, 1978).

13. For an extensive discussion of Schlegel in this context, see: Günter Oesterle, "Entwurf einer Monographie des ästhetisch Hässlichen. Die Geschichte einer ästhe-

tischen Kategorie von Friedrich Schlegels *Studium*-Aufsatz bis zu Karl Rozenkranz' *Ästhetik des Hässlichen* als Suche nach dem Ursprung der Moderne," in Dieter Bänch, ed. *Literaturwissenschaft und Sozialwissenschaften 8: Zur Modernität der Romantik* (Stuttgart: Metzler, 1977), 217–97.

14. Hans Robert Jauss, "Die klassische und christliche Rechtfertigung des Hässlichen in mittelalterischer Literatur," in Idem, *Alterität und Modernität der mittelalterischen Literatur* (Munich: Fink, 1977), 143–68.

15. Victor Hugo, *Préface de Cromwell* (Paris: Larousse, 2006).

16. Karl Rozenkranz, *Ästhetik des Hässlichen* (Stuttgart: Reclam, 1996).

17. For a discussion of the ugly in Baudelaire, consult: Michelle Hannoosh, *Baudelaire and Caricature: From the Comic to an Art of Modernity* (University Park: Pennsylvania State University Press, 1992).

18. "Infatti, mi pare che c'è qualche cosa nel futurismo che è già passata, già morta ossia nata morta ed è specialmente quell'umorismo ironico e giocarellone dinnanzi alla realtà, cosa stantivissima che si trova tale e quale nei romantici specialmente tedeschi." "Può essere che un giorno a l'altro io scriva un articolo interpretative sul Futurismo." A letter of Vossler to Marinetti from July 28, 1914, preserved in Yale University's Beinecke Rare Books Library. For more on the context of this letter, consult: Jeffrey T. Schnapp, "Gorilla Art: On an Unpublished Letter from Karl Vossler to Filippo Tommaso Marinetti," *Modernism/Modernity*, 9(4) (2002), 667–73.

19. "Veneziani, schiavi del passato, non urlate contro la pretesa bruttezza delle locomotive, dei tramways e degli automobili, da cui sappiamo trarre, a colpi di genio, la grande estetica futurista!" Marinetti, *Teoria e invenzione futurista*, 270.

20. "[N]oi essaltamo ad un tempo il Patriottismo, la Guerra—sola igiene del mondo—il gesto distruttore dei libertarî, e le belle idee per cui si muore, gloriosamente opposte alle brutte idee per cui si vive." Marinetti, *Teoria e invenzione futurista*, 444–45.

21. For a survey, see: Günter Berghaus, *Italian Futurist Theatre, 1909–1944* (Oxford: Clarendon Press, 1998).

22. Touching nonetheless many of the issues raised here, is Mark Antliff's essay "Cubism, Futurism, Anarchism: The 'Aestheticism' of the *Action d'art* Group, 1906–1920," *Oxford Art Journal*, 21(2), 1998, 99–120.

23. Benedetto Croce, "Fatti politici e interpretazioni storiche," *La Stampa*, May 15, 1924; reprinted in Idem, *Cultura e vita morale* (Bari: Laterza, 1955), 268–69.

24. I am of course referring here to Benjamin's essay "Das Kunstwerk im Zeitalter seiner technischen Reproduzierbarkeit," in Walter Benjamin, *Gesammelte Schriften I, 2* (Werkausgabe Band 2), ed. Rolf Tiedemann & Hermann Schweppenhäuser (Frankfurt a.M.: Suhrkamp, 1980), 471–508.

25. See Sascha Bru, *Democracy, Law and the Modernist Avant-Gardes: Writing in the State of Exception* (Edinburgh: Edinburgh University Press, 2009), 41–86. Compare: Enzo Santarelli, *Fascismo e neofascismo: Studi e problemi di ricerca* (Rome: Editori Riuniti, 1974), 3–50; Niccolò Zapponi, "La politica come espediente e come utopia: Marinetti e il Partito Politico Futurista," in Sergio Lambiase and Gian Battista Nazzaro, *F.T. Marinetti futurista: Inediti, pagine disperse, documenti e antologia critica*

(Naples: Guida, 1977), 221–39; Günter Berghaus, "The Futurist Political Party," in Sascha Bru and Gunther Martens, eds., *The Invention of Politics in the European Avant-Garde, 1906–1940* (Amsterdam; New York: Rodopi, 2006), 153–82. A brief yet interesting historical account can be found in: Emilio Settimeli, "Storia del partito politica futurista," *Oggi e domani*, 23(3), 1931, 27.

26. Ferruccio Vecchi, *Arditismo civile* (Milan: L'Ardito, 1920), 54.

27. Marinetti, *Teoria e invenzione futurista*, 476.

28. ". . . gran libro del Futurismo." Marinetti, *Teoria e invenzione futurista*, 999.

29. Tellingly, in his monograph for the exhibition, Joshua Taylor cautioned the viewer that "[t]he nature of the [Italian] Futurist impulse in politics . . . should not influence the assessment of its achievement in art." Joshua Taylor, *Futurism* (New York: The Museum of Modern Art, 1961), 17.

30. Pontus Hulten, "Futurism and Futurists" and "Futurist Prophecies," in Idem, ed., *Futurism and Futurisms*, trans. Asterisco e.a. (New York: Abbevill Press, 1986), 13–21. Renzo de Felice's often elliptic note on "Ideology" in the same catalogue (448–91), was the only text to really tackle practical political issues. As many have observed, by linking Italian Futurism to its Russian and other counterparts, the exhibition above all depoliticized Italian as well as other Futurisms. See, among others, Anne Bowler, "Politics as Art: Italian Futurism and Fascism," *Theory and Society*, 20(6), 1991, 763–94, here 790.

31. Didier Ottinger e.a., eds., *Le futurisme à Paris. Une avant-garde explosive* (Paris: Editions du Centre Pompidou, 2008).

32. Artist Vincent Trasov is one example. After having studied modern languages, Trasov launched an oeuvre that has consistently explored the plastic and other qualities of language. Working in British Columbia in the 1970s, he designed a campaign meant to get a famous icon from Anglo-American pop culture, Mr. Peanut, into the seat of mayor in Vancouver. "A Nut for Mayor," was one of his slogans, and when appearing in public Trasov wore a costume designed to make him look like a life-size Mr. Peanut. Mr. Peanut drew more votes than Marinetti's entire *Fascio*: 3, 4 percent. The fate of Trasov's performance in art history is doubly tragic, however. Not only was his game that of the prank, it is also remembered as just that. A show commemorating these events, *The Mr. Peanut Mayorality Campaign of 1974*, was organized by the Morris and Helen Belkin Art Gallery at the University of British Columbia in Summer 2005.

33. For a concise survey here, consult: Günter Berghaus, *Futurism and Politics: Between Anarchist Rebellion and Fascist Reaction, 1909–1944* (Oxford: Berghahn Books, 1996).

34. For a study of Beuys' relation to other modernist avant-gardes, see: Herwig Duschek, *Die Anti-Kunst: Beuys und die Moderne* (Westerstetten: Dittmar, 2005).

35. "Krawall in Aachen. Interview mit Joseph Beuys," *Kunst*, no. 4 (October-November, 1964), 96. See also Götz Adriani, Winfried Konnertz and Karin Thomas, *Joseph Beuys. Leben und Werk* (Cologne: DuMont, 1981), 139. I rely heavily on the latter here.

36. Interview with Joseph Beuys by Imerline Lebeer, in *Cahiers du Musée national d'art moderne*, no. 4 (1980), 176, my translation.

37. Beuys' developed his intricate theory of "Soziale Plastik" in a number of publications, including *Ein kurzes erstes Bild von dem konkreten Wirkungsfelde der sozialen Kunst* (Wangen: FIU-Verlag, 1987), and *KUNST = KAPITAL—Achberger Vorträge* (Wangen: FIU-Verlag, 1992).

38. For details, see: Joseph Beuys, *Jeder Mensch ein Künstler: Gespräche auf der Dokumenta 5*, ed. Clara Bodenmann-Ritter (Berlin: Ullstein, 1994).

39. Umberto Eco, *Storia della bruttezza* (Milan: Bompiani, 2007), 421–40.

40. This is not the place to rehearse Hegel's views at length. To get a good sense of the issues raised here, see: Dino Formaggio, *La "morte dell'arte" e estetica* (Bologna: Il Mulino, 1983).

41. For more on Adorno's view of the ugly, see: Peter Uwe Hohendahl, "Aesthetic Violence: The Concept of the Ugly in Adorno's *Aesthetic Theory*," *Cultural Critique*, no. 60 (Spring, 2005), 170–96.

42. An overview of their actions is given in the documentary film *The Yes Men Fix the World* (2009), written, produced and directed by Andy Bichlbaum and Mike Bonanno, codirected by Kurt Engfehr, and distributed by Shadow Distribution. The Yes Men's actions have not gone unnoticed in art reviews. *Art in America*, for instance, has been keeping track of their progress in shorter articles; see e.g. the 2009 vol. 97, no. 1 (p. 28), and no. 10 (p. 36). The French translation of their book *Les Yes Men. Comment démasquer (en s'amusant un peu) l'imposture néoliberale* (Paris: La Découverte, 2005), has been widely reviewed, even in the *Canadian Journal of Political Science* [39(1), 2005] published by Cambridge University Press. Their most fervent critics so far work in the domains of cultural and performance studies. A most insightful article on the "aesthetic" of the Yes Men, for instance, is: Maria Hynes, Scott Sharpe, and Bob Fagan, "Laughing with the Yes Men: the Politics of Affirmation," *Continuum. Journal of Media and Cultural Studies*, 21(1), 2007, 107–21.

~

CHAPTER EIGHTEEN

Futurism and the Manifesto in the 1960s

Florian Mussgnug

"With bright, irritating intellectual clarity, Marinetti announced the birth of Futurism. We have not come to terms with this movement so far, or with its creator, but we will have to do so."[1] Giorgio Manganelli's belated homage to Filippo Tommaso Marinetti, written in 1987, reveals an ambivalence that was common among Italian artists and intellectuals during the 1960s. Despite their self-image as advocates and heirs to Futurism, the authors and critics of Gruppo 63 did little to celebrate Italy's earliest and more influential avant-garde.[2] To embrace the label of "new avant-garde" ("neoavanguardia"), according to Angelo Guglielmi, meant above all to recognize that futurist celebrations of violent change were an inadequate response to the highly specialized means and media of the electronic age. Avant-garde culture, according to Guglielmi, was a mere relic of the past, which contemporary artists did well to reject in favour of a more pragmatic and ideologically neutral "experimentalism" ("sperimentalismo"):

> The condition of contemporary culture is like that of a city, which the enemy has fled after covering it with mines. The winners are at the gates, but what will they do? Send assault troops to conquer a city that has already been conquered? But this would only increase the chaos, and cause unnecessary new ruins and deaths. Rather, they will send specialized units through the backstreets. And these troops will enter the abandoned city, not with machine guns but with geiger counters.[3]

Guglielmi's playful enquiry into the etymology of "avant-garde" makes futurist visions of heroic rebellion appear anachronistic. As a form of social
critique, avant-garde culture is obsolete, since its alleged enemy—the for-
merly dominant and supposedly monolithic system of bourgeois values—has
ceased to exist. Unlike the futurists, who directed their scorn against a largely
homogeneous and solidly conservative establishment, Italy's *neoavanguardisti*
perceived themselves at the heart of a rapidly modernizing economy, sur-
rounded by quickly developing and highly flexible mass media, and faced
with a seemingly endless appetite for cultural novelty.[4] Fears of "neutraliza-
tion" were not uncommon, and feelings of inadequacy may have prompted
at least one member of Gruppo 63, Fausto Curi, to describe his group as
a "cold avant-garde" ("avanguardia fredda"), in evident contrast with the
revolutionary "heat" of Futurism.[5] In a similar spirit, Umberto Eco remarked
on the contrast between a "generation of Vulcan" and a "generation of Neptune" while Edoardo Sanguineti deplored the inevitable transition from a
heroic to a cynical age, sanctioned by the triumph of the culture industry and
its most tangible avatar, the museum.[6] Manganelli, one of the group's most
eclectic members, went further than most in suggesting the following, radical
re-definition of avant-garde culture:

> In my opinion . . . avant-garde writers are men of letters: meticulous creators
> of artifice, a little pedantic, naturally inclined . . . towards the austere, com-
> binatory delights of language. . . . The avant-garde, then, may offer us, and
> in fact already offers, a literature of artifice: not sentimental, not private, not
> even demonic, not moral, not social, but highly arbitrary and at the same time
> rigorous. Arbitrary is the choice of the ritual to which I devote myself, strict
> my observance of the rite chosen in this manner.[7]

Instead of launching attacks against particular social conventions or artistic
canons, Italy's new avant-garde found its vocation in a careful scrutiny of the
ambiguities and contradictions of language: "The avant-garde, then, quite
logically, in my opinion, concentrates on structural research, on research
into language."[8] In political terms, this attention to language coincided with
an overt diffidence towards *all* full-fledged ideologies. In order to realize its
subversive potential, Manganelli suggests, the avant-garde had to question
all hegemonic norms and extend its challenge to every possible set of linguistic conventions.

Manganelli's celebration of pure subversion and Guglielmi's reflections
concerning the future of *neosperimentalismo* mark the range of Gruppo 63's
critical attitudes towards Futurism. While both authors call for a radical re-

thinking of avant-garde theory, their specific proposals appear diametrically opposed. Where Guglielmi endorses the political zeal of earlier avant-garde movements but not their strategies, Manganelli accepts the form but not the content of avant-garde politics. Despite these differences, however, the authors' concern with language is symptomatic of a wider change: a shift away from the futurists' focus on political antagonism and the male body as a site of heroic defiance, and towards precarious, disembodied subjectivity. Personal identity and embodiment, as Manganelli points out in one of his earliest published statements, do not precede language, but are the result of specific and contingent linguistic conventions:

> Every universe is primarily a linguistic universe: a morphology, and therefore subject to the rigour and arbitrariness of all morphologies. We can thus affirm that language is not what makes the universe thinkable (what can we say? how is the world made of language?), but rather, I would say, inhabitable.[9]

Manganelli's claim that every universe is primarily a linguistic universe affirms that linguistic meaning cannot be explained in relation to "inner" mental representations or through direct reference to an extra-linguistic sphere. Spoken and written language are not an approximate translation of an autonomous mental discourse, since the structure of thought is not independent from the structure of language. As a consequence, language cannot be contemplated from the outside—the linguistic universe is not "thinkable"—it can only be experienced, as it were, from within ("inhabited"). In his early, unfinished text *Scrivere libri e altre cose* (1953–1955) Manganelli opts for a different, more unusual paraphrase: "Nothing needs to be clarified, in fact. We must make the universe chewable. For the universe that chews us we are clear enough."[10] To speak a language, then, does not mean to establish a connection between two distinct spheres, language and reality, but to be part of a universe which is already, and always, intrinsically linguistic. Or, as Manganelli puts it, somewhat more laconically, in a 1988 interview with Graziella Pulce: "The ideas never come. First come words, then more words, then again words. Then we all go home."[11]

The political implications of Manganelli's poetics must not be ignored. For the author of *Hilarotragoedia*, the linguistic universe is essentially a prison-house of norms: "A game: but nothing, when it comes down to it, is more vexatious than a game."[12] Since its existence rests on a totally arbitrary basis—the contingent rules of the language game—it can easily be replaced by another system of linguistic conventions. In fact, every linguistic universe is haunted by its own contingency: "Every language 'knows' that other languages challenge its totality; that infinitely many 'as if's present themselves as alternative possibilities, that somehow they all occupy the same space."[13] Threatened by the possibility of other, equally arbitrary norms and rites, the linguistic universe seeks to deny their existence and claims to be an absolute and inescapable social reality. Indeed, the inhabitants of the linguistic universe do not only suffer from its semantic restrictions, they are also victims of the linguistic universe's ambition to present itself as the only true reality: "its true vocation to act as something definitive, as 'reality,' and therefore its guilty conscience. To sustain its members, it relies on two weapons: terrorism and euphemism. That is to say, the State and History."[14] Language is thus perceived as a hostile force, and artistic invention becomes an impossible demand. Every heroic rebellion against the dictatorship of language is haunted by a tragic awareness of its inevitable contingency; instead of putting an end to anxiety, the struggle for an absolute and ultimate revolution only reveals our inescapable state of confinement.

The contrast with Marinetti could not be more marked. For the inventor of Futurism, antagonism is always creative and productive; it affirms the importance of virility and celebrates the hero's victory over the debilitating constraints of nature, sentiment, cultural tradition. Self-sacrifice—the most extreme expression of heroic defiance—is seen as a paradoxical source of authenticity: a radical gesture of self-invention and self-creation. As Christine Poggi remarks, Marinetti and his peers were driven by a deep suspicion of the liberal, humanist subject—the rational mind "in possession of a body"—and rejected its alleged universality in favor of a new idea of embodiment: the superhuman hybrid, "intended to obliterate traditional distinctions between the organic and the inorganic, between sentient beings and the physical and mechanical world."[15] The boundaries of this new, fantasized fusion of male body and machine are uncertain. For Marinetti, the death of the authorial self is only the beginning of a utopian transformation of subjectivity, which converts human emotions into a set of forces of compression, dilation, cohesion, and disaggregation, a crowd of massed molecules and whirling electrons: "We systematically destroy the literary I, and will scatter it among universal vibrations; we will be able to express the infinitely small, the movement of molecules."[16] Marinetti's "multiple man" ("uomo moltiplicato"), however, does not threaten the hierarchical categories of male and female, self and other. Quite on the contrary: the fusion of steel and flesh bestows new, unlimited potency. As Jeffrey Schnapp observes, Marinetti's hybrid of man and machine is inherently unstable, but his / its instability is described by the poet as a violent vitality: the erotic energy of a centaur.[17]

For Marinetti, the ideal futurist—sportsman, aviator, and warrior—has a consciousness, which resembles a smoothly running motor: there is no space for sentimentality, nostalgia or inner conflict, and every form of tension is directed outwards. Even in its most overtly tragic or ironic formulation— Marinetti's description of Mafarka's death, Palazzeschi's *Il codice di Perelà* (1911)—Futurism conceives of poetic practice as an aggressive, violent affirmation of the autonomous subject. In Manganelli's literary works, this fantasy of absolute transgression—Marinetti's belief that the author must accept the risk of annihilation to achieve immortality—is frequently evoked as a target of gentle parody. In *Hilarotragoedia* (1964), for instance, the un-named narrator's musings about anxiety, decline and despair, prompt the objection of an idealistic youth—addressed as "beloved Caliban, my passion-ate and desperate friend"—who offers a fervent, Marinettiesque appeal to the ultimate harmony that stems from death:[18]

> Impassioned in your speech; your boyish face flushed and exasperated with the error of birth: this is how you paced up and down in the narrow room, gesticulating with your thin arms, the length of your legs, and continuing: but there exists a condition which puts an end to all repugnant alternatives, . . . it is death: the solecism that tightens the vocabulary of mathematics; the error, which gives meaning to impeccable speech; the daily apocalypse; the portable end of the world; the annihilation of every scheduled universe.[19]

While Marinetti's celebration of heroic subjectivity defers anxieties about mortality to an unspecified future, Manganelli's bleak vision of non-existent readers and perpetually dying authors foregrounds and intensifies such anxieties, bringing them to bear directly on the reader's experience: "Writing can find an audience, but . . . it is only a temporary recipient. [Literature] is made for inaccurate readers, for the unborn, for those intended not to be born, or already born and dead, also for impossible readers."[20] Manganelli's literature for "impossible readers," unreadable and unread, thus presents itself as "opaque writing" ("scrivere oscuro"), in evident contrast with the "irritat-ing intellectual clarity" ("irritante chiarezza intellettuale") associated with Marinetti: it has a shadowy, ghostly quality; its singular force consists in its resistance to all definitive interpretations.

The full implications of this shift from heroic embodiment to precarious, disembodied subjectivity are nowhere more obvious than in Gruppo 63's attitude towards the manifesto. No other form of artistic expression is as intrinsically linked to the historical avant-gardes; no genre as representative of their profound and lasting concern with politics and the public sphere.

The manifesto, as Andrew J. Webber points out, is "a textual act of public showing, a making manifest of a challenge towards historical conventions," and as such it tends towards the modes of spectacle and politics.[21] Unlike most forms of artistic production, the manifesto transcends the traditional focus on the individual work, setting it instead within the context of a public performance. Its mode of production presupposes the existence of a viewing subject, which takes an active part in public interpellation, or rather in the material offering to the reader/spectator. In the cultural context of the 1960s this strongly deictic stance was seen by many as politically suspicious and impossible to reconcile with the neoavanguardia's most cherished cultural practices: openness and creative suspicion. For Edoardo Sanguineti, the political and cultural influence of Gruppo 63 could not be summarized in programmatic statements or public declarations, but expressed itself in the group's exemplary, discursive practice. As Sanguineti recalled in 1993, Gruppo 63 never presented itself as an artistic movement based on a manifesto, but—following the example of the German *Gruppe 47*— defined itself as an open forum for discussion and artistic exchange: "In short, the existence of different positions was in line with the structure of the group, and this was appropriate to the times: there was no poetic manifesto and we did not want one."[22] According to Eco, openness was not only a necessary response to the political and cultural context of the 1960s, but also a guarantee for plurality and true creativity:

> [Gruppo 63] was not a Masonic lodge which you could join with the right recommendations, albeit in secret (and at risk of not being accepted by the majority of members). It was more like a village festival, which included all those who were present and who took part in the general atmosphere and the genius loci.[23]

More than two decades earlier, Manganelli evokes the same idea—the group's self-image as an "open laboratory" ("laboratorio aperto")—when he recalls the atmosphere at the group's second meeting in Reggio Emilia, in 1964:

> In our group there are no alternative views, because the group has no manifesto, it has no theory, no orthodoxy, it is a club for angry people . . . no, I should rather say, for dishonest people: dishonest at various levels of consciousness, but certainly dishonest, otherwise there would be no need to form a club.[24]

In 1986, Manganelli confirms this impression in one of his rare retrospective judgments on the neoavanguardia: "Gruppo 63 never developed any aesthetic principles. In fact, please excuse the expression, it was a big mess. Inside, there was everything and the contrary of everything: people who cheated and people who did not cheat, and even people who counted from one to five thousand. But counting from one to five thousand was not compulsory for everybody."[25]

Heterogeneity, constructive criticism and ongoing debate, then, were important preconditions for Italy's new avant-garde. And yet, retrospective accounts do not give an exhaustive impression of the group's history. In a recent recollection Giorgio Celli draws a very different picture, which underlines the decisive influence of some key figures:

> Nanni Balestrini, the winged messenger of the newborn Group 63 . . . invited the Gozzis [Louis and Alberto Gozzi] to the first meeting in Palermo. For reasons that I will leave to the speculations of posterity, but that were not noble, I was left at home, and had to swallow my pride. I did not swallow in silence, though, because one day I went to Milan to complain to Balestrini about my exclusion.[26]

A similar idea of the group—based on investiture rather than mere coexistence—also features in Renato Barilli's and Angelo Guglielmi's 1976 preface to the anthology *Gruppo 63. Critica e teoria*, which suggests that the group's tolerance towards a wide range of different theoretical approaches and artistic attitudes never expressed itself in a neutral, unbiased atmosphere, but provoked heated debates and more or less permanent disagreements between the group's more outspoken members.[27] Openness, in this context, does not denote a wholesale acceptance of every theoretical stance, but rather a methodological *tabula rasa*, against which new theories and poetics flourished and competed for primacy.

In this context, the neoavanguardia's apparent suspicion of the manifesto also acquires a new and more complex meaning. Influential and well-known texts such as Alfredo Giuliani's introduction to *I Novissimi*, Sanguineti's "Il trattamento del materiale verbale nei testi della nuova avanguardia" ("The Treatment of Verbal Material in the Works of the New Avant-garde") and Eco's "L'avanguardia in vagone letto" ("The Avant-garde in the Wagon-lits") are not only a reaction against the strident rhetoric of Futurism; they also mark an attempt to define the goals and self-image of Italy's new avant-garde. Sanguineti clearly articulates this ambivalence—and his only thinly disguised nostalgia for the manifesto— when he calls Enrico Baj's and Sergio Dangelo's *Manifeste de la peinture nucléaire* (1952) "the last manifesto" ("l'ultimo manifesto"):

> In fact, [this manifesto] marks the definitive end of the movements that shaped the avant-garde's long history: all those avant-gardes, which would soon be

called "historical." It closes an epoch by almost literally citing the genre's traditional modes and styles, which (moving from romantic prototypes), are anchored in Symbolism, and . . . Futurism.[28]

More self-conscious and self-ironic than their early twentieth-century counterparts, the "pseudo-manifestos" of Gruppo 63 were not always immune to the more overt theatricality of Futurism. This may be seen, for instance, in Manganelli's "La letteratura come menzogna," ("Literature as Deception") which states the author's polemical concern with the supposed ideological and aesthetic inadequacy of literary realism and philosophical humanism. Belligerent, passionate and indiscriminately hostile to any form of tradition, "La letteratura come menzogna" is clearly reminiscent of what Renato Poggioli described as the "avant-garde posture."[29] But Manganelli's pamphlet is also a playful and ironic parody of the manifesto, a re-writing of the genre, which gently mocks the exhibitionism and sensationalism of avant-garde rhetoric. This is particularly evident in the opening paragraph of "La letteratura come menzogna":

> Some time ago, during a discussion, someone quoted: "As long as there are children in the world who die of hunger, it is immoral to write literature." Someone else glossed: "Then it has always been immoral." Suppose that the wisdom of our rulers, the systematic wrath of the governed, the pious collaboration of winds and rains, will allow us, within a few generations, to announce: "From today, Monday, no more children will die of hunger." Is it not likely that some honest and lucid thinker will step forward to remind us of suicides, untimely deaths, crimes of passion, alcoholics?[30]

It is easy to recognize Manganelli's ironic homage to Marinetti's *Manifesto del futurismo*. Like Marinetti, Manganelli rejects the aesthetic restraint of conventional literary criticism, opting instead for a combination of pseudo-philology and rhetorical excess. His stylistic cacophony exploits the subtle distinctions of rhetoric ("we may define literature as *adunaton*" / "possiamo definire la letteratura un *adunaton*"), and relies on erudite quotations in Latin ("*Ciceronianus sum*"), German ("a mushy white slurry, which is *Weltanschauung*" / "un liquame molliccio biancastro, che è la *Weltanschauung*") and English ("Where we witness the triumph of that ridiculous, middle-aged figure: Man" / "Dove trionfa quel risibile *middle aged*, l'Uomo").[31] Moreover, "La letteratura come menzogna" imitates Marinetti's disregard for systematic declarations and endorses his apparently spontaneous and anecdotal narrative style—what Marjorie Perloff has described as "Marinetti's master stroke."[32] Like the *Manifesto del futurismo* Manganelli's text opens with a seemingly casual reference to a recent discussion among friends: "We had been awake all night—my friends and I" / "some time ago, during a discussion, someone quoted" ("Avevamo vegliato tutta la notte—i miei amici ed io" / "qualche tempo fa, durante una discussione, qualcuno citò").[33]

Subtle differences, however, are as important as apparent similarities. While Marinetti opts for buffoonery and grandeur, Manganelli shies away from a head-on discussion of literature and social commitment, opting instead for a slightly ironic, intertextual *falsetto*. His unnamed interlocutors discuss a question of great social relevance, yet their dialogue has a disturbingly theatrical quality. Ideas are not stated with sincere conviction, but "quoted" ("citò") as humanist platitudes and immediately commented upon ("chiosò") like literary texts. More importantly, the anonymity of Manganelli's interlocutors ("qualcuno"; "qualcun altro") and their ironically ceremonial tone contrast with the idea of urgency normally associated with the avant-garde. By stripping contemporary debates about literature's social role of their immediate political and ethical relevance, Manganelli is able to present them as unchanging philosophical *topoi*: "For centuries, [literature] has been accused of fraud, corruption, wickedness. It is either pointless or poisonous."[34] Blurring the boundaries between historical periods, Manganelli evokes the idea of an archaic and never-ending hostility to literature, and thus introduces an idea that will dominate the remaining part of the manifesto and that has since come to be seen as the core of his poetics: literature is essentially and irredeemably fraudulent and insincere. Marinetti, it can be assumed, would have appreciated the rhetorical force of Manganelli's sweeping generalization.

Since the mid-1980s, literary scholarship has been dominated by an argument—first put forward in Peter Bürger's influential *Theorie der Avantgarde*—which associates "genuine" avant-garde culture with the social conditions of the early twentieth century and which treats subsequent artistic practice as mostly derivative mimicry.[35] In Italy, where a translation of Bürger's study was first published in 1990, this vision of the new avant-garde has given new credibility and support to traditional Marxist detractors of Gruppo 63 such as Gianni Scalia and Franco Fortini.[36] At the same time, an increasing interest in Postmodernism has prompted many former *neoavanguardisti* to reconsider (and often to re-write) their ideas in relation to new critical paradigms.[37] As a result, earlier debates about avant-garde art as a direct contestation of dominant socio-political conditions have been replaced by more anxious reflections about the logic of representation or the artist's alleged loss of oppositional force. Anti-historical, theoretical definitions of avant-garde practice, which enjoyed an almost axiomatic importance, are now largely absent from critical debates. With the single exception of Edoardo Sanguineti, Italian scholars seem to prefer more historically specific, *post-hoc* definitions.[38]

British and North American scholars have been equally critical of simplistic, allegedly comprehensive definitions of avant-garde practice. This awareness, however, has not lead, as in Italy, to a categorical rejection of avant-garde theory. Instead, critics like Susan Suleiman and Peter Wollen—and, more recently, Richard Murphy and Marjorie Perloff—have stressed the importance of differential assessments, while at the same time affirming the need for comprehensive critical definitions.[39] As Hal Foster points out, the works of recent avant-garde artists display a high degree of cultural self-awareness, which is mostly overlooked by postmodern approaches, but also by traditional, anti-historical avant-garde theory.[40] In order to acknowledge the new avant-garde's iconoclastic energy as well as its lasting political relevance, artists and scholars have therefore moved beyond simplistic notions of absolute rupture—what Rosalind Krauss describes as the "modernist myth" of the originality of the avant-garde—and towards a self-reflective stance, which acknowledges both historical debts and internal contradictions.[41]

Gruppo 63's ambivalent attitude towards Futurism and the genre of the manifesto are exemplary of this wider trend. As Antoine Compagnon has pointed out, the avant-garde's rhetoric of absolute rupture provoked shifts and tensions within the cultural field of modernism.[42] Self-assured and optimistic proclamations of the necessity of revolutionary progress were often contrasted by a nostalgic, darkly prophetic and deeply pessimistic anti-modernism, which saw cultural transformation as arbitrary and which emphasized the negative consequences of change. Despite Renato Barilli's efforts to label the neoavanguardia as a postmodern movement, this attitude is best described as a form of late modernism—with a deliberate emphasis on the tragic as well as playful aspects of lateness.[43] Modernist concerns—formalism, self-questioning, the radical displacement of established conventions—survive as a deliberate self-constraint; what Edward Said has called "a self-imposed exile from what is generally acceptable."[44] For the futurists, originality was necessarily projected into the future: the aesthetic and political value of the great work of art consisted in its appearance *before* its time. The pseudo-manifestos of Italy's Gruppo 63, by contrast, look *back* to the avant-garde and endorse its style and concerns with a retrospective, but not entirely ironic self-awareness. The new starting point envisaged here, finally, is neither transgression nor pure restoration, but an attempt to endorse each of these opposed attitudes, or rather to embrace the tension between them.

Notes

1. "Con luminosa, irritante chiarezza intellettuale, Marinetti annunciava la nascita del Futurismo. Con codesto nome, con il suo progettista, mal si sono fatti i conti fino a oggi; ma si dovranno pur fare." Giorgio Manganelli, *Salons* (Milan: Adelphi, 2000), 91–92. All translations are mine, unless otherwise indicated. Some sections of this essay have been adapted from Florian Mussgnug, *The Eloquence of Ghosts: Giorgio Manganelli and the Afterlife of the Avant-garde* (Oxford: Peter Lang, 2010).

2. See Andrea Barbato e.a., *Avanguardia e neo-avanguardia*, introduction by Giansiro Ferrata (Milan: Sugar, 1966).

3. "La situazione della cultura contemporanea è simile a quella di una città dalla quale il nemico, dopo averla cosparsa di mine, è fuggito. Il vincitore che è alle porte della città cosa farà? Invierà delle truppe d'assalto a conquistare una città già conquistata? Se lo facesse aggraverebbe il caos, provocando nuove inutili rovine e morte. Piuttosto farà arrivare dalle retrovie i reparti specializzati che avanzeranno nella città abbandonata non con le mitragliatrici ma con gli apparecchi Geiger." Angelo Guglielmi, *Avanguardia e sperimentalismo* (Milan: Feltrinelli, 1964), 56. On the poetics of "sperimentalismo" see Vincenzina Levato, *Lo sperimentalismo tra Pasolini e la neoavanguardia (1955–1965)* (Soveria Mannelli: Rubbettino, 2002); Nicola Turi, *Testo delle mie brame: Il metaromanzo italiano del secondo Novecento (1957–1979)* (Florence: Società Editrice Fiorentina, 2007); Luigi Weber, *Con onesto amore di degradazione: Romanzi sperimentali e d'avanguardia nel secondo Novecento italiano* (Bologna: Il Mulino, 2007); Salvatore Ferlita, *Sperimentalismo e avanguardia* (Palermo: Sellerio, 2008). Matei Calinescu's insightful reading compares Guglielmi's passage to Hans Magnus Enzensberger's "Aporias of the avant-garde" (1962) and suggests that Guglielmi concentrates on the changing social context of avant-garde literature, while Enzensberger draws attention to the movement's self-contradictory premises and attitudes. Matei Calinescu, *Five Faces of Modernity: Modernism, Avant-garde, Decadence, Kitsch, Postmodernism* (Durham, NC: Duke University Press, 1987), 120–25.

4. See Renato Barilli, *La neoavanguardia italiana: dalla nascità del "Verri" alla fine di "Quindici"* (Bologna: Il Mulino, 1995).

5. Fausto Curi, *Ordine e disordine* (Milan: Feltrinelli, 1965).

6. See Nanni Balestrini and Alfredo Giuliani, eds., *Gruppo 63: la nuova letteratura: 34 scrittori* (Milan: Feltrinelli, 1964), 413–14; Edoardo Sanguineti, *Ideologia e linguaggio*, ed. by Erminio Risso (Milan: Feltrinelli, 2001), 55–58.

7. "A mio avviso . . . gli scrittori d'avanguardia sono dei letterati, puntigliosi escogitatori di artifici, un poco pedanti, intelligenze naturalmente inclini . . . agli austeri estri combinatori del linguaggio. . . Dunque l'avanguardia potrà proporre, e di fatto già propone, una letteratura come artificio; fatto non sentimentale, non privato, e nemmeno demonico, non morale, non sociale, ma sommamente arbitrario e insieme, rigoroso. Arbitraria è la scelta del rito cui mi dedico, rigorosa l'osservanza del rito scelto a quel modo (Giorgio Manganelli, *Il rumore sottile della prosa*, ed. Paola Italia [Milan: Adelphi, 1994], 72–73).

8. "Dunque l'avanguardia, del tutto logicamente, a mio avviso, si concentra nelle ricerche di ordine strutturale; nelle ricerche di linguaggio." Manganelli, *Rumore sottile*, 73.

9. "Ogni universo è in primo luogo un universo linguistico in quanto è proprio una morfologia ed è sottoposto a tutto il rigore e a tutta l'arbitrarietà delle morfologie. Così noi possiamo parlare del linguaggio come di ciò in cui l'universo stesso diventa non direi pensabile (cosa possiamo dire? in che modo l'universo è linguaggio?), direi: abitabile." Giorgio Manganelli e.a., "La carne è l'uomo che crede al rapido consumo," *Grammatica*, 1. 1964: 1.

10. "Nulla deve chiarirsi, in realtà. Si tratta di rendere masticabile l'universo. Per l'universo che ci mastica siamo chiari abbastanza." Marco Belpoliti and Andrea Cortellessa, eds., *Giorgio Manganelli*, Riga 25 (Milan: Marcos y Marcos, 2006), 115.

11. "Le idee non vengono mai. Prima vengono le parole, poi vengono ancora le parole, poi vengono ancora le parole. Poi si va a casa." Graziella Pulce, *Lettura d'autore: conversazioni di critica e di letteratura con Giorgio Manganelli, Pietro Citati e Alberto Arbasino* (Rome: Bulzoni, 1988), 102.

12. "Un gioco: ma nulla è più minutamente vessatorio di un gioco." Giorgio Manganelli, *Encomio del tiranno: scritto all'unico scopo di fare dei soldi* (Milan: Adelphi, 1990), 21.

13. "Ciascun linguaggio 'sa' che altri sistemi linguistici sfidano la sua totalità; che infiniti possibili 'come se' si pongono come alternativi; che in qualche modo occupano tutti il medesimo spazio." Giorgio Manganelli, *La letteratura come menzogna* (Milan: Adelphi, 1985), 49.

14. "La sua vera vocazione a porsi come definitivo, come la 'realtà' e quindi la sua cattiva coscienza. Per reggere le proprie membra, esso ricorre a due armi: al terrorismo e all'eufemismo. Cioè, allo Stato e alla Storia." Manganelli, *Letteratura come menzogna*, 47.

15. Christine Poggi, *Inventing Futurism: The Art and Politics of Artificial Optimism* (Princeton: Princeton University Press, 2009), 151.

16. "Noi distruggeremo sistematicamente l'io letterario perché si sparpagli nella vibrazione universale, e giungiamo ad esprimere l'infinitamente piccolo e le agitazioni molecolari." Filippo Tommaso Marinetti, "Uccidiamo il Chiaro di Luna!" (1909) in Luciano De Maria, ed., *Marinetti e i futuristi* (Milan: Garzanti, 1994), 9–20.

17. Jeffrey T. Schnapp, "Propeller Talk," *Modernism/Modernity* 1, September 1994, 153–78, here 161.

18. "Diletto Calibano, mio passionale e disperato amico." Giorgio Manganelli, *Hilarotragoedia* (Milan: Adelphi, 1987), 73.

19. "Infervorato nel discorso, congestionato il volto di ragazzo inciprignito dall'errore della nascita, passeggiavi per l'angusta stanza, articolando le braccia magre, la lunghezza delle gambe, e continuavi: ma esiste, esiste una condizione in cui cessa la repugnanza delle alternative . . . ; esiste la morte, solecismo che rigorizza il lessico matematico, errore che dà senso all'impeccabile discorso, quotidiana apocalisse, portatile fine del mondo, azzeramento di ogni programmato universe." Manganelli,

Hilarotragoedia, 75. More humorously, "In onore dei dinosauri" depicts the great reptiles as avant-garde artists *ante litteram*, perennially in search of a perfect, collective death: Giorgio Manganelli, *Antologia privata* (Milan: Rizzoli, 1989), 217–20.

20. "Scrivere può trovare un pubblico; tuttavia . . . esso non è che il provvisorio destinatario. [La letteratura] viene creata per lettori imprecisi, nascituri, destinati a non nascere, già nati e morti; anche, lettori impossibili." Manganelli, *Letteratura come menzogna*, 219.

21. Andrew Webber, *The European Avant-garde 1900–1940* (Cambridge: Polity, 2004), 18.

22. "Insomma, l'esistenza di posizioni diverse era in sintonia con la struttura del gruppo che poi era quella adeguata alla situazione: non c'era un manifesto di poetica e non lo si voleva fare." Fabio Gambaro, *Colloquio con Edoardo Sanguineti: quarant'anni di cultura italiana attraverso i ricordi di un poeta intellettuale* (Milan: Anabasi, 1993), 70–71.

23. "[Il Gruppo 63] non era una massoneria in cui, con buone raccomandazioni, ci si potesse iscrivere, sia pure in segreto (e a rischio di non essere accettati dalla maggioranza dei soci). Era piuttosto come una festa di paese, in cui fa parte chi è presente e partecipa dello spirito generale e del genius loci." Umberto Eco, *Sugli specchi e altri saggi* (Milan: Bompiani, 1985), 94.

24. "Nel nostro Gruppo non ci sono posizioni alternative ad altre, anche perché il Gruppo non ha un Manifesto, non ha una teoria, non ha mica una ortodossia, è un club di persone irritate . . . no, di persone disoneste, direi, di persone disoneste a vari livelli di coscienza ma disoneste, altrimenti non ci sarebbe alcun motivo di fare un club." Eugenio Battisti, ed., *Gli amici dissidenti. Il Gruppo 63 a Reggio Emilia,* "Marcatrè," 11–12–13, 1965, 48.

25. "Il Gruppo 63 non ha mai elaborato dei suoi precetti estetici. In realtà, mi si passi l'espressione, era un gran casino. C'era dentro tutto e il contrario di tutto: gente che barava e gente che non barava e perfino gente che contava i numeri da uno a cinquemila. Ma contare da uno a cinquemila non era mica obbligatorio per tutti." Giorgio Manganelli, *La penombra mentale: Interviste e conversazioni 1965–1990,* ed. Roberto Deidier (Rome: Editori Riuniti, 2001), 169.

26. "Nanni Balestrini, l'alato messaggero del nascente Gruppo 63 . . . invitò così i Gozzi [Luigi e Alberto Gozzi] alla prima riunione . . . a Palermo, mentre io, per ragioni che lascio all'investigazione dei posteri, ma che non furono nobili, rimasi a casa, a mandar giù un grossissimo rospo. Non lo inghiottii in silenzio, però, perché un bel giorno andai a Milano per lamentarmi con Balestrini di quella mia esclusione." Renato Barilli, Fausto Curi e.a., *Il Gruppo 63: Quarant'anni dopo. Bologna, 8–11 maggio 2003. Atti del convegno* (Bologna: Pendragon, 2005), 69–70.

27. See Mario Moroni, Luca Somigli and Paolo Chirumbolo, eds., *Neoavanguardia: Italian Experimental Literature and Arts in the 1960s* (Toronto: University of Toronto Press, 2010), 128–30.

28. "Per un verso, infatti, [il manifesto] certamente chiude tutti i movimenti che avevano segnato la lunga vicenda di quelle avanguardie che, in breve, saranno

chiamate storiche. E chiude quasi commemorando citazionalmente i modi e gli stili tradizionali del genere, ancorati segnatamente (muovendo dai prototipi romantici) al simbolismo e . . . al futurismo." Edoardo Sanguineti, *Cultura e realtà*, ed. by Erminio Risso (Milan: Feltrinelli, 2010), 254.

29. Renato Poggioli, *The Theory of the Avant-Garde* (Cambridge: Harvard University Press, 1968), 30.

30. "Qualche tempo fa, durante una discussione, qualcuno citò: 'Finché c'è al mondo un bimbo che muore di fame, fare letteratura è immorale'. Qualcun altro chiosò: 'Allora lo è sempre stato.' Supponiamo che la saggezza dei governanti, la sistematica collera dei governati, la pia collaborazione dei venti e delle piogge consentano, tra qualche generazione, di annunciare: 'Da oggi, lunedì, nessun bambino morirà più di fame'. Non sorgerà allora qualche onesto e lucido raziocinatore a rammentarci i suicidi, le morti precoci, i delitti passionali, gli alcolizzati?" Manganelli, *Letteratura come menzogna*, 215.

31. Manganelli, *Letteratura come menzogna*, 217–18.

32. Marjorie Perloff, *The Futurist Moment: Avant-Garde, Avant Guerre, and the Language of Rupture* (Chicago: University of Chicago Press, 2003²), 86.

33. On the originality of Marinetti's opening, see Perloff, *The Futurist Moment*, 82–90; Poggi, *Inventing Futurism*, 4–16.

34. "Da secoli [la letteratura] viene accusata di frode, di corruzione, di empietà. O è inutile o è velenosa." Manganelli, *Letteratura come menzogna*, 216.

35. See Peter Bürger, *Theorie der Avantgarde* (Frankfurt a.M.: Suhrkamp, 1974).

36. Franco Fortini, *Verifica dei poteri: scritti di critica e di istituzioni letterarie* (Milan: Il Saggiatore, 1965); Gianni Scalia, *Critica, letteratura, ideologia: 1958–1963* (Padua: Marsilio, 1968).

37. For an authoritative overview of the Italian debate about *neoavanguardia* and postmodernism, see Monica Jansen, *Il dibattito sul postmoderno in Italia: in bilico tra dialettica e ambiguità* (Florence: Franco Cesati, 2002); Vittorio Spinazzola, *Dopo l'avanguardia* (Ancona: Transeuropa, 1989) treats Italian postmodernism as a consequence of the decline of the new avant-garde. Matteo Di Gesù, *La tradizione del postmoderno* (Milan: Franco Angeli, 2003) by contrast, describes the poetics of Gruppo 63 as an early manifestation of Italian postmodernism.

38. Sanguineti, *Ideologia e linguaggio*, 55–58. See also Edoardo Sanguineti and Jean Burgos, *Per una critica dell'avanguardia poetica in Italia e in Francia* (Turin: Bollati Boringhieri, 1995).

39. See Peter Wollen, "The Two Avant-Gardes" in Idem, *Readings and Writings: Semiotic Counter-Strategies* (London: Verso, 1982), 92–104; Susan Rubin Suleiman, *Subversive Intent: Gender, Politics, and the Avant-garde* (Cambridge, MA: Harvard University Press, 1990); Richard Murphy, *Theorizing the Avant-garde. Modernism, Expressionism and the Problem of Postmodernity* (Cambridge: Cambridge University Press, 1999); Perloff, *The Futurist Moment*.

40. Hal Foster, *The Return of the Real: The Avant-garde at the End of the Century* (Cambridge, MA: MIT Press, 1996), 5–6.

41. Rosalind Krauss, *The Originality of the Avant-Garde and Other Modernist Myths*, (Cambridge, MA: MIT Press, 1985).

42. Antoine Compagnon, *Les Antimodernes: De Joseph de Maistre à Roland Barthes* (Paris: Gallimard, 2005).

43. Renato Barilli, "Una generazione postmoderna," *Il Verri*, 1–2, 1984, 15–55; Idem, *Il ciclo del postmoderno: la ricerca artistica negli anni '80* (Milan: Feltrinelli, 1987); Idem, "Tre definizioni diverse del postmoderno," *Allegoria*, 17, 1994, 133–37.

44. Edward Said, *On Late Style: Music and Literature Against the Grain* (London: Bloomsbury Publishing, 2006), 16.

~

CHAPTER NINETEEN

No Man's Land

From Free-Word Tables to Verbal-Visual Poetry

Teresa Spignoli

In the spring of 1972, Luigi Ballerini—at that point a professor of Italian Literature at the City University of New York—realized, for the eighth Tri-Annual Congress of the International Association for Italian Studies, an exhibit entitled *Italian Visual Poetry 1912–1972*.[1] This exhibit was the first ever to propose a critical trajectory that distinguished a continuation of futurist work and the verbal-visual experimentation of the second half of the twentieth century. The show had notable success, so much so that it was shown again in the Fall of that same year at the Galleria d'Arte Moderna in Turin, now with the title *Scrittura visuale in Italia, 1912–1972*.[2] The apparently innocuous substitution of the term "poetry" with that of "scrittura" (writing) ("rejected" in New York, the same Ballerini reveals) indicates, rather, the inclusion of a series of experiences, such as music[3] and painting that had been excluded from the American exhibition:

> I hope that the formula for visual writing, handed down by the futurists, and the meeting of that lineage in the 1950s and 1960s with the semantizing tendencies of certain types of painting[4]—and, rather, of certain pictography—and the developments that resulted from that meeting, suffice to justify in Turin just as in New York, the specifically Italian environment of the initiative and the 'determination' of its destiny.[5]

And so Ballerini, in the brief preface to the catalogue, immediately distin-guishes the two dialectic poles upon which the verbal-visual[6] writing bases its principles in Futurism and in the pictorial experimentation of the 1950s and 1960s. This stance traced a critical trajectory that would require future re-readings of both periods in light of the other. In that sense, one would think of, among the more important events,[7] the exhibit organized at the end of the 1980s by Achille Bonito Oliva—*La parola totale: una tradizione futurista, 1909–1986* (The Total Word: a Futurist Tradition, 1909–1986), and, in the following decade, the show produced by Sarenco and Mascelloni, *Poesia totale 1897–1997: dal colpo di dadi alla poesia totale* (Total Poetry 1897–1997: from 'Un coup de dés' to Total Poetry). In regards to the last decade, one could look to the exposition held at MART at Rovereto in 2007—*La parola nell'arte. Ri-cerche d'avanguardia nel '900, dal futurismo a oggi attraverso le collezioni del Mart*, curated by Gabriella Belli—and the exhibit organized in Milan by Giovanni Lista and Ada Masoero, as part of celebrations dedicated to Futurism's centen-nial, *Futurismo 1909–2009*.[8] The last section, *Velocità+Arte+Azione*, is dedi-cated in its entirety to *L'eredità del futurismo* (The Legacy of Futurism), giving particular attention precisely to verbal-visible research.

The interpretive prospect suggested by the Turinese exhibit (*Scrittura visuale in Italia, 1912–1972*), moreover, stimulated the same protagonists of verbal-visual experimentation to reckon with a legacy—precisely that of Futurism—that was often concealed, when not actually openly dismissed because of the heavy ideological mark that still scarred the Marinettian movement. Despite the fundamental contributions of Luciano De Maria,[9] this prejudice impeded objective critical assessment of the movement's principles,[10] as well as of a serious analysis of its historical association with fascism.[11] It is not, in fact, a coincidence that in the anthology *Tavole parolibere futuriste (1912–1944)* [12] published by Luciano Caruso and Stelio Maria Martini in 1974 in parallel to the Ballerini exhibit[13]—taken explicitly as its point of departure[14]—addresses precisely this problematic knot.[15] The anthology proposes to trace a first bal-ance of the futurist production, which is already on its way as far as its pictorial dimension is concerned,[16] whereas an accomplished definition seems still to be awaited in regards to the literary production—with reference to the free-word tables[17]—and distinguishes the fundamental contribution of the futurist avant-garde to the questioning of the artistic canon and to the resulting opening up of literary experimentation to new and diverse outcomes:

> The truth is that the futurists continue to be weighed down by a series of acts of condemnation and ostracism, in Italy and abroad . . . which explains why for-eign avant-gardes lacked direct references to the Italian futurists . . .; this also

explains the strange phenomena in Italy after Futurism in which individual or collective events pertaining to an Italian avant-garde that from the start and in a totally autonomous manner seemed to have discovered the contradictions, nodes and paths to be followed, out of a necessity to face the extreme attrition of the expressive means already possessed by the futurists. This, for the first time in history, set back into play the very elements of that mode of communication and expression, reabsorbing them as material for invention and creative objects.[18]

In fact, Caruso and Martini discern precisely in the reaction to the "extreme attrition of the expressive-communicative means," the common feature, if not the "last reason" of the first and second avant-garde waves of the twentieth century, which instigate the "setting back into play of the means themselves, which therefore becomes the privileged place of invention—at once both the object and the goal of the activity." If it follows that an aspect of Futurism is the indisputable merit of having elaborated upon, for the first time, "a new conception of literature"—one that no longer configures itself as a "means of the expressive-communicative function of language" but now becomes itself an "object of invention and of imagination"—the function of having carried to maturation the core principles of Futurism is then, rather, assigned to the neo-avantgarde movements of the 1960s: "the historical avant-garde movements . . . will have to await the neo-avantgarde movements, as it is their fundamental motivations, not always unconscious, that emerged consciously and made themselves concrete according to what their own intimate reasons were requesting of them."[19]

In this way, the two curators reconducted the verbal-visual experimentation of the latter half of the twentieth century, at that point marginalized by critics of contemporary literary and artistic panorama, to a particular avant-garde tradition. For the rest, Martini and Caruso, entrenched directly in this environment of verbal-visual writing, were occupied by the term "neo-avantgardes" ("neoavanguardie"); this term, opportunely termed in the plural, does not only refer to Gruppo 63,[20] which is commonly associated with the definition of neo-avantgarde. Rather, the plural term "neo-avantgardes" ("neoavanguardie"), refers to a complex group of experiences, which counts very diverse movements within it, categorized by their basic thesis of verbal-visual poetry or verbo-visual writing. This group, in totality, includes those experiments aimed at investigating the "no-man's land" between word and image, and pushing categorical limits in a way that leads to a cross-media effect, in the pre-futurist and absolutely romantic reproposition of the mirage of a totally unified art ("arte totale").[21]

Therefore it was in the critical trajectory traced by the two curators the predilection accorded to the analysis of the free-word tables originated; of the free-word tables, following Ballerini's reading, the works collected in Marinetti's anthology came to be considered above all the "most mature": *Les Mots en liberté futuristes*, with particular attention to the compositions *Le soir; couchée dans son lit; Elle relisait la lettre de son artilleur au front; Après la Marne Joffre visita le front en auto; Une assemblée tumultueuse (sensibilité numérique).*[22]

The pivot on which the system of the free-word tables turns is to be found in the typographic revolution.[23] Other than having influence on the way of the artistic product's fruition—of which are appreciated the visual and musical merits, besides the literary—this typographic revolution also positions itself in contrast to the rules of the editorial market due to the difficulty of reproducing the poem in series, leading to the works' total editorial failure, in spite of the impressive publishing apparatus set up by Marinetti. In this way, Martini and Caruso present this as Futurism puts into action—"despite itself"—a "claim of language and of writing like spaces of the invective and of the aesthetics" against a market that is the principal cause precisely of that language attrition of which has been said before.[24] It is also in opposition to this market that Futurism presents its transgressive position, in the first place against the societal restrictions that seem to be mirrored by the typographical restrictions of the page. It is therefore not by chance that Stelio Maria Martini's same creative production picks up on these trends in his use of cut-outs from daily newspapers and magazines, spread across the page, resulting in poem-collages (figure 19.1), of which the author underlines implicitly the affiliation to the futurist free-word tables; in the preface to his collection, *Schemi*, published in 1962 for "Documento Sud" he affirms:

> The visual element is nothing else but the development of the possibilities offered in this way by the word, if not its completion (if only I had been able to put it in a way as practical, I would not have hesitated to add auditory elements such as sounds of instruments, random sounds or human voices, etc. . . . elements in relief, mobiles, olfactory elements, etc. . . .)[25]

The reference to Marinettian manifestos is obvious, in which is theorized precisely a development of graphic symbols, in an auditory, olfactory and visual sense, by means of the adoption of a "multilinear lyricism" ("lirismo multilineo") and by adopting the typographical print revolution,[26] often by insertion of external elements such as newspaper clippings and advertising slogans, used by the futurists, whether it be applied in visual art (for example, a work such as *Manifestazione interventista* by Carlo Carrà) or whether it be

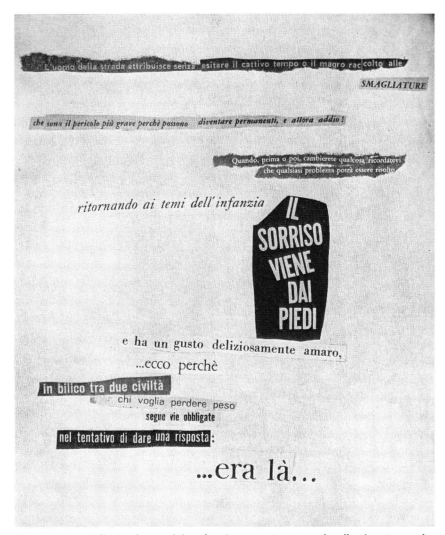

Figure 19.1. Stelio Maria Martini, *Schemi*, 1962. Courtesy of Collection Centre for Contemporary Art Luigi Pecci, Prato. Donation Carlo Palli.

applied in a literary way (for example, see *Bombardamento sola igiene* by Marinetti, constructed with contemporary newspaper clippings). If this is not the place for tracing a history of the utilization of collage techniques,[27] from the cubist *papier collé* up until the avant-garde movements of the 1960s, passing by the famous polemic between Papini and Boccioni in *Lacerba*,[28] it should nevertheless be noted that many of the artistic research outcomes that lie between the 1950s and 1960s, started from a rethinking of this technique—this is the case for example of the famous *décollage* of Rotella—developed simultaneously with the verbal-visual poetry, with which it sometimes intersected.[29]

That which begs analysis here is, rather, the persistence and developments of styles in the futurist avant-garde in the second half of the twentieth century, giving particular attention to the verbal-visual production of the Gruppo 70, in which is particularly evident the use of futuristic language, configured in terms of an operation that aims to undermine the languages of mass communication using, in an alienating way, techniques and sub-codes belonging to advertising, to magazines, the newspapers, and to specialized language.

Literature and New Media

In the same years in which Stelio Maria Martini composed *Schemi*, in other cultural centers—such as that of Genoa with its group of "Ana Eccetera," and in Rome with the magazine *Ex* by Emilio Villa and Mario Diacono—similar experiments came to fruition. In the city of Florence, Lamberto Pignotti created Gruppo 70,[30] with the organization of the conference *Arte e comunicazione*,[31] dedicated to the analysis of the relationship between new media and poetic production, according to an ideological perspective, however alien, at least in part, to Neapolitan and Genovese experiences. This ideological line of thought also represents the crux of reflection for the Gruppo 63, which was formed in October of that year at the conference organized in Palermo.[32] Besides, precisely in that period modern semiotic studies were developed, the precursor of which was Barthes's *Mythologies*, to which can be added the studies of the Frankfurt School, Max Bense's aesthetic algebra, and McLuhan's communication theory. Pignotti constantly refers to these studies in his theoretical essays, from the first ones published in 1962 in the journal *Questo e Altro* (This and More),[33] in which he conducts a close analysis of the relationship between the artistic activity, the new industrial realities and mass communication channels.

Placing himself in the debate instigated by *Menabò*[34] with his essay "L'industria che non si vede" ("The unseen industry"), Pignotti analyzes the evolution of the industry from the nineteenth century to contemporary times, pointing out that it is no longer to be a tangible and verifiable reality. Rather, to Pignotti, the industry is a "way" ("una maniera"), that pervades every aspect of life itself, by changing "any and every relationship that can be established between the poet and the object of his aesthetic considerations."[35] From this, the need arises to update the fundamental artistic tools in the face of the technological innovations promoted by the new industrial society, developing a style which will impact on this reality: "Under the pressure of technology"—Pignotti says—"the language of poetry, not to perish, had to be renewed."

This has led to what Max Bense defines as a "technological style," or rather a style in which is found "the transplantation and manipulation of technological, linguistic elements," such as "journalism, the logical-mathematical language, sporting, scientific, humorous, telegraphic, bureaucratic and commercial, advertising language and so on."[36] The assumption of this style, according to Pignotti, would also beg consideration of a reappropriation of contents:[37] "It will not be about sending stars into retirement in order to appoint the spacecrafts. We must be able to know how to speak about the moon, even when we have installed with our satellite a regular service line."[38]

To achieve this result, after a first period of linear poetry production, the technique of making collages from newspaper clippings is indicated, and then in a second instance illustrations from glossy magazines, fashion magazines and advertisements from that period are introduced. The slogans and images become decontextualized and inserted in the compositions in order to convey a contradictory message that uses the effectiveness of advertising—the surprise and shock—to impose a "product" of a cultural nature onto a recipient. An example of this would be, in a work of Eugenio Miccini, *Meglio del mondo non c'è che il mondo* (There's nothing better of the world than the world) in which, on a page that bears the phrase "Campagna per l'incremento dei consumi" (campaign to increase consumption) as its frame, places this advertising slogan (probably written on a previous painting) at is center:[39]

Speak poetry you all will understand each other/ better read poetry if you want / seize the world / the one you have at hand is no use // With little expense and minimal passion / our Company gives you in exchange for the old one/ (that which we are not, that which we do not want)[40]/ a new world on discount / don't wait until tomorrow it's a purchase / to be done now / best of the world / the better of the world/ there is nothing but the world.[41]

Miccini's work is included in the anthology *Poesie visive* (Visual Poetry) published by Edizioni Sampietro,[42] in which also appears a "Cancellatura" ("Erasure") by Emilio Isgrò—similar in this first phase, to the work of Gruppo 70—which is composed of an article entitled *Ideologia della sopravvivenza* (Ideology of Survival) (figure 19.2), where, among the blackened words, it is possible to discern a sentence that seems to evoke the words of Pignotti: "it is absurd to 'describe' the launch of a spacecraft with the same words that once served Flaubert to describe the bed and the skirts of Madame Bovary."[43]

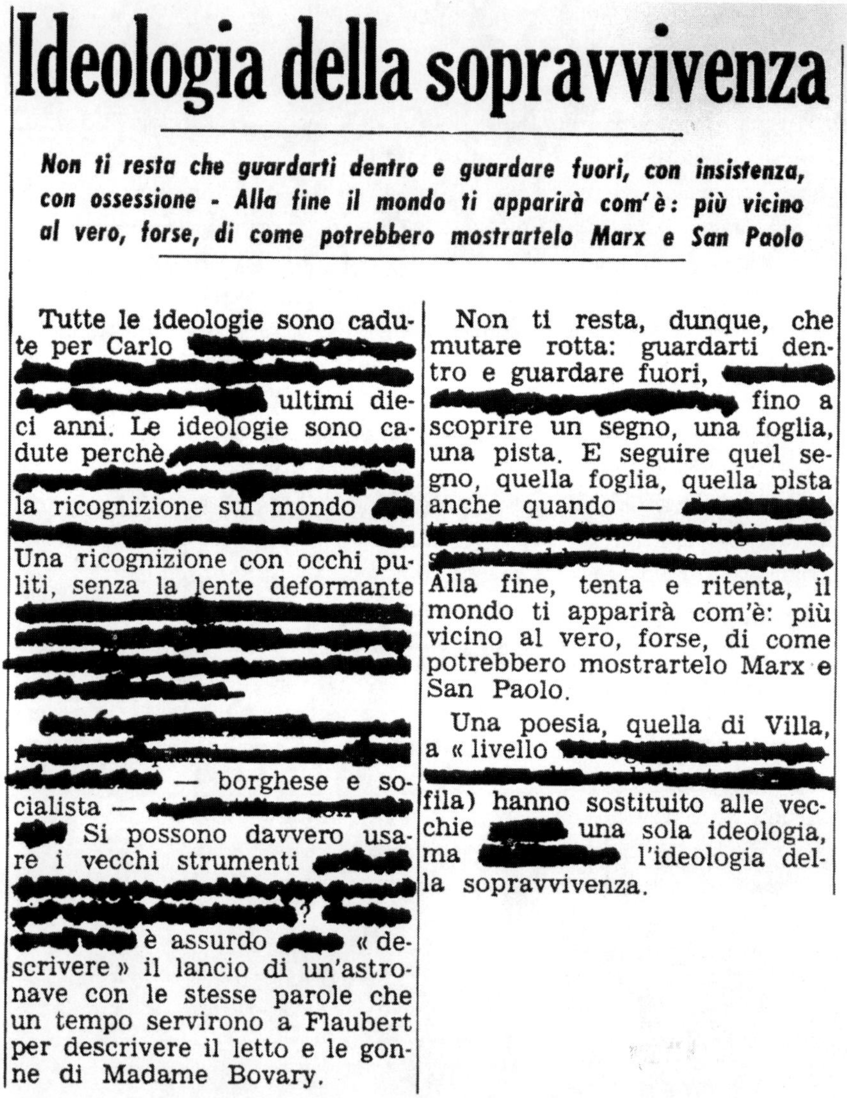

Ideologia della sopravvivenza

Non ti resta che guardarti dentro e guardare fuori, con insistenza, con ossessione - Alla fine il mondo ti apparirà com'è: più vicino al vero, forse, di come potrebbero mostrartelo Marx e San Paolo

Tutte le ideologie sono cadute per Carlo ▮▮▮▮▮▮ ▮▮▮▮▮▮ ultimi dieci anni. Le ideologie sono cadute perchè ▮▮▮▮▮▮ la ricognizione sul mondo ▮▮

Una ricognizione con occhi puliti, senza la lente deformante ▮▮▮▮▮▮ ▮▮▮▮▮▮

▮▮ — borghese e socialista — ▮▮▮▮ ▮▮ Si possono davvero usare i vecchi strumenti ▮▮▮▮

▮▮▮▮ è assurdo ▮▮▮ « descrivere » il lancio di un'astronave con le stesse parole che un tempo servirono a Flaubert per descrivere il letto e le gonne di Madame Bovary.

Non ti resta, dunque, che mutare rotta: guardarti dentro e guardare fuori, ▮▮▮▮ fino a scoprire un segno, una foglia, una pista. E seguire quel segno, quella foglia, quella pista anche quando — ▮▮▮▮▮▮

Alla fine, tenta e ritenta, il mondo ti apparirà com'è: più vicino al vero, forse, di come potrebbero mostrartelo Marx e San Paolo.

Una poesia, quella di Villa, a « livello ▮▮▮▮ fila) hanno sostituito alle vecchie ▮▮▮ una sola ideologia, ma ▮▮▮ l'ideologia della sopravvivenza.

Figure 19.2. Emilio Isgrò, *Cancellatura (Ideologia della sopravvivenza)*, 1965. Courtesy Archivio Emilio Isgrò, Milan.

The theme of scientific and technological advances, of which research carried out for space missions—that in a few years from then would send man to the moon—constituted a symbolic aspect, is at the heart of a work by Lucia Marcucci *Il fidanzato in fuga* (The Fleeing Fiancé) (figure 19.3), in which the words taken from newspapers and pasted on the image of three

Figure 19.3. Lucia Marcucci, *Il fidanzato in fuga*, 1964. Courtesy Lucia Marcucci.

space suits, make an ironic phrase that casts a sarcastic shadow on the "magnificent and progressive fate" that would have led mankind to conquer space.

In essence we are witnessing, on the one hand, the development of a language that expresses a new reality configured by scientific progress, and, on the other hand, the questioning of the value and significance of that progress. The production of Gruppo 70 is framed in a very specific historical and social context: between 1958 and 1963, Italy was undergoing a phase of great economic expansion, with as a result the perfection of the modern capitalist system. This system was supported by a massive, previously unknown, use of radically revised means of communication that adopted new techniques and languages while constantly moving product advertising in the media closer to center stage.

For the rest, an analogous situation, mediated by Futurism, occurs at the beginning of the century when the industrial boom following the second industrial revolution creates profound social and economic changes, as well as a first and unscrupulous use of the emerging media. Indeed, both Futurism and verbal-visual poetry attempt to update the role and function of artistic activity in relation to the evolution of the historical and social processes in place, obviously each one offering diametrically opposed answers, but with the same determination to take on the emerging social reality, above all in regards to the relationship between art and new media. In an essay published in 1982—"Paroliberismo. Modelli di scrittura verbo-visiva futurista negli anni Dieci" (Paroliberismo. Models of Verbal-visual Futurist Writing 1910–1920)—the same Pignotti refers to the new "modalities of reading," and to road-side billboards and posters, pages of newspapers, and marketing campaigns, when he underlines:

> Futurist attention to the visual angle of literature and the complementary inclination of art toward the verbal side do not arise, do not manifest and no longer develop as expressions defined in an exclusively literary or artistic environment, but rather are related to the early twentieth century expansion of the technological civilization and its languages, the mass media and its messages.[44]

Since Pignotti's early theoretical works, it is in fact easy to note similarities and differences with the tenets of Futurism, whereas in the founding manifesto of 1909 Marinetti refers explicitly to the need to update the tools of artistic production to reflect the new industrial realities,[45] postulating that a substantial change should be seen in the role of the artist—from that of witness and interpreter to that of an active proponent of the transformation processes affecting society, becoming a social agent[46] able simultaneously to represent and to affect the historical and cultural realities changed.

The same ambivalence of Pignotti's early theoretical work, in relation to the futurist lessons, seems on the contrary to reaffirm its contents, in an attempt to establish a new aesthetic beyond the futurist: "In respect to art technology, the so-called avant-garde art is art of the past. In fact, times of the past are as well the simple past as the present perfect. The so-called avant-garde artists have become 'classics' and as such should be categorized and studied."[47] In the same way, in his essay "La suggestione di Gordon Flash" ("The Suggestion of Flash Gordon"), Pignotti takes a certain distance from the historical avant-garde by putting it in the past, yet at the same time recreates the lesson by replicating literally the lexicon: "For we prefer the living over the dead, we prefer our brothers over our fathers. And rather than the yellowed pages of the first twentieth-century avant-garde we prefer the pages fresh off the presses with news of the morning."[48] Pignotti proposes, in essence, the abolition of the old aesthetic in favor of an update on the new sensibility of contemporary art making: "Nor no one of us blushes about declaring the junk dealer Proust to be boring, or about having been more aesthetically influenced by Flash Gordon than by James Joyce."[49]

From this also follows an assumption of the languages of modernity (such as, for instance, comics and graphic novels) with a particular focus on advertising, of which the futurists were the first to identify the fundamental mechanisms. It achieves this by means of an artistic operation which, at the same time that it acquired the overriding principles, escaped the economic laws of the market, in particular the reproducibility of art in series, and promoted, rather, the making of a spectacle out of the artistic act, that extended to all aspects of the contemporary social and cultural reality (theater, music, painting, sculpture, architecture, radio, cinema, etc . . .).

In this context we have already mentioned the importance of new printing solutions adopted from newspapers, widely used by futurists in the graphic revolution. Even more important, however, is the contribution of advertising techniques upon the artistic production, both from the "formal" point of view, in the composition of the *tavole parolibere*, and from a "content oriented" point of view, in the application of advertising as an epiphenomenon of modernity and the new metropolitan scenario which it wishes to represent.[50] The *Passeggiata* (Stroll) by Palazzeschi[51] appears emblematic in this regard; here the urban landscape is described as "a succession of advertisements, newspaper titles, shop signs, house numbers, signs in shop windows,"[52] juxtaposed to each other according to the technique of verbal collage, in a manner not unlike that made by Boccioni in the *parolibera* text *Scarpetta da società + orina con slogan*. In Boccioni's work, advertisements and house numbers are framed and insolated from the text, already foreshadowing a compository solution in the interaction between word and image such as that obtained by Soffici in *Chimismi lirici* of *Bif § ZF + 18*, or for example that of a real free-word table such as *Buffet di Stazione*.[53] The marketing techniques also indicate different graphic methods to lay out a page, with innovative solutions such as the use of different fonts, heavy use of uppercase and lowercase letters, bold, italics, columns, and creative spacing,[54] using the mechanisms of industrial new linotype; an example of this is in the choice of the title *Bif § ZF + 18*, which is actually a typographical error randomly selected by the composing machine on the table of the typesetter.[55]

As early as 1916, Terenzio Grandi, in an article in *L'Arte Tipografica* with the title "Futurismo tipografico"—which was in fact very critical of the futurist movement, equated to "the whim of fashion of women's hats"[56]—argued that the words-in-freedom were in fact greatly indebted to the "capable womb of the art that is advertising,"[57] which was then functionalized and bent to assist the development of a completely new artistic language. This new artistic language adopted the techniques of the nascent mass media in its attempt at commanding that the artistic process be seen as a phenomenon that affects all aspects of reality. Its tangible manifestation, in the amazing and spectacularized multiplicity of reality's forms, is the same as the futurist reconstruction of the universe. If in fact, as pointed out by Giovanni Anceschi, there is no denying the influence of the avant-garde language on the language of advertising—and we will focus on this later—it is equally true that this has been preceded "by a phenomenon, in an opposite sense, of the borrowing on the part of the avant-garde, of advertising techniques of communication."[58] It is therefore no coincidence that the modulation of poetic language based upon the new technological reality, promoted by Pignotti, makes use of techniques that were drawn from mass media and that stem from studies conducted in those years by Bense and Dorfles,[59] in particular those on the efficiency of the advertisement message, obtained through the degree of novelty and "unexpectedness" ("inaspettatezza") that it contains, with a deviation from the norm in order to capture the attention of the viewer.[60]

By resorting to war terminology drawn largely from Marinetti's manifestos, Pignotti convincingly clarifies the ambivalence of the relationship with the mass media, in which the visual poetry is compared to "a modern Trojan Horse."[61] Adopting the approach of contemporary means of communication, this horse leads to a tight "semiological guerrilla warfare" against the alienation of contemporary language, codes and the iconographic repertoire of the consumer society in order to "overturn its meanings," returning the "goods to sender," thus conveying a message, in an opposite way, short circuiting the relationship between signifier and sign, and mobilizing speech to go in the direction of a new signification.

In short, as Miccini summarized quite well, the discussion is about transforming *mass media* into *mass culture*,[62] both working on their own ground. Assuming, therefore, mass *culture* to the subject of Pignotti's artistic works, he mediates also the resulting system of diffusion. Pignotti defiantly announces in his essay "La suggestione di Gordon Flash," that the poems would have been transmitted to stadium audiences by loudspeakers between sports matches, shown on television as part of the popular show *Carosello*, posted as manifestos on street posters, or displayed as billboards along highway shoulders.[63]

A proposal not dissimilar, but obviously marked by an opposite intention, from what Depero had already called for in the 1931 manifesto *Il futurismo e l'arte pubblicitaria*, published in *Numero unico futurista Campari*. Here the wish to assimilate *tout court* art into advertising—"the art of the future will mightily be advertising"—mobilizes the powerful fascination of advertising systems "that audaciously imposed itself on the walls, sides of buildings, shop windows, in trains, on sidewalks everywhere," in the making of a mass distribution of the *artistic* product. This mass distribution is in line with the rest of the powerful publicity machine that Marinetti brought into focus by means of the spectacles of his artistic and cultural happenings (e.g., the famous *serate futuriste*), the spread of futurist aesthetic programs by means of leaflets, books launched and publicized via advertisements in newspapers and magazines, or via newspaper wrappers meant to increase circulation.

This goal was picked up again, but with much less success, by Gruppo 70 with its promotion of real performances that took place near the highway exit of Florence-North;[64] in these performances, the group integrated poetry, music, film and painting, as in *Poesie e no* in *Luna Park*, or in *Approdo*. In an attempt to "bring poetry into the square" ("portare la poesia in piazza"), stepping out from the traditional circuits of art products' dissemination, this movement supported the use of widely distributed popular genres, such as graphic novels and comic strips (figure 19.4), or even puzzles and postage stamps (figure 19.5). So, Gruppo 70—consciously adopting a code of communication with the intention that this code would be easily deciphered by a mass audience and would simultaneously ensure a wider dissemination of the art work—tread a precariously thin line that marked the anti-market from the commercial market. Gruppo 70 proceeded with the conscious theoretical assumption that it is the fate of mass codification to inevitably run counter

Figure 19.4.   Eugenio Miccini, *USA. Rebus gestis*, 1967. Courtesy Alessandro Miccini.

Figure 19.5. Lamberto Pignotti, *A casa mia*, 1968. Courtesy Lamberto Pignotti.

to the aims of the avant-garde, as well as the mixture of aesthetic language and the language of advertising, the latter of which Gruppo 70 appropriates the innovations set forth in the arts and literature.

In fact, if on the one hand the aesthetic operation makes use of techniques drawn from mass media to strike the imagination of the recipient (through a standard deviation from the current codes of communication), on the other hand it is advertising itself that reabsorbs many of the innovations proposed by the avant-garde, translating its intellectual messages into banal and normalized forms. Essentially Pignotti underlines the delineation of "an area within which the values of mass communication open themselves toward the avant-garde . . . the values of the avant-garde open symmetrically toward mass communications."[65]

If advertising's modus operandi—"to depart from the norm generally given by the total of all the advertisements in circulation"—recurs in a generalized way as "forms of the artistic avant-gardes" which are then to be emptied of their original meaning and their subversive connotations, this then involves "a work of indirect disclosure," "against a mass audience, often unaware of current art trends." The attempt to promote a new aesthetic that involves every aspect of society and cultural reality (poetry, painting, cinema, theater, music, advertising), through the revival of avant-garde forms, therefore, presupposes the assumption in the theoretical domain of the contradictions to which every avant-garde is fatally subject: "Today, as happens in Gruppo 70, one can still 'scream' in the manner of the futurists, the dadaists and the surrealists, but only after acquiring thorough knowledge of structuralism and communication theory."[66]

Notes

1. Translation by Claudia M. Clemente.

2. Luigi Ballerini, *Italian Visual Poetry, 1912–1972*. New York: Finch College Museum; Istituto Italiano di Cultura, 1973; *Scrittura visuale in Italia, 1912–1972*. Introduction by Aldo Passoni; Catalogue for the exhibit held at the Galleria Civica d'Arte Moderna, Turin, September 27–October 28, 1973.

3. Present in the catalogue are, in fact, works by Sylvano Bussotti (*Sette fogli*; *La Passion selon Sade*; *Rara*; *Rara si pettina*; *Sciogliere un voto a Gianfranco*; *Julio Organum Julii*) and Giuseppe Chiari (*Teatrino*; *Don't Trade Here*; *La folla solitaria*; *Frase* [1971]; *Frase* [1973]).

4. Ballerini refers above all to "pittura alfabetizzante" ("alphabetizing visual art") by Gastone Novelli, of which the following works are included in the catalogue: *Et les obligations*; *Le monde est accablant*; *Sankhaara*; *Il vocabolario*; *Senza titolo* [1965].

5. "Spero che la formula della paternità futurista della scrittura visuale, e dell'incontro di tale paternità, negli anni Cinquanta e Sessanta, con le tendenze semantizzanti di certa pittura—e anzi di certa pittografia—e gli sviluppi che da tale incontro sono risultati, bastino a giustificare, a Torino come a New York, l'ambito soltanto italiano dell'iniziativa e a 'determinarne' il destino."

6. Ballerini, in the introduction to the catalogue *Scrittura visuale in Italia*, traces back in fact to the genesis of "writing with a meta-verbal tendency which has been configured in recent years in Italy," and to "the almost coincidental meeting of dissatisfied energies that the Futurist visual writing had recklessly abandoned, and by the renewed cultural tension running through the painting of the late 1950s."

7. Mentioned in the margin is the exhibit *Parola immagine oggetto* (Word, image, object), organized by the Istituto Italiano di Cultura of Tokyo (January 22 to February 11, 1976), at the occasion of what would have been Marinetti's 100th birthday. To this show a special edition of the journal *317* is dedicated, in which futurist free-word tables are reproduced alongside contemporary works of authors such as Lamberto Pignotti, Eugenio Miccini, Luciano Caruso, Martino Oberto.

8. Achille Bonito Oliva, *La Parola totale: una tradizione futurista, 1909–1986*. Catalogue of the exhibition held at Modena, Galleria Fonte d'Abisso, May 10–July 5, 1986. Modena: Mucchi, 1986. Enrico Mascelloni and Sarenco. *Poesia totale 1897–1997: dal colpo di dadi alla poesia totale*. Catalogue of the exhibition held at Mantova, Palazzo della Ragione, June–September 1998. Verona: Adriano Parise, 1998. Belli, Gabriella. *La parola nell'arte. Ricerche d'avanguardia nel '900, dal Futurismo a oggi attraverso le collezioni del Mart*. Catalogue of the exhibition held at Rovereto, Museo di Arte Moderna e Contemporanea di Trento e Rovereto (MART), November 10, 2007–April 6, 2008. Milano: Skira, 2007.

9. Luciano De Maria, ed., *Teoria e invenzione futurista* (Milan: Mondadori, 1968).

10. On the reception of Futurism, see the essay by Günter Berghaus in this volume.

11. This calls to mind the fundamental study by Renzo De Felice, *Mussolini il rivoluzionario* (Turin: Einaudi, 1965).

12. A more comprehensive volume followed this in 1977, that also included a "Postfazione a commento" (Postscript with commentary) by Christopher Wagstaff, in Luciano Caruso and Stelio Maria Martini, eds., *Tavole parolibere futuriste (1912–1944)* (Naples: Liguori, 1977). That same year, furthermore, Caruso and Martini began to promote two exhibits dedicated to, respectively, *Tavole parolibere e tipografia futurista* (Free-word Tables and Futurist Typography) Exhibition Catalogue, Venice, Ca' Corner della Regina, October 15–November 20, 1977, and *Scrittura visuale e poesia sonora futurista* (Visual Writing and Sonorous Futurist Poetry) Exhibition Catalogue, Florence, Palazzo Medici Riccardi, November 4, 1977–December 15, 1977.

13. In Ballerini's exhibit, among other, were shown works by Caruso (two pages from *Tabulae*; two pages from *De invenzione linguarum*; two pages from *Syn-Scriv*), and by Martini (*Felice chi può*; *Una finestra*; *Una lezione per l'Occidente*; *Una logica*; *Un meccanismo*; *Il tema speciale di chiusura*; *Un teste che si contraddice*; *L'uomo della strada attribuisce*).

14. In reference to the editorial note by Luciano Caruso: "The idea and the need to conduct more research was prompted by Ballerini's exhibit *Scrittura visuale in Italia, 1912–1972*, held in the rooms of the Museo Civico of Turin."

15. In reference to the connection between Futurism and the fascist movement, Luciano Caruso and Stelio Maria Martini point out contradictory aspects, noting how *de facto* fascism had not used the futurist movement: "what remains to be explained is the perfect lack of use of Futurism by the fascists, the little or no consideration about the fact that fascism addressed the futurists, Futurism as a movement, and the reasons of Futurism" ("resta da spiegare la perfetta inutilizzazione del futurismo da parte del fascismo, la scarsa o nessuna considerazione che il fascismo rivolse ai futuristi, al futurismo come movimento, alle istanze del futurismo"). "La fuga in avanti del futurismo" ("The Forward Flight of Futurism"), introduction to *Tavole parolibere futuriste* (1974), 6. In an even more explicit way, in the presentation "La luce del sensibile" ("The light of the senses") to *Scrittura visuale e poesia sonora*, 12, Caruso and Martini affirm: "We say that it is no longer legitimate to implicate a critique of Futurism along with a general condemnation of fascism; indeed, despite its

ostentatious support of fascism, Futurism itself rejected the rhetorical and cultural restoration adopted by fascism, resulting in a mis-match in which Futurism found itself unused by fascist dogma" (12); ("Noi diciamo che non è più lecito coinvolgere nella condanna del fascismo un movimento negatore della tradizione come il futurismo, che di fatto costituì [ad onta della adesione anche troppo ostentata al fascismo] la negazione della restaurazione retorica e culturale che il fascismo operò, lasciando il futurismo assolutamente inutilizzato.")

16. One thinks of the volume by Maurizio Calvesi, *Le due avanguardie. Dal futurismo alla pop art* (Milan: Lerici, 1966); and of the works by Enrico Crispolti about the second wave of Futurism, *Il secondo futurismo. Torino 1923–1938* (Turin: Pozzo, 1961); *Il mito della macchina e altri temi del futurismo* (Bologna: Pendragon, 1995), as well as of the exhibits dedicated to Enrico Prampolini (Exhibition Catalogue, Turin, Galleria Narciso, October 31– November 20, 1963) and Giacomo Balla (Exhibition Catalogue, Turin, Galleria Civica d'Arte Moderna, from April 4, 1963).

17. On this, see Caruso and Martini, *Le tavole parolibere ovvero la "rivoluzione culturale" dei futuristi* (1977), 37: "As far as we know, in regards to how many studies to this day have been dedicated to the literary aspect of Futurism, among which are those brought into being by the desire to comprehend and also reevaluate Futurism, not one addresses the central question of words-in-freedom and the free-word tables, and when these topics are brought up, the question is dealt with (or evaded) in few words, and not very enthusiastically at that." ("A nostra notizia, per quanti studi siano comparsi a tutt'oggi sul futurismo letterario, tra quelli animati dalla volontà di comprendere ad anche rivalutare il futurismo, nessuno affronta la centrale questione delle parole in libertà e delle tavole parolibere, e dove di esse ci si occupa, la questione è sbrigata (o elusa) con poche parole non propriamente entusiaste.")

18. "La verità è che sui futuristi continuano a pesare una serie di condanne e di ostracismi, in Italia e all'estero . . . ed in tali condanne ed ostracismi sono da rintracciare sia le ragioni dei mancati accenni ai futuristi . . . da parte della neoavanguardia straniera, sia anche la spiegazione degli strani fenomeni per cui, dopo il futurismo, in Italia le vicende singole o collettive dei fenomeni d'avanguardia sembrano aver scoperto come daccapo ed in maniera autonoma le contraddizioni, i nodi e le strade da prendere a seguito della constatata necessità di far fronte all'estremo logoramento del mezzo espressivo comunicativo e dalla quale i futuristi avevano già, essi per primi nella storia, rimesso in gioco gli elementi costitutivi del mezzo stesso riassumendoli come materia d'invenzione ed oggetti di creazione." Caruso and Martini, "La luce del sensibile," introduction to Idem, *Scrittura visuale e poesia sonora*, 9.

19. "Le avanguardie storiche . . . dovranno attendere le neoavanguardie perché i loro motivi di fondo, non sempre inconsci, emergessero consapevolmente e si concretassero secondo che le loro intime ragioni richiedevano." Caruso and Martini, "La fuga in avanti del futurismo" (The Forward Flight of Futurism), introduction to Idem, *Tavole parolibere futuriste* (1975), 6.

20. On the legacy of Futurism in the theoretical and creative production of Gruppo 63, see the essay by Florian Mussgnug in this volume.

21. I take the concept of "no-man's land" from a quote by Lamberto Pignotti: "Put aside the fictitious lines of demarcation what will be required is an exploration far and wide of that no-man's land that is for now between written and visual language, between word and image." ("Accantonate le fittizie linee di demarcazione occorrerà allora esplorare per lungo e per largo quella terra di nessuno che sta per ora fra il linguaggio scritto e quello visivo, fra parola e immagine.")

22. An analysis of these free-word tables in Caruso and Martini's *Tavole parolibere* (1977), 54–56.

23. See Mario Diacono, "L'oggettipografia futurista," in Caruso and Martini, *Tavole parolibere futuriste* (1975), 9–15.

24. See Caruso and Martini, "La fuga in avanti del futurismo," *Tavole parolibere futuriste* (1975), 3: "The total editorial failure of almost all futurist production is, above all, revealed and one needs to pause to consider for one moment this particular aspect of the production, the reasons why it did not work on the part of the editorial industry, are evidently traceable to the difficulty and costs of the typographical reproduction, carrying also, for a good part of what was printed, an implication about the domestification and the deformation of the product." ("Va innanzitutto rilevata l'assenza totale di successo editoriale di quasi tutta la produzione futurista ed occorre soffermarsi sul particolare aspetto di detta produzione, le cause di rifiuto della quale, da parte dell'industria editoriale, di per sé già evidentemente rintracciabili nelle difficoltà [e nei costi] della riproduzione tipografica, comportano anche, per buona parte di quanto fu stampato, un risvolto di addomesticamento e di deformazione del prodotto.")

25. "L'elemento visivo non è che il potenziamento delle possibilità così offerte dalla parola, quando non il completamento (se appena l'avessi potuto in maniera altrettanto pratica, non avrei esitato ad aggiungere elementi uditivi quali suoni di strumenti, accidentali o voci umane ecc . . . , elementi di rilievo, mobili, olfattivi, ecc . . .)."

26. The reference is obviously to *Technical Manifesto of Futurist Literature* (*Manifesto tecnico della letteratura futurista*) (1912), and to these texts that followed: *Destruction of Syntax, Imagination Without Threads, Parole in Libertà* (1913); *The Geometric and Mechanic Splendor and the Numerical Sensibility* (1914). (*Distruzione della sintassi. Immaginazione senza fili. Parole in libertà* [1913]; *Lo splendore geometrico e meccanico e la sensibilità numerica* [1914].)

27. See Maria Mimita Lamberti and Maria Grazia Messina, *Collage/Collages, dal Cubismo al New Dada* (Milan: Electa, 2008).

28. The polemics took place in three parts, with Papini's article "Il cerchio si chiude" ("The Circle is Closed") in *Lacerba* 4 (1914), Boccioni's response, "Il cerchio non si chiude!" ("The Circle is not Closed!") in *Lacerba* 5 (1914), and Papini continues the discussion with "Cerchi aperti cerchi chiusi" ("Open Circles, Closed Circles ") in *Lacerba* 6 (1914).

29. Of particular interest are the frequent cases of collaboration between painters and poets, one thinks, for example of Bueno (*Homo technologicus*, produced

with Pignotti), Scialoja (*Il giardino*, produced with Giuliani), Ragazzi (*Sono biglie di vetro*; *E poi non c'è*, produced with Porta) and Novelli (*Prototeatro 2*, produced with Giuliani).

30. The group's name refers to "the future beyond the 1970s, and is composed of poets, painters, musicians that are aware of the phenomena of contemporary mass communication, experiment with artistic genres with various topical interests: they aim to place their works in their current society of technology of the masses." The quote, presumably by Pignotti—is from the brochure of the *Festival dei Popoli* (Florence: Edizioni 70, 1967).

31. The conference took place on May 24, 25, and 26, 1963, and was organized by Lamberto Pignotti, Eugenio Miccini, Sergio Salvi and Silvio Ramat, with the collaboration from the artists of the "Nuova Figurazione" ("New Figuration ")—Antonio Bueno, Silvio Loffredo, Alberto Moretti e Venturino Venturi—who were joined by Vinicio Berti, Gualtiero Nativi, Carlo Cioni, Riccardo Guarnieri. Other than these the following musicians contributed to the initiative: Pietro Grossi, Giuseppe Chiari and Sylvano Bussotti. Notable among the participants were: Gillo Dorfles, Cesare Vivaldi, Renato Barilli, Roman Vlad, Klaus Metzger, Umberto Eco, Luciano Anceschi, Elio Pagliarani, Aldo Rossi, Edoardo Sanguineti. A transcription of the proceedings is published in the first volume of *Dopotutto*, part of *Letteratura*, 67–68 (1963): 104–76. For more comprehensive information on the activity of Gruppo 70 see Lucilla Saccà, *La parola come immagine e come segno* (Pisa: Pacini, 2000); Lucia Fiaschi, *Parole contro* (Siena: Carlo Cambi, 2009).

32. The exchanges between the two groups were frequent and ongoing; this makes one think of the activity of Balestrini, Giuliani and Porta that composed works of visual poetry, on more than one occasion, such as those inserted by Pignotti in the 1965 anthology *Poesie visive* (Bologna: Sampietro, 1965)—or of those of the members of Gruppo 70 at the meetings organized by Gruppo 63, with the organization of shows and performances. Of these, one recalls the exhibit of visual poetry in which participated: Balestrini, Bueno, Diacono, Giuliani, Manieri, Martini, Miccini, Pedio, Pignotti, Porta, Spatola, Villa, organized on the occasion of the second convention of Gruppo 63 held in Reggio Emilia (November 1 through 3, 1964). For more information on this, see Pignotti, "Per la mostra di poesia visiva del Gruppo 63," *Dopotutto*, an insert in *Letteratura* 73 (1965): 74–75.

33. Lamberto Pignotti, "L'industria che non si vede," *Questo e Altro* 1 (1962): 59–61; "La Poesia tecnologica," *Questo e Altro* 2 (1962): 60–68 .

34. The debate on literature and industry, *Letteratura e industria*, took place in volume 4 of *Il Menabò* (1961), in which Lamberto Pignotti's poetry appeared, collected under the title *L'uomo di qualità* (*The Man of Quality*).

35. Pignotti, "L'industria che non si vede," 60.

36. Pignotti, "La Poesia tecnologica," 61.

37. In "L'industria che non si vede" (61), Pignotti defines the technological style as a sort of third way between the realistic hypothesis and that of the avant-garde, or, rather, as "a possible fusion and usage of their positive implications that

are firstly the need of linguistic communication and secondly that of a syntactic-semantic updating."

38. "Non si tratterà di mandare in pensione le stelle per assumere le astronavi. Bisognerà saper parlare della luna anche quando sarà istituito col nostro satellite un regolare servizio di linea." Pignotti, "L'industria che non si vede," 60.

39. As explained by Lucia Marcucci in an interview, often "the first works of technological poetry were made thanks to the support (of artistic funding) by Antonio Bueno, Lastraioli, Barni, Moretti and Roberto Malquori. I possess a work by Barni, in which Miccini has added a few sentences, dated 1965" (Interview with Lucia Marcucci, in Fiaschi, *Parole contro*, 31).

40. The reference is obviously to the famous poem of Eugenio Montale, *Non chiederci la parola*, implicitly brought up as a reference in order to represent par excellence the Italian literary tradition, indeed, in order to "liquidate" it.

41. "Parlate poesia vi intenderete / meglio leggete poesia se volete / prendete il mondo al balzo / quello che avete a mano non serve. // Con modica spesa e minima passione / la ns. Società vi dà in cambio del vecchio / (ciò che non siamo, ciò che non vogliamo) / un mondo nuovo con lo sconto / Non rimandate a domani è acquisto / da farsi subito / meglio del mondo / non c'è che il mondo."

42. The anthology *Poesie visive*, edited in four volumes, numbered 5 to 8, each annotated with an introduction by Pignotti includes works by Nanni Balestrini, Bonito Oliva, Danilo Giorgi, Luca Sampietro, Emilio Isgrò, Eugenio Miccini, Lamberto Pignotti, Lucia Marcucci, Stelio Maria Martini, Luciano Ori, Antonio Porta, Alfredo Giuliani, Adriano Spatola, Luigi Tola, and Guido Ziveri.

43. "È assurdo 'descrivere' il lancio di un'astronave con le stesse parole che un tempo servivano a Flaubert per descrivere il letto e le gonne di Madame Bovary."

44. "L'attenzione futurista al versante visivo della letteratura e la complementare inclinazione al versante verbale dell'arte non sorgono, non si manifestano e non si sviluppano più come espressioni definibili nell'ambito esclusivamente letterario o artistico, ma sono connesse all'espansione, ai primi del Novecento, della civiltà tecnologica e dei suoi linguaggi, della comunicazione di massa e dei suoi messaggi." Lamberto Pignotti, "Paroliberismo. Modelli di scrittura verbo-visiva futurista negli anni Dieci" (1982), in Idem, *Figure scritture. Su certi segni delle arti e dei mass media* (Udine: Campanotto, 1987), 17.

45. This concept is underlined by Marinetti in the opening to the manifesto: *Distruzione della sintassi. Immaginazione senza fili. Parole in libertà* (1913) (*Destruction of Syntax. Imagination without Lines. Words in Liberty*), cited by the same Pignotti as *incipit* to his essay "Paroliberismo": "Those that today use the telegraph, the telephone, the gramophone, the train, the bicycle, the motorcycle, the auto, the transatlantic ship, the dirigible, the airplane, the cinema, the major newspapers (which are the synthesis of one day on Earth), do not think that these diverse forms of communication, transportation, and of information wield a decisive influence on their psyches." ("Coloro che usano oggi del telegrafo, del telefono e del grammofono, del treno, della bicicletta, della motocicletta, dell'automobile, del transatlantico, del dirigibile,

dell'aeroplano, del cinematografo, del grande quotidiano (sintesi di una giornata del mondo) non pensano che queste diverse forme di comunicazione, di trasporto e d'informazione esercitano sulla loro psiche una decisiva influenza").

46. Fausto Curi, "Una stilistica della materia" (1994), in Idem *Tra mimesi e metafora. Studi su Marinetti e il futurismo* (Bologna: Pendragon, 1995), 47–49.

47. "Rispetto all'arte tecnologica la cosiddetta arte d'avanguardia è arte del passato. Sono infatti tempi del passato sia il passato remoto che il passato prossimo. I cosiddetti artisti d'avanguardia sono ormai dei 'classici' e come tali vanno inquadrati e studiati." Lamberto Pignotti, "La suggestione di Gordon Flash," *Marcatrè* 11–13 (1965): 107. In regards to this, it is necessary to recall a passage of the 1909 *Manifesto*—cited among others by Caruso and Martini in the introduction to *Tavole parolibere futuriste* (1977), 30—in which Marinetti afferms: "when we'll be forty, other younger and more able men than we are will throw us into the wastepaper basket, like useless texts. We want that!" ("quando avremo quarant'anni, altri uomini più giovani e più validi di noi, ci gettino pure nel cestino, come manoscritti inutili. Noi lo desideriamo!").

48. "Ai morti preferiamo i vivi, ai padri preferiamo i fratelli. Alle pagine ingiallite dell'avanguardia primo novecentesca preferiamo le pagine ancora odorose d'inchiostro tipografico con le notizie del mattino." Pignotti, "La suggestione di Gordon Flash," 107.

49. "Né qualcuno di noi arrossisce dichiarando di trovar noioso il rigattiere Proust o di essere stato più suggestionato esteticamente da Gordon Flash che da James Joyce." Ibidem.

50. On the nexus between Futurism and advertising, see, specifically Giovanni Fanelli and Ezio Godoli, *Il futurismo e la grafica* (Milan: Edizioni Comunità, 1988).

51. Pignotti, "Letteratura e pubblicità" in *Scritture convergenti. Letteratura e mass media* (Udine: Campanotto, 2005), 19, in the *incipit* of which are inscribed some of Palazzeschi's verses: "Brusquely proposing this passage from Aldo Palazzeschi's *La passeggiata* (and it is not out of place to point out that the composition dates to before World War I) we would be tempted to pose this question—as brusquely if not brutally—to unwary readers—does this pertain to poetry or to advertising? This question would be sure to elicit, quite understandably, a certain confusion—so weak at times is the distinction between these two expressive areas in language." ("Proponendo bruscamente questo brano tratto dalla poesia di Aldo Palazzeschi, *La passeggiata* ['e non è fuor di luogo far rilevare che la composizione è anteriore alla prima guerra mondial'] saremmo tentati di porre—altrettanto bruscamente e anzi brutalmente—agli sprovveduti lettori la domanda se si tratti qui di poesia o di pubblicità, certi di suscitare in loro una qualche e comprensibile perplessità, così labile a volte è attualmente il confine fra questi due ambiti espressivi del linguaggio.") Yet, one also sees an analogous observation made by Pignotti on the works of visual poetry: "it can happen to you, for example to come across in visual poetry (or almost) when looking at a commercial poster, or a magazine, or the pages of a cartoon . . . " ("vi potrà capitare per esempio di imbattervi in poesie visive (o quasi) guardando un cartellone pubblicitario, o la

copertina di un rotocalco, o la pagina di un fumetto"). Lamberto Pignotti, introduction to "Antologia di Poesia visiva," *Il Portico* 7 (July 1966): 34.

52. Pignotti, *Scritture convergenti*, 19.

53. Balla and Soffici's works are reproduced in the catalogue curated by Ballerini , *Scrittura visuale in Italia*, presented as examples of free-word tables, commented upon in the introduction of *Ottico ideottico* (pages not numbered).

54. See Domenico Cammarota, "La rivoluzione tipografica futurista" ("The Futurist Typographical Revolution"), in Gabriella Belli, *La parola nell'arte* (Milan: Skira, 2007), 55–59.

55. An analysis of the *parolibera* production is conducted by Pignotti and Stefania Stefanelli in the volume *La scrittura verbo-visiva* (Rome: Editoriale l'Espresso, 1980); on this subject see also the careful study by Francesca Polacci and Dario Tomasello, *Bisogno furioso di liberare le parole* (Florence: Le Lettere, 2009).

56. "L'alterno variare di moda dei cappelli femminili." Grandi, "Futurismo tipografico," in *L'Arte Tipografica* 4 (June 1916): 27; also see Terenzio Grandi, "Futurismo tipografico: breve postilla," *L'Arte Tipografica* 5 (July 1916).

57. Grandi, "Futurismo tipografico," 29: "Meanwhile, I do not know how to refrain from pointing out how the hidden bonds should be strong . . . between the words in *libertà* and those used in advertisement. Ties between them, I say, that are essential, since they are formal, absolutely certain, and place Futurism in direct dependence upon the art of appealing to the public; let this be explained on the last pages of a newspaper, or in its vastest applications, up to the top of the tallest towers. . . . Ah, yes! The capable womb of the art of advertising; here you find discovered one of the most major sources of Futurism." ("Intanto, non so trattenermi dal rilevare come debbano essere forti i legami occulti . . . tra le parole in libertà e la *réclame*. Dico legami essenziali, poiché quelli formali vi sono, indubbi, e pongono il futurismo in dipendenza diretta dell'arte del richiamo; si esplichi questa sulle ultime pagine d'un giornale, o nelle sue applicazioni vastissime, fin sulla cima delle più alte torri. . . . Ah, si! Il capace grembo dell'arte reclamistica; ecco scoperto donde si parte una fra le maggiori scaturigini del futurismo.")

58. Giovanni Anceschi, "Preavanguardie commerciali," *Linea Grafica* 5 (1986): 30–39.

59. Gillo Dorfles, *Simbolo, comunicazione, consumo* (Turin: Einaudi, 1962).

60. Pignotti, "La poesia tecnologica," 60: ". . . information (whether it be linguistic or literary) reaches its maximum effect via a signal, that for its novelty, its unexpectedness, and its unpredictability yields a maximum effect of surprise. The more this signal is repeated, the efficacy of the reaction and the consequent informative degree of the sign tend to zero. In order to restore efficient information, one should modify or change the signal." (" . . . l'informazione (linguistica o letteraria) raggiunge la sua massima efficacia tramite un segnale che per la sua novità, inaspettatezza e imprevedibilità procura il massimo di sorpresa. Al progressivo ripetersi del segnale l'efficacia della reazione e il conseguente grado informativo tendono a zero. A un'efficiente informazione si ritornerà solo modificando o cambiando il segnale.")

61. In the introduction to the anthology *Poesie visive* (Visual Poetry), Pignotti uses a lexicon clearly derived from Futurism: ". . . more than of an anthology, this has to do with a bulletin about a cultural battle in progress; do not expect an arrogant procession of battalions on parade but rather the discontinuous and uncertain advance of assault groups. The belligerent metaphors suit visual poetry perfectly—a poetry that stands for some time on the battle field, on no-man's land." (". . . più che di un'antologia si tratta . . . di un bollettino relativo a una battaglia culturale in corso: non aspettatevi una pettoruta sfilata di battaglioni in parata ma piuttosto il discontinuo e incerto avanzare di manipoli d'assalto. Le bellicose metafore si addicono perfettamente alla poesia visiva, una poesia che sta da qualche tempo in zona di operazioni, nella terra di nessuno.")

62. Eugenio Miccini, "Trasformare i mass-media in mass culture," *Marcatrè* 11–13 (1965): 107.

63. Pignotti, "La suggestione di Gordon Flash," 108; but also see the introductory note Lamberto Pignotti, "Inchiesta sulla letteratura d'avanguardia," *Dopotutto*, in *Letteratura* 73 (1965): 51–52.

64. Photographic documentation of the events promoted by Gruppo 70 has been included in the volume by Miccini and Pignotti *Poesie in azione* (Florence: Giubbe Rosse, 2001). For more information, see my essay "Le performance di poesia visiva e lo spazio urbano (1960–1970)," *Poeti e Poesia* 22 (April 2011): 172–81.

65. Lamberto Pignotti, *Il discorso confezionato* (Florence: Vallecchi, 1979), 29, from which the following quotes are also extracted.

66. "Oggi, come avviene appunto nell'ambito del gruppo 70, è possibile sì ancora 'urlare' alla maniera dei futuristi, dei dadaisti e dei surrealisti, ma solo coi volumi della teoria della comunicazione e dello strutturalismo sotto il braccio." Lamberto Pignotti, "Un rilancio del surrealismo?" *Marcatrè* 26–29 (1966): 247.

CHAPTER TWENTY

～

The Postwar Reception of Futurism

Repression or Recuperation?

GÜNTER BERGHAUS

For the last fifteen years, I have been collecting material for a bibliographical handbook of Italian Futurism and its international offshoots. A first install-ment was published, in a concise fashion, in the year 2000.[1] An enlarged version of it, containing some 25,000 entries, is expected for 2012/2013. This project has given me an insight into the ups and downs, the strengths and weaknesses of Futurism scholarship. Some of this I should like to highlight in this essay. I want to discuss some of the material published in the years 1945–1960, but not for the sake of reviewing the early history of Futurism Studies; rather, I want to suggest a need for a thorough analysis of postwar research into Futurism and a revision of the historiography of Futurism.

To this day, the prevailing view of the reception of Futurism after 1945 is that the anti-fascist consensus in Italian politics cast a political anathema on Marinetti's movement. We are always given to understand that we had to wait until the 1970s before the significance of Futurism was fully understood; we are told that it was the generation of 1968 who discovered the left-wing side of Futurism, particularly in Russia, and subsequently unearthed the radical, anti-establishment politics and aesthetics of the movement. I have no doubt that Marinetti's accommodation with the fascist regime cast a long and dark shadow on Futurism. However, the more than 1,600 publications I am listing in my bibliography for the years 1945–1969 suggest that long before 1968 a large number of initiatives were underway to recover, re-assess and re-evaluate the role of Futurism in the development of avant-garde and modern art.

Futurism and Its Critics, 1945–1950

Some of the first studies of Futurism came from former members of the movement itself. And the first to be exhibited were Futurists who had distanced
themselves from Marinetti during the period of *secondo futurismo*. Already in
1945, Carrà began to occupy an elevated position in the cultural establishment of liberated Italy. Severini, who had spent most of his creative life in
Paris, was above suspicion as far as fascist sympathies were concerned, and
was regularly exhibited and written about. In January 1947, he was for the
first time reunited with his former Futurist colleagues in the exhibition "Boccioni Carrà Severini (1910–1914)" at the Galleria La Margherita in Rome.
Also Balla and Russolo re-appeared on the scene, although I cannot say at
the moment whether any of the images exhibited in the late 1940s belonged
to their futurist period. Depero made a second attempt at gaining a foothold
in the American market and published for this purpose *So I Think, So I Paint:
Ideologies of an Italian Self-made Painter*.[2] Of course, it is one thing for a living artist to promote his work and to organize retrospective exhibitions that
support his claim for a prominent position in the chronicles of twentieth-
century art. But it is an altogether different matter to have a public institution opening its doors to former members of the futurist movement. This is
what happened in 1948 when the Quadriennale di Roma organized its first
postwar exhibition, entitled *Rassegna nazionale di arti figurative*. The show in
the Galleria d'Arte Moderna included twenty-six works by ten futurist artists. For understandable reasons, the emphasis was placed on the first phase of
Futurism. The fascist heritage in both Futurism and the Ente Quadriennale
was sidelined, also physically, in as much as works from the *secondo futurismo*
period were relegated to a small side room.

The critical response to this first postwar edition of the Quadriennale
indicated that, on the whole, the curators' strategy was successful. The
public still possessed a living memory of fascist propaganda art dressed up
in futurist attire and was therefore more than pleasantly surprised to see
the dynamic and vibrant works of the movement's founding fathers. Piero
Scarpa, for example, praised the Quadriennale's executive committee for
having mounted a retrospective of the "first phase of Futurism, which many
people don't know," and Walter Guidi expressed his genuine excitement
with the words: "These dead artists are more alive than living artists." Piero
Girace spoke for many when he wrote: "Amongst the most interesting
aspects of this Quadriennale is the retrospective of the futurist painters. It
has a tremendous importance and will serve as a yardstick for certain recent
experiments in the fine arts."[3]

Another institution that considered it opportune to offer the public a fresh chance to judge and review the historical significance of Futurism was the Venice Biennale. To test the waters, they put together a show called "forty years of Italian art from Futurism to the present day" and presented it in Lausanne and Lucerne.[4] Encouraged by the response this exhibition received, the Biennale presented, at its twenty-fifth edition in 1950, thirty-nine works by Balla, Boccioni, Carrà, Russolo and Severini.[5] The person in charge was Umbro Apollonio, a young lecturer in contemporary arts at the University of Padua and from 1950 director of the Archivio Storico della Biennale. He was the mastermind behind a plethora of activities that fostered and stimulated the early phase of revisitations and revaluations of Futurism.

Apollonio's engagement for a re-assessment of Futurism found a loyal supporter in Carlo Cardazzo, who ran the Venetian Galleria del Cavallino on Riva degli Schiavoni.[6] In 1945, he was the first to present a "Mostra del futurismo," and in 1950 he issued a first series of reprints of futurist manifestos, accompanied by studies on Boccioni and on the "heroic phase" of the futurist movement.[7] Before I return to Apollonio and the Biennale, a few other activities of historical significance need to be mentioned. In 1949, the Museum of Modern Art in New York mounted a seminal Futurism exhibition as part of a show on twentieth-century Italian Art, which was followed by similar events in Brussels, Zurich, London and Paris.[8] These exhibitions prompted, both in the popular press and in scholarly journals, a large number of reviews and critical reassessments of futurist aesthetics. Publishing houses observed this trend and engaged some prominent art historians to investigate the history of Futurism and to portray its most significant representatives. From the more than 100 publications some stand out, such as Raffaele Carrieri's history of avant-garde art that went through several editions and formed the basis of a splendid tome on Futurism. Equally impressive was the magnificent issue of *Cahiers d'art* edited by Christian Zervos, and two well-informed Futurism numbers of art magazines from Switzerland and Germany.

The Reception of Futurism, 1950–1960

After this encouraging start in the immediate postwar period, the significance of Futurism for experimental art and literature came to be presented in a number of books, such as:

- Fortunato Bellonzi, ed.: *F.T. Marinetti e il movimento futurista*. Special issue of *Fiera letteraria* 9:7 (14 febbraio 1954).

- Libero De Libero, ed: *Antologia futurista*. Torino: "Civiltà delle Macchine," 1954.
- Libero Altomare: *Incontri con Marinetti e il futurismo*. Roma: Corso, 1954.
- René Berger, ed.: *Le Mouvement dans l'art contemporain*. Lausanne: Association Pour l'Art, 1955.
- Guy Weelen: *Le Problème du mouvement dans l'art contemporain*. Paris: Synthèses, 1955.
- Guido Ballo: *Pittori italiani dal futurismo a oggi*. Roma: Edizioni Mediterranee, 1956. German edition *Italienische Malerei vom Futurismus bis heute*. Köln: Kiepenheuer & Witsch, 1958. English edition *Modern Italian Painting from Futurism to the Present Day*. London: Thames & Hudson, 1958.
- *Futurismo*. Special issue of *Il Tevere: Quindicinale diretto da Walter Gentili* 1:4 (30 June 1956).
- *Futurismo*. Special issue of *L'osservatore politico letterario* 4:9 (September 1958).
- Alberto Frattini: *Marinetti e il futurismo*. Milano: Marzorati, 1958.
- Umbro Apollonio: *Antonio Sant'Elia: Documenti, note storiche e critiche*. Milano: Il Balcone, 1958.
- Enrico Falqui: *Bibliografia e iconografia del futurismo*. Firenze: Sansoni, 1959.
- Walter Vaccari: *Vita e tumulti di F.T. Marinetti*. Milano: Omnia, 1959.
- Mario De Micheli: *Le avanguardie artistiche del Novecento*. Milano: Feltrinelli, 1959. Translated into Czech, Spanish, Portuguese, Serbo-croatian and Hungarian.

The effect of these critical studies and of the exhibitions that took place in the early 1950s was that Futurism came to be seen as more than just a fascist or para-fascist art movement. This shift of opinion was largely due to the initiative of a number of influential critics, historians and curators, some of them old enough to have experienced the scintillating force of Futurism when it first burst onto the scene in the 1910s. They were now able to place Futurism in the context of an international avant-garde and to demonstrate that Marinetti and his followers had been a driving force behind the renewal of the visual and literary arts in the early twentieth century. And it is largely the work of these critics that to this day conditions our understanding of the historical role of Futurism:

- 1878 Paolo D'Ancona
- 1885 Raffaele De Grada

- 1885 Lionello Venturi,
- 1901 Enrico Falqui
- 1905 Raffaele Carrieri
- 1907 Fortunato Bellonzi
- 1909 Giulio Carlo Argan
- 1910 Carlo Ludovico Ragghianti
- 1911 Carlo Bo
- 1911 Umbro Apollonio
- 1914 Guido Ballo
- 1917 Mario Verdone
- 1920 Ruggero Jacobbi
- 1922 Carlo Belloli
- 1927 Maurizio Calvesi
- 1928 Luciano de Maria
- 1933 Enrico Crispolti

Many of these men are long deceased, but they often left their private archive to public institutions. I believe that it would be a most valuable task to investigate the manifold activities of these scholars, as it would give us important insights into the manner in which Futurism came to be rediscovered and re-presented in the postwar period. It may also shed light on how Futurism influenced the experimental arts of the 1950s and how historical continuities were created between *primo futurismo* and the neo-avant-garde of the post-WWII period. We all know that history is not served to us on a plate. History is a reconstruction of facts and forces of the past. And each historian brings to this task his or her personal concerns and partisan interests. These, of course, must be critically analyzed by later generations. I cannot do this here, but I must stress that the historiography of Futurism is a topic yet to be investigated.

So far, I have primarily dealt with critics creating a new image of Futurism and evaluating its role in the formation of modern art. But one should not forget that, in the 1950s, many members of the futurist movement were still alive. They observed with great interest the re-awakening interest in Futurism, began to organize themselves and attempted to demonstrate to a skeptical public the artistic achievements of the futurist movement. In 1951, they mounted a first *Mostra nazionale della pittura e della scultura futuriste*, followed, a few years later, by a *Mostra antologica del futurismo*. In an interesting letter of 1954, Palazzeschi described to Vallecchi a serious re-awakening of interest in Futurism and suggested that his novel *Perelà* should be re-issued with the label "futurist" attached to it: "I advise you to furnish the book with a *wrapper that says:* 'A futurist novel by Aldo Palazzeschi.' I think that at present it would prove to be an advantageous advertisement for the book."[9] In Rome, Enzo Benedetto set up a journal (*Arte-Viva*) and an Istituto Internazionale di Studi sul Futurismo to prepare the ground for the fiftieth anniversary of Futurism in 1959.

Before I return to the *cinquantenario del futurismo*, I want to briefly mention some other exhibitions of the 1950s. First of all, there were dozens of ex-futurists who were given retrospective shows, far too many to be enumerated here. To begin with, the initiative came from private galleries, but soon the public institutions followed suit. The first major event of this kind was the *Mostra dell'arte nella vita del Mezzogiorno d'Italia* at the Palazzo delle Esposizioni, organized by the Quadriennale in 1953. It included two retrospectives of works by Umberto Boccioni and Pippo Rizzo and an accompanying catalogue / anthology of writings by Boccioni. The next "regular" Quadriennale was held in 1955–1956. Fortunato Bellonzi organized, together with Maria Drudi Gambillo, a show that included many Futurists and because of its success was later transferred to Germany.[10] A year later, in 1957, they issued as the ninth volume of their *Quaderni* a critical study on Prampolini by Pierre Courthion.

With the *Cinquantenario* now looming on the horizon, in Rome the Galleria Nazionale d'Arte Moderna instituted a series of lectures, which included Angelo Maria Ripellino speaking on Russian Futurism, Nello Ponente on futurist theater, and Maurizio Calvesi on cubist influences in early Futurism. In preparation for the fiftieth anniversary of the foundation of Futurism in 1909, the Quadriennale charged Drudi Gambillo with the editing of the two-volume *Archivi del futurismo* and the mounting of a major retrospective dedicated to futurist painting, which subsequently transferred to Switzerland and Germany:

> *Il futurismo.* Presentazione di Aldo Palazzeschi. Saggi critici di Giorgio Castelfranco, e Jacopo Recupero. Roma: Ente Premi, Palazzo Barberini, 6 giugno—6 settembre 1959. Roma: De Luca, 1959. Swiss edition *Il futurismo.* Winterthur: Kunstverein Winterthur, 4. Oktober–15. November 1959. German edition *Futuristen.* München: Städtische Galerie im Lenbachhaus, 5. Dezember 1959–14. Februar 1960.

In Venice, the Biennale showed even more initiative in presenting Futurism as the great Italian contribution to the renewal of the arts in the twentieth century.[11] The edition of 1954 set aside a room for twenty-one works by Enrico Prampolini. For the *cinquantenario*, they edited a special Futurism issue of their house journal, *La Biennale di Venezia: Arte, cinema, musica, teatro,*[12] mounted a historical survey (*Peintres et sculpteurs italiens du futurisme à nos jours*) and sent it to four French museums before presenting it in Italy. These activities were only the highlights of an assiduous effort undertaken throughout the 1950s. At the second Bienal de São Paulo (8 December 1953–8 February 1954), Apollonio presented a Futurism show that was subsequently touring to great acclaim in various other Latin American countries:

- *II Bienal do Museu de Arte Moderna de São Paulo. Sala especial: Futurismo. A cargo de Umbro Apollonio.* São Paulo: Bienal, 1954.
- *Futuristas e artistas italianos de hoje na segunda Bienal de São Paulo, Brasil. Exposicão organizada pela Bienal de Veneza, 8 de dezembro de 1953– 8 de fevereiro de 1954.* Prefazione di Antonio Segni; testo di Rodolfo Pallucchini. Venezia: Ferrari, 1953.
- *Futuristas e artistas italianos de hoje na segunda Bienal de São Paulo, Brasil.* Exposicão organizada pela Bienal de Veneza a cargo do Ministerio de relações esteriores e do Ministerio da educacão, 8 de dezembro de 1953– 8 de fevereiro de 1954. Traducão de Laura Marchiori. Venezia: Esposizione Biennale Internazionale d'Arte [Venezia: Officine Grafiche, 1953]; São Paulo: Bienal do Arte Moderna, 1953.

Futurism also featured prominently in two government-sponsored travel exhibitions of the Art-Club in Rome, *Italian Art of the 20th Century*, curated by Enrico Prampolini. The Australian edition was furnished with informative notes by his brother Vittorio Orazio on Balla, Boccioni, Prampolini, Severini and Sironi:

- *Italian Nykytaidetta / Italiensk Nutidskonst.* Näyttelyn järjestäneet = Anordnad av Nykytaide—Nutidskonst r.y., Art Club, Direzione delle Belle Arti. Helsinki: Taidehalli, 14.3.-27.3.1951. Helsinki: Taidehalli, 1951.
- *Italian Artists of To-day: Exhibition of Italian Contemporary Art.* Göteborg: Konsthallen, February 1951; Helsinki: Konsthallen, March 1951; Oslo: Kunstnernes Hus, April 1951; Copenhagen: Frie udstilling, May 1951. Rome: Bestetti, 1951.
- *Italian Art of the 20th Century.* Introduction Enrico Prampolini. Biographical notes by Vittorio Orazio. Perth: Art Gallery of Western Australia, March–April 1956; Adelaide: National Gallery of South Australia, May–June, 1956; Melbourne: National Gallery of Victoria, July 1956; Hobart: Tasmanian Museum, August–September 1956; Brisbane: Queensland Museum, November–December 1956; Canberra: Australian National Galleries. Melbourne: McLaren, 1956.

A similar event was the touring show, *Diez años de pintura italiana*, of 1957.[13] It left a lasting impression on the artistic communities and should be considered, together with the other travel shows of futurist paintings, as a significant contribution to the revival of a critical interest in Futurism:

> Italy found itself in the second half of the nineteenth century in a cultural isolation. Her intellectual preoccupations were based on hollow and rhetoric traditions which were in urgent need of renewal and more legitimate precepts. It was due to Futurism that the country freed herself, absorbed European artistic trends and opened her doors to modern art. Thus occurred the profound transformation of language that would relegate simple technical skills to a secondary position. It set in motion a process that was to characterize modern figurative art, i.e. a categorical rejection of the notion of art as object and a foregounding of the reactions experienced by the viewer. Futurism was to introduce to art the great technological achievements of the time and the living practices of human beings, and it replaced the idyllic landscapes with cities inhabited by modern man.[14]

Back in Italy, the Galleria Blu in Milan began a series of Futurism shows that was of historical significance as it hailed in a re-evaluation of the period of *secondo futurismo*.[15] At this point, of course, the name of Enrico Crispolti needs to be mentioned who, more than anyone else, widened the spectrum of Futurism scholarship, by incorporating the period of *secondo futurismo*, and became one of the protagonists of Futurism Studies for the next fifty years. And with him, a new generation of critics and curators appeared on the scene that produced hundreds of exhibitions as well as dozens of major studies and anthologies.

One of these was Mario Verdone (1917–2009), a film and theater historian who in his youth had been a close friend of many futurists. In the 1960s, he started a campaign against the pervasive state of misinformation and prejudice that still prevailed in Italy with regard to Futurism. Consequently, with several hundred publications to his name,[16] he became one of the founding fathers of Futurism Studies. Another man from that generation was Maurizio Calvesi, who in 1953 had presented a first selection of writings by Umberto Boccioni[17] and subsequently published more than twenty books and catalogues on Boccioni, Balla and other leading Futurist artists. In 1967, he published for the Edizioni Fratelli Fabbri *Dinamismo e simultaneità nella poetica futurista*, a series of nine volumes on Futurism, and a popular history of the avant-garde in the first half of the twentieth century (see below). A third scholar who should be mentioned here, is Luciano de Maria (1928–1993), an expert on French literature who became editor of the series "I Meridiani" at the publishing house Mondadori[18] and who first attempted to issue the collected works of Marinetti. De Maria also became the author of numerous critical studies of Marinetti's literary œuvre and of various mass-circulation editions, such as *Marinetti e il futurismo* and *Filippo Tommaso Marinetti e il futurismo*.[19]

Futurism in the 1960s: Theater and Music

In the 1960s, Futurism came to be seen as having been more than a movement in the fine arts and in literature. Giovanni Calendoli's three-volume edition of Marinetti's plays[20] reminded Italian audiences that Futurism had also been an active force in the theater. To follow suit, the publishing house Ceschina in Milan issued in 1961 a fresh edition of Francesco Cangiullo's *Le serate futuriste*, originally published in 1930. To complement this book of theatrical memoirs, Cangiullo began a long series of newspaper articles and issued, towards the end of his life, an anthology of texts, *Teatro della sorpresa*.[21]

Throughout the 1960s, essays on futurist theater appeared in journals such as *Sipario*, *Marcatré*, *Fenarete*, *Il caffè*, *Il dramma*, *Il verri* and *Palatino*. At the University of Padna, Giovanni Calendoli, Umberto Artioli and Flores D'Arcais set up a Centro di Studi del Teatro e dello Spettacolo and published a new journal, *Studi teatrali*, which dedicated its first issue of March 1966 to the subject of futurist theater. A year later, *Sipario: Rassegna mensile dello spettacolo* followed suit.[22] The already mentioned Mario Verdone, who since 1965 was teaching at the Centro Sperimentale di Cinematografia in Rome and had issued an anthology of texts and documents, *Ginna e Corra: Cinema e letteratura del futurismo*,[23] published his influential study, *Il teatro del tempo futurista* (Rome: Lerici, 1969), and a year later the anthology, *Teatro italiano d'avanguardia: Drammi e sintesi futuriste* (Roma: Officina, 1970).[24]

Around the same time, another rediscovery took place: Russian Futurism.[25] This also included the futurist activities in the domain of theater, which became the topic of books such as Angelo Maria Ripellino: *Majakovskij e il teatro russo d'avanguardia*,[26] Konstantin Rudnitskii: *Rezhisser Meierkhol'd* and editions such as *The Complete Plays of Vladimir Mayakovsky*.[27] In the United States, the Kirby "family" laid the foundation for the rediscovery of Futurism in the experimental theater movement, first by Ernest Theodore Kirby in his anthology, *Total Theater*, and then by Michael and Victoria Nes Kirby in *Futurist Performance*.[28]

Needless to say, the professional theater made productive use of the material that became newly available. In France, Futurism arrived on the scene when Michel Corvin, an important promoter of an experimental theater practice that was inspired by the Art et Action Group, who before the war had shown futurist *sintesi* in Paris,[29] decided to mount a spectacle in honor of Louise Lara and Édouard Autant and presented, on November 28, 1966, at the Théâtre du Tertre four *sintesi* by Marinetti and Cangiullo (*Le basi, Ritornerò, Il donnaiuolo e le quattro stagioni* and *Gelosia*).[30] Maurice Lemaître, who in 1959 had set up a group called Le Théâtre Neuf and in 1962 had published a manifesto, *Pour un Théâtre Neuf*, founded an "école d'auteurs" at the *Conservatoire d'Art Dramatique in Paris* and a *café-théâtre*, in which works from the historical avant-garde and the neo-avant-garde were presented in new productions. For this purpose, he published the volume, *Le Théâtre futuriste italien et russe*,[31] and announced in a hectographed circular of November 1965 "une découverte des théâtres futuristes italien et russe et proposait de remonter probablement *Les Poupées électriques* et *Le Roi Bombance* de Marinetti, ainsi que *Zanguezi* de Khlebnikov."[32] On March 18, 1967, he gave a practical demonstration of the two latter pieces at the Conservatoire National d'Art Dramatique, entitled *Hommage au théâtre futuriste italien et russe*.[33] After this scenic reading of excerpts, Lemaître acquired the rights from SIAE (March 29, 1967) for a full staging of Marinetti's play, and on April 11, 1967, was appointed to act as sole representative of Marinetti's theatrical œuvre in France. When he heard that the Théâtre L'Echiquier, run by Roland Sabatier, planned to perform *Le Roi Bombance* on April 19, he sent a protest note against this unauthorized production to SIAE, but could not prevent it from taking place. As a consequence, he mounted a production of Khlebnikov's *Nochnoy obysk* (Night Search) at the café-théâtre of the Lettristes circle, La Cave, (May 2–31, 1967), followed by *Le Roi Bombance*:

- Présentation à la Cave des Lettristes, café-théâtre créé par Isidore Isou, de deux pièces de Francis Picabia, *Festival-Manifeste-Presbyte* et *Le Refrain, de quoi?*, une pièce de Vélémir Khlebnikov, *Perquisition de nuit*, et deux œuvres de Maurice Lemaitre, *Kréach ou le Phare de l'homme-colombe* et *Dit Lemaitre*, œuvre ouverte avec participation des spectateurs.
- Création au café-théâtre La Cave des Lettristes de la pièce de F.-T. Marinetti, *Le Roi Bombance*, mise en scène par Pierre Hoffman.
- Ouverture du nouveau café-théâtre de L'Echiquier, animé par Roland Sabatier, avec une reprise du *Boudoir de la Philosophie*, puis de la pièce de F.-T. Marinetti, *Le Roi Bombance*.[34]

The latter occasion was seized by the Istituto Italiano di Cultura to organize a public debate on the topic of "Movimento futurista," in which Enrico Falqui,

Michel Décaudin, René Jullian, Bruno Romani and the theater director Nicolas Bataille participated.[35] Nicolas Bataille had been involved with the Art et Action homage to Futurism of 1966 and had directed fifteen *sintesi* in a *Spectacle futuriste italien* of high professional quality that ran from February 9 to March 4, 1967, at the Théâtre de l'Épée de Bois in Vincennes.[36] As Bataille was partly living in Tokyo at the time, he re-mounted the production there and won with it in 1969 the Prix Kinokunya "pour la meilleure mise en scène de l'année."

In Italy, the practical recuperation of the futurist heritage began in 1967. A group of students undertook a *Serata futurista* on January 27, 1967, at the Casa Internazionale dello Studente in Rome. Under the direction of Francesco Marenga, the Compagnia del Teatro degli Universitari di Villa Flaminia performed a number of *sintesi* by Marinetti, Cangiullo, Corradini, Corra, Buzzi, Folgore and others.[37] In Livorno, the Jesuit father Valentino Davanzati organized another futurist evening at the Centro Culturale "Il Grattacielo."[38] Also in Livorno, Paolo Belforte and Luciano Caruso presented in the Libreria Belforte a scenic recitation of various short plays from the *Teatro sintetico* repertoire.[39] In Turin, the Teatro delle Dieci, a group of young actors from the Teatro Stabile under the directorship of Massimo Scaglione, had taken over a cinema, the Ridotto del Romano on piazza Castello. In 1967, the company was joined by Gian Renzo Morteo, who was undertaking research into the theater of the historical avant-garde and created with them an evening of futurist *sintesi* (April 1967) and a Dada spectacle (December 1967–January 1968). In Rome, at the Teatro Arlecchino, Luigi Pascutti premièred on January 20, 1968, a futurist collage, *Nessuno in casa di Filippo Tommaso Marinetti*. In 1968, the Teatro Stabile di Torino undertook a professional production of Marinetti's *Il suggeritore nudo*, directed by Paolo Poli (premièred on March 22, 1968, at the Sala Gobetti). Subsequently, it traveled to the Festival di Spoleto and became incorporated into the repertoire of the 1968–1969 season at the Teatro delle Muse in Rome.[40] The spectacle in Turin was accompanied by a collage of futurist scenes (including a reconstruction of Balla's *Fuochi d'artificio*), called *Futur/ Realtà*, directed by Gabriele Oriani (son of the Turinese Futurist, Pippo Oriani) and performed at the Festival Teatrale Venezia (October 10–11, 1968), at the Sala Gobetti (October 13–18, 1968), at the *Experimenta 3* festival at the Deutsche Akademie der Darstellenden Künste, Frankfurt, June 3–6, 1969, the open-air theater of the Scuola Clotilde di Savoia in Turin (July 14, 1969) and the Tecnoteatro in Turin on July 26, 1969.[41] And in Milan, the theater group Gli Improvvisati dedicated an evening to the *Teatro sintetico futurista* at the Istituto Leone XIII, performing, amongst other pieces, Marinetti's *Bambole elettriche* (Poupées électriques).[42]

These early attempts to recuperate the futurist heritage in the theater have to be seen in conjunction with the *Retrospettiva di Umberto Boccioni* at the 33rd Biennale di Venezia (June 18–October 16, 1966) and the *Mostra speciale, Quattro maestri del primo futurismo italiano* at the 34th Biennale di Venezia (June 22–October 20, 1968), the publication of Luigi Scrivo's anthology *Sintesi del futurismo: Storia e documenti* and the first volume of Marinetti's "opera omnia," *Teoria e invenzione futurista*.[43] These exhibitions and books did not only cause extensive discussion in Italian newspapers and magazines, but were also accompanied by public debates between critics and ex-futurists in cultural centers, and a series of "serate futuriste" dedicated to poetry recitations and readings from futurist manifestos. Tullio Crali, who had learned the art of declamation from Marinetti in the 1930s and 40s, was particularly active in this respect and provided an important link between historical Futurism and the younger generation's rediscovery of Futurism.[44]

It was not only the futurist plays that began to inspire young theater artists. The new developments in stage design and staging techniques fostered an interest in their futurist predecessors and led to exhibitions such as the *Mostra delle scenografie di Enrico Prampolini nel Salone Napoleonico dell'Accademia di Brera* (1969), and *Avanguardia a teatro dal 1915 al 1955 nell'opera scenografica di Depero, Baldessari, Prampolini*, which ran at the Museo Teatrale alla Scala from November 29, 1969, to January 10, 1970.

In the musical sphere, the rediscovery of futurist composers was rung in with Francesco Balilla Pratella's memoirs, "Marinetti e il suo futurismo in Romagna"[45] and Giovanni Seganti's chronicle of the first futurist meetings in Lugo, "Futurismo lughese: I simpatici pazzi."[46] Luigi Russolo, who after the war had continued to exhibit as a painter, saw a first reprint of his seminal manifesto, *L'arte dei rumori*, in a French translation: *L'Art des bruits: Manifeste futuriste 1913*.[47] Following the short brochure, *Russolo*, by Giuseppe Cartella Gelardi, the artist's wife, Maria Zanovello Russolo, published in 1958: *Russolo: L'uomo, l'artista*.[48] That the musical avant-garde of the postwar period took notice of these publications is testified in an essay by the great exponent of *musique concrète*, Pierre Schaeffer: "La galleria sotto i suoni, ovvero il futuro anteriore," and by the Dutch composer Lilien Ignace: "Soniek anno 1914: 'L'arte dei rumori' van Luigi Russolo."[49] The musicologist Claudio Marabini dedicated an essay, "Per una storia del futurismo," to Balilla Pratella. Fred K. Prieberg's paper, "Der musikalische Futurismus," was followed by his influential study, *Musica ex machina: Über das Verhältnis von Musik und Technik*.[50] Also in other countries, interest in musical Futurism was re-awakened, as the English edition of Russolo's *The Art of Noise: Futurist Manifesto, 1913* (Translated by Robert Filliou. New York: Something

Else Press, 1967) and John C. G. Waterhouse's article, "A Futurist Mystery." (*Music and Musicians* 15:8 [April 1967]: 26–30), demonstrate.[51] Even in Japan, where noise music was to become an important element of avant-garde sound art, the pioneering role of Futurism was recognized, as the following installment of a series of essays on "Heretical composers" showed: Kuniharu Akiyama: "Itan no sakkyokuka -3- Sōon no shisō no senkusha Ruiji Russorō" [The Precursor of the Idea of Noise: Luigi Russolo].[52] Back in Italy, Armando Gentilucci published a long paper, "Il futurismo e lo sperimentalismo musicale d'oggi" (*Convegno musicale* 1:3–4, July–December 1964: 275–303) and re-issued it later as a brochure, *Il futurismo e lo sperimentalismo musicale d'oggi* (Turin: Edizioni del Convegno, 1965).[53] And for years to come, Giovanni Lugaresi's edition of Pratella's correspondence, first published in the *Osservatore politico letterario* and then as a volume, remained a trough of information on all aspects of Futurism.[54]

Futurism in the 1960s: The Fine Arts

Finally, I should like to return to the Fine Arts and highlight some of the most significant exhibitions and publications of the 1960s. I mentioned above Maria Drudi Gambillo's work for the Quadriennale, which included her magisterial edition of the *Archivi del futurismo*, and the exhibition, *Il futurismo*, held at the Palazzo Barberini, the Kunstverein Winterthur and the Städtische Galerie München. A smaller sequel to the *Archivi* was *Dopo Boccioni: Dipinti e documenti futuristi dal 1915 al 1919*.[55] Her work on the *Archivi* had been given practical support by the young art historian Enrico Crispolti, who also helped with mounting the first Balla exhibition after the artist's death in 1958 and four years later with the extensive retrospective at the Galleria Civica d'Arte Moderna in Turin.[56] Crispolti was at that time engaged in a major re-assessment of futurist art of the 1920s and 1930s, that is, the "post-heroic" phase that was supposedly so tainted by fascism that it deserved little more than a footnote in history books. Crispolti's fresh assessment of the works of Filia, Prampolini, Rosso, Diulgheroff, Oriani, etc. brought to light some extraordinary works, which he wrote about in *Notizie*, a journal he was editing at the time with Luciano Pistoi.[57] His collaboration with Drudi Gambillo led in 1960 to the historical exhibition *Secondo futurismo* at the Galleria Blu,[58] which was followed by *Aspetti del secondo futurismo torinese: Cinque pittori ed uno scultore. Fillia, Mino Rosso, Diulgheroff, Oriani, Alimandi, Costa* (Turin: Galleria Civica d'Arte Moderna, March 27–April 30, 1962) and *Mostra a quattro protagonisti del "secondo futurismo": Fillia, Farfa, Diulgheroff, Oriani* (Venice: Galleria Il Canale, October 6–20, 1964).

Due to the research carried out by Crispolti and Drudi Gambillo, resistance toward Futurism began to subside. It became more and more an accepted fact that Futurism under Mussolini had been more than fascist art and that there had been some significant artistic developments after Futurism's "heroic years" of 1909–1915. Popular interest in Futurism grew year by year and was suitably fuelled by museums, galleries and publishing houses. All major painters and sculptors of the futurist movement received retrospectives in prominent museums, and galleries were busily trading in futurist pictures that came in ever-rising numbers on the market. From the group shows, a few stand out because of their popular and critical success:

- *Futurism.* New York: The Museum of Modern Art, 31 May–5 September 1961. Detroit: Institute of Arts, 18 October–19 December 1961. Los Angeles: County Museum, 14 January–19 February 1962.
- *Italien 1905–1925: Futurismus und Pittura metafisica.* Hamburg: Kunstverein, September 28–November 3, 1963. Frankfurt am Main: Steinernes Haus Römerberg, November 16, 1963–January 5, 1964. Offenbach: Graphische Werkstätte Offenbach, 1963.
- *Arte moderna in Italia 1915–1935.* Florence: Palazzo Strozzi, February 26–May 28, 1967.
- *G. Balla prefuturista.* Rome: Galleria dell'Obelisco, as of January 19, 1968. Followed in the same gallery by *G. Balla: Luce e movimento.* As of February 23, 1968. *G. Balla: Gli stati d'animo.* As of April 20, 1968. *Giacomo Balla: Il giardino futurista, 1916–1930.* As of June 3, 1968. *G. Balla: Sculture, 1913–1915.* July 1968. *Fortunato Depero: Opere 1914–1918.* As of December 5, 1969. *Omaggio a Balla.* As of December 1971.
- *Quattro maestri del primo futurismo italiano: Linee della ricerca— dall'informale alle nuove strutture.* XXXIV Biennale di Venezia, June 22–October 20, 1968.
- *Cento opere d'arte italiana dal futurismo ad oggi.* Rome: Galleria Nazionale d'Arte Moderna, December 20, 1968–January 20, 1969. German edition *Italienische Kunst des XX. Jahrhunderts.* Bochum: Städtische Kunstgalerie, May 5–30, 1968. Berlin: Kunstamt Berlin-Charlottenburg, June 8–29, 1968. Cologne: Kunsthalle am Neumarkt, May–September 1968.

Visitors to these shows needed to be fed with easily digestible and inexpensive publications. Thus, several portfolios dedicated to individual futurist painters came on the market, as well as albums such as *Il futurismo.*[59] More upmarket were Maurizio Calvesi's illustrated volumes, *Dinamismo e simulta-*

neità nella poetica futurista, published as part of a series on modern art (L'arte moderna: Settimanale, 37–45): [60]

Vol. 1: *Il manifesto del futurismo e i pittori futuristi*.
Vol. 2: *Boccioni e il futurismo milanese*.
Vol. 3: *I futuristi e la simultaneità: Boccioni, Carrà, Russolo e Severini*.
Vol. 4: *Penetrazione e magia nella pittura di Balla*.
Vol. 5: *Il futurismo romano*.
Vol. 6: *Futurismo e arte meccanica: Il comico, l'automatico, il casuale*.
Vol. 7: *Futurismo e orfismo*.
Vol. 8: *Il futurismo russo*.
Vol. 9: *Antologia critica, bibliografia e indici*.

Reissued in various forms of adaptation as:

- *Il futurismo*. Vols. 1–3. L'arte moderna 13–15. Milan: Fabbri, 1967.
- *Il futurismo*. Mensili d'arte 39. Milan: Fabbri, 1970. German edition *Futurismus*. Munich: Schuler, 1975. *Galerie der klassischen Moderne: Futurismus von Giacomo Balla bis Gino Severini*. Herrsching: Pawlak, 1988. French edition *Le futurisme*. Paris: Éditions Tête de Feuilles, 1976.
- *Il futurismo: La fusione della vita nell'arte*. L'arte moderna 5. Milan: Fabbri, 1975. German edition *Der Futurismus: Kunst und Leben*. Cologne: Taschen, 1987.
- *Il futurismo*. L'arte nella società 1. Milan: Fabbri, 1976.

A different type of mass-circulation publication was:

- José Pierre. *Il futurismo e il dadaismo*. Lausanne; Geneva: Rencontre; Edito Service, 1965. Milan: Orpheus Libri, 1965. Milan: Il Saggiatore, 1968. French edition *Le Futurisme et le dadaisme*. Lausanne: Rencontre, 1966. Reprint 1967, 1968, 1973, 1974, 1981. Lausanne: Ed. du Rionzi, [1970]. German edition *Futurismus und Dadaismus*. Lausanne: Rencontre, 1967. Dutch edition *De schilderkunst van het futurisme en dadaïsme*. Utrecht: Het Spectrum, 1968. Spanish edition *El futurismo y el dadaismo*. Madrid: Aguilar, 1968. English edition *Futurism and Dadaism*. Geneva: Edito Service, 1969. London: Heron, 1969. Swedish edition *Futurismen och dadaismen*. Hälsingborg: Concert Hall, 1969.
- Maurizio Calvesi. *Le due avanguardie dal futurismo alla pop art*. Saggi 37. Milan: Lerici, 1966. Second edition Vols. 1–2, Universale Laterza

176–177. Bari: Laterza, 1971. Third edition Biblioteca Universale Laterza, 17. Bari: Laterza, 1981. Reprinted in 1984, 1991, 1998, 2001, 2004, and 2008.

Also the scholarly book market was furnished by a number of surveys such as:

- Pär Bergmann. *"Modernolatria" et "Simultaneità": Recherches sur deux tendances dans l'avant-garde littéraire en Italie et en France à la veille de la première guerre mondiale.* Uppsala: Svenska Bokförlaget, 1962.
- Christa Baumgarth. *Geschichte des Futurismus.* Reinbek: Rowohlt, 1966.
- René Jullian. *Le Futurisme et la peinture italienne.* Paris: Société d'Édition d'Enseignement Supérieur, 1966.
- Gabriele Mandel. *La Peinture italienne du futurisme à nos jours.* Milan: Institut Européen d'Histoire de l'Art, 1967.
- Marianne W. Martin. *Futurist Art and Theory 1909–1915.* Oxford: Clarendon Press, 1968.
- Enrico Crispolti. *Il mito della macchina e altri temi del futurismo.* Trapani: Celebes, 1969.

Somewhere placed between popular and scholarly target audiences were the special issues on Futurism published by periodicals such as:

- *Notizie* 3:10 (January 1960).
- *Civiltà delle macchine* 9:1 (January–February 1961).
- *Il caffè politico e letterario* 10:3 (June 1962).
- *La fiera letteraria* (March 21, 1965).
- *Bianco e Nero* 10–12 (October–December 1967).
- *Il castoro* 34 (October 1969).
- *Il caffè* 16: 2–3 (June–July 1969).
- *Quaderni del osservatore* 2: 8 (December 1969).
- *Le arti: Mensile di cultura e di attualità* 19: 7–8 (July–August 1970).
- *Il verri: Rivista di letteratura* 15: 33–34 (October 1970).

Also the commercial galleries began to mount group shows of Futurism (rather than exhibitions of individual futurist artists), no doubt sensing lucrative business opportunities here:

- 1968. *Le Futurisme: Balla, Boccioni, Carrà, Russolo, Severini, Zatkova, Soffici, Sironi, Rosso.* Geneva: Galerie Krugier & Co., May 2–June 8, 1968. Geneva: Dumaret & Golay, 1968.

- 1968. *Aspects du futurisme*. Basel: Galerie d'Art Moderne Marie-Suzanne Feigel, June 15–August 1968.
- 1968. *The Futurism: Balla, Boccioni, Carrà, Russolo, Severini, Soffici, Sironi, Rosso*. New York: Albert Loeb & Krugier Gallery, November–December 1968.

As a result of this revival of interest, the futurist veterans also made their voice heard, partly to stimulate research into Marinetti's movement, partly to boost their own reputation. In June 1967, Enzo Benedetto's periodical *Arte-Viva* published a declaration signed by twelve surviving futurists, which became the "Manifesto di Futurismo Oggi" and the starting signal for *Futurismo-Oggi: Periodico mensile per i giovani futuristi italiani*. It ran for twenty-five years, at the best of times as a bi-monthly, and acted as a mouthpiece for the Centro Iniziative Culturali Futurismo Oggi.[61] It also published a book series, Quaderni di Futurismo-oggi, of which altogether thirty-eight volumes appeared (plus four "fuori numerazione").

Statistical Analysis

It needs to be stressed here that the list of publications presented in this essay is anything but complete. What I have selected for discussion only highlights some significant exhibitions and books that may have had an influence on and possibly changed people's perception of Futurism. However, if we want to assess the question of "recuperation or rejection of Futurism" in a more representative manner, we must look at more than just the tip of the iceberg. For this reason I have undertaken a statistical analysis that is shown in figure 20.1.[62]

As one can see, toward the end of the 1960s, more than one hundred publications a year dealing with Italian Futurism came on the market. This hardly squares with what an "authoritative" critic recently wrote about that period: "There was a deafening silence about futurism in Italy. Only after important critical and popular editions appeared a decade later did the scholarship take off. Among the pioneers was Maurizio Calvesi, . . ."[63] This may be what Calvesi, Crispolti, etc. want us to believe, as it puts them into the position of "Founding Fathers of Futurism Studies." But my bibliographical investigations show that this is not historically correct. Furthermore, there was a distinct rise of interest in Futurism coming from the fields of music, theater and cinema. A growing number of publications demonstrated that the movement had had an influence in every branch of the avant-garde and had made an impact in countries as far apart as Japan, Brazil, and the United

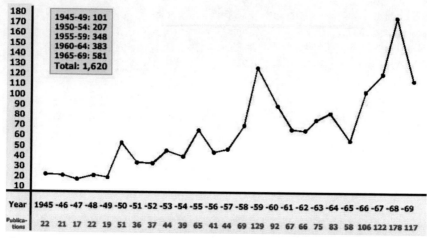

Figure 20.1. Preliminary Count of Publications on Italian Futurism, 1945–1969.

States. In the case of Russia they also showed that Futurism was able to inspire many left-wing artists.

From the end of the 1960s onwards, a new phase set in. The old equation "Futurism = Fascism" lost ground; politics came to be sidelined; and the full spectrum of futurist activities became the subject of more than 9,000 publications in the following forty years (1970–2009). And I am consciously leaving out here the more than 5,000 publications dealing with Futurism in countries other than Italy!

Finally, I should like to make a tentative comparison between the postwar fate of Italian Futurism and that of two comparable avant-garde movements (see table 20.1). For this I have used three databases: my *Bibliographic Handbook of Futurism*, The University of Iowa International Dada Archive, and the world's largest online library catalog, WorldCat.

Table 20.1. Comparative Publication Figures for Futurism, Dada, and Surrealism, 1945–2009.

	1945–2009	1945–1950 (%)[1]	1951–1960 (%)	1961–1970 (%)	1945–1970 (%)
Berghaus Futurism	10,620	101 (0.9 %)	555 (5.2 %)	964 (9.1 %)	1,620 (15.3%)
Iowa Dada Archive	7,479	46 (0.6 %)	386 (5.2 %)	742 (9.9 %)	1,108 (14.8 %)
WorldCat Surrealism	8,129	267 (3.3 %)	313 (3.9 %)	968 (11.9 %)	1,511 (18.6 %)

The percentage figures given here relate to the overall figure of 1945–2009.

The fact that Surrealism still attracted quite a sizeable number of publications in the period 1945–1950 is easily explained by the fact that the movement was still active at that time, whereas Futurism ended in 1944 and Dada in 1923. Otherwise, the overall development was fairly similar, with a few exceptions, as one can gather from these yearly figures in table 20.2.

Whereas Surrealism declined between 1945 and 1955 and then rose fairly steadily from year to year, Dada experienced a growth until 1955 that was similar to that of Futurism, albeit with smaller absolute figures. It then peaked in 1957 (probably due to the fortieth anniversary in 1956 of the founding of the Cabaret Voltaire), just like Futurism did in 1959 because of the *cinquantenario*. In the course of the 1960s, both Dada and Futurism experienced peaks and troughs, yet despite these oscillations the overall growth figures averaged out at some seventy-five (Dada) and ninety-five (Futurism) publications per year. In the ten-year period 1961–1970, Futurism fared similarly to Surrealism, yet over the following twenty-five years, Surrealism kept a plateau of some 150–180 publications a year, whereas Futurism increased its appeal until yearly figures reached 300 publications and more (see figure 20.2).

In view of these figures, I feel inclined to reject the popular belief that Futurism was ostracized in the postwar period. It is without question that in some quarters Futurism was looked upon with suspicion or disapprobation. That surviving veterans of the futurist movement were not granted the exhibition possibilities they would have liked to have obtained is also indisputable. However, it was also understandable that in the postwar world, when the European art world was dominated by neo-avant-garde trends such as Abstract Expressionism, Concrete Art, Tachism, Kineticism, Pop-Art, etc., young artists searching for inspiration and models to follow were turning their attention towards the contemporary USA rather than prewar Italy. To this new generation it mattered little whether the futurists had been fascists or not; to them, Futurism was simply "old hat" and they did not want to be seen the company of rearguard artists. Therefore, the mantra of complaints that rang from the pages of *Futurismo-oggi* has be treated with caution. In my view, the recuperation of the historical avant-garde (and Surrealism only became "historical" after Breton's death in 1966) was a slow process, both in Italy and in other parts of the world.

The important role of Futurism within the matrix of modernist art was recognized early on; yet, due to the movement's tainted history in the 1930s and 1940s, ideological barriers had to be removed before the full spectrum of futurist creativity could be appreciated. This happened slowly but steadily in the period 1950–1970. From then on, the historical avant-garde in its main

Table 20.2. Annual Publication Figures for Futurism, Dada and Surrealism, 1945–1969.

	1945	1946	1947	1948	1949	1950	1951	1952	1953	1954	1955	1956	1957
Futurism	22	21	17	22	19	51	36	37	44	39	65	41	44
Dada	3	9	10	8	8	12	12	16	13	6	18	11	117
Surrealism	55	27	69	54	28	44	15	33	29	22	22	35	27

	1958	1959	1960	1961	1962	1963	1964	1965	1966	1967	1968	1969
Futurism	69	129	92	67	66	75	83	58	106	122	178	117
Dada	106	26	65	57	23	97	52	70	155	52	116	75
Surrealism	32	35	66	53	51	54	75	76	101	128	128	176

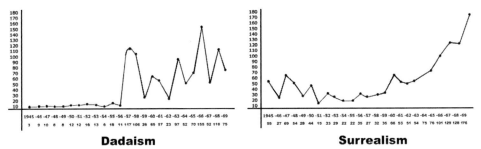

Figure 20.2.   Annual Publication Figures for Dada and Surrealism, 1945–1969.

manifestations, including the manifold facets of futurist art, became an auspicious market proposition, both in the publishing and in the gallery world. Futurism Studies profited from that situation and experienced rapid growth rates in the years 1970–2010. Looking back at these last forty years, we can now discern that it was in this period that some 85 percent of the existing literature on Futurism came to be published.

Notes

1. "Futurism: A Bibliographic Reference Shelf," in *International Futurism in Arts and Literature*, ed. Günter Berghaus (Berlin: De Gruyter, 2000), 487–597.

2. This was largely an English adaptation of *Fortunato Depero nelle opere e nella vita*, trans. Raffaella Lotteri (Trento: Mutilati e Invalidi, 1940). English edition by same publisher (Trento: Mutilati e Invalidi, 1947). However, apart from a presentation in his studio on MacDougal Street, Greenwich Village, the only exhibition he had in the United States was in 1948 at the New School for Social Research in New York.

3. My quotes here are taken from Gino Agnese and Alessandro Sagramora, eds., *I futuristi e le Quadriennali* (Milan: Electa, 2008), 105–6. Unless otherwise noted, all translations are my own.

4. *Quarante ans d'art italien du futurisme à nos jours*. Lausanne: Musée Cantonal des Beaux Arts, February 15–March 15, 1947. *40 Jahre italienischer Kunst: Die Erneuerungsbewegungen vom Futurismus bis heute*. Lucerne: Kunstmuseum, March 29–June 1, 1947.

5. Umbro Apollonio, "I firmatari del 10 manifesto futurista." *XXV Biennale di Venezia: Catalogo* (Venice: Alfieri, 1950), 57–60. See also Giulio Carlo Argan, "Aspects of the Venice Biennale: Futurism," *Burlington Magazine* 92: 570 (September 1950), 265–76.

6. This important curator and cultural manager has been the subject of several studies and exhibitions: *Omaggio a Cardazzo*. Testi di Raffaele Carrieri, e Umbro Apollonio (Milan: Edizioni Galleria del Naviglio, November 16–30, 1964). Tullio D'Albisola, *Carlo Cardazzo amico di Albisola* (Milan: All'insegna del pesce d'oro, 1964). Antonella Fantoni, *Il gioco del Paradiso: La collezione Cardazzo e i primi anni della Galleria del Cavallino* (Venice: Edizioni del Cavallino, 1996). Luca Massimo Barbero, ed., *L'officina del*

contemporaneo: Venezia '50–'60. Venice, Palazzo Fortuny, June 15–November 9, 1997 (Milan: Charta, 1997). Giovanni Bianchi, *Un cavallino come logo: Storia delle Edizioni del Cavallino* (Venice: Edizioni del Cavallino, 2007). Luca Massimo Barbero, ed., *Carlo Cardazzo: Una nuova visione dell'arte.* Venice: Peggy Guggenheim Collection, November 1, 2008–February 9, 2009 (Milan: Electa–Mondadori, 2008). Angelica Cardazzo, ed., "*Caro Cardazzo . . .*": *Lettere di artisti, scrittori e critici a Carlo Cardazzo dal 1933 al 1952* (Venice: Edizioni del Cavallino, 2008).

7. Marco Valsecchi, *Umberto Boccioni* (Venice: Edizioni del Cavallino, 1950). Giampiero Giani, *Il futurismo, 1910–1916* (Venice: Edizioni del Cavallino, 1950).

8. James Thrall Soby and Alfred Hamilton Bar, eds., *Twentieth-Century Italian Art.* New York: Museum of Modern Art, June 28–September 18, 1949. Giuseppe Raimondi, ed., *Art italien contemporain: Campigli, Carrà, Casorati, De Chirico, De Pisis, Marini, Martini, Modigliani, Morandi, Scipione, Severini, Sironi, Tosi.* Brussels: Palais des Beaux-Arts, January 28–February 26, 1950 (Brussels: Éditions de la Connaissance, 1950). *Futurismo & pittura metafisica: Balla, Baldessari, Boccioni.* Zurich: Kunsthaus Zürich, November–December, 1950 (Zurich: Das Kunsthaus, 1950). Paolo D'Ancona, ed., *Modern Italian Art: An Exhibition of Paintings and Sculpture Held under the Auspices of the Amici di Brera and the Italian Institute.* London: Tate Gallery, June 28–July 30, 1950 (London: Arts Council of Great Britain, 1950). Paolo D'Ancona and Gabrielle Vienne, eds., *Exposition d'art moderne italien.* Organisée sous les auspices de l'Association Française d'Action Artistique par les Associazione degli Amici di Brera e dei Musei Milanesi. Paris: Musée National d'Art Moderne, May–June 1950 (Paris: Presses Artistiques, 1950). *Futurism and Later Italian Art.* Palm Beach: The Society of the Four Arts, February 9–March 4, 1951. *Futurism: Balla, Boccioni, Carrà, Russolo, Severini.* New York: Sidney Janis Gallery, March 22–May 1, 1954.

9. *Perelà: Uomo di fumo.* Nuova edizione (Florence: Vallecchi, 1954). The letter of July 30, 1954, can be found in Aldo Palazzeschi, *Tutti i romanzi,* vol. 1 (Milan: Meridiani Mondadori, 2004), 1511.

10. *Pittura e scultura italiane dal 1910 al 1930.* Edited by Giorgio Castelfranco and Marco Valsecchi. Rome: De Luca, 1956. *I maestri della mostra antologica della pittura e scultura italiane dal 1910 al 1930.* Edited by the Centro di Documentazione della Presidenza del Consiglio dei Ministri. Rome: Quadriennale, 1956. *Arte italiana dal 1910 ad oggi.* Esposizione organizzata dalla Quadriennale di Roma per la Haus der Kunst, Monaco di Baviera. Munich: Haus der Kunst, June 6–September 15, 1957 (Rome: Tipografia Istituto Grafico Tiberino, 1957). German edition *Ausstellung italienischer Kunst von 1910 bis zur Gegenwart.* Organisiert von der Quadriennale di Roma für das Haus der Kunst. Munich: Haus der Kunst, June 6–September 15, 1957 (Rome: Tipografia Istituto Grafico Tiberino, 1957).

11. See *Peintres et sculpteurs italiens du futurisme à nos jours.* Catalogue de l'exposition organisée par la Biennale de Venise. Charleroi: Palais des Beaux-Arts; Dijon: Musée des Beaux-Arts; Saint Étienne: Musée d'Art et d'Industrie; Lyon: Musee des Beaux-Arts 1959; the special issue on Futurism of *La Biennale di Venezia: Arte, cinema, musica, teatro* 9:36–37 (July–December, 1959); and the major retrospective *Il*

futurismo ed il suo tempo: XXX Biennale di Venezia. Mostra storica del futurismo. Edited by Pierre Francastel (Venice: La Biennale di Venezia, Stamperia di Venezia, 1960).

12. *La Biennale di Venezia: Arte, cinema, musica, teatro* 9, nos. 36–37 (July–December 1959).

13. *Diez años de pintura italiana: Exposición circulante en Sur América.* Organizada por la Bienal de Venecia, por encargo del Ministerio de Asuntos Exteriores y del Ministerio de Educación. Caracas: Museo de Bellas Artes, January 27–February 17, 1957; Bogotà: Museo Nazionale, March 7–21, 1957; Lima: Museo de Arte Italiano, as of April 15, 1957; Santiago de Chile: Museo de Arte Contemporáneo, s.d.; Rio de Janeiro: Museu de Arte Moderna, s.d., Buenos Aires: Museo Nacional de Bellas Artes, June 18–July 19, 1957 (Venice: Arti Grafiche Sorteni, 1957). Portuguese edition *Dez anos de pintura italiana, 1945–1955: Exposicão itinerante na América do Sul e na Península Ibérica.* Organizada pela Bienal de Veneza, por iniciativa do Ministério dos Negócios Estrangeiros e do Ministério da Educacão Nacional da Itália. Lisbon: Palácio Foz, April 5–25, 1958 (Lisbon: Secretariado Nacional da Informacão, 1958).

14. Luis Vargas Saavedra: "Exposición 'Diez años de pintura italiana.' Museo de Bellas Artes, del 18 de junio al 19 de julio." *Anales de la Universidad de Chile* 115:45 (1957), 374–80, here: 376.

15. From these, one should mention the exhibitions on Sironi (1957); Balla (1959); Farfa (1959); *Il secondo futurismo* (1960); Severini (1963); Depero (1965 and 1969); Boccioni (1966) and *Aeropittura futurista* (1970).

16. See Sofia Corradi and Isabella Madia, eds., *Un percorso di auto-educazione: Materiali per una bio-bibliografia di Mario Verdone = Materials for a Bio-bibliography of Mario Verdone: With an Abstract in English* (Rome: Aracne, 2003). Other presentations of his life and œuvre include Eusebio Ciccotti, *Omaggio a Mario Verdone.* Special issue of *Il lettore di provincia* 131 (Ravenna: Longo Angelo, 2009). Stelio Cro, "Theater, Cinema and Futurism in the Writings of Mario Verdone," *Canadian Journal of Italian Studies* 9:32 (1986): 93–97. Claudio Marchi, "Una rilettura di 'Cinema e letteratura del futurismo,' 1968–2008," *Il lettore di provincia* 131 (2008): 119–28. Paolo Perrone Burali d'Arezzo, "Mario Verdone e il futurismo." Mario Verdone, *Il mio futurismo* (Milan: Nuove Edizioni Culturali, 2006), 9–14. Roberto Salsano, "Mito, biografia, letteratura nella radiofonia di Mario Verdone," *Rivista di studi italiani* 19:2 (2001): 233–42. Roberto Salsano, *Avanguardia e tradizione: Saggi su Mario Verdone* (Florence: Cesati, 2007).

17. Umberto Boccioni, *Scelta degli scritti, regesti, bibliografia e catalogo delle opere.* Ed. Maurizio Calvesi (Rome: De Luca, 1963).

18. See *I meridiani: Catalogo generale, 1969–1991* (Milan: Mondadori, 1990).

19. Luciano De Maria, *Marinetti e il futurismo* (Milan: Mondadori, 1973, 1977, 1981, 1994); Luciano De Maria, *Filippo Tommaso Marinetti e il futurismo* (Milan: Mondadori, 2000).

20. *Teatro* (Rome: Bianco, 1960).

21. Francesco Cangiullo, *Teatro della sorpresa* (Livorno: Belforte, 1968).

22. *Sipario: Rassegna mensile dello spettacolo,* no. 260 (December 1967).

23. It first appeared as a special Futurism number of *Bianco e Nero* 10–12 (October–December 1967), was then reissued as a book by Bianco e Nero, 1968, and reprinted under the title *Cinema e letteratura del futurismo* (Calliano: Manfrini, 1990).

24. Mario Verdone, *Il teatro del tempo futurista* (Rome: Lerici, 1969); Mario Verdone, *Teatro italiano d'avanguardia: Drammi e sintesi futuriste* (Rome: Officina, 1970).

25. See the issues of *Rassegna sovietica* 16:3 (July–September 1965); 18:2 (April–June 1967); 19:1 (January–March 1968); and *Ricerche slavistiche* 12 (1964). From the book publications one needs to mention Dmitrij Chyzhevskyi, *Die Anfänge des russischen Futurismus* (Wiesbaden: Harrassowitz, 1963). Curzia Ferrari, *Poesia futurista e marxismo: Russia 1910–1920* (Milan: Editoriale Contra, 1966). Vladimir Markov, *Manifesty i programmy russkikh futuristov = Die Manifeste und Programmschriften der russischen Futuristen* (Munich: Fink, 1967), and *Russian Futurism: A History* (Berkeley: University of California Press, 1968). Benedikt Lifscitz, *L'arciere dall'occhio e mezzo: Autobiografia del futurismo*. Edited by Giorgio Kraiski (Bari: Laterza, 1968). *Poesie di Chlébnikov*. Edited by Angelo Maria Ripellino (Turin: Einaudi, 1968).

26. Angelo Maria Ripellino, *Majakovskij e il teatro russo d'avanguardia* (Turin: Einaudi, 1959; 1968²). This influential study was also translated: German edition *Majakowskij und das russische Theater der Avantgarde* (Cologne: Kiepenheuer & Witsch, 1959, 1964²). French edition *Maiakovski et le théâtre russe d'avant-garde* (Paris: L'Arche, 1965). Brazilian edition *Maiakóvski e o teatro de vanguard* (São Paulo: Editora Perspectiva, 1971, 1986²).

27. Konstantin Rudnitskii, *Rezhisser Meierkhol'd* (Moscow: Nauka, 1969); Vladimir Mayakovsky, *The Complete Plays*. Transl. Guy Daniels (New York: Simon and Schuster, 1968).

28. Michael Kirby, Victoria Nes Kirby, *Futurist Performance*. New York: Dutton, 1971, reprinted New York: PAJ, 1986. Michael Kirby had acquired his knowledge as part of his PhD dissertation, *The History and Theory of Futurist Performance* (New York University, 1970). Victoria was largely in charge of translating the plays and manifestos.

29. See Corvin's influential and many times reprinted book, *Le Théâtre nouveau en France* (Paris: Presses Universitaires de France, 1963), and *Le Laboratoire de théâtre, Art et Action: Étude sur le théâtre de recherche entre les deux guerres* (Lille: Université de Lille, 1973).

30. See *Cahier de l'Association Internationale pour L'Étude de DADA et du Surréalisme* 2 (1968), 258. Pasquale A. Jannini e.a., *La fortuna del futurismo in Francia* (Rome: Bulzoni, 1979), 96.

31. Maurice Lemaître, ed., *Le Théâtre futuriste italien et russe* (Paris: Éditions Lettristes, 1965; 1967²).

32. Personal communication of Roland Sabatier.

33. The Bibliothèque National preserves a programme, *Le Théâtre neuf . . . animateur: Maurice Lemaître, présente un hommage au théâtre futuriste italien et russe: Filippo-Tomaso [sic] Marinetti . . . etc. Conservatoire national d'art dramatique, 18 mars 1967*. Giovanni Lista described it as "*Le Roi Bombance a été l'objet d'une lecture a l'italienne exécutée par Maurice Lemaître selon la technique du 'théâtre discrépant*

et ciselant' des lettristes." (*La Scène futuriste*, 72, n. 75). In *La Lettrisme devant Dada et les nécrophages de Dada* (Paris: Centre de Créativité, 1967), 25, Lemaître wrote: "*Zanguezi*, la pièce de Khlebnikov, dont j'ai donné récemment des extraits au Conservatoire, après *Le Roi Bombance* de Marinetti, dans une soirée d'Hommage et Redécouverte des théâtres futuristes italien et russe." As Lemaître wrote to me in a personal communication, the excerpts were presented by actors and with scenery. But there was no cooperation between him and the Théâtre L'Echiquier over the performance of Marinetti's *Roi Bombance*.

34. Maurice Lemaître: "Le Point de vue de l'animateur," *Paris-Théâtre* 21:257–58 (1968), 38–45, here: 44.

35. See Paolo Maroni, "Il futurismo riscoperto dagli intellettuali francesi," *Il messaggero*, May 9, 1967.

36. It was preceded in the first part of the evening by Ribemont-Dessaigne's *L'Empereur de Chine*, directed by Jacques Legré. The Futurist part of the evening consisted of 15 *sintesi* by Marinetti, Cangiullo, Boccioni, Settimelli and Pratella. See *Cahier de l'Association Internationale pour l'Étude de DADA et du Surréalisme 2* (1968), 258, Giovanni Lista's interview with Bataille ("Nicolas Bataille: La riscoperta del teatro futurista italiano") in *Sipario* 315–16 (August–September 1972), 30–31 and "Teatro futurista visto da Nicola Bataille," *Futurismo-oggi* 4:32–33 (September–October 1972), 237. Bataille seems to have been introduced to Futurism by Claude Autant-Lara and Akakia Viala (Marie-Antoinette Allévy) of the Art et Action group. His presentation of the four *sintesi* at the Théâtre du Tertre in 1966 was supported by Marie-Louise Van Veen, who in 1927 had premièred Ruggiero Vasari's *Angoscia delle macchine*.

37. See *Quaderni di Futurismo-oggi. Due* (Rome: Arte-Viva, [1967]), 19.

38. This appears to have been in 1967, followed in March 1968 by a debate on Futurism with the participation of Francesco Cangiullo, who on December 19, 1968 premièred in the centre's small theater *La cura delle rose*, performed by the Compagnia dei Giovani del Centro Artistico Il Grattacielo. See Mario Verdone, *Teatro del tempo futurista* (Rome: Bulzoni, 1988), 207, n. 60.

39. See Francesco Cangiullo's preface to *Teatro della sorpresa* (Livorno: Belforte, 1968), 19.

40. See Mario Verdone, *Teatro del tempo futurista* (Rome: Bulzoni, 1988), 173. Bartolucci discussed the production in the programme *Il suggeritore nudo: Introduzione al futurismo* (Turin: Teatro Stabile, [1968]), 41–47, reprinted in Giuseppe Bartolucci, ed.: *Il "gesto" futurista: Materiali drammaturgici* (Rome: Bulzoni, 1969), 55–62.

41. See Elena Gigli, *Giochi di luce e forme strane di Giacomo Balla: Feu d'artifice al Teatro Costanzi, Roma 1917* (Rome: De Luca, 2005), 65–73.

42. See *Quaderni di Futurismo-oggi 6* (1969), 16.

43. Luigi Scrivo, ed., *Sintesi del futurismo: Storia e documenti* (Rome: Bulzoni, 1968); Filippo Tommaso Marinetti, *Teoria e invenzione futurista* (Milan: Mondadori, 1968).

44. See the column "Notizie e pareri altrui" in the *Quaderni di Futurismo-Oggi* of 1967–1969.

45. *La piê: Rassegna di illustrazione romagnola* 20:1–2 (January–February 1951): 5–8; 20:7–8 (July–August 1951): 153.

46. *Lugo nostra: Culturale—Artistica—Letteraria.* Special issue for Christmas 1956. Lugo: Randi, 1956. 5–7.

47. Luigi Russolo, *L'Art des bruits: Manifeste futuriste 1913.* Introduction by Maurice Lemaître (Paris: Richard-Masse, 1954).

48. Giuseppe Cartella Gelardi, *Russolo* (Portogruaro: Tipografia Biasutti, 1949); Maria Zanovello Russolo, *Russolo: L'uomo, l'artista* (Milan: Cyril Corticelli, 1958).

49. Pierre Schaeffer, "La galleria sotto i suoni, ovvero il futuro anteriore." *La Biennale di Venezia: Arte, cinema, musica, teatro* 9:36–37 (July–December 1959): 65–71; Lilien Ignace, "Soniek anno 1914: 'L'arte dei rumori' van Luigi Russolo," *Mens en melodie* 18 (1963): 203–6.

50. Claudio Marabini, "Per una storia del futurismo," *Nuova antologia: Rivista di lettere, scienze ed arti* 98, no. 1953 (September–December 1963); Fred K. Prieberg, "Der musikalische Futurismus," *Melos* 25 (1958): 124–27; Fred K. Prieberg, *Musica ex machina: Über das Verhältnis von Musik und Technik* (Berlin: Ullstein, 1960); Italian edition *Musica ex machina* (Turin: Einaudi, 1963).

51. Luigi Russolo, *The Art of Noise: Futurist Manifesto, 1913.* Transl. by Robert Filliou (New York: Something Else Press, 1967); John C. G. Waterhouse, "A Futurist Mystery," Music and Musicians 15:8 (April 1967): 26–30.

52. Kuniharu Akiyama, "Itan no sakkyokuka -3- Sōon no shisō no senkusha Ruiji Russorō" [The Precursor of the Idea of Noise: Luigi Russolo], *Ongaku geijutsu* [*Musical Art*] 26:10 (September 1968): 44–49.

53. Armando Gentilucci, "Il futurismo e lo sperimentalismo musicale d'oggi," *Convegno musicale* 1:3–4 (July–December 1964): 275–303, reissued later as a brochure: Armando Gentilucci, *Il futurismo e lo sperimentalismo musicale d'oggi* (Turin: Edizioni del Convegno, 1965).

54. "Lettere di Marinetti a F. Balilla Pratella," edited by Giovanni Lugaresi, *Osservatore politico letterario* 15:7 (July 1969): 53–82; 15:8 (August 1969): 63–91; 15:9 (September 1969): 81–94. "Lettere a F. Balilla Pratella di Severini, Russolo, De Pisis," edited by Giovanni Lugaresi, *Osservatore politico letterario* 15:10 (October 1969): 80–95. *Lettere ruggenti a F. Balilla Pratella,* edited by Giovanni Lugaresi with a comment by Giuseppe Prezzolini (Milan: Quaderni dell'Osservatore, 1969).

55. Maria Drudi Gambillo and Teresa Fiori, eds., *Archivi del futurismo.* 2 vols. (Rome: De Luca, 1958–1962); Maria Drudi Gambillo, *Dopo Boccioni: Dipinti e documenti futuristi dal 1915 al 1919* (Rome: Edizioni Mediterranee "La Medusa," 1961).

56. *Futurballa, 1871–1958.* Edited by Enrico Crispolti. Milan: Galleria Blu, 1959; *Giacomo Balla.* Edited by Enrico Crispolti and Maria Drudi Gambillo. Turin: Galleria Civica d'Arte Moderna, as of April 4, 1963 (Turin: Pozzo-Salvati-Gros Monti & C., 1963).

57. "Appunti sul problema del secondo futurismo nella cultura italiana fra le due guerre," *Notizie: Arti figurative* 2:5 (April 1958): 34–52.

58. See *Notizie: Arti figurative* (Turin) 3:1 (January 1960), which contained a section by Crispolti: "Indicazioni per una cronologia del secondo futurismo" (12–16), and one by Drudi Gambillo: "Documenti per la poetica della seconda generazione futurista" (18–36). Concurrently, Crispolti published the essay, "Il secondo futurismo," *Le arti* 11:1–2 (January–February 1960): 22–23.

59. Renzo Modesti, ed., *Il futurismo* (Casatenovo Brianza: Vister, 1960).

60. Maurizio Calvesi, ed., *Dinamismo e simultaneità nella poetica futurista* (Milan: Fabbri, 1967).

61. See Benedetto's "Storia di Futurismo-oggi," *Futurismo-oggi* 19:7–12 (July–December 1987): 3–4. The first issue of *Futurismo-oggi* appeared in December 1969.

62. These statistics cover books, catalogues and essays in scholarly journals, but exclude book and exhibition reviews. The census date is November 2009, that is, before completing my bibliographic handbook.

63. Walter L. Adamson: "Fascinating Futurism: The Historiographical Politics of an Historical Avant-garde," *Modern Italy* 13:1 (February 2008): 69–85; here: 71.

General Bibliography of Futurism

Adamson, Walter L. *Avant-Garde Florence: From Modernism to Fascism* (Studies in Cultural History). Cambridge: Harvard University Press, 1993.

———. *Embattled Avant-Gardes: Modernism's Resistance to Commodity Culture in Europe*. Berkeley: University of California Press, 2007.

Affron, Matthew, and Mark Antliff, eds. *Fascist Visions: Art and Ideology in France and Italy*. Princeton: Princeton University Press, 1997.

Agnese, Gino, and Alessandro Sagramora, eds. *I futuristi e le Quadriennali*. Milan: Electa, 2008.

Amatori, Franco. *Storia della Lancia: impresa, tecnologie, mercati: 1906–1969*. Milan: Fabbri, 1992.

Anceschi, Giovanni. "Preavanguardie commerciali." *Linea Grafica* 5 (1986): 30–39.

Antonucci, Giovanni. *Cronache del teatro futurista*. Rome: Abete, 1975.

Antonucci, Giovanni, ed. *Il futurismo e Roma*. Rome: Istituto di Studi Romani, 1978.

Apollinaire, Guillaume. *Oeuvres en prose complètes*. Paris: Gallimard, 1993.

Apollonio, Umbro, ed. *Futurist Manifestos*. London: Thames and Hudson, 1973.

Baldazzi, Anna, ed. *Contributo a una bibliografia del futurismo letterario italiano*. Archivio italiano. Rome: Cooperativa Scrittori, 1977.

Ballerini, Luigi. *Italian Visual Poetry, 1912–1972*. New York: Finch College Museum/ Istituto Italiano di Cultura, 1973.

———. *Scrittura visuale in Italia, 1912–1972*. Introduction by Aldo Passoni; Catalogue of the Exhibition at the Galleria Civica d'Arte Moderna, Turin, 27 settembre–28 ottobre 1973.

Barbato, Andrea e.a. *Avanguardia e neo-avanguardia*, introduction by Giansiro Ferrata. Milan: Sugar, 1966.

Bartram, Alan. *Futurist Typography and the Liberated Text*. New Haven: Yale University Press, 2006.

Bartsch, Ingo, and Maurizio Scudiero, eds. *—auch wir Maschinen, auch wir mechanisiert!—: die zweite Phase des italienischen Futurismus 1915–1945*. Bielefeld: Kerber, 2002.

Beccaria, Gian Luigi. *Le forme della lontananza*. Milan: Garzanti, 1989.

Belli, Gabriella. *La parola nell'arte. Ricerche d'avanguardia nel '900, dal futurismo a oggi attraverso le collezioni del Mart*. Milan: Skira, 2007.

Bellini, Dario, ed. *Con Boccioni a Dosso Casina: i testi e le immagini dei futuristi in battaglia*. Rovereto: Nicolodi, 2006.

Bellini, Eraldo. *Studi su Ardengo Soffici*. Milan: Vita e Pensiero, 1987.

Benesch, Evelyn, and Ingried Brugger, eds. *Futurismus: Radikale Avantgarde*. Vienna; Milan: Kunstforum; Mazzotta, 2003.

Berghaus, Günter. *Futurism and Politics: Between Anarchist Rebellion and Fascist Reaction, 1909–1944*. Providence, RI: Berghahn Books, 1996.

———. *Futurism and the Technological Imagination* (Avant Garde Critical Studies) 24. New York: Rodopi, 2009.

———. *The Genesis of Futurism: Marinetti's Early Career and Writings 1899–1909*. Leeds: Society for Italian Studies, 1995.

———. *International Futurism in Arts and Literature*. European Cultures 13. New York: Walter de Gruyter, 2000.

———. *Italian Futurist Theatre, 1909–1944*. Oxford: Clarendon Press, 1998.

———. *Theatre, Performance, and the Historical Avant-Garde* (*Palgrave Studies in Theatre and Performance History*). New York: Palgrave Macmillan, 2005.

Berghaus, Günter, ed. *Fascism and Theatre: Comparative Studies on the Aesthetics and Politics of Performance in Europe, 1925–1945*. Providence, RI: Berghahn Books, 1996.

Bertini, Simona. *Marinetti e le eroiche serate*. Novara: Interlinea, 2002.

Bertoni, Alberto. *Dai simbolisti al Novecento. Le origini del verso libero italiano*. Bologna: Il Mulino, 1995.

Blum, Cinzia Sartini. *The Other Modernism: F.T. Marinetti's Futurist Fiction of Power*. Berkeley: University of California Press, 1996.

Blumenkranz-Onimus, Noëmi. *La poésie futuriste italienne: essai d'analyse esthétique*. Collection d'esthétique 43. Paris: Klincksieck, 1984.

Bohn, Willard. *The Aesthetics of Visual Poetry, 1914–1928*. Cambridge: Cambridge University Press, 1986.

———. *The Other Futurism: Futurist Activity in Venice, Padua, and Verona* (Toronto Italian Studies). Toronto: University of Toronto Press, 2004.

Bohn, Willard, ed. *Italian Futurist Poetry* (Toronto Italian Studies). Translated by Willard Bohn. Toronto: University of Toronto Press, 2005.

Bonadeo, Alfredo. *D'Annunzio and the Great War*. Madison, NJ: Fairleigh Dickinson University Press, 1995.

Bonito Oliva, Achille. *La parola totale: una tradizione futurista, 1909–1986.* Modena: Mucchi, 1986.

Bontempelli, Massimo. *Odi.* Modena: A. F. Formíggini, 1910.

———. *Opere Scelte.* Edited by Luigi Baldacci. Milan: Mondadori, 1978.

———. *Il purosangue.* Milan: Edizioni "La Prora," 1933.

———. *Il purosangue. L'ubriaco.* Milan: Facchi, 1919.

———. *Settenari e sonetti: 1904.* Ancona: Puccine e figli, 1910.

Bowlt, John E., ed. *Russian Art of the Avant-Garde: Theory and Criticism, 1902–1934* (*The Documents of 20th-Century Art*). New York: Viking Press, 1976.

Bragaglia, Anton Giulio. *Fotodinamismo futurista.* Turin: Einaudi, 1980.

Braun, Emily. *Mario Sironi and Italian Modernism: Art and Politics under Fascism.* Cambridge: Cambridge University Press, 2000.

Bru, Sascha. *Democracy, Law and the Modernist Avant-Gardes: Writing in the State of Exception.* Edinburgh: Edinburgh University Press, 2009.

Bru, Sascha, and Gunther Martens, eds. *The Invention of Politics in the European Avant-Garde* (*1906–1940*). Avant garde critical studies 19. Amsterdam; New York: Rodopi, 2006.

Bru, Sascha, Jan Baetens, Benedikt Hjartson, Peter Nicholls, Tanja Ørum, and Hubert van den Berg, eds. *Europa! Europa?: The Avant-Garde, Modernism, and the Fate of a Continent.* European avant-garde and modernism studies = Ètudes sur l'avant-garde et le modernisme en Europe 1. Berlin: De Gruyter, 2009.

Buelens, Geert. *Europa Europa!: Over de dichters van de Grote Oorlog.* Amsterdam; Antwerp: Ambo; Manteau, 2008.

Buzzi, Maria, ed. *Bibliografia generale di Paolo Buzzi.* With a Foreword by Lino Montagna and a Speech Transcription by Emilio Guicciardi. Turin: Tipi dell'Impronta, 1959.

Buzzi, Paolo. *Futurismo: scritti, carteggi, testimonianze.* Edited by Mario Morini and Giampaolo Pignatari. I Quaderni di Palazzo Sormani 7. Milan: Palazzo Sormani, 1983.

Calinescu, Matei. *Five Faces of Modernity: Modernism, Avant-garde, Decadence, Kitsch, Postmodernism.* Durham, NC: Duke University Press, 1987.

Calvesi, Maurizio. *Le due avanguardie Tal futurismo alla pop art.* Milan: Lerici, 1966.

———. *Il futurismo.* Mensili d'arte 39. Milan: Fabbri, 1970.

———. *Il futurismo: la fusione della vita nell'arte.* Milan: Fabbri, 1977.

Cammarota, M. Domenico. *Futurismo: bibliografia di 500 scrittori italiani.* Documenti del MART 10. Milan: Skira, 2006.

Campbell, Timothy C. *Wireless Writing in the Age of Marconi.* Electronic mediations 16. Minneapolis: University of Minnesota Press, 2006.

Cappelli, Vittorio, and Luciano Caruso, eds. *Calabria futurista.* Soveria Mannelli: Rubbettino, 1997 and 2009.

Carli, Mario, and Giuseppe Attilio Fanelli, eds. *Antologia degli scrittori fascisti.* Florence: Bemporad, 1931.

Carriero, Marcello. *Volt futurista, Viterbo 1888–Bressanone 1927.* Immagine 8. Viterbo: Sette Città, 2006.

Caruso, Luciano, ed. *L'Italia futurista: Firenze, 1916–1918.* Florence: SPES, 1992.

———. *Manifesti, proclami, interventi e documenti teorici del futurismo, 1909–1944,* 4 vols. Florence: Coedizioni SPES-Salimbeni, 1990.

Caruso, Luciano, and Stelio Maria Martini, eds. *Scrittura visuale e poesia sonora futurista.* Catalogue of the Exhibition at Palazzo Medici Riccardi, Florence, November 4– December 15, 1977.

———. *Tavole parolibere futuriste (1912–1944): Antologia.* Le Forme del significato 8, 10. Naples: Liguori, 1975.

———. *Tavole parolibere e tipografia futurista,* Catalogue of the Exhibition at Ca' Corner della Regina, Venice, October15–November 20, 1977.

Caspar, Marie-Hélène, ed. *Il futurismo italiano.* In *Narrativa* 9. Nanterre: Université Paris X, 1996.

Cescutti, Tatiana. *Les origines mythiques du futurisme. Marinetti poète symboliste (1902–1908).* Jalons. Paris: Presses de l'Université Paris-Sorbonne, 2009.

Cigliana, Simona. *Futurismo esoterico: contributi per una storia dell'irrazionalismo italiano tra Otto e Novecento.* Critica e letteratura 33. Naples: Liguori, 2002.

Contarini, Silvia. *La femme futuriste: mythes, modèles et représentations de la femme dans la théorie et la littérature futuristes (1900–1919).* Nanterre: Presses Universitaires de Paris, 2006.

Crispolti, Enrico. *Il futurismo e la moda: Balla e gli altri.* Venice: Marsilio, 1986.

———. *Il mito della macchina e altri temi del futurismo.* Trapani: Celebes, 1969.

———. *Il secondo futurismo. Torino 1923–1938.* Turin: Pozzo, 1961.

———. *Storia e critica del futurismo.* Rome; Bari: Laterza, 1986.

Crispolti, Enrico, ed. *Casa Balla e il futurismo a Roma.* Rome: Istituto Poligrafico e Zecca dello Stato, 1989.

———. *Enrico Prampolini.* Catalogue of the Exhibition at Galleria Narciso, Turin, October 31–November 20, 1963.

———. *Futurismo: 1909–1944: Arte, architettura, spettacolo, grafica, letteratura—.* Milan: Mazzotta, 2001.

———. *Futurismo e meridione.* Naples: Electa, 1996.

———. *Giacomo Balla.* Catalogue of the Exhibition at the Galleria Civica d'Arte Moderna, Turin, April–May 1963.

———. *Nuovi archivi del futurismo.* Rome: De Luca, 2010.

Crispolti, Enrico, and Franco Sborgi, eds. *Futurismo: I grandi temi, 1909–1944.* Milan: Mazzotta, 1997.

Curi, Fausto. *Tra mimesi e metafora. Studi su Marinetti e il futurismo.* Bologna: Pendragon, 1995.

D'Ambrosio, Matteo. *Le "Commemorazioni in avanti" di F.T. Marinetti: futurismo e critica letteraria.* Naples: Liguori, 1999.

———. *Futurismo a Napoli.* Naples: Liguori, 1995.

———. *Futurismo e altre avanguardie.* Critica e letteratura 13. Naples: Liguori, 1999.

———. *Nuove verità crudeli: Origini e primi sviluppi del futurismo a Napoli.* Naples: Guida, 1990.

———. *Roman Jakobson e il futurismo italiano*. Domini 86. Naples: Liguori, 2009.

D'Ambrosio, Matteo, ed. *Marinetti e il futurismo a Napoli*. Rome: De Luca, 1996.

David, Emilia. *Interventismo e anti-interventismo nelle produzioni grafico-tipografiche del futurismo e del dadaismo*. Rome: Aracne, 2009.

Décaudin, Michel. *La crise des valeurs symbolistes*. Genève-Paris: Slatkine, 1981.

De Felice, Renzo. *Mussolini il rivoluzionario*. Preface by Delio Cantimori. Turin: Einaudi, 1965.

De Felice, Renzo, ed. *Futurismo, cultura e politica*. Turin: Fondazione Giovanni Agnelli, 1988.

De Maria, Luciano, ed. *Filippo Tommaso Marinetti e il futurismo*. Milan: Mondadori, 2000.

———. *Marinetti e i futuristi*. Milan: Garzanti, 1994.

Demetz, Peter. *Worte in Freiheit: der italienische Futurismus und die deutsche literarische Avantgarde (1912–1934). Mit einer ausführlichen Dokumentation*. Munich; Zurich: Piper, 1990.

Depero, Fortunato. *Depero futurista*. Milan: Dinamo Azari, 1927.

De Turris, Gianfranco. *Le aeronavi dei Savoia: protofantascienza italiana 1891–1952*. Milan: Nord, 2001.

Dombroski, Robert S. *L'esistenza ubbidiente. Letterati italiani sotto il fascismo*. Naples: Guida, 1984.

Dorfles, Gillo. *Nuovi riti, nuovi miti*. Turin: Einaudi, 1965.

Drudi Gambillo, Maria, and Teresa Fiori, eds. *Archivi del futurismo*. 2 vols. Archivi dell'arte contemporanea. Rome: De Luca, 1958.

Fanelli, Giovanni, and Ezio Godoli. *Il futurismo e la grafica*. Milan: Edizioni Comunità, 1988.

Febbraro, Paolo. *Saba, Umberto*. Rome: Gaffi, 2008.

Fiaschi, Lucia. *Parole contro, 1963–1968. Il tempo della poesia visiva*. Siena: Carlo Cambi Editore, 2009.

Finter, Helga. *Semiotik des Avantgardetextes: gesellschaftliche und poetische Erfahrung im italienischen Futurismus*. Studien zur allgemeinen und vergleichenden Literaturwissenschaft 18. Stuttgart: Metzler, 1980.

Fossati, Paolo. *La realtà attrezzata. Scena e spettacolo dei futuristi*. Turin: Einaudi, 1977.

Foster, Hal. *The Return of the Real: The Avant-Garde at the End of the Century*. Cambridge, MA: MIT Press, 1996.

Futurismo e agro pontino. Quaderno del Novecento 9. Latina: Novecento, 2000.

Garafola, Lynn. *Diaghilev's Ballets Russes*. Cambridge, MA: Da Capo, 1998.

Gentile, Emilio. *"La nostra sfida alle stelle": futuristi in politica*. Rome: Laterza, 2009.

———. *The Struggle for Modernity: Nationalism, Futurism, and Fascism*. Italian and Italian American studies. Westport, CT: Praeger, 2003.

Gigli Marchetti, Ada, and Luisa Finocchi, eds. *Stampa e piccola editoria tra le due guerre*. Studi e ricerche di storia dell'editoria 2. Milan: Franco Angeli, 1997.

Giroud, Vincent, and Paola Pettenella, eds. *Futurism: From Avant-Garde to Memory: Papers*. Documents of MART 8. Milan: Skira, 2006.

Godoli, Ezio, ed. *Il dizionario del futurismo*. 2 vols. Florence: Vallecchi, 2001.

Gruber, Klemens. *Die zerstreute Avantgarde: strategische Kommunikation im Italien der 70er Jahre*. 2nd ed. Maske und Kothurn Beihefte15. Vienna; Cologne; Weimar: Böhlau, 2010.

Guerri, Giordano Bruno. *Filippo Tommaso Marinetti: Invenzioni, avventure e passioni di un rivoluzionario*. Le scie. Milan: Mondadori, 2009.

Guglielmi, Guido. *L'invenzione della letteratura: Modernismo e avanguardia*. Naples: Liguori, 2001.

Guzzetta, Lia Fava, ed. *Tra simbolismo e futurismo*. *Verso sud*. Segni del Moderno 4. Pesaro: Metauro, 2009.

Hanson, Anne. *The Futurist Imagination: Word & Image in Italian Futurist Painting, Drawing, Collage, and Free-Word Poetry*. New Haven, CT.: The Gallery, 1983.

Härmänmaa, Marja. *Un patriota che sfidò la decadenza: F.T. Marinetti e l'idea dell'uomo nuovo fascista, 1929–1944*. Suomalaisen Tiedeakatemian toimituksia nide 310. Helsinki: Academia Scientiarum Fennica: Distribuzione Libreria Tiedekirja, 2000.

Hewitt, Andrew. *Fascist Modernism: Aesthetics, Politics, and the Avant-Garde*. Stanford: Stanford University Press, 1993.

Higgins, Lesley. *The Modernist Cult of Ugliness. Aesthetic and Gender Politics*. New York: Palgrave Macmillan, 2002.

Hinz, Manfred O. *Die Zukunft der Katastrophe: Mythische und rationalistische Geschichtstheorie im italienischen Futurismus*. Berlin; New York: De Gruyter, 1985.

Hultén, Pontus. *Futurismo & Futurismi*. Milan: Bompiani, 1986.

Humphreys, Richard. *Futurism*. Cambridge: Cambridge University Press, 1999.

Jakobson, Roman. *My Futurist Years*. Edited by Bengt Jangfeldt; Translated by Stephen Rudy. New York: Marsilio, 1992.

Jannini, Pasquale-Anjel e.a., *La fortuna del futurismo in Francia*. Rome: Bulzoni, 1979.

Kern, Stephen. *The Culture of Time and Space 1880–1918*. Cambridge: Harvard University Press, 1983.

Krauss, Rosalind. *The Originality of the Avant-Garde and Other Modernist Myths*. Cambridge, MA: MIT Press, 1985.

Lacerba: Firenze, 1913–1915. Rome: Archivi d'arte del XX secolo: Milan: Mazzotta, 1970.

Lamberti, Maria Mimita, and Maria Grazia Messina. *Collage/collages, dal cubismo al new dada*. Milan: Electa, 2008.

Lambiase, Sergio, and Gian Battista Nazzaro. *F.T. Marinetti futurista: Inediti, pagine disperse, documenti e antologia critica*. Naples: Guida, 1977.

Lapini, Lia. *Il teatro futurista italiano*. Milan: Mursia, 1977.

Lawton, Anna, ed., *Russian Futurism through Its Manifestoes, 1912–1928*. Translated by Anna Lawton and Herbert Eagle. Ithaca: Cornell University Press, 1988.

Lear, Jonathan. *Therapeutic Action: An Earnest Plea for Irony*. New York: Other Press, 2003.

Lemaire, Gérard-Georges. *Les mots en liberté: futuristes, Marinetti, Boccioni, Carrà, Cangiullo, Depero, Severini, Soffici, etc, etc-- = Parole in libertà*. Paris: Damase, 1986.

Lista, Giovanni. *Arte e politica: il futurismo di sinistra in Italia*. Milan: Multhipla, 1980.

———. *Cinema e fotografia futurista*. Milan: Skira, 2001.

———. *F.T. Marinetti: L'anarchiste du futurisme: Biographie*. Paris: Séguier, 1995.

———. *Futurism*. New York: Universe Books, 1986.

———. *Futurism*. Paris: Terrail, 2001.

———. *Giacomo Balla, futuriste*. Lausanne: L'Age d'Homme, 1984.

———. *La scène futuriste*. Paris: Éditions du Centre national de la recherche scientifique, 1989.

———. *Le livre futuriste de la libération du mot au poème tactile*. Modena: Panini, 1984.

———. *Marinetti et le futurisme: études, documents, iconographie*. Lausanne: L'Age d'Homme, 1977.

Lista, Giovanni, ed. *Futurisme. Manifestes, Proclamations, Documents*. Lausanne: L'Age d'Homme, 1974.

Lista, Giovanni, Paolo Baldacci, and Livia Velani, eds. *Balla. La modernità futurista*. Milan: Skira, 2008.

Lista, Giovanni, and Ada Masoero, eds. *Futurismo 1909–2009: velocità+ arte+ azione*. Milan: Skira, 2009.

Livi, François. *Tra crepuscolarismo e futurismo: Govoni e Palazzeschi*. Milan: IPL, 1980.

Livi, François, ed. *"Poesia" (1905–1909)*. Naples: Edizioni Scientifiche Italiane, 1992.

Lombardi, Daniele. *Il suono veloce: Futurismo e futurismi in musica*. Le Sfere 27. Milan; Lucca: Ricordi; Libreria Musicale Italiana, 1996.

Luisetti, Federico, and Luca Somigli, eds. *A Century of Futurism, 1909–2009*. In *Annali d'Italianistica* 27. Chapel Hill: University of North Carolina Press, 2009.

Magro, Franco. *Catanzaro vento futurista*. Soveria Mannelli: Calabria Letteraria, 2004.

Manifesti, proclami, interventi, e documenti teorici del futurismo, 1909–1944. Florence: Coedizioni SPES-Salimbeni, 1980.

Mann, Paul. *Masocriticism*. The SUNY series in postmodern culture. Albany: State University of New York Press, 1999.

———. *The Theory-Death of the Avant-Garde*. Bloomington: Indiana University Press, 1991.

Marcadé, Jean-Claude, ed. *Malévitch, 1878–1978: Actes du colloque international tenu au Centre Pompidou, Musée National d'art Moderne, les 4 et 5 Mai 1978*. Cahiers des Avant-gardes. Lausanne: L'Age d'Homme, 1979.

———. *Présence de F.T. Marinetti: actes du colloque international tenu à l'UNESCO*. Lausanne: L'Age d'Homme, 1982.

Marchioni, Nadia. *La Grande Guerra degli artisti: Propaganda e iconografia bellica in Italia*. Florence: Pagliai Polistampa, 2005.

Mariani, Gaetano. *Poesia e tecnica nella lirica del Novecento*. Padua: Liviana Editrice, 1958.

———. *Il primo Marinetti*. Florence: Le Monnier, 1970.

Marinetti, Filippo Tommaso. *Le "Commemorazioni in avanti" di F.T. Marinetti: futurismo e critica letteraria*. Edited by Matteo D'Ambrosio. Teorie & oggetti della letteratura 22. Naples: Liguori, 1999.

——. *Critical Writings*. Edited by Günter Berghaus. New York: Farrar, Straus, and Giroux, 2006.

——. *Le premier manifeste du futurisme: édition critique avec, en fac-similé, le manuscrit original de F.T. Marinetti*. Ottawa: Éditions de l'Université d'Ottawa, 1986.

——. *Scritti francesi*. Milan: Mondadori, 1983.

——. *Selected Writings*. Edited and translated by Robert Willard Flint. New York: Farrar, Straus and Giroux, 1972.

——. *Taccuini 1915–1921*. Edited by Alberto Bertoni, Introduction by Renzo De Felice and Ezio Raimondi. Bologna: Il Mulino, 1987.

——. *Teatro*. Edited by Jeffrey T. Schnapp. Milan: Mondadori, 2004.

——. *Teoria e invenzione futurista*. Edited by Luciano De Maria. 2 vols. Milan: Mondadori, 1968.

Marinetti, Filippo Tommaso, and Aldo Palazzeschi. *Carteggio: con un'appendice di altre lettere a Palazzeschi*. Introductory note by Luciano De Maria. Edited by Paolo Prestigiacomo. Milan: Mondadori, 1978.

Marinetti, Filippo Tommaso, Emilio Settimelli, and Mario Carli. *Che cos'è il futurismo: nozioni elementari*. Milan: Direzione del movimento futurista, 1920.

Marinetti, Filippo Tommaso, and Francesco Cangiullo, *Lettere (1910–1943)*. Edited by Ernestina Pellegrini. Florence: Vallecchi, 1989.

Markov, Vladimir. *Russian Futurism: A History*. Berkeley: University of California Press, 1968.

Martin, Marianne W. *Futurist Art and Theory 1909–1915*. Oxford: Clarendon Press, 1968.

Mascelloni, Enrico, and Sarenco. *Poesia totale 1897–1997: Dal colpo di dadi alla poesia totale*. Verona: Adriano Parise, 1998.

Masi, Alessandro, ed. *Zig zag: Il romanzo futurista*. Milan: Il Saggiatore, 1995.

Masoero, Ada, ed. *Universo meccanico: Il futurismo attorno a Balla, Depero, Prampolini*. Milan: Mazzotta, 2003.

Masoero, Ada, and Renato Miracco, eds. *Futurismo 1909–1926. La bellezza della velocità*. Milan: Mazzotta, 2003.

Meazzi, Barbara. *Le futurisme entre l'Italie et la France: 1909–1919*. Chambéry: Université de Savoie, 2010.

Mengaldo, Pier Vincenzo. *Poeti italiani del Novecento*. Milan: Mondadori, 1994.

——. *La tradizione del Novecento*. Milan: Feltrinelli, 1975.

Miccini, Eugenio, and Lamberto Pignotti. *Poesie in azione*. Introduction by Pietro Favari. Florence: Giubbe Rosse, 2001.

Miligi, Giuseppe. *Prefuturismo e primo futurismo in Sicilia*. Messina: Sicania, 1989.

Mitchell, Bonner. *Les manifestes littéraires de la Belle Époque, 1886–1914. Anthologie critique*. Paris: Seghers, 1966.

Mondello, Elisabetta. *Roma futurista*. Milan: Franco Angeli, 1990.

Moroni, Mario, Luca Somigli, and Paolo Chirumbolo, eds. *Neoavanguardia: Italian Experimental Literature and Arts in the 1960s*. Toronto Italian Studies. Toronto: University of Toronto Press, 2010.

Mussgnug, Florian. *The Eloquence of Ghosts: Giorgio Manganelli and the Afterlife of the Avant-Garde*. Oxford: Peter Lang, 2010.

Nicholls, Peter. *Modernisms: A Literary Guide*. Berkeley: University of California Press, 1995.

Ottingier, Didier e.a., eds. *Le futurisme à Paris. Une avant-garde explosive*. Paris: Éditions du Centre Pompidou, 2008.

Pacini, Piero, ed. *Esposizioni futuriste, 1912–1918: 26 cataloghi originali*. Florence: Studio per edizioni scelte, 1978.

Palazzeschi, Aldo. *Tutte le poesie*. Edited by Adele Dei. Milan: Mondadori, 2002.

Panzera, Lisa, ed. *La Futurista: Benedetta Cappa Marinetti*. Philadelphia, PA: Goldie Paley Gallery, Moore College of Art and Design, 1998.

Papini, Giovanni, and Ardengo Soffici. *Carteggio*. Edited by Mario Richter. Rome; Fiesole: Edizioni di Storia e Letteratura; Fondazione Primo Conti, 1991.

Papini, Maria, ed. *L'Italia futurista (1916–1918)*. Rome: Edizioni dell'Ateneo & Bizzarri, 1977.

Pavel, Thomas G. *Fictional Worlds*. Cambridge: Harvard University Press, 1986.

Perloff, Marjorie. *The Futurist Moment: Avant-Garde, Avant Guerre, and the Language of Rupture*. Chicago: University of Chicago Press, 1986, 2003.

Pickering-Iazzi, Robin, ed. *Mothers of Invention: Women, Italian Fascism, and Culture*. Minneapolis: University of Minnesota Press, 1995.

Pignotti, Lamberto. *Il discorso confezionato. Informazione arte cultura nella società dei consumi*. Florence: Vallecchi, 1979.

———. *Figure scritture. Su certi segni delle arti e dei mass media*. Udine: Campanotto, 1987.

———. *Scritture convergenti. Letteratura e mass media*. Udine: Campanotto, 2005

Pignotti, Lamberto, and Stefania Stefanelli. *La scrittura verbo-visiva. Le avanguardie del Novecento tra parola e immagine*. Rome: Editoriale l'Espresso, 1980.

Piscopo, Ugo. *Futurismo a Napoli 1915–1928*. Naples: Tullio Pironti, 1981.

Poggi, Christine. *In Defiance of Painting: Cubism, Futurism, and the Invention of Collage*. New Haven: Yale University Press, 1992.

———. *Inventing Futurism: The Art and Politics of Artificial Optimism*. Princeton: Princeton University Press, 2009.

Poggioli, Renato. *The Theory of the Avant-Garde*. Cambridge: Harvard University Press, 1968.

Puchner, Martin. *Poetry of the Revolution: Marx, Manifestos, and the Avant-Gardes*. Translation/transnation. Princeton: Princeton University Press, 2006.

Ragazzi, Franco, ed. *Liguria futurista*. Milan: Mazzotta, 1997.

———. ed. *Marinetti e il futurismo in Liguria*. Genoa: De Ferrari, 2006.

Rainey, Lawrence S., Christine Poggi, and Laura Wittman, eds. *Futurism: An Anthology*. New Haven: Yale University Press, 2009.

Richard de la Fuente, Véronique. *Valentine de Saint Point (1875–1953): une poétesse dans l'avant garde futuriste et méditerranéiste*. Céret: Éditions des Albères, 2003.

Richter, Mario. *La formazione francese di Ardengo Soffici*. Milan: Vita e Pensiero, 1969.

————. *Papini e Soffici. Mezzo secolo di vita italiana* (1903–1957). Florence: Le Lettere, 2005.

Roche-Pézard, Fanette. *L'aventure futuriste, 1909–1916.* Rome: École française de Rome, 1983.

Rosà, Rosa. *Una donna con tre anime: Romanzo futurista.* Edited by Claudia Salaris. Milan: Edizioni delle Donne, 1982.

Rothenberg, Jerome, and Pierre Joris, eds. *Poems for the Millennium: The University of California Book of Modern & Postmodern Poetry.* Vol. 1, From *Fin-de-Siècle* to *Negritude.* Berkeley: University of California Press, 1995.

————. *Poems for the Millennium: the University of California Book of Modern & Postmodern Poetry.* Vol. 2, From *Postwar* to *Millennium.* Berkeley: University of California Press, 1998.

Russell, Charles. *Poets, Prophets, and Revolutionaries: The Literary Avant-Garde from Rimbaud through Postmodernism.* New York: Oxford University Press, 1985.

Ruta, Anna Maria. *Il futurismo in Sicilia.* Marina di Patti: Silvana, 1991.

Saccà, Lucilla. *La parola come immagine e come segno. Firenze: storia di una rivoluzione colta* (1960–1980). Pisa: Pacini Editore, 2000.

Saccone, Antonio. *La trincea avanzata e la città dei conquistatori: Futurismo e modernità.* Naples: Liguori, 2000.

Saítta, Sylvia. *Regueros de tinta: el diario "Crítica" en la década de 1920.* Colección Historia y Cultura. Buenos Aires: Editorial Sudamericana, 1998.

Salaris, Claudia. *Dizionario del futurismo: idee, provocazioni e parole d'ordine di una grande avanguardia.* Rome: Editori Riuniti, 1996.

————. *Filippo Tommaso Marinetti.* Immagini 2. Florence: La Nuova Italia, 1988.

————. *Luciano Folgore e le avanguardie.* Florence: La Nuova Italia, 1997.

————. *Marinetti: arte e vita futurista.* Rome: Editori Riuniti, 1997.

————. *La Roma delle avanguardie. Dal futurismo all'underground.* Rome: Editori Riuniti, 1999.

————. *Sicilia futurista.* Palermo: Sellerio, 1986.

————. *Storia del futurismo: Libri, giornali, manifesti.* Rome: Editori Riuniti, 1985.

Salaris, Claudia, ed. *Le futuriste: donne e letteratura d'avanguardia in Italia* (1909–1944). Milan: Edizioni delle Donne, 1982.

Sanguineti, Edoardo. *Tra liberty e crepuscolarismo.* Milan: Mursia, 1977.

Schnapp, Jeffrey T. *Staging Fascism: 18 BL and the Theater of Masses for Masses.* Stanford: Stanford University Press, 1996.

Schnapp, Jeffrey T, ed. *Speed Limits.* Miami Beach, FL; Montréal; Milan: Wolfsonian-Florida International University; Canadian Centre for Architecture; Skira, 2009.

Scimé, Giuliana. *Il laboratorio dei Bragaglia 1911–1932.* Ravenna: Agenzia Editoriale, 1986.

Scriboni, Giancarlo. *Tra nazionalismo e futurismo: Testimonianze inediti di Volt.* Venice: Marsilio, 1980.

Scrivo, Luigi, ed. *Sintesi del futurismo: Storia e documenti.* Rome: Bulzoni, 1968.

Somigli, Luca. *Legitimizing the Artist: Manifesto Writing and European Modernism, 1885–1915.* (Toronto Italian Studies). Toronto: University of Toronto Press, 2003.

Somigli, Luca, and Mario Moroni, eds. *Italian Modernism: Italian Culture between Decadentism and Avant-Garde*. (Toronto Italian Studies). Toronto: University of Toronto Press, 2004.

Spackman, Barbara. *Fascist Virilities: Rhetoric, Ideology, and Social Fantasy in Italy*. Minneapolis: University of Minnesota Press, 1996.

Spagnoletti, Giacinto. *Palazzeschi*. Milan: Longanesi, 1971.

Strauven, Wanda. *Marinetti e il cinema: tra attrazione e sperimentazione*. Zeta cinema 14. Udine: Campanotto, 2006.

Tallarico, Luigi. *Il futurismo e la Calabria*. Reggio Calabria: Iiriti, 2003.

Taylor, Joshua. *Futurism*. New York: The Museum of Modern Art, 1961.

Tisdall, Caroline, and Angelo Bozzolla. *Futurism*. London: Thames and Hudson, 1977.

Tomasello, Dario. *Oltre il Futurismo. Percorsi delle avanguardie in Sicilia*. Rome: Bulzoni, 2000.

Tomasello, Dario, and Francesca Polacci. *Bisogno furioso di liberare le parole: Tra verbale e visivo. Percorsi analitici delle tavole parolibere futuriste*. Florence: Le Lettere, 2010.

Toni, Anna Caterina, ed. *I luoghi del futurismo (1909–1944)*. Rome: Multigrafica, 1986.

Vanden Berghe, Dirk. *Ardengo Soffici dal romanzo al "puro lirismo."* 2 vols. Florence: Olschki, 1997.

Verdone, Mario. *Anton Giulio Bragalia*. Rome: Centro Sperimentale di Cinematografia, 1965.

———. *Cinema e letteratura del futurismo*. Rome: Edizioni di Bianco e Nero, 1968.

———. *I fratelli Bragaglia*. Rome: Lucarini, 1991.

———. *Il teatro del tempo futurista*. Rome: Lerici, 1969.

Verdone, Mario, ed. *Teatro italiano d'avanguardia: Drammi e sintesi futuriste*. Rome: Officina, 1970.

Vetri, Lucio. *Letteratura e caos. Poetiche della "neo-avanguardia" italiana degli anni Sessanta*, Milan: Mursia, 1992.

Viazzi, Glauco, ed. *I poeti del futurismo, 1909–1944*. Milan: Longanesi, 1978.

Volt. *Archi voltaici: Parole in libertà e sintesi teatrali*. Milan: Poesia, 1916.

———. *La fine del mondo: Romanzo di fantascienza futurista*. Florence: Vallecchi, 2003.

———. *Programma della destra fascista*. Florence: La Voce, 1924.

Webber, Andrew. *The European Avant-Garde 1900–1940*. Cambridge: Polity, 2004.

Weber, Luigi. *Romanzi del movimento, romanzi in movimento: La narrativa del futurismo e dintorni*. Massa: Transeuropa, 2010.

Wells, Herbert G. *Four Complete Novels*. New York: Barnes & Noble, 1994.

White, John J. *Literary Futurism: Aspects of the First Avant Garde*. Oxford; New York: Clarendon Press; Oxford University Press, 1990.

Index

~

About the Contributors

Walter L. Adamson is Samuel Candler Dobbs professor of history at Emory University and the author of four books, most recently *Embattled Avant-gardes: Modernism's Resistance to Commodity Culture in Europe* (2007). In 2011 he was named a John S. Guggenheim Fellow for a project on fascism and religion in Italy. His earlier books include *Hegemony and Revolution: A Study of Antonio Gramsci's Political and Cultural Theory* (1980), which won the Society for Italian History's Howard Marraro Prize for the best book in Italian history in 1981; and *Avant-Garde Florence: From Modernism to Fascism* (1993), which won the American Historical Association's Marraro Prize for the best book in Italian history in 1995.

Günter Berghaus was, for many years, a reader in Theatre History and Performance Studies and is now a senior research fellow at the University of Bristol. He has directed numerous plays from the classical and modern repertoire and has been organizer of several international conferences. He has published some twenty books on various aspects of theatre history, performance studies, and the avant-garde. He is a leading expert on Italian Futurism and edits the International Yearbook of Futurism Studies. His current project is a bibliographic handbook, *International Futurism, 1945–2009*, which lists some 25,000 studies related to artists who were active in the movement and to aesthetic genres and media in which Futurism exercised a particularly noteworthy influence.

Monica Biasiolo is a lecturer in Italian at the University of Erlangen-Nuremberg, where she earned her PhD with a thesis on the antifascist intellectual Giaime Pintor: *Giaime Pintor und die deutsche Kultur* (2010). Her research focuses on twentieth-century Italian, French, and German literature, gender studies, and the avant-garde. She is the author of articles and book chapters on Renato Guttuso, Giuseppe Ungaretti, and Paul Éluard.

Francesca Bravi is a lecturer in Italian at the Christian-Albrechts University of Kiel. She graduated in German and English literature as well as in Intercultural Studies at the University "Carlo Bo" of Urbino. Her PhD dissertation on the representation of dreams in German and French literature of the 1970s was published as *Sogno e romanzo. Tra fisiologia e filologia. La rappresentazione del sogno in romanzi degli anni '70 in DDR e Francia* (2011).

Sascha Bru is professor of literary theory at the University of Leuven and codirector opf mdrn, a research scheme that aims to devise new ways of writing the history of modernist literature (www.mdrn.be). His most recent book is *Democracy, Law and the Modernist Avant-Gardes. Writing in the State of Exception* (2009). Recently coedited books include *The Cultural and Critical History of Modernist Magazines, III, Europe 1880–1940* (2012). With Peter Nicholls he is the editor of the book series European Avant-garde and Modernism Studies.

Geert Buelens is professor of modern Dutch literature at the University of Utrecht and guest professor at the University of Stellenbosch. In 2008 he was a Kluge Fellow at the Library of Congress. He has published widely on the Flemish avant-garde writer Paul van Ostaijen and on twentieth-century avant-garde poetry, nationalist literature, and poetry of the First World War. He is editor of *Avant-Garde Critical Studies*.

Silvia Contarini is professor of Italian studies and director of the Centre de Recherches Italiennes at the University of Paris Ouest Nanterre. Her work on Italian Futurism, and particularly on futurist women, has made her one of the leading scholars on Futurism. Her publications include *Le futurisme et les avant-gardes littéraires et artistiques au début du XXe siècle* (edited with Karine Cardini, 2002), and *La Femme futuriste. Mythes, modèles et représentations de la femme dans la théorie et la litérature futuriste* (2006).

Eleonora Conti is a specialist in twentieth-century Italian literature at the University of Bologna, where she co-directs the electronic journal on modern and contemporary Italian literature *Bollettino '900*. She completed her PhD at the University of Paris IV-Sorbonne with a dissertation on Giuseppe Ungaretti's mediation between Italian and French culture in the 1920s. She is the editor of *Giuseppe Ungaretti, Lettere a Giuseppe Raimondi (1918–1966)* (2004), and has authored numerous articles on modern Italian literature published in journals such as *Allegoria, Filologia e Critica, Intersezioni, Italianistica, Lingua e stile, Revue des Études Italiennes, Il verri*, and in various edited volumes.

Patricia Gaborik held the Paul Mellon Postdoctoral Rome Prize at the American Academy in Rome in 2005–2006 and is currently based in that city. She has published essays on Italian theatre in translation, Futurism, Massimo Bontempelli, and various aspects of nationalist and fascist performance in edited volumes: *Metamorphoses, Modern Drama, National Theatres in a Changing Europe* (2012), *Il futurismo nelle avanguardie* (2010), *Avant-Garde Performance and Material Exchange: Vectors of the Radical* (2011), and the third volume of Einaudi's *Atlante della letteratura italiana* (2012).

Laura Greco is a PhD student at the University of Palermo, where she is completing a dissertation on the literary works (poetry, novels, essays, and theater) and projects of Federico De Maria.

Kyle Hall is completing the doctoral program in Italian studies at Harvard University. His research focuses on the development of political biographies during the nineteenth century, particularly as they regard the unification of Italy and the formation of a national consciousness.

Harald Hendrix is professor of Italian studies and head of the Department of Modern Languages at the University of Utrecht. He has published on the European reception of Italian Renaissance culture, on the early modern aesthetics of the non-beautiful, and on the intersections of literature, memory, and tourism. Amongst his recent books are the edited volumes *Writers' Houses and the Making of Memory* (2008), *Officine del nuovo* (with Paolo Procaccioli, 2008), *Dynamic Translations in the European Renaissance* (with Philiep Bossier and Paolo Procaccioli, 2011), *The Turn of the Soul* (with Lieke Stelling and Todd Richardson, 2012), and *Le butin intellectuel de Chypre, 1450–1600* (with Evelien Chayes and Benjamin Arbel, 2012).

Monica Jansen is a lecturer in Italian studies at the University of Utrecht and editor-in-chief of *Incontri. Rivista europea di studi italiani*. Her publications include *Il dibattito sul postmoderno in Italia* (2002), *The Value of*

Literature in and after the Seventies: The Case of Italy and Portugal (coedited with Paula Jordao, 2006), *Contemporary Jewish Writers in Italy: A Generational Approach* (coedited with Reinier Speelman and Silvia Gaiga, 2007), *Noir de noir: un'indagine pluridisciplinare* (coedited with Dieter Vermandere and Inge Lanslots, 2010), and *Memoria in noir: un'indagine pluridisciplinare* (coedited with Yasmina Khamal, 2010).

Federico Luisetti is associate professor of Italian studies, comparative literature, and communication studies at the University of North Carolina at Chapel Hill. He is the author of *Una vita. Pensiero selvaggio e filosofia dell'intensità* (2011), *Estetica dell'immanenza. Saggi sulle parole, le immagini e le macchine* (2008), and *Plus Ultra. Enciclopedismo barocco e modernità* (2001). He has edited with Luca Somigli a special issue on Italian Futurism of the journal *Annali d'italianistica*, 27, 2009: *A Century of Futurism: 1909–2009* and with Giorgio Maragliano two volumes on museum studies: *Dopo il museo* (2006) and *Museo*, a special issue of the *Rivista di estetica*, ns 16, 1/2001.

Stefano Magni lectures on Italian literature at the University of Provence Aix-Marseille. His main field of research is twentieth-century Italian narrative. He has worked on WWI and WWII memoirists, historical avant-garde, late 1960s and 1970s rebellion literature, and postmodernism.

Florian Mussgnug is a lecturer in Italian literature at University College London. He has published widely on twentieth-century Italian literature. His recent publications include a book on *The Eloquence of Ghosts. Giorgio Manganelli and the Afterlife of the Avant-Garde* (2010) and an edited volume on *Postmodern Impegno. Ethics and Commitment in Contemporary Italian Literature* (with Pierpaolo Antonello, 2009).

Marjorie Perloff is Sadie D. Patek Professor Emerita of Humanities at Stanford University. She is the author of many books on twentieth- and twenty-first-century poetry and poetics, including *The Futurist Moment: Avant-Garde, Avant-Guerre, and the Language of Rupture* (1986; revised ed. 2003), and, most recently, *Unoriginal Genius: Poetry by Other Means in the New Century* (2010).

Davide Podavini graduated in Italian literature at the University of Pavia with a thesis on Marinetti's anthology *Poeti futuristi*. His research focuses on Italian twentieth-century poetry. He is the editor of Giovanni Raboni's last work, *Ultimi versi* (2006), and is preparing, in collaboration with Patrizia Valduga, the catalogue of Giovanni Raboni's private archive.

Jeffrey T. Schnapp is professor of romance languages and literatures and director of the metaLAB at Harvard University. A cultural historian with research interests ranging from antiquity to the present, he has published widely on Italian twentieth-century culture, including *Staging Fascism: 18 BL and the Theater of Masses for Masses* (1996), *Anno X. La Mostra della rivoluzione fascista del 1932* (2003), and *Building Fascism, Communism, Democracy* (2003). He is the editor of *Filippo Tommaso Marinetti, Teatro* (2 vols., 2004). His recent publications include *Speed Limits* (2009), *The Electric Information Age Book* (with Adam Michaels, 2012), *Digital Humanities* (with Anne Burdick and others, 2012), *Modernitalia* (coedited with Francesca Santovetti, 2012), and *Italiamerica* (coedited with Emanuela Scarpellini, 2012).

Beatrice Sica is a lecturer in Italian literature at University College London. She received her MA in modern and contemporary Italian literature from the Scuola Normale Superiore in Pisa and her PhD in Italian studies from New York University, where she was also a research fellow at the Humanities Initiative. She held post-doctoral fellowships at the Collège de France in Paris (2010–2011) and at Harvard University (2011–2012).

Teresa Spignoli is a postdoctoral researcher in twentieth-century Italian literature at the University of Florence. Her research focuses on the study of archival materials, particularly epistolary correspondences between modern Italian authors, on the hermetic elements in the poetry of Giuseppe Ungaretti as well as on the intersections of literature, visual arts, and theatre in the 1970s. Her most recent book is *Caffè letterari a Firenze* (2009). She is the editor of *Carlo Betocchi & Antonio Pizzuto, Lettere 1966–1971* (2006), *Il romanzo di formazione nell'Otto e nel Novecento* (2007) (with Maria Carla Papini and Daniele Fioretti), and of Piero Bigongiari & Giuseppe Ungaretti, *"La certezza della poesia." Lettere 1942–1970* (2008).

Dirk Vanden Berghe is a lecturer in Italian literature at the Vrije Universiteit in Brussels. His research focuses on stylistic and intertextual aspects of early nineteenth and early twentieth-century Italian literature. He has published on the work of poet-translators both of proto-romantic works and of classics. On the Florentine pre-WWI avant-garde he has published various articles, entries in the *Routledge Encyclopedia of Italian Literary Studies* (2007), as well as the two-volume *Ardengo Soffici dal romanzo al "puro lirismo"* (1997).